Lecture Notes in Computer Science

Lecture Notes in Computer Science

Edited by G. Goos and J. Hartmanis

69

F. L. Bauer, E. W. Dijkstra,
S. L. Gerhart, D. Gries, M. Griffiths,
J. V. Guttag, J. J. Horning, S. S. Owicki,
C. Pair, H. Partsch, P. Pepper,
M. Wirsing, H. Wössner

Program Construction

International Summer School

Edited by F. L. Bauer and M. Broy

Springer-Verlag
Berlin Heidelberg New York 1979

AMS Subject Classifications (1970): 68-02, 68 A 05
CR Subject Classifications (1974): 4.12, 4.20, 4.22, 4.30, 4.31, 4.32, 4.34
5.24

ISBN 3-540-09251-X Springer-Verlag Berlin Heidelberg New York
ISBN 0-387-09251-X Springer-Verlag New York Heidelberg Berlin

Library of Congress Cataloging in Publication Data. Main entry under title: Program
construction, International Summer School. (Lecture notes in computer science ; 69)
"Sponsored by the NATO Scientific Affairs Division." Bibliography: p. Includes
index. 1. Electronic digital computers--Programming--Addresses, essays, lectures.
I. Bauer, Friedrich Ludwig, 1924- II. Broy, M., 1949- III. North Atlantic Treaty Organization. Division of Scientific Affairs. IV. Series. QA76.6.P75117 001.6'42 79-13704

Printing and binding: Beltz Offsetdruck, Hemsbach/Bergstr.
2141/3140-54321

PREFACE

In a series of Summer Schools at Marktoberdorf, problems of programming methods and techniques have been dealt with. This fifth undertaking has the general theme of Program Construction. Constructing reliable software at calculable risks is the main concern of Software Engineering. Verification methods have drastically influenced the scene. Only correct programs can be verified, however. Analytic verification techniques have been developed recently into a method of joint construction of program and proof. This more synthetic approach in full consequence leads to general methods for Program Development by Successive Transformations. Both techniques have relative merits in particular situations; a general comparison seems to be difficult, although the transformation approach may be more promising. Moreover, each one method may be viewed as a border case of the other one.

More important than this technical competition is the general observation made at this Summer School as well as at the previous ones: Any reasonable effort in programming needs human thinking more than anything else. The Thinking Programmer knows about the Interplay between Invention and Formal Techniques. Mastering complexity is his aim, and while he needs powerful tools to achieve this, his best assets are the wisdom of knowing his limits.

F. L. Bauer

The International Summer School took place from July 26 to August 6, 1978, in Markt-oberdorf. This Summer School was organized under the auspices of the Technical University Munich, and was sponsored by the NATO Scientific Affairs Division under the 1978 Advanced Study Institutes Programme. Partial support for this conference was provided by the European Research Office, the National Science Foundation and the Bund der Freunde der Technischen Universität München.

CONTENTS

I. THE THINKING PROGRAMMER

Interplay Between Invention and Formal Techniques - The Thinking Programmer

As we all know, the programmable computer, with its current speed and storage, is a gadget without precedent. It is a gadget that we may appreciate in many different ways: in this series of lectures I would like to appreciate it as the embodiment of an intellectual challenge that is also without precedent, viz. the challenge to program the gadgets. This challenge seems unique in the combination of the possibility for unmastered complexity - programs are among the most complex things ever conceived - and the ultimate, but misleading, simplicity of a world of zeros and ones alone.

Programmable computers present an environment in which all unmastered complexity has not been forced upon us by unruly nature, but is most definitely man-made: if the programming community finds itself in a mess, it is a mess it has most definitely created itself. It is the circumstance that makes the activity of programming an ideal proving ground for the investigations concerning the effectiveness of all sorts of thinking habits and patterns of reasoning. On closer scrutiny the world of programming should provide us with a wealth of examples, both of effective and of clumsy thinking, while the fact that the programmer deals with artefacts should present the examples with greater clarity than almost any other intellectual activity. To such a scrutiny the series of lectures will be devoted.

If our personal thinking habits have been acquired in our past, we are responsible for our thinking habits in a more distant future, as we have still to live through part of what then will be our past. The lectures will be given under the assumption that the participants will acknowledge this responsibility.

As our examples from computing science are intended to cover a wide range we may hope to establish in passing a more explicit appreciation of why some techniques have been so successful and of why certain concepts indeed deserve the important role they play in our field.

E. W. Dijkstra

A more formal treatment of a less simple example

Edsger W.Dijkstra

For obvious reasons, most programming experiments that have been carried out in the exploration of formal techniques, dealt with simple, algebraic examples. For equally obvious reasons, the examples shown in tutorial texts on this subject are mostly of the same nature. (There has been a time when all of Computing Science seemed to boil down to massaging Euclid's Algorithm for the greatest common divisor!) This paper is primarily directed at remedying this situation.

*   *   *

Our ultimate goal is to develop a program that will transform expressions from infix notation to postfix notation. The subject matter to be manipulated by our program are therefore not integers, but strings of characters that may, or may not belong to certain syntactic categories. For variables of type "character string" we have to have at our disposal the analogon of high-school algebra (such as $(a > b \text{ and } c > d) \Rightarrow a + c > b + d$, etc.) that sufficed for the well-known numerical examples. Before embarking on our problem proper, we shall first introduce the necessary formal apparatus and the notation needed for its description.

We assume our syntax given in BNF. Let $< pqr >$ denote a syntactical category. We shall then express the fact that a string named K belongs to the syntactical category $< pqr >$ by

$$pqr(K) \quad .$$

For strings (named K , L , ...) and characters (named y , z , ...) we shall denote concatenation by juxtaposition, e.g. KL , Ky , Ky; etc.. If L may be any string and y may be any character, any non-empty string may be denoted by yL or Ly .

With any syntactic category $< pqr >$ we may associate the syntactic category $< bopqr >$ --"begin of a $< pqr >$"-- consisting of all the strings that either are a $< pqr >$ or can be extended at the right-hand side so as to become a $< pqr >$ or both. According to that definition the statement that the syntactic category $< pqr >$ is not empty --i.e. contains, as most useful syntactic categories, at least one string-- is equivalent with the predicate

$$bopqr(\text{ empty string}) \quad .$$

The formal definition of the predicate bopqr in terms of pqr --with
K and L denoting arbitrary strings-- is

$$bopqr(K) <=> (\underline{E} \ L: pqr(KL)) \qquad (1)$$

Separating the case that L is empty and the case that L is not empty, we
can rewrite (1) as

$$bopqr(K) <=> (pqr(K) \ \underline{or} \ (\underline{E} \ yL: pqr(KyL)))$$

which, thanks to (1), can be reduced to

$$bopqr(K) <=> (pqr(K) \ \underline{or} \ (\underline{E} \ y: bopqr(Ky))) \qquad (2)$$

from which we immediately derive

$$(bopqr(K) \ \underline{and} \ (\underline{A} \ y: \underline{non} \ bopqr(Ky))) => pqr(K) \qquad (3)$$

From (1) we derive further

$$bopqr(Ky) <=> (\underline{E} \ L: pqr(KyL))$$
$$= (\underline{E} \ yL: pqr(KyL))$$
$$=> bopqr(K) .$$

From this result

$$bopqr(Ky) => bopqr(K) \qquad (4)$$

follows that $< bopqr > = < bobopqr >$.

Because $pqr(K) => (\underline{E} \ L: pqr(KL))$ --L = the emptystring does the job--
a further consequence of (1) is

$$pqr(K) => bopqr(K) \qquad (5)$$

From our informal description of what we intended the notion "begin of"
to mean, the above is all intuitively obvious, and by now the reader may wonder
what all the fuss is about. The point is that we need such formulae as soon as
we wish to give a more rigorous treatment of a parser.

*   *   *

We intend to develop a mechanism called "sentsearch" that is intended
to recognize strings from the syntactical category $< sent >$. More precisely,
we assume that the input string can be scanned in the order from left to right
and reserve the identifier "x" for the next visible character of the input
string. If the input string starts with "a + b ...." , then we have initially

x = "a" ; after the execution of "move" the relation x = "+" will hold. Besides
assigning a new value to x , the primitive "move" can be viewed as also appending the old value of x to the right to "the strings of characters moved over"
or "the string of characters read" or "the string of characters that are no longer
visible."

Let S be the string of characters "moved over" by an activation of
sentsearch .

Note 1. When developing the body of sentsearch we may assume that a local
so-called "ghost variable" S is initialized at the beginning as the empty
string, that each call on "move" is implicitly preceded by "S:= Sx" , and
that upon termination S is handed back as a "ghost function value" to the
calling environment. (End of Note 1.)

In the case that the input sequence does not start with a < sent > ,
we want S to be the sequence that is insufficient to establish this fact,
while Sx is long enough to make this conclusion. That is, upon termination

bosent(S) and non bosent(Sx)

will hold. The first term expresses that not too much has been moved over, the
second term expresses that enough has been moved over. In the case that the
input string does start with a < sent > , we wish S to be equal to that
< sent > and assume our syntax for < sent > --about which nothing has been
given yet-- to satisfy

$$sent(L) \Rightarrow non \ (E \ y: bosent(Ly)) \tag{6}$$

Whether or not a < sent > has been found is to be recorded in the
global boolean c --short for "correct"-- and our complete specification of
sentsearch is that it has to establish Rs(S, x, c) , where Rs(S, x, c) is given
by

$$bosent(S) \ and \ non \ bosent(Sx) \ and \ c = sent(S) \tag{7}$$

Note 2. The consequence of assumption (6) is that when the input string starts
with a < sent > and the analysis has progressed to S equal to that < sent > ,
the term non bosent(Sx) is true for all possible values of x , i.e. sentsearch
can then terminate without inspecting the next visible character. The end of a
< sent > is assumed to be detectable without looking beyond it. (End of Note 2.)

We now give the syntax for $<\text{sent}>$:

$$<\text{sent}> ::= <\text{exp}> ; \qquad\qquad (8)$$

From this we have to derive the syntax for the syntactical category $<\text{bosent}>$:

$$<\text{bosent}> ::= <\text{sent}> \mid <\text{boexp}> \qquad\qquad (9)$$

Each $<\text{bosent}>$ can be derived by taking a $<\text{sent}>$ and removing at the right-hand side zero or more characters from it. Removal of zero characters gives the first alternative, removal of one or more charachters from "$<\text{exp}> ;$" boils down --because the semicolon is a single character-- to the removal of zero or more characters from $<\text{exp}>$: but that is by definition the syntactic category called $<\text{boexp}>$. Hence (9). The two alternatives are mutually exclusive, for we have for any string L :

$$\text{boexp}(L) \Rightarrow \underline{\text{non}} \ \text{sent}(L) \qquad\qquad (10)$$

This can be proved by deriving a contradiction from $\text{boexp}(L)$ $\underline{\text{and}}$ $\text{sent}(L)$. From $\text{boexp}(L)$ follows --according to (2)--

$$\text{exp}(L) \ \underline{\text{or}} \ (\underline{E} \ y\colon \text{boexp}(Ly))$$

We deal with both term separately:

$$\text{exp}(L) \Rightarrow \text{(on account of (8))}$$
$$\text{sent}(L;) \Rightarrow \text{(on account of (5))}$$
$$\text{bosent}(L;) \Rightarrow (\underline{E} \ y\colon \text{bosent}(Ly)) \qquad ;$$

the second term gives

$$(\underline{E} \ y\colon \text{boexp}(Ly)) \Rightarrow \text{(on account of (9))}$$
$$(\underline{E} \ y\colon \text{bosent}(Ly)) \ .$$

As both terms of the disjunction imply the same, we conclude that also

$$\text{boexp}(L) \Rightarrow (\underline{E} \ y\colon \text{bosent}(Ly)) \ .$$

According to (6), however,

$$\text{sent}(L) \Rightarrow \underline{\text{non}} \ (\underline{E} \ y\colon \text{bosent}(Ly)) \ .$$

The desired contradiction has been established and (10) has been proved.

Syntax rule (8) strongly suggests that the body of sentsearch should start with a call of expsearch. In order to design sentsearch in terms of expsearch we only need to know the net effect of expsearch and we propose in analogy to (7) that --when E is the string of characters moved over by expsearch-- the primitive expsearch will establish $\text{Re}(E, x, c)$, where $\text{Re}(E, x, c)$ is given by boexp(E) and non boexp(Ex) and c = exp(E)   (11)

Designing sentsearch in terms of expsearch means that we would like
to have theorems, such that from the truth of a relation of the form Re the
truth of relations of the form Rs can be concluded. There are three such
theorems.

Theorem 1.   (Re(L, x, c) and non c) ⇒ Rs(L, x, c)

Proof. Assumed:

0.   Re(L, x, c) and non c
       Derived:
1.   boexp(L)   with (11) from 0
2.   bosent(L)   with (9) from 1
3.   c = exp(L)   with (11) from 0
4.   non c   from 0
5.   non exp(L)   from 3 and 4
6.   non sent(Lx)   with (8) from 5
7.   non boexp(Lx)   with (11) from 0
8.   non bosent(Lx)   with (9) from 6 and 7
9.   non sent(L)   with (10) from 1
10.   c = sent(L)   from 4 and 9
11.   Rs(L, x, c)   with (7) from 2, 8 and 10
                                       (End of Proof of Theorem 1.)

Theorem 2.   (Re(L, x, c) and c and non semi(x)) ⇒ Rs(L, x, false)

Proof. Assumed:

0.   Re(L, x, c) and c and non semi(x)
       Derived:
1.   boexp(L)   with (11) from 0
2.   bosent(L)   with (9) from 1
3.   non semi(x)   from 0
4.   non sent(Lx)   with (8) from 3
5.   non boexp(Lx)   with (11) from 0
6.   non bosent(Lx)   with (9) from 4 and 5
7.   false = sent(L)   with (10) from 1
8.   Rs(L, x, false)   with (7) from 2, 6 and 7
                                       (End of Proof of Theorem 2.)

Theorem 3.   (Re(L, x, c) and c and semi(x)) => Rs(Lx, y, c)

Proof.   Assumed:

0.   Re(L, x, c) and c and semi(x)

        Derived:

1.   c = exp(L)   with (11) from 0
2.   c   from 0
3.   exp(L)   from 1 and 2
4.   semi(x)   from 0
5.   sent(Lx)   with (8) from 3 and 4
6.   c = sent(Lx)   from 2 and 5
7.   bosent(Lx)   with (5) from 5
8.   non bosent(Lxy)   with (6) from 5
9.   Rs(Lx, y, c)   with (7) from 7, 8 and 6.

                                    (End of Proof of Theorem 3.)

        And now a possible body of sentsearch is evident, when we realize
that its call on expsearch implies for the ghost variable S the assignment
"S:= SE"

proc sentsearch: { S = empty string}
                 expsearch {Re(S, x, c)};
                 if non c → skip
                 ▯ c and non semi(x) → c:= false
                 ▯ c and semi(x) → move
                 fi {Rs(S, x, c)}
corp

Note 3. Instead of Theorems 1 and 2 we could have discovered
Theorem 1'. (Re(L, x, c) and non c) => Rs(L, x, false)
Theorem 2'. (Re(L, x, c) and non semi(x)) => Rs(L, x, false).
This would have directed us towards the design of the body

proc sentsearch: expsearch;
                 if non c or non semi(x) → c:= false
                 ▯ c and semi(x) → move
                 fi
corp

which, thanks to de Morgan's Theorem, has no aborting alternative construct.
(End of note 3.)

We now consider for $<\exp>$ the following syntax

$$<\exp> ::= <\text{adder}> <\text{term}> \qquad (12)$$
$$<\text{adder}> ::= \{ <\text{term}> <\text{adop}> \} \qquad (13)$$
$$<\text{adop}> ::= + \mid - \qquad (14)$$

where the braces indicate a succession of zero or more instances of the enclosed. Because each instance of the syntactic category $<\text{adop}>$ is a single character, we derive

$$<\text{boexp}> ::= <\text{adder}> <\text{boterm}> \qquad (15)$$

from which follows
$$(\text{adder}(L) \text{ and } \text{boterm}(K)) \Rightarrow \text{boexp}(LK) \qquad (16)$$

But this gives us no way of proving that a string is not of the syntactic category $<\text{boexp}>$. In particular, the conclusion

$$(\text{adder}(L) \text{ and } \text{non } \text{boterm}(K)) \Rightarrow \text{non } \text{boexp}(LK) \qquad \text{is not justified.}$$

We must make --in analogy to (6)-- an assumption about $<\text{term}>$ and $<\text{adop}>$, and we assume
$$(\text{term}(L) \text{ and } \text{adop}(y)) \Rightarrow \text{non } \text{boterm}(Ly) \qquad (17)$$

This means, to start with, that with $\text{term}(L)$, $\text{term}(L')$, $\text{adop}(y)$, and $\text{adop}(y')$, we can conlude from $LyS = L'y'S'$, that $L = L'$ and $y = y'$. In other words, for every $<\text{boexp}>$ that starts with an instance of $<\text{term}> <\text{adop}>$, that instance is uniquely defined. By removing it from the front end , we are still left with a string from the syntactic category $<\text{boexp}>$, and therefore we are allowed to conclude

$$(\text{adder}(L) \text{ and } \text{non } \text{boexp}(K)) \Rightarrow \text{non } \text{boexp}(LK) \qquad (18)$$

This does not solve our problems yet, because, in order to use (18) in order to prove $\text{non } \text{boexp}(LK)$, we still have to prove $\text{non } \text{boexp}(K)$, be it only for a possibly shorter string K . We can do it, however, for a string related to the syntactic category $<\text{term}>$, as we can prove

$$(\text{boterm}(L) \text{ and } \text{non } \text{boterm}(Ly) \text{ and } \text{boexp}(Ly)) \Rightarrow (\text{term}(L) \text{ and } \text{adop}(y)) \quad (19)$$

The nonempty string Ly , satisfying $\text{boexp}(Ly)$ can have one of three different forms:

1) $<\text{term}> <\text{adop}> <\text{nonempty boexp}>$

This would imply, that L itself is of the form

$<\text{term}> <\text{adop}> <\text{boexp}>$

which, on account of its first two elements and (17) is incompatible with boterm(L)

2)   < term > < adop >

Because all instances of < adop > are single characters, this case implies

indeed   term(L) and adop(y)

3)   < boterm >

This case is incompatible with non boterm(Ly).

Hence, formula (19) has been proved.

Similarly, we should ask ourselves how to prove that some string is
not an element of the syntactic category < exp > . From (12) we can derive

$$(adder(L) \text{ and } term(K)) \Rightarrow exp(LK) \tag{20}$$

but, again, the conclusion

$$(adder(L) \text{ and non } term(K)) \Rightarrow non \ exp(LK) \quad \text{ is not justified,}$$

only --similar to (18)--

$$(adder(L) \text{ and non } exp(K)) \Rightarrow non \ exp(LK) \tag{21}$$

Analogous to (19) we have

$$(boterm(L) \text{ and } exp(L)) \Rightarrow term(L) \tag{22}$$

The term exp(L) tells us that the string L can have one of two different forms:

1)   < term >

This case indeed implies term(L)

2)   < nonempty adder > < term >

On account of (17) --and also (4)-- this case is exluded by boterm(L).

Hence formula (22) has been proved.

Finally we can conclude that

$$(exp(L) \text{ and } adop(y)) \Rightarrow adder(Ly) \tag{23}$$

The left-hand side tells us on account of (12) that Ly is of the form

< adder > < term > < adop >

and therefore (13) alows us to conclude adder(Ly) , and (23) has been proved.

Syntax rules (12) and (13) strongly suggest that the body of expsearch
should call --possibly repeatedly-- a new primitive termsearch. In order to
design expsearch in terms of termsearch we only need to know the net effect

of termsearch and we propose --in analogy to (7) and (11)-- that, when T is defined as the string of characters moved over by termsearch , the primitive termsearch will establish Rt(T, x, c) , where Rt(T, x, c) is given by

$$\text{boterm}(T) \text{ and } \underline{\text{non}} \text{ boterm}(Tx) \text{ and } c = \text{term}(T) \tag{24}$$

Designing expsearch in terms of termsearch means that we would like to have theorems allowing us to draw conclusions from the truth of a relation of the form Rt .

Theorem 4. (adder(L) and Rt(T, x, c) and c and adop(x)) $\Rightarrow$ adder(LTx)

Proof. Assumed:

0.　　adder(L) and Rt(T, x, c) and c and adop(x)

　　　Derived:

1.	c = term(T)	with (24) from 0
2.	c	from 0
3.	term(T)	from 1 and 2
4.	adder(L)	from 0
5.	exp(LT)	with (20) from 3 and 4
6.	adop(x)	from 0
7	adder(LTx)	with (23) from 5 and 6
		(End of Proof of Theorem 4.)

Theorem 5. (adder(L) and Rt(T, x, c) and non c) $\Rightarrow$ Re(LT, x, c)

Proof. Assumed:

0.　　adder(L) and Rt(T, x, c) and non c

　　　Derived:

1.	c = term(T)	with (24) from 0
2.	non c	from 0
3.	non term(T)	from 1 and 2
4.	boterm(T)	with (24) from 0
5.	non boterm(Tx)	with (24) from 0
6.	non boexp(Tx)	with (19) from 3, 4, and 5
7.	adder(L)	from 0
8.	non boexp(LTx)	with (18) from 6 and 7
9.	boexp(LT)	with (16) from 4 and 7
10.	non exp(T)	with (22) from 3 and 4
11.	non exp(LT)	with (21) from 7 and 10
12.	c = exp(LT)	from 2 and 11

13.   Re(LT, x, c)   with (11) from 8, 9, and 12

                                    (End of Proof of Theorem 5.)

__Theorem 6.__   (adder(L) __and__ Rt(T, x, c) __and__ __non__ adop(x)) $\Rightarrow$ Re(LT, x, c)

__Proof.__   Assumed:

0.   adder(L) __and__ Rt(T, x, c) __and__ __non__ adop(x)

        Derived:

1.   ~ boterm(T)   with (24) from 0
2.   adder(L)   from 0
3.   boexp(LT)   with (16) from 1 and 2
4.   __non__ boterm(Tx)   with (24) from 0
5.   __non__ adop(x)   from 0
6.   __non__ boexp(Tx)   with (19) from 1, 4, and 5
7.   __non__ boexp(LTx)   with (18) from 2 and 6
8.   c = term(T)   with (24) from 0
9.   c $\Rightarrow$ term(T)   from 8
10.   c $\Rightarrow$ exp(LT)   with (20) from 2 and 9
11.   __non__ c $\Rightarrow$ __non__ term(T)   from 8
12.   __non__ c $\Rightarrow$ __non__ exp(T)   with (22) from 1 and 11
13.   __non__ c $\Rightarrow$ __non__ exp(LT)   with (21) from 2 and 12
14.   c = exp(LT)   from 10 and 13
15.   Re(LT, x, c)   with (11) from 3, 7, and 14

                                    (End of Proof of Theorem 6.)

A corollary of Theorems 5 and 6 is

        (adder(L) __and__ Rt(T, x, c) __and__ __non__(c __and__ adop(x))) $\Rightarrow$ Re(LT, x, c)   .

A possible body for expsearch is by now pretty obvious when we realize that its
calls on termsearch imply for its ghost variable E   the assignment E:= ET (as
"move" implies E:= Ex). In the post-assertions for calls on termsearch the
relation E = LT has been given in order to define L in terms of E and   T.

__proc__ expsearch: {adder(E) because E = empty string}
                termsearch {E = LT __and__ adder(L) __and__ Rt(T, x, c)};
                __do__ c __and__ adop(x) $\rightarrow$ {adder(Ex)}
                      move {adder(E)};
                      termsearch {E = LT __and__ adder(L) __and__ Rt(T, x, c)}
                __od__ {Re(E, x, c)}

__corp__

We now consider for < term > the following syntax

$$< term > ::= < plier > < prim > \qquad (25)$$
$$< plier > ::= \{ < prim > < mult > \} \qquad (26)$$
$$< mult > ::= * \qquad (27)$$

and assume about < prim > and < mult >

$$(prim(L) \ \underline{and} \ mult(y)) \Rightarrow \underline{non} \ boprim(Ly) \qquad (28)$$

Formulae (25), (26), (27), and (28) are similar to (12), (13), (14), and (17) respectively, and all our conclusions since then carry over. With P as the string of characters moved over by a primitive primsearch that establishes —in analogy to (24)— $Rp(P, x, c)$, where $Rp(P, x, c)$ is given by

$$boprim(P) \ \underline{and} \ \underline{non} \ boprim(Px) \ \underline{and} \ c = prim(P) \qquad (29)$$

we can write immediately (!)

<u>proc</u> termsearch: $\{plier(T) \text{ because } T = empty \text{ string}\}$
        primsearch $\{T = LP \ \underline{and} \ plier(L) \ \underline{and} \ Rp(P, x, c)\}$;
        <u>do</u> c <u>and</u> $mult(x) \rightarrow \{plier(Tx)\}$
            move $\{plier(T)\}$;
            primsearch $\{T = LP \ \underline{and} \ plier(L) \ \underline{and} \ Rp(P, x, c)\}$
        <u>od</u> $\{Rt(T, x, c)\}$
<u>corp</u>

It is time to "close" our syntax:

$$< prim > ::= < iden > \mid < paren > \qquad (30)$$
$$< iden > ::= \{ < letter > \} < letter > \qquad (31)$$
$$< paren > ::= < open > < exp > < close > \qquad (32)$$
$$< open > ::= (\qquad (33)$$
$$< close > ::=) \qquad (34)$$
$$< letter > ::= a \mid b \mid c \mid d \mid e \mid f \qquad (35)$$

The important conclusions from (35) are:

1)   that the syntactic category < letter > is nonempty

2)   that all instances of the syntactic category < letter > are all single characters

3)   that these characters differ from the six previously introduced

characters.

From the nonemptiness of the syntactic category $<$ letter $>$ we draw
the same conclusion for $<$ iden $>$, hence for $<$ prim $>$, hence for $<$ term $>$,
hence for $<$ exp $>$, and hence for $<$ sent $>$. In particular we shall need to refer to

$$\text{boprim(empty string)} \tag{36}$$

From (30) we derive

$$< \text{boprim} > ::= < \text{boiden} > \mid < \text{boparen} > \tag{37}$$

From (31) and (32) respectively, we derive

$$(\text{boiden}(y) = \text{letter}(y)) \quad \underline{\text{and}} \ \underline{\text{non}} \ \text{iden(empty string)} \tag{38}$$
$$(\text{boparen}(y) = \text{open}(y)) \quad \underline{\text{and}} \ \underline{\text{non}} \ \text{paren(empty string)} \tag{39}$$

and hence

$$\text{boprim}(y) = (\text{letter}(y) \ \underline{\text{or}} \ \text{open}(y)) \tag{40}$$
$$\underline{\text{non}} \ \text{prim(empty string)} \tag{41}$$

From (31) we derive

$$< \text{boiden} > ::= \{ \ < \text{letter} > \ \} \tag{42}$$

and, because instances of $<$ letter $>$ are single characters

$$\underline{\text{non}} \ \text{letter}(y) \Rightarrow \underline{\text{non}} \ \text{boiden}(Ly) \tag{43}$$

From (32) we derive

$$< \text{boparen} > ::= \text{empty string} \mid < \text{open} > < \text{boexp} > \mid < \text{paren} > \tag{44}$$

The three alternatives for $<$ boparen $>$ are mutually exclusive: for
the first one versus the two others, it is obvious. For the last two I can
prove the mutual exclusion only by using the technique of the bracket count.

Lemma 1. exp(L) implies that the number of instances of $<$ open $>$ in L
equals the number of instances of $<$ close $>$ in L .

Lemma 2. boexp(L) implies that the number of instances of $<$ open $>$ in L
equals at least the number of instances of $<$ close $>$ in L .

Lemma 1 follows from the fact that in the original syntax --i.e. without the
"begin-of"-derivations-- the only rule using $<$ open $>$ or $<$ close $>$, viz.
(32), introduces them pairwise. Lemma 2 follows from the observation that
in this only introduction, the instance of $<$ open $>$ precedes that of $<$ close $>$.

(Presumably official syntactic theory has more formal proofs for these two Lemmata; I am fully convinced of their correctness by the preceding four lines of argument.)

The last two alternatives of (44) are mutually exclusive, because from Lemma 2 we can conclude that in a string of the form $<$ open $><$ boexp $>$ the number of instances of $<$ open $>$ exceeds the number of instances of $<$ close $>$, while in a string of the form $<$ paren $>$ these numbers are equal on account of Lemma 1. In other words:

$$(\text{open}(y) \ \underline{\text{and}} \ \text{boexp}(L)) \Rightarrow \underline{\text{non}} \ \text{paren}(yL) \tag{45}$$

or, equivalently

$$\text{paren}(yL) \Rightarrow (\text{open}(y) \ \underline{\text{and}} \ \underline{\text{non}} \ \text{boexp}(L)) \tag{45'}$$

Expressed in terms of paren and boparen only, also holds

$$\text{paren}(L) \Rightarrow \underline{\text{non}}(\underline{E} \ z : \text{boparen}(Lz)) \tag{46}$$

This formula can be derived by deriving a contradiction from the truth of the left-hand side and the falsity of the right-hand side. From paren(L) and (39) we conclude that L is nonempty, and we may write L = yK , such that, on account of (45'), we deduce

$$\text{open}(y) \ \underline{\text{and}} \ \underline{\text{non}} \ \text{boexp}(K)$$

On the other hand, $(\underline{E} \ z : \text{boparen}(yKz))$ is, according to (1), equivalent to

$$(\underline{E} \ z, M : \text{paren}(yKzM))$$

or

$$(\underline{E} \ M, z : \text{paren}(yKMz))$$

Rule (32) then allows us to conclude

$$\text{open}(y) \ \underline{\text{and}} \ (\underline{E} \ M : \text{exp}(KM)) \ \underline{\text{and}} \ (\underline{E} \ z : \text{close}(z)) \ .$$

The second term is equivalent to boexp(K), we have the contradiction we were looking for, and hence, (46) has been proved.

<u>Theorem 7</u>. (L = empty string <u>and</u> <u>non</u>(letter(x) <u>or</u> open(x))) $\Rightarrow$ Rp(L, x, false)
<u>Proof</u>. Assumed:

0.   L = empty string <u>and</u> <u>non</u>(letter(x) <u>or</u> open(x))
       Derived:
1.   L = empty string   from 0
2.   boprim(L)   with (36) from 1
3.   <u>non</u>(letter(x) <u>or</u> open(x))   from 0

4.	non boprim(x)	with (40) from 3
5.	x = Lx	from 1
6.	non boprim(Lx)	from 4 and 5
7.	false = prim(L)	with (41) from 1
8.	Rp(L, x, false)	with (29) from 2, 6, and 7
		(End of Proof of Theorem 7.)

Theorem 8. (iden(yL) and letter(x)) $\Rightarrow$ iden(yLx)

Proof. Evident from (31)

Theorem 9. (iden(yL) and non letter(x)) $\Rightarrow$ Rp(yL, x, true)

Proof. Assumed:

0.	iden(yL) and non letter(x)	
	Derived:	
1.	iden(yL)	from 0
2.	boiden(yL)	with (5) from 1
3.	boprim(yL)	with (37) from 2
4.	boiden(y)	with (4) from 2
5.	letter(y)	with (38) from 4
6.	non open(y)	from 5
7.	non boparen(y)	with (39) from 6
8.	non boparen(yLx)	with (4) from 7
9.	non letter(x)	from 0
10.	non boiden(yLx)	with (43) from 9
11.	non boprim(yLx)	with (37) from 8 and 10
12.	true = prim(yL)	with (30) from 1
13.	Rp(yL, x, true)	with (29) from 3, 11, and 12
		(End of Proof of Theorem 9.)

See Note 4 on page **17**

Theorem 10. (open(y) and Re(E, x, c) and c and close(x)) $\Rightarrow$ Rp(yEx, z, c)

Proof. Assumed:

0.	open(y) and Re(E, x, c) and c and close(x)	
	Derived:	
1.	c = exp(E)	with (11) from 0
2.	c	from 0
3.	exp(E)	from 1 and 2
4.	open(y)	from 0
5.	close(x)	from 0
6.	paren(yEx)	with (32) from 3, 4, 5

7.	prim(yEx)	with (30) from 6
8.	boprim (yEx)	with (5) from 7
9.	non boparen(yExz)	with (46) from 6
10.	non letter(y)	from 4
11.	non boiden(y)	with (38) from 10
12.	non boiden(yExz)	with (4) from 11
13.	non boprim(yExz)	with (37) from 9 and 12
14.	c = prim(yEx)	from 2 and 7
15.	Rp(yEx, z, c)	with (29) from 8, 13, and 14
		(End of Proof of Theorem 10.)

Theorem 11. (open(y) and Re(E, x, c) and non c) $\Rightarrow$ Rp(yE, x, c)

Proof. Assumed:

0. open(y) and Re(E, x, c) and non c

Derived:

1.	boexp(E)	with (11) from 0
2.	open(y)	from 0
3.	boparen(yE)	with (44) from 1 and 2
4.	boprim(yE)	with (37) from 3
5.	non letter(y)	from 2
6.	non boiden(y)	with (38) from 5
7.	non boiden(yEx)	with (4) from 6
8.	non boexp(Ex)	with (11) from 0
9.	c = exp(E)	with (11) from 0
10.	non c	from 0
11.	non exp(E)	from 9 and 10
12.	non paren(yEx)	with (32) from (2 and) 11
13.	non boparen(yEx)	with (44) from 8 and 12
14.	non boprim(yEx)	with (37) from 7 and 13
15.	non boiden(yE)	with (4) from 6
16.	non iden(yE)	with (5) from 15
17.	non paren(yE)	with (45) from 1 and 2
18.	non prim(yE)	with (30) from 16 and 17
19.	c = prim(yE)	from 10 and 18
20.	Rp(yE, x, c)	with (29) from 4, 14 and 19
		(End of Proof of Theorem 11.)

Theorem 12. (open(y) and Re(E, x, c) and non close(x)) ⇒ Rp(yE, x, false)

Proof. Assumed:

0.   open(y) and Re(E, x, c) and non close(x)

Derived:

1.	boexp(E)	with (11) from 0
2.	open(y)	from 0
3.	boparen(yE)	with (44) from 1 and 2
4.	boprim(yE)	with (37) from 3
5.	non letter(y)	from 2
6.	non boiden(y)	with (38) from 5
7.	non boiden(yEx)	with (4) from 6
8.	non boexp(Ex)	with (11) from 0
9.	non close(x)	from 0
10.	non paren(yEx)	with (32) from 9
11.	non boparen(yEx)	with (44) from 8 and 10
12.	non boprim(yEx)	with (37) from 7 and 11
13.	non boiden(yE)	with (4) from 6
14.	non iden(yE)	with (5) from 13
15.	non paren(yE)	with (45) from 1 and 2
16.	false = prim(yE)	with (30) from 14 and 15
17.	Rp(yE, x, false)	with (29) from 4, 12, and 16

Note 4. In proofs 9 through 12, I refer a number of times to formula (4), but it is not really that one that is needed, but the obvious generalization

$$bopqr(KL) \Rightarrow bopqr(K) \quad ;$$

sometimes it is used in the inverted, but equivalent, form

$$non \; bopqr(K) \Rightarrow non \; bopqr(KL) \quad .$$

Furthermore I offer my apologies for the great similarity between the proofs of Theorem 11 and Theorem 12. The total text could have been shortened by first stating a Lemma 3 that captures the intersection of the two proofs. It is just too expensive to change in this respect this document, which is not intended to be submitted for publication. (End of Note 4.)

With Theorems 7 through 12 we have prepared the way for the following design of a body for primsearch .

```
proc primsearch : {P = empty string}
        if non(letter(x) or open(x)) → {Rp(P, x, false)}
              c:= false {Rp(P, x, c)}
        ▯ letter(x) → move {P ≐ yL and iden(P)};
              do letter(x) → {P = yL and iden(Px)}
                    move {P = yL and iden(P)}
              od {Rp(P, x, true};
              c:= true {Rp(P, x, c)}
        ▯ open(x) → move {P = y and open(y)};
              expsearch {P = yE and open(y) and Re(E, x, c)};
              if c and close(x) → {Rp(Px, z, c)}
                    move {Rp(P, x, c)}
              ▯ non c → skip {Rp(P, x, c)}
              ▯ non close(x) → {Rp(P, x, false}
                    c:= false {Rp(P, x, c)}
              fi {Rp(P, x, c)}
        fi {Rp(P, x, c)}
corp
```

Now our syntax has been "closed" by (30) through (35), we can at last
fulfill our obligation of proving what up till now have been assumptions, viz.

$$sent(L) \Rightarrow non (E\ y: bosent(Ly)) \tag{6}$$
$$(term(L)\ and\ adop(y)) \Rightarrow non\ boterm(Ly) \tag{17}$$
$$(prim(L)\ and\ mult(y)) \Rightarrow non\ boprim(Ly) \tag{28}$$

Relation (6) follows from the fact that $bosent(Ly)$ implies $boexp(L)$, and
from our syntax for $< exp >$, $< term >$, $< prim >$, and $< iden >$, this
implies that L does not contain a semicolon; $sent(L)$ implies according to
(8) that L does contain a semicolon. This is the contradiction that follows
from the assumption that (6) does not hold; hence (6) has been proved. In
order to prove (17) --under the assumption of (28)!-- we observe that with

$$< term > ::= < plier > < prim >$$
$$< boterm > ::= < plier > < boprim >$$

the negation of (17)

$$term(L)\ and\ adop(y)\ and\ boterm(Ly)$$

would imply that $< prim > < adop >$ could be of the form $< boprim >$. It therefore suffices to prove that

$$(\text{prim}(L) \ \underline{\text{and}} \ \text{op}(y)) \Rightarrow \underline{\text{non}} \ \text{boprim}(Ly) \qquad \text{with}$$
$$< \text{op} > ::= < \text{adop} > \ | \ < \text{mult} > \ .$$

This last implication can be proved by deriving a contradiction from its negation:

$$\text{prim}(L) \ \underline{\text{and}} \ \text{op}(y) \ \underline{\text{and}} \ \text{boprim}(Ly) \ ;$$

it can be done using Lemma 1 and Lemma 2, and I gladly leave this detail to
the reader.

* * *

In view of the lenth of this report, the transformation from infix to
postfix notation --- on page 2 announced as "our ultimate goal"! --- will
be postponed and left for some later document.

History.

Nearly three years ago I wrote a seven-page report, EWD375 "A non
algebraic example of a constructive correctness proof." in which (essentially)
the same problem has been tackled as here. Last January, while I was lecturing
in La Jolla, Jack Mazola urged me to show a more complicated example; I tried
to reconstruct the argument of EWD375 on the spot and failed.

Last February, when I was home again, I reread EWD375 and it left me
greatly dissatisfied. I remembered that EWD375 had been a cause for great enthusiasm when it was written, and I could not understand that enthusiasm anymore.
I found EWD375 very hard to read and hardly convincing: what three years ago I
had considered as "a proof" now struck me at best as "helpful heuristics". (A
strange experience to be nearly ashamed of what had been a source of pride only
a few years ago!)

It was now clear why, last January in La Jolla, I was unable to give
on the spot a formal treatment of the syntax analyzer: it was not just a failure
of memory, it was also a profound change in my standards of rigor (undoubtedly
also caused by the fact that over the last few years I burned a few fingers!).
I decided to forget EWD375 and to start again from scratch. This document is
the result of that effort.

It has been surprisingly hard to write. After the first six pages had been written --I had only dealt with sentsearch-- there has been a long pause before I gathered the strength and the courage to tackle expsearch, and for a few weeks I put the unfinished document away. To undertake the treatment of primsearch proved to be another hurdle.

What the final document does not show is that the notation eventually used for the assertions, the theorems and the proofs is the result of many experiments. Before we invented, for instance, the trick to use the predicate $pqr(K)$ to denote that the string K belongs to the syntactic category $< pqr >$ all our formulae became unwieldy; so they did, as long as we indicated concatenation of strings with an explicit operator instead of --as eventually-- just by juxtaposition. I hesitated, when I wrote --as on the middle of page 5-- $sent(L;)$ because I saw problems coming by the time that I had to write such predicates for strings containing unmatched parentheses; the trick of introducing $< open >$ and $< close >$ solved that problem. Instead of (8) I should have written

$$< sent > ::= < exp > < semi >$$
$$< semi > ::= \; ;$$

Again, at the time of writing, also this report has been a source of great excitement. This is somewhat amazing as it does not contain a single deep thought! Is it, because we now still remember how much more beautiful it is than all the rejected efforts? I wonder how I shall feel about it in a few years time!

Acknowledgement.

I am greatly indebted to W.H.J.Feijen, M.Rem, A.J.Martin and C.S.Scholten, whose encouragement and active participation have been absolutely essential. And I am grateful to Jack Mazola for prividing me with the incentive.

19th of March 1976   prof.dr.Edsger W.Dijkstra
Burroughs   Burroughs Research Fellow
Plataanstraat 5
NUENEN - 4565
The Netherlands

Stationary behaviour of some ternary networks

Edsger W.Dijkstra

We consider a graph of N vertices in which each vertex has a multiplicity three, i.e. in which three edges meet at each vertex. Because the number of edges equals $3N/2$, we conclude that N must be even.

Each edge connects two different vertices --i.e. no "auto-cycles"--; the graph is partially directed, more precisely: each vertex has an outgoing edge, an undirected edge, and an ingoing edge. (Such graphs exist for all even $N \geq 4$.)

In the initial situation, 3N numbers --which can be assumed to be all different from each other-- are placed at the vertices, three at each vertex. A move consists of sending for each vertex:
1)   its maximum value to the neighbour vertex at the other end of its outgoing edge,
2)   its medium value to the neighbour vertex at the other end of its undirected edge,
3)   its minimum value to the neighbour vertex at the other end of its ingoing edge,
4)   and of accepting three new values from its neighbours.
(We can also view a move as $3N/2$ simultaneous swaps of values at the end of each edge.)

After the move, again three values are placed at each vertex, and, therefore, a next move is possible. We are interested in the periodic travelling patterns as will occur in infinite sequences of moves.

Suppose that, before distributing the 3N values among the vertices, we had painted the N largest values red, the N smallest values blue, and the N remaining values in between white; then we are interested in final patterns in which at each vertex a red, a white, and a blue value can be found. Note that such a distribution of colours is stable: in each move two white values will be swapped along each undirected edge, and along each directed edge a red and a blue value will be swapped --the red one will go in the direction of the arrow, the blue one will travel in the opposite direction-- ; after the move, again all three colours will be present in each vertex.

We furthermore require that the period of the stationary behaviour is exactly N moves. Below we shall give constructions of such networks for each $N \geq 4$ with the property that the desired stationary behaviour as described above will be established after a finite number of moves, independently of the initial distribution of the 3N values. The cases N = 4Z and N = 4Z + 2 are treated separately.

<u>N = 4Z</u> .

The directed edges form a single directed cycle; the 2Z undirected edges connect the pairs of in this directed cycle diametrically opposite vertices. (If the vertices are numbered from O through N-1 , then a directed edge goes from vertex nr.i to vertex nr.$(i+1)$<u>mod</u> N , and undirected edge connects vertex nr.i and vertex nr.$(i+2Z)$<u>mod</u> N .)

<u>Proof of stabilization</u>. Let k be the maximum value, such that the k largest values are all placed in different vertices; initially we have $1 \leq k \leq N$. We shall first show that within a finite number of moves, k = N by showing that, if $k < N$, within a finite number of moves k will be increased by at least 1 . In each move the k largest values will each be moved to the next vertex in the cycle: as long as k does not increase, the definition of k implies that the k+1st largest must share a vertex with exactly one of the k largest ones. It is, therefore, the medium value in that vertex and will be sent away along the undirected edge: relative to the rotating pattern of the k largest ones, it advances in the cycle over 2Z-1 places. Because $gcd(4Z, 2Z-1) = 1$, the k+1st largest value, while oscillating along an undirected edge, must find itself within at most N-1 moves in a vertex that is not also occupied by one of the k largest values: that is the moment that k is increased by at least one. Hence, eventually each vertex will have exactly one red value.

For reasons of symmetry, eventually each vertex will also have exactly one blue value. But when both red and blue values are evenly distributed among the vertices, so will the white ones be. Hence the stable state will have been reached. The period of the cyclic behaviour obviously equals N . (End of proof of stabilization.)

N = 4Z + 2 .

Here the directed edges of the graph form two cycles of length 2Z+1 each.
The 2Z+1 undirected edges each connect one vertex of the one cycle with one
vertex of the other cycle. (Note that the way in which each vertex of the one
cycle is paired with exactly one vertex of the other cycle, is arbitrary.)

Proof of stabilization.   Let k be defined as in the previous proof
and assume k $<$ N . The k largest values are in general divided over the
two cycles; in each they form a pattern that will rotate and will return in
its original position in 2Z+1 moves. Within at most N-1 moves, however,
k will have been increased. Consider again the k+1st largest one. As long
as it shares a vertex with one of the k largest ones, it will oscillate
along an undirected edge. During two moves it returns to a vertex of a cycle
in which in the meantime the subset of the k largest values has moved over
2 places. Because gcd(2Z+1, 2) = 1, from one of the cycles at most 2Z double
moves, or in toto N-1 single moves are possible, and it must find itself in
a vertex that is not also occupied by one of the k largest ones. Eventually, each vertex will have exactly one red value, etc.. The period is
the smallest common multiple of 2Z+1 --the period of the red and the blue
values-- and 2 --the period of the white ones--; because 2Z+1 is odd,
the total period = N . (End of proof of stabilization.)

The above problem and solution emerged during my "Tuesday afternoon
discussion" of May 17, 1977, with Feijen, Prins, Peeters, Martin, and Bul-
terman. It was Feijen who posed the problem as a generalization of the
binary network --without undirected edges-- that I had shown in my lectures
that morning. The solution has been recorded because we liked the argument,
in spite of the fact that it is far from giving a sharp upper bound on the
number of moves needed.

Plataanstraat 5   prof.dr.Edsger W.Dijkstra
5671 AL NUENEN   Burroughs Research Fellow
The Netherlands

Finding the correctness proof of a concurrent program

Edsger W.Dijkstra

Introduction.

In this paper we want to do more than just giving another --be it un-
usual-- example of the utility of the first-order predicate calculus in
proving the correctness of programs. In addition we want to show how,
thanks to a systematic use of the first-order predicate calculus, fairly
general --almost "syntactic"-- considerations about the formal manipulations
involved can provide valuable guidance for the smooth discovery of an otherwise surprising argument.

For proofs of program correctness two fairly different styles have
been developed, "operational" proofs and "assertional" proofs. Operational
correctness proofs are based on a model of computation, and the corresponding
computational histories are the subject matter of the considerations. In
assertional correctness proofs the possibility of interpreting the program
text as executable code is ignored and the program text itself is the subject
matter of the formal considerations.

Operational proofs --although older and, depending on one's education,
perhaps more "natural" than assertional proofs-- have proved to be tricky to
design. For more complicated programs the required classification of the
possible computational histories tends to lead to an exploding case analysis
in which it becomes very clumsy to verify that no possible sequence of events
has been overlooked, and it was in response to the disappointing experiences
with operational proofs that the assertional style has been developed.

The design of an assertional proof --as we shall see below-- may present problems, but, on the whole, experience seems to indicate that assertional
proofs are much more effective than operational ones in reducing the gnawing
uncertainty whether nothing has been overlooked. This experience, already
gained while dealing with sequential programs, was strongly confirmed while
dealing with concurrent programs: the circumstance that the ratios of the
speeds with which the sequential components proceed is left undefined greatly
increases the class of computational histories that an operational argument
would have to cover!

In the following we shall present the development of an assertional correctness proof of a program of N-fold concurrency. The program has been taken from the middle of a whole sequence of concurrent programs of increasing complexity --the greater complexity at the one end being the consequence of finer grains of interleaving-- . For brevity's sake we have selected here from this sequence the simplest item for which the assertional correctness proof displays the characteristic we wanted to show. (It is not the purpose of this paper to provide supporting material in favour of the assertional style: in fact, our example is so simple that an operational proof for it is still perfectly feasible.)

*   *   *

In the following y denotes a vector of N components y[i] for $0 \leq i < N$. With the identifier f we shall denote a vector-valued function of a vector-valued argument, and the algorithm concerned solves the equation

$$y = f(y) \tag{1}$$

or, introducing f_0, f_1, f_2,... for the components of f

$$y[i] = f_i(y) \quad \text{for } 0 \leq i < N \quad . \tag{2}$$

It is assumed that the initial value of y and the function f are such that repeated assignments of the form

$$< y[i] := f_i(y) > \tag{3}$$

will lead in a finite number of steps to y being a solution of (1). In (3) we have used Lamport's notation of the angle brackets: they enclose "atomic actions" which can be implemented by ensuring between their executions mutual exclusion in time. For the sake of termination we assume that the sequence of i-values for which the assignments (3) are carried out is (the proper begin of) a sequence in which each i-value occurs infinitely often. (We deem this property guaranteed by the usual assumption of "finite speed ratios"; he who refuses to make that assumption can read the following as a proof of partial correctness.)

For the purpose of this paper it suffices to know that functions f exist such that with a proper initial value of y equation (1) will be solved

by a finite number of assignments (3). How for a given function f and
initial value y this property can be established is not the subject of
this paper. (He who refuses to assume that the function f and the initial
value of y have this property is free to do so: he can, again, read the
following as a proof of partial correctness that states that when our
concurrent program has terminated, (1) is satisfied.)

Besides the vector y there is --for the purpose of controlling ter-
mination-- a vector h , with boolean elements $h[i]$ for $0 \leq i < N$, all
of which are true to start with. We now consider the following program of
N-fold concurrency, in which each atomic action assigns a value to at most
one of the array elements mentioned. We give the program first and shall
explain the notation afterwards.

The concurrent program we are considering consists of the following
N components $cpnt_i$ $(0 \leq i < N)$:

$cpnt_i$:
    LO: do $< (E\ j: h[j]) > \rightarrow$
    L1: $< \underline{if}\ y[i] = f_i(y) \rightarrow h[i] := false >$
                   $[\ y[i] \neq f_i(y) \rightarrow y[i] := f_i(y) > $;
    L2j: $(\underline{A}\ j: < h[j] := true >)$
            fi
      od

In line LO , "$(E\ j: h[j])$" is an abbreviation for

$$(E\ j: 0 \leq j < N: h[j])\qquad ;$$

for the sake of brevity we shall use this abbreviation throughout this paper.
By writing $< (E\ j: h[j]) >$ in the guard we have indicated that the inspection
whether a true $h[j]$ can be found is an atomic action.

The opening angle bracket " < " in L1 has two corresponding closing
brackets, corresponding to the two "atomic alternatives"; it means that in
the same atomic actions the guards are evaluated and either "$h[i] := false$"
or "$y[i] := f_i(y)$" is executed. In the latter case, N separate atomic
actions follow, each setting an $h[j]$ to true: in line L2j we have used

the abbreviation "$(\underline{A} \; j: \; < h[j]:= true >)$" for the program that performs
the N atomic actions $< h[0]:= true >$ through $< h[N-1]:= true >$ in some
order which we don't specify any further.

In our target state y is a solution of (1), or, more explicitly

$$(\underline{A} \; j: \; y[j] = f_j(y)) \tag{4}$$

holds. We first observe that (4) is an invariant of the repeatable statements,
i.e. once true it remains true. In the alternative constructs always the
first atomic alternative will then be selected, and this leaves y , and
hence (4) unaffected. We can even conclude a stronger invariant

$$\underline{non} \; (\underline{E} \; j: \; h[j]) \; \underline{and} \; (\underline{A} \; j: \; y[j] = f_j(y)) \tag{5}$$

or, equivalently $\quad (\underline{A} \; j: \; \underline{non} \; h[j]) \; \underline{and} \; (\underline{A} \; j: \; y[j] = f_j(y)) \tag{5'}$

for, when (5) holds, no assignment $h[i]:= false$ can destroy the truth of
$(\underline{A} \; j: \; \underline{non} \; h[j])$. When (4) holds, the assumption of finite speed ratios
implies that within a finite number of steps (5) will hold. But then the
guards of the repetitive constructs are false, and all components will terminate
nicely with (4) holding. The critical point is: can we guarantee that none
of the components terminates too soon?

We shall give an assertional proof, following the technique which has
been pioneered by Gries and Owicki [1]. We call an assertion "universally
true" if and only if it holds between any two atomic actions --i.e. "always"
with respect to the computation, "everywhere" with respect to the text-- .
More precisely: proving the universal truth of an assertion amounts to showing
1)   that it holds at initialization
2)   that its truth is an invariant of each atomic action.

In order to prove that none of the components terminates too soon, i.e.
that termination implies that (4) holds, we have to prove the universal truth of

$$(\underline{E} \; j: \; h[j]) \; \underline{or} \; (\underline{A} \; j: \; y[j] = f_j(y)) \quad . \tag{6}$$

Relation (6) certainly holds when the N components are started because
initially all $h[j]$ are true. We are only left with the obligation to
prove the invariance of (6); the remaining part of this paper is devoted
to that proof, and to how it can be discovered.

We get a hint of the difficulties we may expect when trying to prove the invariance of (6) with respect to the first atomic alternative of L1:

$$< y[i] = f_i(y) \rightarrow h[i] := false >$$

as soon as we realize that the first term of (6) is a compact notation for

$$h[0] \; \underline{or} \; h[1] \; \underline{or} \; \ldots \; \underline{or} \; h[N-1]$$

which only changes from true to false when, as a result of "h[i]:= false" the <u>last</u> true h[j] disappears. That is ugly!

We often prove mathematical theorems by proving a stronger --but, somehow, more manageable-- theorem instead. In direct analogy: instead of trying to prove the invariant truth of (6) directly, we shall try to prove the invariant truth of a stronger assertion that we get by replacing the conditions $y[j] = f_j(y)$ by stronger ones. Because <u>non</u> R is stronger than Q provided (Q <u>or</u> R) holds, we can strengthen (6) into

$$(\underline{E} \; j: h[j]) \; \underline{or} \; (\underline{A} \; j: \underline{non} \; R_j) \tag{7}$$

provided

$$(\underline{A} \; j: y[j] = f_j(y) \; \underline{or} \; R_j) \tag{8}$$

holds. (Someone who sees these heuristics presented in this manner for the first time may experience this as juggling, but I am afraid that it is quite standard and that we had better get used to it.)

What have we gained by the introduction of the N predicates R_j ? Well, the freedom to choose them! More precisely: the freedom to <u>define</u> them in such a way that we can <u>prove</u> the universal truth of (8) --which is structurally quite pleasant-- in the usual fashion, while the universal truth of (7) --which is structurally equally "ugly" as (6)-- follows more or less directly from the <u>definition</u> of the R_j's : that is the way in which we may hope that (7) is more "manageable" than the original (6).

In order to find a proper definition of the R_j's, we analyse our obligation to <u>prove</u> the invariance of (8).

If we only looked at the invariance of (8), we might think that a definition of the R_j's in terms of y :

$$R_j = (y[j] \neq f_j(y))$$

would be a sensible choice. A moment's reflection tells us that that
definition does not help: it would make (8) universally true by definition,
and the right-hand terms of (6) and (7) would be identical, whereas under the
truth of (8), (7) was intended to be stronger than (6).

For two reasons we are looking for a definition of the R_j's in which
the y does not occur: firstly, it is then that we can expect the proof of
the universal truth of (8) to amount to something --and, thereby, to contribute
to the argument-- , secondly, we would like to conclude the universal truth
of (7) --which does not mention y at all!-- from the definition of the
R_j's . In other words, we propose a definition of the R_j's which does not
refer to y at all: only with such a definition does the replacement of
(6) by (7) and (8) localize our dealing with y completely to the proof
of the universal truth of (8).

Because we want to define the R_j's independently of y , because
initially we cannot assume that for some j-value $y[j] = f_j(y)$ holds, and
because (8) must hold initially, we must guarantee that initially

$$(\underline{A} \; j: R_j) \tag{9}$$

holds. Because, initially, all the $h[j]$ are true, the initial truth of
(9) is guaranteed if the R_j's are defined in such a way that we have

$$(\underline{E} \; j: \underline{non} \; h[j]) \; \underline{or} \; (\underline{A} \; j: R_j) \; . \tag{10}$$

We observe, that (10) is again of the recognized ugly form we are trying to
get rid of. We have some slack --that is what the R_j's are being introduced for-- and this is the moment to decide to try to come away with a
stronger --but what we have called: "structurally more pleasant"-- relation
for the definition of the R_j's , from which (10) immediately follows. The
only candidate I can think of is

$$(\underline{A} \; j: \underline{non} \; h[j] \; \underline{or} \; R_j) \tag{11}$$

and we can already divulge that, indeed, (11) will be one of the defining
equations for the R_j's .

From (11) it follows that the algorithm will now start with all the

. R_j's true. From (8) it follows that the truth of R_j can be appreciated as "the equation $y[j] = f_j(y)$ need not be satisfied", and from (7) it follows that in our final state we must have all the R_j's equal to false.

Let us now look at the alternative construct

$$L1: \quad < \underline{if}\ y[i] = f_i(y) \rightarrow h[i] := false >$$
$$[\!]\ y[i] \neq f_i(y) \rightarrow y[i] := f_i(y) > ;$$
$$L2j: \qquad\qquad (\underline{A}\ j: < h[j] := true >)$$
$$\underline{fi} \qquad .$$

We observe that the first alternative sets $h[i]$ false, and that the second one, as a whole, sets all $h[j]$ true. As far as the universal truth of (11) is concerned, we therefore conclude that in the first alternative R_i is allowed to, and hence <u>may</u> become false, but that in the second alternative as a whole, all R_j's <u>must</u> become true.

Let us now confront the two atomic alternatives with (8). Because, when the first atomic alternative is selected, only $y[i] = f_i(y)$ has been observed, the universal truth of (8) is guaranteed to be an invariant of the first atomic alternative, provided it enjoys the following property (12):

In the execution of the first atomic alternative

$$< y[i] = f_i(y) \rightarrow h[i] := false >$$

<u>no</u> R_j for $j \neq i$ changes from true to false. $\qquad\qquad$ (12)

Confronting the second atomic alternative

$$< y[i] \neq f_i(y) \rightarrow y[i] := f_i(y) >$$

with (8), and observing that upon its completion <u>none</u> of the relations $y[j] = f_j(y)$ needs to hold, we conclude that the second atomic alternative itself must already cause a final state in which all the R_j's are true, in spite of the fact that the subsequent assignments $h[j] := true$ --which would each force an R_j to true on account of (11)-- have not been executed yet. In short: in our definition for the R_j's we must include besides (11) <u>another</u> reason why an R_j should be defined to be true.

As it stands, the second atomic alternative only modifies y , but we had decided that the definition of the R_j's would not be expressed in terms

of y ! The only way in which we can formulate the additional reason for an
R_j to be true is in terms of an <u>auxiliary</u> variable (to be introduced in a
moment), whose value is changed in conjunction with the assignment to $y[i]$.
The value of that auxiliary variable has to force each R_j to true until the
subsequent assignment $< h[j]:= true >$ does so via (11). Because the second
atomic alternative is followed by N subsequent, separate atomic actions
$< h[j]:= true >$ --one for each value of j -- , it stands to reason that we
introduce for the i-th component $cpnt_i$ an auxiliary local boolean array
s_i with elements $s_i[j]$ for $0 \le j < N$. Their initial (and "neutral")
value is true. The second atomic alternative of L1 sets them all to false,
the atomic statements L2j will reset them to true one at a time.

In contrast to the variables y and h , which are accessible to
all components --which is expressed by calling them "global variables"-- ,
each variable s_i is only accessible to its corresponding component $cpnt_i$
--which is expressed by calling the variable s_i "local" to component
$cpnt_i$ -- .

Local variables give rise to so-called "local assertions". Local
assertions are most conveniently written in the program text of the individual components at the place corresponding to their truth: they state
a truth between preceding and succeeding statements in exactly the same way
as is usual in annotating or verifying sequential programs. If a local
assertion contains only local variables, it can be justified on account of
the text of the corresponding component only.

In the following annotated version of $cpnt_i$ we have inserted local
assertions between braces. In order to understand the local assertions about
s_i it suffices to remember that s_i is local to $cpnt_i$. The local
assertion $\{R_i\}$ in the second atomic alternative of L1 is justified by
the guard $y[i] \ne f_i(y)$. in conjunction with (8). We have further incorporated in our annotation the consequence of (12) and the fact that the
execution of a second alternative will never cause an R_j to become false:
a true R_i can only become false by virtue of the execution of the first
alternative of L1 by $cpnt_i$ itself! Hence, R_i is true all through the
execution of the second alternative of $cpnt_i$.

$cpnt_i$:

L0: $\underline{do} < (\underline{E} \ j: h[j] > \rightarrow \{(\underline{A} \ j: s_i[j])\}$

L1: $< \underline{if} \ y[i] = f_i(y) \rightarrow h[i]:= false > \{\underline{A} \ j: s_i[j]\}$

   $\| \ y[i] \ne f_i(y) \rightarrow$

    $\{R_i\} \ y[i]:= f_i(y);$

    $(\underline{A} \ j: s_i[j]:= false) > \{R_i \ \underline{and} \ (\underline{A} \ j: \underline{non} \ s_i[j])\};$

L2j: $(\underline{A} \ j: \{R_i \ \underline{and} \ \underline{non} \ s_i[j]\} < h[j]:= true; \ s_i[j]:= true >)$

   $\underline{fi} \ \{(\underline{A} \ j: s_i[j])\}$

  $\underline{od}$

On account of (11) R_j will be true upon completion of L2j . But
the second atomic alternative of L1 should already have made R_j true,
and it should remain so until L2j is executed. The precondition of L2j,
as given in the annotation, hence tells us the "other reason besides

$$(\underline{A} \ j: \underline{non} \ h[j] \ \underline{or} \ R_j) \tag{11}$$

why an R_j should be defined to be true":

$$(\underline{A} \ i, \ j: \underline{non} \ R_i \ \underline{or} \ s_i[j] \ \underline{or} \ R_j) \qquad . \tag{13}$$

Because it is our aim to get eventually all the R_j's false, we $\underline{define}$
the R_j's as the $\underline{minimal}$ solution of (11) and (13), minimal in the sense
of: as few R_j's true as possible.

The existence of a unique minimal solution of (11) and (13) follows
from the following construction. Start with all R_j's false --all equations
of (13) are then satisfied on account of the term "$\underline{non} \ R_i$" -- . If all
equations of (11) are satisfied as well, we are ready --no true R_j's at
all-- ; otherwise (11) is satisfied by setting R_j to true for all j-values
for which h[j] holds. Now all equations of (11) are satisfied, but some
of the equations of (13) need no longer be satisfied: as long as an (i, j)-
pair can be found for which the equation of (13) is not satisfied, satisfy it
by setting that R_j to true: as this cannot cause violation of (11) we
end up with the R_j's being a solution of (11) and (13). But it is also
the minimal solution, because any R_j true in this solution must be true
in any solution.

For a value of i , for which

$$(\underline{A} \; j: \; s_i[j]) \tag{14}$$

holds, the above construction tells us that the truth of R_i forces no
further true R_j's via (13); consequently, when such an R_i becomes false,
no other R_j-values are then affected. This, and the fact that the first
atomic alternative of L1 is executed under the truth of (14) tells us,
that with our definition of the R_j's as the minimal solution of (11) and (13),
requirement (12) is, indeed, met.

We have proved the universal truth of (8) by defining the R_j's as
the minimal solution of (11) and (13). The universal truth of (7), however,
is now obvious. If the left-hand term of (7) is false, we have

$$(\underline{A} \; j: \; \underline{non} \; h[j]),$$

and (11) and (13) have as minimal solution all R_j's false, i.e.

$$(\underline{A} \; j: \; \underline{non} \; R_j)$$

which is the second term of (7). From the universal truth of (7) and (8),
the universal truth of (6) follows, and our proof is completed.

Concluding remarks.

This note has been written with many purposes in mind:

1)   To give a wider publicity to an unusual problem and the mathematics
involved in its solution.

2)   To present a counterexample contradicting the much-propagated and hence
commonly held belief that correctness proofs for programs are only laboriously
belabouring the obvious.

3)   To present a counterexample to the much-propagated and hence commonly
held belief that there is an antagonism between rigour and formality on the
one hand and "understandability" on the other.

4)   To present an example of a correctness proof in which the first-order
predicate calculus is used as what seems an indispensable tool.

5)   To present an example of a correctness proof in which the first-order
predicate calculus is a fully adequate tool.

6)   To show how fairly general --almost "syntactic"-- considerations about
the formal manipulations involved can provide valuable guidance for the discovery of a surprising and surprisingly effective argument, thus showing how
a formal discipline can assist "creativity" instead of --as is sometimes
suggested-- hampering it.

7)   To show how also in such formal considerations the principle of
separation of concerns can be recognized as a very helpful one.

    I leave it to my readers to form their opinion whether with the above
I have served these purposes well.

Acknowledgements. I would like to express my gratitude to both IFIP WG2.3 and
"The Tuesday Afternoon Club", where I had the opportunity to discuss this
problem. Those familiar with the long history that led to this note, however,
know that in this case I am indebted to C.S.Scholten more than to anyone else.
Comments from S.T.M.Ackermans, David Gries, and W.M.Turski on an earlier version
of this paper are greatfully acknowledged.

[1]   Owicki, Susan and Gries, David, "Verifying Properties of Parallel
        Programs: An Axiomatic Approach". Comm.ACM 19, 5 (May 1976), pp.279-285.

Plataanstraat 5   prof.dr.Edsger W.Dijkstra
5671 AL NUENEN   Burroughs Research Fellow
The Netherlands

ON THE INTERPLAY BETWEEN MATHEMATICS AND PROGRAMMING

E.W. Dijkstra

This talk is delivered under confusing circumstances. And the only way I can think of, of assisting you in not getting confused by these complicating circumstances is describing them explicitly in my introduction. The complication is that, while I would prefer to give a completely technical talk, its moral is heavily loaded from a political point of view: it is a technical talk to be delivered against almost overwhelming political odds. In order to make you understand all this we have to go back to about ten years ago, when Programming Methodology became a topic of explicit concern.

In the history of programming October 1968 has been a turning point. In that month a conference on the topic denoted by the newly coined term "software engineering" was held in Garmisch-Partenkirchen. The conference was sponsored by the NATO Science Committee. The conference was remarkable because a large fraction of the participants had positions so high in their local hierarchy that they could afford to be honest. As a result this was the first sizeable conference at which the existence of the so-called "software crisis" was openly admitted. The gloomy atmosphere of doom at that conference has been a severe shock for some of the participants; some left the place very depressed indeed. The majority, however, left the conference with a feeling of relief, some even in a state of great excitement: it had been admitted at last that we did not know to program well enough. I myself and quite a few others had been waiting eagerly for this moment, because now at last something could be done about it. For years we had already been worried by the consequences of the proliferation of error-loaded software, but there is very little point in trying to urge the world to mend its ways as long as that world is still convinced that its ways are perfectly adequate. It was at that conference in Garmisch-Partenkirchen, that the whole climate changed. Now, nearly a decade later, we can only conclude that the excitement was fully justified: it was indeed a turning point in the histo-

ry of programming. Since that conference, programming has never been the
same again.

In reaction to the recognition that we did now know how to program
well enough, people began to ask themselves how a really competent programmer would look like. What would we have to teach if we wanted to educate a
next generation of really competent programmers? This became the central
question of the study that later would become known as "programming methodology". A careful analysis of the programmer's task was made, and programming emerged as a task with a strong mathematical flavour. As I have once
put it "Programming is one of the hardest branches of applied mathematics
because it is also one of the hardest branches of engineering, and vice
versa". Why the programming task has such a strong mathematical flavour is
something I shall indicate later.

A lower bound for what the adequate education of a really competent
programmer should comprise was very convincingly established, but it was
not an easy message to sell, because it demonstrated by necessity the total inadequacy of the education of what is known as "the average programmer". The world today has about a million "average programmers", and it is
frightening to be forced to conclude that most of them are the victims of
an earlier underestimation of the intrinsic difficulty of the programmer's
task and now find themselves lured into a profession beyond their intellectual capabilities. It is a horrible conclusion to draw, but I am afraid
that it is unavoidable.

The conclusion that competent programming required a fair amount of
mathematical skills has been drawn on purely technical grounds and, as far
as I know, has never been refuted. On emotional grounds which are only too
understandable, many people have refused to draw the conclusion, and the
conclusion is opposed to, not because its validity is challenged, but because its social consequences are so unpleasant.

The situation is immensely aggravated by changes in attitude towards
science and technology in general, that took place during the sixties. In
that decade we have seen a growing distrust of technology, a disillusion
with science, which by the end of that decade caused political outbursts
from which most universities haven't fully recovered yet.

For those who had hoped that the explosive growth of universities and
other research establishments would automatically bear fruits in proportion
to that growth, the results have indeed been disappointing, because, while

the quantity grew, the average quality declined. Browsing through a scientific journal or attending a conference is nowadays rather depressing; there is no denying it: there is just an awfull lot of narrow mediocrity, of downright junk even. Many people seem to have failed to see, that it was not science itself, but only the explosive growth of the institutions that was to blame. Throwing away the child with the bathwater, they have declared war on science in its best tradition. They are openly antiscientific, antiacademic, very much against rigour and formal techniques, and they propose to be agressively creative, gloriously intuitive and nobly interdisciplinary instead. The cruel love of perfection and excellence, that used to characterize the hard sciences, are but elitist relics to be abolished as quickly as possible, and progressive from now onwards shall mean soft. The political slogans of the late sixties cast these views in a jargon that is still alive and still causes confusion.

The result of all this is that the message that "software", in spite of its name, requires a very hard discipline, is in many environments now politically unacceptable, and therefore fought by political means. In characteristically anonymous blurbs in periodicals of the Computer Weekly variety I find myself under political attack. "Dijkstra articulates the voice of reaction" is a mild one. "I am inclined to view Dijkstra [...] as intellectual product of the Germanic system" is much worse. And I arouse the "suspicion that [my] concepts are the product of an authoritarian upbringing" coming as I do from a country having "social philosophies touched by authoritarianism and the welfare state" etc. Nice is also the choice of adjectives when my efforts are described as "directed into turning a noble art into a rigid discipline". The first time I found myself confronted with the opinion that adhering to a formal discipline hampers creativity I was completely baffled, because it is absolutely contrary to my experience and the experience of the people I have worked with. I found the suggestion so ludicrous that I could not place it at all: it is so terribly wrong. Since then I have learned that as symptom of a political attitude it is quite well interpretable.

Having thus -I hope- cleared the sky from political encumbrances, I shall now turn to the technical part of my talk.

Why is programming intrinsically an activity with a strong mathematical flavour? Well, mathematical assertions have three important characteristics.

1) Mathematical assertions are always general in the sense that they are applicable to many -often even infinetely many- cases: we prove something for *all* natural numbers or *all* nondegenerate Euclidean triangles.

2) Besides general, mathematical assertions are very precise. This is already an unusual combination, as in most other verbal activities generality is usually achieved by vagueness.

3) A tradition of more than twenty centuries has taught us to present these general and precise assertions with a convincing power that has no equal in any other intellectual discipline. This tradition is called Mathematics.

The typical program computes a function that is defined for an incredibly large number of different values of its arguement; the assertion that such and such a program corresponds to such and such a function has therefore the generality referred to above.

Secondly: the specification of what a program can achieve for us must be pretty precise, if it is going to be a safe tool to use. Regarded as a tool its usage can only be justified by an appeal to its stated properties, and if those are not stated properly its usage cannot be justified properly. And here we have the second characteristic.

Thirdly: the assertion that such and such a program corresponds to such and such a function, although general and precise, is not much good if it is wrong. If the program is to be regarded as a reliable tool, our least obligation is a convincing case, that that assertion is correct. That program testing does *not* provide such a convincing case is well-known. The theoretically inclined can deduce this from the indeed incredibly large number of different argument values for which the function is typically defined; the more experimentally inclined can conclude this from more than twenty years of experience in which program testing as main technique for quality control has not been able to prevent the proliferation of error-loaded software. The only alternative that I see is the only alternative mankind has been able to come up with for dealing with such problems, and that is a nice convincing argument. And that is what we have always called Mathematics.

Here we touch upon the major shift in the programmer's task that took place during the last ten years. It is no longer sufficient to make a program of which you hope that it is correct -i.e. satisfies its specifications- you must make the program in such a way that you can give a convincing argument for its correctness. Superficially it may seem that this shift

has made the task of the poor programmer only more difficult: besides making a program he has to supply a correctness argument as well. It may indeed be hard to supply a nice correctness argument for a *given* program; if,
however, one does not add one's correctness concerns as an afterthought,
but thinks about the correctness argument right at the start, the correctness concerns have proved to be of great heuristic value. And the wise
programmer now develops program and correctness argument hand in hand; as
a matter of fact, the development of the correctness argument usually runs
slightly ahead of the development of the program: he first decides how he
is going to prove the correctness and then designs the program so as to fit
the next step of the proof. That's fine.

You may think that I have introduced a more serious difficulty by stating that the programmer should make his program in such a way that he can
give "a convincing argument" for its correctness. Convincing to whom? Well,
of course, only to those who care. But couldn't those have very, very different notions of what to regard as "convincing"? Has the programmer to
provide as many different arguments as there may be people caring about
the correctness of his program? That would make his task clearly impossible.

The task is, indeed, impossible as long as we don't distinguish between "conventional" and "convenient". What different people from different
parts of the world have been used to varies so wildly, that it is impossible to extract a guiding principle from trying to present your argument
in the most "conventional" way: their usual patterns of thinking are most
likely inadequate anyhow. About convenience of a notation, about effectiveness of an argument, about elegance of a mathematical proof, however, I
observed among mathematicians a very strong consensus -the consensus was,
as a matter of fact, much greater than most of the mathematicians I spoke
suspected themselves- and it is this consensus among mathematicians that
has proved to be a very valuable guiding principle in deciding towards what
type of "convincing argument" the programmer should be heading.

Let me now try to sketch to you the type of mathematics involved in
arguing about programs. One way of viewing a program is as the rules of behaviour which can be followed by an automatic computer, which is then said
"to execute" the program. The process taking place when a computer executes
a program is called a "computation", and a computation can be viewed as a
time-sequence or a long succession of different machine states. The part of
the machine in which its current state is recorded is called the store -or:

the memory-; the store is very large because it must be able to distinguish between a huge number of different states.

In arguing about programs we have to characterize the set of machine states that are possible at various stages of the computational process. Individual states are characterized by the values of variables in very much the same way as the position of a point in a plane can be characterized by the value of its coordinates in a well-chosen coordinate system. There are in this analogy only two differences: while the coordinates in the Euclidean plane are usually viewed as continuous, the variables characterizing the state of the machine are discrete variables that can only take on a finite number of different values. And secondly: while in Euclidean plane geometry two coordinates suffice to fix the position of a point, in computations we typically need thousands or millions of different variables te record the current machine state.

In spite of the fact that that last difference is a drastic one, the analogy is yet a useful one. Everybody familiar with analytic geometry knows how specific figures, lines, circles, ellipses etc. can be characterized by *equations*: the figures are regarded as the subset of the points whose coordinates satisfy the equation. The analogy to the figure in analytic geometry is the subset of possible states at a certain point of progress of the computation, and in analogy to analytic geometry, such a subset is characterized by an equation: the subset comprises all states of the machine in which the values of the variables satisfy that equation.

The analogy can even be carried a little bit further: we all know how the ease with which a proof in analytical geometry can be carried out often depends on the choice of our coordinate system. The program designer has a similar freedom when he chooses the conventions according to which the variables he introduced shall represent the information to be manipulated. He can use this freedom to speed up the computation; he can also use it to simplify the equations characterizing the sets of states he is interested in. If he is lucky, or gifted, or both, his choice of representation serves both goals.

So much for the analogy; now for the difference. The number of variables he is dealing with is much larger than the two coordinates of plane geometry, and the subsets of machine states he needs to characterize have very seldomly an obvious regularity as the straight line, the circle, and the ellipse that analytic geometry is so good at dealing with. This has two immediate consequences.

First of all we need a much richer framework and vocabulary in which we can express the equations than the simple algebraic relations that carry analytic geometry. The framework is provided by the first-order predicate calculus, and the vocabulary by the predicates the programmer thinks it wise to introduce. That the first-order predicate calculus was the most suitable candidate for the characterization of sets of machine states was assumed right at the start; early experiences, however, were not too encouraging, because it only seemed practicable in the simplest cases, and we discovered the second consequence: the large number of variables combined with the likely irregularity of the subsets to be characterized very quickly made most of the formal expressions to be manipulated unmanageably long.

Let me put it in other words. The programmer is invited to apply the first-order predicate calculus; I am even willing to make a stronger statement: not knowing of any other tool that would enable to do the job, the programmer *must* apply the first-order predicate calculus. But he has to do so in an environment in which he is certain to create an unmanageable mess unless he *carefully* tries to avoid doing so (and even then success is not guaranteed!). He has to be constantly consciously careful to keep his notation as adequate and his argument as elegant as possible. And it is only in the last years that we are beginning to discover what that care implies. Let me give you a simple example to give you some feeling for it.

To begin with we consider a finite undirected graph at each vertex of which a philosopher is located: philosophers located at vertices that are directly connected by one edge of the graph are called each other's neighbours and no philosopher is his own neighbour. For the time being the life of a philosopher exists of an endless alternation of two mutually exclusive states, called "thinking" and "tabled".

In our next stage we allow edges to be marked or not, a marked edge meaning that the two philosophers at its two ends are both tabled, more precisely

P1: For any pair (A, B) of neighbours
   "both A and B are tabled" = "the edge between A and B is marked".

We assume that the system is started in an initial state in which

1) all edges are unmarked

2)   all philosophers are thinking.

As a result, P1 initially holds. Therefore P1 will continue to hold indefinitely, provided no philosopher transition from thinking to tabled introduces a violation of it. This is obviously achieved by associating with these transitions the following "point actions" -where no two different point actions are assumed to take place simultaneously-

T1:   < mark the edges connecting you to tabled neighbours and switch from thinking to tabled >

T2:   < unmark your marked edges and switch from tabled to thinking >.

The first transition now introduces a mark for every pair of tabled neighbours introduced by it, the second one removes a mark for every pair of tabled neighbours disappearing as a result of it. With these conventions the permanent truth of P1 is guaranteed.

From the above we see that a mark on the edge between the neighbours A and B has either been placed by A or by B. In our next stage we shall indicate which of the two has placed the mark by representing a marked edge between A and B by a directed edge, i.e. by placing an arrow along the edge. In this representation relation P1 is rephrased as

P1:   For any pair (A, B) of neighbours
      "both A and B are tabled" = "the edge between A and B is directed".

The direction of the arrow is fixed, by rephrasing the transitions as

T1:   < direct arrows pointing towards your tabled neighbours and switch from thinking to tabled >

T2:   < make all your edges undirected and switch from tabled to thinking >.

We observe that transitions T1 create arrows and only transitions T2 destroy them. More precisely: each arrow is created as an outgoing arrow of its creator, hence,

      a philosopher without outgoing arrows remains without outgoing arrows until it performs itself its *own* transition T1.

      We now subdivide the state "tabled" into the succession of two substates "hungry" followed by "eating", where the transition is marked by the observation of absence of outgoing arrows, more precisely

      "philosopher A is tabled" = "philosopher A is hungry or eating"

and the life of a philosopher now consists of a *cyclic* pattern of transitions

T1: < direct arrows pointing towards your tabled neighbours and switch
from thinking to hungry >

T1.5: < observe that you have no outgoing arrows and switch from hungry to
eating >

T2: < remove all your incoming arrows and switch from eating to thinking >

and we establish the permanent truth of

P2: For any philosopher A we have

"philosopher A has no outgoing arrows" or "philosopher A is hungry".

In transition T1 the first term P2 may become false, but the second one becomes certainly true; in transition T1.5 the second term becomes false at
a moment when the first term is true, a truth that cannot be destroyed by
the other philosophers. In T2 the fact that initially the philosopher is
eating tells us in combination with P2 that its arrows, if any, must be incoming arrows; hence, removal of your incoming arrows is the same as removal of all your arrows.

Relations P1 and P2 guarantee that no two neighbours can be eating simultaneously: if they were, they would both be tabled, hence there would be
an arrow between them (on account of P1), for one of them it would be an
outgoing arrow, but P2 excludes that an eating philosopher, which by definition is not hungry, has outgoing arrows.

(In addition we can prove that if the graph is finite and each eating
period for each philosopher is finite, then each hungry period for each
philosopher will be finite. This follows from the fact that the arrows never form a directed cyclic path.)

The way in which the above argument has been described illustrates one
of the aspects of the "care" which is becoming typical for the competent
programmer: "step-wise refinement" is one of the catchwords. Note that we
have started the argument in terms of the still very simple concepts "tabled" and "marked". Only after the exhaustion of these two concepts, the
state "marked" was split up into two mutually exclusive substates as represented by the two possible directions of an arrow along the edge. And only
when the consequences of that refinement had been explored, the state "tabled" was subdivided into two mutually exclusive states, viz. "hungry" and
"eating".

In the simple example shown such a cautious approach may seem exagger-
ated, but for the trained programmer it becomes a habit. In a typical program so many different variables are manipulated that the programmer would

lose his way in his argument if he tried to deal with them all at once. He
has to deal with so many concerns that he would lose his way if he did not
separate them fairly effectively. He tries to keep his arguments simple
compared to the final program by abstracting from all sorts of details
that can be filled in later.

In yet another respect the above argument is typical. I did not tell
you the original problem statement, but that was phrased as a synchronization problem, in which no two neighbours were allowed to eat simultaneously. The notion "hungry" has to be invented by the programmer; and then the
argument is introduced by abstracting from the difference between "hungry"
and "eating", in terms of the notion "tabled" that did not occur in the
original problem statement at all. Such abstractions *must* be performed:
instead of "tabled" one can say "hungry" or "eating", but the translation
of "a pair of tabled neighbours" gives you some hint of the clumsiness thus
engendered.

One last detail worth noticing is provided by our arrows. We had to
introduce two different forms of marking: we could have done that with colours, say red edges and blue edges, but then we would have lost that my incoming arrows are my neighbours outgoing arrows, and the whole argument
would have lost its clarity.

So much for the care needed to keep the arguments manageable: we can
summarize it by stating that in programming mathematical elegance is not a
dispensable luxury, but a matter of life and death.

In the example sketched the argument could be rendered nicely and com-
pactly essentially thanks to the introduction of the proper nomenclature,
but quite often more drastic steps have to be taken. In order to formulate
the equations characterizing sets of possible machine states it is quite
often necessary to change the program by the insertion of additional operations on so-called "auxiliary variables". They are not necessary for the
computation itself, they are hypothetical variables whose values we can
view as being changed in the course of the computational process studied.
They record some aspect of the progress of the computation that is not
needed for the answer, but for the argument justifying the program. Their
values can appear in the characterizing equations in terms of which the
correctness argument is couched. The introduction of the appropriate auxiliary variables is a next step in the progress of "choosing an adequate
nomenclature"; the role of the auxiliary variables in proofs of program

correctness is very similar to the role of auxiliary lines or points in geo-
metrical proofs, and their invention requires each time a similar form of
creativity. This is one of the reasons why I as a computing scientist can
only regret that the attention paid to Euclidean geometry in our secondary
school curricula has been so drastically reduced during the last decades.

In a recent correctness proof I had to go still one step further. I
had to introduce auxiliary variables, but their values did not occur directly in our characterizing equations: in those equations occurred terms which
had to be defined as the minimal solution of two sets of equations in which
the auxiliary variables appeared as constants. As far as I am aware, that
proof was the first one of its kind, but its discovery was a pure joy. It
showed a counterexample to the commonly held but erroneous belief that formal correctness proofs for programs are only belabouring the obvious; it
showed how the first-order predicate calculus was an indispensable and adequate tool, but, most important of all, it showed how a careful analysis of
the syntactic structure of the predicates quite naturally led to all the
additional logical gear to be invented.

In the interplay between mathematics and programming during the last
ten years programming as an intellectual discipline has clearly been at the
receiving end. A new area of intellectual activity has been discovered to
be amenable to mathematical treatment, and thanks to the introduction of
mathematical techniques we can now design programs that are an order of
magnitude better than the ones we could design ten years ago. In the past
the discovery of a new area of applicability of mathematics has always influenced and stimulated mathematics itself, and it is reasonable to wonder
about the question what influence on mathematics may be expected this time.

I expect that the influence will be very wholesome. The programmer applies mathematical techniques in an environment with an unprecedented potential for complication; this circumstance makes him methodologically very,
very conscious of the steps he takes, the notations he introduces etc.
Much more than the average mathematician he is explicitely concerned with
the effectiveness of this argument, much more than the average mathematician he is consciously concerned with the mathematical elegance of his argument. He simply has to, if he refuses to be drowned in unmastered complexity. From the programmer's exposure and experience I can expect only
one influence on mathematics as a whole: a great improvement of the taste
with which formal methods are applied. This improvement may very well turn

out to be drastic. In texts about the philosophy of science from the first
half of this century it is quite common to encounter a postulated antagonism between formal rigour on the one hand and "understandability" on the
other. Already now, whenever I see such a text it strikes me as hopelessly
out of date, arguing as it does against formal rigour instead of against
ugliness: in those days the two were evidently often regarded as synonymous.
And I have some indication that this improvement in taste is not only the
dream of an optimist. I have conducted a little experiment with students
from all over the world, in which I asked them to prove a nice little theorem from number theory that, although everyone can understand what the
theorem states, happens to be unknown: the mathematicians with programming
experience did markedly better than the mathematicians without that experience.

A theorem about odd powers of odd integers

Edsger W. Dijkstra

<u>Theorem</u>. For any odd $p \geq 1$, integer $K \geq 1$, and odd r such that
that $1 \leq r < 2^K$, a value x exists such that

R: $1 \leq x < 2^K$ <u>and</u> $2^K | (x^P - r)$ <u>and</u> $odd(x)$.

<u>Note</u>. For "$a|b$" read: "a divides b". (End of note.)

<u>Proof</u>. The existence of x is proved by designing a program computing x
satisfying R .

Trying to establish R by means of a repetitive construct, we must
choose an invariant relation. This time we apply the well-known technique
of replacing a constant by a variable, and replace the constant K by the
variable k . Introducing $d = 2^k$ for the sake of brevity, we then get

P: $d = 2^k$ <u>and</u> $1 \leq x < d$ <u>and</u> $d | (x^P - r)$ <u>and</u> $odd(x)$.

This choice of invariant relation P is suggested by the observation that
R is trivial to satisfy for $K = 1$; hence P is trivial to establish
initially. The simplest structure to try for our program is therefore:

    x, k, d := 1, 1, 2 $\{P\}$;
    <u>do</u> $k \neq K \rightarrow$ "increase k by 1 under invariance of P" <u>od</u> $\{R\}$.

Increasing k by 1 (together with doubling d) can only violate the
term $d | (x^P - r)$. The weakest precondition that $d := 2*d$ does <u>not</u> do so
is --according to the axiom of assignment-- $(2*d) | (x^P - r)$. Hence an
acceptable component for "increase k by 1 under invariance of P"
is
            $(2*d) | (x^P - r) \rightarrow k, d := k+1, 2*d$.

In the case <u>non</u> $(2*d) | (x^P - r)$ we conclude from $d | (x^P - r)$ that $x^P - r$ is
an odd multiple of d . Because d is even, and p and x are odd, the
binomial expansion tells us that $(x+d)^P - x^P$ is an odd multiple of d ,
and that hence $(x+d)^P - r$ is a multiple of $2*d$. Because also d is doubled,
$x < d$ remains true under $x := x+d$, because d is even $odd(x)$ obviously
remains true, and our program becomes:

```
x, k, d := 1, 1, 2 {P};
do k ≠ K → if (2*d)|(x^P-r) → k, d := k+1, 2*d {P}
        ▯ non (2*d)|(x^P-r) → x, k, d := x+d, k+1, 2*d {P}
      fi {P}
od {R}
```

Because this program obviously terminates, its existence proves the theorem.
(End of proof.)   *   *   *

     With the argument as given, the above program was found in five minutes.
I only mention this in reply to Zohar Manna and Richard Waldinger, who wrote
in "Synthesis: Dreams ⇒ Programs" (SRI Technical Note 156, November 1977)

> "Our instructors at the Structured Programming School have urged us
> to find the appropriate invariant assertion before introducing a loop.
> But how are we to select the successful invariant when there are so
> many promising candidates around? [...] Recursion seems to be the ideal
> vehicle for systematic program construction [...]. In choosing to
> emphasize iteration instead, the proponents of structured programming
> have had to resort to more dubious (sic!) means."

Although I haven't used the term Structured Programming any more for at least
five years, and although I have a vested interest in recursion, yet I felt
addressed by the two gentlemen. So it seemed only appropriate to record that
the "more dubious means" have --again!-- been pretty effective. (I have
evidence that, despite the existence of this very simple solution, the problem
is not trivial: many computing scientists could not solve the programming
problem within an hour. Try it on your colleagues, if you don't believe me.)

Plataanstraat 5   prof.dr.Edsger W.Dijkstra
5671 AL Nuenen   Burroughs Research Fellow
The Netherlands

In honour of Fibonacci

Edsger W. Dijkstra

Studying an artificial intelligence approach to programming the other day --I read the most weird documents!-- I was reminded of the Fibonacci sequence, given by

$$F_1 = 0 , \quad F_2 = 1 ,$$
$$F_n = F_{n-1} + F_{n-2} \qquad (-inf < n < +inf) .$$

For $N \geq 2$ the relation

R: $\quad x = F_N$

is trivially established by the program

$$y, x, i := 0, 1, 2 \ \{y = F_{i-1} \ \underline{and} \ x = F_i \ \underline{and} \ 2 \leq i \leq N\}; \qquad (1)$$
$$\underline{do} \ i \neq N \rightarrow y, x, i := x, x + y, i + 1 \ \underline{od} \ \{R\}$$

a program with a time-complexity proportional to N; I remembered --although I did not know the formulae-- that R can also be established in a number of operations proportional to $\log(N)$ and wondered --as a matter of fact: I still wonder-- how proponents of "program transformations" propose to transform the linear algorithm (1) into the logarithmic one.

Yesterday evening I was wondering whether I could reconstruct the logarithmic scheme for the Fibonacci sequence, and whether similar schemes existed for higher order recurrence relations (for a $k \geq 2$):

$$F_1 = F_2 = \ldots = F_{k-1} = 0 , \quad F_k = 1$$
$$F_n = F_{n-1} + \ldots + F_{n-k} \qquad (-inf < n < +inf) \qquad (2)$$

Eventually I found a way of deriving these schemes. For $k = 2$, the normal Fibonacci numbers, the method leads to the well-known formulae

$$F_{2j} = F_j^2 + F_{j+1}^2$$
$$F_{2j+1} = (2F_j + F_{j+1}) * F_{j+1} \quad or \quad F_{2j-1} = (2F_{j+1} - F_j) * F_j .$$

This note is written, because I liked my general derivation. I shall describe it for $k = 3$.

Because for $k = 3$ we have $F_1 = F_2 = 0$ and $F_3 = 1$ we may write

$$F_n = F_3 * F_n + (F_2 + F_1)* F_{n-1} + F_2 * F_{n-2} \qquad . \qquad (3)$$

From (3) we deduce the truth of

$$F_n = F_{i+3}* F_{n-i} + (F_{i+2} + F_{i+1})* F_{n-i-1} + F_{i+2}* F_{n-i-2} \qquad (4)$$

for $i = 0$. The truth of (4) for all positive values of i is derived by mathematical induction; the induction step consists of

1) substituting $F_{n-i-1} + F_{n-i-2} + F_{n-i-3}$ for F_{n-i}

2) combining after rearrangement $F_{i+3} + F_{i+2} + F_{i+1}$ into F_{i+4} .

(The proof for negative values of i is done by performing the induction step the other way round.)

Substituting in (4) $n = 2j$ and $i = j-1$ we get

$$F_{2j} = F_{j+2}* F_{j+1} + (F_{j+1} + F_j)* F_j + F_{j+1}* F_{j-1}$$

and, by substituting $F_{j+2} - F_{j+1} - F_j$ for F_{j-1} , and subsequent rearranging

$$F_{2j} = F_j^2 + (2F_{j+2} - F_{j+1})* F_{j+1} \qquad . \qquad (5)$$

Substituting in (4) $n = 2j+1$ and $i = j-1$ we get

$$F_{2j+1} = F_{j+2}^2 + (F_{j+1} + F_j)* F_{j+1} + F_{j+1}* F_j$$
$$= (2F_j + F_{j+1})* F_{j+1} + F_{j+2}^2 \qquad (6)$$

Formulae (5) and (6) were the ones I was after.

<u>Note</u>. For $k = 4$ the analogue to (4) is

$$F_n = F_{i+4}* F_{n-i} + (F_{i+3} + F_{i+2} + F_{i+1})* F_{n-i-1} +$$
$$(F_{i+3} + F_{i+2})* F_{n-i-2} + F_{i+3}* F_{n-i-3}$$

(End of note.)

Plataanstraat 5   prof.dr.Edsger W.Dijkstra
5671 AL Nuenen   Burroughs Research Fellow
The Netherlands

On the foolishness of "natural language programming"

Edsger W.Dijkstra

Since the early days of automatic computing we have had people that
have felt it as a shortcoming that programming required the care and accuracy that is characteristic for the use of any formal symbolism. They
blamed the mechanical slave for its strict obedience with which it carried
out its given instructions, even if a moment's thought would have revealed
that those instructions contained an obvious mistake. "But a moment is a
long time, and thought is a painful process." (A.E.Housman). They eagerly
hoped and waited for more sensible machinery that would refuse to embark
on such nonsensical activities as a trivial clerical error evoked at the
time.

Machine code, with its absence of almost any form of redundancy,
was soon identified as a needlessly risky interface between man and machine.
Partly in response to this recognition so-called "high-level programming
languages" were developed, and, as time went by, we learned to a certain
extent how to enhance the protection against silly mistakes. It was a
significant improvement that now many a silly mistake did result in an
error message instead of in an erroneous answer. (And even this improvement wasn't universally appreciated: some people found error messages they
couldn't ignore more annoying than wrong results, and, when judging the
relative merits of programming languages, some still seem to equate "the
ease of programming" with the ease of making undetected mistakes.) The
(abstract) machine corresponding to a programming language remained, however, a faithful slave, i.e. the nonsensible automaton perfectly capable
of carrying out nonsensical instructions. Programming remained the use
of a formal symbolism and, as such, continued to require the care and accuracy required before.

In order to make machines significantly easier to use, it has been
proposed (to try) to design machines that we could instruct in our native
tongues. This would, admittedly, make the machines much more complicated,
but, it was argued, by letting the machine carry a larger share of the
burden, life would become easier for us. It sounds sensible provided you
blame the obligation to use a formal symbolism as the source of your dif-

ficulties. But is the argument valid? I doubt.

We know in the meantime that the choice of an interface is not just
a division of (a fixed amount of) labour, because the work involved in co-
operating and communicating across the interface has to be added. We know
in the meantime --from sobering experience, I may add-- that a change of
interface can easily increase at both sides of the fence the amount of
work to be done (even drastically so). Hence the increased preference
for what are now called "narrow interfaces". Therefore, although changing
to communication between machine and man conducted in the latter's native
tongue would greatly increase the machine's burden, we have to challenge
the assumption that this would simplify man's life.

A short look at the history of mathematics shows how justified this
challenge is. Greek mathematics got stuck because it remained a verbal,
pictorial activity, Moslem "algebra", after a timid attempt at symbolism,
died when it returned to the rhetoric style, and the modern civilized
world could only emerge --for better or for worse-- when Western Europe
could free itself from the fetters of medieval scholasticism --a vain
attempt at verbal precision!-- thanks to the carefully, or at least consciously designed formal symbolisms that we owe to people like Vieta,
Descartes, Leibniz, and (later) Boole.

The virtue of formal texts is that their manipulations, in order
to be legitimate, need to satisfy only a few simple rules; they are, when
you come to think of it, an amazingly effective tool for ruling out all
sorts of nonsense that, when we use our native tongues, are almost impossible to avoid.

Instead of regarding the obligation to use formal symbolisms as a
burden, we should regard the convenience of using them as a privilege:
thanks to them, schoolchildren can learn to do what in earlier days only
genius could achieve. (This was evidently not understood by the author
that wrote --in 1977-- in the preface of a technical report that "even
the standard symbols used for logical connectives have been avoided for
the sake of clarity". The occurrence of that sentence suggests that the

author's misunderstanding is not confined to him alone.) When all is said and told, the "naturalness" with which we use our native tongues boils down to the ease with which we can use them for making statements the non-sense of which is not obvious.

It may be illuminating to try to imagine what would have happened if, right from the start, our native tongues would have been the only vehicle for the input into and the output from our information processing equipment. My considered guess is that history would, in a sense, have repeated itself, and that computer science would consist mainly of the indeed black art how to bootstrap from there to a sufficiently well-de-fined formal system. We would need all the intellect in the world to get the interface narrow enough to be usable, and, in view of the history of mankind, it may not be overly pessimistic to guess that to do the job well enough would require again a few thousand years.

<u>Remark</u>. As a result of the educational trend away from intellectual disci-pline, the last decades have shown in the Western world a sharp decline of people's mastery of their own language: many people that by the stan-dards of a previous generation should know better, are no longer able to use their native tongue effectively, even for purposes for which it is pretty adequate. (You have only to look at the indeed alarming amount of on close reading meaningless verbiage in scientific articles, technical reports, government publications etc.) This phenomenon --known as "The New Illiteracy"-- should discourage those believers in natural language programming that lack the technical insight needed to predict its failure. (End of remark.)

From one gut feeling I derive much consolation: I suspect that machines to be programmed in our native tongues --be it Dutch, English, American, French, German, or Swahili-- are as damned difficult to make as they would be to use.

Plataanstraat 5   prof.dr.Edsger W.Dijkstra
5671 AL NUENEN   Burroughs Research Fellow
The Netherlands

Program inversion

Edsger W.Dijkstra

Let the integer array $p(0..M-1)$ be such that the sequence
$p(0)$, $p(1)$,..., $p(M-1)$ represents a permutation of the numbers from 0
through M-1 and let the integer array $y(0..M-1)$ be such that
$(\underline{A}\ i: 0 \leq i < M: 0 \leq y(i) \leq i)$. Under those constraints we are interested in the relation

$$(\underline{A}\ i: 0 \leq i < M: y(i) = (\underline{N}\ j: 0 \leq j < i: p(j) < p(i))\ ) \qquad (1)$$

(Legenda: "$(\underline{N}\ j: 0 \leq j < i: p(j) < p(i))$" should be read as "the number
of mutually different values j in the range $0 \leq j < i$, such that
$p(j) < p(i)$".)

We can now consider the two --solvable-- problems

A)   Given p , assign to y a value such that (1) is satisfied.
B)   Given y , assign to p a value such that (1) is satisfied.

Because we want to consider programs the execution of which may modify the
given array, we rephrase:

A)   Given p , assign to y a value such that (1) holds between the
initial value of p and the final value of y .
B)   Given y , assign to p a value such that (1) holds between the
initial value of y and the final value of p .

If A transforms p into a (standard) value which is its initial
value in B , and if B transforms y into a (standard) value which is
its initial value in A , then transformations A and B are <u>inverse</u>
transformations on the pair (p,y). We are interested in these inverse
transformations because in general problem A is regarded as easier than
B : we have solved problem B as soon as we have for A a reversible
solution!

Our first effort.

Let the standard value for p be such that $(\underline{A}\ i: 0 \leq i < M: p(i) = i)$.
From (1) we immediately deduce that a permutation of the values $p(0)$,...,
$p(k-1)$ does not affect the values of $y(i)$ for $i \geq k$. This suggests

the computation of the values $y(k)$ in the order of increasing k , each time combining the computation of $y(k)$ with a permutation of $p(0),\ldots,$ $p(k)$. Because the final value of p should be sorted, we are led most naturally to a bubble sort:

```
k:= 0; {p(0),...,p(k-1) is ordered}
do k ≠ M → "make  p(0),.., p(k) ordered";
            k:= k + 1 {p(0),..., p(k-1) is ordered}
od
```

The standard program for the bubble sort is

```
k:= 0;
do k ≠ M → j:= k;
            do j > 0 cand p(j-1) > p(j) → p:swap(j-1,j);
                                          j:= j - 1
            od {here  j = the value  y(k)  should get};
            k:= k + 1
od {A i: 0 ≤ i < M : p(i) = i}
```

We initialize via $y:=(0)$ the array variable y as the empty array with $y.lob = 0$, each time extending it with a new value as soon as that has been computed. Because $k = y.dom$ would be an invariant, the variable k can be eliminated.

Program A1:
```
y:=(0); {y.dom = 0}
do y.dom ≠ M → j:= y.dom {this is an initialization}; {j = y.dom}
                do j > 0 cand p(j-1) > p(j) → p:swap(j-1,j);
                                              j:= j - 1 {j < y.dom}
                od; y:hiext(j) {j's value is no longer relevant} {y.dom > 0}
od {A i: 0 ≤ i < M: p(i) = i}
```

Inverting it we construct

Program B1:
```
p:=(0); do p.dom ≠ M → p:hiext(p.dom) od; {A i: 0 ≤ i < M: p(i) = i }
do y.dom ≠ 0 → j,y:hipop {this is an initialization of  j };
                do j ≠ y.dom → j:= j + 1; p:swap(j-1,j) od
                    {j's value is no longer relevant}
od
```

This inversion was easy because the post-condition of each repeatable statement implies the negation of the stated precondition of the repetitive construct as a whole; furthermore we have used that y:hiext(j) and j,y:hipop are each other's inverse, that j:= j + 1 and j:= j - 1 are each others inverse, and that p:swap(j-1,j) is its own inverse.

We leave to the reader the insertion of provable assertions in program B1 that would justify the derivation of A1 from B1 by inversion.

Our second effort.

We can also compute the values $y(k)$ in the order of decreasing k . (Here it is as if our standard value of p is the empty array with p.lob = 0 and the standard value of y is the empty array with y.hib = M - 1 .) We make three observations:

1)   As soon as the $y(i)$ for $i \geq k$ have been computed, the $p(i)$ for $i \geq k$ no longer matter, i.e. we can work with a single array, $v(0..M-1)$ say, where in A/B , in relation (1) p refers to the initial/final value of v , and y refers to the final/initial value of v .

2)   Denoting with $Q(k)$: "the sequence $p(0), p(1),...,p(k)$ represents a permutation of the numbers $0,...,k$ " we can write $Q(k) \Rightarrow y(k) = p(k)$.

3)   Decreasing in the range $0 \leq i < k$ all $p(i)$ such that $p(i) > p(k)$ by 1 leaves all $y(i)$ with $0 \leq i < k$ unaffected.

These observations lead to the following program (in which we can view the elements $v(i)$ with $i < k$ as the corresponding elements of (a changing) p and the $v(i)$ with $i \geq k$ as the corresponding elements of a growing y .)

```
k:= M; {k = M and Q(k-1) and v = p}
do k ≠ 0 → k:= k - 1; {Q(k)}
            i:= 0; do i ≠ k → if v(i) > v(k) → v:(i)= v(i) - 1 {v(i) ≥ v(k)}
                             ▯ v(i) < v(k) → skip {v(i) < v(k)}
                             fi; i:= i + 1
                   od {i = k and Q(k-1)}
od {k = 0 and v = y}
```

In the alternative construct the postconditions have been added in order to ease the inversion:

Program B2:

k:= 0 $\{v = y\}$;

$\underline{do}$ k $\neq$ M $\rightarrow$ i:= k;

$\qquad$ $\underline{do}$ i $\neq$ 0 $\rightarrow$ i:= i - 1;

$\qquad\qquad$ $\underline{if}$ $v(i) \geq v(k)$ $\rightarrow$ v:(i)= $v(i)$ + 1

$\qquad\qquad$ $[\![$ $v(i) < v(k)$ $\rightarrow$ skip

$\qquad\qquad$ $\underline{fi}$

$\qquad$ $\underline{od}$ $\{i = 0\}$;

$\qquad$ k:= k + 1

$\underline{od}$ $\{k = M \underline{and} v = p\}$

$$* \qquad * \qquad *$$

The problems A and B I had invented for examination purposes.
After the students had handed in their work, it was W.H.J.Feijen who suggested that it would be nice to derive the one program from the other via
inversion. Because in this case we have a deterministic program in which
no information is destroyed, the inversion is a straightforward process.
What remains of these techniques in the general situation remains to be
seen. Is it possible to show that a program with nondeterministic elements
leads to a unique answer because in its inverse no information is destroyed?
Who knows.... In the meantime I have derived a program --B2 to be precise--
that was new for me.

Plataanstraat 5

5671 AL NUENEN

The Netherlands

prof.dr.Edsger W.Dijkstra

BURROUGHS Research Fellow

The Schorr-Waite Graph Marking Algorithm

David Gries*
Department of Computer Science
Cornell University
Ithaca, N.Y. 14853

Abstract

An explanation is given of the Schorr-Waite algorithm for marking all nodes of a directed graph that are reachable from one given node, using the axiomatic method.

1. The graph-marking problem

Consider an array node(1:n) of n nodes, each of which consists of four fields: a value field, which need not concern us, a field m with a value in the set {0:3}, and two fields ℓ and r (for left and right) with values in the set {0:n}.

value	m	ℓ	r
?	0:3	{0:n}	{0:n}

We sometimes refer to node(i) by its index only (e.g. node i, or simply i) and to its subfields as m(i), ℓ(i) and r(i).

Consider a fixed value root, 1≤root≤n. Using fields ℓ and r in the conventional fashion as "pointers", "links" or indices of other nodes, root defines a directed graph G of nodes "reachable" from root, where, as usual, node i is reachable from node j if there is a path (e0, e1, ...,em) with

(1)   m≥0, j=e0, i=em

(2)   ($\underline{A}$k: 0≤k≤m: $e_{k+1} = \ell(ek)$ $\underline{or}$ $e_{k+1} = r(ek)$)

Throughout, we discuss only noncyclic paths--no node appears twice on a path--although the graph may contain cycles. In addition, we use the following notation:

ispath(j,i) ≡ there exists a path from node j to node i.

Node j is called the head of the path.

G   = {i:ispath(root,i) }

---

*This research was supported by the National Science Foundation under grant MCS76-22360.

If a <u>nil</u> pointer is desired, one can use the value 0. We then let
the array be node(0:n) and set ℓ(0)=r(0)=0. This standard trick eliminates superfluous tests for <u>nil</u>.

The purpose of a marking algorithm is to mark in some fashion all
nodes in graph G. In the case presented here, we assume initially that
m(i)=0 for all nodes i and that execution of the marking algorithm sets
the m field of the nodes in G to 3, thus establishing the truth of

$$(\underline{A}i:\ i\,\epsilon\,G:\ m(i)=3)\ \underline{and}\ (\underline{A}i:\ i\,\notin G:\ m(i)=0)$$

It is assumed that all other fields of all nodes retain their original
values.

2. The Schorr-Waite idea

A marking algorithm traverses G in some fashion, marking nodes as
it goes. It is necessary to keep track of the part of G still to be
traversed, and one often uses a stack to do this. Fig. 1a shows a partially traversed graph and a stack S=(s1,s2,s3).

Stack S describes a path from <u>root</u> to the node p currently being
"visited", and this path serves to define those nodes still to be marked,
as follows:

(1) All the nodes in stack S have been marked (shaded).

(2) Any unmarked node in the graph lies on a path of unmarked
     nodes, the head of this path being p itself or the node r(s)
     for some s in S.

With this as the invariant of the loop of the following algorithm, it
is easy to see that the algorithm marks all the nodes of the graph.
The invariant is initially true and is maintained true by execution of
each guarded command. Upon termination, the invariant, m(p)≠0 and
S=φ together imply that all nodes are marked. And it is easy to argue
that the loop terminates.

```
p,S:= root, φ;
do m(p)=0              → m(p):=3;   push(p,S); p:=ℓ(p)
☐ m(p)≠0 and S≠φ      → pop(S,p);  p:= r(p)
od
```

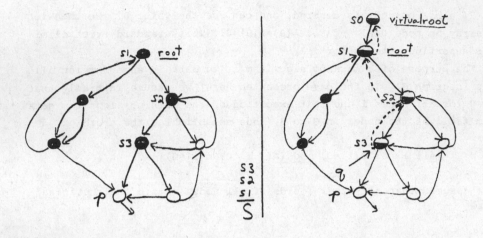

(a) Using a stack   (b) Using Schorr-Waite idea

Figure 1. Partially Traversed Graph

It can be seen that this algorithm generates a <u>spanning</u> <u>tree</u> of the
directed graph. The Schorr-Waite algorithm performs the same service,
marking nodes in the same order, but instead of using a stack to maintain the path from <u>root</u> to p the graph is altered so that the path can
be determined from p, another simple variable q, and the graph itself.

Let p be the node currently being visited and, as Fig. 1b shows,
let q contain the value s3. Since we know in this context that $\ell(q)$
<u>should</u> be p, this allows us to use field $\ell(q)$ for a different purpose --
for example, to hold q's predecessor on the path, s2. Similarly, in
node s2 we can indicate its predecessor s1 and in node s1 its predecessor
s0. Thus the path is determined and the stack is unnecessary. Our task
is to decide exactly what $\ell(i)$ and $r(i)$ should contain for nodes i on
the path, and to make sure that the ℓ and r fields are restored to
their original value upon termination.

As indicated in Fig. 1b, we have introduced a virtual root <u>virtual-</u>
<u>root</u>, solely to simplify the algorithm given later. The fields of
node(<u>virtualroot</u>) are never referenced, and thus we can assume they contain whatever we desire. The value <u>virtual root</u> itself, however, must
be assignable to the ℓ and r fields of a node.

3. The Schorr-Waite Algorithm

The algorithm manipulates the values of the ℓ and r fields, and this forces us to name their initial values. Thus we postulate the initial conditions

$$(\underline{A}i: \quad 0 \leq i \leq n: \quad m(i)=0 \ \underline{and} \ \ell(i)=Li \ \underline{and} \ r(i)=Ri)$$

i.e., Li and Ri are the initial values of the ℓ and r fields of node i. For the virtual root we postulate

$$\ell(\underline{virtualroot})=r(\underline{virtualroot})=\underline{root} \ \underline{and} \ m(\underline{virtualroot})=2.$$

We will need to mention the predecessor of a node on a particular path in the $\underline{original}$ graph. Generally speaking, a node has several predecessors, but at this time we need not designate which one is meant. We use Pi to designate $\underline{a}$ predecessor of i, and thus

$$\text{for any node i reachable from } \underline{root}, \ L_{Pi}=i \ \underline{or} \ R_{Pi}=i.$$

Let us now give the algorithm; its description follows.

```
p,q:= root,virtualroot;
do p≠virtualroot →
      m(p):= m(p)+1
      if m(p)=3 cor m(ℓ(p))=0 → p,ℓ(p),r(p),q:= ℓ(p),r(p),q,p
      ▯ m(p)≠3 cand m(ℓ(p))≠0 →  ℓ(p),r(p),q:= r(p),q,ℓ(p)
      fi
od
```

Invariant I1

Each iteration of the algorithm is said to "visit the current node p", and each node of the graph is visited three times. After the first visit to node i all unmarked nodes in its left subgraph determined by Li are visited three times and fully marked. Node i is then visited a second time. Its right subgraph Ri is visited and marked. Node i is then visited a third time.

Field $m(i)$ is used to keep track of how often node i has been visited -- thus it may have a value 0,1,2, or 3. Secondly, depending on how often the node has been visited, fields $\ell(i)$ and $r(i)$ each contain one

of the three values Li, Ri and Pi. As shown in Fig. 2, these three
values "rotate" through the fields in a simple manner. In addition, for
the node p currently being visited, q contains the link Lp, Rp or PP
that is <u>not</u> currently contained in node p itself.

	m(i)	ℓ(i)	r(i)	q
(0)	0	Li	Ri	Pp
(1)	1	Ri	Pi	Lp
(2)	2	Pi	Li	Rp
(3)	3	Li	Ri	

Fig. 2. Possible Content of Node i, and q when i=p

We have indicated the content of individual nodes; we also need to
describe the relationship among nodes on the path from <u>virtualroot</u> to p.
Any node t on this path satisfies the following property $\mathcal{P}$(t). An
important point is that the nodes on the path have their mark fields 1
or 2 -- they are partially marked. Please note that in a subscription
of a vector the lower bound is 0; e.g. (a,b,c)[0] = a and (a,b,c)[1] = b.

$\mathcal{P}$(t) $\equiv$ there is a path S(t)=(e1,...,ek,e_{k+1})=(<u>virtualroot</u>,...,ek,t)
of the original graph, where k≥0 and each ej, 1≤j≤k,
currently satisfies

1. 1≤m(ej)≤2
2. e_{j+1} = (P_{ej}, L_{ej}, R_{ej})[m(ej)] <u>and</u> $P_{e_{j+1}}$ = ej

We now collect these facts in an invariant I1 of the loop of the
algorithm.

I1: 1. for each node i: (a) 0≤m(i)≤3,
                    (b) ℓ(i)=(Li,Ri,Pi,Li)[m(i)],
                    (c) r(i)=(Ri,Pi,Li,Ri)[m(i)],
     2. for node p: 0≤m(p)≤2 <u>and</u> q=(Pp,Lp,Rp)[m(p)] <u>and</u> $\mathcal{P}$(p)

It is easy to see that execution of p,q:= <u>root</u>, <u>virtualroot</u> establishes the truth of I1. We now show that I1 is indeed an invariant of
the loop. We can verify this informally and "operationally", since the
cases are few and the statements simple. We do this now; formal verification of one of the cases is discussed later.

Using $\tilde{p}$ to denote the value of p prior to execution of the loop body, we consider execution of the loop body with Il <u>and</u> p≠virtualroot true and show that Il is true afterwards. The precondition implies $0 \le m(\tilde{p}) \le 2$. Execution always adds 1 to $m(\tilde{p})$ and assigns $r(\tilde{p})$ to $\ell(\tilde{p})$ and q to $r(\tilde{p})$. This "rotates values" one position through the fields $\ell(\tilde{p})$ and $r(\tilde{p})$ as required. Thus, with the help of precondition Il, Il.1 is seen to be true after execution.

We now show that Il.2 is invariantly true. Table 1 describes execution of the loop body in five cases, based on the values $m(\tilde{p})$ and $m(\ell(\tilde{p}))$ before execution. Each line gives the initial conditions, the path $S(p) = S(\tilde{p})$ (that is defined in relation $\mathcal{P}(p)$) before execution and the path $S(p)$ after execution of the loop body. It should be noted that execution alters the contents only of node $\tilde{p}$; hence the properties required of nodes el,...ek in $S(p)$ remain true.

In the first two cases of Table 1, a <u>new</u> node $L\tilde{p}$ or $R\tilde{p}$ with mark field 0 is added to the path (by execution of $p:=\ell(p)$). Since $1 \le m(\tilde{p}) \le 2$ after execution, we see that the properties of p required in $\mathcal{P}(p)$ are satisfied: $p=(P\tilde{p},L\tilde{p},R\tilde{p})[m(\tilde{p})]$ and $Pp = \tilde{p}$. Hence $\mathcal{P}(p)$ remains true. Moreover, execution leaves $m(p)=0$ and $q = \tilde{p} = Pp$, and Il.2 is true after execution.

Consider next the two cases given by $(m(\tilde{p})<2$ <u>and</u> $m(\ell(p))\ne0)$. Execution leaves $p=\tilde{p}$ and hence $\mathcal{P}(p)$ remains true. Note that execution adds 1 to $m(\tilde{p})$, leaving $1 \le m(\tilde{p}) \le 2$, and sets q to the initial value of $\ell(\tilde{p})$, which yields $q=(Pp,Lp,Rp)[m(p)]$. Hence Il.2 **re**mains invariantly true.

Consider the last case, with $m(\tilde{p})=2$. Variable p is set to the value $ek=\ell(\tilde{p})$, thus deleting a node from path $S(p)$. $\mathcal{P}(p)$ remains true. Note that $m(ek)$ is not changed, so that upon termination $1 \le m(p)=m(ek) \le 2$. Moreover, q is set to the value $\tilde{p}$, thus satisfying $q=(Pp,Lp,Rp)[m(p))]$, and Il.2 is true upon termination.

Initial Condition	Consequence	S(p) after execution
$m(\tilde{p})=0$, $m(\ell(\tilde{p}))=0$	$\ell(\tilde{p})=L\tilde{p}$	$(el,...,ek,\tilde{p},p)$, $p=L\tilde{p}$
$m(\tilde{p})=1$, $m(\ell(\tilde{p}))=0$	$\ell(\tilde{p})=R\tilde{p}$	$(el,...,ek,\tilde{p},p)$, $p=R\tilde{p}$
$m(\tilde{p})=0$, $m(\ell(\tilde{p}))\ne0$	$\ell(\tilde{p})=L\tilde{p}$	$(el,...,ek,\tilde{p})$, $p=\tilde{p}$
$m(\tilde{p})=1$, $m(\ell(\tilde{p}))\ne0$	$\ell(\tilde{p})=R\tilde{p}$	$(el,...,ek,\tilde{p})$, $p=\tilde{p}$
$m(\tilde{p})=2$	$\ell(\tilde{p})=P\tilde{p}=ek$	$(el,...,ek)$, $p=ek$

Table 1. Outline of execution of loop body
with (initially) $S(p)=S(\tilde{p})=(el,...,ek,\tilde{p})$

This shows informally the invariance of Il. For those whose tastes run to more formal proof, we now show that Il remains invariantly true when the second multiple assignment is executed. The guard of this assignment is $(m(p) \neq 3$ cand $m(\ell(p)) \neq 0)$, and since we are assuming it to be true just before execution of the multiple assignment the following weakest precondition must be true before execution of the loop body:

$$wp("m(p) := m(p)+1", \; m(p) \neq 3 \text{ cand } m(\ell(p)) \neq 0)$$
$$= \quad (m; \; p:m(p)+1)(p) \neq 3 \text{ cand } (m; \; p:m(p)+1)(\ell(p)) \neq 0$$
$$= \quad m(p)+1 \neq 3 \text{ cand } (m; \; p:m(p)+1)(\ell(p)) \neq 0 \tag{2}$$

Here we have used the definition of array assignment (see [3] or [7]), and the conventional notation $(m; \; j:r)$ to denote the array (or function) that is the same as m except that its value at the point j is r. Writing

$$ass \equiv "m(p) := m(p)+1; \; \ell(p),r(p),q := r(p),q,\ell(p)"$$

we must prove that

$$Il \text{ and } p \neq virtualroot \text{ and } (2) \Rightarrow wp(ass,Il)$$

Let us prove this in parts. We have

$$wp(ass, \mathcal{P}(p)) = \mathcal{P}(p)$$

and this is implied by Il. Secondly,

$$wp(ass, 0 \leq m(p) \leq 2 \text{ and } q=(Pp,Lp,Rp)[m(p)]$$
$$= 0 \leq m(p)+1 \leq 2 \text{ and } \ell(p)=(Pp,Lp,Rp)[m(p)+1]$$
$$= -1 \leq m(p) \leq 1 \quad \text{ and } \ell(p)=(Lp,Rp,Pp)[m(p)]$$

and this is implied by Il and assertion (2). Finally,

$$wp(ass, Il.1) = \text{for each node } i,$$
$$\text{(a)} \quad 0 \leq (m; \; p:m(p)+1)(i) \leq 3,$$
$$\text{(b)} \quad (\ell; \; p:r(p))(i) = (Li,Ri,Pi,Li)[(m; \; p:m(p)+1)(i)],$$
$$\text{(c)} \quad (r; \; p:q)(i) \quad = (Ri,Pi,Li,Ri)[(m; \; p:m(p)+1)(i)].$$

For i=p this yields

        (a) $0 \leq m(p)+1 \leq 3$,

        (b) $r(p) = (Lp, Rp, Pp, Lp)[m(p)+1]$,

        (c) $q = (Rp, Pp, Lp, Rp)[m(p)+1]$,

which is implied by I1 and assertion (2). For i≠p this yields simply what I1 indicates:

        (a) $0 \leq m(i) \leq 3$,

        (b) $\ell(i) = (Li, Ri, Pi, Li)[m(i)]$,

        (c) $r(i) = (Ri, Pi, Li, Ri)[m(i)]$.

Hence I1 is invariant.

The invariant I2

Thus far we have determined the possible content of the individual nodes and the form of the path S(p) from <u>virtualroot</u> to node p. We must also indicate possible m values of nodes not on the path. More importantly, we need to show the following: any unmarked node in the graph is on a completely unmarked path, and further the head of that path is either p or Rs for some node s on the path S(p). It is this property that will help us prove that upon termination all nodes are marked. Note the similarity between this and the invariant used in the algorithm of Section 2. The complete invariant is given below.

I2. 1. (Ai: i ∉ G: m(i)=0)

     2. (Ai: i ∉ S(p): m(i)=0 <u>or</u> m(i)=3)

     3. (Ai: i ∉ G <u>and</u> m(i)=0: there is a path of the original graph, all of whose nodes are unmarked (mark field 0), with one of the forms

          a) (Rp,...,i)   (only if m(p)=1)

          b) (p,...,i)   (only if m(p)=0)

          c) (Rs,...,i)   (s ∈ S(p),s≠p, p not on the
                                                                   path)

That I2.1 is invariant is obvious; the algorithm only traverses nodes in G. Part I2.2 is initially true, since all nodes are initially unmarked. Secondly, only the last node in S(p), that is, p itself, has its m field changed. Hence I2.2 could be falsified only by having a

node p with $m(p)=1$ or $m(p)=2$ deleted from the path; but p is deleted
from $S(p)$ only when $m(p)=3$. Thus I2.2 remains true.

We now show that I2.3 is invariant as follows; we consider any
unmarked node i that is "reachable" by some path as described in I2.3
and show that execution of the loop body with p having the initial
value $\tilde{p}$ terminates either with $m(i)\neq0$ or with i reachable by some path
as described in I2.3. There are three paths described in I2.3 and
five cases to consider for execution of the loop body, as described in
Table 1. This yields 15 combinations, but many of those are impossible
and need not be considered.

case a: $m(\tilde{p})=1$ and the path to i has form $(R\tilde{p},\ldots,i)$.

Only one case given in Table 1 arises: $m(\tilde{p})=1$, $m(\ell(\tilde{p}))=0$ and $\ell(\tilde{p})=R\tilde{p}$.
Execution transforms path $S(p)$ into $(e1,\ldots,ek,\tilde{p},p)$ with $p=R\tilde{p}$ and $m(p)=0$;
hence i is reachable using the path $(p,\ldots,i)$ -- case b of I2.3.

case b: $m(\tilde{p})=0$ and the path to i has the form $(\tilde{p},\ldots,i)$.

If the path consists of a single node $\tilde{p}$, $\tilde{p}$ is marked ($m(\tilde{p})$ becomes 1).
Otherwise the path to i has the form $(\tilde{p},L\tilde{p},\ldots,i)$ or $(\tilde{p},R\tilde{p},\ldots,i)$. The
three possible initial conditions (based on Table 1), the initial path
to i, the path $S(p)$ after execution, and the path that makes i reachable
according to I2.3 after execution, are listed below.

condition	old path to i	S(p)	new path to i
$m(p)=0$, $m(\ell(\tilde{p}))=0$	$(\tilde{p},L\tilde{p},\ldots,i)$	$(e1,\ldots,ek,\tilde{p},p)$	$(p,\ldots,i),p=L\tilde{p},m(p)=0$
$m(p)=0$, $m(\ell(\tilde{p}))=0$	$(\tilde{p},R\tilde{p},\ldots,i)$	$(e1,\ldots,ek,\tilde{p},p)$	$(Rs,\ldots,i),s=\tilde{p}\,\epsilon\,S(p)$
$m(p)=0$, $m(\ell(\tilde{p}))\neq0$	$(\tilde{p},R\tilde{p},\ldots,i)$	$(e1,\ldots,ek,\tilde{p})$	$(Rp,\ldots,i),m(p)=1$

case c: $s\,\epsilon\,S(\tilde{p})$, $s\neq\tilde{p}$ and the path has the form $(Rs,\ldots,i)$.

Execution in the first two cases of Table 1 can affect this path only
if the new node p is on it. But since $m(p)=0$ after execution, this means
i would be reachable after execution using a path $(p,\ldots,i)$. Execution
in cases 3,4 of Table 1 do not affect the path $(Rs,\ldots,i)$. Finally,
consider the 5th case. The path $(Rs,\ldots,i)$ is not affected by execution
unless $s=ek$. Suppose that $s=ek$: the path is $(R_{ek},\ldots,i)$. There are
two possible situations before execution:

(1) $m(\tilde{p})=2$, $\ell(\tilde{p})=ek$, $m(ek)=1$, $\tilde{p}=L_{ek}$;

(2) $m(\tilde{p})=2$, $\ell(\tilde{p})=ek$, $m(ek)=2$, $\tilde{p}=R_{ek}$; this is a contradiction: $\tilde{p}=R_{ek}$, $m(\tilde{p})=2$, but $m(R_{ek})=0$.

In the former case the path $S(p)$ is changed to $(el,...,ek)$ with $p=ek$, $m(p)=1$, and i can be reached from the path $(Rp,...,i)$, which satisfies I2.3b. This completes the proof of the invariance of I2.3.

Showing termination

Let g be the number of nodes in the graph reachable from <u>root</u>. The function t,

t=3*g-(sum of the m fields of nodes reachable from <u>root</u>),

satisfies $(I1 \Rightarrow t \geq 0)$. It is decreased by one with each iteration of the loop. Hence, after a finite number of iterations the loop must be terminated.

Showing the result upon termination

Upon termination we should have established the truth of

(<u>A</u>i: i ∉ G: m(i)=0) <u>and</u> (<u>A</u>i: i ∈ G: m(i)=3)

The first part is always true, so it remains to show that the second part is true upon termination. Upon termination (p=<u>virtualroot</u> <u>and</u> $\mathcal{P}$(p)) holds. Hence the path $S(p)$ consists of the single node <u>virtualroot</u> and m(<u>virtualroot</u>) = 2. This, together with I2.2, implies that there are no unmarked nodes in G. Further, I2.1 implies that all nodes of G have their mark fields 3, while I1 indicates that the ℓ and r fields of all nodes have their initial values.

4. Variations on the theme

We have shown that the algorithm traverses and marks all nodes of the graph. The conditions were that each node of the graph have exactly two successors, and that marking consists of changing the m field of each node from 0 to 3. One can easily modify the algorithm to cover various other cases, as follows. We leave these to the reader:

1. Instead of using a virtual root, one can initialize with p,q:= <u>root</u>, <u>root</u> and replace "p≠<u>virtualroot</u>' by "m(p)≠3 in the algorithm.

2. One can allow a real <u>nil</u> pointer in the ℓ and r fields if one suitably tests ℓ(p) in the guards of the alternative statement before testing
m(ℓ(p)).

3. The mark field is sometimes a single bit that must be set to 1, but
a second bit field in each node can be used. This field is 0 initially
and upon termination.

4. One can allow two kinds of nodes: "interior" nodes have a two-bit
m field and ℓ and r fields; "atomic" nodes contain a one-bit m field
and a value field. Atoms should be visited only once, interior nodes
three times.

5. One can modify the algorithm to traverse any arbitrary graph and
generate a spanning tree for it. The m field must then be large enough
to contain 1 plus the maximum number of outgoing edges from a node. In
this case, it may be better not to "rotate" the values through the link
fields. Instead use the convention that the outgoing-edge fields from
node i are e(i,1),...,e(i,n) and that if 1≤m(i)≤n then e(i,m(i)) contains
the predecessor Pi of node i.

6. <u>Discussion</u>

I have given a proof -- a convincing argument -- of the correctness
of the Schorr-Waite marking algorithm using the "axiomatic" proof method.
(The algorithm itself was discovered by Schorr and Waite [4] and independently by L.P. Deutsch.) I developed the proof first because I wanted
to discuss the algorithm in a class and secondly because the feeling had
been that this algorithm was too difficult or unsuitable for application
of the method; others felt that the "intermittent assertion" method,
used informally by Knuth in his volumes and later developed by Burstall
[5] and Manna and Waldinger [6], was more suitable. (I don't mean to
imply that developing this proof was easy. I went through many versions;
it took time to develop a good notation in which to describe the ideas
clearly.)

The suitability of the methods is left to the reader to judge, but
I would like to make two comments.

First, in all the published literature on the intermittent assertion
method that I have seen so far, the algorithms used to illustrate the
method have been quite "unstructured" and therefore difficult to comprehend. It is as if the authors felt that the method gave them license

to dish up raw spaghetti to the reader to digest, with the feeling that
the sauce (the proof method) poured over the spaghetti would compensate.
To my taste, it doesn't. This is a comment on how the method has been
used thus far, and not a comment on the method itself. In time one
might learn to cook the spaghetti and sauce so that both are palatable.

Secondly, with the axiomatic method, one is forced to develop an
invariant for each loop, and I feel this is a great advantage rather
than a disadvantage. The invariant is a handle by which one can hold
on to the loop. Quite often, one will forget the algorithm but remember
the essential parts of the invariant, and from this one can usually
reconstruct the full invariant and then the algorithm. The fact that
the algorithm itself is given in a simple, structured form can help.

In the marking algorithm presented, one has to remember a few essential points about the invariant: First, the field m(i) indicates
which values Li, Ri and Pi are in ℓ(i) and r(i). The symmetry and the
way the values "rotate through" should help. Secondly, one must remember
that q and p help define a path S(p) of partially marked nodes from the
root to p. Thirdly, each unmarked node of the graph is reachable on an
unmarked path from p or from a node Rs for some node s on the path S(p).
Remembering these basic facts should allow one to reconstruct the invariant and algorithm.

Acknowledgements. I am grateful to Gary Levin for carefully reading
and commenting on several drafts of this article, and to Edsger W. Dijkstra for some value criticism on the last draft.

References

[1] Floyd, R.W. Assigning meanings to programs. Proc. Amer. Math.
     Soc. Symp. in Applied Math 19 (1967), 19-31.

[2] Hoare, C.A.R. An axiomatic basis for computer programming. CACM
     12 (Oct. 1969), 576-580, 583.

[3] Dijkstra, E.W. A Discipline of Programming. Prentice-Hall, 1976.

[4] Schorr, H. and W.M. Waite. An efficient machine-independent pro-
     cedure for garbage collection in various list structures. CACM 10
     (Aug. 1967), 501-506.

[5] Burstall, R.M. Program proving as hand simulation with a little
     induction. Proc. IFIP Congress 1974, 308-312.

[6] Manna, Z. and R. Waldinger. Is "sometime" sometimes better than
     "always"? Intermittent assertions in proving program correctness.
     CACM 21 (Feb. 1978), 159- 172.

[7] Gries, D. The multiple assignment statement. IEEE Trans. Software
     Engineering, SE-4 (March 1978), 89-93.

Eliminating the Chaff

a Sermon[1] by

David Gries

Cornell University

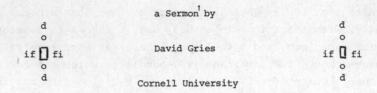

The Scripture

The scripture for this morning's sermon is taken from Knuth's first epistle[2] to the Structurians (page 6, paragraphs 2 and 3). This particular part of the epistle concerns Knuth's attempt to develop an algorithm discussed in the first book of the old testament,[3] and the problems that Knuth faced:

> "Whenever I'm trying to write a program without go to statements, I
> waste an inordinate amount of time in deciding what type of iterative
> clause to use (while or repeat,etc.) ... I know in my head what I
> want to do, but I have to translate it painstakingly into a notation
> that often isn't well-suited to the mental concept....
> (I wrote the program while) ... I was in bed with a pad of paper,...,
> at about 1:00 am; I expect I finished 15 or 20 minutes later. About
> 2 minutes were wasted trying to think of a suitable iteration statement."

Here endeth the reading of the scripture.

The Technical Lesson

Keeping in mind the scripture for the day, let us develop a small algorithm in the methodological way and see what can be learned from it. Given are fixed $n \geqslant 1$, $p \geqslant 0$, and $s = n \cdot p$. Given is an array $b[1:n]$ with initial values

```
b[i] = Bi  for 1≤i≤n.
```

An algorithm is desired that will establish the truth (and remember, truth is always our goal) of

```
R:  b[i] = Bi + p·(i-1)   for 1≤i≤n.
```

Now, the heathen will simply write as fast as he can. Using a simple variable t in order to avoid the necessity for a multiplication within the loop, he scribbles

```
t = 0;
DO i = 1 TO n;;
   b[i]  = b[i] +t;;
   t = t+p; END;;
```

We of the faith, however, shudder at such a shoddy proceeding. Divine inspiration leads us to first write an invariant that captures the idea of first calculating b[1], then b[2], and so on, but avoiding the multiplication:

```
P:  1≤k≤n+1  and  t = p·(k-1)  and  s = n·p  and
    b[i] = Bi + p·(i-1) for 1≤i<k   and
    b[i] = Bi  for k≤i≤n.
```

We also divine the variant function f ≡ n-k, and then develop the guarded command loop with the guard B still missing:

```
k,t:= 2,p;
do  ? →b[k]:= b[k]+t;
       k,t:= k+1,t+p
od
```

Knowing that B can often be determined from (P and B)⇒wp("loop body", P) and (P and not B)⇒R, we develop the pertinent part of the aforementioned weakest pre-condition:

```
1≤k+1≤n+1  and  t = p·(k-1)  and  s=n·p.
```

We see that the guard B ≡ (k≠n+1) will be satisfactory. But being experienced in these matters, we know that a second, a third, or even fourth effort can help. Success is the result of one's own hard efforts and is neither the gift of God nor a spontaneous natural product.

We note that if initially p=0 there is no need to add anything to the elements of array b at all. The heathen, when approached with this fact (he rarely is careful enough to note such things himself), will no doubt awkwardly embed his loop in an IF:

```
IF p=0 THEN DO:  t=0;
                 DO I=...
                 END;;END;
```

Shunning such an immoral approach, we pray for guidance, investigate P and R again, and note that

$$P \text{ and } p \cdot (k-1) = t = s = p \cdot n$$

yields either p=0, in which case the result R is established, or k=n+1, in which case R is also established. Hence we take not B ≡ (t=s) and proudly write

```
k,t:= 2,p;
do t≠s → b[k]:= b[k]+t;
        k,t:= k+1, t+p
od
```

A prayer of thanks completes the task.

Note that the resulting algorithm seems to have two so-called counters or index-variables, and that one might attempt to rewrite it as

```
k:= 2;
for t:= p step p until s do  k,b[k]:= k+1, b[k]+t .
```

But this doesn't work because the loop, in most languages, is either ill-defined or nonterminating when p=0! The poor heathen, his thoughts dangerously impaired by devilishly inadequate control structures, is simply unable to write the algorithm in its simplest and most elegant form.

A Moralistic Discussion

Searchers for simplistic beauty, we gather here today to discuss the fate of those who wallow in self-indulgent complexity, who revel in difficult and wrong solutions to simple problems, who insist on following outmoded, archaic or even modern but untested religions, who stubbornly refuse to admit the superiority of the one true one. These souls will live a long, harsh life in the hell of unreliability. Burdened by the complexity of their own notations, plagued by undisciplined thoughts, they will suffer in the computer rooms for eons. But I do foresee that one day they will judge again, the predicated transformation will take place, and the world will be in harmony.

The fate of Knuth, the author of today's reading, is a good example for all of us. An excellent mind, a great creative thinker, the fastest pen in the West, Knuth still has his troubles. You see, he has taken upon himself the task of describing Computer Science in seven volumes, but it looks like a never-ending task. The faster he writes, the further behind he is! Knuth could be likened to Job; blameless and upright, he has enormous misfortune, being saddled with more page proofs to read than anyone in history. But unlike Job, it is his own fault. It is his own Job Control Language that has caused much of his misfortune; this archaic, outmoded creation causes programs and their description to be twice, nay even thrice as long and complicated as necessary.

Just listen to the cry of a man who recognizes his problem but is incapable of transforming himself: "I waste an inordinate amount of time deciding what type of iterative clause to use!" "About 2 minutes were wasted?" "I was in bed with a pad of paper!"

Is he not just like the heathen in the technical lesson, who breaks under the strain of so many inadequate control structures, so many outmoded algorithmic thoughts? Friends, Knuth's problems could be so simply solved just by casting out old habits and accepting the guarded commandments from above.

Colleagues in clearness and conciseness, on my way here this morning I had the occasion to walk through a vegetable garden with our leader, and he taught me a lesson I will never forget. The sun was shining brightly, a light breeze was blowing. We meandered through bushes bearing bright green beans, around vines of crisp cucumbers, every plant bore its luscious fruit for the fulfillment of our stomachs -- except the tomato plant. This poor tomato plant was actually quite large and sprawling, with some of its branches hungrily lapping up the space between it and its neighbors, even flowing over and covering them. And yet, it had only a few, pitiful tomatoes.

Our leader saw its condition and began snapping off the sprawling branches and pinching off new shoots, and slowly the tomato plant was pruned to a manageable size. As he did this, our leader caressed the plant and gently said:

"Sucker the tomatoes to come unto me."

His idea was that the plant growth was going into those unproductive, ungainly, sprawling offshoots, and by suckering the plant, by pinching off awkwardness, the growth could be given where needed, so that the tomatoes themselves could grow and prosper.

Ah, my friends, I saw the analogy at once and resolved then and there to spread the word far and wide. Our own programs, our programming languages, nay, even our own thoughts should be purged of all life-sapping, useless growth. And I urge you to begin immediately to release those complexities, to burn those whiles, untils and repeats, to exorcise those daemonic indexed dos, to prune those PL/Is, and instead to concentrate on the simple, the elegant, the sweet. And soon, you will find yourself able to grow more luscious, tasteful fruit in the form of the heavenly algorithms we all long for. As you eliminate the chaff, bit by bit you will find your memory expanding, your intuition intuiting, you real creative ability showing itself. And you will find the peace, the tranquility, the harmony you so much desire.

My colleagues in simplicity, in closing let me implore you to guard your commands well. Lately I notice a number of false prophets intermittently asserting themselves. Before tasting the fruit of their labors, make sure it is manna from heaven, and not from elsewhere. Even now, in a distant land the old god of wine and other pleasures, Bacchus, has emerged again, and is enticing others to indulge in heathenish notational orgies.

And in addition, pretenders are claiming unsubstantiated practicality of transubstantiations from recursion to iteration. Many of these pretenders have the audacity

to use Shakespeare's name when they rail at iteration: "Oh! thou hast damnable iteration, and art indeed able to corrupt a saint," when we all know that what Shakespeare
really said was

> Oh FORTRAN! thou hast damnable iteration, and art indeed able
> to corrupt a saint like Knuth!

This of course he said when discussing Knuth's plight with our leader; the repetitive
guarded command construct was so much praised in this conversation. We all also remember their other discussion, part of which has become known as "As You Like It",
in which Shakespeare said of the alternative construct:

> Your "if" is the only peacemaker; much virtue in "if".

Oh my friends, it is up to you, and you alone, to stand steadfast against these frauds,
against pollution by awkward notation, against constructs that limit the possibilities
for algorithmic expression, and I urge you to lead a clean, static, assertional life,
exorcising all those sinful, operational feelings.

Let us Supplicate

Oh leader, we all know what fools mortals are, but help us, we beseech you, to break
our bad habits, to put our houses in order. Teach us that every why needs a wherefore
but not a watfor. Help us to learn that knowledge is lost unless it is turned into
wisdom. Help us to learn that correctness lies within a little and certain compass,
but that error is immense. Teach us that the ideal is the union of the mathematician
with the poet, of correctness with a passion. Let us become doers and not just hearers
of the word, so that we become invariantly true to you and thus invariantly one with
you.   doodiffi.

Notes

1) I have often been accused (jokingly, of course) of "preaching the religion". Here
   is a taste of my real preaching. I leave the reader to judge how serious my message is.
2) Knuth, D.E. A Review of "Structured Programming". STAN-CS-73-371, Computer Science
   Department, Stanford University, June 1973.
3) Dahl, O.-J., E.W. Dijkstra and C.A.R. Hoare. Structured Programming. Academic
   Press, 1972.
4) Various passages from other authors have been appropriately misquoted.
5) Don Knuth's single comment on a draft of this sermon was "Amen!".

II. PROGRAM VERIFICATION

Proofs, Programs and their Development - The Axiomatic Approach

The idea of proving properties of programs (e.g., correctness) was mentioned as early as 1961 by McCARTHY; diligent searching would possibly uncover earlier references. The idea began to come of age in 1966 and 1967, through the work of NAUR and FLOYD. In 1969 HOARE published a paper that, building on Naur's and Floyd's work, laid the foundations for much of the current work in programming methodology, program proving, and programming language design. Hoare's approach, known currently as the "axiomatic" approach, was to define language constructs in terms of how programs containing them could be proved correct, instead of in terms of how they were to be executed. The definitions consisted of a logical system of axiom schemata and inference rules.

Such a language definition makes sense; if we want to really understand programs we need to know what "correctness" means and we need to know how to formally prove correctness. But the idea of such a language definition had other advantages as well. It allowed us to think of defining constructs to make proofs involving them easier to understand, instead of making their execution easy. Thus understanding, instead of execution, was pushed to the fore. Secondly, it led quite naturally to a clear separation of concerns; the programmer could consciously but separately pursue his main concerns: correctness and efficiency.

At first, the major problem seemed to be to produce correctness proofs for existing programs, and indeed it was a difficult if not impossible task. But gradually it was recognized that the program and its proof should be developed hand-in-hand, with the proof ideas leading the way. In other words, concern for correctness - and the arguments used in proving correctness - should influence the development of a program from the beginning. This led DIJKSTRA to develop a calculus for the derivation of programs.

We are now at a stage where sound knowledge of the axiomatic approach (including the above mentioned calculus), together with conscious application of the principles involved, can indeed enhance the effectivity of the programmer.

We are learning how to temper the formalisms with common sense, we are learning how to master the complexity involved in programming, as we are slowly learning how to teach others to do so.

A glance through the lecture notes in this volume will illustrate how much the concern for understandable correctness has influenced us. We find it playing a role in the specification of algorithms, in work on abstract data types, in the definition of programming languages and their constructs, in discussions of concurrent programming, and in examples of program development. These notes, however, contain no introduction to the axiomatic method or the calculus mentioned earlier. These topics have been in the literature long enough to be part of the culture of any computer scientist. Each of the articles will refer the reader to necessary introductory material, should the reader feel it necessary to read introductory material.

D. Gries

CURRENT IDEAS IN PROGRAMMING METHODOLOGY

David Gries
Cornell University

1. Introduction

1.1 Topic definition

This contribution attempts to review and assess research in the area of programming methodology. Programming actually covers the management, planning, design, implementation or development, verification, debugging and evaluation of programs. Since most of these topics are treated in other articles of this book, I concentrate here on one aspect of programming: the design and development of small (up to five pages long) correct programs.

Does it make sense to discuss programming such small programs? Definitely. Experience shows that the production of a small, correct program is itself a difficult task, which relatively few people have mastered. It is hard to understand how we can expect to effectively develop large programs when an understanding of the development of small programs has to a large extent eluded us. We can even argue that the ability to regularly produce small, correct programs is necessary for the development of large programs, as follows (Dijkstra):

A large program or software system is ultimately composed of n (say) small programs or program "modules". Suppose each of these n independent modules has a probability p of being correct. Then the probability P that the whole system is correct surely satisfies $P \leq p^n$. Since n is large, in order to have any confidence in the reliability of the system at all, p must be <u>very</u> close to one.

Thus, I feel justified in concentrating on one single aspect of programming: the development of small, correct programs.

[+]Excerpts from an article to appear in <u>Research Directions In Software Technology</u> (P. Wegner, editor)

This article will <u>not</u> pinpoint numerous deep, detailed results, theorems or mechanical tools that, if only brought to the attention of the programmer, would cause an immediate rise in productivity and reliability. Instead, I hope to give an overall impression of the important ideas that have been emerging over the past ten years. Hopefully, the reader will come to the conclusion that while the ideas behind good programming seem simple, their conscious application is not. Any real rise in programmer effectivity will require education, a change of attitude on the part of the programmer, and much practice. Let us begin by assessing the past in order to provide a perspective on our current thoughts about programming.

1.2. A Very Short History of Programming

During the early years of computing, computers were relatively expensive, limited in power, and often unreliable. The main emphasis was on the computer: keeping it in working order and using it as efficiently as possible. The programmer's task was to code simple (by today's standards), small algorithms in the machine language of a particular computer, using as many clever tricks and techniques as possible in order to overcome restrictions on memory and speed. The fact that programs could modify themselves was thought to be a significant achievement, and sharing of memory for different purposes within a program, sometimes even first as data and then as instructions, was considered a clever way to beat the machine.

A program was a personal thing, rarely to be read by others. Programs were written for one machine, and for one purpose; rarely were they transported to other installations for use elsewhere.

With the emergence of FORTRAN and other high-level languages, programming methodology changed little. True, it became easier to program, but the idea was still to squeeze memory and time out of the machine, using as many clever tricks as possible. The good programmer knew FORTRAN on his machine well enough to "get at" the machine in spite of FORTRAN!

Programming in FORTRAN could be taught in one or two weeks to produce good programmers, depending on their ability to solve puzzles. Little attention was given to readability, adaptability, or even to correctness in the general sense; learning the language and coping with machine-oriented output seemed more important.

As computers became more powerful and flexible, as the cost of
hardware decreased, as the problems given to programmers became more
complex and large, and as programmers discovered that clever tricks
used earlier were not enough, emphasis changed from hardware to software. The appetite of programmers and those who posed problems for
complexity outgrew their ability to digest it. More and more time was
spent debugging, deadlines were missed more frequently, and cost
overruns became the rule rather than the exception.

I have painted a rather bleak picture of the past, based on
retrospection on my own training and experiences and on looking at
texts and journals, both old and new. There were, of course, many
good experiences and exciting events, too. Wilkes points out
that the closed subroutine was invented in 1949; that some early texts
discussed and advocated what could be regarded as a primitive form of
structured programming (e.g. Wilkes [51]), and that in those ancient
times some programmers found no need to make use of flow
charts in designing programs -- a big advance over many of today's
programmers. Macro-assembly languages, FORTRAN, ALGOL and LISP were
significant achievements. Moreover, most programs did tend to work
after a fashion.

Nevertheless, the state of affairs in programming per se had
deteriorated so much by the late 1960's that two NATO conferences
were convened in 1968 and 1969 to discuss the problem of producing
reliable software at a reasonable cost (Buxton [68,69]). While not
all participants agreed to the use of the term "software crisis," all
agreed that we really did not know how to produce software in a
reasonable manner. Today, we recognize that programming is a difficult
task, and much research in programming methodology is being performed.
This research has already had an effect on the programming world,
enough to warrant more research in both theoretical and practical
areas.

2. Significant Past Research in Programming Methodology

The task of organizing one's thoughts in a way that leads, in a
reasonable amount of time, to an understandable expression of a
computing task, has come to be called structured programming. The

term, first used by Dijkstra in his monograph Notes on Structured
Programming [72], has shaken the programming world. Used in its
narrowest sense (don't use gotos), it has of course been shouted down
by most intelligent people. Used in the broader sense given above, it
has influenced research and practice of programming methodology.

One might well ask whether programmers naturally practice
structured programming. The answer is no, on three counts. First, the
average programmer does not complete his task in a reasonable amount of
time, as is evidenced by the frequent cost overruns and misssing of
deadlines. Second, his final program is not understandable; others
have trouble reading it and later modifying it. Third, most programs
do not satisfy the original specifications and are replete with errors,
some of which are not found for years.

Important research has been directed towards answering the following
questions:

1. How should (could) the process of developing a program be
    organized?

2. How should (could) the program be organized?

3. How do we know a program is correct?

4. How should (could) the documentation be written so as to best
    describe the program?

A discussion of research directed towards answering these questions
will make more sense if we first attempt to understand what problems
the programmer faces, why programmers have difficulties, and what
(mental) tools he has available to overcome them. I attempt this briefly
in the next two subsections, interpreting ideas first presented by
Dijkstra [72].

2.1. The Programmer's Attitude

We must acknowledge that programming is a difficult intellectual
task, due to the size and complexity of the problem we tackle. Size
is certainly a factor. Compilers have 5,000 to 50,000 lines of high-
level language code, and operating systems sometimes 20 times that
amount! Hence, any single person can only hope to remember or even

read the details of only a small part of the programming system.

However program size is not the only culprit. A program of five or six lines can be difficult to understand if not organized and explained well. Two kinds of "complexity" confront us even in such small programs. First, we have the complexity of the computations effected by execution of the program. This kind of complexity we try to overcome by partly "structuring" the program and its description in some way (to be described later).

The second kind of complexity has to do with the "mathematical system" on which the proof of correctness (and other properties) of the program lies. For example, consider a hash-coding scheme, where for a table of size n elements the successive probes for a key K will be at the elements numbered $H1(K), H2(K)..., Hn(K)$. We usually desire these $Hi(K)$ to be all different, so that if necessary all the elements of the table will be tested for the presence of key K. Furthermore, we usually desire other properties of the Hi, such as the absence of primary or secondary "clustering". Such properties can depend on very deep mathematical theorems, which the programmer must discover or at least understand.

The programmer is faced with problems of size and complexity, but there are limits to the amount of material and the degree of complexity he can digest. The programmer must first of all recognize his limitations, rather than ignore them, and seek ways to overcome them. Without this recognition of the difficulty of the task, failure must result.

The wise programmer restricts himself to intellectually manageable programs -- those that can be understood in time proportional to their lengths. This rule actually helps the programmer. If he finds himself incapable of easily understanding something he has written, he immediately redoes it so that it is understandable. He has others read his program before committing it to the computer, so that he can be sure that others understand it. He welcomes their criticism. The ability to understand guides him in his choice of program structures and method of organization.

In other words, the programmer attempts to organize the chaos of details into an understandable program. He attempts to find notation and organization to simplify the complexity. In a sense, we might call structured programming <u>computational</u> <u>simplicity</u>, as opposed to computer science's already existing field, computational complexity.

I should also like to discuss the programmer's attitude toward program errors. The historic attitude is that errors are a necessary evil, and that finding and fixing them naturally requires a good (30-60%) percentage of the programmer's time. Hence the emergence of the terms <u>bugs</u> and <u>debugging</u>. Bugs, like mosquitoes, are always present and must be swatted when found.

The futility of such an attitude was aptly pointed out by Dijkstra, when he said that program testing can never reveal the <u>absence</u> of errors (which is what we want) but only their presence. Others have noted the relatively high cost of fixing a detected error late in the testing process, as opposed to the cost of spending more time on program design and implementation (before testing) so that the error is detected much earlier or so that it never even enters the program.

Thus, while testing it necessary, the responsible programmer writes his program so that the detection of an error during testing is the exception rather than the rule. He develops and organizes his program so that he <u>knows</u> that it is correct, before testing begins.

What emerges from this discussion is that the programmer's <u>attitude</u> towards programming is extremely important. He must recognize his limitations and discover ways to overcome them. He must realize that his job is to produce a correct, readable program <u>before</u> testing. He understands that only through an intensive, ongoing study of the programming process and of the mental tools available to him can he learn to perform his job well.

2.2. Our Mental Aids

In order to know what he can intellectually manage, the programmer must know what mental tools are available to help him. Dijkstra [72] discusses three important ones: enumerative reasoning, mathematical induction and abstraction.

We use <u>enumerative</u> <u>reasoning</u> to understand sequences of statements, conditional statements and some uses of the goto. In effect, we try

to look at each possible execution path and understand that it works
correctly. Enumeration is only an adequate tool when the number of
cases to be considered is moderately small.

Mathematical induction is used to understand iteration (loops)
and recursive procedures. The typical loop can be iterated zero times,
once, twice, or any number of times, and we use induction to see that
all of these work correctly just as we use induction to prove properties
of the integers. The use of induction will be illustrated in section
2.3. For now we just mention that induction is an indispensible tool
and that programmers must learn how to handle it formally. Programmers
need much more mathematical maturity than is currently recognized.

Abstraction can be thought of as the process of singling out one
or more qualities or properties of an object for further use. The
purpose is to be able to concentrate only on relevant properties of
the situation and to ignore irrelevant ones. Abstraction permeates
the whole of programming. The concept of a variable is an abstraction
from its current value. When we write a procedure and then write
several calls we are using abstraction. That is, when we write it we
are concerned with how it works; afterwards, we can forget completely
about the how and concern ourselves only with what it does. In effect,
we have extended our programming language with another operation. When
we implement a new data type, say complex variables or linked lists, we
again think of these data types as abstract objects that we can use.

Abstraction is a most powerful tool, used also in mathematics,
and the programmer must be aware of how and why he uses it.

Now if enumerative reasoning (in small quantities), induction
and abstraction are our main mental aids, then we should restrict
ourselves to constructs and organizations that allow us to use them
efficiently. Sequencing and alternation we understand through
enumerative reasoning; iteration through induction. Procedures, macros,
and programmer-defined data types are mechanisms that help us in using
abstraction. Should we wish to use other program constructs, we must
be sure beforehand that we can effectively understand them.

2.3. On Proving the Correctness of Programs

A proof of a theorem is an argument that convinces the reader

that the theorem is correct. The proof may be formal, arising from
axioms as a step-by-step application of inference rules as in logic;
on the other hand it may be composed entirely of informal reasoning.

Evidence supports the statement that typical, informal reasoning
used for programs is insufficient, and because of this debugging takes
a major portion of the total project -- from 30% to 60% of the total
time.

With simple problems or theorems, informal reasoning often
suffices, but as problems become more complex, informal reasoning
becomes less and less helpful, and we must rely on more systematic,
formal techniques. Programs are by nature complex, detailed objects,
and even a five or six line program can be incomprehensible unless
explained correctly. Therefore, it is necessary to develop formal
techniques for proving properties of programs. However, they must be
practical enough to be used by programmers on "real life" problems,
and hopefully should shed light on the programming process as a whole.

This idea of proving programs correct has been simmering for some
time. For example, in a most stimulating paper, which first stated
the goals and benefits of a mathematical science of computation,
McCarthy [61] said that "instead of trying out computer programs on
test cases until they are debugged, one should prove that they have
the desired properties." Naur [66] emphasized the importance of program
proofs and provided an informal technique for specifying them. Floyd
[67] suggested that specification of proof techniques could provide
an adequate definition of a programming language. Influenced by this
suggestion, Hoare [69] provided the first axiomatic approach for
computer programming. This paper laid the foundations for much of the
current work in programming methodology, program proving, and program
language design. Indeed, the approach forms a good part of the foundation of "structured programming," and I would like to outline it here.

Hoare [69] formally defines a programming language -- a fragment
of ALGOL. The definitions of the language constructs are designed
precisely to indicate how to prove properties of programs using the
constructs. The meaning of a construct is given in terms of assertions
about the input variables and output variables of the construct. As
an example, suppose P is an assertion, x:=e an assignment statement,
and P[e->x], the result of textually substituting (e) for every

occurrence of x in P. Then the <u>definition</u> of the assignment statement
is

$$\{P[e->x]\} \quad x:=e \quad \{P\}$$

which informally reads: if P[e->x] is true before executing the
assignment x:=e, then P is true afterwards. As an example, we have
$\{(a+b)+c>0\}$ d:=a+b $\{d+c>0\}$.

Note that this definition indicates nothing about <u>how</u> to execute
the assignment statement. It describes only assertions or relations
between variables that hold before and after the execution. Thus our
attention is turned away from how to execute things, and towards the
more static and easier-to-observe objects, the assertions.

The <u>while</u> loop is defined as follows:

Under the assumption {P <u>and</u> B} S {P} the following holds:
{P} <u>while</u> B <u>do</u> S {P <u>and</u> (<u>not</u> B)}   (1)

In English, we read (1) as follows. Suppose execution of the loop
body S under the precondition B leaves a particular assertion P invariantly true. Then, if the loop <u>while</u> B <u>do</u> S is executed with P true
initially, upon termination P will still be true and moreover B will
be false.

Remember, (1) is the <u>definition</u> of the loop. It teaches us to
understand a particular loop within a program in several steps, as
follows.

1. Show that P is true initially, before execution of the loop;

2. Show that the desired result R of execution follows from P
    <u>and</u> <u>not</u> B;

3. Show that {P <u>and</u> B} S {P};

4. Show that the loop halts (by other means, although this can
    be included in the formal loop definition also).

The power of this definition can be seen on the following oft-used but
simple example. Suppose we have integers a, b>0, and suppose we want

a program segment to calculate $z=a^b$. A simple program segment for this
is

```
z,x,y:= 1,a,b;
while y ≠ 0 do
    begin s1: while even(y) do y,x:= y/2, x·x;
          s2: y,z:= y-1,z·x
    end
```

This is a short program segment. Yet, as given it is difficult to
understand; even the comments given by the average programmer would not
help, for they would attempt to explain from an operational point of
view what is happening. Suppose however that we give the following
assertion P and appeal to the definition of the while loop:

$$P: \quad y \geq 0 \;\text{and}\; (z \cdot x^y = a^b)$$

It is easy to verify (1) that P is true initially; (2) that (P and
y=0) implies the desired result; (3) that execution of the sequence
s1;s2 leaves P true; and finally (4) that the loop halts, since each
execution of the loop body decreases y by at least one.

Thus the introduction of the single comment $\{P: \quad y \geq 0 \;\text{and}\; z \cdot x^y = a^b\}$
is enough to help any educated reader understand the program.

Hoare's work is theoretical; formal proofs of correctness of a
program are like proofs in logic, leading from the axioms or definitions
of the basic statement types, through a step-by-step application of
inference rules, to the program with assertions as a proved theorem.
Yet his technique can be appled informally, with the amount of formality
and detail needed being directly proportional to the complexity of the
program. The practicality of the method cannot be refuted; whether it
will be accepted in the near future by programmers, or whether the
average programmer has the education and ability to understand and use
it, is another question.

The axiomatic method teaches us to work with assertions or
relations about values of variables instead of the actual values themselves. Thus we begin to think more about the static, mathematical
aspects of programs -- the assertions -- instead of the dynamic behavior,
which is difficult to understand. We learn to think less in terms of

test cases; we have an alternative to hand simulation of the program, which for one particular test case does little to help us prove correctness. We learn how to understand loops in terms of the loop invariant. The loop is the most difficult programming construct to use and understand; finally we can control it. Introductory programming texts, for example Conway and Gries [73], McGowan and Kelly [75] and Wirth [73], are beginning to incorporate ideas stemming from work on correctness proofs and structured programming.

Some people have cited the need to produce an invariant relation for a loop as a major disadvantage of the axiomatic method. I claim this as a major _advantage_, for it forces the programmer to make explicit -- both to _himself_ and to the reader -- that which he has been doing implicitly, vaguely, imprecisely and incorrectly all along.

Several examples of proofs of program correctness have appeared in the literature. These show that proofs of correctness can be given for complicated programs of 2-3 pages, and not just small ones as the program given above. The examples show that, if done judiciously, a proof of correctness leads to better understanding in less time. As primary examples, we cite Gries [73,75,76], and Dijkstra [76], which will be discussed later.

Research is also being performed on the mechanical verification of program correctness, mostly with the aid of interactive systems in which the programmer plays a role. This research is important because it can help shed more light on the programming process and our understanding of it and thus can help us develop programming methodology and mental tools for the programmer himself to use. Whether such systems will actually be used in a productive fashion by programmers remains to be seen.

2.4. Developing Programs and Their Proofs

An important point is that a program and its correctness proof must be developed hand-in-hand, with the proof ideas generally leading the program development. One cannot expect to produce a whole program and then prove it correct. Instead, at each stage of development, the programmer must know that what he has done is correct.

Just how proof ideas could lead program development has not been at all clear. Recently, Dijkstra has published a new book (Dijkstra [76]), which provides some exciting, new insight on this problem. Dijkstra provides a "calculus" -- a set of rules -- for deriving programs. Successful application of these rules leads to a correct program. Of course, as with the integral calculus, we may not be able to apply it successfully. Success depends on the ability of the applier and the program to which the rules are applied.

Dijkstra's new twist comes from reasoning that the definition of a statement type should reflect how the definition is to be used in <u>deriving</u> programs. Thus, he defines a statement type S by giving the rule for deriving the weakest assertion (the precondition) wp(S,R) for which execution of S will establish the desired precondition R. [Jim Horning has pointed out that we really want to define ws(P,R), which, for any precondition P and postcondition R would yield the statement S to connect P and R, but he doesn't know how to define ws.]

For example, the assignment statement defined earlier as {P[e->x]} x:=e {P} is redefined using

$$wp("x{:}=e", P) \equiv P[e->x]$$

This subtle change is enough to give us deeper insight. No longer are P, S and R treated equally in {P} S {R}. Instead, the definitions say that the precondition P must be derived from S and R.

That is actually the reverse of what most programmers think and it may indeed be difficult for them to break the habit of always thinking in a purely operational manner -- in terms of how the computer executes a program. The typical programmer thinks he works "forward" by developing a statement S that, given precondition P, will establish the postcondition R. Dijkstra's more "goal-oriented" approach advises us to develop the statement S by concentrating on the postcondition R, and by looking on S as a statement that transforms the postcondition R into the precondition P.

An example will illustrate the extreme importance of the postcondition R (instead of the precondition) in developing a program. Let us attempt to find a statement S that assigns to variable z the maximum of <u>fixed</u> variables x and y, under all circumstances. Thus, given

$R \equiv z = max(x,y)$, or equivalently

$$R \equiv (z=x \text{ and } x \ge y) \text{ or } (z=y \text{ and } y \ge x) \qquad (2)$$

we want to determine S satisfying {true} S {R}.

We will first attempt to derive S <u>solely from definition (2) of R</u>. How can we assign to z to establish R? One obvious way is to set z:=x, but from the first term of R we see this establishes R only if x≥y. Another obvious way is to set z:=y, which establishes R only if y≥x. This leads us to construct the following conditional statement in (Dijkstra's notation).

$$\begin{array}{l}\text{if } x \ge y \rightarrow z:=x \\ [] \ y \ge x \rightarrow z:=y \\ \underline{fi}\end{array} \qquad (3)$$

Both formal and informal reasoning leads to the conclusion that execution of (3) will <u>always</u> establish R -- that is, the precondition is <u>true</u>. Hence (3) is one solution to the problem.

Given R, we developed statement S, and then found indeed that for the desired precondition P we had {P} S {R}. The reader is now invited to do the reverse: begin with the <u>precondition</u> P ≡ {true} <u>only</u>, and develop S from P only (without recourse to R). Once S is developed, see whether the desired precondition R defined by (2) is established:

    Given: {true}
    Develop: S
    <u>Then</u> check whether {true} S {R} holds.

The reader will agree that the chance of arriving at a correct statement S in this manner is remote.

Dijkstra [76] is filled with examples of idealized versions of proof-and-program development: another example appears in Gries [76]. Dijkstra [76] represents one of the most significant advances in programming in the 1970's.

3. <u>Discussion</u>

That even small programs can exhibit astonishing complexity and
that we do have intellectual limitations is patently clear. That testing
can only show the presence of errors and not their absence is obvious.
In presenting such an overview we run the risk of turning the reader
away from delving further into the subject. The reader must realize
that we cannot go much deeper without getting into too many details.
In addition, I would like to say the following.

First, before 1968 (or thereabouts), a few people realized these
so-called obvious facts; only around the time of the emergence of
Dijkstra's <u>Notes on Structured Programming</u> did the computer science
community, as a whole, begin to become aware of the problems of programming and their possible solutions.

Secondly, the best research is not that which confounds us with its
complexity, but that which impresses us with its simplicity and naturalness. The discovery of hitherto unknown simple ideas whose practical
application leads to significant advances is what we need, especially
in a field like programming. However, we must realize that although
the ideas may be simple, we cannot always expect their practical
application to be an easy task. In this regard, I like the following
saying -- I don't know to whom I should attribute it.

Never dismiss as obvious any fundamental principle, for it is
only through <u>conscious application</u> of such principles that success
will be achieved.

Recognizing a principle and consciously applying it are two different things. One of our human shortcomings is that we want simplified,
easy solutions to our difficult problems. Because of this, we tend to
forget about the fundamental principle we should be following, and we
concentrate instead on some single, sometimes trivial, idea that sup-
posedly implies the principle. For example, many have simplified the
principle "make the program text reflect the structure of computations
evoked by it" into "don't ever use gotos". Naturally, people presented
<u>only</u> with the latter statement balk at it.

Another example from Tony Hoare is the following. When loading programs for execution we want flexibility _and_ efficiency. Since the early 1960's we have attempted to achieve this by having the compiler produce object modules, and by having a linking loader link modules together and load them for execution. Gradually, the principle of efficiency with flexibility has been replaced by the requirement "the compiler must produce an object module, and there must be a linking loader." This latter requirement appears in the specification for every new compiler or system, completely _excluding_ the idea that other solutions to the problem of efficiency with flexibility might be found in a particular context.

As a third example, the _seemingly_ easiest solution to the ever increasing cost and time of testing and debugging is to develop more and better mechanical debugging aids and mechanical verifiers. However, the _real_ solution, which is difficult, is to learn enough about programming so that we can teach the programmer not to put bugs into his program in the first place.

I am supposed to speculate on future research in this article, but I really don't feel capable of doing so. I have difficulty predicting my own particular area of research in two years, much less that of others. I do feel that though we have made fantastic progress in the past ten years, much still remains to be done. We have identified some important principles; we must now learn how to apply them effectively. We have a framework for proving programs correct and a formal calculus for the development of programs; the methods must be developed and refined and extended and made digestible for the programmer. We still do not have practical methods for understanding huge areas of programming, (e.g., pointers), nor do we have practical replacements for them.

Up to this point, there has been some "impact of research on software technology." Most programmers have heard of "structured programming" -- even if they do not understand it completely -- and they try to organize their programs more effectively.

But practicing programmers do not understand the deeper issues involved in programming, as discussed in this article. Many programmers have not even heard of (and few use) important concepts that they should be using daily in their work, like "proof of correctness", "precondition", "invariant relation of a loop", and "axiomatic basis for a programming language."

Our main hope of further advancement in the practice of software development lies not with better management techniques or better automated tools, but with the programmer himself. His attitudes and habits must change. He must have the feeling that he can develop small correct algorithms before testing begins, and that as a professional programmer it is his duty to do so. At the same time, he must realize that he cannot hope to develop a correct algorithm unless he learns to curb complexity -- unless he learns to organize and present a program as simply and clearly as possible. This will not obviate the need for testing, but the detection of errors during testing should tend to become the exception rather than the rule. Furthermore, if he has done his job well, the errors detected will be trivial to fix, arising more from simple transcription errors rather than from gross logical inconsistencies and bad design.

Such a change of attitude requires education, and this is difficult to implement. For example, I daresay that the majority of programming teachers do not (yet?) agree with me when I say that the programmer must produce a correct algorithm before he begins testing. More practical experience must be gained with these new ideas, and this experience documented in a convincing manner. The experience must influence the content of textbooks. This is happening now to some extent -- see the annotated bibliography -- but I would hope that 20 years from now new texts will show the same order of improvement over current texts as current texts show over those produced in and before 1955.

Such a radical change also requires new attitudes on the part of managers. Productivity can no longer be measured only in terms of lines of code produced -- irrespective of how good they are. Attention must be given to different techniques, and to radical ideas such as having programmers read each others' programs.

Above all, programmers must be given time to study programming (2-3 hours per week?). Programming methodology has changed radically in the past, and will continue to grow and develop. The only way to lessen the time gap between research and the application of its results is to allow the study of research results on a regular basis.

References

Buxton, J.N., P. Naur, and B. Randell (eds.) _Software Engineering Concepts and Techniques_. Petrocelli/Charter, New York. (Reports on NATO conferences held in Garmisch, Oct. 1968, and Rome, Oct. 1969)

Conway, R. and D. Gries. _An Introduction to Programming: a structured approach_. Winthrop, Cambridge, Mass. 1973 (3rd edition, 1978).

Dahl, O.J., E.W. Dijkstra, and C.A.R. Hoare. _Structured Programming_. Academic Press, London, 1972.

Dijkstra, E.W. "Notes on Structured Programming". In Dahl [72].

——— _A Discipline of Programming_. Prentice Hall, Englewood Cliffs, 1976.

Floyd, R.W. "Assigning meanings to programs". In Math. Aspects of Computer Science, XIX American Math. Society (1967), 19-32.

Gries, D. "Describing an algorithm by Hopcroft". Acta Informatica, 1973.

——— "An exercise in proving parallel programs correct". CACM 20 (Dec 1977), 921-930.
"Proof of correctness of Dijkstra's on-the-fly garbage collector". Lecture Noted in Computer Science 46, Springer Verlag 1976, 57-81.

——— "An illustration of current ideas on the derivation of correctness proofs and correct programs". IEEE Transactions on Software Engineering 2 (Dec 76), 238-243.

Hoare, C.A.R. "An axiomatic approach to computer programming". CACM 12 (Oct 69), 576-580, 583.

McCarthy, J. "A basis for a mathematical theory of computation". Proceedings, Western Joint Computer Conference, Los Angeles, May 1961, 225-238, and Proceedings of IFIP Congress 1962, North Holland Publishing Company, Amsterdam, 1963.

McGowan, C.L. and J.R. Kelly. _Top-down Structured Programming Techniques_ Petrocelli Charter, New York, 1975.

Naur, P. "Proofs of algorithms by general snapshots". BIT 6(1966), 310-316.

——— "Programming by action clusters". BIT 9(1969), 250-268.

Wilkes, M.V., D.J. Wheeler, and S. Gill. _The Preparation of Programs for an Electronic Digital Computer_ Addison-Wesley Press, Inc., Cambridge, Mass., 1951.

Wirth, N. _Systematic Programming: an Introduction_. Prentice Hall, Englewood Cliffs, N.J., 1973.

BASIC AXIOMATIC DEFINITIONS

by

David Gries
Cornell University

This is intended only as a reference to the basic ideas and facts used in proving programs correct. It gives axiomatic definitions for assignment, sequencing, alternation and iteration. It outlines Dijkstra's calculus for the derivation of programs: it describes what a "predicate transformer" is, states   properties a predicate transformer should enjoy, and defines assignment, etc., in terms of such predicate transformers.

The student who is not versed in this topic should not assume that this material is sufficient. After the course, he should study Dijkstra's A Discipline of Programming or other suitable material.

Basic Terminology and Hoare-like Proof Rules

Let P and Q be predicates, or statements about variables
of a program that are either true or false. Let S be a program
statement. Then

$$\{P\} \ S \ \{Q\} \tag{1}$$

is interpreted as: if execution of S is begun in a state such
that P is true, then it is guaranteed to terminate in a state
such that Q is true.

We gave a set of axioms and inference rules that define
programming language constructs and that allow us to formally
__prove__ statements such as (1). An axiom (scheme) has the form
$\{P\} \ S \ \{Q\}$, an inference rule the form

$$\frac{a,b,\ldots,c}{\{P\} \ S \ \{Q\}}$$

which means: if conditions $a,b,\ldots,c$ hold, then so does $\{P\} \ S \ \{Q\}$.
P, Q, and R represent predicates, B and Bi logical expressions
of the language, S and Si statements. The statements in question
are:

(1) __skip__

(2) __abort__

(3) x:=e   (x a simple variable, e an expression)

(4) IF   ≡ __if__ B1→S1 ☐ ... ☐ Bn→Sn __fi__

(5) DO   ≡ __do__ B1→S1 ☐ ... ☐ Bn→Sn __od__

In addition BB ≡ B1 __or__ B2 __or__ ... __or__ Bn.

A1: Axiom of skip: $\{P\}$ skip $\{P\}$ (for all P)

A2: Axiom of abort: $\{false\}$ abort $\{P\}$ (for all P)

A3: Axiom of assignment: $\{P[e{\rightarrow}x]\}$ x:=e $\{P\}$ (for all P)

where $P[e{\rightarrow}x]$ is the result of simultaneously replacing all occurrences of x in P by e.

R1: Rule of Consequence

$$\frac{P \Rightarrow P1,\ Q1 \Rightarrow Q,\ \{P1\}\ S\ \{Q1\}}{\{P\}\ S\ \{Q\}}$$

R2: Rule of Composition(;)

$$\frac{\{P\}\ S1\ \{Q1\},\ \{Q1\}\ S2\ \{Q\}}{\{P\}\ S1;S2\ \{Q\}}$$

R3: Rule of Alternation.

BB,

$$\frac{\{P\ and\ Bi\}\ Si\ \{Q\},\ for\ 1{\leq}i{\leq}n}{\{P\}\ IF\ \{Q\}}$$

R4: Rule of Iteration

$\{P$ and $Bi\}$ Si $\{P\}$, for $1{\leq}i{\leq}n$, $n>0$,

$(P$ and $Bi) \Rightarrow t>0$, for $1{\leq}i{\leq}n$, t an integer function,

$$\frac{\{P\ and\ Bi\}\ T:=t;\ Si\ \{t{\leq}T-1\},\ for\ 1{\leq}i{\leq}n,\ T\ a\ new\ variable}{\{P\}\ DO\ \{P\ and\ not\ BB\}}$$

Note 1. In addition, one uses the conventional rules of the predicate calculus.

Note 2. One can prove that evaluation of an expression e or execution of an assignment statement x:=e may not have "side effects" -- i.e. may not change the value of any variable that may be referenced in the context where e or x:=e occurs (except, of course, for x).

Note 3. The assignment statement axiom appears "backward" to those unfamiliar with it. A more "forward-looking" (operational) but equivalent definition is:

{P} x:=e {(Ev: P[v→x] and x=e[v→x])}

Note 4. The assignment statement should properly include the restriction that it be possible to evaluate e, but we typically leave this implicit:

{domain(e) cand P[e→x] } x:=e {P}.

Note 5. B→S is called a guarded command. B is the guard, S the command.

Note 6. The rule of iteration expresses total correctness -- execution of the loop is guaranteed to terminate. The rule for partial correctness, which guarantees only the result provided termination is achieved, is

$$\frac{\{P \text{ and } Bi\} \ Si \ \{P\}, \text{ for } 1 \leqslant i \leqslant n, \ n>0}{\{P\} \ DO \ \{P \text{ and not } BB\}}$$

A Calculus For the Derivation of Programs

The following is extracted from Dijkstra's A Discipline of Programming. Given a statement S and a predicate R,

wp(S,R)

is to be interpreted as the largest set of states (the weakest precondition) such that execution of S begun in one of these states is guaranteed to terminate in a state satisfying R. A (programming) language is defined by defining wp(S,R) for statement types S and all predicates R.

The connection between this and the Hoare-like formalism is:

If   {Q} S {R} then Q ⇒ wp(S,R).

For a fixed statement S, given a postcondition R, wp(S,R)
delivers a predicate denoting the corresponding weakest precondition; wp(S,R) is called a predicate transformer, since
it transforms R into wp(S,R).

In order to satisfactorily have the interpretation given
above, any statement (mechanism) S must have the following
four properties:

Property 1 (Law of the Excluded Miracle)

> wp(S,false) = false

Property 2 (Monotonicity) For all Q, R,

> if   Q ⇒ R
>
> then wp(S,Q) ⇒ wp(S,R)

Property 3 For all Q, R,

> (wp(S,Q) and wp(S,R)) = wp(S,Q and R)

Property 4 For all Q, R,

> (wp(S,Q) or wp(S,R)) ⇒ wp(S,Q or R)

Property 4' For deterministic S, for all Q, R,

> (wp(S,Q) or wp(S,R)) = wp(S,Q or R)

Definitions of language constructs

1. skip   wp(skip,R)   = R   for all R

2. abort   wp(abort,R) = false   for all R

3. assignment wp("x:=e",R) = R[e→x]   for all R

4. Composition wp("S1;S2",R) = wp(S1,wp(S2,R)) for all R

5. Alternation wp(IF,R) = (Ej: 1≤j≤n: Bj) and

> (Aj: 1≤j≤n: Bj ⇒ wp(Sj,R))

6. <u>Iteration</u>   Define conditions $Hk(R)$ by

$$H0(R) = R \text{ \underline{and} \underline{not}} (\underline{E}j: 1 \leq j \leq n: Bj)$$

and for $k > 0$:

$$Hk(R) = wp(IF, H_{k-1}(R)) \text{ \underline{or}} H0(R))$$

Then $wp(DO, R) = (\underline{E}k: k \geq 0: Hk(R))$

<u>Note 1</u>. <u>if</u> <u>fi</u> (an alternative statement with <u>no</u> guarded commands), if allowed, is equivalent to <u>abort</u>. Similarly <u>do</u> <u>od</u> is equivalent to <u>skip</u>.

<u>Note 2</u>. One can prove the following about the alternative statement IF. Suppose there is a predicate Q satisfying

$$Q \Rightarrow BB$$

and $(\underline{A}j: 1 \leq j \leq n: (Q \text{ \underline{and}} Bj) \Rightarrow wp(Sj, R))$

Then $Q \Rightarrow wp(IF, R)$

<u>Note 3</u>. One can prove the following about the iterative statement DO. Suppose there exists a predicate P such that

$$(P \text{ \underline{and}} BB) \Rightarrow wp(IF, P)$$

Suppose further that there exists an integer function t satisfying

$$(P \text{ \underline{and}} BB) \Rightarrow (t > 0)$$

and

$$(P \text{ \underline{and}} BB) \Rightarrow wp("T:=t; IF", T \leq t-1)$$

where T is a new variable. Then

$$P \Rightarrow wp(DO, P \text{ \underline{and} \underline{not}} BB)$$

THE MULTIPLE ASSIGNMENT STATEMENT

by

David Gries

Cornell University

Abstract

The conventional axiomatic definitions are given for multiple assignment to simple variables and for assignment to a single subscripted variable, along with examples to illustrate their use. The original contributions of this paper are the extension of the definition to include
multiple assignment to several subscripted variables, and the development
of a nontrivial, practical algorithm in which multiple assignment to
several subscripted variables is indeed useful. Arguments are given to
support the conjecture that the use of subscripted variables, like the
use of pointers, can lead to exponential explosion of the length of a
proof (and thus of the time needed to understand a program) unless the
programmer is careful.

1. Assignment to Simple Variables

Let $R[x \to e]$ denote the simultaneous textual replacement of free occurrences of x in assertion R by e. Using the notion of "weakest precondition" developed by Dijkstra [1], Hoare's [3] axiomatic definition
of assignment x:=e to a simple variable x is written as [2]

$$wp("x:=e", R) = R[x \to e] \tag{1}$$

As an example, we have $wp("x:=x+1", x>0) = (x+1>0)$.

Following Dijkstra [1], this is easily extended to a multiple or

---

[1]
Copyright 1978 by the Institute of Electrical and Electronics Engineers,
Inc. Reprinted by permission from IEEE Trans. on Software Engineering
SE-4 (March 1978), 89-93. This research was supported in part by the
National Science Foundation under Grants NSF GJ-425 and MCS76-22360.

[2]
For clarity and brevity, we omit necessary requirements on types of
variables, domains of expressions, etc. ·For the same reasons, we restrict our attention to one-dimensional arrays.

concurrent assignment $x1,\ldots,xn:=e1,\ldots,en$ where all the xi are different
simple variables, as follows. Using $\bar{x}$ to denote the list $x1,\ldots,xn$ (and
$\bar{e}$ in a similar fashion), denote by $R[\bar{x}{\to}\bar{e}]$ or $R[x1,\ldots,xn{\to}e1,\ldots,en]$ the
simultaneous replacement of all free occurences of the xi in assertion R
by the corresponding ei. Then

$$wp("\bar{x}:=\bar{e}", R) \equiv R[\bar{x}{\to}\bar{e}] \tag{2}$$

As an example, the weakest precondition for the statement $s,i:= s+i,i+1$
with precondition $(i>2$ and $s=1+2+\ldots+ (i-1))$ is

$$i+1>2 \text{ and } s+i=1+2+\ldots+(i+1-1) \equiv i{>}1 \text{ and } s=1+2+\ldots+(i-1).$$

One implementation of $\bar{x}:=\bar{e}$ consistent with definition (2) is to first
evaluate all expressions ei to produce a set of values vi, and then to
assign each vi to the corresponding variable xi, in any order.

II. Assignment to a Subscripted Variable

The definition of assignment to an array element given by Hoare and
Wirth [4] can be interpreted as treating an array as a (partial) function
and assignment as a change in the whole function. We now discuss their
definition.

Given a function f, let the notation $(f;i:v)$ denote a new function
defined by

$$(f;i:v)[j] \equiv \underline{if}\ j=i\ \underline{then}\ v\ \underline{else}\ f[j] \tag{3}$$

In a similar manner, we extend the notation to allow redefinition at
several values of the domain. For example,

$$(f;i1:v1;i2:v2)[j] \equiv \begin{cases} j=i2 & {\to}v2 \\ j{\neq}i2 \text{ and } j=i1 & {\to}v1 \\ j{\neq}i2 \text{ and } j{\neq}i1 & {\to}f[j]. \end{cases} \tag{4}$$

Note that the ordering of the pairs i1:v1 and i2:v2 is important when
i1=i2. We use the following notation if we do not want to consider the
ordering of these pairs:

$$(f;il,\ldots,im:vl,\ldots,vm)[j] \equiv \begin{cases} j=il \longrightarrow vl \\ \quad \vdots \\ j=im \longrightarrow vm \\ j\neq il \text{ and}\ldots\text{and } j\neq im \to f[j]. \end{cases} \quad (5)$$

However, this defines a function only if ik=ih implies that vk=vh, for
$1 \le k < h \le m$.

   An assignment b[r] := e where b is an array and r and e are expressions is then defined as

$$wp("b[r] := e", R) \equiv R[b \leftarrow (b;r:e)] \quad (6)$$

The precondition is thus the postcondition R, with every occurrence of
function (array) b replaced by another function. This definition may be
understood as follows. Assertion R, which contains a reference b[i]
(say), must be true after execution of the assignment. If i=r (the value
of r before execution of the assignment) then b[i] in R refers to the
value of e (before execution); otherwise b[i] in R refers to the value
of b[i] before execution of the assignment. Hence, the precondition is
the same as the postcondition R except that b[i] is replaced by (b;r:e)[i].
This is achieved simply by replacing b by (b;r:e).

   Some examples will help. The reader would do well to try to determine the weakest precondition himself using his own informal techniques
before studying our solutions, in order to gain appreciation for the use
of the definition.

$$wp("x[j]:=j", x[j]=j) \equiv (x;j:j)[j]=j$$
$$\equiv j=j \equiv \underline{true}$$

$$wp("x[i]:=1", x[i]=x[j]) \equiv (x;i:1)[i]=(x;i:1)[j]$$
$$\equiv 1=(x;i:1)[j]$$
$$\equiv 1=(\underline{if}\ i\ =\ \ j\ \underline{then}\ 1\ \underline{else}\ x[j])$$
$$\equiv i=j\ \underline{or}\ x[j]=1$$

$$wp("x[i]:=a", x[x[i]]=b) \equiv (x;i:a)[(x;i:a)[i]]=b \ (a,b\ \text{are con-}$$
$$\text{stants})$$
$$\equiv (x;i:a)[a]=b$$
$$\equiv (\underline{if}\ i=a\ \underline{then}\ a\ \underline{else}\ x[a])=b$$
$$\equiv i=a=b\ \underline{or}\ (i\neq a\ \underline{and}\ x[a]=b)$$

$$wp("x[x[j]]:=j", x[j]=j) \equiv (x;x[j]:j)[j]=j$$
$$\equiv (\underline{if}\ x[j]=j\ \underline{then}\ j\ \underline{else}\ x[j])=j$$
$$\equiv (x[j]=j\ \underline{and}\ j=j)\ \underline{or}\ (x[j]\neq j\ \underline{and}$$
$$x[j]=j)$$
$$\equiv x[j]=j$$

By viewing an array as a function, Hoare and Wirth were able to arrive at the simple and elegant definition (6). As can be seen from the examples, however, a fair amount of work may be required to simplify the precondition into an understandable form. Fortunately, this is simply manipulation of static expressions, which we should all be able to perform if we are careful and persistent. And, as we discuss in Section VI, we feel that this amount of complexity will appear in any definition of assignment to arrays.

III. Multiple Assignment to Arrays

Let us consider first an assignment

$$b[r1],...,b[rm]:=e1,...,em \tag{7}$$

or

$$\overline{b[r]}:=\overline{e}$$

where b is an array, and the ri and ei are expressions. The usual implementation evaluates first all the ri and ei, and then makes the assignments based on these values, in any order. We would like to develop a proof rule consistent with this implementation.

The first attempt at extending the single-assignment statement definition (6) to cover assignment (7) is to define $wp("\overline{b[r]}"="\overline{e}", R)$ to be R with b replaced by $(b;\overline{r}:\overline{e})$. This makes sense because then neither the implementation nor the proof rule determines a particular ordering of assignment to b[r1],...,b[rm]. However $(b;\overline{r}:\overline{e})$ may not be a function-if for example r1=r2 but e1≠e2-and we must make sure that this does not lead to a precondition that is not well defined.

We want to develop a formula for the weakest precondition such that execution of the assignments in any order will establish the postcondition R. This we do by simply forming the conjunction of the weakest precondition of all possible orderings of assignments:

$$wp("\overline{b[r]}:=\overline{e}", R) \equiv \bigwedge_{\substack{(i1,...,im)}} R[b \to (b;r_{i1}:e_{i1};...;r_{im}:e_{im})]$$

a permutation of (1,...,m)

This rule is consistent (although we have not formally proved it so) with the intended implementation of evaluating the ri and ei and then assigning in any order. However, it looks quite formidable and in the interests of the programmer, we feel it advisable to simplify the rule. One way to simplify it is to elide the nondeterminism by having the proof rule implicitly specify the order of assignment. This we do in proof rule (9), our choice for the definition of multiple assignment. An implementation consistent with this rule will evaluate the ri and ei, then assign in left-to-right order: el to b[rl], e2 to b[r2], etc.

$$wp("\overline{b[r]}:=\bar{e}", R) \equiv R[b \rightarrow (b;rl:el;...;rm:em)] \tag{9}$$

We shall not give the formal definition of an arbitrary assignment to several different simple variables and array elements, since it is notaionally messy but conceptually simple-it calls for the simultaneous substitution of the simple variables [as given by (2)] and the array names [as given by (9)]. As an example, we have

$$wp("xl,x2,a[rl],a[r2],b[r3]:=el,e2,e3,e4,e5",R)$$
$$\equiv R[xl,x2,a,b \rightarrow el,e2,(a;rl:e3;r2:e4), (b;r3:e5)]$$

IV. An Example

We now illustrate with a multiple assignment whose purpose is to establish the fact that a simple variable p together with some elements of an array b[1:n] form a linked list f ending in 0. Thus, the following picture should be established:

$$\tag{10}$$

where we use the notation $b^0[p]=p, b^1[p]=b[p], b^k[p]=b[b^{k-1}[p]]$ for $1 \leq k$. The restrictions on the linked list values $f=(t0,...,tm)$ are captured in the following assertion I:

$I \equiv$

   $f=(t0,...,tm)$ __and__   [f is the sequence of linked list values.]
  $m \geq 0$ __and__   [f contains at least one value.]
  $tm=0$ __and__   [The last value is 0.]

$(j \neq k \Rightarrow tj \neq tk)$ and [All linked list values are different]

$0 \leq j \leq m \Rightarrow 0 \leq tj \leq n$ [and are 0 or are in the domain of b.]   (11)

The fact that p and b contain the linked list values is indicated by the following assertion R:

$$R \equiv I \text{ and } t0=p \text{ and } (Aj:1 \leq j \leq m:tj=b[t_{j-1}]) \tag{12}$$

We would like to determine the conditions under which execution of

$$p,b[p],b[i]:=b[p],b[i],p$$

will yield a linked list (12). Using (9) and (1), the weakest precondition such that execution of this assignment will establish postcondition (R and $1 \leq i \leq n$) is

$$I \text{ and } 1 \leq i \leq n \text{ and } t0=b[p] \text{ and } (Aj:1 \leq j \leq m:tj=(b;p:b[i];i:p)[t_{j-1}]).$$

$$\tag{13}$$

In order to make sense out of this precondition, we break it into cases based on the relation between i, p, and the values of list f. In doing so we are aided immensely by the fact that each $tk \in f$ is different, so that at most one can be equal to each of i and p. Moreover, we have managed to arrange it so that all references to function $(b;p:b[i];i:p)$ are in one place-on the second line of the precondition (13). Had we earlier replaced the tj in I by their definition $b^j[p]$, then the many occurrences of $(b;p:b[i];i:p)^j[p]$ in the precondition would have increased the confusion enormously.

We break the precondition into three cases:

1) $i \notin f, p \notin f$.
2) $i=t_{k-1} \in f$. We have $tk=(b;p:b[i];i:p)[i]=p$.

    Hence p=tk is also in f.
3) $i \notin f, p=t_{k-1} \in f$. Assuming $p=t0=b[p]$ leads to m=0, t0=0,p=0, so

    that b[p] is not defined. Hence $1 \leq k-1 \leq m$.

Rewriting the precondition in terms of these three cases and simplifying yields the following:

I <u>and</u> 1≤i≤n <u>and</u>

$\quad$(($i \notin f$ <u>and</u> $p \notin f$ <u>and</u> $f=(b[p],b^2[p],b^3[p],...)$) <u>or</u>

$\quad$($i=b^k[p]$ <u>and</u> $f=(b[p],...,b^k[p],p, b[i],b^2[i],...)$) <u>or</u>

$\quad$($i \notin f$ <u>and</u> $p=b^k[p]$ <u>and</u> $f=(b[p],...,b^k[p],b[i],b^2[i],...)$))) $\quad$ (14)

We sketch these three cases in (15) below. Thus, if initially array b and variables p and i have values that fit one of these three, execution of p, b[p], b[i]:=b[p], b[i], p establishes (12).

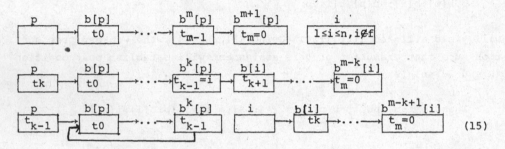

$\quad$(15)

V. Proof of Correctness of an Algorithm

$\quad$Consider an array c[1:n] of integers, whose sorted order is indicated by a linked list defined by a simple variable p and an integer array b[1:n]. Thus, $c[p] \leq c[b[p]] \leq c[b^2[p]] \leq ... \leq c[b^{n-1}[p]]$ and $b^n[p]=0$. As an example, we have

			1	2	3	4	5
n	5	c	23	22	25	21	24
p	4	b	5	1	0	2	3

We wish to write an algorithm that sorts array c [changes it to c=(21,22,23,24,25) in this example]. The values of p and array b may be changed during execution of the algorithm. Knuth [5, exercise 12, pp. 81, 596] presents a version of the following linear algorithm due to McClaren (we use Dijkstra's [1] guarded command notation):

```
      i:=0;
      do i<n-1 → i:=i+1;
                  c[p],c[i]:=c[i],c[p];
                  p,b[p],b[i]:=b[p],b[i],p;
                  do p≤i → p:=b[p] od
      od
```

Note that the algorithm uses two multiple assignments, one of which was discussed in detail in Section IV.

Let us try to understand this informally. Just before (and after) each loop iteration, we assert that c[1:i] is sorted and that it contains the i smaller values of c[1:n]. Secondly the linked list determines the order of elements in c[i+1:n], with p>i, and with c[p] being the smallest value in c[i+1:n]. The linked list may contain indices in the range 1:i, but for the purposes of describing the order of elements of c[i+1:n], these indices may be ignored. This is certainly true initially, with i=0, and upon termination with i=n-1 it implies that c[1:n] is sorted.

Now look at the body of the loop. After execution of i:=i+1, c[p] is the smallest value in c[i:n]. Execution of the swap c[p], c[i]:=c[i], c[p] reestablishes the fact that c[1:i] contains the i smaller values. The purpose of the three-way interchange of values p, b[p], b[i] is to reestablish the fact that the linked list determines the order of elements in c[i+1:n] (how this works will be seen later). But the linked list may contain indices in the range 1:i, and the purpose of the inner loop is to reestablish p>i, so that b[p] is again the smallest value in b[i+1:n].

Let us now go into more detail. We use the notation

    f=list(p,b)

to denote that sequence f is a linked list of values $f=(p,b[p], b^2[p],...)$ ending in 0, from the set {0,...,n}. We describe part of the invariant just discussed informally in (16).

$I(i) \equiv$ 1) $0 \le i < n$.

    2) $c[1:i]$ is sorted.

    3) $(y \in c[i+1:n]$ and $i \ne 0)$ implies $c[i] \le y$.

    4) f is a linked list $f=(t0,\dots,tm)$ with the following properties:

       a) $m>0$ and $tm=0$,

       b) all elements of f are different,

       c) $\{i+1:n\} \subset f \subset \{0:n\}$,

       d) Suppose $k<j$ and $i<tk$, $tj \le n$. Then $c[tk] \le c[tj]$.   (16)

An important part to note is 4d) It indicates that linked list f always indicates the ordering of elements in $c[i+1:n]$ [as it does initially, with $f=$list (p,b)]. Sequence f may contain other values from $\{1:i\}$, but these are simply ignored.

The complete invariant is

$$I(i) \text{ and } f=\text{list}(p,b) \text{ and } p>i \tag{17}$$

It is initially true, with $i=0$. Secondly, upon termination $I(i)$ and $i=n-1$ implies that $c[1:n]$ is sorted. Hence we need only show that (17) is indeed an invariant of the loop. To do this, we study the effect of the statements of the body of the loop:

    $\{I(i)$ and $p>i$ and $f=$list(p,b) and $i<n-1\}$

    $i:=i+1$

    $\{A1:I(i-1)$ and $p \ge i$ and $f=(p,b[p],b^2[p],\dots)\}$

This is fairly obvious. Secondly:

    $\{A1\}$

    $c[p],c[i]:=c[i],c[p]$

    $\{A2:(I(i)$ and $p=i$ and $f=(p,b[p],b^2[p],\dots))$ or

        $(I(i)$ and $p>i$ and $f=(i=b^{k+1}[p],b[p],\dots,b^k[p],p,$

                      $b[i],b^2[i],\dots))\}$

The case p=i is obvious, since p=i implies no real effect and implies
that c[i] is the smallest of c[i:n]. If p>i then c[p] and c[i] are
interchanged so that c[i] is the smallest of c[i:n]. This has neces-
sitated the interchange of i and p in f, as indicated.

Thirdly, assertion A2 implies A3, where

A3: $(I(i)$ and $p=i$ and $f=(b[p],b^2[p],\ldots))$ or
      $(I(i)$ and $p>i$ and $f=(b[p],\ldots,b^{k+1}[p]=i,p,$
      $b[i],b^2[i],\ldots))$

Why does A2 imply A3? Suppose p=i. In this case p is not needed in
the sequence f and has been deleted-remember, f must describe the
ordering of elements of c[i+1:n] and entries k in f with $1 \le k \le i$ are
superfluous. Suppose p>i. In this case, entry i in f is also superfluous, and all we have done to get from A2 to A3 is exchange the
position of i in f.

      {A3}
      p,b[p],b[i]:=b[p],b[i],p
      {A4:I(i) and f=list(p,b)}

To see why the preceding statement is true, note that A4 contains
essentially the postcondition R described in (12), while A3 consists
of two of the three cases of the weakest precondition given in (13).
Hence, this is just an application of what we showed in Section IV.

Finally, we have the following obvious fact that establishes that
(17) is indeed a loop invariant.

      {A4}
      do $p \le i \longrightarrow p:=b[p]$ od
      {I(i) and f=list(p,b) and p>i}

It remains to show that the algorithm terminates (and is linear
in n). That the outermost loop terminates in n-1 iterations is obvious.
To show termination and linearity we need only show that the body
p:=b[p] of the inner loop can be executed at most n times. That this
is so follows from: 1) the linked list initially contains n+1 elements,
2) no part of the algorithm increases the length of the list, 3) execution of p:=b[p] reduces the length by 1, and 4) 0 is always in the
linked list.

VI. Discussion

We were led to study the multiple assignment by noticing that in
the algorithm of Section V, execution of p,b[p], b[i]:=b[p], b[i], p,
performed satisfactorily even in the case p=i and b[i]≠p. Typical
operational arguments had always led to the conclusion that this must
be an error because one would not know which of b[i] and p to store in
b[p]. This study led to definition (8) and its simplification (9),
which forces a left-to-right assignment.

The multiple assignment statement is preferable to equivalent
sequences of assignments in cases like the one discussed in this paper.
Two sequences equivalent to p, b[p], b[i]:=b[p], b[i], p are

```
        t:=p;                              t:=p;
        p:=b[t];                           t2:=b[i];
        b[t]:=b[i];          and           t3:=b[p];
        b[i]:=t                            b[i]:=t;
                                           b[i]:=t2;
                                           p:=t3.
```

Calculating the precondition for such sequences is certainly going to
be more work than for the multiple assignment. More importantly, it
is easier to understand the use of the multiple assignment, since it
is more concise and straightforward. Consider for example the algorithm
of Section V. Each statement of the loop body is quite clear-once one
understands the invariant. The purpose of the exchange of c[p] and
c[i] is just to put the smallest of c[i:n] in c[i]. The purpose of
the next exchange is to rearrange the linked list to satisfy the required properties. And it is clear from this assignment that it is
only rearranging the linked list.

The examples of the use of Hoare's definition of assignment to
arrays, and the discussion of the assignment in Section IV should make
it clear that understanding such assignments can be tricky. The proof
rule is simple, but its simplification is messy. How much work does
it require to simplify? Suppose the postcondition contains n references
b[i1], b[i2],..., b[in] and the assignment is b[j]:=e. Then the precondition will contain n references (b;j:e)[i1],...,(b;j:e)[in]. Thus
this precondition could be broken down into 2^n cases:

1) $j \neq i1, j \neq i2, j \neq i3, \ldots, j \neq in$
2) $j = i1, j \neq i2, j \neq i3, \ldots, j \neq in$
3) $j \neq i1, j = i2, j \neq i3, \ldots, j \neq in$
4) $j = i1, j = i2, j \neq i3, \ldots, j \neq in$
5) $\ldots$

So we see that understanding the precondition may require work exponential in the number of different references in the postcondition to the array being changed. A different definition of assignment to arrays in [2] supports this conjecture.

We can control this complexity by keeping the number of references to the array to a minimum, and secondly by maintaining enough restrictive information so as to allow us to treat many of the subcases in a similar fashion. We did this effectively in Section IV. Although there were in total 2^{m+1} subcases, we were able to describe them in just three different assertions because we knew that none of the tk were the same.

The astute reader will recognize that the problem that causes complexity with arrays (as used in this paper) also causes complexity with pointer **var**iables dynamic aliasing. Two different variables i and j used as indices can yield two different names b[i] and b[j] for the same array element, and moreover the names change dynamically as i and j change.

Finally, it should be noted that when we first began this work, we knew that the first two situations described in (15) implied the precondition (13). That a third situation existed, the last one of (15), came as an unexpected, pleasant surprise solely from the formal construction of the precondition.

REFERENCES

[1] E.W. Dijkstra, A Discipline of Programming. Englewood Cliffs,
     N.J.: Prentice-Hall, 1976.

[2] D. Gries, Assignment to subscripted variables, Computer Science
     Department, Cornell University, Tech. Rep. 77-305, Sept. 1976.

[3] C.A.R. Hoare, An axiomatic approach to computer programming,
     CACM 12 (Oct 69), 576-580, 583.

[4] C.A.R. Hoare and N.Wirth, An axiomatic definition of the programming

     language PASCAL, Acta Informatica 2 (1973), 335-355.

[5] D.E. Knuth, The Art of Computer Programming, vol. 3. Reading,
     MA: Addison-Wesley, 1973.

IS SOMETIMES EVER BETTER THAN ALWAYS?

David Gries*
Department of Computer Science
Cornell University
Ithaca, New York 14853

Abstract

The "intermittent assertion" method for proving programs correct is explained and compared to the conventional axiomatic method. Simple axiomatic proofs of iterative algorithms that compute recursively defined
functions, including Ackermann's function, are given. A critical examination of the two methods leads to the opinion that the axiomatic method
is preferable.

1. Introduction

The so-called "intermittent assertion" method for proving programs
correct [1] has begun to attract a good deal of attention, so much that
it can no longer be ignored. The purpose of this paper is to compare
the method -- as it is explained in [1] -- with the more conventional
axiomatic method. It is assumed that the reader is familiar with the
axiomatic method [2], together with the concept of total correctness --
see e.g. [3].

The intermittent assertion method is used in [4] to argue informally
about several algorithms. The method involves associating an assertion
with a point in the algorithm with the intention that at _some_ _time_ during
execution control will pass through that point with the assertion true,
but that it need not be true _every_ time control passes that point. Based
on the fact that at some time control will be at that point with the
assertion true, one then argues that control will later reach another
point (e.g. the end of the algorithm) with another assertion true (e.g.
the output assertion).

Burstall discusses the idea in [5], while Manna and Waldinger [1]
are responsible for the current wave of interest in the technique.
Topor [6] also uses it to prove correct a version of the Schorr-Waite

---

*This research was supported by the National Science Foundation under
Grant MCS76-22360.

algorithm for marking nodes of a directed graph; an axiomatic proof appears in [7].

The intermittent assertion method has been mainly used to reason about iterative algorithms that compute recursively defined functions, and in this setting it has been thought to be more "natural" than the axiomatic method. In fact, [1] contains a challenge to use the axiomatic method on an iterative algorithm that computes Ackermann's function. Sections 2 and 3 contain proofs of this algorithm using the two methods, which the reader is invited to compare. Section 4 shows how to transform a particular recursive definition scheme into an equivalent iterative algorithm using the axiomatic method. The scheme was taken from [1]. Section 5 gives arguments that lead to the conclusion that the axiomatic method is to be preferred.

2. The Intermittent Assertion Method

Ackermann's function $A(m,n)$ is defined for $m,n \geq 0$ by

$$A(m,n) = \begin{cases} m=0 & \to \quad n+1 \\ m \neq 0, n=0 & \to \quad A(m-1, 1) \\ m \neq 0, n \neq 0 & \to \quad A(m-1,\ A(m,n-1)) \end{cases}$$

The following algorithm to compute $A(m,n)$ uses a "sequence" variable s. Each element si of sequence $s = \langle sn, \ldots, s2, s1 \rangle$ satisfies $si \geq 0$, and $n = size(s) \geq 0$ is the length of the sequence. Numbering the elements in reverse order, as I have done, simplifies later notation. Element si of s will be referenced within the algorithm by $s(i)$, while $s(..i)$ refers to the possibly empty sequence $\langle sn, s_{n-1}, \ldots, si \rangle$. Operation $s|x$ denotes the concatenation of element x to sequence s. For example, if $size(s) \geq 2$, then $s = s(..3) \mid s(2) \mid s(1)$. The algorithm contains labels needed to discuss the "flow of control" in the intermittent assertion method.

```
    start:  s:= <m,n>;
    do test:  size(s) ≠ 1 →
        if  s(2)=0                    → s:= s(..3) | s(1)+1
        ▯ s(2)≠0 and s(1)=0          → s:= s(..3) | s(2)-1 | 1
        ▯ s(2)≠0 and s(1)≠0          → s:= s(..3) | s(2)-1 | s(2) | s(1)-1
        fi
    od;
    finish: skip
```

Remark   The above algorithm is a paraphrase of that given in [1], which
was written in terms of conditional and goto statements and arrays. The
use of guarded commands and sequences, together with the label test on
the guard of the loop, leads to a clearer algorithmic description and
proof. end of remark

The intermittent assertion method allows one to use an assertion
that is true at a point of a program, but only sometimes. A typical
example is contained in the following lemma.

Lemma 2.1.   If sometime size(s)≥2 and s = ŝ|a|b at test,
          then sometime s = ŝ|A(a,b) at test.

Proof. Suppose s = ŝ|a|b at test. The lemma is proved by induction
on the lexiocographic ordering ⪞ on pairs of nonnegative integers,
which is defined as follows:

<a,b> ⪞ <â,b̂> if and only if a>â or (a=â and b>b̂).

Thus we assume the lemma holds for any sequence ŝ and pair <â,b̂> satisfying <a,b> ⪞ <â, b̂>, and show that it holds for any sequence ŝ and
<a,b>. The reasoning is based on an informal understanding of how pro-
grams are executed. There are three cases to consider, corresponding
to the three guarded commands of the alternative statement of the loop
body.

case a=0: s = ŝ|0|b at test: Since size(s)≠1 the loop body is
executed, the first guarded command is executed, s is changed to
s = ŝ | b+1, and control returns to test with s = ŝ | b+1 = ŝ|A(0,b).

case a≠ 0, b=0: s = ŝ|a|0 at test: Note that A(a,0)=A(a-1,1).
Execution of the second guarded command changes s to ŝ|a-1|1 and control
returns to test. Since <a,0> ⪞ <a-1,1>, by induction control will at
some point reach test with s = ŝ|A(a-1,1) = ŝ|A(a,0). Thus the lemma
is established in this case.

case a,b≠0: s = ŝ|a|b at test: The third guarded command is exe-
cuted, s becomes ŝ|a-1|a|b-1, and control returns to test. Since
<a,b> ⪞ <a,b-1>, by induction control will return to test at some point
with s = ŝ|a-1|A(a,b-1). Since <a,b> ⪞ <a-1,A(a,b-1)>, by induction
further execution is guaranteed to cause control to reach test again,
with s = ŝ|A(a-1,A(a,b-1)) = ŝ|A(a,b). The lemma is established.

This is typical of the reasoning used with intermittent assertions.

Now suppose execution of the algorithm begins with $m, n \geq 0$. Control reaches <u>test</u> with $s = \langle m, n \rangle$. By the lemma, control will reach <u>test</u> again with $s = \langle A(m,n) \rangle$, the loop will terminate because size$(s) = 1$, and control will reach <u>finish</u> with $s(1) = A(m,n)$. Thus we have proved:

<u>Theorem 2.2.</u> If some time $m, n \geq 0$ at <u>start</u>, then some time $s(1) = A(m,n)$ at <u>finish</u>.

This proof is a paraphrase of that in [1]; I have tried to make the reasoning as concise and clear as possible.

3. The Axiomatic Method

We now give a proof of correctness of the algorithm using the axiomatic approach. We first define a relation $\succ$ on sequences. The reader will note that $p \succ q$ if and only if one execution of the loop body with $s = p$ transforms s into q.

<u>Definition 3.1.</u> The relation $\succ$ on sequences is defined by
 (a) $s|0|b \succ s|b+1$ for $b \geq 0$, any sequence s
 (b) $s|a|0 \succ s|a-1|1$ for $a > 0$, any sequence s
 (c) $s|a|b \succ s|a-1|a|b-1$ for $a, b > 0$, any sequence s

Note that for any sequence p with size$(p) > 1$ there exists exactly one sequence q such that $p \succ q$. For p with size$(p) \leq 1$ there is no such q. Most of the work in proving correctness is contained in the following

<u>Lemma 3.2.</u> Given $a, b \geq 0$ for any sequence s there exists $t \geq 0$ such that $s|a|b \overset{t}{\succ} s|A(a,b)$ (i.e. one gets from $s|a|b$ to $s|A(a,b)$ by t applications of $\succ$).

<u>Proof.</u> The proof is by induction on the lexicographic ordering of pairs of nonnegative integers. We assume the lemma true for $\hat{a}, \hat{b}$ satisfying $\langle a, b \rangle \gtrsim \langle \hat{a}, \hat{b} \rangle$ and prove it true for a, b. There are three cases to consider, based on the definition of $\succ$.

 <u>case $a = 0$</u>: $s|0|b \succ s|b+1 = s|A(0,b)$, and $t = 1$.

 <u>case $a \neq 0, b = 0$</u>: $s|a|0 \succ s|a-1|1$. Since $\langle a, 0 \rangle \gtrsim \langle a-1, 1 \rangle$, by

induction there exists t1 such that $s|a-1|1 \overset{t1}{\succ} s|A(a-1,1) = s|A(a,0)$.
Thus $s|a|0 \overset{t}{\succ} s|A(a,0)$ with $t = t1+1$.

case $a,b \neq 0$: $s|a|b \succ s|a-1|a|b-1$. Since $<a,b> \succapprox <a,b-1>$, by induction
there is a t1 such that $s|a-1|a|b-1 \overset{t1}{\succ} s|a-1|A(a,b-1)$. Since
$<a,b> \succapprox <a-1,A(a,b-1)>$, by induction there is a t2 such that
$s|a-1|A(a,b-1) \overset{t2}{\succ} s|A(a-1,A(a,b-1)) = s|A(a,b)$. Hence $s|a|b \overset{t}{\succ}$
$s|A(a,b)$ with $t=1+t1+t2$. This ends the proof.

For convenience, we give the algorithm again, without the labels.

```
{m,n≥0}
s:= <m,n>;
do size(s)≠1 →
    if s(2)=0                    → s:=s(..3) | s(1)+1
    ▯ s(2)≠0 and s(1)=0          → s:=s(..3) | s(2)-1 | 1
    ▯ s(2)≠0 and s(1)≠0          → s:=s(..3) | s(2)-1 | s(2) | s(1)-1
    fi
od
{s = <A(m,n)>}
```

One way to derive a useful loop invariant is to weaken the result
assertion (i.e. $s=<A(m,n)>$) to include the initial condition (i.e.
$s=<m,n>$). To do this we make use of relation $\succ$. Note that there is a
$t \geq 0$ such that $<m,n> \overset{t}{\succ} <A(m,n)>$. Furthermore, t is unique, since for
any sequence p there is at most one q such that $s \succ q$, and there is no
q such that $<A(m,n)> \succ q$. Hence, for any sequence p such that $<m,n> \overset{*}{\succ} p$
there is a unique $T(p)$, $T(p) \geq 0$, an integer function of p, such that
$<m,n> \overset{*}{\succ} p \overset{T(p)}{\succ} <A(m,n)>$. We therefore take as our loop invariant P:

$$P: \quad <m,n> \overset{*}{\succ} s \overset{T(s)}{\succ} <A(m,n)>.$$

P is initially true with $s=<m,n>$ and $T(s)=T(<m,n>)$; upon termination
(P and size(s)=1) implies the desired result. That P remains true is
almost trivial to show, since $\succ$ was expressly defined so that execution
of the loop body with variable s containing a value p would change s to
the unique value q satisfying $p \succ q$. For a termination function we take
$T(s)$ that was just defined, which is decremented by 1 each time the
loop body is ececuted.

Remark 1. The invariant P was not as easy to derive as the above description indicates, although it should have been. <u>end of remark 1</u>.

<u>Remark 2</u>. Reference [1] says that the axiomatic approach requires two separate proofs to establish total correctness, one to show partial correctness and the other to show termination. While this is true, the example indicates that a proper choice of invariant can make the proof of termination almost trivial. <u>end of remark 2</u>.

<u>Remark 3</u>. The formalization of the method for proving termination has previously been done in two ways, which we summarize here. (1) derive an integer function $t(\tilde{x})$ of the program variables $\tilde{x}$; show that $t \geq 0$ whenever the loop is still executing; and show that each execution of the loop body decreases t by at least 1. For a loop <u>do</u> B → S <u>od</u> with invariant P, this means prove that

$$(P \text{ \underline{and} } B) => t \geq 0 \qquad\qquad \text{and}$$
$$\{P \text{ \underline{and} } B \text{ \underline{and} } t=c\} \quad S \quad \{t \leq c-1\} \quad \text{for all c.}$$

(2) Choose a "well-founded" set $(W, \succ)$ -- i.e. $\succ$ is a partial ordering with the property that for any w in W there is no infinite chain $w \succ w1 \succ w2 \succ \ldots$. Then choose a function $f(\tilde{x})$ of the program variables x and prove that

$$\{P \text{ \underline{and} } B \text{ \underline{and} } f(\tilde{x})=w\} \quad S \quad \{w \succ f(\tilde{x})\} \quad \text{for any w in W.}$$

The two methods are equivalent. The first induces a function $f(\tilde{x})=t(\tilde{x})$ and a well-founded ordering $\succ$ defined by $f(\tilde{x}) \succ f(\tilde{y})$ if (P <u>and</u> B) implies $t(x) > t(y) \geq 0$. Given a proof by the second method, under the reasonable assumption that nondeterminism is bounded (see [3]), choosing $t(\tilde{x})$ to be the length of the longest sequence $f(\tilde{x}) \succ w1 \succ \ldots$ yields a proof by the second method.

In this situation, I prefer the first method to the second; it is easier to state, just as easy to use, and makes more sense to the majority of programmers. <u>end of remark 3</u>.

4. A Transformation Scheme

In [1] it is proved using intermittent assertions that a recursive definition (or algorithm) of the form

$$F(x) = \begin{cases} p(x) & \rightarrow \quad f(x) \\ \underline{not}\ p(x) & \rightarrow \quad h(F(g1(x)),\ F(g2(x))) \end{cases}$$

under the assumptions

   (1) p, f, g1, g2 and h are total functions;
   (2) h is associative: $h(u,h(v,w)) = h(h(u,v),w)$ for all u,v,w;
   (3) e is the left identity of h: $h(e,u) = u$ for all u

is equivalent to the following iterative algorithm. The algorithm uses
a sequence variable s and a simple variable z.

```
{F(x) well-defined}
  s,z:= <x>,e;
  do s≠ <> →
     if      p(s(1)) → s,z:= s(..2), h(z,f(s(1)))
     ▯ not p(s(1)) → s:=s(..2) | g2(s(1)) | g1(s(1))
     fi
  od
  {z=F(x)}
```

We want to prove the same thing using the axiomatic method. It is
tempting to apply the technique used to prove the Ackermann algorithm
correct, and indeed it works like a charm.

   We first note that there must be a well-founded ordering $\gtrless$ defined
by

   (F(x) well-defined $\underline{and}$ $\underline{not}$ p(x)) implies
   $(x \gtrless g1(x)\ \underline{and}\ x \gtrless g2(x))$.

This means that there is no infinite chain $x \gtrless x1 \gtrless \ldots$ if F(x) is well-
defined, and that we can use the ordering $\gtrless$ to prove something by induction, the way $\gtrless$ was used in Section 3.

   In attempting to define an ordering on sequences as in Section 3,
we find that we must also take into account the value of simple variable
z. So we define a relation $\gt$ on pairs (s;z), where s is a sequence and
z a value.

Definition 4.1. Relation $\gt$ is defined for any sequence s and values x
and z as follows:

(a) if $p(x)$, then $(s|x;\ z) \succ (s;\ h(z,f(x)))$

(b) if <u>not</u> $p(x)$, then $(s|x;\ z) \succ (s|g2(x)|g1(x);\ z)$

<u>Lemma 4.2</u>. Given x for which $F(x)$ is well-defined, for any sequence s and value z there exists a $t \geqslant 0$ such that

$$(s|x;\ z) \overset{t}{\succeq} (s;\ h(z,F(x))).$$

<u>Proof</u>. The proof is by induction on the ordering $\tilde{>}$ described above. There are two cases, corresponding to the cases in definition 4.1:

  <u>case $p(x)$</u>: $(s|x;\ z) \succ (s;\ h(z,f(x))) = (s;\ h(z,F(x)))$, and $t=1$.

  <u>case not $p(x)$</u>: We have:

$(s|x;\ z)$
$\succ (s|g2(x)|g1(x);\ z)$ by definition
$\overset{t1}{\succeq} (s|g2(x);\ h(z,F(g1(x))))$ by induction, since $x \tilde{>} g1(x)$
$\overset{t2}{\succeq} (s;\ h(h(z,F(g1(x))),\ F(g2(x))))$ by induction, since $x \tilde{>} g2(x)$
$= (s;\ h(z,h(F(g1(x)),F(g2(x)))))$ by associativity of h
$= (s;\ h(z,F(x)))$ by definition of F.

Thus $(s|x;\ z) \overset{t}{\succeq} (s;\ h(z,F(x)))$ with $t = 1+t1+t2$. This completes the proof of Lemma 4.2.

  Now note that Lemma 4.2 implies the existence of a $t \geq 0$ such that

$$(<x>;e) \overset{t}{\succeq} (<>;\ h(e,F(x))) = (<>;\ F(x));$$

we define a function $\mathcal{T}$ as in Section 3, and use the loop invariant

  P: $(<x>;\ e) \overset{*}{\succeq} (s;z) \overset{\mathcal{T}((s;z))}{\underline{\hspace{1.2cm}}} (<>;\ F(x))$.

We leave the simple proof that P is indeed the desired invariant to the reader; the necessary termination function is $\mathcal{T}$ of the invariant P. To the reader we also leave the proof that if $F(x)$ is not well-defined then the algorithm does not terminate.

5. Discussion of the Methods

Reference [1] said that all known proofs of the Ackermann algorithm using conventional methods were extremely complicated. The proof in Section 3 is offered to support my conjecture that axiomatic proofs need be no more complicated than intermittent assertion proofs. The material in Section 4 offers hope that iterative algorithms that compute recursively defined functions -- a major stronghold of the intermittent assertion method -- will quietly succumb to the axiomatic method. It is simply a matter of learning the necessary techniques. The authors of [1] quite rightly imply that a proof method should be "natural", but "naturalness" in any field of endeavor must be learned.

The reader should note that the intermittent assertion method has not yet been formalized. The major reference on the subject, [1], explains the method by example only, and the examples are based only upon an informal understanding of how programs are executed. This is not a criticism; it takes time and thought to make progress in research. But it does mean that one should regard claims made about the method as only enthusiastic opinion. For example, in [1] it is proven that any axiomatic proof can be mechanically translated into an intermittent assertion proof, but it is claimed without proof that going the other way is impossible. It is also maintained that the intermittent assertion method is strictly more powerful than the axiomatic method. To argue against these statements is pointless until the intermittent assertion method has been properly defined.

Let us now compare the two methods, where our knowledge of the intermittent assertion method is based solely on the examples given in [1]. We can begin by comparing the two proofs of the Ackermann algorithm. Here one notices a strong similarity. Lemmas 2.1 and 3.2 lie at the heart of the proofs, and both are proved by induction over the ordering $\gtrless$. Each proof breaks down into 3 similar cases. The main difference is that one proof requires a detailed analysis of an algorithm, while the other requires an analysis only of a simple relation that took 4 lines to define. And herein lies what I would call a major drawback to the intermittent assertion method, which I will now try to explain.

Any algorithm is based on certain properties of the objects it manipulates, and it seems to me desirable to keep a clear distinction between these properties and the algorithm that works on the objects. Thus, in the axiomatic proof of Section 3, Definition 3.1 and Lemma 3.2 define, describe, and prove properties of sequences in a completely mathematical setting. Then the proof of the algorithm follows easily

by considering the algorithm together with these properties. A change
in the algorithm does not destroy the neat mathematical properties, but
only perhaps how they are used in the proof. In addition, one can work
with mathematical properties that have been proven by others, without
having to understand their proof. The principle of separation of concerns is being adhered to clearly in the axiomatic approach.

The intermittent assertion method on the other hand, as explained
in current proofs, seems to encourage confusion of properties of the
objects and the algorithm itself. Thus, in Section 2 the fact that there
is a nice ordering of sequences is hopelessly entangled in the proof of
algorithmic correctness. It should be noted that the proof given in
Section 2 is a paraphrase of that given in [1], and it is designed to
clarify and not obscure the method. This proof seems to be typical of
intermittent assertion proofs.

It is true that an axiomatic proof may have more parts to it. For
example, once the mathematical properties were stated and proved in Section 3, it was necessary to relate them to the algorithm itself using
a loop invariant and termination function. I gladly accept this "extra"
work, for in return I gain a better understanding and have a proof that
is clearly structured into its component parts.

Through programming, we hope to learn to cope with complexity (and
to teach others how to cope) using principles like abstraction and separation of concerns. The axiomatic method encourages the use of and
gives insight into these principles; the intermittent assertion method
seems by its very nature to discourage their use, and thus seems to be
a step backward.

A symptom of this backward step is the reintroduction of time.
The beauty and elegance of Hoare's axiomatic method was that it taught
us to understand an algorithm as a mathematical entity instead of as a
program to be executed by a computer, and we can now bring to bear on
the programming task all our mathematical training. The reintroduction
of time confuses the issue and appears to be a step backward.

It has been asserted that time must be introduced in order to formally prove concurrent nonterminating programs correct. Reference [1]
goes so far as to say that "the standard tools for proving correctness
of terminating programs, input-output specifications, and invariant
assertions, are not appropriate for continuously operating programs."
Having myself participated in extending the axiomatic techniques to
this class of programs (see e.g. [8]) I fail to see how the authors can
make this claim.

Let us briefly discuss possible formalization of the intermittent

assertion method. One way to do this would be to give "axiomatic"
proof rules for the various constructs -- an attempt in this direction
has already been made [9]. My opinion (not a claim) is that this will
likely lead to complex, unmanageable proof rules. This opinion is based
on the complexity of the argument used in the proof in Section 2. The
argument had to include not only the normal kind of induction typical
for loops, but also two successive induction steps based on the ordering
$\gtrless$. A proof rule to formalize the method as explained in this example
is going to be more complex than in the axiomatic approach. Another
way to formalize is to introduce "dynamic logic;" I fear this will be
too complex for the gain it achieves.

Again, the beauty of the axiomatic approach is partly in the simplicity of the proof rules, although much mathematical manipulation may
be necessary in order to simplify assertions, etc. For example, the
proof rule for the simple loop do B → S od is

$$\frac{\{P \text{ and } B\} S \{P\} \qquad\qquad\qquad\qquad P: \text{ loop invariant}}{\{P\} \text{ do } B \to S \text{ od} \quad \{P \text{ and not } B\}}$$

$\{P \text{ and } B\} S \{P\}$	P:	loop invariant
$(P \text{ and } B) \Rightarrow t \geq 0$	t:	termination function
$\{P \text{ and } B\} T:=t;S \quad \{t \leq T-1\}$	T:	extra variable

$$\{P\} \text{ do } B \to S \text{ od} \quad \{P \text{ and not } B\}$$

Finally, let me comment on the difficult of deriving useful loop
invariants. It is true that deriving the invariant for the Ackermann
algorithm was not as easy as might be inferred from the discussion, and
I am grateful to Manna and Waldinger for challenging me to find it.
However, finding loop invariants is becoming easier and easier to those
who practice the method. More and more complicated algorithms are suc-
cumbing to the approach. It is simply a matter of experience, as illustrated by the steady progress being made.

For me, the loop invariant is a crisp, clear way of understanding
a loop, and for me finding an invariant is the prime way to develop or
understand a loop. I believe that all good programmers use loop invariants, in that they look at the "general picture" or state of affairs
before each loop iteration. All we are requiring when asking for an
invariant is a precise definition of what the programmer has up till
now been doing in a vague, imprecise way.

To conclude, all the arguments seem to me to be on the side of that
axiomatic method, and it remains the method that I will teach and practice, until other arguments convince me otherwise.

Acknowledgements. I wish to thank Bob Constable and Gary Levin for discussions that led to the invariant used in the Ackermann algorithm. I am indebted to Jim Donahue, Gary Levin and John Williams for critically reading drafts of this paper.

References

[1]   Manna, Z. and R. Waldinger. Is "sometime" sometimes better than
      "always"? CACM 21 (February 1978), 159-171.

[2]   Hoare, C.A.R. An axiomatic basis for computer programming. CACM
      12 (October 1969), 576-580, 583.

[3]   Dijkstra, E.W. A Discipline of Programming, Prentice Hall, 1976.

[4]   Knuth, D.E. The Art of Computer Programming, Vol. I, Addison-Wesley,
      Reading, Mass. 1968.

[5]   Burstall, R.M. Program proving as hand simulation with a little
      induction. Proc. IFIP Congress 1974, Amsterdam. (308-312).

[6]   Topor, R.W. A simple proof of the Schorr-Waite garbage collection
      algorithm. to appear in Acta Informatica?

[7]   Gries, D. The Schorr-Waite graph marking algorithm. Computer
      Science, Cornell University, 1977. Submitted to Acta Informatica.

[8]   Gries, D. An exercise in proving parallel programs correct. CACM
      20 (December 1977), 921-930.

[9]   Soundararajan, N. Axiomatic proofs of total correctness of pro-
      grams. NCSDCT, Tata Inst. of Fundamental Research, Bombay, India,
      1978.

A Case Study in Language Design: Euclid

J. J. Horning

Xerox Palo Alto Research Center

INTRODUCTION

Euclid [Lampson *et al.* 1977] is a language for writing system programs that are to be verified. Its design proceeded in conjunction with the development of a set of proof rules [London *et al.* 1978] in the style of Hoare. It provides a good illustration of the practical consequences of attempting to design a realistic language for which proofs will be feasible. I was a member of the Euclid design team, and am hence more familiar with its successes and failures than with those of the other languages to be discussed. Most of the following material is extracted from "Notes on the Design of Euclid" [Popek *et al.* 1977]. Further commentary can be found in *SIGPLAN Notices*, March 1978.

GOALS, HISTORY, AND RELATION TO PASCAL

Euclid was evolved from Pascal by a series of changes intended to make it more suitable for verification and for system programming. We expect many of these changes to improve the reliability of the programming process, firstly by enlarging the class of errors that can be detected by the compiler, and secondly by making explicit in the program text more of the information needed for understanding and maintenance. We see Euclid as a step along one of the main lines of current programming language development: transferring more and more of the work of producing a correct program, and of verifying that it is consistent with its specification, from the programmer and the verifier (human or mechanical) to the programming language and its compiler.

The basic design of Euclid took place at four two-day meetings of a five-man committee (J. J. Horning, B. W. Lampson, R. L. London, J. G. Mitchell, G. J. Popek) in 1976, supplemented by a great deal of individual effort and uncounted Arpanet messages. Almost all of the basic changes to Pascal were agreed upon during the first meeting; most of the effort since then has been devoted to smoothing out unanticipated interactions among the changes and to developing a suitable exposition of the language.

Our changes to Pascal generally took the form of restrictions, which allow stronger statements about the properties of programs to be based on the rather superficial, but quite reliable, analysis that a compiler can perform. In some cases, we introduced new constructions whose meaning could be explained by expanding them in terms of existing Pascal constructions. These were not merely "syntactic sugaring": we had to introduce them, rather than leaving the expansion to the programmer, because the expansion would have been forbidden by our restrictions. Breaking the restrictions in these controlled

J. J. HORNING

ways did not violate the protection offered, because the new constructions were sufficiently restrictive in some other way.

EUCLID AND VERIFICATION

One of the fundamental assumptions in the design of Euclid is that (in principle) all Euclid programs are to be verified before use. That is, relatively formal proofs of the consistency between programs and their specifications will be done before reliance is placed on the operation of those programs; the proofs could be either manual or automatic. We used the axiomatic definition of Pascal for guidance.

Perhaps the most obvious consequence of this assumption is the provision within the language of syntactic means for including specifications and intermediate assertions. Routines are specified by pre- and post-assertions; modules by a pre-assertion, an invariant, an abstraction function, and specifications for exported routines and types. In addition, assertions may be placed at any point in the flow of control.

To assist in testing programs prior to completion of verification, any scope in Euclid can be prefixed by checked, which will cause the compilation of run-time checks for all *basic assertions* (Boolean expressions not enclosed in comment brackets) within the scope; this includes all *legality assertions*, which will be discussed later. If any assertion evaluates to *False* when it is reached in the program, execution will be terminated with a suitable message.

Because we expect all Euclid programs to be verified, we have made no special provisions for exceptional condition handling, as discussed in Part II. Run-time software errors should not occur in verified programs, and we know of no efficient general mechanisms by which software can recover from unanticipated failures of current hardware. Furthermore, we did not understand how to develop proof rules for exception handling mechanisms; more recent work by Levin [1977] provides some hope in this area.

We have also been led to a somewhat unorthodox position on uninitialized variables (except pointer variables). We do not forbid these syntactically (cf. [Dijkstra 1976] for a rather elaborate proposal), nor, for reasons of efficiency, do we require a default initialization. Our reasoning is as follows: verification generally places stronger constraints on variables than that they merely have values of appropriate types when they are used—they must have *suitable* values. Thus, the symptom of an uninitialized variable will generally be the inability to prove an assertion involving that variable. However, if a program can be verified without reference to the initial value of a variable, than *any* value is acceptable and initialization is superfluous.

Relying so heavily on verification has an obvious pitfall: suppose that the proof rules and the implementation don't agree? (Indeed, for Pascal, they do not.) Aside from some omissions and known technical difficulties, the major discrepancies between the Pascal definition and implementation take the form of restrictions needed by the proof rules, but not enforced by the implementation. For example, "The axioms and rules of inference ... explicitly forbid the presence of certain 'side effects' in the evaluation of functions and execution of statements. Thus programs which invoke such side-effects are, from a formal point of view, undefined. The absence of such side-effects can in principle be checked by a textual (compile-time) scan of the program. However, it is not obligatory for a Pascal implementation to make such checks" [Hoare and Wirth 1973].

A CASE STUDY IN LANGUAGE DESIGN: EUCLID

In the design of Euclid, we have made a major effort to ensure that there are no gaps between what is required by the definition and what must be enforced by any implementation, and that such enforcement is a reasonable task. Gaps have been eliminated by a variety of means: removing features from the language, extending the formal definition, placing more definite requirements on the implementation, and finally, introducing *legality assertions* as messages from the compiler to the verifier about necessary checking.

LEGALITY ASSERTIONS

There are many language-imposed restrictions that must be satisfied by every legal Euclid program. In addition to syntactic constraints, many of them (e.g., declaration of identifiers before use) are easily checked by the compiler, and it would be silly to ask the verifier to duplicate this effort. Others (e.g., type constraints) can usually be checked rather easily by the compiler, but may occasionally depend on dynamically generated values. Still others (e.g., array indices within bounds, arithmetic overflow), will usually depend on dynamic information, although the compiler can often use declared ranges or flow analysis to do partial checking. (For example, $i := i + 1$ will obviously never assign a value that is too small if i was previously in range.) Our philosophy is that the verifier should rely as much as possible on the checking done by the compiler. In fact, unless the compiler indicates differently, the verifier is entitled to assume that the program has been determined by the compiler to be completely legal. The compiler is to augment the program with a *legality assertion* (which the verifier is to prove) whenever it has not fully checked that some constraint is satisfied. Any program whose legality assertions can all be proved valid is a legal program, with well-defined semantics.

The compiler may produce legality assertions only for certain conditions specifically indicated in the Euclid Report. They always take the form of Boolean expressions within the language, and are usually quite simple (e.g., $i < 10$, $i = j$, p not $= C.nil$). Some typical situations where legality assertions are required will be discussed in the next section. Note that legality is a more fundamental property than correctness, since:

> Legality is defined as consistency with the language specification, rather than consistency with a particular program specification. A program could be consistent with one specification and inconsistent with another.

> A program that is illegal has no defined meaning, and hence cannot be said to be correct or incorrect.

Also note that a particular program is not sometimes legal and sometimes illegal (e.g., depending on whether $i = j$ on some run): the verifier must prove that the legality assertions are *valid* (true for all possible executions).

ALIASING

In most languages the rules connecting names (identifiers) to what they denote (e.g., variables) give rise to some subtle, but serious, problems for both programmers and verifiers. Probably the worst problem occurs when, at some point in the program, some variables (e.g., those passed as variable parameters to a procedure) are accessible by more than one name. Thus, assignment to x may change y. We call this *aliasing*.

The disadvantages of aliasing for programmers, readers, verifiers, and implementors

J. J. HORNING

have been well-documented [Hoare 1973, 1975][Fischer and LeBlanc 1977]. When assignment to x has the "side effect" of changing y it is likely to cause surprise and difficulty all around. However, programmers and language designers have been reluctant to eliminate all features that can give rise to aliasing, e.g., pointer variables and passing parameters by reference. In designing Euclid, we took a slightly different approach: we kept the language features, but banned aliasing. Essentially, we examined each feature that could give rise to aliases, and imposed the minimum restrictions necessary to prevent them. Every variable starts with a single name; if no aliases can be created, then by induction aliasing will not occur.

The case of variable parameters to procedures is typical. All of the actual **var** parameters in a call must be *nonoverlapping*. If the actual parameters are simple names ("entire variables"), this requirement merely means that they must all be distinct. However, we must also prohibit passing a structured variable and one of its components (e.g., A and $A(1)$). What about two components of the same variable? This is allowed if they are distinct (e.g., $A(1)$ and $A(2)$), and disallowed if they are the same (e.g., $A(1)$ and $A(1)$). Since subscripts may be expressions, it may be necessary to generate a legality assertion (e.g., i not$= j$ in the case of $A(i)$ and $A(j)$) to guarantee their distinctness.

It may appear that structured variables, such as arrays, violate our rule that assignment to one entire variable can never change another. After all, assignment to $A(i)$ may sometimes change $A(j)$. We adopt the view of [Hoare and Wirth 1973, p. 345] that "assignment to an array component" is actually an assignment to the containing array. Thus $A(i) := 1$ is an assignment to A, and can be expected to change $A(j)$ if $j = i$.

Pointers appear to pose a more difficult problem. Assignment to $p\uparrow$ (i.e., to the variable to which p refers) may change the value of x if pointers are allowed to point at program variables, or may change the value of $q\uparrow$ if p and q happen to point to the same variable (i.e., if $p = q$). We avoided the former problem by retaining Pascal's restriction that pointers may only point to dynamically generated (and anonymous) variables. The usual treatment of the latter problem is to consider pointers as indices into "implicit arrays" (one for each type of dynamic variable), and to treat dereferencing of pointers as subscripting into the corresponding arrays [Luckham and Suzuki 1976][Wegbreit and Spitzen 1976]. We adopted a variant of this solution in which each pointer is bound to a *collection*, which is an explicit program variable that plays the role of the implicit array. Thus $p\uparrow$ is just shorthand for $C(p)$, where C denotes p's collection, and the proof rules for arrays can be carried over directly. In particular, assignment via a dereferenced pointer is considered to be an assignment to its collection. From the verifier's standpoint, the situation is slightly better than that for arrays, since the decision of whether two subscripts are equal may involve arbitrary arithmetic expressions, while the decision of whether two pointers are equal reduces to the question of whether they resulted from the same dynamic variable generation (*New* invocation).

We have not yet discussed passing dereferenced pointers as variable parameters. If $p\uparrow$ and $q\uparrow$ (really $C(p)$ and $C(q)$) are both passed, the nonoverlapping requirement demands p not$= q$. Passing both p and $p\uparrow$ is not a problem unless the formal parameter corresponding to p can be dereferenced (i.e., unless C is also passed), but the nonoverlapping requirement forbids passing both $p\uparrow$ and C. In fact, passing pointers themselves as parameters (like passing array indices) never creates aliasing problems, since dereferenced pointers (like subscripted arrays) are not entire variables; assignment to one of them is considered as assignment to its collection.

We allow any number of collections to have elements of the same type, with no more difficulty than arises from multiple arrays of the same type. Thus, the programmer can partition his dynamic variables and pointers into separate collections to indicate some of his knowledge about how they will be used; the verifier is assured that pointers in different collections can never point to overlapping variables. [The astute reader will have noted that we have essentially returned to the "class variables" that were in the original Pascal, but dropped in the revised version.]

One consequence of our complete elimination of aliasing is that "value-result" and "reference" are completely equivalent implementation mechanisms for var parameters, and a compiler is free to choose between them strictly on the basis of efficiency.

SCOPE OF NAMES

In traditional block-structured languages, the intimate connection between a variable's lifetime and the scope in which it is declared is a frequent source of problems. A variable whose use is intended to be narrowly confined (e.g., to a set of operations on a data structure), may have to be declared more globally, simply to ensure its continued existence. That, combined with the automatic inheritance of names into inner scopes may mean that its name is "known" over a considerable extent of the program text. Any proof that all assignments to the variable preserve a certain property may require examination of all that text.

Euclid treats routines (procedures and functions) and modules as *closed scopes*, and restricts the inheritance of names into such scopes to those *imported* by the programmer. Furthermore, names declared within a module are known outside only if they are explicitly *exported*. The basic idea is that a module should "package up" a data structure and a related set of routines for its manipulation, and should hide the internal details from the outside world. The "protection" provided by control over exported names serves as a useful first step towards abstract data types [SIGPLAN 1976]. In addition, they make it possible to separate concerns in the development and verification of data structures. Properties of the (non-exported) variables of a module can be ensured and verified solely on the basis of the inside of the module, with no concern for its use. The user of the module, on the other hand, is solely concerned with these properties (the module's interface), and not with the mechanism that ensures them.

TYPES

One of Pascal's principal contributions was its treatment of data types. Despite certain deficiencies [Habermann 1973], this treatment is more satisfactory than that of competitive languages. Pascal's types provide a flexible and convenient set of efficient data structuring mechanisms, and are useful conceptual tools for partitioning and organizing data within programs. It is a major undertaking to develop a new approach to data types that is both consistent and useful, and we did not attempt to do so for Euclid. Nevertheless, we felt compelled to try some small changes in the direction of safety.

Almost all type-checking in Pascal can be done at compile-time; the major exceptions are due to the incomplete specification of formal parameters that are functions and procedures and to problems with variant records [Fischer and LeBlanc 1977]. The former are not a problem in Euclid, since more serious problems of specification and verification led us to eliminate such parameters entirely, but Euclid retains variant records. The problems in Pascal arise from aliasing (which we have already dealt with), from the treatment of the *tag* (which indicates the current variant) as an ordinary, assignable field of a variant record, and from the accessibility of variant field selectors even when they do not apply to the current variant.

J. J. HORNING

In Pascal, uncontrolled assignment to the tag field can change the current variant without ensuring that the corresponding fields contain values of appropriate types. We have eliminated this possibility in Euclid by making the tag a constant component of a variant record, and hence not assignable. If a variable is of a variant record type, its current variant can only be changed by assignment of a record of one of the other variant record types; this assignment supplies a complete set of fields appropriate to that variant.

Variant field selectors are only accessible within the alternatives of a *discriminating case* statement, where the alternative is selected by the current tag. In the case statement, a local name is provided for the variant record (as either a constant or a variable); within any alternative, that name has the (nonvariant) type selected by the corresponding tag value, and all field selectors of that type are accessible. If the local name is bound to a variable, the nonaliasing rule makes its more global name unusable within the scope; hence there is no danger that its type may be changed within the scope (e.g., by calling a procedure that does so surreptitiously). If the local name is a constant, the variable may still be changed, but this will not affect the (discriminated) constant in any way, so access to its fields remains safe. Thus, variant records cannot be used to circumvent Euclid's type-checking. As a minor benefit, we avoid the need for the Pascal restriction that the same field names may not be used in separate variants.

CONTAINMENT OF MACHINE DEPENDENCIES

Euclid contains most of the "escape hatches" (providing direct access to machine features) typical of system implementation languages [MOHLL 1975]. There is provision for machine-code routine bodies, for placing variables at fixed addresses, for specifying the internal representation of a record, and for explicitly overriding type-checking. Many of these features are difficult to define formally, and all of them pose problems for verification, yet they seem necessary in small portions of operating systems. We have not solved the verification problems; we have merely provided a mechanism for containing their effects.

Some modules in a Euclid program may be explicitly declared to be machine-dependent; these are the only modules that are allowed to contain the various machine-dependencies mentioned above, or to contain machine-dependent modules. Machine-dependent modules serve to isolate these features textually, and to encapsulate their use; they may be imported into modules that are not machine-dependent (and rely only on the specifications, not the implementations, of the imported modules). This does not simplify the process of verifying that machine-dependent modules actually do meet their specifications; it merely means that the verification of all other modules can proceed in a machine-independent manner.

We expect machine-dependent modules to be used for two different purposes:

to provide efficient machine-dependent implementations for packages whose specification is machine-independent (e.g., string manipulation, high-level input-output), and

to provide controlled access to machine features (e.g., channels, clocks, page tables).

Programs using only the former type of machine-dependent modules should be quite portable, requiring changes to (and re-verification of) only the bodies of the machine-dependent modules. However, modules of the latter type will have machine-dependent specifications that will work against portability of either programs or proofs.

Contributions of Euclid

Even though Euclid does not represent a dramatic advance in the state of the art, we have accomplished several things:

Firstly, we have designed a useful language (Euclid minus machine-dependent modules) all of whose features are (in principle) verifiable in their full generality by existing techniques.

Secondly, we have demonstrated that it is possible to completely eliminate aliasing in a practical programming language.

Thirdly, we have made variant records completely type-safe without destroying their utility.

By and large, the changes that we made to Pascal could be justified without reference to verification, and would be useful even in situations where verification is not a formal requirement. However, it is unlikely that many of them would have been made had verification not been one of our primary concerns. Furthermore, we seem to have been somewhat more successful at "getting it right the first time" when we started from a verification issue than when we worked back from an implementation concern. Perhaps this is because the construction of proof rules is a useful discipline that makes it necessary to be very explicit about the interactions of language features.

References

Dijkstra, E. W. [1976]. *A Discipline of Programming*. Prentice–Hall, Englewood Cliffs.

Fischer, Charles N., and Richard J. LeBlanc [1977]. "Efficient implementation and Optimization of run–time checking in Pascal." *SIGPLAN Notices* 12, no. 3, pp. 19–24.

Habermann, A. N. [1973]. "Critical comments on the programming language Pascal." *Acta Informatica* 3, pp. 47–57.

Hoare, C. A. R. [1973]. "Hints on programming language design." Technical Report STAN–CS–73–403, Stanford University Computer Science Department.

——[1975]. "Recursive data structures." *Int. J. Comp. Inf. Sci.* 4, p. 105.

——and Wirth [1973]. "An axiomatic definition of the programming language Pascal." *Acta Informatica* 2, pp. 335–355.

Lampson, B. W., J. J. Horning, R. L. London, J. G. Mitchell, and G. J. Popek [1977]. "Report on the programming language Euclid." *SIGPLAN Notices* 12, no. 2.

London, R. L., J. V. Guttag, J. J. Horning, B. W. Lampson, J. G. Mitchell, and G. J. Popek [1978]. "Proof rules for the programming language Euclid." *Acta Informatica* 10, pp. 1–26.

Luckham, D., and N. Suzuki [1976]. "Automatic program verification V: Verification-oriented proof rules for arrays, records, and pointers." Technical Report STAN–CS–76–549, Stanford University Computer Science Department.

J. J. HORNING

MOHLL [1975]. *Machine Oriented Higher Level Languages.* ed. W. L. van der Poel and L. A. Maarssen, North–Holland, Amsterdam.

Popek, G. J., J. J. Horning, B. W. Lampson, R. L. London, J. G. Mitchell [1977]. "Notes on the design of Euclid." *SIGPLAN Notices* 12, no. 3, pp. 11–18.

SIGPLAN [1976]. Special issue on data: abstraction, definition, and structure. *SIGPLAN Notices* 11.

Wegbreit, B., and J. Spitzen [1976]. "Proving properties of complex data structures." *J. ACM* 23, no. 2, pp. 389–396.

PROOF RULES FOR THE PROGRAMMING LANGUAGE EUCLID

by

R. L. London[1], J. V. Guttag[2], J. J. Horning[3],
B. W. Lampson[4], J. G. Mitchell[4], and G. J. Popek[5]

April 7, 1978

Accepted for Publication in *ACTA INFORMATICA*

Summary. In the spirit of the previous axiomatization of the programming language Pascal, this paper describes Hoare-style proof rules for Euclid, a programming language intended for the expression of system programs which are to be verified. All constructs of Euclid are covered except for storage allocation and machine dependencies.

Authors' addresses and support:

1. USC Information Sciences Institute, 4676 Admiralty Way, Marina del Rey, CA 90291. Supported by the Defense Advanced Research Projects Agency under contract DAHC-15-72-C-0308.

2. Computer Science Department, University of Southern California, Los Angeles, CA 90007. Supported in part by the National Science Foundation under grant MCS-76-06089 and the Joint Services Electronics Program monitored by the Air Force Office of Scientific Research under contract F44620-76-C-0061.

3. Computer Systems Research Group, University of Toronto, Toronto, Canada M5S 1A4. Supported in part by a Research Leave Grant from the University of Toronto and a grant from the National Research Council of Canada. Current address: Xerox Research Center.

4. Xerox Research Center, 3333 Coyote Hill Road, Palo Alto, CA 94304.

5. 3532 Boelter Hall, Computer Science Department, University of California, Los Angeles, CA 90024. Supported in part by the Defense Advanced Research Projects Agency under contract DAHC-73-C-0368.

The views expressed are those of the authors.

*"The symbolic form of the work has been forced upon
us by necessity: without its help we should have
been unable to perform the requisite reasoning."*
> A. N. Whitehead and B. Russell,
> *Principia Mathematica,*
> p. vii

"Rules are rules."
> Anonymous

Introduction

The programming language Euclid has been designed to facilitate the
construction of verifiable system programs. Its defining report [11]
closely follows the defining report [15] of the Pascal language (see
also [10]). The present document, giving Hoare-style proof rules
applicable only to legal Euclid programs, owes a great deal to (and is
in part identical to) the axiomatic definition of Pascal [9]. Major
differences from [9] include the treatment of procedures and functions,
declarations, modules, collections, escape statements, binding,
parameterized types, and the examples and detailed explanations in
Appendices 1-3. Other semantic definition methods are certainly
applicable to Euclid. We have used proof rules for two
reasons: familiarity and the existence of the Pascal definition.
Readers unfamiliar with proof rules may want to read [6, 7].

One may regard the proof rules as a definition of Euclid in the same
sense as the Pascal axiomatization defines Pascal. By stating what can
be proved about Euclid programs, the rules define the meaning of most
syntactically and semantically legal Euclid programs, but they do not
give the information required to determine whether or not a program is
legal. This information may be found in the language report. Neither
do the proof rules define the meaning of illegal Euclid programs
containing, for example, division by zero or an invalid array index.
Finally, explicit proof rules are not provided for those portions of
Euclid defined in the report by translation into other legal Euclid
constructs. This includes pervasive, implicit imports through thus, and
some uses of return and exit. All such transformations must be applied
before the proof rules are applicable.

As is the case with Pascal, the Euclid axiomatization should be read in
conjunction with the language report, and is an almost total
axiomatization of a realistic and useful system programming language.
While the primary goal of the Euclid effort was to design a practical
programming language (not to provide a vehicle for demonstrating proof
rules), proof rule considerations did have significant influence on
Euclid [13]. All constructs of the language are covered except for
storage allocation (zones and collections that are not
referenced-counted) and machine dependencies. In a few instances rules
are applicable only to a subset of Euclid; the restrictions are noted
with those rules.

Conventions and Notation

In describing these Euclid proof rules we have used as much as possible of the Pascal axiomatization. We have also deliberately followed the same order and style of presentation and tried to use the same terminology.

The notation P(y/x) to denote substitution is used for the formula which is obtained by systematically substituting y for all free occurrences of x in the predicate P. If this introduces conflict between free variables of y and bound variables of P, the conflict is resolved by systematic change of the latter variables. The notation P(y/x) may be read "P with y for x."

$$P(y_1/x_1, \ldots, y_n/x_n)$$

denotes simultaneous substitution for all occurrences of any x_i by the corresponding y_i. Thus occurrences of x_i within any y_j are *not* replaced. The expressions $x_1, \ldots, x_n$ must be distinct; otherwise the simultaneous substitution is not defined. The meaning of substitution for subscripted and qualified expressions is defined in Sections 4 and 5.

Euclid expressions in assertions must be legal Euclid expressions. Assertions may contain, outside of expressions, non-Euclid notations such as quantifiers or set constructors.

In the proof rules, S and S_j denote a sequence of zero or more statements. As is done in the Pascal axiomatization, we refer to values of a type as elements of that type. Also, the rule of consequence

$$P \supset Q, \ Q\{S\}U, \ U \supset R$$
$$\text{-----------------------}$$
$$P\{S\}R$$

may be used in proofs.

Data Types

The axioms presented in this and the following sections display the relationship between a type declaration and the axioms which specify the properties of values of the type and operations defined over them. The treatment is not wholly formal, and the reader must be aware that:

1. Free variables in axioms are assumed to be universally quantified over the appropriate type.

2. The expression of the "induction" axiom is always left informal.

3. The types of variables used in the axioms have to be deduced either from the section heading or from the more immediate context.

4. The name of a type is used as a transfer function constructing a value of the type (such a use of the type identifier is not available in Euclid).

5. The verifier can assume that everything will be type-checked by the compiler or that the compiler will generate the necessary legality assertions.

6. In defining Euclid's types we will not be presenting proof rules that may be directly applied to Euclid programs. Rather, we will provide a set of assertions, denoted by H, about the values of the type being defined. These assertions are incorporated into proof rules in Section 9 on constant, variable, and type declarations. Rule 9.1, for example, tells us that in the case of an identifier declaration, x:T, we may use the fact that $x \in T$, i.e., x has the attributes associated with values of type T.

Parameterized types are covered in Section 9.5. The rules for type compatibility in Euclid are defined in the language report.

Scalar Types

$\underline{\text{type}}$ $T=(c_1, c_2, \ldots, c_n)$

1.1. $c_1, c_2, \ldots, c_n$ are distinct elements of T.

1.2.   These are the only elements of T.

1.3. $c_{i+1} = T.\text{succ}(c_i)$ for $i=1, \ldots, n-1$

1.4. $c_i = T.\text{pred}(c_{i+1})$ for $i=1, \ldots, n-1$

1.5. $\neg(x<x)$

1.6. $(x<y) \land (y<z) \supset (x<z)$

1.7. $(x \neq c_n) \supset (x < T.\text{succ}(x))$

1.8. $x>y \equiv y<x$

1.9. $x \leq y \equiv \neg(x>y)$

1.10. $x \geq y \equiv \neg(x<y)$

1.11. $x \neq y \equiv \neg(x=y)$

1.12. $T.\text{first} = c_1$

1.13. $T.last = c_n$

1.14. $T.ord(c_i) = i-1$ for $i = 1, \ldots, n$

The standard scalar type Boolean is defined as

<u>type</u> Boolean = (False, True).

The Boolean operators <u>not</u>, <u>and</u>, <u>or</u>, and -> (implication) are those of the conventional logical calculus except that some operands may possibly not be evaluated. Specifically, in terms of conditional expressions,

x <u>and</u> y means <u>if</u> x <u>then</u> y <u>else</u> false, i.e., x cand y,
x <u>or</u> y means <u>if</u> x <u>then</u> true <u>else</u> y, i.e., x cor y,
x -> y means <u>if</u> x <u>then</u> y <u>else</u> true.

(Note, however, that conditional expressions are not included in Euclid.)

The standard type integer stands for the set of the whole numbers. The arithmetic operators $+, -, *$, and <u>div</u> are those of whole number arithmetic. The modulus operator <u>mod</u> is defined by the equation

$$m \bmod n = m - (m \operatorname{div} n) * n$$

whereas div denotes division with truncated fraction, i.e., move toward zero. Implementations are permitted to refuse the execution of programs which refer to integers outside the appropriate range, signedInt or unsignedInt.

Type char

2.1.   The elements of type char are the 26 (capital) letters, the 10 (decimal) digits, and possibly other characters defined by particular implementations. In programs, a constant of type char is denoted by preceding the character with a $.

The sets of letters and digits are ordered, and the digits are coherent, i.e.,

2.2.

$A < $B	$a < $b	$1 = char.succ($0)
$B < $C	$b < $c	$2 = char.succ($1)
...	...	...
$Y < $Z	$y < $z	$9 = char.succ($8).

Axioms 1.5-1.13 apply to the char type. The functions char.ord and Chr are defined by the following additional axioms:

2.3. If u is an element of char, then char.ord(u) is a non-negative integer (called the ordinal number of u), and

$$Chr(char.ord(u))=u$$

2.4. $$u<v \equiv char.ord(u)<char.ord(v).$$

These axioms have been designed to make possible an interchange of programs between implementations using different character sets. It should be noted that the function char.ord does not necessarily map the characters onto consecutive integers.

Subrange Types

type $T=m..n$

Let m,n be elements of scalar type T_0.

3.1. $T.first=m$

3.2. $T.last=n$

3.3. For all i in T_0 such that $m \le i \le n$, i is an element of T.

3.4. These are the only elements of T.

3.5. $T.first \le i < T.last \supset T.succ(i)=T_0.succ(i)$

3.6. $T.first < i \le T.last \supset T.pred(i)=T_0.pred(i)$

Note that since all elements of T are elements of T_0, all operators of T_0 apply to them.

Array Types

type $T=$ array I of T_0

Here I is a scalar or subrange type. Let $m=I.first$ and $n=I.last$.

4.1. If x_i is an element of T_0 for all i such that $m \le i \le n$, then $T(x_m,...,x_n)$ is an element of T.

4.2. These are the only elements of T.

4.3. $T(x_m,...,x_n)(i)=x_i$ for $m \le i \le n$

Letting x stand for $T(x_m,\ldots,x_n)$ we introduce the following abbreviation:

$$(x,i:y) \text{ stands for } T(x_m,\ldots,x_{i-1},y,x_{i+1},\ldots,x_n).$$

The formula

$$P(y/x(i)),$$

denoting a substitution for an array reference, is then defined to be

$$P((x,i:y)/x).$$

To extend this definition to substitution for a multiply-subscripted array reference, we define

$$(x,<i_1,\ldots,i_n>:y), \text{ where } n\geq 2$$

to be equal to

$$(x,<i_1,\ldots,i_{n-1}>:(x(i_1)\ldots(i_{n-1}),i_n:y))$$

and the formula

$$P(y/x(i_1)\ldots(i_n)), \text{ where } n\geq 2$$

is equivalent to

$$P((x,<i_1,\ldots,i_n>:y)/x).$$

4.4. $x.\text{IndexType}=I$, $x.\text{ComponentType}=T_0$.

Record Types

$$\underline{\text{type}}\ T=\underline{\text{record}}\ s_1:T_1,\ldots,s_m:T_m\ \underline{\text{end}}\ T$$

where each s_i must be preceded by $\underline{\text{const}}$ or $\underline{\text{var}}$.

Let x_i be an element of T_i for $i=1,\ldots,m$.

5.1. $T(x_1,x_2,\ldots,x_m)$ is an element of T.

5.2. These are the only elements of T.

5.3. $T(x_1,\ldots,x_m).s_i=x_i$ for $i=1,\ldots,m$
$(x,s_i:y)$ stands for $T(x_1,\ldots,x_{i-1},y,x_{i+1},\ldots,x_m)$.

The formula $P(y/x.s_i)$ is defined analogously to arrays (see definitions following 4.3).

Variant Records

$$\underline{type}\ T_\theta(c) = \underline{record}\ s_1:T_1,\ldots,s_n:T_m;$$
$$\underline{case}\ c\ \underline{of}$$
$$k_1 => s'_1:T'_1\ \underline{end}\ k_1$$
$$k_2 => s'_2:T'_2\ \underline{end}\ k_2$$
$$\ldots$$
$$k_n => s'_n:T'_n\ \underline{end}\ k_n$$
$$\underline{end}\ \underline{case}$$
$$\underline{end}\ T$$

where the type of c is a scalar or subrange type with elements $k_1,\ldots,k_n$. Note that $k_a,k_b,\ldots,k_m => S$ stands for $k_a => S; k_b => S;\ldots; k_m => S$.

Consider type $T = T_\theta(k_j)$, and let x'_j be an element of T'_j for $j=1,\ldots,n$.

5.1a $T(x_1,\ldots,x_m,k_j,x'_j)$ is an element of T.

5.2a These are the only elements of T.

5.3a $T(x_1,\ldots,x_m,k_j,x'_j).s_i = x_i$ for $i=1,\ldots,m$

5.4a $T(x_1,\ldots,x_m,k_j,x'_j).s'_j = x'_j$ for $j=1,\ldots,n$

5.5a Letting z stand for $T(x_1,\ldots,x_m,k_j,x'_j)$, the standard Euclid component itsTag is defined by $z.itsTag = k_j$.

A variant record may also contain an otherwise clause

$$\underline{otherwise} => s'_{n+1}:T'_{n+1}$$

in which case the type of c may contain elements in addition to $k_1,\ldots,k_n$. If there is such a clause, we have the following additional axioms for the otherwise (n+1) situation:

Let k_j be an element of the type of c such that $k_j \ne k_i$ for $1 \le i \le n$, and let x'_{n+1} be an element of T'_{n+1}.

5.1b $T(x_1,\ldots,x_m,k_j,x'_{n+1})$ is also an element of T.

5.4b $T(x_1,\ldots,x_m,k_j,x'_{n+1}).s'_{n+1} = x'_{n+1}$

5.5b Identical to 5.5a.

The case with a field list containing several fields

$$k_j => s_{j1} : T_{j1}, \ldots, s_{jh} : T_{jh} \text{ end } k_j$$

is to be interpreted as

$$k_j => s'_j : T'_j \text{ end } k_j$$

where s'_j is a fresh identifier, and T'_j is a type defined as

$$\underline{type} \ T'_j = \underline{record} \ s_{j1} : T_{j1}, \ldots, s_{jh} : T_{jh} \ \underline{end} \ \underline{record}.$$

In this case $x.s_{jt}$ is interpreted as $x.s'_j.s_{jt}$.

Now consider type $T = T_0(\underline{any})$.

5.1c $T(x_1, \ldots, x_m, y, x')$ is an element of T for $(y, x') = (k_1, x'_1), \ldots,$
(k_n, x'_n), (k_d, x'_{n+1}) where $k_d \neq k_i$ for $i = 1, \ldots, n$.

5.2c These are the only elements of T.

5.3c $T(x_1, \ldots, x_m, y, x').s_i = x_i$ for $i = 1, \ldots, m$

There is no 5.4c since access to the variant part of the record may only be done using the discriminating case statement (see Section 12.5).

Machine-dependent records do not change verification properties. The additional information supplied can be ignored (unless the machine interprets certain locations specially).

Set Types

$$\underline{type} \ T = \underline{set} \ \underline{of} \ T_0$$

Let x_0 be an element of T_0.

6.1. $T(\ )$ is an element of T.

6.2. If x is an element of T, then $x + T(x_0)$ is an element of T (the operator $+$ is defined below).

6.3. These are the only elements of T.

6.4. $T(x_1, x_2, \ldots, x_n)$ means $T(([T(\ ) + T(x_1)] + T(x_2)] + \ldots + T(x_n))$.

6.5. $T.BaseType = T_0$

$T(\ )$ denotes the empty set, and $T(x_0)$ denotes the singleton set containing x_0. The operators $+, *, -, \underline{xor}$, and $\underline{in}$, applied to elements whose type is set, denote the conventional operations of set union, intersection, difference, symmetric difference, and membership. The operators <= and >= denote set inclusion. The specific axioms defining these operators are omitted.

Note that Euclid allows implementations to restrict set types to be built only on base types T_0 with a specified maximum number of elements.

Module Types

Because modules are by far the most complex part of Euclid, this section contains a large amount of explanation as well as the technical details of the module rule. The explanatory material can be read now. However, we recommend that Section 10 on procedures and functions be read before reading the rule and the technical details. An example of the use of the module rule appears as Appendix 3. Additional comments on the module construct appear in the Epilogue. The material on modules appears here because modules, like subrange types and array types, are type constructors.

```
type T(const C) = pre P1; post Q1; module t invariant Q0;
     imports (var Y const D readonly R)
     exports (const (K1, p, f) var V1 readonly R1)
     const K; var V
     procedure p(var X2 nonvar C2) = imports (var Y2 nonvar D2)
          pre P2; post Q2; begin S2 end
     function f(nonvar C3) returns G = imports (nonvar D3)
          pre P3; post Q3; begin S3 end
     initially imports (var Y4 nonvar D4) post Q4; begin S4 end
     abstraction function A returns t0 = imports (nonvar D5)
          begin S5 end
     invariant Q
     finally imports (var Y6 nonvar D6) pre P6; begin S6 end
end T
```

The parts of a module definition are explained in the section on module types in the Euclid report. We assume that equality is not exported. Nonvar denotes the list of const and readonly identifiers. Each of c, y, d, r, k1, v1, r1, k, v, x2, c2, y2, d2, c3, d3, y4, d4, d5, y6, and d6 denotes the list of identifiers in the corresponding upper case declaration (p and f denote declared routines). As the Euclid report requires, the lists k1, v1, and r1 are sublists of k, v, and v (yes, v, not r), respectively. The declarations K and V may not include identifiers from y or r. The list d5 is a sublist of c, d, k, and v-v1. The arguments of P1 and Q1 may include as free variables only identifiers from c, y, d, and r. Similarly, the arguments of P2, Q2, P3, Q3, Q4, and P6 may only include t and their respective formal parameter and import lists; Q3 may also include g. Q, the "concrete invariant," may only include c, d, k, and v-v1, that is to say, the same identifiers as d5. Q0, the "abstract invariant," may include c, d, and t.

The exported identifiers of k1, v1, and r1 are treated as if they were fields of a record type named T. The abstraction function A maps the identifiers in d5 into a value of type T(c); its body may contain constructs outside Euclid. The function A is for verification purposes and is not callable from a Euclid program.

The module is a mechanism for providing encapsulation and the support of data abstractions. There are two points from which it may be viewed: The users of the module see only the abstract pre- and postconditions associated with module routines and the pre- and postcondition of the module itself. The implementor of the module also sees the bodies of the routines and the (concrete) identifiers declared within the module. The connection between the concrete and abstract identifiers is the abstraction function, A, which transforms a set of concrete identifiers to an abstract identifier. See [8] for a more complete discussion of the role of A.

The module rule given below contains a conclusion and eight premises. We shall explain the structure of the rule, describe the purpose and workings of each premise, and finally give the rule itself.

The conclusion of the rule involves the instantiation of a module identifier and the use of that identifier in a scope. Premises 1-6 are properties required of the module definition; these verifications need be done only once per module definition. Premise 7 discharges the instantiation precondition; this must be proved each time a module is instantiated. Premise 8, itself in five parts, uses the verified definitions (formulas 8.1-8.4 which depend on premises 1-6) to verify the uses, in premise 8.5, of the module identifier in the scope. Thus the module rule has the structure

$$1,2,3,4,5,6,$$
$$7,$$
$$[8.1, 8.2, 8.3, 8.4] \vdash 8.5$$
$$\text{------------------------------}$$
$$P\{var\ x:T(a);\ S\}\ R \wedge Q1$$

We now describe each premise in more detail. In premises 1-6 the substitution of a call of the abstraction function, A, for the name of the module, t, converts a predicate on the abstract identifier t to one involving concrete identifiers. Premise 1: concrete invariant implies abstract invariant. Premise 2: module precondition across declaration of module's local variables and body of __initially__ establishes the postcondition of __initially__ and the concrete invariant. Premise 3: verification of each exported procedure body, i.e., precondition and concrete invariant across body establishes postcondition and preserves concrete invariant. Premises 4-5: these two premises are for each exported function body. Premise 4 is analogous to premise 3 except (a) the concrete invariant is automatically preserved since functions have no side effects, and (b) the single-valued requirement described following Rule 10.2 is included. Premise 5 also concerns functions and is the consistency clause described after Rule 10.2. Premise 6: finally establishes the postcondition of the module.

Premise 7: instantiation environment implies module precondition with actuals substituted for formals.

Premise 8: shows how the instantiated module variable x is used in the scope S. It must be shown in premise 8.5 that the instantiation environment across _initially_, S, and _finally_ establishes R. In showing premise 8.5 one may use the four formulas 8.1-8.4, which give the properties of the module procedures, functions, _initially_, and _finally_, respectively. Formulas 8.1 and 8.2 correspond to the conclusions of the procedure and function call rules; the only difference is that the abstract invariant may be used in proving the preconditions and is assumed following the calls. (This is the source of much of the utility of the module construct. It allows us to prove theorems using data type (generator) induction.) Formula 8.3 treats x.Initially as a parameterless procedure call that establishes the abstract invariant. Formula 8.4 treats x.Finally as a parameterless procedure call for which the abstract invariant may be used in establishing its precondition. (If x is declared to be an array of modules or a record containing modules, then x.Initially and x.Finally must each be replaced in 8.3, 8.4, and 8.5 by a sequence of calls to initialization and finalization routines, respectively. These sequences are defined in the report.)

Here, then, is the full module rule.

7.1. (module rule)

(1) $Q \supset Q0(A/t)$,
(2) $P1 \{const\ K;\ var\ V;\ S_4\} Q4(A/t) \wedge Q$,
(3) $P2(A/t) \wedge Q \{S_2\} Q2(A/t) \wedge Q$,
(4) $\exists g1 (P3(A/t) \wedge Q \{S_3\} Q3(A/t) \wedge g=g1(A,c,d))$,
(5) $\exists g (P3(A/t) \wedge Q \supset Q3(A/t))$,
(6) $P6(A/t) \wedge Q \{S_6\} Q1$,
(7) $P \supset P1(a/c)$,

(8.1) $[\ Q0(a/c,\ x/t,\ x'/t') \supset (P2(x/t,\ x'/t',\ a2/x2,\ e2/c2,\ a/c) \wedge$
         $(Q2(x2\#/t,\ x'/t',\ a2\#/x2,\ e2/c2,\ a/c,\ y2\#/y2,\ a2/x2',\ y2/y2') \supset$
         $R1(x2\#/x,\ a2\#/a2,\ y2\#/y2))) \{x.p(a2,\ e2)\} R1 \wedge Q0(a/c,\ x/t,\ x'/t')$,
(8.2) $(Q0(a/c,\ x/t) \supset P3(x/t,\ a3/c3,\ a/c)) \supset$
         $Q3(x/t,\ a3/c3,\ a/c,\ f(a3,\ d3)/g) \wedge Q0(a/c,\ x/t)$,
'8.3) $P1(a/c) \wedge (Q4(x4\#/t,\ x'/t',\ a/c,\ y4\#/y4,\ y4/y4') \supset R4(x4\#/x,\ y4\#/y4))$
         $\{x.Initially\} R4 \wedge Q0(a/c,\ x/t,\ x'/t')$,
(8.4) $(Q0(a/c,\ x/t,\ x'/t') \supset P6(x/t,\ x'/t',\ a/c)) \wedge (Q1(a/c,\ y6\#/y6,\ y6/y6')$
         $R(y6\#/y6)) \{x.Finally\} R\ ]$
         $\vdash$
(8.5) $P(x\#/x) \{x.Initially;\ S;\ x.Finally\} R(x\#/x)$

         $P \{var\ x:T(a);\ S\} R \wedge Q1$

where the "#" denotes fresh identifiers and the scope of x is exactly S. As noted above, calls in S to module routines use formulas 8.1-8.4. Although not written, calls in S_2, S_3, S_4, and S_6 to module routines are similarly handled, but using the A/t substitution ("x." is missing) and without assuming Q0(a/c, x/t) or Q0(a/c, x/t, x'/t'). Since a module may not import its own name, premise 2 is never "recursively applied" in T. In the interest of simplicity, the formulas for recursion, <u>return</u>, and H are omitted in premises 3-5. Non-exported routines follow the rules for routines in Section 10.

In the simple case where the module T imports no var variables, i.e., <u>initially</u> and <u>finally</u> can have no side effects outside T, premise 6 and Q1 are missing (finally can have no visible effect) and premise 8 can be just

$$[8.1, 8.2]\ |\!-\!-\ P(x\#/x) \land Q4(x/t) \land Q0(x/t)\ \{S\}\ R(x\#/x)$$

where 8.1 and 8.2 contain no #'s on identifiers from y.

This formulation of the module rule follows [8]. Other approaches [14, 5], which use different specification methods, might have been substituted and, of course, may be used to verify programs containing modules. With these alternative approaches there would be changes only to the verification information of the module.

Pointer and Collection Types

$$\underline{type}\ T_\theta = \underline{collection\ of}\ T'$$
$$\underline{var}\ C\!:\!T_\theta$$
$$\underline{type}\ T = \uparrow C$$

8.1. C.nil is an element of T.

8.2. There are an unbounded number of elements of T: $\pi_1, \pi_2, \ldots$ (see 8.7).

8.3. If $\beta_1, \ldots, \beta_n$ are elements of T' and $\pi_1, \ldots, \pi_n$ are distinct members, $\neq$ C.nil, of T, then

$$T_\theta(\{\pi_1\!:\!\beta_1, \ldots, \pi_n\!:\!\beta_n\})\ \text{is an element of}\ T_\theta.$$

Note that $\pi_i\!:\!\beta_i$ indicates that π_i denotes the component β_i in the collection.

8.4. These are the only elements of T_θ.

8.5. If $C = T_\theta(\{\pi_1\!:\!\beta_1, \ldots, \pi_n\!:\!\beta_n\})$ then $C(\pi_i) = \beta_i$.

8.6.   For any element $\pi \neq C.nil$ of type T, $\pi\uparrow = C(\pi)$.

We introduce the following abbreviation:

If $C = T_\emptyset(\{\pi_1:\beta_1,\ldots,\pi_n:\beta_n\})$ then $(C,\pi_i:y)$ stands for

$\quad T_\emptyset(\{\pi_1:\beta_1,\ldots,\pi_n:\beta_n\} - \{\pi_i:\beta_i\} + \{\pi_i:y\})$.

No operations are defined on the elements of T except test of equality, $\uparrow$, and the standard function $C.Index$. The only defined property of $C.Index$ is that it is one-to-one. For every collection there are two standard procedures, $C.New(t)$ and $C.Free(t)$, involving the elements of T. Assume the declaration <u>var</u> $t:T$, and that $C = T_\emptyset(\{\pi_1:\beta_1,\ldots,\pi_n:\beta_n\})$.

8.7. $C.New(t)$ means $t := \pi$

where π is an element of T, $\pi \neq \pi_i$ for $i = 1,\ldots,n$,

and $C := T_\emptyset(\{\pi_1:\beta_1,\ldots,\pi_n:\beta_n\} + \{\pi:\beta\})$ where β is undefined (and may not be referenced).

8.8. $C.Free(t)$ means

$C := T_\emptyset(\{\pi_1:\beta_1,\ldots,\pi_n:\beta_n\} - \{t:C(t)\})$ (recall $C(t)$ means $t\uparrow$)

$t := C.nil$.

Declarations

The purpose of a declaration is to introduce a named object (constant, type, variable, function, or procedure) and to prescribe its properties. These properties may then be assumed in any proof relating to the scope of the declaration.

Constant, Variable, and Type Declarations

If D is a sequence of variable and type declarations, then

$$D;S$$

is called a scope, and the following are its rules of inference (some expressed in the usual notation for subsidiary deductions):

9.1.
$$\frac{x\#.itsType = T, \; x\# \in T \;\vert\!-\; P\{S(x\#/x)\}Q}{P\{\underline{var}\; x:T;\; S\}Q}$$

where $itsType$ is the standard Euclid component. The substitution of the fresh identifier x# for x expresses the fact that x is a "local" variable. T is any type except a module (see Section 7) or a structured type (record or array) involving modules whose initially or finally clauses modify imported var identifiers. The separate rules required to cover these structured types are omitted.

9.2. $P(e/x)$ (const x:=e} P

This axiom also applies to structured constants according to the order of the components.

9.3a $x=y \land P(x\#/x)$ {S} $Q(x\#/x, \ x/y)$

P {underline{bind} varBindingCondition x to y; S} Q

9.3b $i=i_0 \land x=y(i) \land P(x\#/x)$ {S} $Q(x\#/x, \ (y, i_0:x)/y)$

P {underline{bind} varBindingCondition x to y(i); S} Q

where, in all cases, i_0 and x# are fresh variables; and where varBindingCondition is readonly, var or empty.

9.4.   H |-- P {S} Q

                    P {underline{type} T=...; S} Q

where H is the set of assertions derived from the type declaration of T in the manner described in Sections 1-6 and 8.

Parameterized Types

                    type T(c) = pre P1; Defn

9.5. $P \supset P1(a/c)$, P {underline{const} c:=a; type T'=Defn; var x:T'; S} Q

                    P {underline{var} x:T(a); S} Q

                    type T'(...,x,...) = ...
                    type T_0 = collection of T'(...,unknown,...)
                    var C:T_0
                    type T = ↑C
                    var t:T

If T is referenced as the object type of a collection, then one or more of the actual parameters may be specified as <u>unknown</u>. In such cases the component of H (in Rule 9.4) associated with t is the disjunction

$$^{+}_{a \ in \ \underline{x}+(\underline{any})} \ t \ \epsilon \ \uparrow \underline{collection \ of} \ T'(\ldots,a,\ldots).$$

9.6. C.New(t,y) means all of Section 8.7 except that the type of β is T'(...,y,....).

Procedure Declarations and Calls

<u>procedure</u> p(<u>var</u> X, nonvar C) = <u>imports</u> (<u>var</u> Y, nonvar D)
     <u>pre</u> P; <u>post</u> Q; <u>begin</u> S <u>end</u>

Nonvar denotes the list of <u>const</u> and <u>readonly</u> identifiers. Let x, c, y, and d be the identifiers declared in X, C, Y, and D, respectively. P and Q are each predicates involving as free variables only x, c, y, and d. Q may also involve x' and y', fresh variables which denote the initial values of x and y on entry to the procedure body.

10.1. (procedure-call rule)

[P(a1/x, e1/c) ∧ (Q(a1#/x, e1/c, y#/y, a1/x', y/y') ⊃
        R1(a1#/a1, y#/y)) {p(a1, e1)}R1, Q{<u>return asserting</u> Q} false, H]
    I--
x=x' ∧ y=y' ∧ P{S}Q

P(a/x, e/c) ∧ (Q(a#/x, e/c, y#/y, a/x', y/y') ⊃ R(a#/a, y#/y))
    {p(a, e)}R

This rule, which is similar to the adaptation rules in [7, 3], assumes the above declaration of procedure p. If the procedure p is nonrecursive, the premise of 10.1 can be just

[Q{<u>return asserting</u> Q} false, H] I-- x=x' ∧ y=y' ∧ P{S}Q.

In 10.1 a and e are the list of actual parameters which correspond respectively to the formal parameters specified as variable and nonvariable parameters. Note that the elements of a and y will, in any legal Euclid program, all be distinct in the sense that none can overlap any other. H is the conjunction of the assertions for each x∈X and c∈C, that they are elements of their declared type. (The members of Y and D need not be included in this H, but are covered by 9.1 and 9.4.) The "#" indicates that fresh variables are to be used. Recall that the prime symbol (') denotes initial value of the corresponding formal parameter at procedure body entry. By convention, P and R do not contain primes. An example of the application of Rule 10.1 is contained in Appendix 1. A full discussion of this rule appears in [4] which compares this rule to several other rules, including those contained in [7, 9].

It should be noted that if two or more of the actuals, a, are components of the same array, a slight complication arises in substituting for the actuals. $R(a\#/a, y\#/y)$ may evaluate to a formula of the form

$$R(a1\#/B(i_1)\ldots(i_m), \ a2\#/B(j_1)\ldots(j_n)).$$

Since the non-overlapping rule guarantees that there exists a k where $1 \leq k \leq m \leq n$ such that $i_k \neq j_k$, the substitution is well-defined. Applying the rule for array element substitution will reduce this to

$$R((B,<i_1,\ldots,i_m>:a1\#)/B, \ (B,<j_1,\ldots,j_n>:a2\#)/B).$$

At this point simultaneous substitution is no longer well-defined. We therefore define *extended simultaneous substitution* with the rule

$$R((B,<i_1,\ldots,i_m>:a1\#)/B, \ (B,<j_1,\ldots,j_n>:a2\#)/B) =$$
$$R(((B,<i_1,\ldots,i_m>:a1\#),<j_1,\ldots,j_n>:a2\#)/B).$$

Note that in verifying Euclid programs this situation can only arise in connection with substitutions generated by application of the procedure-call rule. In this environment, we know, because of the non-overlapping restriction, that replacing the simultaneous substitution with sequential substitutions produces identical results regardless of the order in which they are performed.

Note that we do not have an independent rule covering the return statement. Rather, we have embedded it in the above rule for procedure calls, which allows us to use the axiom

$$Q\{\underline{return} \ \underline{asserting} \ Q\}false$$

in proving P{S}Q for p. Informally the rule states that any return causes us to exit the statically enclosing procedure. Although the syntax of Euclid is just "return," we have added the "asserting Q" clause in order to state succinctly the axiom for return. We assume a preprocessor, if necessary, that determines the statically enclosing procedure associated with each return and adds to each return the corresponding Q. This addition is necessary to ensure against making an unsound inference about a return from an internally nested procedure with a different postcondition. The statement return when B may be replaced (as specified in the Euclid report) by the statement

$$\underline{if} \ B \ \underline{then} \ \underline{return} \ \underline{end} \ \underline{if}.$$

Beware, the axiom involving return may not be used immediately if the procedure p contains an instantiation of a module whose finally clause falsifies Q. In such cases, the expansion described in the Euclid report for moving the finally clause must be first applied.

Rule 10.1 may be used in proving assertions about calls of the procedure p, including those occurring within S itself or in other declarations in the same scope. The rule is applicable to all recursive calls because of the clause in the premise to the left of the turnstile, |--. In this "recursion" clause note that the symbols are deliberately different from those in the rule's conclusion: R1 replaces R, and a1 and e1 replace a and e to allow different formulas and actual parameters to be used for recursive calls. The entire premise of Rule 10.1 need be proved only once for each procedure declaration, not once for each call.

For a procedure declaration itself we have

10.1a   R {procedure p...begin S end} R

Function Declarations and Calls

function f(nonvar C) returns G = imports (nonvar D)
     pre P; post Q; begin S end

The same notation is used as in procedures. Nonvar denotes the list of const and readonly identifiers; P is a predicate involving c and d; Q involves c, d, and g. A rule similar to 10.1a applies to function declarations:

10.2a   R {function f...begin S end} R

Function calls, unlike procedure calls, appear in expressions which are part of statements. There is no function-call statement corresponding to a procedure-call statement. The proof rule for functions depends crucially on the fact that Euclid functions have no side effects, a consequence of the absence of var in a function declaration. Therefore, the order of evaluation of functions within an expression does not matter.

Suppose in an expression, possibly within S itself or in other declarations in the same scope, there is a call f(a) of the function f with actual parameters a. The rule

10.2. (function-call rule)

$$[P(a1/c) \supset Q(a1/c, f(a1, d)/g), Q\{return \; asserting \; Q\} false, H]$$
$$|-- \; [P\{S\}Q, \exists g1\,(P\{S\} g=g1(c,d))]],$$
$$H \supset \exists g(P \supset Q)$$
$$\rule{8cm}{0.4pt}$$
$$P(a/c) \supset Q(a/c, f(a, d)/g)$$

may be used in verifying the properties of the expression involving f(a). Since the term f(a,d), rather than f(a), occurs in the conclusion of the rule, applying this rule to an assertion R will first require the verifier to apply the substitution f(a,d)/f(a) to R. This rule is due to David Musser; a full discussion is in [12].

The second premise, called the consistency clause, ensures that the lemma in the conclusion of the rule will not be inconsistent. In the first premise, the P{S}Q part gives the relation which the function's declared body, S, and its single precondition, P, and single postcondition, Q, must satisfy. The part involving ∃g1 is a requirement that the function be single-valued; it is discussed below. These, like the second premise, need be proved only once per function declaration. The other three parts of the premise (before the |--) are the recursion clause, the definition of the return statement, and the type information for each c ∈ C and g, respectively. The return statement is the same as in procedures, including the "asserting Q" clause. The statements

$$\text{return expr when B}$$
$$\text{return expr}$$

are equivalent to

$$\text{if B then g := expr; return end if}$$
$$\text{g := expr; return,}$$

respectively.

In ∃g1(P{S}g=g1(c,d)), g1 is a mathematical function of c and d. The premise is thus equivalent to requiring that S defines a mathematical function, i.e., that it be single-valued. Note that the implicit universal quantifiers associated with formulas in the Hoare logic go inside the existential quantifier in this formula. If the function contains no module variables in its parameter or import lists, the ∃g1 part is automatically true because Euclid is a deterministic langauge.

The standard equality of Euclid modules (if equality is exported) is, informally, component-by-component (bitwise) equality of the modules' concrete representations. With respect to this equality, Euclid functions of modules are also single-valued and thus the ∃g1 part is again true. However, other equality relations may be needed in the verification of programs which use Euclid modules. In particular, the abstraction function of a module, A, may be used to induce an equality relation on the concrete objects, a relation that is different from the standard equality. For example, suppose a stack module uses for its concrete representation an array and a top-of-stack pointer. The stack operations push, a second push, and then a pop ought to yield the same stack as does just the first push. Using an abstraction function that ignores the "unused" part of the array (where the second pushed element remains), the single push will give a stack equal to that of push-push-pop; using the standard equality, this will not be true. Thus always using the standard equality will not suffice to verify certain programs. As another example, consider sets represented by arrays. Equal sets, by a useful abstraction function, contain identical elements although not necessarily in the same order within the array. The abstract operation of choosing an arbitrary element from the set can be implemented by returning the first element from the array. According to set equality defined by the abstraction function, this operation is not single-valued. In such a situation, the standard algebraic simplification rules may fail since f(s')=f(s) is not necessarily true. Accordingly, before using the function-call rule on Euclid functions of modules, it is necessary to prove that the function is single-valued with respect to the equality relation induced by A.

A pseudo-function type-converter is treated as a function with appropriate precondition and postcondition as defined in the Euclid report. Examples involving function calls are in Appendix 2.

Statements

Statements are classified into simple statements and structured statements. The meaning of all simple statements (except procedure calls) is defined by axioms, and the meaning of structured statements (and procedure calls) is defined in terms of rules of inference permitting the properties of the structured statement to be deduced from properties of its constituents. However, the rules of inference are formulated so as to facilitate the reverse process of deriving necessary properties of the constituents from postulated properties of the composite statement. The reason for this orientation is that in deducing proofs of properties of programs it is most convenient to proceed in a "top-down" direction.

Simple Statements

Assignment Statements

11.1.   P(y/x) {x:=y}P

The substitution definitions given in Sections 4, 5, and 8 apply here.

Procedure Statements

Procedure statements are explained in Section 10 on procedure declarations and calls.

Escape Statements

Return statements are explained in Section 10. Exit statements are explained in Section 12.6.

Empty Statements

11.2. $\qquad$ P{ }P

Assertion Statements

11.3. $\qquad$ P $\wedge$ Q{assert P}P $\wedge$ Q

11.4.   If the checked option is specified, we may use

$$Q\{\underline{assert}\ B\}Q \wedge B$$

where B is a Boolean expression.

Structured Statements

Compound Statements

12.1. $\qquad$
$$\frac{P_{i-1}\{S_i\}P_i \quad \text{for } i=1,\ldots,n}{P_0\{S_1;S_2;\ldots;S_n\}P_n}$$

If Statements

12.2. $\qquad$
$$\frac{P \wedge B\{S_1\}Q,\ P \wedge \neg B\{S_2\}Q}{P\{\underline{if}\ B\ \underline{then}\ S_1\ \underline{else}\ S_2\ \underline{end\ if}\}Q}$$

12.3. $\qquad$
$$\frac{P \wedge B\{S\}Q,\ P \wedge \neg B \supset Q}{P\{\underline{if}\ B\ \underline{then}\ S\ \underline{end\ if}\}Q}$$

Case Statements

12.4a $\qquad$
$$\frac{P \wedge (x=k_i)\ \{S_i\}Q,\ \text{for } i=1,\ldots,n}{P\{\underline{case}\ x\ \underline{of}\ k_1 \Rightarrow S_1;\ldots;k_n \Rightarrow S_n\ \underline{end\ case}\}Q}$$

12.4b $\qquad$
$$\frac{P \wedge (x=k_i)\{S_i\}Q\ \text{for } i=1,\ldots,n,\ P \wedge x\ \underline{not\ in}\ (k_1,\ldots,k_n)\ \{S_{n+1}\}Q}{P\{\underline{case}\ x\ \underline{of}\ k_1 \Rightarrow S_1;\ldots;k_n \Rightarrow S_n;\underline{otherwise} \Rightarrow S_{n+1}\ \underline{end\ case}\}Q}$$

Note that $k_a,k_b,\ldots,k_m \Rightarrow S$ stands for $k_a \Rightarrow S;k_b \Rightarrow S;\ldots;k_m \Rightarrow S$. The type of x is constrained as in the section on variant records.

12.5. $P\{\underline{var}\ anyx:T(k_i);\ S;\ \underline{begin}\ \underline{var}\ x:T(k_i):=anyx;\ S_i\ \underline{end}\}Q$,
            for $i=1,\ldots,n$

            $P\{\underline{var}\ anyx:T(\underline{any});\ S;\ \underline{case}\ x:=anyx\ of$
            $k_1=>S_1;\ldots;k_n=>S_n\ \underline{end}\ \underline{case}\}Q$

There may be other formal parameters in T besides the single any (see
the expansions in the procedure declarations section of the Euclid
report). The case

            $\underline{var}\ anyx:T(\underline{any});\ S;\ anyx:=y$

is already covered by the assignment axiom (Rule 11.1).

Loop Statements

12.6. $Q\{\underline{exit}\ \underline{asserting}\ Q\}\ false\ \mid--\ P\{S\}P$

            $P\{\underline{loop}\ S\ \underline{end}\ \underline{loop}\}Q$

Note that exit plays the same role with respect to loops that return
plays with respect to procedures and functions (among other things, it
is associated with the nearest enclosing loop and a corresponding exit
assertion; and the axiom involving exit may not be used directly with
certain module instantiations). Like return when B, the statement exit
when B may be replaced by the statement

            if B then exit end if.

For Statements

For statements may always be expanded as explained in the Euclid report.
However, for simplified cases the following rules are available, where
the loop body S may not contain an escape statement:

Let T be a subrange type.

12.7. $(T.first \le x \le T.last)\ \wedge\ P([T.first..x))\ \{S\}P([T.first..x])$

            $P([\ ])\ \{\underline{for}\ x\ \underline{in}\ T\ \underline{loop}\ S\ \underline{end}\ \underline{loop}\}P([T.first..T.last])$

12.8. $(T.first \le x \le T.last)\ \wedge\ P((x..T.last])\ \{S\}P([x..T.last])$

            $P([\ ])\ \{\underline{for}\ x\ \underline{decreasing}\ \underline{in}\ T\ \underline{loop}\ S\ \underline{end}\ \underline{loop}\}P([T.first..T.last])$

$[u..v]$ denotes the closed interval $u,\ldots,v$, i.e., the set $\{i\mid u\le i\le v\}$, and
$[u..v)$ denotes the half-open interval $u,\ldots,v$, i.e., the set $\{i\mid u\le i<v\}$.

Similarly, [u..v] denotes the set {i|u<i≤v}. Note that [u..u)=(u..u] is the empty set. Since x, T.first, and T.last are constants, S cannot change x, T.first, or T.last.

Let T be a set type.

12.9.
$$\frac{T_1 \leq T \wedge x \text{ in } T-T_1 \wedge P(T_1) \ \{S\} P(T_1+(x))}{P(()) \ \{\text{for } x \text{ in } T \text{ loop } S \text{ end loop}\} P(T)}$$

Recall that ( ) are used for set brackets. Since x and T are constants, S cannot change x or T.

Epilogue

We would like to note a few points about our experiences in constructing these proof rules.

We began to axiomatize Euclid in early 1976, and essentially ended over a year later. At the start we expected an interesting but not terribly challenging project. We were half-right--it was for us interesting *and* challenging. We learned a great deal about both proof rules and Euclid--two topics we were not nearly so well versed in as we thought.

Our increased understanding of Euclid paid a clear and immediate dividend. A number of improvements to the language were made as a direct result of facts discovered during the axiomatization. (This in turn meant the need for new proof rules.) The long-term payoff of our increased understanding of proof rules is less certain. We would like to believe that were we to begin a similar project today, we would find it considerably less painful. It is, however, far from clear to us that it would be the routine task it must eventually become if rigorous definitions of new programming languages are to be the norm. We would surely try to write the proof rules in parallel with the design rather than afterward, as we did in some instances with Euclid. We spent an inordinate amount of time and effort on problems related to modules. Had we felt free to make substantial changes to this part of Euclid, much of this time and effort could have been avoided, and the proof rules themselves simplified substantially.

A somewhat disturbing aspect of these proof rules is our lack of complete confidence in them. There are some rules with which we are still unhappy, although we know of no errors in them. Nevertheless, it would be naive for us to believe that there are no remaining errors; many bugs were found in earlier versions, and we have too much programming experience to interpret this as a good sign. Our approach to "verifying" these proof rules has been to study each rule in (as much as possible) isolation. We have informally presented (to ourselves and others) the reasons we believe each rule to be appropriate, and have tested each rule on as many distinct cases as we had the energy to look at. The inadequacies of this approach have been cogently argued in the literature on programming. What is needed is a more formal approach to validating proof rules. The work by Donahue [2] on "verifying" soundness via a complementary definition and by Clarke [1] on completeness seems a step in this direction. We would very much encourage and be happy to talk with anyone who wishes to examine rigorously the soundness and completeness of these proof rules.

Acknowledgments

We are greatly indebted to C.A.R. Hoare and Niklaus Wirth for their axiomatization of Pascal. We are grateful to them, and to Springer-Verlag, for permission to use sections of the Pascal axiomatization [9] in this paper. Suggestions, comments, and criticisms by numerous colleagues and the referees have greatly aided us; David Musser has been especially helpful. As always, responsibility for errors and problems remains with us. We appreciate the efforts of Betty Randall and Lisa Moses in typing and formatting the various versions of this work.

Appendix 1

Procedures

Consider the trivial procedure, with only one var parameter, one const parameter, and no imported variables

procedure p(var a:signedInt, b:signedInt) = pre true; post a≤2∗b;

begin var c:signedInt; c:=2∗b; if a>c then a:=c end if end.

Letting S stand for the body of this procedure, it is easy to prove

$$true \; \{S\} \; a≤2∗b.$$

The invocation of this procedure will (in general) change the value of a in some manner dependent on the initial values of a and b (and, if present and referenced from within S, on values of imported variables).

Now the effect of any call of p(z,w) is to change z such that z≤2∗w, and using the procedure-call rule (10.1) we may validly conclude for any R that

$$true \land (z\#≤2∗w \supset R(z\#/z)) \; \{p(z,w)\}R.$$

In particular, R might be just z≤2⋇w or R might involve variables other than z and w if the call p(z,w) followed statements involving those other variables. The properties of a call of p are contained solely in the postcondition a≤2⋇b.

The given postcondition is not the only property that can be proved about p. For example, if the postcondition a=min(a',2⋇b), where the prime denotes the initial value of a, had been supplied with p, we could validly conclude that

$$\text{true} \land (z\#=\min(z,2⋇w) \supset R(z\#/z)) \{p(z,w)\}R.$$

It is important to see how the rule accommodates a structured actual variable in a var position. For a call p(d(i), i) where d is an array and R is d(i)≤2⋇i we may validly conclude, using the original postcondition, that

$$\text{true} \land (d\#(i)≤2⋇i \supset d\#(i)≤2⋇i) \{p(d(i), i)\}d(i)≤2⋇i.$$

If the formal parameter b were also a var parameter, we may validly conclude

$$\text{true} \land (d\#(i)≤2⋇i\# \supset d\#(i\#)≤2⋇i\#) \{p(d(i), i)\}d(i)≤2⋇i$$

which uses i# in place of i in *three* places. In the var b case, by the rules of simultaneous substitution (see discussion following Rule 10.1), Q(d#(i)/a, i#/b) is d#(i)≤2⋇i# while R(d#(i)/d(i), i#/i) is d#(i#)≤2⋇i#. In the const b case, Q(d#(i)/a, i/b) and R(d#(i)/d(i)) are both d#(i)≤2⋇i.

Note that while making the second formal var has no effect on the behavior of the program, it does reduce the number of things we can prove. Though the procedure does not change the second parameter, this cannot be deduced from the postcondition associated with p.

Appendix 2

Functions

Suppose we have the function declarations

function f(c:signedInt) returns m:signedInt =
    pre $P_f(c)$; post $Q_f(c,m)$; begin S_f end

function g(c:signedInt) returns m:signedInt =
    pre $P_g(c)$; post $Q_g(c,m)$; begin S_g end

and suppose that we have proved of the two bodies

$$P_f \{S_f\}Q_f \quad \text{and} \quad P_g \{S_g\}Q_g$$

and proved of the pre- and postconditions

$$\exists m(P_f \supset Q_f) \text{ and } \exists m(P_g \supset Q_g).$$

The axiom for the assignment statement

$$x := f(g(x))+1$$

leads to

$$R([f(g(x))+1]/x) \{x := f(g(x))+1\} R.$$

The two function calls $g(x)$ and $f(g(x))$ appear in the expression $f(g(x))+1$. The function-call rule applied to g requires that the precondition $P_g(x)$ be established which in turn yields the postcondition $Q_g(x,g(x))$. The latter may be used is applying the function-call rule to f to establish $P_f(g(x))$ which yields $Q_f(g(x),f(g(x)))$. The two postconditions $Q_f(g(x),f(g(x)))$ and $Q_g(x,g(x))$ may be used to establish the substituted R term. Having done all the above, we may conclude that R holds after the assignment.

As another simpler example, to show

$$P\{\underline{if}\ f(x) > 0\ \underline{then}\ S_1\ \underline{else}\ S_2\ \underline{end\ if}\}Q,$$

it suffices to show the three premises

$$P \supset P_f(x),$$

$$P \wedge f(x)>0 \{S_1\}Q,$$

$$P \wedge \neg f(x)>0 \{S_2\}Q.$$

The first premise shows that it is legal to call $f(x)$ and, by the function-call rule applied to f, to use the postcondition $Q_f(x,f(x))$ as an additional hypothesis in establishing the second and third premises of the if rule. As a concrete example of this schema, suppose we have the function declaration

$$\underline{function}\ power(x,y:signedInt)\ \underline{returns}\ z:signedInt = \\ \underline{pre}\ y{\geq}0;\ \underline{post}\ z=x{**}y;\ \underline{begin}\ S\ \underline{end}$$

and suppose that we have proved

$$y{\geq}0\ \{S\}\ z=x{**}y,$$

$$\exists z(y{\geq}0 \supset z=x{**}y).$$

We wish to show

b≥1 {if power(a,b)>0 then c:=true else c:=false end if}c=(a✲✲b>0).

Since

$$b≥1 ⊃ b≥0,$$

the function-call rule applied to power(a,b) yields the conclusion power(a,b)=a✲✲b. Using this equation it is easy to show

$$b≥1 ∧ power(a,b)>0 \{c:=true\} c=(a✲✲b>0),$$

$$b≥1 ∧ power(a,b)≤0 \{c:=false\} c=(a✲✲b>0),$$

that is,

$$b≥1 ∧ a✲✲b>0 ⊃ a✲✲b>0,$$

$$b≥1 ∧ a✲✲b≤0 ⊃ false=(a✲✲b>0).$$

Note that if the formal parameter y were of type unsignedInt, the precondition of power could be just the constant true. In this case the compiler, rather than the verifier, would have to be satisfied that b≥0. The compiler might, of course, produce a legality assertion for the verifier.

Appendix 3

Modules

As an example of the use of the module rule, we shall use a variant of the smallIntSet example in [8]. Our module smallIntSet provides the abstraction of a set of integers in the range 1..100. The abstract operations are insertion and removal of individual elements and a membership test. When a variable of type smallIntSet is declared, it is initialized to the empty set. The set will be represented by a Boolean array, S, of 100 elements,

S: array 1..100 of Boolean.

S(i)=true iff i belongs to the set. In this example { } are used for set brackets. Comment brackets around non-Euclid pre and post are omitted.

```
type smallIntSet =
    pre true
    module smallSet
    invariant true
    exports (insert, remove, has, :=)
    var S: array 1..100 of Boolean
```

```
procedure insert (i:integer) =
     pre 1≤i≤100 ∧ smallSet=smallSet'
     post smallSet=smallSet' ∪ {i}
     begin S(i):=true end insert

procedure remove (i:integer) =
     pre 1≤i≤100 ∧ smallSet=smallSet'
     post smallSet=smallSet' ~ {i}
     begin S(i):=false end remove

function has (i:integer) returns hasResult:Boolean =
     pre 1≤i≤100
     post hasResult=(i ∈ smallSet)
     begin hasResult:=S(i) end has

initially
     post smallSet=emptySet
     begin for j in S.IndexType loop S(j):=false end loop end

abstraction function setValue returns resultSet = imports (S)
     begin resultSet = {j | S(j) ∧ 1≤j≤100} end

invariant true
```

```
end smallIntSet
```

At the point where we encounter this module definition program, we verify the asserted properties of the definition. The necessary formulas to be verified here are derived from the module definition and the first six premises of the module rule:

(1)   true ⊃ true

(2)   true {var S:array 1..100 of Boolean
          begin for j in S.IndexType
                loop S(j):=false end loop end} setValue(S)=emptySet ∧ true

(3) (insert)   1≤i≤100 ∧ setValue(S)=setValue(S') ∧ true {S(i):=true}
                setValue(S)=setValue(S') ∪ {i} ∧ true

(3) (remove)   1≤i≤100 ∧ setValue(S)=setValue(S') ∧ true {S(i):=false}
                setValue(S)=setValue(S') ~ {i} ∧ true

(4)   ∃g1 (1≤i≤100 ∧ true {hasResult:=S(i)}
                hasResult=(i ∈ setValue(S)) ∧ hasResult=g1(setValue(S)))

(5)   ∃hasResult (1≤i≤100 ∧ true ⊃ hasResult=(i ∈ setValue(S)))

(6)   there is no finally, so this premise is missing.

In the above formulas the abstraction function setValue has its imported identifier S included as an argument. We shall not go through the exercise of proving these. They are all trivially verifiable.

Now, to show

$x=2$ {var x:smallIntSet; x.insert(3); x.insert(5); y:=x.has(3); x.delete(3); z:=x end} $z=\{5\} \wedge y=$true$\wedge x=2$,

where y and z have been declared prior to x, we can use the remainder of the module rule.

First, to verify the declaration var x:smallIntSet, we need only show

(7) $x=2 \supset$ true.

Having verified this, and premises 1-6, we may now derive and, by premise 8 in the module rule, assume and use the formulas (where x1, x2, x3, and x4 are fresh variables)

(8.1a) true $\supset$ ($1 \leq 3 \leq 100 \wedge (x1=x \cup \{3\} \supset x1=\{3\} \wedge x\#=2)$)
{x.insert(3)} $x=\{3\} \wedge x\#=2$

(8.1b) true $\supset$ ($1 \leq 5 \leq 100 \wedge (x2=x \cup \{5\} \supset x2=\{3,5\} \wedge x\#=2)$)
{x.insert(5)} $x=\{3,5\} \wedge x\#=2$

(8.1c) true $\supset$ ($1 \leq 3 \leq 100 \wedge (x3=x \sim \{3\} \supset x3=\{5\} \wedge x\#=2 \wedge y=$true$)$)
{x.delete(3)} $x=\{5\} \wedge x\#=2 \wedge y=$true

(8.2) true $\supset$ ($1 \leq 3 \leq 5 \supset x.has(3)=3 \in x$)

(8.3) true $\wedge$ ($x4=$emptySet $\supset x4=$emptySet $\wedge x\#=2$) {x.Initially} $x=$emptySet $\wedge x\#=2$,
i.e., $x\#=2$ {x.Initially} $x=$emptySet $\wedge x\#=2$

(8.4) This premise is missing because there is no finally.

We now instantiate premise 8.5 by setting S to be

x.insert(3); x.insert(5); y:=x.has(3); x.delete(3); z:=x end

and R to be

$x=\{5\} \wedge y=$true$\wedge x=2$

obtaining

(8.5) $x\#=2$ {x.Initially; S} $z=\{5\} \wedge y=$true$\wedge x\#=2$.

We now prove premise 8.5 using the formulas 8.1a-8.3. Using (8.3) we reduce the formula to be proved to

$x\#=2 \wedge x=$emptySet {S} $z=\{5\} \wedge y=$true$\wedge x\#=2$.

Next, using (8.1a), we get

$x\# = 2 \land x = \{3\}$ {x.insert(5); y:=x.has(3); x.delete(3); z:=x}
$z = \{5\} \land y = true \land x\# = 2.$

Then, by (8.1b), we get

$x\# = 2 \land x = \{3,5\}$ {y:=x.has(3); x.delete(3); z:=x}
$z = \{5\} \land y = true \land x\# = 2.$

By (8.2) and the assignment axiom, the problem reduces to

$x\# = 2 \land x = \{3,5\} \land y = true$ {x.delete(3); z:=x} $z = \{5\} \land y = true \land x\# = 2.$

By (8.1c) we get

$x\# = 2 \land x = \{5\} \land y = true$ {z:=x} $z = \{5\} \land y = true \land x\# = 2$

which, by the assignment axiom, is true.

Since the module smallIntSet imports no _var_ variables, the instantiation of premise 8.5 could have been from the simpler form of premise 8. If this were done, there would be no formula 8.3 to be used.

References

1. Clarke, E. M. Jr.: Programming language constructs for which it is impossible to obtain good Hoare-like axiom systems. Conference Record of the Fourth ACM Symposium on Principles of Programming Languages, Los Angeles, pp. 10-20. New York: ACM 1977

2. Donahue, J. E.: _Complementary Definitions of Programming Language Semantics._ Lecture Notes in Computer Science, Vol. 42. Berlin-Heidelberg-New York: Springer 1976

3. Ernst, G. W.: Rules of inference for procedure calls. _Acta Informatica_ 8, 145-152 (1977)

4. Guttag, J. V., Horning, J. J., and London, R. L.: A proof rule for Euclid procedures. _Working Conference on Formal Description of Programming Concepts, Preprints of Technical Papers,_ (E. Neuhold, ed.), St. Andrews, New Brunswick, pp. 10.1-10.8. Publication by North Holland forthcoming. Also USC Information Sciences Institute, Technical Report ISI/RR-77-60, May 1977

5. Guttag, J. V., Horowitz, E., and Musser, D. R.: Abstract data types and software validation. USC Information Sciences Institute, Technical Report ISI/RR-76-48, August 1976

6. Hoare, C. A. R.: An axiomatic basis for computer programming. *Comm. ACM* 12, 576-580 and 583 (1969)

7. Hoare, C. A. R.: Procedures and parameters: An axiomatic approach. In: *Symposium on Semantics of Algorithmic Languages* (E. Engeler, ed.), Lecture Notes in Mathematics, Vol. 188, pp. 102-116. Berlin-Heidelberg-New York: Springer 1971

8. Hoare, C. A. R.: Proof of correctness of data representations. *Acta Informatica* 1, 271-281 (1972)

9. Hoare, C. A. R. and Wirth, N.: An axiomatic definition of the programming language PASCAL. *Acta Informatica* 2, 335-355 (1973)

10. Jensen, K. and Wirth, N.: *PASCAL User Manual and Report.* Lecture Notes in Computer Science, Vol. 18, 2nd ed. Berlin-Heidelberg-New York: Springer 1975

11. Lampson, B. W., Horning, J. J., London, R. L., Mitchell, J. G., and Popek, G. J.: Revised report on the programming language Euclid (to appear). An earlier version appeared in *SIGPLAN Notices*, 12, No. 2, February 1977

12. Musser, D. R.: A proof rule for functions. USC Information Sciences Institute, Technical Report ISI/RR-77-62, October 1977

13. Popek, G. J., Horning, J. J., Lampson, B. W., Mitchell, J. G., and London, R. L.: Notes on the design of Euclid. Proceedings of an ACM Conference on Language Design for Reliable Software, Raleigh, North Carolina, *SIGPLAN Notices*, 12, No. 3, 11-18 (1977)

14. Spitzen, J. and Wegbreit, B.: The verification and synthesis of data structures. *Acta Informatica* 4, 127-144 (1975)

15. Wirth, N.: The programming language PASCAL. *Acta Informatica* 1, 35-63 (1971)

Verification of Euclid Programs

J. J. Horning

Xerox Palo Alto Research Center

ABSTRACT

The proof rules for the programming language Euclid are closely modelled on the axiomatic definition of Pascal. However, there is intended to be a much closer correspondence between the language as actually implemented and the proof rules. This has been achieved by a combination of language changes, more stringent requirements on the compiler, and modifications of the proof rules. Several novel features of Euclid were introduced specifically in response to problems and limitations of the Pascal definition.

Typical proof rules and proofs for programs using basic language constructs are very similar in Euclid and Pascal. We discuss some of these as a review of Hoare's methodology.

The proof rules for Euclid functions and procedures deviate from those for Pascal, and avoid some of their problems. We discuss the reasons for some of the changes.

Some parts of the Euclid language, such as modules and zones, were motivated by application or implementation considerations. These have been more difficult to axiomatize, and have proved to be some of the most troublesome parts of the language. We mention a few of the problem areas.

These notes should be read in conjunction with the published proof rules.

TYPICAL EUCLID PROOF RULES SIMILAR TO THOSE FOR PASCAL

The notation used in the proof rules for Euclid [London *et al.* 1978] was taken directly from that used for Pascal [Hoare and Wirth 1973]. If P and Q are predicates, and S a statement, then

P { S } Q

represents the assertion that if P holds prior to the execution of S *and* execution of S terminates, then Q will hold upon termination. This is sometimes called a "partial correctness" assertion, to distinguish it from assertions that also imply termination.

J. J. HORNING

The proof rules consist of axiom schemas for the basic statement types of the programming language, axioms about data types that may be used within the scopes of declarations, and rules of inference for proving assertions about compound statements (and ultimately about programs) from assertions about their components. Rules of inference are stated in the form

$$\frac{A, B, \dots, C}{P \ \{ \ S \ \} \ Q} \qquad (Premises) \\ (Conclusion)$$

which indicates that if premises A, B, ... , C (generally involving elements of P, S, and Q) can all be demonstrated, then P { S } Q follows.

Rule of consequence

There is one basic, language-independent rule of inference, which allows us to freely strengthen preconditions, or weaken postconditions

$$\frac{P \supset Q, \quad Q \ \{ \ S \ \} \ U, \quad U \supset R}{P \ \{ \ S \ \} \ R.}$$

Axiom of assignment

The basic axiom schema describes the effect of the assignment statement

$$P(e/x) \ \{ \ x := e \ \} \ P$$

where $P(e/x)$ represents the result of textually substituting e for all "free" occurrences of x in P. An assignment to a component of a structured variable (a record or an array) is treated as an assignment to the variable itself of a structured value that differs from the previous value only in the selected component.

Compound statement

$$\frac{P \ \{ \ S1 \ \} \ Q, \quad Q \ \{ \ S2 \ \} \ R}{P \ \{ \ S1 \ ; \ S2 \ \} \ R.}$$

This rule of inference explains the effect of composing statements. Alternatively, it allows us to decompose the proof of an assertion about a compound statement into two proofs, one about each component. Although Q is formally arbitrary, in practice, Q will be chosen to simplify the verification process; generally it will be the *weakest* Q such that Q { S2 } R.

Conditional statement

$$\frac{P \land B \ \{ \ S1 \ \} \ Q, \quad P \land \neg B \ \{ \ S2 \ \} \ Q}{P \ \{ \ \text{if B then S1 else S2 end if} \ \} \ Q.}$$

Again, we have a rule with multiple premises, each involving a simpler statement. The Boolean expression in the conditional statement and its negation are used to strengthen the preconditions of the premises.

VERIFICATION OF EUCLID PROGRAMS

THE PROCESS OF PROOF

In practice, proofs generally proceed "backwards" in two senses:

We work from a desired conclusion to obtain a set of premises that are sufficient
to establish it—and use these premises in turn as subgoals of the verification
process, until we finally arrive at a set of premises that can be proved directly.

We work from the desired postcondition to find a sufficient precondition, and
then show that this precondition is implied by the program's precondition, rather
than starting from the precondition, deriving the strongest postcondition, and
then showing that this postcondition implies the desired postcondition.

For most programming language constructs, including those discussed in the previous
section, given a statement and desired pre- and postconditions, it is straightforward to
determine a set of sufficient premises. The premises so generated will generally
themselves contain program text, and require further analysis. Ultimately axiom schemas
such as the one for assignment make it possible to eliminate all program text from the
assertions, leaving a collection of formulas of the predicate calculus whose validity is
sufficient to establish the originally asserted properties of the program. These program-
free formulas are generally called *verification conditions*. The generation of these
verification conditions from program text annotated with assertions is a straightforward,
but tedious, process of formula manipulation. Since it is completely formal, there is no
reason not to automate it, and a verification condition generator is an important part of
any system for assisting in program proofs.

Note. There are significant notational differences between the Hoare-style proof
rules used in Euclid and Pascal, and the *predicate transformers* used by Dijkstra,
which are functions from programs and postconditions to preconditions.
However, in practice the difference is not as large as it might seem. Useful
inference rules do not seem to take arbitrary forms, and the greater generality
allowed by Hoare's notation is not often needed in practice. In fact, rules that
seem to exploit this generality often have to be modified somewhat to permit
mechanical generation of verification conditions. We adopted the style of Hoare
because of the availability of the formal Pascal definition; in retrospect, this may
not have been sufficient to outweigh the advantages of the predicate transformer
style.

After the generation of the verification conditions, what is left is a set of proofs to be
performed in the predicate calculus. The original program no longer appears, and in
principle the proof of the verification conditions is a theorem-proving exercise that need
not take account of their origin. Of course, theorem-proving is itself a hard problem
(indeed, a problem that is unsolvable in general). However, experience is beginning to
indicate that most verification conditions that arise from understandable correct programs
are rather trivial; in fact, good algebraic simplification programs reduce most of them to
obvious tautologies. Again, there is no reason not to perform this simplification
automatically.

Exercise. Generate the verification conditions for

true { if X > Y then z := X else z := Y end if }
$$z \geq X \wedge z \geq Y \wedge (z = X \vee z = Y)$$

by first using the rule for conditional statements and then the axiom of
assignment twice. Simplify the predicates obtained. Finally, use the rule of
consequence to complete the verification of this assertion.

J. J. HORNING

In the verification of most "interesting" programs, a few "hard" theorems remain unproven by algebraic simplification. These generally correspond to the mathematical facts about the domain of the program that are needed anyhow to understand why the program works properly. There are a variety of ways of dealing with such proof obligations. Whether we rely on previously published proofs, an automatic theorem-prover, or proof "by hand" will depend largely on what the problem domain is, how much is already known about it, and how well our theorem-prover performs in that domain.

Limitations

There are some programming language constructs for which an automatic verification condition generator requires some help. An obvious example is loops, where the proof rule is stated in terms of a "loop invariant," which is not in general deducible from the pre- and postconditions and the loop body. However, it is now widely believed that the choice of a loop invariant is an important part of systematic program construction, and we have taken the position that such assertions should be included in the text of the program, for reasons of documentation (and possibly even optimization) as well as verification.

Another example is provided by procedures and functions. It is generally not easy to infer the minimal specification that would ensure correctness by inspecting all the calls on a routine. But, for methodological reasons, we would like to *separate* our proofs about a routine from our proofs about programs that may call it, and do the former only once. This separation is made possible by stating a specification of the routine itself, independently of its calls. Again, we take the position that the general pre- and postconditions of a routine form a proper part of its program text, and need not be inferred as part of the process of generating verification conditions.

ITERATION

Euclid provides several forms of iteration. The most general, to which the others can all in principle be rewritten, is the **loop** with embedded exit statements.

Loop

$$Q \ \{ \ exit \ asserting \ Q \ \} \ false \ \vdash \ P \ \{ \ S \ \} \ P$$
$$P \ \{ \ loop \ S \ end \ loop \ \} \ Q.$$

The additional notation here, $\vdash$, is the logical connective asserting that the formulas to the left are sufficient to enable the proof of the formulas to the right. In this case, we have a specialized form of the well-known proof rule for program jumps [Clint and Hoare 1972]. Note that exit statements may be embedded anywhere within S, they need not be textually first (as in while and **do - od** loops) or last (as in **repeat - until** loops). P is the loop invariant, and we have previously noted that it should be supplied as part of the program to be verified. Thus, our proof obligation for the loop with precondition P (or, by the rule of consequence, any stronger precondition) and postcondition Q reduces to the need to demonstrate that S preserves P if it does not exit, and that it only exits if Q has been established.

Exercise. Generate the verification conditions for

    i = 0
    { loop assert P(i)
        b(i) := i;
        if i = N-1 then exit asserting P(N)
        else i := i+1
        end loop }
    P(N)

where $P(x) = (\forall k)[k < 0 \lor k \geq x \lor b(k) = k]$

using $P(i)$ as the loop invariant. (A key step will be the derivation of the assertion $P(i) \{ b(i) := i \} P(i+1)$ and its verification.)

EUCLID PROOF RULES FOR FUNCTIONS AND PROCEDURES

An extensive discussion of the proof rule for procedures, and the reasons for the form chosen for Euclid has been published by Guttag *et al.* [1978]; the form of the proof rule for functions has been explained by Musser [1977]. Here we will sketch at a more abstract level some issues and their resolution.

Soundness

There are two senses in which it is important that each proof rule for a programming language be "sound." Firstly, it is important that it be *logically sound*, i.e., it must not introducing any contradictions into the proof theory for the language. Secondly, it must be *consistent with the intended implementation*, so that proofs that use it are indeed applicable to real programs (or at least, if they are not, the fault can be traced to the implementation). The proof rules published for Pascal [Hoare and Wirth 1973] contain examples of both kinds of unsoundness; considerable effort was expended to ensure that the Euclid proof rules would not share these problems.

A problem of the first sort in the Pascal proof rule for functions was first pointed out by Ashcroft [Ashcroft *et al.* 1976]. The problem is technical and obscure, but basically the Pascal rule allows $P \supset Q$ to be used as an axiom within the scope of a function declaration, where P and Q are predicates derived from the pre- and postconditions of the function. Of course, one of the proof obligations associated with the function declaration is the requirement to show that the precondition is sufficient to ensure the postcondition after termination of the function body. Unfortunately, for function bodies that do not terminate, it is possible to discharge this obligation for the precondition **true** and the postcondition **false**, allowing **true** $\supset$ **false** to be used as an axiom *even for programs that never call the function*, thereby making the proof theory inconsistent. The Euclid function-call rule includes the premise $H \supset \exists g (P \supset Q)$ specifically to ensure that the pre- and postconditions are consistent regardless of whether the function body always terminates.

A problem of the second sort arises in the implicit treatment of scope rules in the Pascal proof rules. The names of global variables used in a routine will generally appear as free variables in the pre- and postconditions of the routine. When these assertions are used in proofs about particular calls, each free variable in the assertions is "bound" to the

J. J. HORNING

variable *at the point of call* that has the same name. This is not a logically unsound rule—languages such as APL, LISP, and SNOBOL actually implement "dynamic binding" for global variables—but it is clearly not the scope rule intended by Wirth [1971] [cf. Wirth and Jensen 1974], nor is it the binding implemented by the standard Pascal compilers. This unfortunate discrepancy means that there are programs for which it is possible to prove some invalid assertions, and impossible to prove some valid assertions. This difficulty is avoided in Euclid by what may seem like a trick: The "dynamic binding" proof rule and the "static binding" implementation are both retained; the unsoundness is avoided by ensuring that all programs that would be sensitive to the difference are illegal. In particular, in Euclid it is illegal to redeclare a name in a scope within which it is known, and illegal to import a routine without also importing everything it imports; these restrictions are sufficient to prevent static and dynamic bindings from producing different results.

Relative completeness

Since even comparatively simple domains within programs, such as the integers, have undecidable proof theories, it is too much to demand that our proof rules make it possible to generate a proof for every program that is, in fact, correct. Cook, however, has introduced the notion of *relative completeness*, which, informally, means that the proof theory of the language is "no more undecidable" than that of its underlying data types. Clark [1977] has shown that there are some combinations of common programming language constructs for which even this weak form of completeness is impossible to obtain with Hoare-like axiom systems. Fortunately, however, Euclid omits some of the problem constructs (for quite other reasons) and the proof rules are believed to be relatively complete—although no proof of this claim has been attempted.

Tractability

Of course, it is not enough for our proof rules for functions and procedures to be sound and complete, they must also be usable. In particular, the generation of verification conditions for programs containing functions and procedures should be straightforward. At first glance, the Euclid rules [London *et al.* 1978, pp. 13, 15] appear quite intimidating, and even after long study they can scarcely be called lucid. But it is possible to trace their use step-by-step. Consider the prototypical procedure declaration

procedure p (var X, nonvar C) =

    imports (var Y, nonvar D)

    pre P

    post Q

    begin S end

What would we like to prove once about such a declaration, independent of particular calls? Essentially, just

$$x = x' \wedge y = y' \wedge P \{ S \} Q$$

where x' and y' are just convenient notations that allow Q to refer to initial values of variable parameters and imported variables. In this proof of the body of p, we can make free use of the consequences of declarations (denoted H), and we may also use the axiom for return

    Q { return asserting Q } false

Finally, if the procedure is recursive, we may also need to assume that any recursive calls on the procedure satisfy its specification.

> *Note.* If you have not previously encountered this aspect of proving recursive procedures, it may seem to be circular reasoning; it is well worth a few minutes thought to discover why it is not, even in the special case where S is just $p(X, C)$.

Having verified the procedure body, we have effectively added another axiom schema to our stock, which can be instantiated to handle particular procedure calls. Again, for each call we work from the postcondition to the precondition, but using the specifications of the procedure to characterize its effect. The basic form is

$$P \land (Q \supset R) \; \{ \; p \; \} \; R$$

but, of course, we must substitute actual for formal parameters and perform a few other "housekeeping" transformations, giving

$$P(a/x, \; e/c) \land (Q(a\#/x, \; e/c, \; y\#/y, \; a/x', \; y/y') \supset R(a\#/a, \; y\#/y)) \; \{ \; p(a, \; e) \; \} \; R$$

Although this rule, in its general form, is somewhat clumsy for manipulation by humans, it presents no difficulty for verification condition generation programs.

TWO PROBLEM CONSTRUCTS

Modules

Modules were introduced into Euclid for methodological reasons. We wanted to support "data abstractions" in general, and to ensure the validity of data type induction in particular. We believed that another unit of *information hiding* [Parnas 1971] was needed to supplement routines. The basic idea was that a module should encapsulate a data structure and a related set of routines for its manipulation, and should hide its internal details from the outside world. Unlike Modula [Wirth 1977], Euclid treats modules as full-fledged data types, and allows them to take formal parameters, have multiple instantiations, etc., but this added generality seemed like useful "power."

We also started from an implementation trick to make modules easy to implement. We viewed them as somewhat glorified records, with some extra components (routines, types, initialization, finalization) and control over the external visibility of their names (export lists). The idea was to compile them just like records, but to remove the non-exported names from the symbol table after processing the module body.

Unfortunately, we did not worry too much about the proof rule for modules until the language design was essentially complete. By then it was almost too late. We finally arrived at a rule that we hope is both sound and complete, but it is long and complex. The rule has eight separate premises, one of which extends over twelve printed lines, and "in the interest of simplicity, the formulas for recursion, return, and H are omitted in premises 3-5." Fortunately, the rule does simplify significantly for restricted forms of modules; much of its complexity is due to the large number of different kinds of components that may be included in a general module. Furthermore, the proof obligations for an equivalent program without modules would be very similar, but somewhat larger because of the difficulty of using data type induction to establish module invariants; the module rule just collects them together. Mechanical verification condition generators should have little difficulty dealing with each of the premises of this rule.

J. J. HORNING

It is difficult to be pleased with such a complex proof rule, but we should avoid confusing the symptom with the problem. Although it is fashionable to discuss "data abstractions" [SIGPLAN 1976] and to suggest that they offer advantages analogous to control abstractions, we don't yet know how to incorporate them into programming languages in a way that gives the programmer and the verifier as much conceptual leverage as subroutines do. Even in retrospect, we are not sure how to make significant improvements in Euclid modules and their proof rules. The proof rules for data abstractions in other languages with which we are familiar also seem unsatisfactorily complex.

Interestingly enough, our implementation trick turned out to require a number of non-obvious restrictions that were overlooked when the language was first designed. For example, we now disallow the use of variables imported into a module for anything except further importation into nested routines and modules. (Use of free variables in record types is also prohibited for the same reasons, but this seems like less of a restriction.) The need for some restrictions was discovered when developing the proof rules, for others, when planning the implementation; however, in the end it became clear that both verification and implementation considerations led to essentially the same set of restrictions.

Zones

In many of the applications for which Euclid is intended, it is unacceptable for the programming language to preempt the implementation of storage allocation. There will be some parts of some programs where precise control of the storage allocation is required. Nevertheless, the abstraction that storage is managed "automatically" is a very useful one, and most of the time it is important to be able to program—and to reason about programs—without concern for the precise details of storage management. Euclid provides a mechanism for separating these concerns. *Dynamic variables* are associated with *collections*, and in normal programming the only relevant characteristic of a collection is that c.New always returns a pointer to a variable that is guaranteed not to overlap with any other variable. However, each collection may be associated with a *zone*, which manages its storage.

Zones are special modules that provide procedures to allocate and deallocate regions of memory on demand. The correctness of a program that uses a zone does not depend on the zone's internal data structures and algorithms—only on its correctness. Similarly, the correctness of a zone's implementation does not depend on the use to which its storage is being put (or even on the type of the variables stored in it). Of course, efficiency concerns cannot be so easily decoupled.

Programmer-supplied storage management requires some breaches in Euclid's type system. The zone has a pool of "raw storage," from which it must allocate space for variables of a number of different types in unpredictable patterns. This does not imply that the zone must be programmed without the benefit of *any* type-checking, as in LIS [Ichbiah *et al.* 1973, 1974]; rather it requires that the same storage be treated as having different types at different levels in the program. This is reflected by the existence of high-level procedures New and Free, which deal with dynamic variables of the type specified by their collection, and low-level procedures Allocate and Deallocate, which deal with storageBlocks within the zone. The compiler converts calls on New and Free to calls on Allocate and Deallocate (converting the type information into size information on the way). Both levels are strictly type-checked; the "magic" happens in this behind the scenes conversion.

VERIFICATION OF EUCLID PROGRAMS

Despite the considerable amount of special machinery built into Euclid to make zones possible, we have no examples of verified zones. It proved surprisingly difficult to write a zone example that appeared to be correct while remaining within legal Euclid. Despite more care and re-writing than any other example, the zone in the Euclid Report [Lampson *et al.* 1977] still contains some illegalities. More importantly, no one has set down in convincing form a module specification for zones that captures the intent given informally above. Thus, the possibility of verifying useful zones remains to be demonstrated. However, we still believe that this aspect of the language represents an advance over the more straightforward technique of abandoning all hope of formal verification by simply dropping into assembly language for the storage allocator.

WHY AREN'T WE BUILDING A EUCLID VERIFICATION SYSTEM?

We are frequently asked "If Euclid was designed for verifiable system programming, why aren't you building a program verification system for Euclid?" There are basically two answers: 1) That wasn't our job, and 2) "Everyone" is.

The Euclid committee was assembled for a brief (two-month) language definition effort. It was never intended that this group form an ongoing Euclid Project; we all have other responsibilities. Production of a Euclid Verifier was no more part of our task than production of a Euclid Compiler, and only one of us (Ralph London) was qualified to undertake such an assignment had we been asked to.

The verification process for programs written in Euclid (or Pascal, or any other similar language) will involve three phases:

> generation of verification conditions,
>
> algebraic simplification of the resulting predicate calculus formulas, and
>
> theorem-proving for the verification conditions that do not simplify to **true**.

As we have previously noted, verification condition generation is the easiest and most straightforward of the three phases; it depends on the syntax and semantics of the particular programming language, but it appears that large parts of the compiler can be borrowed for this analysis. The second and third phases are the objects of considerable attention in many research projects, and are language-independent. Once the verification conditions have been generated, the programming language has disappeared entirely. Hence, any of these systems will work as well for Euclid as for whatever language is currently being used by its developers—even better, if Euclid corresponds more closely to its proof rules than does the other language.

REFERENCES

Ashcroft, E. A., M. Clint, and C. A. R. Hoare [1976]. "Remarks on 'Program proving: Jumps and functions' by M. Clint and C. A. R. Hoare." *Acta Informatica* 6, pp. 317–318.

Clarke, E. M. Jr. [1977]. "Programming language constructs for which it is impossible to obtain good Hoare-like axiom systems." Conference Record, Fourth ACM Symposium on Principles of Programming Languages, Los Angeles, pp. 10–20.

J. J. HORNING

Clint, M., and C. A. R. Hoare [1972]. "Program proving: Jumps and functions." *Acta Informatica* 1, pp. 214–224.

Guttag, John V., James J. Horning, and Ralph L. London [1978]. "A proof rule for Euclid Procedures." In *Formal Description of Programming Concepts*, ed. E. J. Neuhold, pp. 211–220, North-Holland, Amsterdam.

Hoare, C. A. R. and N. Wirth [1973]. "An axiomatic definition of the programming language Pascal." *Acta Informatica* 2, pp. 335–355.

Ichbiah, J. D., J. P. Rissen, and J. C. Heliard [1973]. "The two-level approach to data definition and space management in the LIS system implementation language." *SIGPLAN Notices* 8, no. 9, pp. 79–81.

——, ——, and —— [1974]. "The two-level approach to data independent programming in the LIS system implementation language." In *Machine Oriented Higher Level Languages*, ed. W. L. van der Poel and L. A. Maarssen, pp. 161–174, North-Holland, Amsterdam.

Lampson, B. W., J. J. Horning, R. L. London, J. G. Mitchell, and G. J. Popek [1977]. "Report on the programming language Euclid." *SIGPLAN Notices* 12, no. 2.

London, R. L., J. V. Guttag, J. J. Horning, B. W. Lampson, J. G. Mitchell, and G. J. Popek [1978]. "Proof rules for the programming language Euclid." *Acta Informatica* 10, pp. 1–26.

Musser, David R. [1977]. "A proof rule for functions." University of Southern California Information Sciences Institute Technical Report ISI/RR-77-62.

Parnas, D. L. [1971]. "Information distribution aspects of design methodology." In *Proc. IFIP Congress 71*. pp. 339–344, North-Holland, Amsterdam.

SIGPLAN [1976]. Special issue on data: abstraction, definition, and structure. *SIGPLAN Notices* 11.

Wirth, N. [1971]. "The programming language Pascal." *Acta Informatica* 1, pp. 35–63.

—— [1977]. "Modula: A language for modular multiprogramming." *Software—Practice and Experience* 7, pp. 3–35.

——, and K. Jensen [1974]. *Pascal—User Manual and Report*, Springer-Verlag, New York.

SPECIFICATIONS AND PROOFS FOR ABSTRACT DATA TYPES

IN CONCURRENT PROGRAMS

by

Susan S. Owicki

Digital Systems Laboratory

Departments of Electrical Engineering and Computer Science

Stanford University

Stanford, California 94305

ABSTRACT

Shared abstract data types, such as queues and buffers, are useful tools for building well-structured concurrent programs. This paper presents a method for specifying shared types in a way that simplifies concurrent program verification. The specifications describe the operations of the shared type in terms of their effect on variables of the process invoking the operation. This makes it possible to verify the processes independently, reducing the complexity of the proof. The key to defining such specifications is the concept of a private variable: a variable which is part of a shared object but belongs to just one process. Shared types can be implemented using an extended form of monitors; proof rules are given for verifying that a monitor correctly implements its specifications. Finally, it is shown how concurrent programs can be verified using the specifications of their shared types. The specification and proof techniques are illustrated with a number of examples involving a shared bounded buffer.

INDEX TERMS: Program verification, program proving, concurrency, parallel programs, abstract data types, shared types, and operating system design.

1. INTRODUCTION

An important development in structured programming is the use of data abstractions. An abstract data type defines a class of abstract objects and the set of operations on those objects. Considerable effort has been devoted to issues related to data abstraction: specification of the abstract type ([Guttag 75], [Guttag et al 76], [Liskov and Zilles 75], [Liskov and Berzins 76], [Parnas 72]), programming languages for expressing data abstractions (notable are CLU [Liskov 76] and Alphard [Wulf 76]), and proof methods for data abstractions ([Hoare 72], [Neumann 75], [Schorre, 75], [Shaw 76], [Spitzen 75], [Wulf 76]). In this paper these issues are considered as they arise in concurrent programs, where data abstractions are shared between parallel processes. The major focus will be on axiomatic proof techniques, in the style suggested by Hoare [69]. Verification of both the implementation of an abstract data type and the processes that use it will be considered.

The only feasible way to verify a complex system is to compose the system proof from independent proofs of its modules. Abstract data types facilitate this approach. One can first specify and verify the type and its implementation, then use the specifications, rather than the detailed implementation, in verifying higher-level modules. It is also possible to verify each process in a concurrent system independently, provided that the processes access shared data in a disciplined manner (as with monitors or critical regions). This is accomplished by proving each process using only variables that can not be modified by other processes. This separation of processes greatly simplifies the proof (for comparision see [Lamport 75] and [Owicki and Gries 76b], where process proofs are not so completely separated).

To make such proofs possible, each operation of a shared type must be described in terms of its effect on variables of the process invoking the operation. Section 2 shows how a new concept, private variables, can be used to obtain such specifications; private variables are components of a shared object, but belong to just one process. Section 3 discusses the implementation of shared data types by an extended form of monitors, in which private and auxiliary variables are included for

the sake of proofs. Section 4 presents the rules for proving that a
monitor satisfies its specifications, and sections 5 and 6 discuss the
verification of concurrent processes that use shared data types.

Throughout the paper the abstract type "bounded buffer" will be
used as an illustrative example. It consists of a buffer capable of
holding N elements, and two operations:

append(a): wait until the buffer is not full, then
            add a to the end of the buffer

remove(b): wait until the buffer is not empty, then
            remove its first value and return it in b

More precise specifications are given in the next section.

Although the discussion of the bounded buffer here is primarily
intended to illustrate the specification and proof techniques, it is
also of interest in its own right. Buffers have many uses in concurrent
systems, and other concepts, such as queues and message-passing operations,
can be described in very similar terms. Thus the specification of the
bounded buffer should be applicable to the verification of a number of
concurrent systems.

2. SPECIFICATIONS

The specifications of an abstract data type form the interface
between the program module which implements the type and the modules
which use it. Program verification consists of proving that the implementation satisfies its specifications, and then employing the specifications to verify the modules that use the type. This separation
simplifies verification; it also enhances modularity, since the method
of implementation may be changed without affecting the correctness of the
program, as long as the new implementation also satisfies the specifications.

The specifications for a shared data type are given in the form of
assertions that can be incorporated into the proofs of concurrent processes.
So that the proof of a process is independent of the actions of other
processes, it must contain only safe assertions, i.e. assertions whose

free variables can not be modified by other processes. Thus the assertions
that describe the effect of an abstract operation must also be safe. This
is made possible by including <u>private</u> variables in the abstract type. A
private variable t of type T is declared by <u>var</u> t: <u>private</u> T; this means
that there is one instance of t for each process that uses the shared
object. The instance of t belonging to process S can be changed only by
execution of an operation invoked by S. Thus that instance of t may be
used safely in the proof of S. We will use array notation for private
variables; <u>var</u> t: <u>private</u> T is interpreted as <u>var</u> t: <u>array</u> process id <u>of</u> T,
and t[S] denotes the instance of t for process S. In describing the
effects of an operation, t[#] denotes the instance of t belonging to
the process that invokes the operation.

The table below gives the format for specifications of a shared data
type. Each clause gives the name of an assertion, with the free variables
it may contain indicated in parentheses.

Specifications

typename($\bar{p}$): declaration of component variables
    <u>requires</u>: Requires($\bar{p}$)
    <u>initially</u>: Init(a)
    <u>invariant</u>: I(a)
    <u>operations</u>:
        operation_name (var $\bar{x}$; $\bar{y}$)
            <u>entry</u>: entry($\bar{x}$, $\bar{y}$, $\bar{z}$[#])
            <u>exit</u>: exit($\bar{x}$, $\bar{y}$, $\bar{z}$[#])

where a = parameters and component variables of the type
    $\bar{p}$ = parameters of the type ($\bar{p} \subseteq a$)
    $\bar{z}$ = private variables ($\bar{z} \subseteq a$)
        $\bar{z}$[#] = private variables of calling process
    $\bar{x}$ = var parameters
    $\bar{y}$ = value parameters

Let us consider each clause in turn. First, the name and parameters
of the abstract type are given, followed by its components. Requires is
a condition which must be satisfied when an instance of the type is
created; for example, for the bounded buffer Requires assures that the
buffer size is positive. Init(a) gives the initial value of a newly

created instance of the type. I(a), the invariant, is a consistency assertion about the possible values that can be assumed by a . It is true for the initial value, and is preserved by each operation, although it may fail to hold temporarily during execution of an operation.

Each operation is defined by giving its name and the names and types of its formal parameters. Following Pascal, the formal parameter list contains <u>var</u> parameters, which may be modified by the operation, and value parameters, whose values are not changed. Two assertions describe the effect of the operation. The entry assertion gives the conditions required for correct performance; it is the programmer's responsibility to insure that the entry condition is satisfied each time the operation is invoked. The exit clause describes variable values upon completion. Note that entry and exit describe the operation in terms of private variables and parameters; they are safe assertions and may be used in the proof of a process which invokes the operation.

Specifications for the abstract type bounded buffer are given below; they are adapted from specifications proposed by Good and Ambler [1975] for concurrent programs synchronized with message buffers. The buffer stores values of type message, not defined here. The notation $<x_1, x_2, ..., x_n>$ denotes the sequence whose elements are $x_1, x_2, ...,$ x_n. The empty sequence is written <>. X @ Y is the concatenation of the sequences X and Y. If X is nonempty, its first element is first(X) and X=<first(X)> @ tail(X); similarly, last(X) is the last element in X, and X=head(X) @ <last(X)>. The number of elements in X is length(X). If t is a private variable, ⟨t⟩ denotes the bag containing the values of all instances of t.

Specifications for the Bounded Buffer

bb(N:integer)

 <u>record</u> buf: <u>sequence of</u> message
     <u>comment</u> length (buf) $\leq$ N
   instream: <u>sequence of</u> message
     <u>comment</u> sequence of values appended to bb
   outstream: <u>sequence of</u> message
     <u>comment</u> sequence of values removed from bb

```
in:  private sequence of message
     comment values appended by each process
out: private sequence of message
     comment values removed by each process
```

requires: N > 0

initially: buf = instream = outstream = in = out = <>

invariant: length(buf) ≤ N ∧

instream = outstream @ buf ∧

ismerge(instream, ⌊in⌋) ∧

ismerge(outstream, ⌊out⌋)

operations:

```
append(a:message)
    entry:  in[#] = i' ∧ out[#] = o'
    exit:   in[#] = i' @ <a> ∧ out[#] = o'
remove(var b:message)
    entry:  in[#] = i' ∧ out[#] = o'
    exit:   in[#] = i' ∧ ∃c(b=c ∧ out[#] = o' @ <c>)
```

The bounded buffer has a single parameter N, the buffer size; because of the requires clause, N must be positive. The data for a bounded buffer is a record consisting of sequences buf (the actual buffer), instream, outstream, in, and out. Variables instream and outstream record the global history of buffer operations by storing the sequence of values appended to and removed from the buffer. The private variable in[S] contains the sequence of values appended by process S, while out[S] contains the values removed by S. We will see in section 3 that some of these variables are needed only for proofs, and do not have to be included in an implementation. Initially, all sequences are empty. The invariant states that only N items can be in the buffer (length(buf) ≤ N), that values appended to the buffer either have been removed or are still in the buffer (instream = outstream @ buf), that the global input history is some merge of the private input histories (ismerge(instream, ⌊in⌋)), and that the global output history is a merge of the private output histories (ismerge(outstream, ⌊out⌋)). The predicate ismerge(X,Y), where X is a sequence and $Y = ⌊y_1, y_2, \ldots, y_n⌋$ is a bag of sequences, is defined by ismerge($<>$,Y) = true if y_i = $<>$, $1 \leq i \leq n$

ismerge(X' @ $<x>$, Y) = true if

$\qquad y_k = y_k'$ @ $<x>$ for some $1 \leq k \leq n$

$\qquad$ and ismerge(X', $\langle y_1, \ldots, y_k', \ldots, y_n \rangle$)

ismerge(X,Y) = false otherwise

The behavior of append and remove is defined by their entry and exit assertions. For append, the value a is added to the private input history of the invoking process, while the private output history remains unchanged.

Although append(a) must also change the value of buf and instream, this fact is not explicitly included in the exit clause (it is implied by the exit clause and the invariant, however). This is because the exit assertion will be used in verifying the processes that invoke append, and in that context only the effect on private and local variables is relevant. For remove, the exit condition states that some (unknown) value is returned in b and appended to the process's private output history. One can deduce from the invariant that the value returned must be the first one in buf, but buf, as a shared variable, can not appear in the exit condition. This is an accurate reflection of the fact that, from the viewpoint of a process invoking remove, it is not generally possible to predict what value will be returned.

It is interesting to compare the bounded buffer specification given here to specifications suggested by Hoare [74]. Expressed in our notation, Hoare's specification is

bb2(N): <u>record</u> buf <u>sequence</u> <u>of</u> message

$\quad$ <u>requires</u>: N > 0

$\quad$ <u>initially</u>: buf = $<>$

$\quad$ <u>invariant</u>: length(buf) $\leq$ N

$\quad$ <u>operations</u>:

$\qquad$ append(a:message)

$\qquad\qquad$ <u>entry</u>: buf = buf'

$\qquad\qquad$ <u>exit</u>: buf = buf' @ $<a>$

$\qquad$ remove(<u>var</u> b:message)

$\qquad\qquad$ <u>entry</u>: buf = buf'

$\qquad\qquad$ <u>exit</u>: b = first(buf') $\wedge$ buf = tail(buf')

Hoare's specification is shorter than ours, and it completely describes the effects of the bounded buffer operations. However, it is harder to use in proofs of concurrent programs because it does not provide any private variables. For example, although the effect of bb2.append is buf = buf' @ <x>, one cannot use

{true} bb2.append(x) {x = last(buf)}

in the proof of a process that invokes append. This is because other processes can also append and remove elements from the buffer; in fact, x may not even be in the buffer by the time append(x) returns control to the invoking process.

A valid use of append is

{true} bb2.append(x) {x ∈ buf or x has been removed by another process}.

Our specifications give a convenient way of expressing this:

{true} bb.append(x) {x = last (in[#])}

and

(x ∈ in[#] ∧ bb.I) ⊃ (x ∈ buf ∨ ∃S(x ∈ out[S])).

Howard [76] gives an informal specification of the bounded buffer. He uses variables like instream and outstream, and his specifications include the invariant instream = outstream @ buf. But he has nothing corresponding to the private variables in and out.

3. IMPLEMENTATION

An attractive means of implementing abstract data types in a parallel programming environment is the <u>monitor</u>, as proposed by Hoare [74] and Brinch Hansen [75]. A monitor is a collection of data and procedures shared by several processes in a concurrent program. The monitor data can be accessed only by invoking monitor procedures; thus the monitor presents in a single place a shared data object and all the code that has access to that object. Monitors also facilitate concurrent programming by ensuring that only one process at a time can operate on the shared data and by providing operations for process synchronization.

The general form of a monitor type definition is given below.

```
class classname:  monitor(parameters)
     begin  declaration of monitor data;
            declaration of monitor procedures;
            initialization of monitor data
     end
```

An instance of a monitor is created by the declaration monitor mname: classname(parameters). The notation for a call to a monitor procedure is mname.procedurename (var result parameters; value parameters). To simplify program verification the result parameters must be distinct -- see Hoare [71] for a discussion of parameters and program proofs. The value parameters are not modified by the procedure.

A monitor which implements the bounded buffer type is defined below. Some features of monitors which are important for this example (mutual exclusion, conditions, auxiliary variables, and private variables) will be discussed further. A more complete description of monitors is given in Hoare [74]. Auxiliary and private variables were not in the original definition of monitors; they have been added here because of their usefulness in verification.

```
class bb: monitor (N)
    begin
      BBvar: record m_buffer:  array 0..N-1 of message;
                    last: 0..N-1;
                    count: 0..N;
                    m_instream, m_outstream:
                        auxiliary sequence of message;
                    m_in, m_out:
                        private auxiliary sequence of message end
    nonempty, nonfull: condition;

    procedure append(a:message);
       begin if count = N then nonfull.wait;
       last := last ⊕ 1; m_buffer[last] := a; count := count + 1;
       m_instream := m_instream @ <a>; m_in := m_in @ <a>;
       nonempty.signal
    end append;
```

```
    procedure remove(var b:message);
        begin if count = 0 then nonempty.wait;
            count := count-1; b := m_buffer[last⊖count];
            m_outstream := m_outstream @ <b>; m_out := m_out @ <b>;
            nonfull.signal
        end remove;
    begin count := 0; last := 0; m_instream := <>; m_outstream := <>;
        m_in := <>; m_out := <> end;
    end bounded buffer
    ⊕ and ⊖ are computed modulo N
An instance of the monitor is BB:bb
```

In order to allow a number of processes to share the monitor data
in a reliable fashion, execution of monitor procedures is mutually
exclusive; i.e. only one procedure call at a time is executed. If
a number of calls occur, all but the first are delayed until the monitor
is finished with the first call. This prevents some of the obscure
time-dependent coding errors that can occur with shared data.

Synchronization among concurrent processes is accomplished through
condition variables in monitors. A condition is a queue for processes.
There are two operations on conditions: condition_name.wait and condition_
name.signal. A process which executes condition_name.wait is suspended
and placed at the end of the condition queue. When a process executes
condition_name.signal the first process waiting on the condition queue
is reactivated. In order to insure that only one process at a time may
execute a monitor procedure, the procedure executing the signal must be
suspended while the reactivated procedure uses the monitor.

The bounded buffer monitor uses two conditions, nonempty and nonfull.
If the append operation finds that there is no room in the buffer, it
waits on condition nonfull. After a remove operation there must be room
in the buffer, so remove ends with nonfull.signal. Condition nonempty
is used in a similar way by processes trying to remove an element from
the buffer.

The bounded buffer monitor illustrates two added features of monitors:
private and auxiliary variables. Auxiliary variables are included as aids

for verification; they are not necessary for the correct implementation
of the monitor and may be ignored by a compiler. The importance of
such auxiliary variables for proofs of parallel programs is discussed
in Owicki [76].

In order to insure that the auxiliary variables are truly unnecessary
for a correct implementation, they may appear only in assignment statements x := e, where x is an auxiliary variable and e does not contain
any programmer-defined functions (which might have side effects). This
guarantees that the presence of auxiliary variables does not affect
the flow of program control or the values of non-auxiliary variables.
Thus their presence or absence is invisible to a program which uses the
monitor.

The auxiliary variables m_instream and m_outstream are history
variables in the sense of Howard [76]. In fact, m_instream and m_outstream
play the same role as the history variables A and R in Howard's verification of a bounded buffer monitor.

Private variables in a monitor are used to implement abstract private
variables, and they have essentially the same meaning. The declaration
t: private T creates one instance of the variable t for each process
that uses the monitor; t[S] is the instance belonging to process S. A
reference to t in a monitor procedure is treated as a reference to t[S],
where S is the process which invoked the procedure. Thus it is syntactically impossible for a procedure to modify any private variables except
those belonging to the process that invoked it. In this paper all private
variables are auxiliary variables. Non-auxiliary private variables
might be a useful extension of monitors, but their implementation is
not discussed here.

In the bounded buffer monitor, m_in and m_out are private variables
which implement the abstract private variables in and out. Private
abstract variables must be implemented by private monitor variables,
so that it is impossible for one process to modify the private abstract
variables of another.

4. VERIFYING THE IMPLEMENTATION

The methodology for proving that a monitor correctly implements
its specifications is derived from Hoare's method for abstract data
objects in sequential programs [Hoare 72]; it is also closely related to
generator induction [Spitzen 75]. The main difference is that the proof
must take into account the sharing of the monitor among concurrent
processes. One first defines the relation between the abstract object
a and the monitor variables m by giving a representation function rep
such that $a = \text{rep}(m)$. A monitor invariant must also be defined; it is
called monitorname.I_M or simply I_M, and it gives a consistency condition
on the monitor variables m just as I does for the abstract variables a.
The verification of the monitor consists of proving the following
conditions:

1. $I_M(m) \supset I(\text{rep}(m))$

2. {Requires} monitor initialization $\{I_M(m) \wedge \text{Init}(\text{rep}(M))\}$

3. For each monitor procedure p($\underline{\text{var}}\ \bar{x}; \bar{y}$)
    $$\{p.\text{entry}(\bar{x},\bar{y},\text{rep}(m)) \wedge I_M(m)\}$$
    body of procedure p
    $$\{p.\text{exit}(\bar{x},\bar{y},\text{rep}(m)) \wedge I_M(m)\}$$

The proofs can be accomplished with the usual proof rules for
sequential statements and the following axioms for wait and signal.
With each condition variable b_i associate an assertion B_i describing
the circumstances under which a process waiting on b_i should be resumed.
Then the axioms for wait and signal are

$$\{I_M \wedge P\}\ b_i.\text{wait}\ \{I_M \wedge P \wedge B_i\}$$

$$\{I_M \wedge P \wedge B_i\}\ b_i.\text{signal}\ \{I_M \wedge P\}$$

where the free variables of P are private, local to the procedure,
parameters, or constants. This is an extension of Hoare's original rules
[Hoare74]. The assertion P was added to allow a proof to use the fact
that the values of private and local variables can not change during
wait or signal.

In the bounded buffer example, the relationship between the abstract buffer bb and the monitor data BBvar is given by

    bb = (buf,instream,outstream,in,out)
       = rep(BBvar)
       = (seq(m_buffer,last,count),m_instream,
           m_outstream,m_in,m_out)

where seq(b,ℓ,c) = <> if c=0
                     = seq(b,$\ell\ominus$1,c-1) @ <b[ℓ]> if c>0

In this case, the function rep is almost an identity function, because the abstract variables instream, outstream, in, and out are directly implemented by the corresponding monitor variables. The abstract sequence buf is implemented by the array m_buffer and variables last and count; function seq gives the value of the abstract buffer determined by the monitor variables.

The monitor invariant for the bounded buffer monitor BB is

BB.I_M: $0 \le$ count $\le N \wedge 0 \le$ last $\le N-1 \wedge$
         m_instream = m_outstream @ seq(m_buffer, last, count)
         $\wedge$ ismerge(m_instream, $<$m_in$>$)
         $\wedge$ ismerge(m_outstream, $<$m_out$>$)

The conditions to be verified are

1. BB.$I_M \supset$ bb.I(rep(BBvar)) - obvious from the definition of rep

2. {bb.Requires} initialization {BB.$I_M \wedge$ Init(rep(m))}

This expands to

{N > 0}
count := 0; last := 0;
m_instream := m_outstream := m_in := m_out := <>;
{$I_M \wedge$ seq(m_buffer, last, count) = <> $\wedge$
     m_instream = m_outstream = m_in = m_out = <>}

The proof is trivial.

3. $\{m\_in[\#] = i' \land m\_out[\#] = o' \land I_M\}$
   code for append(a)
   $\{m\_in[\#] = i' @ <a> \land m\_out[\#] = o' \land I_M\}$

   and

   $\{m\_in[\#] = i' \land m\_out[\#] = o' \land I_M\}$
   code for remove(b)
   $\{m\_in[\#] = i' \land \exists c(b = c \land m\_out[\#] = o' @ <c>) \land I_M\}$

A proof outline for remove(b) is given below; append(a) is similar.

        Proof outline for BB.remove

Wait assertion for nonfull: count < N

         for nonempty: count > 0

$\{I_M \land m\_in[\#] = i' \land m\_out[\#] = o'\}$

begin

  if count = 0 **then**

    $\{I_M \land m\_in[\#] = i' \land m\_out[\#] = o'\}$

    nonempty.wait;

    $\{I_M \land count \geqslant 0 \land m\_in[\#] = i' \land m\_out[\#] = o'\}$

  $\{I_M \land count > 0 \land m\_in[\#] = i' \land m\_out[\#] = o'\}$

  count := count - 1; b := m_buffer[last $\ominus$ count];

  m_outstream := m_outstream @ <b>; m_out := m_out @ <b>;

  $\{I_M \land 0 \leq count < N \land m\_in[\#] = i' \land$

       $\exists c(b = c \land m\_out[\#] = o' @ <c>)\}$

  nonfull.signal

  $\{I_M \land m\_in[\#] = i' \land \exists c(b = c \land m\_out[\#] = o' @ <c>\}$

end

$\{remove.exit \land I_M\}$

In addition to proving that a monitor satisfies its specifications, one may wish to show that it has other properties (probably related to performance). Howard [76] is an excellent source of techniques for verifying such properties.

5. PROGRAM PROOFS

In this section we show how to verify concurrent programs given the specifications of shared data types. Concurrent execution is initiated by a statement of the form

$$\underline{\text{monitor}} \ M_1:A_1,\ldots,M_m:A_m \ \underline{\text{cobegin}} \ L_1:S_1 \ //\ldots// L_n:S_n \ \underline{\text{coend}}.$$

The S_i are statements to be executed concurrently, i.e. parallel processes, and L_i is the name of process S_i. The only variables that may appear in S_i are those declared in S_i (its local variables) or constants declared in a block containing the $\underline{\text{cobegin}}$ statement. S_i also has indirect access, through procedure calls, to monitor variables. Thus all variables are protected from the danger of overlapping operations in different processes: they are constants (no modifications), local variables (accessible to only one process), or monitor variables (protected by the monitor mutual exclusion).

The specifications of type A_i are linked to monitor M_i by the convention that M_i.assertionname refers to the named assertion in the specifications of A_i, with the monitor name M_i prefixing each shared variable. Thus, given monitor BB:bb, BB.Init is the assertion BB.buf = BB.instream = BB.outstream = BB.in = BB.out = <>. Then the rule of inference for verifying $\underline{\text{cobegin}}$ statements is

$$\{P_i\} \ S_i \ \{Q_i\}, \ (P_i,Q_i \text{ safe for } S_i, \ 1 \le i \le n)$$

$$\overline{\{(\underset{i}{\wedge} M_j.\text{Init}) \supset (\underset{i}{\wedge} P_i)\} \ \underline{\text{monitor}}..M_j:A_j..\underline{\text{cobegin}}..L_i:S_i..\underline{\text{coend}} \ \{(\underset{j}{\wedge} M_j.\text{I}) \wedge (\underset{i}{\wedge} Q_i)\}}$$

(The notation $\dfrac{P_1,\ldots,P_n}{Q}$ means that Q may be inferred if all P_i have been proved.) Recall that safe assertions can have no free variables which can be changed by other processes, so P_i and Q_i may only refer to constants and local and private variables of S_i. The effect of the cobegin statement on private and local variables is obtained from independent proofs of the individual processes. For shared objects, the initial assertion can be assumed to hold at the beginning of concurrent execution, and the invariant holds at the end.

Monitor procedure calls in S_i are verified using the entry and exit assertions and the usual rules for procedure calls, as described in Hoare [1972]. The basic rule for a procedure call in process S_i is

$$\{M.p.entry \; {\bar{x} \; \bar{y} \; \# \atop \bar{a} \; \bar{e} \; L_i}\} M.p(\bar{a};\bar{e}) \; \{M.p.exit \; {\bar{x} \; \bar{y} \; \# \atop \bar{a} \; \bar{e} \; L_i}\}$$

where the actual var parameters $\bar{a}$ must be distinct from each other and from the actual value parameters $\bar{e}$. $M.p.entry \; {\bar{x} \; \bar{y} \; \# \atop \bar{a} \; \bar{e} \; L_i}$ represents the result of substituting actual parameters $\bar{a}$, $\bar{e}$ for formal parameters $\bar{x}$, $\bar{y}$ and the name of the calling process L_i for the symbol $\#$ in $M.p.entry$.

Hoare's rule of adaptation is also useful: it allows the entry and exit assertions to be adapted to the environment of the procedure call.

$$\frac{\{P\} \; M.p(\bar{a},\bar{e}) \; \{Q\}}{\{\exists \bar{k}(P \wedge \forall \bar{a}, \bar{z}[L_i](Q \supset R))\} \; M.p(\bar{a},\bar{e}) \; \{R\}}$$

where $\bar{k}$ is a list of variables free in P and Q but not R, $\bar{a}$ or $\bar{e}$, and $\bar{z}[L_i]$ is a list of private variables of M belonging to L_i.

For example, given

$$\{BB.in[L_i] = i' \wedge BB.out[L_i] = o'\} \; BB.append(x) \; \{BB.in[L_i] = i' @ <x> \wedge \\ BB.out[L_i] = o'\}$$

the rule of adaptation allows the inference of

$$\{true\} \; BB.append(x) \; \{x = last(BB.in \; [L_i])\}$$

or

$$\{in[L_i] @ <x> = i_0 \wedge out[L_i] = <>\} \; BB.append(x) \; \{in[L_i] = i_0 \wedge \\ out[L_i] = <>\}.$$

As an example of verifying a concurrent program, consider the system of processes illustrated below.

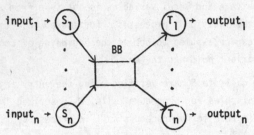

Process S_i reads an input stream, $input_i$, of m elements and feeds them into a bounded buffer BB. T_i removes m elements from the buffer (not necessarily the m elements appended by S_i) and prints them on $output_i$. One can prove

$$\{in[S_i] = out[S_i] = <>\}\ S_i\ \{in[S_i] = input_i \wedge out[S_i] = <>\}$$

as outlined below. Let leading(j,X), where $X = <x_1, x_2, ..., x_k>$ with $k \geq j$, be the initial segment $<x_1, x_2, ..., x_j>$ of X.

Then

$\quad$ $\{BB.in[S_i] = <> \wedge BB.out[S_i] = <>\}$

$\quad$ S_i : **begin**

$\quad\quad$ j,x:integer;

$\quad\quad$ **for** j := 1 **until** m **do**

$\quad\quad\quad$ $\{BB.in[S_i] = leading(j-1,input_i)\ \wedge\ BB.out[S_i] = <>\}$

$\quad\quad\quad$ read x from $input_i$;

$\quad\quad\quad$ $\{BB.in[S_i]\ @\ <x> = leading\ (j,input_i) \wedge BB.out[S_i] = <>\}$

$\quad\quad\quad$ BB.append(x);

$\quad\quad\quad$ $\{BB.in[S_i] = leading(j,input_i) \wedge BB.out[S_i] = <>\}$

$\quad\quad\quad$ **od**

$\quad\quad$ $\{BB.in[S_i] = leading(m,input_i) \wedge BB.out[S_i] = <>\}$

$\quad\quad$ **end**

$\quad$ $\{BB.in[S_i] = input_i \wedge BB.out[S_i] = <>\}$

Note that the assertions for BB.append are similar to the examples given earlier.

A similar proof shows

$\quad$ $\{BB.in[T_i] = BB.out\ [T_i] = <>\}\ T_i\ \{BB.in[T_i] = <> \wedge BB.out[T_i] =$

$output_i \wedge length(output_i) = m$}.

Now suppose these processes are initiated by the statement
L:<u>monitor</u> BB:bb <u>cobegin</u> $S_1//.../S_n//T_1//.../T_n$ <u>coend</u>.

The proof rule for <u>cobegin</u> gives

{BB.Init $\supset \bigwedge_i$ (BB.in$[S_i]$ = BB.out$[S_i]$ = BB.in$[T_i]$ = BB.out$[T_i]$ = <>
$\wedge output_i$ = <> $\wedge length(input_i)=m$)}

<u>monitor</u> BB:bb <u>cobegin</u> $S_1//.../T_n$ <u>coend</u>

{BB.I $\wedge$ ($\bigwedge_i$ BB.in$[S_i]$ = $input_i \wedge$ BB.out$[T_i]$ = $output_i \wedge$ BB.in$[T_i]$ = <>
$\wedge$ BB.out$[S_i]$ = <> $\wedge length(input_i)$ = $length(output_i)$ = m)}

The pre-condition can be simplified to

$$\bigwedge_i (output_i = <> \wedge length(input_i) = m)$$

The post-condition can be rewritten, expanding BB.I, to

ismerge(instream,$\langle input_i \rangle$) $\wedge$ ismerge(outstream, $\langle output_i \rangle$)
$\wedge$ length(instream) = n*m = length(outstream)
$\wedge$ instream = outstream @ buffer.

This implies that instream = outstream, yielding

ismerge(instream,$\langle input_i \rangle$) $\wedge$ ismerge(instream, $\langle output_i \rangle$)

The final theorem is

{($output_i$ = <> $\wedge length(input_i)$ = m, $1 \le i \le n$)}
<u>monitor</u> BB:bb <u>cobegin</u> $S_1//.../T_n$ <u>coend</u>
{values printed on $\langle output_i \rangle$ = values read from $\langle input_i \rangle$}

A slight variation on this system has processes S and T, which use the bounded buffer in the same way as S_i and T_i above, plus processes $R_1...R_n$ whose actions are irrelevant except that they do not use the buffer. For these processes

{BB.in$[S]$ = BB.out$[S]$ = <> $\wedge$ length(input) = m}
S
{BB.in$[S]$ = input $\wedge$ BB.out$[S]$ = <> $\wedge$ length(input) = m}

and

{BB.in$[T]$ = BB.out$[T]$ = <> $\wedge$ output = <>}
T
{BB.in$[T]$ = <> $\wedge$ BB.out$[T]$ = output $\wedge$ length(output) = m}

and

{BB.in$[R_i]$ = BB.out$[R_i]$ = <>} R_i {BB.in$[R_i]$ = BB.out$[R_i]$ = <>}

Using the rule for <u>cobegin</u> statements

$\{length(input) = m \land output = <>\}$
monitor BB:bb <u>cobegin</u> $S//T//R_1//...//R_n$ <u>coend</u>
$\{BB.I \land BB.in[S] = input \land BB.out[T] = output \land$
$length(input) = length(output) = m \land BB.out[S] = BB.in[T] = <>$
$\land(\underset{i}{\land}(BB.in[R_i] = BB.out[R_i] = <>))\}$

After expanding BB.I, this simplifies to

$\{length(input) = m \land output = <>\}$
<u>monitor</u> BB:bb <u>cobegin</u> $S//T//R_1//...//R_n$ <u>coend</u>
$\{input = output\}$

6. SPECIFICATIONS FOR SPECIAL SYSTEMS

   Often a set of processes use a shared data object in a special way, and a stricter set of specifications is appropriate. For example, if PBB.append(a) is only called with positive values of a, then PBB.remove(b) must return a positive value in b; a stronger entry condition for append implies a stronger invariant and a stronger exit condition for remove. It is always possible to deal with such systems by defining a new set of specifications for the shared object and re-verifying the implementation as described in section 4. In many cases, however, it is possible to derive the stronger specifications from the general ones, without examining the monitor implementation.

   Suppose, then, we have already verified that monitor M satisfies a set of specifications, M.Init, M.I, and, for each procedure p, M.p.entry and M.p.exit. Then M must also satisfy the stricter specifications, M.I', M.p.entry', and M.p.exit', provided the following conditions hold:

   1. $M.Init \supset M.I'$
   2. for each procedure p
      a. $\{M.p.entry \land I\}$ $p(\bar{x};\bar{y})$ $\{M.p.exit \land I\}$
         $\vdash \{M.p.pre' \land I'\}$ $p(\bar{x};\bar{y})$ $\{M.p.post' \land I'\}$

         where $P \vdash Q$ means Q can be proved using P as an assumption

      b. p has no wait or signal operations between the first and last modification of variables in M.I'

Condition 1 ensures that the stronger invariant M.I' holds initially. Condition 2a states that each procedure satisfies the stronger entry-exit conditions and preserves M.I'; the fact that it satisfies the original entry and exit and preserves M.I may be used as a hypothesis. The invariant M.I' must also hold at each wait and signal in M; condition 2b ensures that variables in M.I' have either their entry or exit values at a wait or signal, and in either case M.I' holds by rules 1 and 2a. Most monitor procedures seem to follow the pattern described in 2b.

Consider, as an example, the specifications for a positive-value bounded buffer PBB discussed earlier.

$$PBB.I' = PBB.I \land \forall x(x \in instream \supset x > 0)$$
$$PBB.append.entry' = PBB.append.entry \land a > 0$$
$$PBB.append.exit' = PBB.append.exit$$

$$PBB.remove.entry' = PBB.remove.entry$$
$$PBB.remove.exit' = PBB.remove.exit \land b > 0$$

Since the monitor PBB satisfies the restrictions in 2b, the new specifications can be verified by checking conditions 1 and 2a, which clearly hold.

As another example, consider a system in which a producer process adds an increasing sequence of values to a buffer ABB, and no other process executes append. In this system the sequence of values removed by any process must also be increasing. The specifications for ABB are

$$ABB.I' = ABB.I \land \forall \ell(\ell \neq producer \supset in[\ell] = <>)$$
$$\land\ increasing(in[producer])$$

$$ABB.append.entry' = ABB.append.entry \land \# = producer \land (length(in[\#]) = 0 \lor$$
$$a > last(in[\#]))$$
$$ABB.append.exit' = ABB.append.exit$$
$$ABB.remove.entry' = ABB.remove.entry$$
$$ABB.remove.exit' = ABB.remove.exit \land increasing(out[\#])$$

The entry assertion of ABB.append requires that the calling process is the producer (# = producer), and that the value to be appended is greater than the last value appended. This is enough to imply the strengthened invariant. Note that ABB.I' $\supset$ increasing(in[producer]) $\land$

$$instream = in[producer] = outstream @ buffer \land$$
$$ismerge(outstream, \{out\}),$$

which yields ∀ℓ(increasing(out[ℓ])). Thus the stronger exit condition
for ABB.remove can be derived from ABB.I'.

7. CONCLUSIONS

There are two principles underlying the specification and proof methods
presented in this paper. The first is that shared data abstractions provide
a useful tool for building concurrent programs, and that their usefulness is
much increased if they can be precisely specified. The second is that the
proof of any program module should depend on assertions that cannot be affected by the concurrent actions of other modules. An easy way to insure
that assertions have this property is to limit their use of variables.
This not only reduces the complexity of formal verification, but also proves
a helpful discipline for informal proofs. The techniques discussed here are
suitable for automated verification and for human use. People cannot be
expected to produce detailed formal proofs, so it is important that the methods
can be used informally and still be (relatively) reliable. The use of
safe assertions eliminates most of the complex interactions and the time-
dependent error caused by concurrency. Note the importance of private
variables in this methodology, both in specification and monitors. Without
private variables in the specifications it would be impossible for safe
assertions to describe an abstract operation adequately. Private variables
in monitors make it easy to verify that a monitor satisfies its specifications.

Any verification technique is worthwhile only if it is general and
powerful enough to handle a wide range of problems. The examples in this
paper have shown that the proposed methods are adequate for verifying programs
which use a bounded buffer in several different ways. The techniques have
also been used to prove programs which communicate via message-passing monitors.
With slight extensions to handle dynamic resource allocation, it was possible
to verify several complex (though small) systems, including Hoare's structured paging system [Hoare 73]. More experience is necessary, especially
with larger systems, but it appears that these methods will be sufficient
for many concurrent programs.

REFERENCES

[Brinch Hansen 73] P. Brinch Hansen. Operating Systems Principles. Prentice Hall, Englewood Cliffs, New Jersey, (1973).

[Brinch Hansen 75] P. Brinch Hansen. The programming language concurrent Pascal. IEEE Trans. on Software Eng., SE-1 No. 2, (June, 1975), pp. 199-207.

[Good and Ambler 75] D.I. Good and A.L. Ambler. Proving systems of concurrent processes synchronized with message buffers. Draft, (1975).

[Guttag 75] J.V. Guttag. The specification and application to programming of abstract data types. Ph.D. thesis, Computer Science, University of Toronto, (Sept. 1975).

[Guttag et al 76] J.V. Guttag, E. Horowitz, D.R. Musser. Abstract data types and software validation. Univ. of Southern California Information Sciences Institute report 76-48, (August, 1976).

[Hoare 69] C.A.R. Hoare. An axiomatic basis for computer programming. Comm. ACM 12, 10 (Oct. 1969), pp. 576-583.

[Hoare 71] C.A.R. Hoare. Procedures and parameters--an axiomatic approach. Symp. on the Semantics of Algorithmic Languages, Springer, Berlin-Heidelberg-New York, (1971), pp. 102-116.

[Hoare 72] C.A.R. Hoare. Proof of correctness of data representations. Acta Informatica I (1972), pp. 271-281.

[Hoare 73] C.A.R. Hoare. A structured paging system. Computer J. 16, 3 (1973), pp. 209-215.

[Hoare 74] C.A.R. Hoare. Monitors: an operating system structuring concept. Comm. ACM 17, 10 (Oct. 1974), pp. 549-556.

[Howard 76] J.H. Howard. Proving monitors. Comm. ACM 19, 5 (May 1976),
    pp. 273-279.

[Lamport 75] L. Lamport. Formal correctness proofs for multiprocess
    algorithms. Proc. Second Int. Symp. on Programming, April 1976.

[Liskov and Zilles 75] B.H. Liskov and S. Zilles. Specification
    techniques for data abstractions. IEEE Trans. on Software Eng.
    SE-1, 1 (March 1975), pp. 7-19.

[Liskov and Berzins 76] B.H. Liskov and V. Berzins. An appraisal of
    program specifications. Computation Structures Group Memo 141,
    M.I.T. (July 1976).

[Manna 74] Z. Manna and A. Pnueli. Axiomatic approach to total
    correctness of programs. Acta Informatica 3 (1974) pp. 243-263.

[Neumann 75] P.G. Neumann, L. Robinson, K.N. Levitt, R.S. Boyer, A.R.
    Saxena. A provably secure operating system. Stanford Research
    Institute, Menlo Park, California (June 1975).

[Owicki 76] S.S. Owicki. A consistent and complete deductive system
    for the verification of parallel programs. Proc. 8th ACM Symp. on
    Theory of Computing, (May 1976), pp. 73-86.

[Owicki and Gries 76a] S.S. Owicki and D. Gries. Verifying properties of
    parallel programs: an axiomatic approach. Comm. ACM 19, 5 (May 1976),
    pp. 280-285.

[Owicki and Gries 76b] S.S. Owicki and D. Gries. An axiomatic proof
    technique for parallel programs I, Acta Informatica 6 (1976) pp. 319-340.

[Parnas 72] D.L. Parnas. A technique for the specification of software
    modules, with examples. Comm. ACM 15, 5 (May 1972), pp. 330-336.

[Schorre 75] V. Schorre. A program verifier with assertions in terms
    of abstract data. Systems Development Corporation report SP 3841,
    Santa Monica, California.

[Shaw 76] M. Shaw. Abstraction and verification in Alphard: design and
    verification of a tree handler. Computer Science Department,
    Carnegie-Mellon University, (June 1976).

[Spitzen 75] J. Spitzen and B. Wegbreit. The verification and synthesis of data structures. *Acta Informatica* 4 (1975), pp. 127-144.

[Wulf 76] W.A. Wulf, R.L. London, and M. Shaw. An introduction to the construction and verification of Alphard programs. *IEEE Trans. on Software Eng.*, SE-2, 4 (December, 1976), pp. 253-265.

SPECIFICATION AND VERIFICATION OF A NETWORK MAIL SYSTEM

Susan S. Owicki

Digital Systems Laboratory
Stanford University
Stanford, California 94305

ABSTRACT

Techniques for describing and verifying modular systems are illustrated
using a simple network mail problem. The design is presented in a top-down
style. At each level of refinement, the specifications of the higher level
are verified from the specifications of lower level components.

This work was partially supported by the Air Force Office of Scientific
Research under Contract No. F49620-77-C-0045.

1.   Introduction

We wish to consider the design of a mail system that will route messages among users of a computer network. The network under consideration has a ring structure (Figure 1), in which nodes are connected by one-way communication links. Mail from a user at node i to a user at another node j must be passed around the ring from i to j. The problem is to design a subsystem of processes and monitors, running at each node, to handle the forwarding task and to receive and deliver mail for local users.

We have chosen to develop the system design in a top-down fashion. At the highest level (level 1) are the functional specifications of the mail system as a whole. These specifications, which are discussed in section 2, are a precise statement of the partial correctness requirements of the system. The first refinement, described in section 3, decomposes the system into node and link components that match the network architecture. In the next refinement, described in section 4, each node component is further refined to a set of concurrent processes communicating through buffer monitors. Each level of refinement is presented by giving specifications for the new components in the style of [1]. In addition, a partial correctness proof for the system is given as it is designed. Each level is shown to be a correct implementation of the previous level's specifications; in the last step the code of the processes and monitors is verified.

The partial-correctness specifications of the mail system state that any mail delivered is delivered to the appropriate user. Of course, it is also important that messages are eventually delivered. An informal proof that the system can be made to satisfy this requirement is given in section 5.

The network mail system in this paper is primarily intended to serve as an example of modular proof methodology. Although the overall system structure is realistic, many of the problems that arise in networks are ignored. Most of these difficulties, which include real-time constraints, synchronization protocols, and error-handling, would occur in refining the link modules introduced at level 2. They are briefly discussed when the link modules are described in section 3.

2.   Level 1 Specifications: System Requirements

The functional requirements of the network mail system are given

by the specifications in Figures 2 and 3. At this level, the only
concern is what is to be accomplished by the system, i.e. delivery of
messages to the proper destination, and not how that delivery is to
be achieved.

Figure 2 defines some global types that are used in the specifications at all levels. Most important are the formats of user identifiers and messages. A userId includes both a node address and a
local identifier; each user has a unique userId. Messages are passed
through the system in the form of a record containing the names of
the sender and intended receiver, with a text that can be an arbitrary
character string.

Figure 3 gives the system's external specifications in the format
that will be used for all modules: variable declarations, initial and
invariant assertions, and procedure specifications. At level 1 there
are two auxiliary arrays, H and C, which record the history and current
state of the system. (Auxiliary variables are used in the specifications
and proof, but are not actually implemented). H records the history
of messages passed between modules: H[M1,M2,u,v] denotes the sequence
of messages passed from M1 to M2 that have source user u and
destination user v. At level 1, the only modules are the user processes (identified by userId) and the network mail system itself (NMS),
but the array H will be used with other modules at lower levels. The
array C is used to denote the current contents of each module: C[M,u,v]
is the sequence of messages currently in M that have source u and destination v. Initially, all sequences are empty. The system invariant
states that all messages sent by u addressed to v (i.e. those in
H[NMS,v,u,v]) have either been delivered to v (i.e. are in H[NMS,v,u,v])
or are still in the system (i.e. are in C[NMS,u,v]). Moreover, the
order in which messages are sent is preserved by the system.
The specifications for procedures send and receive indicate
that they may only be called by user processes (in procedure specifications, # denotes the name of the module invoking the procedure).
The effect of send is to append a message to the appropriate history.
(Here H' denotes the value of H at procedure entry, and it is assumed
that all elements of H not explicitly mentioned are not modified by
the procedure.) The effect of receive depends on whether any mail is
available for the caller. If there is, the flag valid is set to
true, and a message is returned and appended to the appropriate history.
Otherwise, valid is set to false, and the history is not modified.

The procedure send must also increase the sequence C[NMS,u,v] (the "contents" of the mail system), and receive must likewise shorten C[NMS,u,v]. The effect on C is not part of the procedure entry/ exit conditions, because it is not visible to the module invoking the procedures. However, it can be inferred from the entry/exit conditions and the module invariant.

These specifications illustrate a difference in notation between this paper and [1]. Rather than declaring some variables to be private to a particular module, we will use the idea of safe variables in a more informal style. A variable is safe for a module if it can only be modified by that module. The specifications and proof of a module must involve only variables that are safe for that module. Of the NMS variables, those that are safe for M1 are H[M1,M2,u,v] , H[M2,M1,u,v] , and C[M1,u,v] (for any M2,u,v). The values of these variables can only be changed by an action of M1 , although the form of that action depends on the relationship between M1 and M2. For example, the value of H[M1,M2,u,v] could be modified by M1 calling M2.send, or by M2 calling M1.receive. Likewise, the sequence C[M1,u,v] could be extended by M2 calling M1.send or M1 calling M2.receive; and it could be shortened by M1 calling M2.send or M2 calling M1.receive .

In all cases, module specifications must use variables safely, as described in [1]. This means that free variables in the specifications of module M must obey the following rules:

1) The initial and invariant assertions may refer to any safe variable of M, e.g. C[M,u,v], H[M,M',u,v] and H[M',M,u,v] (for any M',u,v).

2) Procedure entry and exit assertions may refer to variables that are safe for the calling module, i.e. H[M,#,u,v], H[#,M,u,v] and C[#,u,v] (for any u,v).

Note that the specifications in Figure 2 obey these rules. Later refinements will use H and C in much the same way.

The functional requirements in this section are unrealistic in one major aspect: they do not require any action to be taken if mail is sent to an invalid userId . A reasonable requirement would be to return an error message to a user who sent a message with an invalid address.

A specification along these lines might have the invariant

H[u,NMS,u,v] = H[NMS,v,u,v] @ C[NMS,u,v] for valid v,

H[u,NMS,u,v] = HE[NMS,u,u,v] @ CE[NMS,u,v] @ C[NMS,u,v] for inva-

lid v, where HE records the history of error messages between modules,
and CE denotes the error messages contained in a module. The second
clause of the invariant states that, for each erroneous message
sent, either an error message has been received, or an error message
is on its way, or the original message is still in the system.
Such a specification could be implemented by having the error message
initiated at v.node and returned to u using the normal message
delivery system. However, we will not pursue this extension of the
original specifications.

3.   Level 2 Specifications: Network Architecture
      3.1 Specifications

The first decomposition of the mail system fits the program to
the network architecture. At each node i there is a sybsystem
S[i] , and the communication line leaving node i is represented by a
module L[i] . The specifications for these two component types are
given in Figures 5 and 6.

First, consider the link specifications in Figure 5. The specifications are expressed in terms of the global variable H[M,L[i],u,v]
and H[L[i],M,u,v]. As discussed in Section 2, these elements of the
array of histories H are safe to use in the specifications of
L[i] because they can only be modified as a result of actions of
L[i] . The declaration of variables and the initial assertion are
omitted here because no new variables are needed in the specifications.

The invariant for link L[i] states that all messages sent into
the link from S[i] have been sent out to S[i⊕1] . (We will use
i⊕1 and i⊖1 as abbreviations for (i+1) mod (N+1) and (i-1)
mod (N+1) .) There is no buffer capacity in the link, so send and
receive operations must be synchronized. The entry and exit assertions
for link procedures indicate that the history sequences in H are
updated appropriately, much as in the send and receive procedures of
the NMS system in Figure 3. In addition, L[i].send(m) removes
message m from the contents of the calling module (C[#,u,v]), and
L[i].receive(m) adds m to the contents of the calling module.
It way not necessary to modify C[#,u,v] in the NMS procedures send
and receive because the "contents" of user processes are irrelevant to
the mail system.

No further refinements of the link module are given in this paper; but in a real system, the link itself might be a complex subsystem. The link hides the details of communication devices from the rest of the system. This could involve splitting and re-assembling messages to fit a fixed-length format, synchronizing read and write operations, and recovering from transmission errors. Regardless of the complexity of the link implementations, however, the subsystem running at each node may regard the link send and receive operations as no more complex than appending and removing values in a buffer.

Figure 6 gives the specifications of the sybsystem S[i] that runs at node i. Messages arrive at S[i] from local users and from the input link L[i⊖1] . Those addressed to local users are delivered directly; the others are sent to the output link L[i]. The invariant for S[i] states that input messages (those in H[from(u),S[i],u,v]) have either been sent to the appropriate destination (i.e. are in H[S[i],to(v),u,v]) or are still in the sybsystem (i.e. in C[S[i],u,v]). The form of the invariant is quite similar to the invariant for the entire system (Figure 3); the difference is that S[i] interacts with both user processes and the links L[i⊖1] and L[i]. The procedures S[i].send and S[i].receive directly implement the corresponding level 1 procedures, with each user calling the procedures provided at his node. This is indicated by the procedures' entry assertions.

3.2 Verification

Having given specifications for levels 1 and 2 of the mail system, we should show that they are consistent; i.e., that the link and node modules are a valid implementation of the mail system requirements. Consistency of specifications at two levels is verified by defining the variables and procedures of the higher level in terms of the lower, and then proving that the lower level specifications imply the higher. These requirements are stated in the following definition:

Definition 1: Suppose module V is to be implemented by modules W_1, W_2,...W_k. Let the variables of V be $\bar{v}$, the variables of W_1,...,W_k be $\bar{w}$ and the relationship between them be $\bar{v} = f(\bar{w})$. Then W_1,...,W_k correctly implement V if the following consistency conditions are satisfied.

i. $(\underset{i}{\wedge} W_i.\text{invariant}) \supset V.\text{Invariant}\frac{f(\bar{w})}{v}$

ii. For each procedure p in $W_1...,W_k$ that implements a procedure q in V

    a. $q.\text{entry}\frac{f(\bar{w})}{v} \supset p.\text{entry}$

    b. $p.\text{exit} \supset q.\text{exit}\frac{f(\bar{w})}{v}$

(In the mail system, all variables in the specifications are initialized as empty sequences, so we have omitted the <u>initial</u> and <u>requires</u> clauses, described in [1], from module specifications. In the general case, these clauses would also have to be considered in proving that a lower level implementation is correct.)

Theorem 1: The level 2 specifications of modules S[i] and L[i], for i = 0,..,N (Figures 5 and 6) correctly implement the level 1 system requirements (Figure 3).

Proof: The correspondance between the names of variables and procedures of the two levels is given in Figure 7. The history of messages sent between a user u and the mail system NMS is implemented by the history of messages between u and S[u.node]. The sequence of messages in NMS from user u to user v is implemented at level 2 by the concatenation of the contents of sybsystems at v.node , v.nodeΘ1, ..., u.node. This reflects the fact that a message sent from u and not yet delivered to v must be at one of the nodes on the path from u to v. Finally, the send and receive procedures of level 1 are implemented at each node in level 2.

Verifying the consistency criteria for procedure entry and exit conditions is straightforward; after the substitution of variable names, the level 1 assertions are equivalent to the level 2 assertions.

Verifying the consistency of the invariants requires us to prove

(*) $(\underset{i}{\wedge} (S[i].\text{invariant} \wedge L[i].\text{invariant}) \supset$
          $\forall u,v \; (H[u,S[u.\text{node}],u,v] = H[S[v.\text{node}],v,u,v] @$
                                  $C[v.\text{node},u,v] @ ... @ C[u.\text{node},u,v])$

Let i = u.node, j = v.node, and consider two cases for i and j . If i = j, (*) follows from

    $S[i].\text{invariant} \supset (H[u,S[i],u,v] = H[S[i],v,u,v] @ C[S[i],u,v])$

For i ≠ j, assume the left-hand-side of the implication (*). From S[i].invariant we have

H[u,S[i],u,v] = H[S[i],L[i],u,v] @ C[S[i],u,v].

Applying L[i].invariant gives

H[u,S[i],u,v] = H[L[i],S[i⊕1],u,v] @ C[S[i],u,v].

We can repeatedly apply S[k].invariant and L[k].invariant for

K = i⊕1, ...,j⊕1 to derive

H[u,S[i],u,v] = H[L[j⊕1],S[j],u,v] @ C[S[j⊕1],u,v] @...@ C[S[i],u,v]

Finally, from S[j].invariant we can derive

H[u,S[i],u,v] = H[v,S[j],u,v] @ C[S[j],u,v] @...@ C[S[i],u,v]

This completes the proof of (*) and of Theorem 1.

4.   Level 3 Specifications: The Node Subsystems

4.1 Specifications

The last refinement to be presented is the decomposition of the
node subsystems into processes and monitors. Figure 8 illustrates the
components at each node and the flow of messages among them. There
are three concurrent processes at each node, corresponding to three
asynchronous activities. They are the reader process R and writer
process W, which manage link communications, and a switch process
Sw , which routes messages to a local destination or to the output
link. The processes are connected by three buffers, Swbuf , Ubuf ,
and Wbuf , implemented by monitors.

Specifications for level 3 components are given in Figures 9 - 14.
First, consider the reader process R (Figure 9). Its invariant states
that messages received from link L[i⊕1] are passed to the switch
buffer Swbuf[i] . There are no procedure specifications for a process.
The specifications for the other processes (Figures 10 and 11) are
similar. Process Sw[i] takes messages from Swbuf[i] , sending those
addressed to local users to Ubuf[i] and others to Wbuf[i] . Finally,
process W[i] takes messages from Wbuf[i] and sends them to the next
node via L[i] .   .

Specifications of the three buffers are given in Figures 12 - 14.
Swbuf[i] (Figure 12) and Wbuf[i] (Figure 13) are bounded buffers of

the type described in [1]. Swbuf has two "send" procedures: sendnew ,
called by user processes to initiate mail delivery, and send , called
by the reader process to deposit messages from the input link. For
both buffers, the invariant has the usual clause relating histories of
messages in and out of the module, and a clause reflecting the bound
on the buffer's size. In addition, the variable C[Swbuf[i],u,v]
contains the subsequence of messages in Swbuf[i].buf that are addressed
from u to v . (C[Wbuf[i],u,v] and Wbuf[i].buf have the same
relationship.) The last clause states that the buffer only contains
messages between users u and v if it is on the path from u to
v . For Swbuf[i] , this means that i is in the sequence u.node,
u.node⊕1, ..., v.node , abbreviated
          i in [u.node,v.node].
For Wbuf[i], i must be in u.node, u.node⊕1 , ..., v.node⊖1,
abbreviated
          i in [u.node,v.node).
These limits on the buffer contents are enforced by the entry condition
of send and reflected in the exit condition of receive .
        The last buffer, Ubuf[i] , is treated as an array of unbounded
buffers, one for each local user. Presumably, these buffers are implemented using backing store which can be considered unbounded. In other
respects, the specifications resemble those already considered.

4.2 Verifying Level 3 Consistency

        Our next task is to verify that the level 3 specifications correctly
implement the level 2 specifications of a node subsystem.

Theorem 2: The level 3 modules specified in Figures 9 - 14 are a correct
implementation of the subsystem S[i] described in Figure 6.

Proof: We must show that the requirements of definition 1 are met.
The correspondance between variable and procedure names from the two
levels is given in Figure 15. It is easy to see that the procedure
specifications are consistent, since the entry and exit conditions are
identical for both levels. To show that the invariants are consistent,
we must show that the conjunction of invariants for level 3 modules
implies the subsystem invariant for S[i]. The reasoning involves
separate consideration of four cases for u and v:

a. u.node = v.node = i

b. u.node = i ∧ v.node ≠ i

c. u.node ≠ i ∧ v.node = i

d. u.node ≠ i ∧ v.node ≠ i

Since the four cases are treated in much the same way, we give only the proof of case a.

For u.node = v.node = i, the level 2 invariant becomes, after variable substitution,

(*) H[u,Swbuf[i],u,v] = H[Ubuf[i],v,u,v] @ C[Ubuf[i],u,v]
                                        @ C[Sw[i],u,v] @ C[Swbuf[i],u,v]

Now Swbuf[i].invariant implies

H[u,Swbuf[i],u,v] = H[Swbuf[i],Sw[i],u,v] @ C[Swbuf[i],u,v]

Applying Sw[i].invariant to expand the first term on the right-hand-side gives

H[u,Swbuf[i],u,v] = H[Sw[i],Ubuf[i],u,v] @ C[Sw[i],u,v]
                                       @ C[Swbuf[i],u,v]

Finally, applying Ubuf[i].invariant to expand the first term on the right-hand-side gives (*).

The other three cases can be proved in the same way, for example, in case d above, the level 2 invariant, after variable substitution, is

H[L[iθl], R[i],u,v] = H[W[i],L[i],u,v] @ C[W[i],u,v]
                                     @ C[Wbuf[i],u,v] @ C[Sw[i],u,v]
                                     @ C[Swbuf[i],u,v] @ C[R[i],u,v].

This is implied by the invariants of R[i] , Swbuf[i] , Sw[i] , Wbuf[i] , and W[i] .

4.3 Verifying the Level 3 Implementation

Figures 16 - 21 contain proof outlines for the code implementing the processes and monitors of level 3. The process proofs make use of two predicates, empty and contents , defined below.

empty(M: module) ≡ ∀u,v: userId (C[M,u,v] = <>)

contents(M: module; m:message)

≡ ∀u,v: userId (C[M,u,v] = if (u=m.source) and (v=m.dest)
                           then <m>
                           else <>   )

These predicates describe the two possible states of these processes, which can contain at most one message.

For the most part, the verification of the processes and monitors is straightforward, although tedious, and is not presented here. One interesting point is that the entry conditions of Swbuf[i].send(m) requires i in (m.source.node,m.dest.node]. In order to show that this entry condition is met for the procedure call in R[i] , we need to know that the message obtained from L[iθ1] was in the correct range. The original link specifications did not guarantee this; however, in this system the link is used in such a way that it must be true. This can be expressed by deriving specialized specifications for L[i] based on its use in the mail system. In this new specification, given in Figure 22, a stronger entry condition on L[i].send justified a stronger invariant and exit condition for L[i].receive . A formal derivation of the specialized specifications from the original ones can be obtained using techniques described in [1].

At this point we have developed a partial implementation of the mail system (without the link modules) and verified that the implementation meets the system's functional requirements. As a final step, let us consider strengthening the system requirements to imply that messages are eventually delivered.

5. Guaranteed Message Delivery

The mail system specifications given in Figure 2 require only partial correctness; they imply that if a message is received at all, it is received by the correct user. In this section we consiser two further requirements: that deadlock of the system is impossible, and that all messages are eventually delivered. (The second condition implies the first.) A set of sufficient conditions for preventing deadlock are defined and verified, and implementation methods that meet the criteria are outlined. The proofs are quite informal.

First let us consider the requirement that deadlock (a state in which all processes are blocked) cannot occur in the message system. Theorem 3 below states that deadlock is impossible if the number of undelivered messages in the system is kept smaller than its total buffer capacity. There are a number of ways of implementing the mail system to ensure that this condition is always satisfied. One approach is to delay initial processing of a message until it is certain that the network as a whole has enough buffer space to handle one more message. Several strategies have been proposed for determining, from inspection of local data at the node, when a new message can safely be allowed to enter the system (see, for example [2]). Another approach is to provide enough buffer space to hold as much mail as users can generate. In some systems, there are constraints on user behavior that keep this number small. In general, however, the number of outstanding messages may be quite large, requiring that buffers be implemented on backing store. A third approach - discarding messages when the buffer capacity is exceeded - is acceptable in some applications, but it is not consistent with our specifications.

The following theorem shows that deadlock can be avoided using any strategy that prevents the number of undelivered messages from filling all buffers to capacity.

Theorem 3. Suppose the network mail system is implemented in such a way that the number of undelivered messages (those in $C[NMS,u,v]$, but not in any $C[Ubuf[i],u,v]$) is less than $\sum_i (Swbuf[i].bufsize + Wbuf[i].bufsize)$. Then whenever there is undelivered mail in the system, at least one process is not blocked.

Proof: A process can only be blocked at monitor entry (because another process is holding the monitor) or at a monitor wait operation. The first condition can only arise when a process is executing in the monitor, so in this case at least one process is not blocked. So if all processes are blocked, they must all be blocked at wait operations. In the mail system, there are four places where this can occur:
1. At M.send, when length(M.buf) = M.bufsize, for M = Swbuf[i] or Wbuf[i].
2. At M.receive, when length(M.buf) = 0, for M = Swbuf[i] or Wbuf[i].

3. At L[i].send, when no process is executing L[i].receive.

4. At L[i].receive, when no process is executing L[i].send

The processes in the mail system form a cycle, as illustrated in figure 23. Here the processes are labelled p_0, p_1, ..., p_{3N-1}, and the monitors (excluding Ubuf) are labelled b_0, b_1,..., b_{3N-1}. Each p_i consumes messages from b_i and produces messages for $b_{i \oplus 1}$ If deadlock occurs, each process p_i is blocked at a send to $b_{i \oplus 1}$ or a receive from b_i . Now, whether b_i is a buffer or a link, it is not possible to have both $p_{i \oplus 1}$ blocked at b_i.send and p_i blocked at b_i.receive . Since the processes from a cycle, this implies that either all processes are blocked at receive or all are blocked at send . If all are at send , then all buffers are full, and this violates the hypothesis of the theorem. So if deadlock occurs, all processes are blocked at receive . But this can only happen when all buffers are empty, and there are no undelivered messages. This completes the proof.

Even if deadlock is impossible, message delivery may not be guaranteed. For example, if deadlock is avoided by a mechanism that delays message acceptance, then some messages may be passed over repeatedly while the system delivers other messages. To preclude this possibility, the scheduling of processes and monitors must be done fairly.

Definition: A system has <u>fair process scheduling</u> if each process makes progress at a non-zero rate unless it is blocked.

Fair scheduling for processes is natural if each process executes on its own processor. If the processes are multiprogrammed on a single processor, it is up to the multiprogramming system to ensure fair scheduling.

Definition: <u>A buffer implementation is fair</u> if its send operations are guaranteed to terminate unless the buffer remains full forever, and its receive operations are guaranteed to terminate unless the buffer remains empty forever.

To say that a buffer monitor is fair is to imply that a process attempting to send or receive will not be passed over indefinitely in favor of other processes. If processes are competing to send elements

to a buffer, one of them may be delayed for a time, but as long as the
buffer does not remain full, each process will eventually complete its
send. In the network system, fair scheduling of send operations is
necessary for Swbuf[i] , which takes input from R[i] and from local
users. Fair scheduling of receive operations is needed in Ubuf[i] ,
where user processes may compete to receive messages.

Fair buffer implementations are not difficult if the underlying
implementation of monitors is fair (e.g. if monitor entry and removal
from condition queues is done on a first-in-first-out basis). In this
case, the buffer implementations in Figures 19 - 21 are fair. If the
underlying implementation is unfair, or if the buffer scheduling policy
deliberately delays some processes, e.g. in order to prevent deadlock,
then accomplishing a fair buffer implementation may be more difficult.

Theorem 4. Suppose that the network mail system satisfies the conditions of Theorem 3, and that buffers and process scheduling are implemented fairly. Then if user u calls the procedure send(v,t) , the
message <u,v,t> will eventually reach Ubuf[v.node].

Proof: Suppose not, i.e. suppose some message <u,v,t> remains undelivered. It cannot cycle in the message system, since the invariant
for Wbuf[v.node] guarantees that it cannot leave node v.node via
the link. Thus it must remain forever in some buffer b_i or process
p_i . This can only happen if p_i is permanently blocked at $b_{i \oplus 1}$.send .
By fairness, this can only happen if $b_{i \oplus 1}$ remains full forever, which,
in turn, can only occur if $p_{i \oplus 1}$ remains blocked forever at $b_{i \oplus 2}$.send .
Repeating this argument for $p_{i \oplus 2}, \ldots, p_{i \oplus 1}$, we can show that all
processes are blocked. Since there is undelivered mail in the system,
this is impossible, by Theorem 3. Thus all messages must eventually
be delivered.

We have proved that, with fair buffers and fair process scheduling,
each message is eventually delivered to the appropriate Ubuf[i] .
A final requirement is that a message for user v in Ubuf[v.node]
will reach v if v calls Ubuf.receive a sufficient number of times.
This is easily verified, provided that Ubuf[v.node] is implemented
fairly.

Combining the results of this section with those of sections
2 - 4 gives a proof of total correctness: each message is eventually
delivered to the correct destination, so long as the fairness and dead-
lock-avoidance conditions are satisfied.

6. Summary

The purpose of this paper has been to illustrate the use of modular
proofs for systems programs. Although the mail system presented here
does not deal with many of the difficult problems of network communication, its overall structure is realistic. Other mail systems with
modular architectures are defined in [2], [3], and [4].

The modules in this system have a common pattern, which we might
call the message-passing pattern. This same sort of module appears
often in other types of concurrent systems. Another common pattern,
the dynamically allocated resource, is described in [5]. It is my hope
that we will be able to discover a small set of patterns that account
for most module structures in concurrent programs, and identify convenient
ways of specifying and verifying modules which fit the patterns.
If this is possible, the task of verifying large systems should be
considerably simplified.

Acknowledgements: I am grateful to both Edsger Dijkstra and Leslie
Lamport, whose complaints and suggestions about an earlier version
of this paper led to the current form of specifications for message-
passing modules.

References

[1] Owicki, S., Specifications and Proofs for Abstract Data Types in
Concurrent Programs, in this volume.

[2] Brinch Hansen, P., Network, a Multiprocessor Program. IEEE Trans
on Software Engineering, v.4, no.3 (May, 1978) 194-199.

[3] Ambler, A., et al., A Language for Specification and Implementa-
tion of Verifiable Programs. Proc. of an ACM Conference on Language
Design for Reliable Software, SIGPLAN Notices v. 12, n.3 (also
Operating Systems Review v. 11, n.2, and Software Engineering
Notes, v.2, n.2) (1977) 1-10.

[4] Andrews, G., Modula and the Design of a Message Switching Commu-
     nications System. TR78-329, Cornell University, Computer
     Science Dept. (1978)

[5] Owicki, S., Verifying Parallel Programs with Resource Allocation.
     Proc. International Conference on Math. Studies of Information
     Processing, Kyoto, Japan (1978).

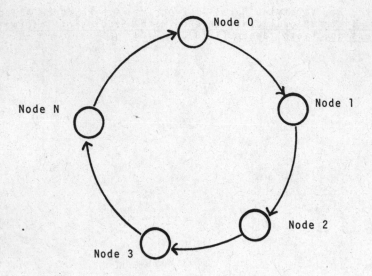

Figure 1.   Ring Network Architecture

```
type nodeId = 0..N;
     localId = sequence of char;
     userId = record
                 node: nodeId;
                 uId: localId
             end;

     cstring = sequence of char;
     message = record
                 source, dest:  userId;
                 text:  cstring
             end;

     messageSequence = sequence of message
```

FIGURE 2. GLOBAL TYPES

```
module NMS

  var H : array [module, module, userId, userId] of messageSequence;
      C : array [module, userId, userId] of messageSequence;

  initial: H = C = <>

  invariant:  ∀u,v:  userId ( H[u,NMS,u,v] = H[NMS,v,u,v] @ C[NMS,u,v] )

  procedures:

    send (u:  userId; t: cstring)
      entry: #: userId
      exit:  H[#,NMS,#,u] = H'[#,NMS,#,u] @ <#,u,t>

    receive (var valid: Boolean; var u: userId; var t: cstring)
      entry: #: userId
      exit:  (valid ∧ H[NMS,#,u,#] = H'[NMS,#,u,#] @ <u,#,t>) v
             (∿valid ∧ H[NMS,#,u,#] = H'[NMS,#,u,#])
```

Figure 3. Network Mail System (NMS) Requirements (Level 1)

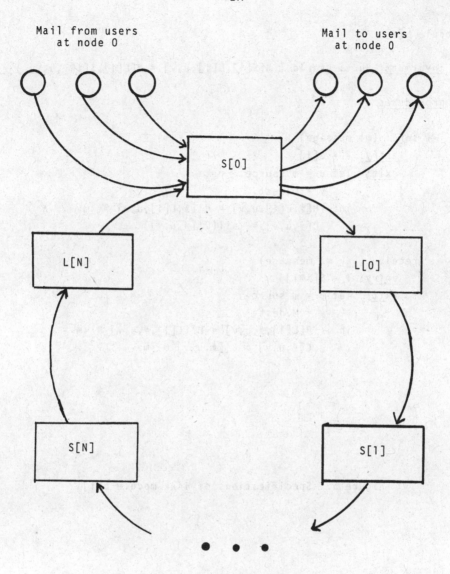

Figure 4.   Level 2 Modules and Message Flow

```
module L[i]

   invariant: ∀u,v: userId ( H[S[i],L[i],u,v] = H[L[i],S[i⊕1,u,v] )

   procedures

      send: (m: message)
         entry: # = S[i]
         exit:  let u = m.source,
                    v = m.dest,
                in  (H[#,L[i],u,v] = H'[#,L[i],u,v] @ <m>      ∧
                     C[#,u,v] = tail(C'[#,u,v])      )

      receive (var m: message)
         entry: # = S[i⊕1]
         exit:  let u = m.source,
                    v = M.dest,
                in  ( H[L[i],#,u,v] = H'[L[i],#,u,v] @ <m>   ∧
                      C[#,u,v] = C'[#,u,v] @ <m>      )
```

Figure 5. Specifications of link module L[i]

```
module S[i]

  invariant: ∀u,v: userId
    (let from(u) = if u.node=i then  u  else  L[iθ1]
         to(u)   = if u.node=i then  u  else  L[i]
      in  H[from(u),S[i],u,v] = H[S[i],to(v),u,v] @ C[S[i],u,v] )


  procedures:

    send (u: userId; t: cstring)
      entry: #: userId  ∧  #.node=i
      exit:  H[#,S[i],#,u] = H'[#,S[i],#,u] @ <#,u,t>

    receive (var valid: Boolean; var u: userId; var t: cstring)
      entry: #: userId  ∧  #.node=i
      exit:( valid  ∧  H[S[i],#,u,#] = H'[S[i],#,u,#] @ <u,#,t>)
            v(∼valid  ∧  H[S[i],#,u,#] = H'[S[i],#,u,#] )
```

Figure 6. Specifications of Node Subsystem S[i]

In all cases u and v range over userId's

Level 1	Level 2

Variables

```
  H[u,NMS,u,v]          H[u,S[u.node],u,v]
  H[NMS,v,u,v]          H[S[v.node],v,u,v]
  C[NMS,u,v]            C[S[v.node],u,v] @ C[S[v.nodeΘ1,u,v]
                              @ ... @ C[S[u.node],u,v]
```

Procedures

```
  NMS.send(u,t)         S[#.node].send(u,t)
  NMS.receive(u,t)      S[#.node].receive(u,t)
```

Figure 7. Level 2 Implementation of Level 1 Variables and Procedures

221

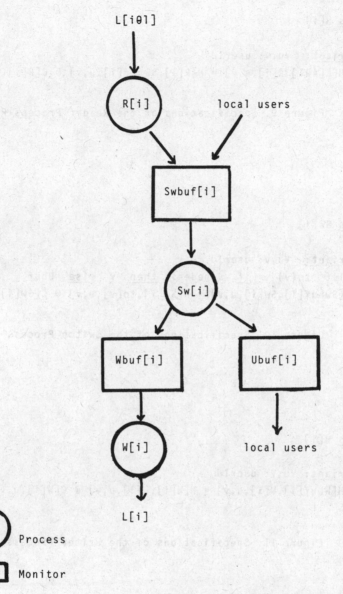

Figure 8. Level 3 Implementations of S[i]

<u>process</u> R[i]

  <u>invariant</u>: ∀u,v: userId
    (H[L[iθ1],R[i],u,v] = H(R[i],Swbuf[i],u,v] @ C[R[i],u,v])

        Figure 9. Specifications of the Reader Process R[i]

<u>process</u> Sw[i]

  <u>invariant</u>: ∀u,v: userId
    (<u>let</u> to(v) = <u>if</u> v.node=i <u>then</u> v <u>else</u> Ubuf   <u>in</u>
    H[Swbuf[i],Sw[i],u,v] = H[Sw[i],to[v],u,v] @ C[Sw[i],u,v])

        Figure 10. Specifications of the Switch Process Sw[i]

<u>process</u> W[i]

  <u>invariant</u>: ∀u,v: userId
    (H[Wbuf[i],W[i],u,v] = H[W[i],L[i],u,v] @ C[W[i],u,v])

        Figure 11. Specifications of the Writer Process W[i]

```
monitor Swbuf[i]

  const bufsize

  var buf: messageSequence

  initial: buf = <>

  invariant: Vu,v: userId
    ( let  from(u) = if u.node=i then u else R[i], in
    H[from(u),Swbuf[i],u,v] = H[Swbuf[i],Sw[i],u,v] @ C[Swbuf[i],u,v]
    ∧ length(buf) ≤ bufsize
    ∧ C[Swbuf[i],u,v] = <buf : source=u ∧ dest=v>
    ∧ ∀m: message (m in buf ⊃ i in [m.source.node,m.dest.node] ) )

  procedures

    sendnew(u: userId; t: cstring)
      entry: #: userId ∧ #.node=i
      exit: (H[#,Swbuf[i],u,v] = H'[#,Swbuf[i],u,v] @ <#,u,t>)

    send(m: message)
      entry: #=R[i] ∧ i in (m.source.node,m.dest.node]
      exit:  let u= M.source ∧ v = m.dest, in
             (H[#,Swbuf[i],u,v] = H'[#,Swbuf[i],u,v] @ <m> ∧
             ∧ C[#,u,v] = tail(C'[#,u,v] )

    receive(var m: message)
      entry: #=Sw[i]
      exit:  let u = m.source ∧ v = m.dest, in
             (H[Swbuf[i],#,u,v] = H'[Swbuf[i],#,u,v] @ <m> ∧
             ∧ C[#,u,v] = C'[#,u,v] @ <m>
             ∧ i in [u.node,v.node] )
```

Figure 12. Specifications of the Buffer Monitor Swbuf[i]

```
monitor Wbuf[i]

  const bufsize

  var buf: messageSequence

  initial: buf = <>

  invariant: ∀u,v: userId
    (H[Sw[i],Wbuf[i],u,v] = H[Wbuf[i],W[i],u,v] @ C[Wbuf[i],u,v]
    ∧ length(buf) ≤ bufsize
    ∧ C[Wbuf[i],u,v] = <buf : source=u ∧ dest=v>
    ∧ ∀m:  message (m in buf ⊃ i in [m.source.node,m.dest.node] )  )


  procedures

    send(m: message)
      entry: # = Sw[i]  ∧ i in [m.source.node, m.dest.node)
      exit:  let u = m.source ∧ v = m.dest, in
             (H[#,Wbuf[i],u,v] = H'[#,Wbuf[i],u,v] @ <m>
              ∧ C[#,u,v] = tail(C'[#,u,v]) )

    receive(var m: message)
      entry:  # = W[i]
      exit:  let u = m.source ∧ v = m.dest, in
             (H[Wbuf[i],#,u,v] = H'[Wbuf[i],#,u,v] @ <m>
              ∧ C[#,u,v] = C'[#,u,v] @ <m>
              ∧ i in [u.node,v.node)  )
```

Figure 13. Specifications of the Buffer Monitor Wbuf[i]

```
monitor Ubuf[i]

  var buf: array [localId] of messageSequence;

  initial: buf = <>

  invariant: ∀u,v: userId

    (H[Sw[i],Ubuf[i],u,v] = H[Ubuf[i],v,u,v] @ C[Ubuf[i],u,v]
    ∧ (v.node=i ⊃ C[Ubuf[i],u,v] = <buf[v.localId] : source = u> )

  procedures

    send(m:  message)
      entry: #=Sw[i]  ∧ m.dest.node=i
      exit:  let u = m.source ∧  v = m.dest, in
               (H[#,Ubuf[i],u,v] = H'[#,Ubuf[i],u,v] @ <m>
                  ∧  C[#,u,v] = tail(C'[#,u,v])  )

    receive(var valid: Boolean; var u: userId; var t: cstring)
      entry: #:userId  ∧  #.node=i
      exit:  let  u = m.source  ∧  v = m.dest,  in
        ( valid  ∧   H[Ubuf[i],#,u,#] = H'[Ubuf[i],#,u,#]@ <u,#,t>
         v(∿valid  ∧   H[Ubuf[i],#,u,#] = H'[Ubuf[i],#,u,#] )
```

Figure 14. Specifications of the Buffer Monitor Ubuf[i]

In all cases u and v range over userId's

Level 2   Level 3

Variables
    H[u,S[i],u,v]   H[u,Swbuf[i],u,v]
    H[L[iΘ1[,S[i],u,v]   H[L[iΘ1],R[i],u,v]
    H[S[i],v,u,v]   H[Ubuf[i],v,u,v]
    H[S[i],L[i],u,v]   H[W[i],L[i],u,v]
    C[S[i],u,v]   Y(v) @ C[Sw[i],u,v] @ C[Swbuf[i],u,v] @ X(u)

                        Where
                      X(u) = if u.node=i
                            then <>
                            else C[R[i],u,v]
                    Y(v) = if v.node=i
                            then C[Ubuf[i],u,v]
                            else C[Wbuf[i],u,v]
                                @ C[W[i],u,v]

Procedures

    S[i].send(u,t)   Swbuf[i].sendnew(u,t)
    S[i].receive(val,u,t)   Ubuf[i].receive(val,u,t)

Figure 15. Level 3 Implementation of Level 2 Variables and Procedures

```
process R[i]

  var m: message;

  begin
    {invariant ∧ empty(R[i]) }
    while true do begin
      {invariant ∧ empty(R[i]) }
      L[i⊕1].receive(m) ;
      {invariant ∧ i in (m.source.node,m.dest.node] ∧
         contents(R[i],m)  }
      Swbuf[i].send(m);
      {invariant ∧ empty(R[i]) }
    end
end
```

Figure 16. Proof Outline for the Reader Process R[i]

```
process Sw[i]

  var m: message

  begin
    {invariant ∧ empty(Sw[i]) }
    while true do begin
    {invariant ∧ empty(Sw[i]) }
    Swbuf[i].receive(m);
    {invariant ∧ i in [m.source,m.dest] ∧
     contents(Sw[i], m )  }
    if m.dest.node = v
       then Ubuf.send(m)
       else Wbuf.send(m)
    {invariant ∧ empty(Sw[i]) }
    end
end
```

Figure 17. Proof Outline for the Switch Process Sw[i]

```
process W[i]

   var m: message;

   begin
      {invariant ∧ empty(W[i]) }
      while true do begin
         {invariant ∧ empty(W[i]) }
         wbuf[i].receive(m);
         {invariant ∧ i in [m.source.node,m.dest.node] ∧
           contents(W[i],m) }
         L[i].send(m);                  '
         {invariant ∧ empty(W[i]) }
      end
   end
end
```

Figure 18. Proof Outline for the Writer Process W[i]

```
monitor Swbuf[i]
  const bufsize =...
  var buf:  messageSequence;
      nonempty, nonfull: condition;
  procedure sendnew(u: userId; t: cstring);
    begin
        {invariant  Λ  sendnew.entry}
        if length (buf) = bufsize  then  nonfull.wait;
        {invariant  Λ  sendnew.entry  Λ  length(buf) < bufsize }
        buf := buf @ <#,u,t>;
        H[#,Swbuf[i],#,u] : = H[#,Swbuf[i],#,u] @ <#,u,t>
        C[Swbuf[i],#,u] : = C[Swbuf[i],#,u] @ <#,u,t>
        {invariant  Λ  sendnew.exit  Λ  length(buf) > 0  }
        nonempty.signal;
        {invariant  Λ  sendnew.exit }
    end


  procedure send(m: message);
    var u,v: userId;
    begin
        {invariant  Λ  send.entry }
        if length(buf) = bufsize  then  nonfull.wait;
        {invariant  Λ  i in (m.source.node,m.dest.node]
         Λ  #=R[i]  Λ  length(buf)<bufsize }
        buf : = buf  @  <#,u,t>;
        u : = m.source;  v := m.dest;
        H[#,Swbuf[i],u,v] := H[#,Swbuf[i],u,v]  @ <m>;
        C[#,u,v] := tail(C[#,u,v]);
        C[Swbuf[i],u,v] := C[Swbuf[i],u,v] @  <m>;
        {invariant  Λ  send.exit  Λ  length(buf) > 0  }
        nonempty.signal
        {invariant  Λ  send.exit}
    end
```

Figure 19. Proof Outline for the Buffer Monitor Swbuf[i]
(Cont. on next page)

```
procedure receive(var m: message);
   var u,v: userId;
   begin
      {invariant  Λ  receive.entry}
      if length(buf) = 0 then nonempty.wait;
      {invariant  Λ  #= Swbuf[i]  Λ  length(buf) > 0 }
      m := head(buf);  buf: = tail(buf);
      u : = m.source;   v := m.dest;
      H[Swbuf[i],#,u,v] := H[Swbuf[i],#,u,v] @ <m>;
      C[#,u,v] := C[#,u,v] @ <m>;
      C[Swbuf[i],u,v] := tail(C[Swbuf[i],u,v]);
      {invariant  Λ  receive.exit  Λ  length(buf) < bufsize }
      nonfull.signal;
      {invariant  Λ  receive.exit }
   end
begin
   buf : = <>
end;
```

Figure 19. Proof Outline for the Buffer Monitor Swbuf[i]

```
monitor Wbuf[i]
    const bufsize = ..
    var buf: messageSequence;
        nonempty, nonfull: condition;
procedure send(m: message);
    var u,v: userId;
    begin
        {invariant ∧ send.entry }
        if length(buf) = bufsize then nonfull.wait;
        {invariant ∧ #=Sw[i] ∧ i in [m.source.node,m.dest.node)
         ∧ length(buf) < bufsize }
        buf := buf @ <m>;
        u := m.source;    v := m.dest;
        H[#,Wbuf[i],u,v]:= H[#,Wbuf[i],u,v] @ <m>
        C[#,u,v] := tail(C[#,u,v])
        C[Wbuf[i],u,v] := C[Wbuf[i],u,v] @ <m>
        {invariant ∧ send.exit ∧ length(buf) > 0 }
        nonempty.signal;
        {invariant ∧ send.exit}
    end;


procedure receive(var m: message)
    var u,v: userId;
    begin
        {invariant ∧ receive.entry }
        if length(buf) = 0 then nonempty.wait;
        {invariant ∧ #=W[i] ∧ length(buf) > 0 }
        m := head(buf);  buf := tail(buf);
        u := m.source;    v := m.dest;
        H[Wbuf[i],#,u,v] := H[wbuf[i],#,u,v] @ <m>;
        C[#,u,v] := C[#,u,v] @ <m>
        C[Wbuf[i],u,v] := tail(Cbuf[i],u,v]);
        {invariant ∧ receive.exit ∧ length(buf) > bufsize}
        nonfull.signal
        {invariant ∧ receive.exit}
    end
begin
    buf := <>
end
```

Figure 20. Proof Outline for the Buffer Monitor Wbuf[i]

```
monitor Ubuf[i]
    var buf: array [localId] of messageSequence;
    procedure send(m: message);
        var u, v: userId;
        begin
            {invariant ∧ send.entry }
            u := m.source;  v := m.dest;
            buf[v.localId] := buf[v.localId] @ <m>;
            H[#,Ubuf[i],u,v] := H[#,Ubuf[i],u,v] @ <m>;
            C[#,u,v] := tail(C[#,u,v]);
            C[Ubuf[i],u,v] := C[Ubuf[i],u,v] @ <m>;
            {invariant ∧ send.exit }
        end;
    procedure receive (var valid: Boolean; var u: userId; var t: cstring)
        var m: message;
        begin
            {invariant ∧ receive.entry }
            if length(buf[#.localId]) = 0
            then valid := false
            else begin
                m := head(buf[#.localId]);
                buf[#.localId] := tail(buf[#.localId]);
                u := m.source;   t := m.text;
                valid := true;
                H[Ubuf[i],#,u,#] := H[ubuf[i],#,u,#] @ <m>;
                C[Ubuf[i],u,#] := tail(C[Ubuf[i],u,#])
            end
            {invariant ∧ receive.exit }
        end;
    begin
        buf := <>
    end
```

Figure 21. Proof Outline for Buffer Monitor Ubuf[i]

```
module L[i]
   invariant:  ∀u,v: userId (H[S[i],L[i],u,v] = H[L[i], S[i⊕1,u,v]
              ∧ ( ( i not in [u.node,v.node)⊃H[S[i],L[i],u,v] =<>))


procedures
   send(m:message)
      entry: # = S[i] ∧ i in [m.source.node,m.dest.node)
      exit: let u = m.source,
                v = m.dest,
            in (H[#,L[i],u,v] = H'[#,L[i],u,v] @ <m> ∧
                C[#,u,v] = tail(C'[#,u,v])


   receive(var m: message)
      entry: # = S[i⊕1]
      exit: let  u = m.source
                 v = m.dest
            in ( i in [u.node,v.node) ∧
                 H[L[i],#,u,v] = H'[L[i],#,u,v] @ <m> ∧
                 C[#,u,v] = C'[#,u,v] @ <m>  )
```

Figure 22. Adapted Specifications of L[i] (for Level 3 Verification)

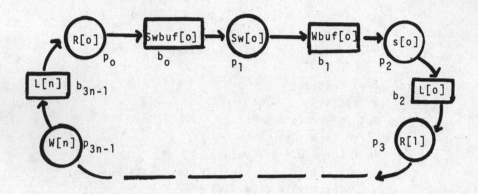

Figure 23. Mail System Processes and Monitors

III. PROGRAM DEVELOPMENT BY TRANSFORMATION

From Specification to Implementation — The Formal Approach

The transformational approach to programming has some roots in the sixties, when LANDIN 1966 showed that certain well-known programming constructs were nothing but notational variants of a Lambda-Calculus formulation, and when GILL 1965 connected go to s (they became harmful shortly afterwards!) to parameterless procedures. A decisive step was made by COOPER 1966 showing how certain linear recursion schemes can be transformed into simpler recursion schemes ('repetitive schemes', 'tail recursion'). Such non-trivial transformations were studied by STRONG 1970 and by DARLINGTON in his 1972 thesis.

The motivation for the transformational approach to program development is "that programs are complicated, hard to understand and prone to errors because we want them to be efficient ... . So the idea is to start with a program which does the right job but entirely sacrifies efficiency in favour of simplicity and modularity. We then transform it by correctness-preserving transformations until a tolerably efficient, though less perspicuous, program is obtained" [1].

Although the simplification of recursion is an important theme in the transformational approach - apart from DARLINGTON and BURSTALL, there are contributions by MANNA and WALDINGER, and by ARSAC - frequently other sorts of transformations are also worthwhile for a 'program manipulation system' as KNUTH envisaged it in 1974. Optimizing compilers comprise many of them, but instead of using them stubbornly, interactive use is to be preferred. Convincing examples of such transformations (albeit done so far by hand) have been given by Susan GERHART and others.

The program with which to start the transformation process is the 'contract' - everything correctly derived from it will be as correct as the contract is. In our view however, the contract does not have the form of a fully algorithmic program; a rigid form of a specification using implicit conditions may serve as a basis as well.

---

[1] R.M. Burstall, Program Development by Transformations: An overview. Proc. CREST Course on Programming, Toulouse 1978, to appear.

Thus, going somewhat beyond BURSTALL and DARLINGTON, transformations may also be applied to pre-algorithmic specifications that use predicates and quantifiers. This ties in very well with the recent development of an abstract specification of data types (ZILLES, GUTTAG, GOGUEN et al.).

Thus, the aim of using transformations in programming is
(i)   the elimination of non-algorithmic particles like quantifiers
(ii) operative amelioration that increases efficiency
(iii) adaptation to make best use of the special capabilities of a given machine.

The basis of the more complex transformations are two elementary ones, called 'unfold' and 'fold'; unfolding means the replacement of a (function) symbol by its definition, folding means the converse. In a versatile system, both these two elementary transformations and a bundle of complex transformations of certain program schemes are to be used, the latter ones being derived within the system by using more elementary ones - a situation strikingly analoguous to working with theorems in mathematics.

It is clear that language questions cannot be neglected in such a transformation system. This has been given special attention in the project CIP. Extensible syntax goes hand in hand with 'defining transformations'; this leads to the idea of 'transformational semantics' based on an applicative core language*. Attempts have been made to include transformations leading to pointers; what the rules are that allow to obtain certain simplifications with the help of selective updating is an open problem.

Program transformation is an important tool for program construction. "Enough work has been done on program transformation to show that it can make a real contribution to systematic program development" (BURSTALL, loc. cit.).

F. L. Bauer

---

*   This core has been extended to include non-deterministic constructs.

Program Development by Stepwise Transformations -

The Project CIP

(This research was carried out within the Sonderforschungsbereich 49
"Programmiertechnik", München)

F. L. Bauer
Institut für Informatik
Technische Universität München

Introduction

The late sixties and early seventies - twenty-five years after the classical work
of ZUSE and VON NEUMANN - have seen the first crisis in the proud development of
computing: large software systems showed alarming deficiencies.

Gradually, it became clear that it was more difficult than expected "to master
complexity"[1] (DIJKSTRA). The cause of the misdevelopment lies in the programming
habits of the great majority of programmers. These had been influenced by the existing programming tools or rather by the lack of appropriate ones. Programming
tools had in turn been corrupted by the arbitrariness of existing hardware, which
indeed ruled the profession. This analysis of the situation was given by DIJKSTRA
at the Rome Conference on Software Engineering (1969) and subsequently led to a movement to establish a discipline of programming.

Another crisis had developed in these years, not totally unrelated to the Software
Crisis: the crisis of programming languages. Seeing 700 of those listed in SAMMET's
book was certainly not what the international ALGOL effort had wanted to produce,but it
was not the number which was an alarming sign: rather, it was the fact that these languages all pretended to be different from each other; their promotors did not want to
understand each other, and language users seemed not to care for a common conceptual
basis. Instead, doctrines were erected.

That the circumstances that led to the Software Crisis were also responsible for this
aberration of the human mind , I could observe even in the work of the group that
developed ALGOL 68. The original ALGOL idea which RUTISHAUSER, SAMELSON, BOTTENBRUCH
and I had propagated: a universal framework of concepts, taken from mathematics and
cast into some language, an idea which had already been spoiled by FORTRAN abracada-
bra and other gimmicks in ALGOL 60, was now completely submerged. I was therefore re-
lieved and started to have new hope when WIRTH said in 1969 [2] "I believe the art of
programming is based on a relatively small number of fundamental concepts ; most of
these concepts are already present in mathematics in some form".

---

[1] This difficulty was frequently circumvented by additional programming efforts,
which only increased the complexity. Apollo programming support,[1] p. 43

[2] [1] p. 20, p. 18, p. 21

WIRTH, however, took the extremely cautious course "to find a compromise which is as close to the machine as possible, while remaining machine independent". While it was certainly practical in the short run to have"features omitted from PASCAL because they appear to be too sophisticated for presently known methods of proof" - and the success PASCAL has had in the most recent years, rather in its middle age, demonstrates this - I was more inclined to look for a long range improvement and I was rather on the side of DIJKSTRA's remark:

"I would like to make a comment on Niklaus Wirth's story. I would like to point out that he starts from a tacit assumption which I wouldn't like to let pass unchallenged. His tacit assumption is that elegance or convenience on the one hand, and efficiency on the other hand, cannot go hand in hand ... I just don't believe it, and I would like to point out that from the point of view of Niklaus Wirth, his assumption is just a belief. If I have any interest in computing science at all it is based on my firm belief that very often the most attractive solution is the most efficient one."[1]
This was in 1969. Working with ALGOL 68, or rather a core of it which is, after all, not as bad as some people had expected from the report, I found therein a basis for a great educational challenge, the build-up of computer science (Informatik) in Germany as a university discipline. I found - and many people concurred - that a stock of concepts common in most of the prevailing programming languages could be conveyed under the notation and terminology of this core of ALGOL 68 as used in [2]. Needless to say that I saw the rough sides, too. They were centered around the ALGOL 68 doctrine of references, and by and large I understood that this, too, was the effect of misguidance by features of existing machines: ALGOL 68 was only masquerading as a high level language, but it is a machine oriented language as much as PASCAL, and was worse because it was unsafe - for example by allowing 'dangling references'.

A further event influenced my approach to a truly algorithmic language: The appearance of a mathematical semantics of programming languages. I had underestimated the importance of MCCARTHY's early, however restricted, attempts, and I was appalled by the clumsiness of the so called Vienna Definition Language, but the work initiated by PETER LANDIN and DANA SCOTT made me think: This was a convincing theory of computation, and nevertheless a gap existed between its merely functional, "applicative" level, the level of the Lambda Calculus on the one side and the prevailing level of constructs with program variables, with its semantics implied by HOARE's 'axioms' (and later by DIJKSTRA's predicate transformers) on the other side.

Moreover, I was not fully satisfied with the idea of proving correctness of a program, i.e. proving that it fits into a problem description. Didn't the whole movement start from the observation that most programs were wrong, and would it make sense to try to prove the correctness of an incorrect program? Programs don't fall from heaven, nor are they the product of omniscient oracles (SINTZOFF). KLAUS SAMELSON and DAVID GRIES appeased me, saying that correctness proof and program construction should go hand in hand. But to me this meant that programming is a transformation process starting from the problem description. LANDIN's work [3] encouraged me in this direction. We will come to this later.

Another misgiving I had was concerned with data structures. Both ALGOL 68 and PASCAL disallowed recursively defined data structures; instead they have to be introduced as a plexus (Geflecht) implementation - sometimes called Lists - with the help of pointers. Although PASCAL provided safe tools using this, it meant a terribly clumsy way of expressing even the simplest operations with sequences, like sorting in of an element. Again, a clean theory of recursive object structures existed in the meantime (DANA SCOTT [4]), based on MCCARTHY's ideas of 1962, and a transformation had to be found from this purely applicative level to the level of Lists. We will also discuss this later.

---

[1] [1] p. 18

Looking at objects and operations simultaneously, there was thus the procedural level of program variables using loops with goto's and of lists with pointers, and
there was the applicative level of recursive definition both of composite operations
and composite objects. But there was a third, still "higher" level, too: The level
of implicit specification, the typical implicit specification of operations being
done with the help of a characteristic property i.e.a predicate which defines it. This
idea generalizes to the joint characterization of objects and operations by a set of
properties, a subject that in the meantime has been studied by ZILLES and GUTTAG.
Naturally, the problem is how to derive from such an implicit specification operative
constructs. We will also come to this later.

So it was necessary to search for transitions between these levels. Such an approach
was endorsed by COOPER having had success [5] in "removing" recursion in particular instances. In order to formulate such transitions, a notation was needed, and
since transitions would always be used locally in the programming process, it was
natural to use one single language throughout, a *Wide Spectrum Language* reaching
from the top level of specification to the fourth, hitherto unmentioned level of data and program addresses.

Work on such a project started in 1972 within the Research Unit 49 of the German Research Council (SFB 49 der DFG) at the Technical University Munich.

The problem of a unique conceptual basis, which I had discussed around 1970 many
times with G. GOOS, and on which I had published first in Russian in the proceedings
of a Novosibirsk Meeting 1970   [6] as a result of ERSHOV's interest in these
questions in connection with his Beta Compiler, were taken up again in my London
lectures in fall 1973 and supplemented by the idea of a transformation system.
DIJKSTRA had seen [1] a program (statically) as a "necklace of pearls". Going a
little step further, I came to the conclusion that programming itself is nothing
else than a transformation process starting from a problem specification, forming
step by step a sequence of programs (corresponding to DIJKSTRA's necklace of pearls)
and ending with a sufficiently efficient, sufficiently machine-oriented program.

Now, if a transformation system - a mental or a programmed one - supports this transformation process, using some wide spectrum language, then the design of such a
language depends on, is guided by and has to take into account the conceptual meaning of these transformations.

Thus, we are not interested in a particular notation, and in order to demonstrate
this I envisaged to have at least say an ALGOL-like version and a PASCAL-like version of one and the same Wide Spectrum Language. Establishing the necessary and worthwhile transformations can be done for a coherent family of languages that can all be
used externally equally well; it will indeed be done for an abstract conceptual language, which is our present understanding of the ALGORITHMIC LANGUAGE. This is ALGOL
in the original sense; "algorithmic language" is a use of words similar to "mathematical language", which also does not mean a specific notation. After all the in-
justice that has been done to ALGOL, SAMELSON and I claim the acronym, also in the
spirit of RUTISHAUSER, for this general and original meaning.

----

[1]   [1] p. 87

Giving the transformation of programs such an importance, it should not be surprising that transformation can be viewed also as defining the semantics of many of the constructs, which are mere extensions (in the sense the word was used e.g. in ALGOL 68). It can be expected to have the semantics of the full Wide Spectrum Language in such a way reduced to an applicative core ("transformational semantics"); some non-trivial investigations in connection with this aim, for example the equivalence with the FLOYD-HOARE-DIJKSTRA Semantics, will be studied in a forthcoming dissertation by PEPPER.

In the following, we shall discuss some particular aspects of a Wide Spectrum Language for Program Transformations and of the transformations themselves. Starting with a discussion of the aims of the process of program evolution, we shall first deal with the applicative core, on which language and transformation are to be based. Next, we go through some examples of usual programming language constructs that can be defined by transformations. We also study mechanisms for joint refinement of objects and operations including the introduction of pointers. In a final section, the techniques of verification versus transformation are discussed. My remarks on the implementation of the system that is to support the mechanical performance of the program development process will be short because actual work has started only recently, and because this part of the project lies in the hands of my friend and colleague KLAUS SAMELSON who will report about details in due course.

When in 1974 a group of people at the Institute of Informatics of the TUM started work along the ideas outlined above, the project has been given the pseudonym CIP, possibly standing for computer-aided, intuition-guided programming. The abstract Wide Spectrum Language is called CIP-L. Its dialect "Algolesian CIP-L" or ALGOL 77 for short, is usually the conversation language; at the time being "Pascalesian CIP-L" is catching up. (In the future, we will give examples in both dialects in order to prevent language prejudice from darkening the issue).

The philosophy presented here is the result of long discussions and detailed studies of a group which started out with R. Gnatz, H. Wössner, U. Hill and H. Kröger; then joined by B. Krieg-Brückner, W. Hesse, F. Geiselbrechtinger on the language side, H. Partsch, P. Pepper, M. Wirsing on transformations, R. Steinbrüggen, F. Erhard, H.-O. Riethmayer, M. Luckmann on the system side; more recently M. Broy, A. Laut, B. Möller joined the group.

The aims of the process of program evolution

Programming lives on the contradiction between problems which are to be solved
and the machines doing it. Both have their particular "languages" - the language
of problems varying very widely, the language of machines showing relatively little
differences [1]. No wonder that these languages usually do not match. But there are
deeper reasons.

*Problem oriented languages are not necessarily fully algorithmic, but machine-
oriented ones are.* A 'problem' just tells what to find without telling how.
Machines that directly elaborate existential.quantifiers are in general intolerably
inefficient and moreover are restricted to finite domains (a search machine would
not terminate if given the problem: "Find all natural numbers x such that
$12x > x^2 + 33$ " and no further information).

*Moreover, problem oriented languages are not necessarily deterministic, but most
machines are.* Problems usually say : "Find s o m e element such that...": Frequently a problem is reduced to a 'simple' one by using some auxiliary problem of the same
kind, e.g. 'find some root of a polynomial' helps to find them all. The sorting problem we will deal with later is of this kind.

*Nondeterministic constructs are useful in the program development process, they allow
to postpone design decisions.* For example, quite a number of sorting and merging algorithms can be derived jointly in this way. There are also other instruments that
allow delaying design decisions. Working with abstract operations on abstract objects is one instance. Subtraction, for example, can be defined at a partial function
on abstract objects with two abstract operations, the unary operation 'successor'
and the nullary operation 0,

$$\underline{funct} \; sub \equiv (\underline{\lambda} \, a, \underline{\lambda} \, b) \; \underline{\lambda} \; :$$
$$\underline{if} \; a = b \; \underline{then} \; 0$$
$$\underline{else} \; succ(sub(a, \; succ(b))) \; \underline{fi}$$

---

[1] At least in the class of von Neumann machines.

Let $\underline{\lambda}$ be a finite set and the mapping succ be expressed by a transition graph like

Recursion terminates, if and only if $a \geq b$ ('a' can be reached from 'b') and if so, the result is obtained by going 'as many steps' starting from 0 (the range is marked in the example by dotted circles). Only by introducing additional properties, the situation is restricted to common subtraction on the natural numbers.

Abstract objects and operations are comprised in an abstract type or abstract computation structure. Thus, *programming is based on expressing some abstract computation structure operatively in terms of another abstract computation structure*. The term 'operatively' means, that descriptive formulations are to be eliminated - this amounts to the elimination of certain quantifiers - and that non-determinism is eliminated.

But even then, an algorithm is frequently not efficient enough. *Programming also means to meliorate the efficiency of algorithms*. Frequently, appropriate development of the descriptive formulation leads directly to ameliorated operative solutions. Even fully operative and deterministic operations can often be improved. Sometimes, one has to go back to the abstract level and has to do mathematics, for example if one wants to accelerate the Fibonacci sequence by calculating F_{2j}, F_{2j+1} from F_j, F_{j+1} [7].

Another example is addition, defined similarly to subtraction above, which works too slowly. We shall find this later as an example of joint refinement both of operations and objects. *As a rule, meliorating an algorithm suggests or even requires a change in the object structure*. And it is clear that *the longer decisions are postponed, the easier it is to make them at the right moment with optimal operative gain*.

So far, it was not necessary to specify a particular class of machines to work with. Now we come to deal with reality. *Although for strictly applicative languages rather efficient machines can be built, prevailing machine languages are not applicative*.

Here we understand a strictly applicative language to be one in which existential quantifiers and non-determinism is disallowed and only recursion is left. Such languages are fully operative and CHURCH-complete. There exist, of course, theoretical text-replacement machines on this level for any given ensemble of primitive computation structures. Particular computation rules lead to the stack machine, which could be built quite economically [1], and there are other proposals for recursive machines [2].

Prevailing machines ('computers') have a number of restrictions. One is that their machine language does not cope with general recursion. This would not be so bad if they would deal at least with linear recursion, but even this is not so: repetitive recursion is all it can handle, and for doing it in the form of iteration, objects are put in containers, program variables are used.

Such an iterative machine - I would like to call it a Babbage-Zuse machine - could still work with general applicative expressions determining the varying contents of the containers. Only techniques for simplifying the control flow of algorithms would be needed to bring algorithms to this level. Due to the fact that other aspects of the von Neumann machine dominate so much the scene, efforts aiming purely in this direction have started relatively late (COOPER [5]); a recent example is PARTSCH and PEPPER's dealing with a class of recursions to which the Towers of Hanoi problem belongs [8]. Some of these techniques look superficially like arithmetization of the control flow; in fact they amount generally to the introduction of suitable abstract computation structures for the 'computation' of the control flow.

We now come to the deteriorating aspects of the von Neumann-machine. They are: complete atomization and complete sequentialization. Atomization expresses the need to decompose objects and operations into atomic particles of some fixed kind or size, sequentialization the need to perform everything in a strict sequential order. Apart from being straightjackets, complete atomization and complete sequentialization amount to a loss of structure [3] and are harmful in the program development process. *The less atomized and sequentialized a program is, the more easily it is transformed for finding operative meliorations* [4].

---

[1] Why can a large computer not have some of the devices even a pocket calculator can have?

[2] Berkling, Mag̃o, Hewitt.

[3] This is the reason for the difficulties of the decompilation process.

[4] Recent technology would allow to avoid sequentialization without great loss in efficiency, this is not (yet) so for atomization.

One way to keep people from passing too early to complete atomization and sequentialization is the use of a language that disallows them, followed by the use of
a compiler. Every language, however, that provides fully for refinement of object
and operation structures - which is needed for melioration - also allows to use
these vehicles for complete atomization and sequentialization. So all we can do is
to preach discipline. *To keep collateral constructs and the block structure as long
as possible seems to be advisable.*

There is another dangerous aspect of the von Neumann machine, which is of quite
subtle nature: organized store. On the applicative level, selective alteration
of a component of a composite object is cumbersome: changing a stack at the remote
end amounts to unraveling the whole stack, changing an array in some element amounts
to building a new array piecemeal (c.f. DIJKSTRA [9], Ch. 11).

Having introduced variables, the step to organized store is done by replacing every
variable for a composite object by a corresponding composition of variables for the
elements of such an object. In connection with atomization this amounts to building
every variable by composing containers for the atomic particles, called storage cells.
This step makes selective updating a most trivial operation: the variable corresponding to the element to be changed is selected and is updated. Selection of this variable is done at the lowest level by an address, if the composition is an array
of variables, or by a pointer. It allows tremendous operative meliorations. Its
danger, which was recognized only lately (DIJKSTRA, HORNING, GRIES) lies in the fact
that now variables are the result of a selection, i.e. a computing process, and therefore can coincide ('aliasing') without having the same name; assignments are then
to be done with special care. This price is usually worth the operative gain, and
we find organized store in all languages devoted to systems programming and in many
other 'low level' languages, like ALGOL 60 (the Report speaks of 'subscripted variables') or PASCAL. Because of the limitations involved, the step to organized store
(i.e. the use of selective updating) should be the last step in a program development before complete atomization and sequentialization (which then in most cases
can be left to an (optimizing) compiler practically with little loss, or even sometimes with marginal gain).

Having outlined this philosophy of the program evolution process, the consequences
for a language to support this process can be seen.

The applicative core of constructs for defining new operations and new object sets

As a matter of principle we treat object structures and operation structures simultaneously. The fundamental concept for doing so is the computation structure, a
conglomerate of object sets and operations defined on these object sets - mathema-
tically a (usually heterogeneous) algebra. In the extreme, the computation structure
is specified only implicitly by its abstract type, i.e. by its signature and by properties of its operations (abstract computation structure). Usually, object sets
and operations of a computation structure are defined, if not by enumeration, then
in terms of other object sets and other operations, i.e. in terms of other computation structures which are said to be primitive with respect to the computation
structure under consideration - a fundamental principle of modularization.

$\mathbb{N} \equiv (\underline{nat}, succ, 0, \leq)$, the set $\underline{nat}$ of natural numbers together with the
successor operation and 0 (a nullary operation) and the linear ordering $\leq$ is
frequently met as a primitive and can be understood to be an abstract computation
structure defined (uniquely!) by nothing but by the laws its operations obey. The
same holds for $\mathbb{B} \equiv (\underline{bool}, \neg , \wedge, \vee)$, the Boolean algebra of truth values, which
can, however, also be defined by enumeration.

McCARTHY discovered in 1962, that branching on condition - the if-then-else-con-
struct - can play the role of the μ-operator of formal logic. This brings $\mathbb{B}$ into
focus; $\mathbb{B}$ becomes a universal computation structure which will always be involved.
Speaking of operations means that the fundamental concept of function application
is available and that this application can be iterated to form general expressions.
These two principles together with the principle of branching on conditions (defined
with the help of boolean expressions) open already the level of recursive functions.

In practice, one rather dislikes partial functions. So-called assertions can be used
to restrict the domain of definition of operations. Thus, an example is the assertion
$a \geq b$ in

        funct sub ≡ (nat a, nat b : a ≥ b) nat :
                    if a = b then 0
                                else succ(sub(a, succ(b))) fi ,

based on $\mathbb{N}$ as a primitive, which specifies a domain such that sub in total.

Branching on condition, however, is only a (deterministic) special case of choice.
Boolean expressions, together with the quantifiers $\forall$ ('for all') and $\exists$ ('there
exists') can be used (as 'characteristic predicates') to characterize subsets to
which the choice operator some can be applied.

$$\underline{some} \ \lambda \ x \ : \ succ(x) = a$$

is such a choice, meaning intuitively

"some element from the set $\{ \lambda \ x \ : \ succ(x) = a \}$ " .

$\underline{some}$ is undefined for the empty set, and it is convenient to have an operator $\underline{that}$, too, which is only defined on singletons and coincides there with $\underline{some}$. Thus,

$$\underline{funct} \ pred \equiv (\underline{nat} \ a \ : \ a \neq 0) \ \underline{nat} \ :$$
$$\underline{that} \ \underline{nat} \ x \ : \ succ(x) = a$$

is the predecessor function, based on $\mathbb{N}$ as a primitive.

For later reference, we note that the equation for $pred$ can be "solved" with the help of sub and the property that $sub \ (a,o) = a$:

$$\underline{funct} \ pred \equiv (\underline{nat} \ a \ : \ a \neq 0) \ \underline{nat} \ : \ sub(a, \ succ(0))$$

Choices are non-deterministic; they comprise guarded expressions similar to DIJKSTRA's guarded commands :

$$\underline{some} \ \sigma \ x \ : \ (p \wedge x \doteq a) \ \vee \ (q \wedge x \doteq b)$$

may be abbreviated to

$$\underline{if} \ p \ \underline{then} \ a$$
$$[] \ q \ \underline{then} \ b \ \underline{fi}$$

provided p , q are defined [1].

Choices do not define mappings, but only correspondences. The mathematical semantics of recursive definitions involving non-deterministic constructs can be based, however, on a fixpoint theory, too [10]. Such recursive definitions may even result in well-determined functions, as is shown by the example

$$\underline{funct} \ pow \equiv (\mu \ a, \ \underline{nat} \ n) \ \mu \ :$$
$$\underline{if} \ n = 0 \ \underline{then} \ e$$
$$[] \ n > 0 \ \underline{then} \ a \ \rho \ pow(a, \ pred(n))$$
$$[] \ n > 0 \wedge \underline{even} \ n \ \underline{then} \ pow(a \ \rho \ a, \ n/2) \ \underline{fi}$$

---

[1] $\doteq$ denotes the so-called 'strong equality', with $a \doteq b$ being $\underline{true}$ if both a and b are undefined or both are defined and equal, $\underline{false}$ otherwise.

with some computation structure (μ, ρ, e) where ρ is an associative binary operation and e an identity with respect to ρ .

Even essentially non-determinate routines may be useful. An example is given by [1]

$$\underline{funct} \text{ diss} \equiv (\underline{string} \ a : a \neq \lozenge)(\underline{string}, \underline{char}, \underline{string}) :$$
$$\underline{some} \ (\underline{string} \ u, \underline{char} \ t, \underline{string} \ v) : a = u \circ t \circ v$$

for the decomposition of a (non-empty) string into a string, a character and a string. It can be used to solve the following problem uniquely:

$$\underline{funct} \text{ insert} \equiv (\underline{string} \ a, \underline{char} \ x : \text{isordered}(a)) \ \underline{string} :$$
$$\underline{some} \ \underline{string} \ b : \text{isordered}(b) \wedge$$
$$\exists \ (\underline{string} \ u, \underline{string} \ v) : a = u \circ v \wedge b = u \circ x \circ v$$

which is nothing but a formalization of the usual verbal explanation of the sorting problem [2]. The predicate isordered is likewise defined by

$$\underline{funct} \text{ isordered} \equiv (\underline{string} \ a) \ \underline{bool} :$$
$$\underline{if} \ a = \lozenge \ \underline{then} \ \underline{true}$$
$$\underline{else} \ \underline{if} \ \text{rest}(a) = \lozenge \ \underline{then} \ \underline{true}$$
$$\underline{else} \ \underline{if} \ \text{top}(a) > \text{top}(\text{rest}(a))$$
$$\underline{then} \ \underline{false}$$
$$\underline{else} \ \text{isordered}(\text{rest}(a)) \ \underline{fi} \ \underline{fi} \ \underline{fi}$$

All this is based on the primitive computation structure $(\underline{string}, \underline{char}, \circ, \text{top}, \text{rest}, \lozenge)$, where $\lozenge$ denotes the empty string.

A recursive solution for insert , based on diss , is

$$\underline{funct} \text{ insert} \equiv (\underline{string} \ a, \underline{char} \ x : \text{isordered}(a)) \ \underline{string} :$$
$$\underline{if} \ a = \lozenge \ \underline{then} \ x$$
$$\underline{else} \ \underline{if} \ x \leq t \ \underline{then} \ \text{insort}(u, x) \circ t \circ v$$
$$[\!] \ x \geq t \ \underline{then} \ u \circ t \circ \text{insort}(v, x) \ \underline{fi}$$
$$\underline{where} \ (\underline{string} \ u, \underline{char} \ t, \underline{string} \ v) \equiv \text{diss}(a) \ \underline{fi}$$

---

[1] $\lozenge$ denotes the empty string.

[2] Not all problems are *ab origine* defined by a characteristic predicate. In axiomatic number theory, for example, addition and multiplication are essentially defined recursively. In particular, it does not make sense to define a predicate by a characteristic predicate.

Such a solution is often found intuitively and then has to be supplemented by a correctness proof. It can, however, also be derived formally, and this requires just the same amount of labor since every formal derivation reflects a proof and vice versa.

The non-determinate function diss allows several well-determined implementations; anyone may be used and gives still a solution. They can be obtained by imposing further conditions, provided these additional conditions introduce no contradiction. In the example above, the requirement $u = \emptyset$ gives linear sorting, the require-ment $0 \leq \text{length}(u) - \text{length}(v) \leq 1$ gives binary sorting. In insort , one of the guards $x \leq t$ and $x \geq t$ can be restricted to $x < t$, $x > t$ resp. Non-determin-ism is a powerful tool for postponing decisions in the program development process.

This example shows us how "structuring a problem" is in the extreme done by replac-ing a descriptive expression by an operative expression in terms of some other des-criptive expression.

On the other hand, "finding a solution" for a problem specified with the help of some (or that), ∀ and ∃ means finally the elimination of these quantifiers [1].

More general than the specification of a routine by a characteristic predicate is the specification of a whole computation structure by a (set of) characteristic predicate(s), i.e. the definition of an abstract type. To give an example:

```
type $tack ≡ (mode μ) stack μ, nullstack, isnull, top, rest,append :
    mode stack μ ,
    funct stack μ nullstack ,
    funct(stack μ) bool isnull ,
    funct(stack μ s : ¬ isnull(s)) μ top ,
    funct(stack μ s : ¬ isnull(s)) stack μ rest ,
    funct(stack μ, μ) stack μ append ,
    law A : ¬ isnull(s) ⇒ append(rest(s), top(s)) = s ,
    law R : rest(append(s,x)) = s ,
    law T : top(append(s,x)) = x ,
    law E : isnull(nullstack) ,
    law NE : ¬ isnull(append(s,x))                        endoftype
```

---

[1] There is no algorithm, no set of rules for doing this in the general case, and it is even hard to find useful classes for which it can be done mechanically. We consider any attempt to achieve this by heuristic methods, by "artificial intelligence", practically worthless.

The computation structure $tack (whose parameter μ denotes some primitive object set) comprises the object set <u>stack</u> μ and the operations isnull, append, top rest , nullstack and is characterized by the laws A , R , T , E, NE . The signature of $tack is expressed by a bipartite graph, the 'signature graph':

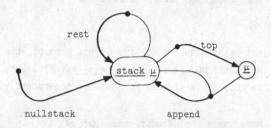

Apart from the requirement that the predicates be not contradictory, practical considerations suggest the requirement that, roughly speaking, the operations of the computation structure, based on nullary operations and primitive object sets, map *onto* the object sets of the computation structure, thus "freely generating" them ('generation principle', a requirement towards uniqueness), and *into* the primitive object sets (GUTTAG's completeness) [1]. In our example, the premise ¬ isnull(s) in A guarantees completeness, while without E , the definition is not monomorphic - although the generation principle selects the "smallest model".

Stacks and their variants: queues, decks, sequences , and object sets of cascade-type: LISP-like lists and trees have so far been the preferred examples of abstract computation structures; but there are many more interesting and practically important examples, like graph-building computation structures [11].

Abstract specifications of computation structures can be transformed into concrete definitions, replacing (partly or totally) the characteristic predicates by (in general recursive) definitions of object sets and operations.

---

[1] More precisely, one considers the set of all terms the outermost operation of which has as its range some object set of the computation structure or some primitive object set. In the first case, the object set in question is identified with the corresponding set of terms ('generated'), in the second case it is requested that equality of any such term with some object from the corresponding primitive object set can be derived from the postulated predicates.

To this end, MCCARTHY again has observed in 1963 that it suffices to have the operations of the (non-associative) direct product

$$(\mu_1, \mu_2, \ldots, \mu_n)$$

of n object sets and of the (associative) direct sum

$$\mu_1 \mid \mu_2$$

of two (disjoint) object sets; with the nullary direct product, the 0-tuple, denoted by $\Diamond$, forming the universal object set mode empty ≡ { $\Diamond$ } . Direct products and direct sums are used in mode declarations, for example non-recursively in

$$\text{mode int} \equiv (\text{nat } credit, \text{ nat } debit)$$

which can be used to construct integers (together with defining an equivalence relation = on int), a rather trivial example. A recursive mode declaration is used in the following sample concretization of $tack ($\mu$) with μ as a primitive:

⌈ mode stack μ ≡ empty | (stack μ trunk, μ item) ,
funct nullstack ≡ stack μ : $\Diamond$,
funct isnull ≡ (stack μ s) bool : s = nullstack ,
funct top ≡ (stack μ s : ¬ isnull(s)) μ : item of s ,
funct rest ≡ (stack μ s : ¬ isnull(s)) stack μ : trunk of s ,
funct append ≡ (stack μ s , μ x) stack μ:(s, x)   ⌋

Here, trunk of and item of are selector functions, defined by the notation (stack μ trunk, μ item) for the direct product; stack μ:(·, ·) is the corresponding constructor. Properties A , R , T , E , NE are wellknown properties of the direct product. For transformation techniques in this area, see [20] .

Less trivial examples are the bounded stack Bstack (μ, n) or cascade-type ('tree-like') computation structures based on

$$\text{mode casc } \mu \equiv \text{empty} \mid (\text{casc } \mu \text{ left}, \mu \text{ node}, \text{casc } \mu \text{ right}) .$$

A given type does by its signature Σ and properties E not always monomorphically characterize computation structures [1]; we may speak of a model of (Σ, E) as "some model of that type", which is again a non-deterministic construct. Again, non-determinism helps to postpone decisions in the design process.

---

[1] There are certain distinguished models, the "initial algebra" and the "terminal algebra"; if they coincide the type is monomorphic.

Constructs defined by transformations

A few kinds of basic transformations of constructs within the applicative core are
to be listed. One is UNFOLD, the substitution of a call by the body of the function
called, which has to be treated with care in non-deterministic situations, and re-
ciprocally FOLD, which has to be handled carefully with respect to termination.

A further example of a basic (one-sided) transformation is RESTRICT, the
restriction of the choice set :

$$\frac{\underline{some}\ \mu\ x\ :\ p(x)}{\underline{some}\ \mu\ x\ :\ q(x)}\qquad \left\{ (\forall\ \underline{\mu}\ x\ :\ q(x) \Rightarrow p(x)) \land (\exists\ \underline{\mu}\ x\ :\ p(x) \Rightarrow \exists\ \underline{\mu}\ x\ :\ q(x)) \right.$$

which in the extreme allows transition to a choice the choice set of which is a
singleton. This is the case where we may write

$$\underline{that}\ \mu\ x\ :\ q(x)\ .$$

Guarded expressions are (see above) notational shorthand for some choices which are
met frequently. This is the first example of a defining transformation.
The alternative (<u>if</u>-<u>then</u>-<u>else</u>-<u>fi</u> construction)

$$\underline{if}\ p\ \underline{then}\ a\ \underline{else}\ b\ \underline{fi}$$

is then defined as the exclusive choice

$$\underline{if}\ \ p\ \underline{then}\ a$$
$$[\!]\ \neg\ p\ \underline{then}\ b\ \underline{fi}$$

The commutativity of guarded expressions and especially the possibility to ex-
change the two branches of an <u>if</u>-<u>then</u>-<u>else</u>-<u>fi</u> - construction under negation
of the condition follow from the definition of guarded expressions using pro-
perties of the universal computation structure ⍰B.

The example of isordered suggests the introduction of McCarthy's sequential alternative in the form

$$\begin{array}{ll}
\underline{if}\ a = 0 & \underline{then}\ \underline{true}\\
\underline{elsf}\ rest(a) = 0 & \underline{then}\ \underline{true}\\
\underline{elsf}\ top(a) > top(rest(a)) & \underline{then}\ \underline{false}\\
& \underline{else}\ isordered(rest(a))\ \underline{fi}
\end{array}$$

with an obvious defining transformation. Now commutativity of the branches is lost.

In recent years, we have even seen the treatment of most of the constructs of programming languages outside the applicative core by mathematical semantics ('denotational semantics') and thus a reduction of these concepts to the applicative core.
If we wish to base programming on program transformation, it would be natural to
define these constructs directly by transformations from and to the core.

Indeed, in a number of cases this is not only possible but quite simple and practical.
An example is the introduction of a block structure through subordinate routines and
auxiliary object declarations.

Let f and g be two different routines out of a system, and let the routine f
have the parameters x_1 , x_2 , ..., x_n .

The parameter x_i of f is said to be *constant* if a call $f(a_1$, a_2 , ... $a_n)$
leads to no other calls of f than   ones which have the object a_i in the
i-th parameter position. If now f is called in some expression within g , we can
'suppress' the parameter x_i of f and 'subordinate' (a copy of) f to the expression; x_i becomes 'global' for this 'scope', which is to be indicated by block
parentheses begin end or rather ⌈ ⌋ for short. This process of parameter suppression is normally done subconciously by a programmer who is familiar with mathematical notation. In a similar way, a system of routines can be subordinated.

Take for example the system of two routines standing side by side (with ≤ , -
and 0 as primitives)

```
funct gcd ≡ (nat a, nat b) nat :
    if b = 0 then a else gcd(b, mod(a, b)) fi ,
funct mod ≡ (nat c, nat d) nat :
    if c < d then c else mod(c - d, d) fi
```

Here, the second parameter d in mod is constant. If we subordinate mod to the
body of gcd , d may be suppressed in a reduced mod' and replaced by a global
parameter.

We obtain as body of gcd a *block with a routine declaration,*

$$\underline{funct} \; gcd \equiv (\underline{nat} \; a, \; \underline{nat} \; d) \; \underline{nat} :$$
$$\lceil \underline{if} \; d = 0 \; \underline{then} \; a \; \underline{else} \; gcd(d, \; mod'(a)) \; \underline{fi}$$
$$\underline{where} \; \underline{funct} \; mod' \equiv (\underline{nat} \; c) \; \underline{nat} :$$
$$\underline{if} \; c < d \; \underline{then} \; c \; \underline{else} \; mod'(c-d) \; \underline{fi} \; \rfloor$$

or even more localised

$$\underline{funct} \; gcd \equiv (\underline{nat} \; a, \; \underline{nat} \; d) \; \underline{nat} :$$
$$\underline{if} \; d = 0 \; \underline{then} \; a \; \underline{else} \; \lceil gcd(d, \; mod'(a))$$
$$\underline{where} \; \underline{funct} \; mod' \equiv (\underline{nat} \; c) \; \underline{nat} :$$
$$\underline{if} \; c < d \; \underline{then} \; c \; \underline{else} \; mod'(c-d) \; \underline{fi} \rfloor \; \underline{fi}$$

Moreover, using again for short $\lceil$ for $\underline{begin}$ and $\rfloor$ for $\underline{end}$, *a block with a collective object declaration* [1]

$$\underline{r} : \lceil (\underline{m}_1 \; x_1 \; , \; ..., \; \underline{m}_n \; x_n) \equiv (E_1 \; , \; ..., \; E_n)$$
$$\underline{within} \; G(x_1 \; , \; ..., \; x_n) \qquad\qquad \rfloor$$

is by definition a shorthand for the application of the routine

$$(\underline{m}_1 \; x_1 \; , \; ..., \; \underline{m}_n \; x_n) \; \underline{r} : G(x_1 \; , \; ..., \; x_n)$$

to the argument set $(E_1 \; , \; ..., \; E_n)$.

Note that the block with parameterless subordinated routines

$$\lceil G(f_1 \; ... \; f_n)$$
$$\underline{where} \; \underline{funct} \; f_1 \equiv \underline{m}_1' : E_1$$
$$\underline{funct} \; f_2 \equiv \underline{m}_2 : E_2$$
$$\vdots$$
$$\underline{funct} \; f_n \equiv \underline{m}_n : E_n \; \rfloor$$

is by definition essentially different from the above construct; G may involve repeated calls of f_1 , ... f_n . It is, of course, always possible to replace an object by a (parameterless) routine, but the converse is only true if $E_1, ..., E_n$ are determinate.

---

[1] The mode specification $\underline{r}$: is usually suppressed.

Object declarations may be used to extract common subexpressions; in any case they can serve to express more explicitly the natural 'stream of evaluation' that results from a 'call by value' computation rule [1]. Iterated use of the transformation

$$f(g(x))$$

$$\downarrow$$

$$\lceil \lambda\, y \equiv g(x)\ \underline{within}\ f(y)\, \rfloor$$

establishes isolation of nested calls. A notational convenience, somewhat similar to the 'sequential alternative', is to write (with an obvious defining transformation)

$$\lceil \underline{real}\ h1 \equiv a - 1\ ;\ \underline{real}\ h2 \equiv h1 \times t - 3\ ;\ \underline{real}\ h3 \equiv h2 \times t - 5\ ;\ h3\, \rfloor$$

instead of the nested, right-aligning construct

$$\lceil \underline{real}\ h1 \equiv t - 1\ \underline{within}\ \lceil \underline{real}\ h2 \equiv h1 \times t - 3\ \underline{within}\ \lceil \underline{real}\ h3 \equiv h2 \times t - 5\ \underline{within}\ h3\, \rfloor\, \rfloor\, \rfloor$$

which isolates the Horner operations of $((t - 1) \times t - 3) \times t - 5$.

The next logical step is the introduction of program variables as a sort of re-usable object names. This step leads definitely outside the applicative level. It can be done by a defining transformation, too. Details of this approach will be found in a forthcoming dissertation by P. PEPPER. It has to be demonstrated that this transformation allows to define the classical 'state-oriented' semantics of constructs with program variables, thus establishing correspondence to the FLOYD-HOARE predicate relations and to DIJSTRA's predicate transformation.

The crucial point is, of course, the phenomenon of repetition and the way it is reflected as iteration when working with program variables. The transformation

```
funct F ≡ (m A) n :                 funct F ≡ (m A) n :
  if P1(A) then F(E1(A))              ⌈var m a := A ; G where
  ▯ P2(A) then E2(A)      fi            proc G ≡ n :
                                           if P1(a) then a := E1(a); G
                                           ▯ P2(a) then E2(a)            fi ⌋
```

---

[1] DE ROEVER [12] has given this alternative to the classical fixpoint theory as used by MANNA; in it the leftmost-innermost ('call by value') computation rule is a safe rule.

(where $P1 \lor P2 = \underline{true}$), shows the essential steps in going from a purely applicative, recursive construct for F to iteration: introduction of a program variable
helps to isolate the call of F . Next, the constant parameter can be suppressed,
which leads to the parameterless procedure G .

This is the essence of the metamorphosis, and what follows is merely notational. It
is widely accepted to write iteration in the <u>while</u> -form; the obvious definitory
transformation results in (*) below. Combining an idea of DIJKSTRA [9] with the
<u>leave</u> -construct already mentioned in [13], an alternative notation (**) can be
used:

```
        proc G ≡ n :                            proc G ≡ n :
(*)   ⌈while P1(a) do a := E1(a) od ;   (**)   do if P1(a) then a := E1(a)
        E2(a)                    ⌋           ▯ P2(a) then E2(a) leave fi od
```

It offers more flexibility, in particular when the recursion occurs together with
multiple branching; possible non-determinism is preserved. It comprises also the
<u>until</u> -form of iteration and the " $(n + 1/2)$ -times iteration". The <u>while</u> -form,
on the other hand, is natural in the case of an <u>if-then-else-fi</u> -situation, i.e.
if in the example above $P2 = \neg P1$. In general, the <u>while</u> -form (*) is a deterministic implementation.

The general <u>do</u> ... <u>od</u> -construct (**) above is a shorthand with the obvious meaning of repetition until leaving. This can be indicated also by interpreting the call
of the parameterless procedure G as a jump to the beginning of G ; a further jump
<u>return</u> , replacing <u>leave</u> , ends the procedure. Thus

```
        proc G ≡ n :
(***)   g : if P1(a) then a := E1(a) ; goto g
            ▯ P2(a) then E2(a) return          fi
```

This gives the loop - form of iteration, a <u>return</u> immediately before the <u>fi</u> being usually suppressed. In this way, systems of recursive definitions can be treated
as well. Whichever of these three notations is used, recursion can be replaced by
iteration fully if and only if every call of a procedure of the system is a *plain
call* [1], i.e. the last action of the surrounding body. A jump is a notational variant
of a plain call of a parameterless procedure - a special case where the calling
mechanism can be utterly simplified (The BLISS compiler did already recognize this
situation).

---

[1]   Germ. "schlichter Prozedurwechsel".

Systems which fulfil the aforementioned requirement are called repetitive. Non-repetitive systems can always be transformed into repetitive ones at the expense of introducing stacks; frequently one can do better, however. To discuss special techniques for this [14] is not possible in the frame of this paper.

Transformation of computation structures

Transformation of computation structures involves not only the modification of routines, but also the modification of mode declarations.

'Structuring the problem' may mean in the extreme to concretize some abstract computation structure in terms of some other abstract computation structure. An example with a situation quite similar to the above treatment of insort with the help of diss is the concretization of the abstract computation structure $N \equiv (nat, succ, 0)$ (the characteristic properties of which, the "Peano axioms", are well known) with the help of the abstract computation structure $\$tack(\mu)$ for some one-element set : $\underline{mode} \ \mu \equiv \{I\}$,

> $\underline{mode} \ \underline{nat} \equiv \underline{stack} \ \{I\}$,
> $\underline{funct} \ succ \equiv (\underline{stack} \ \{I\} \ a) \ \underline{stack} \ \{I\} : append(a, \ I)$
> $\underline{funct} \ 0 \equiv \underline{stack} \ \{I\} : nullstack$

Compared with the clumsy solution given above, pred can now be defined simply by

> $\underline{funct} \ pred \equiv (\underline{stack} \ \{I\} \ a : \neg \ isnull(a)) \ \underline{stack} \ \{I\} : rest(a)$

In such a way, an appropriate change of object structure often simplifies operations. As another example, let us use a stack of binary elements[1] {0, L} for the concretization of natural numbers.

Addition in Nat , which is defined by

> $\underline{funct} \ add \equiv (\underline{nat} \ a, \underline{nat} \ b) \ \underline{nat} :$
> $\quad \underline{if} \ b = 0 \ \underline{then} \ a$
> $\qquad \underline{else} \ succ(add(a, pred(b))) \underline{fi}$

uses pred, which works efficiently in the $\$tack(\{I\})$ implementation. However, with the help of a unary operation double ,

> $\underline{funct} \ double \equiv (\underline{nat} \ a \ ) \ \underline{nat} : add(a, a)$

[1] The English reader may forgive me for using symbols introduced first by KONRAD ZUSE.

and its inverse half defined for even a , using the properties (which can be
proved formally)

$$double(add(m, n)) = add(double(m), double(n))$$

and commutativity of add , the number of recursive invocations of add can be decreased drastically:

<u>funct</u> add ≡ (<u>nat</u> a, <u>nat</u> b) <u>nat</u> :
    <u>if</u> b = 0 <u>then</u> a
    [] a = 0 <u>then</u> b
    [] b ≠ 0 ∧ a ≠ 0 <u>then</u> <u>if</u> even(a) ∧ even(b) <u>then</u> double(add(half(a),half(b)))
                    [] ¬ even(b)   <u>then</u> succ(add(a, pred(b)))
                    [] ¬ even(a)   <u>then</u> succ(add(pred(a), b))   <u>fi</u>[1]

This suggests a change from Nat to $Stack(\{0, L\})$, where the operation double ,
the predicate even, and the operation half are trivially implemented by

<u>funct</u> double ≡ (<u>stack</u> {0, L} a) <u>stack</u> {0, L} : append(a, 0) ,
<u>funct</u> even   ≡ (<u>stack</u> {0, L} a) <u>bool</u> : <u>if</u> isnull(a) <u>then</u> <u>true</u> <u>else</u> top(a) = 0 <u>fi</u>,
<u>funct</u> half   ≡ (<u>stack</u> {0, L} a : even(a)) <u>stack</u> {0, L} : <u>if</u> isnull(a) <u>then</u> a
                                                <u>else</u> rest(a) <u>fi</u>

For the connoisseur, it should be remarked that not only $Stack(\{1\})$ is isomorphic
to the term algebra of (succ, 0) , but $Stack(\{0, L\})$ is also related to the term
algebra of (succ, double, 0) , as is demonstrated by comparing e.g.

$$\underline{succ(}\underline{double(}\underline{succ(}\underline{double(}\underline{succ(}\underline{double(}\underline{double(}\underline{succ(}0)))))))$$
$$\quad L \quad\quad\quad L \quad\quad L \quad\quad\quad\; L \quad\quad\;\; O \quad\;\; L$$

with LOLLL .

The abstract stacks used here may be concretized, on the other hand, by using
McCarthy's recursive definition. This corresponds to replacing functions defined
by a predicate by functions defined recursively.

---

[1]   Note that with <u>true</u> instead of the guards ¬ even(b) and ¬ even(a) , the
    algorithm would be correct, too; the guards speed up the execution, however.

To give a more complicated example, we define an abstract computation structure Grex of aggregates [1]:

> <u>type</u> Grex ≡ (<u>mode</u> μ, <u>mode</u> <u>index</u>) <u>grex</u> μ, put, get, init :
> > <u>mode</u> <u>grex</u> μ ,
> > <u>funct</u> (<u>grex</u> μ, <u>index</u>, μ) <u>grex</u> μ put ,
> > <u>funct</u> (<u>grex</u> μ, <u>index</u>) μ get ,
> > <u>funct</u> <u>grex</u> μ vac ,
> > <u>law</u> S : get(put(a, i, x), j) = <u>if</u> i = j <u>then</u> x
> > > ▯ i ≠ j <u>then</u> get(a, j) <u>fi</u> ,
> >
> > <u>law</u> U : get(vac, j) = ω ,
> > <u>law</u> E : put(a, i, x) ≠ vac ,
> > <u>law</u> I : put(a, i, get(a, i)) = a   endoftype

This structure describes a very archaic form of arrays, of indexed sets with vac being the vacuous set *ab origine*; put and get are operations which are in practice frequently used in connection with background storage (in data bank systems: 'direct access'). The domain of get is defined recursively by

> <u>funct</u> isaccessible ≡ (<u>grex</u> μ a, <u>index</u> i) <u>bool</u> :
> > <u>if</u> a = vac <u>then</u> <u>false</u>
> > ▯ a ≠ vac <u>then</u> (<u>grex</u> μ a', <u>index</u> i') ≡ <u>some</u> <u>grex</u> μ b, <u>index</u> j :
> > > ∃ μ x' : a = put(b, j, x')
> >
> > <u>within</u>   i = i' ∨ isaccessible(a', i)   <u>fi</u>

A structure Flex , which comprises in abstract form what one usually understands to be a (one-sided) flexible array, is defined as follows [2] (<u>index</u> is now a *well-ordered* set with least element min)

> <u>type</u> Flex ≡ (<u>mode</u> μ, <u>mode</u> <u>index</u>) <u>flex</u> μ, init, isinit, ext, rem, hib, alt, sel:
> <u>mode</u> <u>flex</u> μ ,
> <u>funct</u> <u>flex</u> μ init ,
> <u>funct</u> (<u>flex</u> μ) <u>bool</u> isinit ,
> <u>funct</u> (<u>flex</u> μ, μ) <u>flex</u> μ ext ,
> <u>funct</u> (<u>flex</u> μ f : ¬ isinit(f)) <u>flex</u> μ rem ,
> <u>funct</u> (<u>flex</u> μ f : ¬ isinit(f)) <u>index</u> hib ,
> <u>funct</u> (<u>flex</u> μ f, <u>index</u> i, μ : ¬ isinit(f) ∧ i ≤ hib(f)) <u>flex</u> μ alt ,
> <u>funct</u> (<u>flex</u> μ f, <u>index</u> i : ¬ isinit(f) ∧ i ≤ hib(f)) μ sel ,

---

[1] Latin *grex*: flock. GUTTAG: Hoare-like array (HOARE 1973).

[2] For simplicity we use here the one-sided half of Dijkstra's ARRAYs: [9], Ch. 11

law I   : isinit(init) ,

law NI   : ¬ isinit(ext(f,m)) ∧ ¬ isinit(alt(f,i,m))

law HIB1 : hib(ext(f,m)) = if isinit(f) then min
         ▯ ¬ isinit(f) then succ(hib(f)) fi ,

law HIB2 : ¬ isinit(f) ∧ i ≤ hib(f) ⇒ hib(rem(f)) = pred(hib(f)) ,

law HIB3 : ¬ isinit(f) ∧ i ≤ hib(f) ⇒ hib(alt(f,i,m)) = hib(f) ,

law IR   : ¬ isinit(f) ⇒ isinit(rem(f)) = (hib(f) = min) ,

law SEL1 : ¬ isinit(f) ∧ i ≤ succ(hib(f)) ⇒
    sel(ext(f,m), i) = if i = succ(hib(f)) then m
          ▯ i ≠ succ(hib(f)) then sel(f,i) fi ,

law SEL2 : ¬ isinit(f) ∧ i ≤ pred(hib(f)) ⇒
    sel(rem(f) , i) = sel(f, i) ,

law SEL3 : ¬ isinit(f) ∧ i ≤ hib(f) ∧ j ≤ hib(f) ⇒
    sel(alt(f,i,m), j) = if i = j then m
         ▯ i ≠ j then sel(f, j) fi   endoftype

Now, a concretization of Flex in terms of Grex is possible; hib is carried along in the object structure explicitly:

⌈ mode flex μ ≡ (index p, grex μ d) ,
  funct init ≡ flex μ : (ꞷ , vac) ,
  funct isinit ≡ (flex μ a) bool : p of a = ꞷ ,
  funct ext ≡ (flex μ a, μ x) flex μ :
    if isinit(a) then (min, put(d of a, min, x))
        else (succ(p of a), put(d of a, succ(p of a), x))fi,
  funct rem ≡ (flex μ a:¬ isinit(a)) flex μ :
    if p of a = min then init else (pred(p of a), d of a) fi ,
  funct hib ≡ (flex μ a) index : p of a ,
  funct alt ≡ (flex μ a, index i, μ x : ¬ isinit(a) ∧ i ≤ hib(a)) flex μ a :
    (p of a, put(d of a, i, x)) ,
  funct sel ≡ (flex μ a, index i : ¬ isinit(a) ∧ i ≤ hib(a)) μ :
    get(d of a, i)   ⌋

In turn, a concretization of Stack in terms of Flex is possible: init , ext , rem , and sel applied to hib , resp., yield nullstack , append , rest and top, resp.. Bounded stacks can be implemented in this way, too.

Thus, several interesting types of "linear" object structures are reduced to Grex(μ, index) . Implementations 'in bounded homogeneous storage' can be obtained by first restricting

       Grex(μ, index)

to

$$\mathbb{G}rex\ (\mu,\ \underline{index}\ [lwb\ ..\ upb])$$

and then passing to

$$\underline{index}\ [lwb\ ..\ upb]\ \underline{array}\ \mu\ ,$$

the elementary rowing, i.e. to classical arrays (vac is represented by a row all elements of which are ω). However, this makes put and thus alt into complicated operations, since they involve now selective alteration.

In contrast to this "row" technique of implementing linear object structures is the "list" technique. It uses a representation for $\mathbb{F}$lex in terms of $stack :

```
⌈ mode flex μ ≡ (index p, stack μ d) ,
   funct init  ≡ flex μ : (ω , nullstack) ,
   funct isinit≡ (flex μ a) bool : p of a = ω ,
   funct ext   ≡ (flex μ a, μ x) flex μ : (if isinit(a) then min
                                                     else succ(p of a) fi ,
                                      append(d of a, x)                   ) ,
   funct rem   ≡ (flex μ a : ¬ isinit(a)) flex μ :
                    if p of a = min then init
                              else (pred(p of a), rest(d of a)) fi ,
   funct hib   ≡ (flex μ a) index : p of a ,
   funct alt   ≡ (flex μ a, index i, μ x : ¬ isinit(a) ∧ i ≤ hib(a)) flex μ :
                    ⌈(p of a, alt1(d of a, p of a)) where
                     funct alt1 ≡ (stack μ s, index j) stack μ :
                              if j = i then append(rest(s), x)
                                    else alt1(rest(s), pred(j)) fi ⌋ ,
   funct sel   ≡ (flex μ a, index i : ¬ isinit(a) ∧ i ≤ hib(a)) μ :
                    if i = hib(a) then top(d of a)
                              else sel(rem(a), i)                fi        ⌋
```

The final step, which corresponds somewhat to the introduction of $\underline{goto}$s in routines, is the implementation of recursive modes as Lists (with capital L in the sense of KNUTH) with the help of pointers. The transformation is done quite mechanically; we demonstrate this again for $stack :

We represent $stack\ \mu$, defined by

$$\underline{mode}\ \underline{stack}\ \mu \equiv \underline{empty}\ |(\underline{stack}\ \mu\ trunk,\ \mu\ item)$$

by pointers either to $\langle\rangle$ or to a pair $(\underline{stack}\ \mu\ trunk,\ \mu\ item)$.

(A pointer to the 0-tuple $\langle\rangle$ is universally denoted by $\underline{nil}$).

We then have in two steps

mode <u>stack</u> μ ≡ <u>pt stack'</u> μ

mode <u>stack'</u> μ ≡ <u>empty</u> |(<u>stack</u> μ trunk, μ item)

Whenever a stack is formed by the constructor <u>stack</u> μ:(·,·) , we denote the
generation of a pointer to that object by <u>newpt</u>, like <u>newpt stack'</u> μ:(a, x) .
The transcription of append then reads

<u>funct</u> append ≡ (<u>pt stack'</u> μ a, μ x) <u>pt stack'</u>μ : <u>newpt stack'</u>μ:(a, x) ,

top and rest are simply transcribed as

<u>funct</u> top ≡ (<u>pt stack'</u> μ a : a ≠ <u>nil</u>) μ : item <u>of</u> a
<u>funct</u> rest ≡ (<u>pt stack'</u> μ a : a ≠ <u>nil</u>) <u>pt stack'</u> μ : trunk <u>of</u> a ,

nullstack is represented by <u>nil</u> and

<u>funct</u> isnull ≡ (<u>stack</u> μ a) <u>bool</u> : a = nullstack
becomes
<u>funct</u> isnull ≡ (<u>pt stack'</u> μ a) <u>bool</u> : a = <u>nil</u> .

The introduction of pointers, however, presupposes that another transition is made
before: variables for composite objects are represented by a corresponding composition of variables for these objects. This means the introduction of containers,
of organized store. It transforms selective alteration, which is a complicated operation on the applicative level, to selective updating, which is a simple operation.
Selective updating, however, in connection with pointers can be used to replace certain recursions over composite objects by a simple operation. This can be demonstrated
by the operation stalk ,

<u>funct</u> stalk ≡ (μ x, <u>stack</u> μ s) <u>stack</u> μ :
             <u>if</u> isnull(s) <u>then</u> append(nullstack, x)
                     <u>else</u> append(stalk(x, rest(s)), top(s)) <u>fi</u>

which raises a stack at the remote end. Thus, in the iteration

<u>funct</u> convert ≡ (<u>nat</u> A) <u>stack</u> {O, L} :
    ⌈(<u>var nat</u> a, <u>var stack</u> {O, L} s) := (A, nullstack) ;
      <u>while</u> a ≠ 0 <u>do</u> (a,s) := <u>if</u> even(a) <u>then</u> (a/2, stalk(O, s))
                              <u>else</u> ((a − 1)/2, stalk(L, s)) <u>fi od</u> ;

stalk would perpetually run up and down the stack. Using pointers, selective updating
and a pointer variable ss for s as well as an auxiliary pointer variable tt ,
we can replace the particle s := stalk(x, s) by

$$\lceil \underline{pt} \ \underline{stack}' \ \mu \ f \equiv \underline{newpt} \ \underline{stack}' \ \mu : (\underline{nil}, x) \ ; \ next \ \underline{of} \ tt := f \ ; \ tt := f \ \rfloor$$

except for the first step, which is simply

$$\lceil \underline{pt} \ \underline{stack}' \ \mu \ f \equiv \underline{newpt} \ \underline{stack}' \ \mu : (\underline{nil}, x) \ ; \ ss := f \ ; \ tt := f \ \rfloor$$

Finally ss delivers the result $f^{(1)}$, the pointer generated in the first incarnation,all other pointers being used only internally.
For a more detailed discussion, in particular of the pointer representation of 'infinite objects' like ring lists and doubly linked lists, see [15].
For the "row" technique mentioned above, the introduction of containers means transition
to $\underline{index}$ [lwb..upb] $\underline{array}$ $\underline{var}$ μ . It turns put and alt into simple updating
operations on the selected containers.

Verification versus transformation

Verification techniques, based on the FLOYD - HOARE semantics and   DIJKSTRA's predicate transformers, generally work with program variables and usually require
purely iterative situations. If the problem specification is given recursively by a
repetitive system, then the iterative form is a mere transliteration of it. If such
an iterative form falls from heaven, (or is given to a student as an exercise), then
finding the proof amounts to finding "the invariant condition" and this may be quite a
puzzle for the naive programmer. But real programs do not fall from heaven.

Clearly, the postcondition from which to start the verification process corresponds
to the characteristic predicate of the problem description, and the precondition which
stands at the end of the verification process corresponds to an assertion for the descriptive construct.

Moreover, if (as mentioned above) the program and its verification are developed step
by step, there is a corresponding program transformation, too, and vice versa. It may
depend on taste and prejudice what form one prefers. As in mathematics, verification
of a result that is obtained somewhat informally can be technically shorter then the
correct derivation. In particular, verifying that a program fulfils some assertion
can be done 'streamlined', avoiding many corners and eddies into which the bulky program transformation mechanism is going.

We think, however, that derivation of a solution by program transformations, as sketched above, has its merits, too: not only can it be done in one and the same language, it naturally leads to structured solutions and should please the followers of structured programming. It allows in particular to follow several alleys to the solution, side by side.

Program development by stepwise transformation differs from 'stepwise refinement' in the sense of WIRTH and DIJKSTRA in an essential point: "In stepwise refinement, the outline structure of the program, notably the form of recursion/iteration, is fixed, being further specified at each step and never subsequently altered" (BURSTALL [16]). Obviously, the transformational approach does not exclude this, but is much more flexible and powerful.

The transformation system

The design of the language described here (see also [17]) was influenced by the transformations to be accomplished. This created a tendency to make the syntactical and semantical structures of the language simple and transparent, avoiding ornaments and dark corners - important enough in view of the wide spectrum of the language.

Furthermore, the natural idea to introduce the semantics via the transformations turned out to be fruitful. With respect to object declarations, this goes back to LANDIN [3]. Carrying on along this line PEPPER could show how to introduce variables - see a forthcoming thesis [18]. Similar attempts for the introduction of pointers based on [15] (MÜLLER) and of concurrent processes (BROY) are under way. This "transformational semantics" is based upon a core language of simple applicative nature extended to include non-determinism and existential quantifiers like some (GNATZ, WIRSING, BROY). Furthermore, abstract types and computational structures had to be included (PARTSCH, PEPPER, WIRSING, BROY, DOSCH) - the theoretical background for these investigations was to be found in algebra and logic.

We believe that CIP-L contains excellent material for a programming language in the ALGOL tradition, it exceeds both ALGOL 60 and PASCAL in clarity and expressiveness (recursive object structures!). As a side effect, our investigations gave us a deeper understanding of fundamental algorithmic concepts - e.g. the role of the alias ban. These educational aspects will be reflected in a textbook which is about to appear ([19]).

Program development by transformations has to accomplish
(i)   the elimination of mere specifications,
(ii)   operative amelioration which increases efficiency
(iii)   adaption to make best use of the special capabilities of a given machine.
The strategy for achieving this includes 'postponed decisions'; non-determinism and
abstract types are essential instruments in this process.

Program development by transformation can be done mentally, supported by paper and
pencil. Having done so with a great number of examples, we developed a good feeling
of how a programmed support system can be helpful: it takes over the clerical work,
including keeping a record of the development history. Its main advantage seems to
be that all steps can be checked mechanically, and thus genuinely correct versions
will be obtained. The effort may be too expensive when only a dirty one-time program
(throw-away program) is needed - whatever use this may have. The effort is worthwile
for programs that run for a long time, in particular if their reliability is subject
to economic or public requirements.

This includes the fabrication of large programs which are to be placed on one chip in
permanent superhigh-integration technique, one day big enough to comprise a small
compiler or a building block of an operating system, not to speak of arithmetic units
and storage communication units.
It also concerns the fabrication of software which in the public interest should do
exactly what it is intended for and nothing else, i.e. in connection with privacy
regulations.

We realize that it will take a long time until practical results with the programmed
system can be expected. Nevertheless, we see no other way to arrive at techniques
allowing some day the production of quality software - transformation and verification
techniques here going hand in hand.

References

[1] J.N. Buxton, B. Randell(eds.): Software engineering techniques. NATO Scientific Affairs Division, Bruxelles, 1970

[2] F.L. Bauer, G. Goos: Informatik - Eine einführende Übersicht. 2 Vols. 2nd ed. Springer, 1973, 1974

[3] P.J. Landin: The next 700 programming languages. Comm. ACM 9, 157-166 (1966)

[4] D. Scott: Data types as lattices. SIAM Journal of Computing 5, 522-587 (1976)

[5] D.C. Cooper: The equivalence of certain computations. Computer Journal 9, 45-52 (1966)

[6] F.L. Bauer: Programming Languages under Educational and under Professional Aspects (Russian). In: Proceedings 2nd All-Union Conference on Programming, Novosibirsk, February 1970. See also this volume.

[7] E.W. Dijkstra: In honour of Fibonacci. EWD654. This volume.

[8] H. Partsch, P. Pepper: A family of rules for recursion removal related to the Towers of Hanoi problem. Institut für Informatik der Technischen Universität München, Rep. No. 7612, 1976. Also: Information Processing Letters, 5, 1974 - 1977 (1976).

[9] E.W. Dijkstra: A discipline of programming. Prentice-Hall, Englewood Cliffs, N.J., 1976

[10] H. Egli: A mathematical model for nondeterministic computations. ETH Zürich, 1975

[11] T.A. Matzner: Entwicklung eines Algorithmus für Depth-first-search mit einer einfachen Anwendung. In: Algorithmen und Objektstrukturen. Institut für Informatik der Technischen Universität München, Interner Bericht, 1978

[12] W.P. de Roever: Operational, mathematical and axiomatized semantics for recursive procedures and data structures. Mathematisch Centrum, Amsterdam, 1974

[13] W.A. Wulf, D.B. Russell, A.N. Habermann: BLISS: A language for systems programming. Comm. ACM 14, 780-790 (1971)

[14] F.L. Bauer, H. Partsch, P. Pepper, H. Wössner: Techniques for program development. In: Software Engineering Techniques. Infotech State of the Art Report 34. Maidenhead: Infotech International 1977, p. 25-30

[15] F.L. Bauer: Detailization and lazy evaluation, infinite objects and pointer representation. This volume.

[16] R.M. Burstall, M. Feather: Program Development by Transformations: an Overview. In: Proc. Toulouse CREST Course on Programming 1978, to appear.

[17] F.L. Bauer, M. Broy, R. Gnatz, W. Hesse, B. Krieg-Brückner, H. Partsch, P. Pepper, H. Wössner: Towards a Wide Spectrum Language to Support Program Specification and Program Development. SIGPLAN Notices 13 (12), 15-24 (1978). See also this volume.

[18] P. Pepper: A Study on Transformational Semantics. Dissertation, Munich 1978.
See also this volume.

[19] F.L. Bauer, H. Wössner: Algorithmic Language and Program Development. Prentice
Hall International, London 1979

[20] H. Partsch, M. Broy : Examples for Change of Types and Object Structures.
This volume.

APPENDIX:

F. L. Bauer

Programming Languages under Educational and under Professional Aspects*

I. It is an old experience, that sometimes a gap exists between theory
    and practice. This holds also for the field of programming languages.
    I have been involved to some extent both with theoretical and practi-
    cal work in programming languages and I have had my own difficulties
    to bridge the gap. But I am not going to discuss this disharmony to
    great length - I only give for illustration two quotations. One is
    from Alan Perlis and says ironically, that "computer science is able
    to generate its own problems, understood and appreciated by only its
    own people ..., so the thing is quite healthy in the academic sense".
    Indeed, we will have reached soon a point where, in analogy to a fa-
    mous example, "Pure Computer Science" will be an appropriate term.
    The other is from Jerry Feldman: "Practical people do not read the lit-
    erature, even though there are sometimes real solutions to their prob-
    lems to be found there". Related to the topic is the use of the term
    "software engineering" in contrast to computing science.

    My problem is a different one and I think a deeper one: There seems to
    be some contradiction between requirements coming from educational and
    from professional aspects of computing. I want to discuss this for the
    central subject of computing: programming languages.

II. We claim, that programming languages are to be taught conceptually.
    Under educational aspects, they are thus subject to the following
    requirements

    a) There are basic concepts - like parameter, call, branching.

    b) The basic concepts are g e n e r a l and powerful enough,
       that their n u m b e r can be kept small.

    c) It is possible to compose other concepts from basic ones by
       simple and well defined c o m p o s i t i o n   r u l e s.

---

* Lecture, held at the Second All-Union Conference on Programming,
  Novosibirsk, February 1970. A Russian translation has appeared
  in the Conference Proceedings, Siberian Division of the Academy
  of Science, May 1971.

Thus the programming language should not merely be a set of unrelated special cases.

These requirements are not typical for computing science, they hold for many scientific disciplines. They are the result of what is called "the art of simplification". Computing science, similar to mathematics, leads, however, to *very complicated conceptual structures*. Therefore, economical ways for surveying the situation are needed. This leads to

d) The conceptual building should be *recursive* : certain composite concepts should be allowed to be taken for basic ones, from which new concepts may be composed.

As a natural consequence, c o n c e p t s f o r m a l a n - g u a g e. This has not been pointed out strongly enough so far. The conceptual language is fully independent and has its own "natural grammar". Words from the conceptual language are used in the grammar of programming languages and in their semantic definition. There are, of course, many notations possible for the conceptual language. The differences may be manifest in the use of different natural languages.

Some language definition methods n e g l e c t the formation of sufficiently powerful concepts. This does not necessarily weaken the rigour of definition, but usually it leads to less intelligible constructs, with concepts to be formed, if necessary, ad hoc and outside the definition method. The Viennese definition method is a mild example, a terrible one is the use of a compiling program for the definition of a programming language.

It was said above, that programming languages are taught in terms of concepts. Some were listed above. There is plenty of evidence that more concepts are universal, static ones like data and operations on data, standard data classes like integers and Booleans, structured data and corresponding operations, or dynamic ones, like jump, loop and other sequencing tools. Of course, there are more or less fundamental questions connected to all basic concepts, for example to the concept of a program variable. These questions, however, are not so much of

importance in teaching beginners; the parallelism to the role of
axiomatic set theory in the mathematics curriculum is obvious.

A requirement from education is therefore:

e) All programming languages should be based on the s a m e
   basic concepts.

There is no doubt, that this can be done - the question is how complicated it may be in connection with very specific and problem-oriented
concepts. Therefore, we may add

f) The programming language description method should comprise
   that facilitate the formation of *new, composite concepts.*

Nothing would be improved if the mechanism for the formation of new concepts would be ad hoc and not generally understood. Therefore, we may add

g) The rules for building composite concepts should be *universal.*

Summarizing, we require under educational aspects:

> From few, but powerful universal concepts, by universal rules,
> new concepts can be formed as needed and used in programming
> languages of any kind.

Needless to say, that one arrives at similar requirements in connection with the formalization of the semantics of programming languages.

III. Our postulates do not imply that a universal programming language be re-
     quired. Indeed, in order to broaden his conceptual basis and to widen
     his view for the applicability of his knowledge the Computer Science
     student of today is forced to learn as many programming languages as
     possible, and the more different they are, the better.[1] In practice,
     however, there is a discrepancy: only a couple of programming languages
     can be mastered by the beginner, and the fewer, the better from the
     organizational point of view of the computing center, that runs hun-
     dreds of students jobs every day. The answer is at many places a solu-
     tion with two or, at most, three different languages. If then in ad-
     dition the choice is determined by outside influences, as from computer
     manufacturers, the result is pityful.

---

[1] This does not hold, of course, for the simple user.

To have instead *one* conceptually truly universal programming language, allowing variations of style, would be a much better solution.

IV. Students learn programming languages in order to use them professionally. This practical use leads to some obvious observations:

1) The number of programming languages, that can be made available is restricted by economical consideration both with the supplier (who has to pay for the software production) and the user (who has to pay for the time the employee needs to learn and master the language).

2) No programming language can be concocted that is explicitly completely universal: There are always new problem areas, that demand new expressional means not yet available in hitherto existing programming languages.

3) A programming language, that is made quasi-universal by accumulating explicit constructs is usually not very attractive: most professional programmers work for quite a time in the same problem area, they do need only the specific expressional means of this area.

Such a language is most likely to be a nuisance for all user circles, certainly for all but one. Successful languages like ALGOL 60 or APL or LISP are not convincing examples of universal languages: they favour on purpose certain domains and are of little help with others. A solution combining these languages to a quasi-universal set is most likely to end with a mess of mutual inconsistency and correspondingly with difficulties in going from one language to another.

There is a simple answer to these difficulties: to have defined a potentially infinite class of languages, all being conceptually on the same basis, such that every need can be met; to have implemented, maintained and supported a small number of them, that are powerful enough to form together a quasi-universal set.

V. These theoretical considerations of the professional use of programming
languages are usually in conflict with practical   f a c t s .

  a) Programming languages for professional work are judged by the possi-
     bilities for *efficient compilation* both with respect to compile-
     time and run-time demands in storage and computer-time.

The more ambitious in quasi-universality a single programming language is,
the poorer it is with respect to point a).

  b) Programming languages for professional use should make the *best out
     of existing hardware*.

Due to the historical development, there are still more top managers in
manufacturer's headquarters, that came from electrical engineering, than
those, that came from programming; correspondingly, there is not yet much
hope for a change in the arrogant view: let us first design a computer
and then the system people find out how to use it. In my experience, ar-
chitects have very often such an attitude, therefore it is quite appropriate to speak of "computer architecture".

According to experience, point b) is a poison to all conceptual universality. The more it seems to be advantageous to combine things under
one heading for systematic reasons, the more it usually leads to inefficiency of implementation with a given machine. ALGOL 68 suffers to
a great extent from this.

I have always expressed the view, that the implementation should treat
the simple case in a simple way, and should not burden the simple case
with a load coming from the treatment of the general case. The language
designer has to keep this in mind. Even so, frequently a given programming language will not allow us to make the best use of some existing
hardware feature. What is the reason for this? It is because some engi-
neer invented some ad hoc gadget, that gives some advantage in the special
case, and was stupid enough not to see the general case or unable to cope
with it. In this case the inefficiency is wrongly blamed on the programming language; in truth it is caused by an unbalanced hardware design.

Thus, the only way out is to change the hardware of computers and computing systems such, that they are friendlier to the striving for universality. Summarizing, we demand for the professional programmer, that

> computer systems be at hand allowing efficient solutions for a wide
> class of possible programming languages all being in conceptual
> accordance with the language or languages the programmer has been
> exposed to as a student.

VI. Our interest thus comes back to the problem of finding the right set of basic concepts. Experiences with very large programs, or rather disappointment with them, have shown, that the design process has to be broken down into several phases, going into more details step by step. This gives rise to "intermediate concepts" of different depth, quite in parallel to the educational requirements, in particular c) and d). Languages have to be available to accompany these steps, and the design process will be a series of language transformations, all supported by mechanical translations, but involving human interference in a feedback way for checking and improving. Besides languages, that stand side by side, we will now also have a hierarchic subordination of programming languages. Some people believe, that such an approach also leads to safer programming in general, provided we find "reasonable" intermediate concepts. What these concepts are remains to a large extent to be found out, but it should not go unmentioned, that Dijkstra and others have made some remarkable contributions already. It is to be hoped, that the new IFIP Working group 2.3 will contribute a lot to this.

The benefits would be great:
The same programming support system, that is intended to give safer programming, will also be of immense help to the "system analyst" by reducing drastically the time needed for the problem analysis and other preparatory steps needed before the first flow chart is drawn. Very soon, programming manpower could become the bottleneck in computing efforts, and everything should be done to prevent science from being strangulated by this.

Systematics of Transformation Rules [*)]

F.L. Bauer, M. Broy, H. Partsch, P. Pepper, H. Wössner

Institut für Informatik
Technische Universität München
Postfach 20 24 20
D - 8000 München

Abstract

There are essentially two ways to attack the problem of the "correctness" of program
transformations: transformation rules can be given as axioms - thus determining
(parts of) the semantics of the language - or they can be verified with respect to
a particular definition of the semantics. This classification is taken here as a
guide-line for a systematic survey of transformation rules.

[*)] This research was carried out within the Sonderforschungsbereich 49, Programmiertechnik, München

Introduction

In consequence of the much discussed "software-crisis" of the sixties, efforts have been made to improve programming habits. These trends have been supported by a great deal of work on the theoretical aspects of "programming methodology". Nowadays, we can observe a gradual convergence of concepts and ideas towards a generally accepted "discipline of programming" (Dijkstra 1976). Some illustrative catchwords mark this evolution:
- system hierarchy, structured programming, programs as necklaces strung from pearls (Dijkstra 1968, 1969)
- programming by action clusters (Naur 1969)
- iterative multi-level modelling (Zurcher, Randell 1969)
- program development by stepwise refinement (Wirth 1971)
- interactive design of correct programs (Floyd 1971)
- proving structured programs correct (Hoare 1971)
- computer-aided, intuition-guided programming (Bauer 1973)
- top-down program development (Conway, Gries 1973)

These approaches differ in the degree of formal support they provide for the programmer. Some of them are restricted to post-construction verification only; others aim at developing program and proof hand in hand by an interaction of formal and informal methods. The strictest approach, however, is the development of a program by a sequence of formalized steps using verified transformation rules. Thus, the correctness of the final program is guaranteed by construction - relative to the starting point of the development, viz. the original specification of the problem or the very first abstract solution, the "contract". This way of proceeding goes from a conceptually clear formulation of a program to an efficient machine-oriented version and allows to master step by step the complexity of correctness proofs.

The last approach is taken in our project CIP where a system for "computer-aided, intuition-guided programming" is considered, i.e. a programming system that supports and supervises the process of program development (/Bauer 73, 76/).

"Computer-aided" means that the system is designed to take from the programmer the burden of clerical work: any operation, which is of a purely mechanical nature, has to be carried out by the machine. This includes the following tasks:
- Application of formal rules to produce a new (and usually only slightly differing) program version from the actual one.
- Preservation of program versions. In particular, this provides a tool for "backtracking" from blind alleys and for starting anew the development, if some design decisions have to be changed.

- Documentation of the development history.

Methods for developing correct programs in (small) steps are usually based on semantical reasoning. If a mechanical system is used instead, the steps of this development process must be expressed syntactically. Therefore, the transition from one version of a program to another version is described by formal "transformation rules" comparable to the rules of inference in a formal calculus. For these transformation rules it has been proved beforehand that they preserve the meaning of any program they are applicable to. Thus, transformation rules are tools not only for development techniques but also for verification methods, comparable to theorems in mathematics.

Given a contract there exist obviously many programs to fulfil it, even many efficient ones. Which one of these is actually obtained by the transformation process, depends on a number of design decisions. These decisions are guided by intuition, i. e. the system is purely passive (we do not believe in artificial intelligence). By taking away the burden of clerical work, free expression of the programmer's intelligence, ingenuity and intuition is made possible. Design decisions range from the application of simple algebraic identities ("formula manipulation") to more complex transitions between control structures and changes of data structures (cf. /Partsch, Broy 78/).

A first approach to a system for program development by transformations has been undertaken by R.M. Burstall and J. Darlington (see e.g. /Darlington, Burstall 76/, /Burstall, Darlington 75/). Of course, our project has profitted by their experiences. In the meanwhile related efforts have been made elsewhere (/Gerhart 75/, /Standish et al. 76/, /Wegbreit 76/, /Arsac 77/, /Balzer 77/, /Loveman 77/).

Transformation Rules: Representation and Correctness

Basically, a transformation is the generation of a new piece of program from a given one; it is said to be correct, if both programs are semantically equivalent. A transformation rule thus is a mapping between sets of programs. In general, such a mapping is a partial one, as it is only defined for particular kinds of programs.

In principle, there are two possibilities of representing a transformation rule. Both are strictly syntax-oriented as far as its application is concerned:

(i) The transformation rule can be described in the form of an algorithm, which takes a given program as input and produces an equivalent one as output - provided that the input program is in the domain of the rule (compilers behave in this way);

(ii) The transformation rule can be given as an ordered pair of program schemes, the "input template" S and the "output template" T (cf. /Rosen 73/, /DeRemer 74/),

which correspond to the premise and conclusion of a Post production rule. The
application of such a transformation rule to a concrete program therefore resembles a substitution step of a Post system. We denote such rules in the form

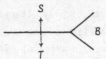

where S and T are the input and output templates mentioned above and B is
a condition, called the applicability condition, mandatory for the application of the transformation; the part B may be missing. If only one of the
two arrows is present, the scheme is applicable in the indicated direction only,
otherwise the scheme is symmetric with respect to S and T. The syntactic form of the input template together with the applicability condition specifies the exact domain of the transformation rule. (For a formal treatment of the
equivalence of programs and program schemes see /Broy et al. 78 b/ and /Pepper
78/.)

Program schemes follow a particular (abstract) syntax, and the correctness of transformation rules depends heavily on a particular definition of the semantics; therefore, we refer to the "wide spectrum language" CIP-L as a formal basis (cf. /Bauer
et al. 78/, /Broy et al. 78 b/, /Pepper 78/). Within CIP-L we distinguish several
"styles" of programming, in particular the applicative level - including descriptive
constructs - and the procedural level - comprising imperative constructs. We will
use this partitioning of the language also as a guide-line for classifying the transformation rules, here. This will also show that many rules which differ in their syntactic particulars exhibit the same underlying idea.

There are certain transformation rules which are characteristic for the semantics of
the applicative kernel of the language ("fundamental transformations"). In addition
to these, so-called "definitional transformations" introduce new language constructs by
explaining them relative to more elementary constructs ("transformational semantics",
cf. e.g. /Pepper 78/). Finally, the abstract data types used in a particular program
provide for "algebraic laws".

Besides these basic transformation rules, we also have derived transformation rules,
which either are abbreviations of sequences of more elementary rules or can be verified by means of the basic transformation rules using induction. Whereas the basic
rules serve as axioms of a transformational calculus, the derived ones are the theorems of this calculus.

Note that transformation rules can be applied not only to programs, but also to program schemes thus producing a new transformation rule consisting of the original prog-

ram scheme as input template and of the generated program scheme as output template. The applicability conditions for the new rule are induced by those of the applied rule. Thus, new transformation rules may be derived within the system.

Basic Transformation Rules

Two fundamental transformation rules play a central role (cf. /Burstall, Darlington 75/)

- UNFOLD substitutes an applied occurrence of a function identifier by the right-hand side of the respective declaration

- FOLD (the inverse operation) substitutes an expression by an application of a function, the declaration of which has a suitable right-hand side.

Note that the presence of non-determinate or undefined expressions as arguments requires certain precautions (in connection with call-by-value semantics).

These rules can be used to prove the correctness of methods for introducing new (auxiliary) functions such as

- functional composition (cf. /Burstall, Darlington 75/, /Partsch, Pepper 77/, /Feather 78/)

- tupling (also called "pairing", or "functional combination"; cf. /Bauer et al. 76/, /Burstall, Darlington 75/, /Friedman, Wise 78/)

- melting (cf. /Bauer et al. 76/)

- embedding (also called "generalization"; cf. /Bauer et al. 76/, /Burstall, Feather 78/, /Wegbreit 76/, /Broy et al. 78 a/)

It will suffice here to present one example e.g. that of embedding on the descriptive level:

$\underline{\text{funct}}$ f $\equiv$ ($\underline{\text{m}}$ x) $\underline{\text{r}}$: $\underline{\text{some}}$ $\underline{\text{r}}$ y : B(x,y)

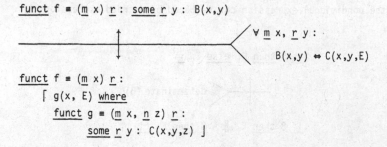

$\forall$ $\underline{\text{m}}$ x, $\underline{\text{r}}$ y :

B(x,y) $\leftrightarrow$ C(x,y,E)

$\underline{\text{funct}}$ f $\equiv$ ($\underline{\text{m}}$ x) $\underline{\text{r}}$:
$\lceil$ g(x, E) $\underline{\text{where}}$
$\quad$ $\underline{\text{funct}}$ g $\equiv$ ($\underline{\text{m}}$ x, $\underline{\text{n}}$ z) $\underline{\text{r}}$:
$\quad\quad$ $\underline{\text{some}}$ $\underline{\text{r}}$ y : C(x,y,z) $\rfloor$

Programs including non-deterministic constructs not only allow for equivalence transformations but also for "implementing transformations", viz. transformations reducing the "breadth" of the programs (i.e. making them less ambiguous) while keeping their definedness (cf. e.g. /Bauer 78 a/, /Bauer, Wössner 79/, /Broy et al. 78 b/) - e.g. the fundamental rule

$$\text{\underline{some} \underline{m} x . } p(x)$$
$$\begin{array}{c} \forall \underline{m} x : (q(x) \Rightarrow p(x)) \\ (\exists \underline{m} x : p(x)) \Rightarrow (\exists \underline{m} y : q(y)) \end{array}$$
$$\text{\underline{some} \underline{m} x : } q(x)$$

describes such an implementation.

The rules of inference of the predicate calculus, of course, hold; e.g.

$$\exists \underline{m} x : B(x)$$

$$\neg \forall \underline{m} x : \neg B(x)$$

can be taken as a definitional transformation introducing (the semantics of) the existential quantifier in terms of the universal quantifier.

Even the semantics of the guarded expression may be defined by definitional transformations

$$\text{\underline{if} } B_1 \text{ \underline{then} } E_1 \; [] \; ... \; [] \; B_n \text{ \underline{then} } E_n \text{ \underline{fi}}$$

$$mode(E_i) = \underline{m} \wedge determinate\,(B_i) \wedge defined\,(B_i)$$
$$\wedge \; determinate\,(E_i)$$
$$\text{\underline{some} \underline{m} x : } (B_1 \wedge x \doteq E_1) \vee ... \vee (B_n \wedge x \doteq E_n)$$

where "$\doteq$" denotes the strong (non-strict) equality.

The semantics of the conditional expression can be based on guarded expressions:

$$\text{\underline{if} } B \text{ \underline{then} } E_1 \text{ \underline{else} } E_2 \text{ \underline{fi}}$$

$$determinate\,(B)$$

$$\text{\underline{if} } B \text{ \underline{then} } E_1 \; [] \; \neg B \text{ \underline{then} } E_2 \text{ \underline{fi}}$$

A collection of definitional transformations, which extend the language by adding program variables, assignments, iterative constructs etc. to the applicative kernel of the language, can be found in /Pepper 78/. A typical example of this kind is

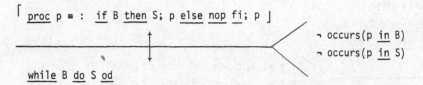

⌐ proc p ≡ : if B then S; p else nop fi; p ⌐

while B do S od

¬ occurs(p in B)
¬ occurs(p in S)

Most systems for program transformations incorporate so-called "algebraic laws" (cf. e.g. /Burstall, Darlington 75/). In connection with abstract data types, which contain tautologies (usually equations) like

∀ nat x : x × 0 = 0´,
∀ stack s, m x : top(append(s,x)) = x ,

this can be generalized: In analogy to the definitional transformations, which give the semantics of new constructs by the corresponding transformation rules, the abstract data types add new functions - and corresponding transformation rules - to a specific program.

Technically, any law of an abstract data type can be used as a transformation rule by means of a "meta-rule" APPLY LAW (cf. e.g. /Bauer et al. 77/).

Derived Transformations

We first regard transformations on the applicative level. Here, a most important class are transformations changing the type of recursion into a simpler one. Usually, this is done in preparation of the transition to imperative program versions. This field of "recursion removal" has been studied intensively in connection with program transformations, as here not only a considerable gain in execution time and storage space is possible, but also because recursive functions are well understood in mathematics (as an - incomplete - sample of papers cf. /Cooper 66/, /Paterson, Hewitt 70/, /Strong 71/, /Darlington, Burstall 76/, /Wegbreit 76/, /Partsch, Pepper 76/, /Loveman 77/).

The execution of a recursive routine may be regarded as the interpretation of a term of primitive operations, the infinite "tree of computation" (cf. /Courcelle, Nivat 76/). In the case of "tail recursion", where the recursive call is the dynamically last action of the routine, recursion can be reduced to iteration.

If one does not have tail recursion, one may try to restructure this term appropriately using algebraic properties of the primitive operations (like associativity, right-commutativity etc.). An example is the rule

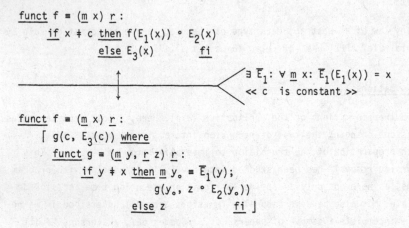

$\underline{funct}\ f \equiv (\underline{m}\ x)\ \underline{r}:$
   $\underline{if}\ B\ \underline{then}\ f(E_1) \circ E_2$
       $\underline{else}\ E_3\ \underline{fi}$

$\forall\ \underline{r}\ a,b,c:\ (a \circ b) \circ c = a \circ (b \circ c)$
$\exists\ \underline{r}\ e:\ \forall\ \underline{r}\ a:\ a \circ e = a$

$\underline{funct}\ f \equiv (\underline{m}\ x)\ \underline{r}:$
  $\lceil\ g(x,e)\ \underline{where}$
    $\underline{funct}\ g \equiv (\underline{m}\ x,\ \underline{r}\ z)\ \underline{r}:$
      $\underline{if}\ B\ \underline{then}\ g(E_1,\ E_2 \circ z)$
         $\underline{else}\ E_3 \circ z\ \ \ \underline{fi}\ \rfloor$

Another possibility is to use special properties of the "decrementing function" E_1 : If there exists an inverse function $\overline{E}_1$, then the arguments can be computed in the reverse order:

$\underline{funct}\ f \equiv (\underline{m}\ x)\ \underline{r}:$
  $\underline{if}\ x \neq c\ \underline{then}\ f(E_1(x)) \circ E_2(x)$
      $\underline{else}\ E_3(x)\ \ \ \ \ \ \ \underline{fi}$

$\exists\ \overline{E}_1:\ \forall\ \underline{m}\ x:\ \overline{E}_1(E_1(x)) = x$
$\ll c\ \text{is constant} \gg$

$\underline{funct}\ f \equiv (\underline{m}\ x)\ \underline{r}:$
  $\lceil\ g(c,\ E_3(c))\ \underline{where}$
    $\underline{funct}\ g \equiv (\underline{m}\ y,\ \underline{r}\ z)\ \underline{r}:$
      $\underline{if}\ y \neq x\ \underline{then}\ \underline{m}\ y_\circ \equiv \overline{E}_1(y);$
             $g(y_\circ,\ z \circ E_2(y_\circ))$
        $\underline{else}\ z\ \ \ \ \ \ \underline{fi}\ \rfloor$

Remarks: (1) This latter transformation can be used for the formal introduction of stacking mechanisms (cf. /Pepper et al. 78/, /Wössner et al. 78/).

        (2) Both rules given above can be verified with the aid of transformations like EMBEDDING, FOLD and UNFOLD (including induction).

A collection of such rules may be found e.g. in /Darlington, Burstall 76/ or in /Bauer et al. 77/ and /Bauer, Wössner 79/.

All these rules can also be applied, if the recursion of the routine f is of a more complex type than linear recursion, i.e. if the expressions E_1, E_2 etc. contain additional calls of f. Then applications of these rules may still bring up some gain, e.g. by generating new versions of f which require smaller stacks (cf. e.g. /Pepper et al. 78/, /Wössner et al. 78/).

Many well-known rules on the imperative level, in particular those that are used in "optimizing compilers" for loops, now can be derived from basic rules and derived rules on the applicative level. As an example one may take the "constant propagation"

while B do m c = E_1 ;
      x := E_2 od

⌈ m c = E_1 ;
    while B do x := E_2 od ⌋

(d)

(a)

(c)

⌈ funct f = (n x) n :
     if B then m c = E_1 ;
           f(E_2)
       else x   fi ;
  x := f(x)   ⌋

⌈ m c = E_1 ;
 ⌈ funct f = (n x) n :
      if B then f(E_2)
        else x fi ;
  x := f(x)   ⌋⌋

(b)

(a): MODE(x) = n ∧ ¬ OCCURS(f in B, E_1, E_2)
(b): ¬ OCCURS(x,f in E_1) ∧ ¬ OCCURS(c in B)
(c): ¬ OCCURS(f in B, E_2) ∧ MODE(x) = n
(d): ¬ OCCURS(x in E_1) ∧ ¬ OCCURS(c in B)

This commuting diagram of transformations is typical of the derivation of rules for imperative constructs.

Another example, the derivation of which requires rather complex proofs by induction, is the "nesting of loops", which e.g. for Dijkstra's guarded commands looks like

do B_1 → S_1
⫿ B_2 → S_2
⫿ C → T
od

∀ R : wp(do ... od, R) ⇒ ¬ C
wp(S_1, C) = false
¬ (C ∧ B_1) ∧ ¬ (C ∧ B_2)

do B_1 → S_1
⫿ B_2 → S_2; do C → T od
od

(the first of the conditions means that C must not be true at the very beginning, the second one ensures that after execution of S_1 the predicate C must not be true, and the third one establishes the disjointness of C and the B_i .)

Besides these complex rules based on induction there also exist simpler ones which are mere abbreviations for sequences of more elementary rules.

Specialized forms of folding and unfolding are e.g.

UNFOLD/FOLD for objects

$$\ulcorner \ (\underline{m}_1 \ x_1, \ \ldots, \ \underline{m}_n \ x_n) \equiv (D_1, \ \ldots, D_n); \ E \ \lrcorner$$

$$\xrightarrow{} \prec \text{determinate } (D_i) \ \wedge \ \text{defined } (D_i)$$

$$E \begin{matrix} D_1, \ \ldots, D_n \\ x_1, \ \ldots, x_n \end{matrix}$$

and

$$E \begin{matrix} D_1, \ \ldots, D_n \\ x_1, \ \ldots, x_n \end{matrix}$$

$$\xrightarrow{} \prec \text{defined } (D_i)$$

$$\ulcorner \ (m_1 \ x_1, \ \ldots, \underline{m}_n \ x_n) \equiv (D_1, \ \ldots, D_n); \ E \ \lrcorner$$

where $E \begin{matrix} D_1, \ \ldots, D_n \\ x_1, \ \ldots, x_n \end{matrix}$ denotes the expression that is generated by simultaneously substituting all free occurrences of $x_1, \ldots, x_n$ in E by $D_1, \ldots, D_n$. (Of course, this substitution operation has to take care of name clashes between the free identifiers of the D_i and bound identifiers within E .)

UNFOLD/FOLD for functions

$$f(A_1, \ \ldots, A_n)$$

$$\xleftarrow{} \prec \underline{\text{funct}} \ f \equiv (\underline{m}_1 \ x_1, \ \ldots, \underline{m}_n \ x_n) \ \underline{r} : E \ \wedge \ \neg \ \text{occurs}(x_i, A_j)$$

$$\ulcorner \ (\underline{m}_1 \ x_1, \ \ldots, \underline{m}_n \ x_n) \equiv (A_1, \ \ldots, A_n); \ \underline{r} : E \ \lrcorner$$

Similar rules exist for procedures, and also rules like "unrolling of a loop" are in principle · UNFOLD-operations.

UNFOLD/FOLD for variables

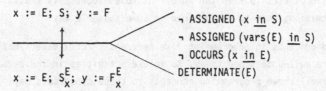

$$x := E; \ S; \ y := F$$

$$x := E; \ S_x^E; \ y := F_x^E$$

¬ ASSIGNED (x in S)
¬ ASSIGNED (vars(E) in S)
¬ OCCURS (x in E)
DETERMINATE(E)

For a calculus of such transformation rules see /Igarashi 64/ and /de Bakker 69/.
Catalogues of rules for imperative constructs may be found in /Weber 76/, /Standish
et al. 76/, /Loveman 77/, /Balzer 77/.

The manipulation system

The project CIP is intended to support top-down development of systems. The design
of the manipulation system for the application of transformation rules follows this principle itself.   Accordingly, transformations are ab initio formulated in the descriptive way of (ii) above, using a pair of templates. There is a general manipulation
algorithm with pairs of templates as parameters which for each given pair turns into
an algorithm in the sense of (i) above, accepting an input program or program scheme
and delivering an output program or program scheme. This manipulation algorithm again
is descriptively defined, see /Rosen 73/. From this abstract definition in several
steps operational versions will be derived after introducing suitable data structures
for representing the programs. This task, tentatively done by hand, will be one of
the first applications of CIP to larger development projects.

Some Areas of Future Research

Some of the previous examples show an important point: The applicability conditions
for the transformations of imperative constructs usually are more complex than those
required on the applicative level. This increased complexity is caused essentially
by the necessary data flow analysis to pay attention to all possible side-effects.

Most of these transformations have counterparts on the applicative level. This means
that they can be applied - generally with less effort - in earlier stages of the
development of a program. This raises the serious question whether the number of
transformations to be offered to the programmer should be drastically reduced by
omitting all rules for imperative constructs for which corresponding rules exist on
the applicative level.

Another problem of transformation systems is strongly related to the previous one:
Often, the same rule exists for several syntactical constructs. For example,

"constant propagation" is possible for certain recursive procedures, for while-loops, until-loops, for-loops etc. To keep the number of rules acceptably small, such classes of transformations have to be combined in some suitable way.

Not all machine-oriented concepts in programming like references (cf. /Bauer 78b/), multi-processing etc. are well-understood today. So future activities in the area of transformations from well-known programming concepts to these constructs may lead to proper formalizations and safe methodologies. This will open the door to a formal discipline of systems programming.

Another aspect can be found in the field of the analysis of algorithms: Since a particular final program is the result of a number of (principally) independent design decisions, program transformations help to elucidate the analogies between related programs. This will lead to the development of program families reflecting a tree of design decisions (cf. e.g. /Darlington 76/, /Broy 78/). Analogously, programs for a whole family of related problems can be treated by developing an appropriate program scheme (cf. e.g. /Gerhart 76/).

Acknowledgement

We thank J.M. Boyle for critical discussions and R. Gnatz and A. Laut for reading drafts of this paper.

Literature

/Arsac 77/

J. Arsac: La Construction de Programmes Structurés. Paris: Dunod 1977

/de Bakker 69/

J. W. de Bakker: Semantics of Programming Languages. In: J. T. Tou (ed.):
Advances in Information System Sciences 2, New York: Plenum Press 1969,
173 - 227

/Balzer 77/

R. M. Balzer: Correct and Efficient Software Implementation via Semi-
Automatic Transformations (Research Proposal, unpublished)

/Bauer 73/

F. L. Bauer: A Philosophy of Programming. A Course of three Lectures
given at the University of London, October 1973. Also in: Proc. Intern.
Summer School on Language Hierarchies and Interfaces, Marktoberdorf 1975.
Lecture Notes in Computer Science 46. Berlin, Heidelberg, New York:
Springer 1976

/Bauer 76/

F. L. Bauer: Programming as an Evolutionary Process. Technische Universität
München, Institut für Informatik, Rep. No. 7617, 1976. Also: Proc 2nd Int.
Conf. on Software Engineering, Oct, 1976, San Francisco, Ca., 223 - 234

/Bauer et al. 76/

F. L. Bauer, H. Partsch, P. Pepper, H. Wössner: Techniques for Program
Development. Technische Universität München, Institut für Informatik,
Interner Bericht, Sept. 1976. Also in: Software Engineering Techniques.
Infotech State of the Art Report 34, 1977, 27 - 50

/Bauer et al. 77/

F. L. Bauer, H. Partsch, P. Pepper, H. Wössner: Notes on the Project CIP:
Outline of a Transformation System. Technische Universität München,
Institut für Informatik, TUM - INFO - 7729, 1977

/Bauer et al. 78/

F. L. Bauer, M. Broy, R. Gnatz, W. Hesse, B. Krieg-Brückner, H. Partsch,
P. Pepper, H. Wössner: Towards a Wide Spectrum Language to Support Program
Specification and Program Development. SIGPLAN Notices 13 (12), 15-24 (1978).
See also this volume.

/Bauer 78 a/
    F. L. Bauer: Program Development by Stepwise Transformations - the Project
    CIP. This volume

/Bauer 78 b/
    F. L. Bauer: Detailization and Lazy Evaluation, Infinite Objects and
    Pointer Representation. This volume

/Bauer, Wössner 79/
    F. L. Bauer, H. Wössner: Algorithmic Language and Program Development.
    London: Prentice-Hall International 1979

/Broy 78/
    M. Broy: A Case Study in Program Development: Sorting. Technische
    Universität München, Institut für Informatik, TUM - INFO - 7831, 1978

/Broy et al. 78 a/
    M. Broy, R. Gnatz, M. Wirsing: Problemspezifikation - eine Grundlage
    für Programmentwicklung. Workshop on Reliable Software, Bonn University,
    September 22 - 23, 1978. To appear in Hanser Verlag.

/Broy et al. 78 b/
    M. Broy, R. Gnatz, M. Wirsing: Semantics for Nondeterministic and
    Noncontinuous Constructs. This volume.

/Burstall, Darlington 75/
    R. M. Burstall, J. Darlington: Some Transformations for Developing
    Recursive Programs. Proc. of 1975 Int. Conf. on Reliable Software,
    Los Angeles 1975, 465 - 472. Also (revised version) J. ACM 24, 1,
    44 - 67 (1977)

/Burstall, Feather 78/
    R. Burstall, M. Feather: Program Development by Transformations: an
    Overview.Proc.of Toulouse CREST Course on Programming, Toulouse, 1978

/Cooper 66/
    D. C. Cooper: The Equivalence of Certain Computations. Comp. J. 9,
    45 - 52 (1966)

/Courcelle, Nivat 76/
    B. Courcelle, M. Nivat: Algebraic Families of Interpretations. 17th
    Symposium on Foundations of Computer Science, Houston 1976

/Darlington, Burstall 76/

J. Darlington, R. M. Burstall: A System which Automatically Improves
Programs. Acta Informatica 6, 41 - 60 (1976)

/Darlington 76/

J. Darlington: A Synthesis of Several Sorting Algorithms. D.A.I. Research
Report no. 23, Dept. of Artificial Intelligence, University of Edinburgh,
1976

/DeRemer 74/

F. L. DeRemer: Transformational Grammars. In: F.L. Bauer, J. Eickel (eds.):
Compiler Construction. An Advanced Course. Lecture Notes in Computer Science
21. Berlin, Heidelberg, New York: Springer 1974, 121 - 145

/Friedman, Wise 78/

D. P. Friedman, D. S. Wise: Functional Combination. Computer Languages 3,
31 - 35 (1978)

/Feather 78/

M. S. Feather: Program Transformations Applied to the Telegram Problem.
In: B. Robinet (ed.): Program Transformations. Proc. of the 3rd International Symposium on Programming, March 28 - 30, 1978, Paris: Dunod 1978, 173-186

/Gerhart 75/

S. L. Gerhart: Correctness-Preserving Program Transformations. Conf. Rec.
Second ACM Symp. on Principles of Programming Languages, Jan. 1975,
54 - 66

/Gerhart 76/

S. L. Gerhart: Control Structure Abstractions of the Backtracking Programming Technique. 2nd Int. Conf. on Software Engineering, 1976, 44 - 49

/Igarashi 64/

S. Igarashi: An Axiomatic Approach to the Equivalence Problems of
Algorithms with Applications. PhD Thesis, University of Tokyo (1964).
Reprinted in: Report of the Computer Center Univ. of Tokyo 1, 1 - 101
(1968)

/Loveman 77/

D. B. Loveman: Program Improvement by Source-to-Source Transformation.
J. ACM 24: 1, 121 - 145 (1977)

/Partsch, Pepper 76/

H. Partsch, P. Pepper: A Family of Rules for Recursion Removal Related to
the Towers of Hanoi Problem. Technische Universität München, Institut
für Informatik, Rep. No. 7612, 1976. Also Inf. Proc. Letters 5: 6,
174 - 177 (1976)

/Partsch, Pepper 77/

H. Partsch, P. Pepper: Program Transformations on Different Levels of
Programming. Technische Universität München, Institut für Informatik,
TUM - INFO - 7715, 1977

/Partsch, Broy 78/

H. Partsch, M. Broy: Examples for Change of Types and Object Structures.
This volume.

/Paterson, Hewitt 70/

M. S. Paterson, C. E. Hewitt: Comparative Schematology. In: Record of the
Project MAC Conf. on Concurrent Systems and Parallel Computation, New
York: ACM 1970, 119 - 127

/Pepper 78/

P. Pepper: A Study on Transformational Semantics. Dissertation, Munich 1978.
See also this volume

/Pepper et al. 78/

P. Pepper, H. Partsch, H. Wössner, F. L. Bauer: A Transformational Approach
to Programming. In: B. Robinet (ed.): Program Transformations. Proc. of the
3rd International Symposium on Programming, March 28 - 30, 1978, Paris:
Dunod 1978

/Rosen 73/

B. K. Rosen: Tree-Manipulating Systems and Church-Rosser Theorems.
Journal ACM 20: 1, 160 - 187 (1973)

/Standish et al. 76/

T. A. Standish, D. C. Harriman, D. F. Kibler, J. M. Neighbors: The Irvine
Program Transformation Catalogue. Dep. Inform. and Comp. Sc., University
of California at Irvine, Irvine, Calif., Jan. 1976

T. A. Standish, D. C. Harriman, D. F. Kibler, J. M. Neighbors: Improving
and Refining Programs by Program Manipulation. Proc. 1976 ACM Annual Conf.,
Oct. 1976, 509 - 516

/Strong 71/

      H. R. Strong: Translating Recursion Equations into Flow Charts. In:
      Proc. 2nd Annual ACM Symposium on Theory of Computing, New York 1970,
      184 - 197. Also J. CSS 5, 254 - 285 (1971)

/Weber 76/

      J. Weber: Programmtransformationen mit Attributierten Transformations-
      grammatiken. Technische Universität München, Institut für Informatik,
      Rep. No. 7604, 1976

/Wegbreit 76/

      B. Wegbreit: Goal-Directed Program Transformation. IEEE Transactions on
      Software Engineering, vol. SE - 2, no. 2, 69 - 80 (1976)

/Wössner et al. 78/

      H. Wössner, P. Pepper, H. Partsch, F.L. Bauer: Special Transformation Techniques.
      This volume

SPECIAL TRANSFORMATION TECHNIQUES *

H. Wössner, P. Pepper, H. Partsch, F. L. Bauer

Institut für Informatik
Technische Universität München
Postfach 20 24 20
D-8000 München 2

Abstract

There are certain simple types of recursion allowing to be transformed immediately into usual iterative language constructs. On the other
hand there are also routines which can only be implemented in full generality by using a stack mechanism. One of the great advantages of
methods for program development is the individual and thus adequate
treatment of routines - especially of recursive ones - by means of
a repertory of transformation techniques. Some of the techniques based on the fundamental method of function inversion are presented in
this paper.

---

* This material will be included in the book "Algorithmic Language
  and Program Development" by F. L. Bauer and H. Wössner, assisted
  by H. Partsch and P. Pepper, to be published by Prentice-Hall International.

> "... the transformation from
> recursion to iteration is
> one of the most fundamental
> concepts of computer science"
> D. E. KNUTH, 1974.

0. Introduction

Starting from the hypothesis that recursive formulation is a useful
conceptual tool in the design of algorithms, the systematic removal
of recursion becomes a decisive step in developing suitable programs
for existing computers.

There are two disadvantages if this step is totally left to a compiler:
First, certain possible improvements are usually not found by compilers;
second, programs are converted immediately into machine code which excludes the further consideration by the programmer, e.g. with regard
to efficiency.

Properly done, the individual development of recursive routines by means
of transformations has a good chance to arrive at programs that are
faster and less storage-consuming (cf. /Auslander, Strong 78/, /Bird 77/,
/Partsch, Pepper 76/). Of course, the transformations become similar
to the standard techniques of compilers if the type of recursion becomes
quite general. In this case, however, an expensive treatment is justified by the complexity of the problems in question.

In the sequel a method of developing repetitive implementations for
arbitrary types of recursive routines is presented. As a base the
principle of function inversion is introduced. The following techniques are then systematically derived from this principle: the introduction of stacks as (additional) parameters, a certain "disentanglement" of the control structure, and subsequently the deparameterization of routines. The application of these techniques finally
leads to special forms of (parameterless) routines where the recursion
only serves the purpose of controlling the flow of computation. In a
last step this control structure now can be analyzed in order to re-
organize it into a repetive form. The programs which result from
this development include, in particular, standard implementations used
in compiler construction.

1.   Function Inversion Techniques

The method of function inversion is introduced as a basic tool for simplifying certain types of recursion. For instance, linear recursion can be restructured into repetitive recursion according to this method. In section 2 the method will be applied to more general types of recursion in order to arrive at "disentangled" descriptions of the control flow.

This method was pioneered by Cooper in 1966 who also introduced the related techniques of operand commutation and of re-bracketing (/Cooper 66/, /Darlington, Burstall 76/).

1.1. Preliminaries

In this section we will concentrate on routines of the form

> funct $L \equiv (\lambda\ m)\ \rho$:
>> if $B(m)$ then $\varphi(L(K(m),\ E(m))$
>>> else $H(m)$ fi

and

> funct $R \equiv (\lambda\ m)\ \rho$:
>> if $B(m)$ then $R(K(m))$
>>> else $H(m)$ fi

with mappings $K: \underline{\lambda} \to \underline{\lambda}$, $\varphi: (\underline{\rho} \times \underline{\nu}) \to \underline{\rho}$, $E: \underline{\lambda} \to \underline{\nu}$, and $H: \underline{\lambda} \to \underline{\rho}$.

Such a "form" is called a scheme of routines: the scheme parameters standing for modes $(\underline{\lambda}, \underline{\rho}, ...)$, expressions $(K, E, H, ...)$, and predicates $(B, C, ...)$, can be instantiated by substituting concrete modes and expressions. An instantiation I associates with each scheme, e.g. L or R, a routine L_I or R_I. If there are no further occurrences of L and R besides the ones explicitly stated then both schemes represent linear recursive routines, the latter being, in particular, repetitive according to the terminal position of the recursive call.

Two schemes are called (strongly) equivalent (/Paterson, Hewitt 70/), if for all instantiations the associated routines are equivalent with respect to the course-of-values, i.e. represent the same mapping from domain to range.

Frequently two schemes are not equivalent for all instantiations but only for those which conform to certain conditions like associativity of operations, existence of neutral elements, etc. In these cases the schemes are called equivalent with respect to a class of instantiations. Thus two schemes P, Q define a class of <u>transformations</u>, summarized in the form of a <u>transformation rule</u> such as

where the <u>applicability condition</u> C indicates the class of instantiations for which Q is equivalent to P. In particular both schemes either terminate or do not terminate. (For further details see /Bauer et al. 78 a,b/.)

1.2. Function Inversion

The basic technique of function inversion can now be represented by a transformation rule changing the type of recursion of L into that of R.

Starting from the value on termination the new routine reconstructs successively the parameter values of all incarnations and performs the "pending" operations with them until the initial parameter value is reached again. The only prerequisite is that the "decrementing" function K is invertible on its range.

If the argument on termination, m_0, can directly be determined from the condition for termination, we have the following transformation: [1]

---

[1] By the way, the first applicability condition can be weakened to the following condition (where λ is the domain of L):
$$\exists \, \overline{K} : \, \forall \, x \in \{K^i(m): i \in \mathbb{N}, \, m \in \underline{\lambda}\}: \, \overline{K}(K(x)) = x \, .$$
Note also that the property $K(\overline{K}(x)) = x$ is not required.

$$\underline{\text{funct}} \ L \equiv (\lambda \ m) \ \rho :$$
$$\underline{\text{if}} \ m \neq m_0 \ \underline{\text{then}} \ \varphi(L(K(m)), E(m))$$
$$\underline{\text{else}} \ H(m) \qquad \underline{\text{fi}}$$

$$\left\{ \begin{array}{l} \exists \ \overline{K}: \forall \ x: \overline{K}(K(x)) = x \\ \text{CONSTANT}(m_0) \end{array} \right.$$

$$\underline{\text{funct}} \ L \equiv (\lambda \ m) \ \rho :$$
$$\lceil \ R(m_0, \ H(m_0)) \ \underline{\text{where}}$$
$$\underline{\text{funct}} \ R \equiv (\lambda \ y, \ \rho \ z) \ \rho :$$
$$\underline{\text{if}} \ y \neq m \ \underline{\text{then}} \ R(\overline{K}(y), \ \varphi(z, E(\overline{K}(y))))$$
$$\underline{\text{else}} \ z \qquad \underline{\text{fi}} \ \rfloor \ .$$

However, if the condition for termination is of the general form $B(m)$, then a "precomputation" of m_0 from the original argument m, $\lambda \ m_0 \equiv P(m)$, may be supplemented to the lower scheme using the function

$$\underline{\text{funct}} \ P \equiv (\lambda \ m) \ \lambda :$$
$$\underline{\text{if}} \ B(m) \ \underline{\text{then}} \ P(K(m))$$
$$\underline{\text{else}} \ m \qquad \underline{\text{fi}} \ .$$

The transformation is intuitively clear, the formal proof, of course, is based on induction.

Remark: If the body of L - e.g. the expression E - contains further calls of L, the transformation is still valid yielding, however, a system of mutually recursive routines (namely L and R).

To get an impression of the effect of this transformation one may consider the simple example of the factorial function which is an obvious instantiation of L according to the correspondences

$$
\begin{array}{ccl}
m_0 & \triangleq & 0 \\
H(m) & \triangleq & 1 \\
\varphi(a,b) & \triangleq & a \times b \\
K(m) & \triangleq & m - 1 \\
E(m) & \triangleq & m \ .
\end{array}
$$

Another kind of example for "function inversion" is provided by the processing of sequences "from left to right" or "from right to left". The first of these two directions is expressed by the pair of operations (top, rest), the second by the pair (bottom, upper). In this case, the inversion does not concern a single function but several complementary functions, instead. We will not go into further details here.

1.3. Function Inversion by Introducing Stacks

There also exist rules for transforming the scheme L into a repetitive (outer) form without requiring any condition. Such a transformation is given in /Paterson, Hewitt 70/; however, it is only of theoretical interest, as it leads to very inefficient computations: the inverse function $\overline{K}$ for the transition from $K^{i+1}(m)$ to $K^{i}(m)$ is realized by computing $K^{i}(m)$ always completely anew.

In this section methods will be developed which, by introducing stacks, generally allow a transition from linear to repetitive recursion, without leading to such inefficient computations.

The property (cf. /Partsch, Broy 78/)

$$rest(append(s, x)) = s$$

is valid for any stack s and any element x. Therefore the operation rest is - with respect to the stack - the inverse function for the operation append. The following development is based on this fact.

To avoid excessive nesting of brackets we write in the sequel

$$s \ \& \ x, \ \underline{top} \ s, \ and \ \underline{rest} \ s \ for$$
$$append(s, x), \ top(s), \ rest(s), \ resp.$$

Our first step is to embed L into an equivalent routine L^{*} with the domain $(\underline{\lambda}, \ \underline{stack} \ \underline{\lambda})$:

$$\underline{funct} \ L \equiv (\underline{\lambda} \ x) \ \underline{\rho} \ :$$
$$\lceil \ L^{*}(x, \ empty) \ \underline{where}$$
$$\underline{funct} \ L^{*} \equiv (\underline{\lambda} \ x, \ \underline{stack} \ \underline{\lambda} \ sx) \ \underline{\rho} \ :$$
$$\underline{if} \ B(x) \ \underline{then} \ \varphi(L^{*}(K(x), \ sx \ \& \ x), \ E(x))$$
$$\underline{else} \ H(x) \qquad \qquad \underline{fi} \ \rfloor \ .$$

The additional parameter sx is at first completely superfluous as it is not yet used anywhere in the body of the routine. Its only purpose is to provide an inverse function

$$\overline{K^*}(x, sx) = (\underline{top}\ sx, \underline{rest}\ sx)$$

for the new decrementing function

$$K^*(x, sx) = (K(x), sx\ \&\ x)\ .$$

Note that $\overline{K^*}$ depends only on its second argument sx .

Applying, therefore, the transformation rule of 1.2 (supplemented by the precomputation) to L^* and subsequently unfolding the call of L^* now yield in a formal way

> funct $L \equiv (\lambda\ x)\ \rho$:
> $\ulcorner$ $R(x_0,\ s_0,\ H(x_0))$ where
> $(\lambda\ x_0,\ \underline{stack}\ \lambda\ s_0) \equiv P(x, empty)$,
>   funct $P \equiv (\lambda\ x,\ \underline{stack}\ \lambda\ sx)(\lambda,\ \underline{stack}\ \lambda)$:
>   if $B(x)$ then $P(K(x),\ sx\ \&\ x)$
>   else (x, sx) fi ,
>
>   funct $R \equiv (\lambda\ y,\ \underline{stack}\ \lambda\ sy,\ \rho\ z)\ \rho$:
>   if $(y, sy) \neq (x, empty)$
>   then $R(\underline{top}\ sy,\ \underline{rest}\ sy,\ \varphi(z, E(\underline{top}\ sy)))$
>   else z fi $\lrcorner$.

The routine R can be considerably simplified by substituting the comparison $(y, sy) \neq (x, empty)$ by the equivalent expression $sy \neq empty$. In this way the parameter y in R becomes superfluous. This also permits a simplification of P by directly returning the value of $H(x_0)$ as a result instead of only x_0 . A summary of the complete development done so far yields the general transformation scheme

<u>funct</u> $L \equiv (\lambda\ x)\ \rho$:
    <u>if</u> $B(x)$ <u>then</u> $\varphi(L(K(x)),\ E(x))$
        <u>else</u> $H(x)$ <u>fi</u>

<u>funct</u> $L \equiv (\lambda\ x)\ \rho$:
  ⌈ $R(P(x,\ empty))$ <u>where</u>
    <u>funct</u> $P \equiv (\lambda\ x,\ \underline{stack}\ \lambda\ sx)(\underline{stack}\ \lambda,\ \rho)$:
        <u>if</u> $B(x)$ <u>then</u> $P(K(x),\ sx\ \&\ x)$
            <u>else</u> $(sx,\ H(x))$ <u>fi</u> ,
    <u>funct</u> $R \equiv (\underline{stack}\ \lambda\ sx,\ \rho\ z)\ \rho$:
        <u>if</u> $sx \neq empty$ <u>then</u> $R(\underline{rest}\ sx,\ \varphi(z,\ E(\underline{top}\ sx)))$
            <u>else</u> z <u>fi</u> ⌋ .

As this transformation does not depend on any condition it represents
a universal method, in particular for transferring linear recursive
routines into repetitive routines. (Note, however, that the non-
repetitive character of the recursion is passed only from the routine
to the data structure.)

The introduction of stacks can also help to increase efficiency in routines which contain abbreviating object declarations. Consider for instance the scheme

<u>funct</u> $L_1 \equiv (\lambda\ x)\ \rho$:
  ⌈ $\mu\ y \equiv G(x)$;
    <u>if</u> $B(x,\ y)$ <u>then</u> $\varphi(L_1(K(x,\ y)),\ E(x,\ y))$
        <u>else</u> $H(x,\ y)$ <u>fi</u> ⌋ .

Three steps are necessary for the treatment of L_1 :
- elimination of the object declaration by consistently replacing y
  by $G(x)$, [1]
- application of the above scheme,
- re-introduction of the object declaration $\mu\ y \equiv G(...)$.

---

[1] Strictly speaking, this is only allowed for determinate G (but
note that the third step repairs this defect).

Hence we obtain

$$
\begin{array}{l}
\underline{\text{funct}}\ L_1 \equiv (\lambda\ x)\ \rho : \\
\lceil\ R(P(x,\ \text{empty}))\ \underline{\text{where}} \\
\quad \underline{\text{funct}}\ P \equiv (\lambda\ x,\ \underline{\text{stack}}\ \lambda\ sx)(\underline{\text{stack}}\ \lambda,\ \rho) : \\
\quad \lceil\ \mu\ y \equiv G(x)\ ; \\
\qquad \underline{\text{if}}\ B(x,\ y)\ \underline{\text{then}}\ P(K(x,\ y),\ sx\ \&\ x) \\
\qquad\qquad\qquad \underline{\text{else}}\ (sx,\ H(x,\ y)) \qquad \underline{\text{fi}}\ \rfloor\ , \\
\quad \underline{\text{funct}}\ R \equiv (\underline{\text{stack}}\ \lambda\ sx,\ \rho\ z)\ \rho : \\
\quad \underline{\text{if}}\ sx \neq \text{empty}\ \underline{\text{then}}\ \mu\ y \equiv G(\underline{\text{top}}\ sx)\ ; \\
\qquad\qquad\qquad\qquad R(\underline{\text{rest}}\ sx,\ \varphi(z,\ E(\underline{\text{top}}\ sx,\ y))) \\
\qquad\qquad\qquad \underline{\text{else}}\ z \qquad\qquad\qquad\qquad \underline{\text{fi}}\ \rfloor\ .
\end{array}
$$

It is obvious that for all parameter values the expression G has to be computed both in the "to" direction in the routine P and in the "fro" direction in the routine R. This double computation should be avoided,[1] especially if it is time-consuming. The introduction of a further (at first superfluous) parameter is again of assistance here:

$$
\begin{array}{l}
\underline{\text{funct}}\ L_1 \equiv (\lambda\ x)\ \rho : \\
\lceil\ L_1^*(x,\ \text{empty},\ \text{empty})\ \underline{\text{where}} \\
\quad \underline{\text{funct}}\ L_1^* \equiv (\lambda\ x,\ \underline{\text{stack}}\ \lambda\ sx,\ \underline{\text{stack}}\ \mu\ sy)\ \rho : \\
\quad \lceil\ \mu\ y \equiv G(x)\ ; \\
\qquad \underline{\text{if}}\ B(x,\ y)\ \underline{\text{then}}\ \varphi(L_1^*(K(x,\ y),\ sx\ \&\ x,\ sy\ \&\ y),\ E(x,\ y)) \\
\qquad\qquad\qquad \underline{\text{else}}\ H(x,\ y) \qquad\qquad\qquad\qquad \underline{\text{fi}}\ \rfloor\rfloor\ .
\end{array}
$$

The decisive property now is, that for the two stacks $\underline{\text{top}}\ sy = G(\underline{\text{top}}\ sx)$ always holds. After transformation by function inversion the declaration $\mu\ y \equiv G(\underline{\text{top}}\ sx)$ in the routine R can be replaced by $\mu\ y \equiv \underline{\text{top}}\ sy$.

This development can also be summarized in a general transformation scheme:

---

[1] In any case this doubling is only allowed for determinate G .

$\underline{funct}\ L_1 \equiv (\lambda\ x)\ \rho :$

$\quad \lceil\ \mu\ y \equiv G(x)\ ;$

$\qquad \underline{if}\ B(x,\ y)\ \underline{then}\ \varphi(L_1(K(x,\ y)),\ E(x,\ y))$

$\qquad\qquad\qquad \underline{else}\ H(x,\ y) \qquad\qquad\qquad \underline{fi}\ \rfloor$

$\underline{funct}\ L_1 \equiv (\lambda\ x)\ \rho :$

$\quad \lceil\ R(P(x,\ empty,\ empty))\ \underline{where}$

$\qquad \underline{funct}\ P \equiv (\lambda\ x,\ \underline{stack}\ \lambda\ sx,\ \underline{stack}\ \mu\ sy)(\underline{stack}\ \lambda,\ \underline{stack}\ \mu,\ \rho) :$

$\qquad \lceil\ \mu\ y \equiv G(x)\ ;$

$\qquad\quad \underline{if}\ B(x,\ y)\ \underline{then}\ P(K(x,\ y),\ sx\ \&\ x,\ sy\ \&\ y)$

$\qquad\qquad\qquad\quad \underline{else}\ (sx,\ sy,\ H(x,\ y)) \qquad\quad \underline{fi}\ \rfloor\ ,$

$\qquad \underline{funct}\ R \equiv (\underline{stack}\ \mu\ sx,\ \underline{stack}\ \mu\ sy,\ \rho\ z)\ \rho :$

$\qquad\quad \underline{if}\ sx \neq empty\ \underline{then}\ \mu\ y \equiv \underline{top}\ sy\ ;$

$\qquad\qquad\qquad\qquad\qquad R(\underline{rest}\ sx,\ \underline{rest}\ sy,\ \varphi(z,\ E(\underline{top}\ sx,\ y)))$

$\qquad\qquad\qquad\quad \underline{else}\ z \qquad\qquad\qquad\qquad\qquad\qquad \underline{fi}\ \rfloor\ .$

This transformation clearly exposes two important situations in which
the introduction of the stack sy is unnecessary:

1. y does n o t occur in the expression E: in the routine R
   the declaration $\mu\ y \equiv \underline{top}\ sy$ and thus also the parameter sy becomes superfluous. This shows quite formally, that a double computation does not take place. The parameter sy disappears in P,
   too.

2. y does n o t occur in the expression K: similar to the first
   case, the object declaration in P now becomes superfluous. With
   the disappearance of the stack sy the object declaration in R
   reads $\mu\ y \equiv G(\underline{top}\ sx)$ again. The one and only computation of $G(x)$
   now occurs in R.

In section 3 such situations - in a slightly more general form - will
play a central role. Therefore, we will concentrate in the next section
on methods for establishing them for arbitrary routines.

2.   Disentanglement of the Control

Function inversion is applicable for more general types of recursion, too, in order to acquire a "disentangled form", such that the flow of control can be directly analyzed.

2.1. Disentangled Routines

In general the execution of recursive routines requires a protocol stack in addition to the parameter stack. In the case of repetitive routines both can be dispensed with by transition to iteration. In the case of linear recursive routines at least the protocol stack becomes very simple, as always the same return point is recorded. It is for this profound reason, that in 1.3, once a stack for parameter values is introduced, we were already able to change over to repetitive routines. The "way back" with the help of the second routine R mirrors precisely the identical return points in the protocol stack. For general recursive routines the role of the protocol stack is no longer trivial, such a simple transition to repetitive routines is no longer possible (cf. e.g. /Paterson, Hewitt 70/). The aim of the subsequent development is to gain a final form where these two stacks are separated and thus can be dealt with independent of each other.

To illustrate first the notion of a "detailed form", we consider the simple case of the scheme L (1.1). By introducing auxiliary object declarations, we get

$$\underline{\text{funct}}\ L \equiv (\lambda\ x)\ \rho :$$
$$\underline{\text{if}}\ B(x)\ \underline{\text{then}}\ \lambda\ x_1 \equiv K(x)\ ;\ \rho\ z \equiv L(x_1)\ ;\ \varphi(z,\ E(x))$$
$$\underline{\text{else}}\ H(x) \hspace{4cm} \underline{\text{fi}}\ .$$

This detailed form of a routine is characterized by the fact that the recursive calls are "isolated" with the help of (possibly hierarchical) object declarations.

The detailed form of a recursive routine is said to be <u>disentangled</u> if
none of the parameters and none of the auxiliary identifiers occurs
both before and after a recursive call - for procedures (section 3)
this will mean that no local variable is allowed to carry its value
over a recursive call.

Obviously, repetitive routines are disentangled. Linear recursive routines which are disentangled but not repetitive can be changed trivially
into a repetitive form.

As an example of a more complex recursive structure consider, e.g., the
following scheme ("Towers of Hanoi", Gray code)

$$\underline{\text{funct}}\ F \equiv (\underline{\text{nat}}\ i,\ \rho\ x)\ \rho\ :$$
$$\underline{\text{if}}\ i > 0\ \underline{\text{then}}\ F(i-1,\ \varphi(i,\ F(i-1,\ x)))$$
$$\underline{\text{else}}\ x \qquad\qquad \underline{\text{fi}}\ .$$

The controlling task of the parameter i becomes clearer if the nested calls are arranged in a detailed form:

$$\underline{\text{funct}}\ F \equiv (\underline{\text{nat}}\ i,\ \rho\ x)\ \rho\ :$$
$$\underline{\text{if}}\ i > 0\ \underline{\text{then}}\ \rho\ x_1 \equiv F(i-1,\ x)\ ;$$
$$\rho\ x_2 \equiv \varphi(i,\ x_1)\ ;$$
$$\rho\ x_3 \equiv F(i-1,\ x_2)\ ;$$
$$x_3$$
$$\underline{\text{else}}\ x \qquad\qquad \underline{\text{fi}}\ .$$

This detailed form turns out to be already disentangled with respect
to x . An analytical treatment of the control flow based on this form
was given in /Partsch, Pepper 76/ ("arithmetization of the protocol
stack"). There is a more general result: The control flow of arbitrary
disentangled routines can be subjected to (individual) analysis. This
will be discussed in section 3 .

2.2. Disentangling Recursive Routines by Means of
Function Inversion

The aim of the following consideration is to produce the disentangled
form of a recursive routine. Function inversion, as it turns out now,
serves exactly this purpose.

In the above scheme L the identifiers x_1 and z satisfy the condition of disentanglement. The parameter x, however, does not. The
decisive step towards disentanglement is to return the actual parameter
value as an additional result. The scheme L then changes into

$$\underline{\text{funct}}\ L \equiv (\underline{\lambda}\ x)\ \rho :$$
$$\lceil\quad b\ \underline{\text{where}}$$
$$(\underline{\lambda}\ a,\ \underline{\rho}\ b) \equiv L^*(x)\ ,$$
$$\underline{\text{funct}}\ L^* \equiv (\underline{\lambda}\ x)(\underline{\lambda},\ \underline{\rho}) :$$
$$\underline{\text{if}}\ B(x)\ \underline{\text{then}}\ \underline{\lambda}\ x_1 \equiv K(x)\ ;$$
$$(\underline{\lambda}\ y,\ \underline{\rho}\ z) \equiv L^*(x_1)\ ;$$
$$(x,\ \varphi(z,\ E(x)))$$
$$\underline{\text{else}}\ (x,\ H(x)) \qquad \underline{\text{fi}}\ \rfloor\ .$$

The additional result has at first no functional use whatever. Nevertheless, the relation

$$y = x_1 = K(x)$$

holds by construction, and conversely - if K possesses the inverse $\overline{K}$ -

$$x = \overline{K}(y)\ .$$

If K does not possess such an inverse, we may use a stack again. In
all the following schemes we then have to substitute

$$(\underline{\lambda}\ x,\ \underline{\text{stack}}\ \underline{\lambda}\ sx) \qquad\qquad \text{for}\quad \underline{\lambda}\ x$$
$$(K(x),\ sx\ \&\ x)\ (\underset{\text{def}}{=}\ K^*(x,\ sx)) \qquad \text{for}\quad K(x)$$
$$(\underline{\text{top}}\ sx,\ \underline{\text{rest}}\ sx)\ (\underset{\text{def}}{=}\ \overline{K^*}(x,\ sx)) \qquad \text{for}\quad \overline{K}(x)$$

If, according to the relation $x = \overline{K}(y)$, x is replaced, a new form of
L^* evolves:

$\underline{\text{funct}}\ L^* \equiv (\lambda\ x)(\lambda,\ \rho)\ :$

$\qquad \underline{\text{if}}\ B(x)\ \underline{\text{then}}\ \lambda\ x_1 \equiv K(x)\ ;$

$\qquad\qquad\qquad (\lambda\ y,\ \rho\ z) \equiv L^*(x_1)\ ;$

$\qquad\qquad\qquad (\overline{K}(y),\ \varphi(z,\ E(\overline{K}(y))))$

$\qquad\qquad \underline{\text{else}}\ (x,\ H(x)) \qquad\qquad \underline{\text{fi}}\ .$

This form is now disentangled. Moreover, a comparison with the repetitive form obtained in section 1.2 shows immediately that the part in
front of the recursive call of L^* has moved to the "precomputing"
routine P and the part after the call of L^* has moved to the main
routine R. Thus the method there is a special case of disentangling
by means of function inversion.

The disentangling method, however, is not restricted to recursions of
the (linear) type of L. We now consider an example for cascade-type
recursion[1]

$\qquad \underline{\text{funct}}\ F \equiv (\lambda\ x)\ \rho\ :$

$\qquad\qquad \underline{\text{if}}\ B(x)\ \underline{\text{then}}\ \varphi(F(K_1(x)),\ F(K_2(x)),\ E(x))$

$\qquad\qquad\qquad \underline{\text{else}}\ H(x) \qquad\qquad\qquad \underline{\text{fi}}\ .$

The detailed form reads

$\qquad \underline{\text{funct}}\ F \equiv (\lambda\ x)\ \rho\ :$

$\qquad\qquad \underline{\text{if}}\ B(x)\ \underline{\text{then}}\ \lambda\ x_1 \equiv K_1(x);\ \rho\ z_1 \equiv F(x_1)\ ;$

$\qquad\qquad\qquad \lambda\ x_2 \equiv K_2(x);\ \rho\ z_2 \equiv F(x_2)\ ;$

$\qquad\qquad\qquad \varphi(z_1,\ z_2,\ E(x)$

$\qquad\qquad \underline{\text{else}}\ H(x) \qquad\qquad\qquad \underline{\text{fi}}\ .$

The parameter x and the auxiliary identifier z_1 here violate the
condition of disentanglement.

---

[1] We can assume, that K_1 and K_2 are not equal, as otherwise we
would have no difference from the scheme L.

It becomes obvious here that care should be taken with the detailization. The form - likewise permissible -

> <u>funct</u> $F \equiv (\lambda\ x)\ \rho$:
>> <u>if</u> $B(x)$ <u>then</u> $\underline{\lambda}\ x_1 \equiv K_1(x)$; $\underline{\lambda}\ x_2 \equiv K_2(x)$;
>>> $\underline{\rho}\ z_1 \equiv F(x_1)$; $\underline{\rho}\ z_2 \equiv F(x_2)$;
>>> $\varphi(z_1, \dot{z}_2, E(x))$
>>
>> <u>else</u> $H(x)$ <u>fi</u>

is not as advantageous as the above form of F because here x_2 violates disentanglement as well as x and z_1. This means - if no inverse functions exist - that a stack of the mode <u>stack</u> λ double the size is needed. For this reason the detailed form should be chosen such that as many auxiliary identifiers as possible already satisfy the condition of disentanglement.

Similar to the method applied to scheme L an additional result of the mode λ is now introduced in F and one obtains the following embedding:

> <u>funct</u> $F \equiv (\lambda\ x)\ \rho$:
> $\lceil$ b <u>where</u>
>> $(\underline{\lambda}\ a,\ \underline{\rho}\ b) \equiv F*(x)$,
>>
>> <u>funct</u> $F* \equiv (\underline{\lambda}\ x)(\underline{\lambda},\ \underline{\rho})$:
>>> <u>if</u> $B(x)$ <u>then</u> $\underline{\lambda}\ x_1 \equiv K_1(x)$; $(\underline{\lambda}\ y_1,\ \underline{\rho}\ z_1) \equiv F*(x_1)$;
>>> $\underline{\lambda}\ x_2 \equiv K_2(x)$; $(\underline{\lambda}\ y_2,\ \underline{\rho}\ z_2) \equiv F*(x_2)$;
>>> $(x, \varphi(z_1, z_2, E(x)))$
>>
>>> <u>else</u> $(x, H(x))$ <u>fi</u> $\rfloor$.

With the inverse functions $\overline{K_1}$ and $\overline{K_2}$ we have the following equivalences

> $y_1 = K_1(x)$ and $x = \overline{K_1}(y_1)$
> $y_2 = K_2(x)$ and $x = \overline{K_2}(y_2)$.

Thus F acquires - apart from z_1 - the desired form

> <u>funct</u> $F* \equiv (\underline{\lambda}\ x)(\underline{\lambda},\ \underline{\rho})$:
>> <u>if</u> $B(x)$ <u>then</u> $\underline{\lambda}\ x_1 \equiv K_1(x)$; $(\underline{\lambda}\ y_1,\ \underline{\rho}\ z_1) \equiv F*(x_1)$;
>> $\underline{\lambda}\ x_2 \equiv K_2(\overline{K_1}(y_1))$; $(\underline{\lambda}\ y_2,\ \underline{\rho}\ z_2) \equiv F*(x_2)$;
>> $(\overline{K_2}(y_2), \varphi(z_1, z_2, E(\overline{K_2}(y_2))))$
>>
>> <u>else</u> $(x, H(x))$ <u>fi</u> .

As there is no possibility of working with an inverse function with respect to z_1 the only viable way is to introduce a stack on parameter and on result position (in the same way as in L_1 in 1.3):

$\underline{funct}\ F \equiv (\lambda\ x)\ \rho\ :$

$\lceil$ b $\underline{where}$

$(\lambda\ a,\ \underline{stack}\ \rho\ sb,\ \rho\ b) \equiv F*(x,\ empty),$

$\underline{funct}\ F* \equiv (\lambda\ s,\ \underline{stack}\ \rho\ sz)(\lambda,\ \underline{stack}\ \rho,\ \rho)\ :$

$\quad \underline{if}\ B(x)\ \underline{then}\ (\lambda\ x_1,\ \underline{stack}\ \rho\ sr_1) \equiv (K_1(x),\ sz)\ ;$

$\qquad\qquad\qquad\quad (\lambda\ y_1,\ \underline{stack}\ \rho\ sz_1,\ \rho\ z_1) \equiv F*(x_1,\ sr_1)\ ;$

$\qquad\qquad\qquad\quad (\lambda\ x_2,\ \underline{stack}\ \rho\ sr_2) \equiv (K_2(x),\ sz\ \&\ z_1)\ ;$

$\qquad\qquad\qquad\quad (\lambda\ y_2,\ \underline{stack}\ \rho\ sz_2,\ \rho\ z_2) \equiv F*(x_2,\ sr_2)\ ;$

$\qquad\qquad\qquad\quad (x,\ sz,\ \varphi(z_1,\ z_2,\ E(x)))$

$\qquad\qquad \underline{else}\ (x,\ sz,\ H(x)) \qquad\qquad\qquad\qquad \underline{fi}\ \rfloor$.

In addition to the above-mentioned equivalences of x and y_1 or x and y_2 the following equivalences now hold

$\qquad sz_1 = sr_1 = sz$

$\qquad sz_2 = sr_2 = sz\ \&\ z_1,\quad$ and $\quad sz = \underline{rest}\ sz_2,\quad z_1 = \underline{top}\ sz_2$.

We take full advantage of these equivalences to produce a disentangled form; e.g. in the result of the $\underline{then}$-branch, sz can be replaced by the equivalent expression $\underline{rest}\ sz_2$, which satisfies the condition of disentanglement. Altogether we obtain:

$\underline{funct}\ F* \equiv (\lambda\ x,\ \underline{stack}\ \rho\ sz)(\lambda,\ \underline{stack}\ \rho,\ \rho)\ :$

$\quad \underline{if}\ B(x)\ \underline{then}\ (\lambda\ x_1,\ \underline{stack}\ \rho\ sr_1) \qquad \equiv (K_1(x),\ sz)\ ;$

$\qquad\qquad\qquad (\lambda\ y_1,\ \underline{stack}\ \rho\ sz_1,\ \rho\ z_1) \equiv F*(x_1,\ sr_1)\ ;$

$\qquad\qquad\qquad (\lambda\ x_2,\ \underline{stack}\ \rho\ sr_2) \qquad \equiv (K_2(\overline{K_1}(y_1)),\ sz_1\ \&\ z_1)\ ;$

$\qquad\qquad\qquad (\lambda\ y_2,\ \underline{stack}\ \rho\ sz_2,\ \rho\ z_2) \equiv F*(x_2,\ sr_2)\ ;$

$\qquad\qquad\qquad (K_2(y_2),\ \underline{rest}\ sz_2,\ \varphi(\underline{top}\ sz_2,\ z_2,\ E(\overline{K_2}(y_2))))$

$\qquad\qquad \underline{else}\ (x,\ sz,\ H(x)) \qquad\qquad\qquad\qquad\qquad \underline{fi}$.

The stack sz is frequently called an (intermediate) result stack. It can be seen, however, that it does not differ from a stack for parameters and local auxiliary identifiers. Its only peculiarity is that it cannot be avoided - even at the cost of multiple computations.

If the routine F has more than two adjacent calls, we can either introduce for each call (except for the last one) a stack of its own with
the mode <u>stack</u> ρ or we can enter all intermediate results z_i successively into a stack sz . In the function φ all z_i are then replaced
by the expressions <u>top</u> sz, <u>top</u> <u>rest</u> sz, <u>top</u> <u>rest</u> <u>rest</u> sz, etc.

We have stated that in general a stack can be used when the inverse
functions $\overline{K_1}$ and $\overline{K_2}$ do not exist. An interesting variant arises if
only one of the two exists, e.g. $\overline{K_1}$. We can then define

$$K_1^*(x, \; sx) = (K_1(x), \; sx) \; , \quad \text{instead of} \quad (K_1(x), \; sx \; \& \; x) \; , \quad \text{and}$$
$$K_2^*(x, \; sx) = (K_2(x), \; sx \; \& \; x)$$

and obtain as inverse functions

$$\overline{K_1^*}(x, \; sx) = (\overline{K_1}(x), \; sx) \; , \quad \text{instead of} \quad (\underline{top} \; sx, \; \underline{rest} \; sx) \; , \quad \text{and}$$
$$\overline{K_2^*}(x, \; sx) = (\underline{top} \; sx, \; \underline{rest} \; sx) \; .$$

This means that as soon as no inverse exists for at least one of the
functions K_i , a stack must be introduced as an additional parameter.
This stack, however, remains constant for all calls for which an inverse function exists, thus reducing the required storage space considerably. (For this reason it is worthwhile to give the programmer "access"
to the stacking mechanism instead of hiding it in a complex compiler.)

Let us now consider schemes for nested recursion. An example is the
scheme

<u>funct</u> $G \equiv (\lambda \; x) \; \rho$:
    <u>if</u> $B(x)$ <u>then</u> $\varphi(G(\psi(G(K_1(x)), \; K_2(x))), \; E(x))$
        <u>else</u> $H(x)$ <u>fi</u> .

In a detailed form it reads

<u>funct</u> $G \equiv (\lambda \; x) \; \rho$:
    <u>if</u> $B(x)$ <u>then</u> $\lambda \; x_1 \equiv K_1(x)$; $\rho \; z_1 \equiv G(x_1)$;
               $\lambda \; x_2 \equiv \psi(z_1, \; K_2(x))$; $\underline{\rho} \; z_2 \equiv G(x_2)$;
               $\varphi(z_2, \; E(x))$
        <u>else</u> $H(x)$ <u>fi</u> .

It can be seen immediately, that this type of recursion is easier to handle than a cascade-type recursion[1], as the intermediate results z_1 and z_2 already satisfy the conditions of disentanglement, but there is no possibility of directly constructing the value of the parameter x from the value x_2 by means of an inverse function. Therefore a stack must definitely be introduced. The routine G thus becomes by strictly applying formal rules

$$\underline{funct}\ G \equiv (\lambda\ x)\ \rho :$$
$$\lceil\ b\ \underline{where}$$
$$(\lambda\ a,\ \underline{stack}\ \lambda\ sa,\ \rho\ b) \equiv G^*(x,\ empty),$$

$$\underline{funct}\ G^* \equiv (\lambda\ x,\ \underline{stack}\ \lambda\ sx)(\lambda,\ \underline{stack}\ \lambda,\ \rho) :$$
$$\underline{if}\ B(x)\ \underline{then}\ (\lambda\ x_1,\ \underline{stack}\ \lambda\ sx_1) \equiv (K_1(x),\ sx)\ ;$$
$$(\lambda\ y_1,\ \underline{stack}\ \lambda\ sy_1,\ \rho\ z_1) \equiv G^*(x_1,\ sx_1)\ ;$$
$$(\lambda\ x_2,\ \underline{stack}\ \lambda\ sx_2) \equiv (\psi(z_1,\ K_2(\overline{K_1}(y_1))),$$
$$sy_1\ \&\ \overline{K_1}(y_1))\ ;$$
$$(\lambda\ y_2,\ \underline{stack}\ \lambda\ sy_2,\ \rho\ z_2) \equiv G^*(x_2,\ sx_2)\ ;$$
$$(\underline{top}\ sy_2,\ \underline{rest}\ sy_2,\ \varphi(z_2,\ E(\underline{top}\ sy_2)))$$
$$\underline{else}\ (x,\ sx,\ H(x)) \qquad\qquad \underline{fi}\ \rfloor\ .$$

Of course, this scheme does not have the most elegant and readable form (in particular, some of the object declarations seem quite superfluous). But these seeming redundancies will ease the later transition to variables and assignments considerably.

2.3. Reshaping the Control Flow Type

Sometimes it is possible to change the control flow into another more efficiently manageable type. The scheme (with an associative operation σ)

$$\underline{funct}\ F \equiv (\lambda\ x)\ \rho :$$
$$\underline{if}\ B(x)\ \underline{then}\ F(K_1(x))\ \sigma\ F(K_2(x))\ \sigma\ E(x)$$
$$\underline{else}\ H(x) \qquad\qquad \underline{fi}$$

may serve as an example.

---

[1] This motivates the transition from one type to the other (if possible) which will be discussed in section 2.3.

This scheme is typical for "processing of trees", where the functions K_1, K_2 mean "left subtree" or "right subtree". In such a case we normally have to use stacks. As shown in 2.2 two stacks are required for such cascade-type recursions, one for the parameters and one for the intermediate results.

However, if the operation σ is associative (as already suggested by the missing brackets in the above scheme) the stack of intermediate results can be avoided. In order to make the notation somewhat simpler a neutral element e for σ is assumed in addition.

With these assumptions the computational terms produced by F can be restructured in order to decrease the amount of pending operations. This is achieved by applying the technique of re-bracketing[1] which leads to

> **funct** $F \equiv (\lambda\ x)\ \underline{\rho}$:
> $\lceil$ $G(x,\ e)$ **where**
>   **funct** $G \equiv (\lambda\ x,\ \rho\ z)\ \underline{\rho}$:
>   **if** $B(x)$ **then** $G(K_1(x),\ (F(K_2(x))\ \sigma\ E(x))\ \sigma\ z)$
>   **else** $H(x)\ \sigma\ z$ **fi** $\rfloor$.

---

[1] The following standard transformation rule is formally applied:

> **funct** $L \equiv (\lambda\ m)\ \underline{\rho}$:
>   **if** $B(m)$ **then** $L(K(m))\ \sigma\ E(m)$
>   **else** $H(m)$ **fi**

$$\left\{ \begin{array}{l} \forall\ \rho\ r,\ s,\ t\ :\ (r\ \sigma\ s)\ \sigma\ t = r\ \sigma\ (s\ \sigma\ t) \\ \exists\ \rho\ e\ :\ \forall\ \rho\ r\ :\ r\ \sigma\ e = r \end{array} \right.$$

> **funct** $L \equiv (\lambda\ m)\ \underline{\rho}$:
> $\lceil$ $G(m,\ e)$ **where**
>   **funct** $G \equiv (\lambda\ m,\ \rho\ z)\ \underline{\rho}$:
>   **if** $B(m)$ **then** $G(K(m),\ E(m)\ \sigma\ z)$
>   **else** $H(m)\ \sigma\ z$ **fi** $\rfloor$.

According to the equivalence $F(x) = G(x, e)$ the inner call of F can be substituted (as the termination of G depends on the first parameter x only, no complications arise); because of the associativity of σ the following evolves

$$\underline{\text{funct}}\ F \equiv (\lambda\ x)\ \rho :$$
$$\lceil\ G(x, e)\ \underline{\text{where}}$$
$$\underline{\text{funct}}\ G \equiv (\lambda\ x,\ \rho\ z)\ \rho :$$
$$\underline{\text{if}}\ B(x)\ \underline{\text{then}}\ G(K_1(x),\ G(K_2(x),\ e)\ \sigma\ (E(x)\ \sigma\ z))$$
$$\underline{\text{else}}\ H(x)\ \sigma\ z \qquad\qquad \underline{\text{fi}}\ \rfloor\ .$$

An important property of G (which can be proved e.g. by computational induction) is, that for arbitrary $\lambda\ a, \rho\ b, \rho\ c$

$$G(a, b)\ \sigma\ c = G(a,\ b\ \sigma\ c)$$

holds. Together with $e\ \sigma\ b = b$ this yields

$$\underline{\text{funct}}\ F \equiv (\lambda\ x)\ \rho :$$
$$\lceil\ G(x, e)\ \underline{\text{where}}$$
$$\underline{\text{funct}}\ G \equiv (\lambda\ x,\ \rho\ z)\ \rho :$$
$$\underline{\text{if}}\ B(x)\ \underline{\text{then}}\ G(K_1(x),\ G(K_2(x),\ E(x)\ \sigma\ z))$$
$$\underline{\text{else}}\ H(x)\ \sigma\ z \qquad\qquad \underline{\text{fi}}\ \rfloor\ .$$

As already shown in 2.2 a nested recursion is more suitable with respect to the stack of intermediate results; this becomes obvious here, too, through the detailed form

$$\underline{\text{funct}}\ G \equiv (\lambda\ x,\ \rho\ z)\ \rho :$$
$$\underline{\text{if}}\ B(x)\ \underline{\text{then}}\ (\lambda\ x_1,\ \rho\ z_1) \equiv (K_2(x),\ E(x)\ \sigma\ z)\ ;$$
$$\rho\ r_1 \qquad\qquad \equiv G(x_1,\ z_1)\ ;$$
$$(\lambda\ x_2,\ \rho\ z_2) \equiv (K_1(x),\ r_1)\ ;$$
$$\rho\ r_2 \qquad\qquad \equiv G(x_2,\ z_2)\ ;$$
$$r_2$$
$$\underline{\text{else}}\ H(x)\ \sigma\ z \qquad\qquad\qquad \underline{\text{fi}}\ .$$

Only the parameter x violates the condition of disentanglement. As nothing should be assumed for K_1 and K_2 the inverse function must be managed with the help of a stack:

<u>funct</u> $F \equiv (\lambda \ x) \ \underline{\rho}$:

$\lceil$ b <u>where</u>

    ($\underline{stack} \ \lambda \ sa, \ \underline{\rho} \ b) \equiv G(x, \ empty, \ e)$,

    <u>funct</u> $G \equiv (\lambda \ x, \ \underline{stack} \ \lambda \ sx, \ \underline{\rho} \ z)(\underline{stack} \ \lambda, \ \underline{\rho})$:

        <u>if</u> $B(x)$ <u>then</u> $(\lambda \ x_1, \ \underline{stack} \ \lambda \ sx_1, \ \underline{\rho} \ z_1) \equiv$

                            $(K_2(x), \ sx \ \& \ x, \ E(x) \ \sigma \ z)$;

                $(\underline{stack} \ \lambda \ sy_1, \ \underline{\rho} \ r_1) \equiv G(x_1, \ sx_1, \ z_1)$;

                $(\lambda \ x_2, \ \underline{stack} \ \lambda \ sx_2, \ \underline{\rho} \ z_2) \equiv$

                        $(K_1(\underline{top} \ sy_1), \ \underline{rest} \ sy_1, \ r_1)$;

                $(\underline{stack} \ \lambda \ sy_2, \ \underline{\rho} \ r_2) \equiv G(x_2, \ sx_2, \ z_2)$;

                $(sy_2, \ r_2)$

            <u>else</u> $H(x) \ \sigma \ z$ <u>fi</u> $\rfloor$.

This example, as well as the preceding disentangled forms, will be further developed in 3.2 by a technique to be discussed in the next section.

3.   Deparameterization and Transition to Iteration

Detailization and disentanglement have been the essential steps in disclosing the control structure of recursive routines as well as in separating it from parameter organization.

This transformation process is now completed by deparameterization:
Parameters and results are eliminated at the cost of introducing variables, assignments and procedures (for a formal treatment of this transition from the applicative to the procedural level see /Pepper 78/).

Finally some "low level" form of recursion will be achieved containing
only commands and calls of procedures without parameters and results.
This form either is already repetitive or is open to a suitable analytical treatment of the control flow - due to the complete separation
from data flow.

3.1. Deparameterization

For certain recursive routines f one can obtain a counterpart with
program variables as parameters by the following steps; the effect of
each step will be illustrated by means of the example of the simple
routine

> funct pow ≡ (int a, nat e) int :
>   if e = 0 then a
>   else sq(pow(a, e − 1)) fi .

a)   Extract the respective expression K from every (direct or indirect) recursive call of the form $f(K(m))$ of the routine f , that
is replace $f(K(m))$ by var λ h := $K(m)$; $f(\underline{val}$ h) with a different
$h = h^{(i)}$ for every occurrence.

Thus pow becomes[1]

---

[1]   The parameter a does not have to be included in the process as it
is fixed. It could also have been suppressed first.

```
funct pow ≡ (int a, nat e) int :
    if e = 0 then a
            else sq( ⌈ var nat h := e - 1 ; pow(a, val h) ⌋ ) fi .
```

b) Introduce now a new routine f* or a new system in which a variable parameter m is used instead of the original parameter.[1]

```
proc pow* ≡ (int A, var nat e) int :
    if val e = 0 then A
            else sq( ⌈ var nat h := val e - 1 ; pow*(A, h) ⌋ ) fi .
```

c) Every auxiliary variable $h^{(i)}$ is replaced by the variable parameter m . The conditions that are necessary for carrying out this
central step of the process will be dealt with in detail below.

```
proc pow* ≡ (int A, var nat e) int :
    if val e = 0 then A
            else sq( ⌈ e := val e - 1 ; pow*(A, e) ⌋ ) fi .
```

d) The original routine f is "embedded" in f* by substituting for
its body a declaration of the program variable m , initialized to
the original parameter M , followed by a call of f* .

```
funct pow ≡ (int A, nat E) int :
    ⌈ var nat e := E ; pow*(A, e) where
      proc pow* ≡ (int A, var nat e) int :
          if val e = 0 then A
                  else sq( ⌈ e := val e - 1 ; pow*(A, e) ⌋ ) fi .
```

e) The parameters of the embedding routine are now fixed and can therefore be "suppressed", i.e. made non-local in this routine.

```
funct pow ≡ (int A, nat E) int :
    ⌈ var nat e := E ; pow* where
      proc pow* ≡ int :
          if val e = 0 then A
                  else sq( ⌈ e := val e - 1 ; pow* ⌋ ) fi ⌋ .
```

---

[1] In order to avoid copying mistakes while changing over to program
variables it has proved practical to use the original parameter
identifiers (lower case) as variable identifiers and to use upper
case for the object identifiers.

With step (e) the parameters have been replaced by non-local variables. Some minor simplifications finally yield for the example

funct pow ≡ (int A, nat E) int :
⌈ var nat e := E ; pow* where
  proc pow* ≡ int : if e = 0 then A else e := e - 1 ; sq(pow*) fi ⌋ .

Now the problem of the parameter stack is solved (it has collapsed into a single non-local program variable), but there still are the "pending" executions of the operation sq . They have to be treated by means of a protocol stack (which in this special case simply can be realized by a counter).

Vital for the success of the method, obviously, is whether in step (c) the "fusion" of the auxiliary variables $h^{(i)}$ and the variable parameter m is possible. A prerequisite is that the value of m is no longer needed "behind" the block in which h is declared (or collateral to it). Thus the main purpose of the disentangling method in section 2 becomes apparent: A disentangled routine fulfills just the conditions for carrying out step (c) ; in other words: every disentangled routine can be deparameterized.

The following routine (/Morris 68/) provides another example of a nested recursion which does not require the introduction of a stack for disentanglement:

funct morris ≡ (int a, int b) int :
    if a = b then b + 1
            else morris(a, morris(a-1, b+1)) fi .

Deparameterization according to the preceding steps results in

```
funct morris ≡ (int A, int B) int :
┌  (var int a, var int b) := (A, B) ;  (a, b) := morris* ; b where
   proc morris* ≡ (int, int) :
        if a = b then (a, b+1)
                 else (a, b) := (a-1, b+1) ;  (a, b) := morris* ;
                      (a, b) := (a+1, b) ;    (a, b) := morris* ;
                      (a, b)                                      fi ┘ .
```

The procedure morris* has no longer a parameter but still has a
(composite) result. Since the result of morris* occurs only in assignments of the form (a, b) := morris*, importing this assignment into
the procedure is permitted and finally yields

```
funct morris ≡ (int A, int B) int :
┌  (var int a, var int b) := (A, B) ; morris** ; b where
   proc morris** ≡
        if a = b then b := b+1
                 else (a, b) := (a-1, b+1) ; morris** ;
                      a := a + 1 ; morris**          fi ┘ .
```

An example of a tree-traversal algorithm is developed in /Pepper et
al. 78/: There the disentanglement either needs a stack or a suitable
change of the data structure, namely the "fusion" of stack and tree
to a "threaded tree" (cf. /Partsch, Broy 78/).

3.2. Examples

The disentangled form was developed for some non-linear recursions
in section 2. To complete this the corresponding deparameterized
version will now be given.

In the cascade-type recursive routine F in 2.2

```
        funct F ≡ (λ x) ρ :
             if B(x) then φ(F(K₁(x)), F(K₂(x)), E(x))
                     else H(x)                          fi
```

the variables v, sv and z can be introduced after disentanglement.
They carry the respective intermediate results and are suppressed as

parameters in F^*. This yields [1,2]

$\underline{funct}\ F \equiv (\lambda\ x)\ \rho\ :$

⌈ $(\underline{var}\ \lambda\ v,\ \underline{var}\ \underline{stack}\ \rho\ sv,\ \underline{var}\ \rho\ z) := (x,\ empty, \text{ω})\ ;$
 $F^*\ ;\ z\ \underline{where}$
 $\underline{proc}\ F^* \equiv\ :$

	v	sv	z
$\underline{if}\ B(v)\ \underline{then}\ v := K_1(v)\ ;$	x_1	sr_1	
$F^*\ ;$	y_1	sz_1	z_1
$v := \overline{K_1}(v)\ ;$	x_1	sz_1	z_1
$(v,\ sv) := (K_2(v)\ ,\ sv\ \&\ z)\ ;$	x_2	sr_2	z_1
$F^*\ ;$	y_2	sz_2	z_2
$v := \overline{K_2}(v)\ ;$			
$(sv,\ z) := (\underline{rest}\ sv,\ \varphi(\underline{top}\ sv,\ z,\ E(v)))$			
$\underline{else}\ z := H(v)$			$\underline{fi}$ ⌋ .

Analogously for the nested recursive routine G in 2.2

$\underline{funct}\ G \equiv (\lambda\ x)\ \rho\ :$
 $\underline{if}\ B(x)\ \underline{then}\ \varphi(G(\psi(G(K_1(x)),\ K_2(x))),\ E(x))$
 $\underline{else}\ H(x)$ $\underline{fi}$

we have a deparameterized form with the variables v, sv and z

$\underline{funct}\ G \equiv (\lambda\ x)\ \rho\ :$

⌈ $(\underline{var}\ \lambda\ v,\ \underline{var}\ \underline{stack}\ \lambda\ sv,\ \underline{var}\ \rho\ z) := (x,\ empty, \text{ω})\ ;$
 $G^*\ ;\ z\ \underline{where}$
 $\underline{proc}\ G^* \equiv\ :$

	v	sv	z
$\underline{if}\ B(v)\ \underline{then}\ v := K_1(v)\ ;$	x_1	sx_1	
$G^*\ ;$	y_1	sy_1	z_1
$v := \overline{K_1}(v)\ ;$	x_1	sy_1	z_1
$(v,\ sv) := (\psi(z,\ K_2(v)),\ sv\ \&\ v)\ ;$	x_2	sx_2	z_1
$G^*\ ;$	y_2	sy_2	z_2
$(v,\ sv,\ z) :=$			
$\quad (\underline{top}\ sv,\ \underline{rest}\ sv,\ \varphi(z,\ E(\underline{top}\ sv)))$			
$\underline{else}\ z := H(v)$			$\underline{fi}$ ⌋ .

---

[1] φ is an insignificant object indicating that the initialization is missing. The use of an uninitialized variable cannot be avoided here as z has pure result character for F^*.

[2] To ease the comparison to the routine F in 2.2 , we have added a margin column. It indicates the current values of the three variables (after execution of the respective statement).

Finally a special case of F in 2.3 was transformed to nested re-cursion (by re-bracketing according to the associativity of σ) and then disentangled. From the final version there we obtain the form-ulation which clearly shows what has been gained in efficiency:

<u>funct</u> $F \equiv (\lambda\ x)\ \rho$:

$\ulcorner$ (<u>var</u> λ v, <u>var</u> <u>stack</u> λ sv, <u>var</u> ρ z) := (x, empty, e) ;

$F*$; z <u>where</u>

<u>proc</u> $F* \equiv$: <u>if</u> $B(v)$

	v	sv	z
<u>then</u> (v, sv, z) := $(K_2(v)$, sv & v, $E(v)\ \sigma\ z)$;	x_1	sx_1	z_1
$F*$;	x_1	sy_1	r_1
(v, sv) := $(K_1(\underline{top}\ sv)$, <u>rest</u> sv) ;	x_2	sx_2	z_2
$F*$;	x_2	sy_2	r_2
<u>else</u> z := $H(v)\ \sigma\ z$ <u>fi</u> $\lrcorner$.			

The result of this deparameterization is in fact the disclosing of the control structure of the algorithm.

3.3. Analysis of the Control Flow

For (direct recursive) repetitive routines of the form

<u>funct</u> $R \equiv (\lambda\ m)\ \rho$:

    <u>if</u> $B(m)$ <u>then</u> $R(K(m))$ <u>else</u> $H(m)$ <u>fi</u>

we obtained in 3.1 the form

<u>funct</u> $R \equiv (\lambda\ M)\ \rho$:

$\ulcorner$ <u>var</u> λ m := M; R^* <u>where</u>

    <u>proc</u> $R^* \equiv \rho$:

        <u>if</u> $B(m)$ <u>then</u> m := $K(m)$; R^*

                  <u>else</u> $H(m)$ <u>fi</u> $\lrcorner$

or, by "extracting" the computation of $H(m)$, a variant using a pure procedure (without result). These forms are, by definition, equivalent to certain iterations (cf. /Wirth 71/, /Dijkstra 73/).

For the more interesting cases we consider the following scheme as a prototype of the result of the above development

$$\underline{proc}\ M \equiv\ :$$
$$\underline{if}\ B\ \underline{then}\ S_1\ ;\ M\ ;\ S_2\ ;\ M\ ;\ S_3$$
$$\underline{else}\ S_4 \qquad\qquad \underline{fi}\ .$$

This scheme can be subjected to an analytical treatment of the flow of computation. Generally, iterative control description is achieved by introducing a label stack for storing the (multiple) return points. Special cases allow this label stack to be simulated by e.g.

- counting the returns, if there is a single return point

- a stack of binary marks or, simpler, a two state counter, if two return points exist

- other possible arithmetic coding of the protocol stack (cf. /Partsch, Pepper 76/, also /Bird 77/).

We will consider here the analytical treatment of the control flow by a stack for binary marks. The basic connection with the other methods is obvious, if we note that a stack of binary marks corresponds to a dual number.

A stack of binary marks is therefore introduced where

$$\underline{mode}\ mark \equiv \{1., 2.\}$$

and M is embedded in the procedure M^* with a mark stack as an additional parameter

$$\underline{proc}\ M\ \equiv\ :\ M^*(empty)\ \underline{where}$$
$$\underline{proc}\ M^* \equiv (\underline{stack}\ \underline{mark}\ p)\ :$$
$$\underline{if}\ B\ \underline{then}\ S_1\ ;\ M^*(p\ \&\ 1.)\ ;\ S_2\ ;\ M^*(p\ \&\ 2.)\ ;\ S_3$$
$$\underline{else}\ S_4 \qquad\qquad\qquad \underline{fi}\ .$$

When a recursive call is terminated we can tell by the stack p where work will be continued: If $\underline{top}\ p = 1.$, then work is continued with S_2, if $\underline{top}\ p = 2.$, work is continued with S_3.

With the help of the information contained in the stack p the recursive calls can be transferred to the branches of a conditional statement
and thus a decisive step has been taken in the direction of a repetitive
form.

However the above formulation "the work is continued with ..." shows
already that additional recursive calls are necessary at those points
where the original routine M terminated. Therefore we must differentiate between two cases of recursive calls: the "real" recursions which
correspond to calls which were already there, and "fake" recursions
which prompt the work to be continued at the points where the recursion
terminated before, i.e. where the previous incarnation was "reactivated".
We can easily distinguish between these two cases by a boolean parameter:
altogether we obtain the following repetitive form for the routine M

proc M ≡ : M*(true, empty) where
proc M* ≡ (bool rec, stack mark p) :
    if rec then if B then S_1 ; M*(true, p & 1.)
                    else S_4 ; M*(false, p) fi
    ▯ ¬ rec then if p ≠ empty
                    then if top p = 1. then S_2 ; M*(true, rest p & 2.)
                        ▯ top p = 2. then S_3 ; M*(false, rest p) fi
                    else skip   fi fi .

The recursion ends exactly when we reach a case of termination
(indicated by ¬rec) and when the stack p is empty. This case is
found in the branch with skip .

It is instructive to consider the special case of linear recursion
once more. The deparameterized form corresponds to the scheme

            proc L ≡ :
                if B then S_1 ; L ; S_2
                    else S_3 fi .

A transformation of the above type thus yields

proc L ≡ : $L*(\underline{true}$, empty) $\underline{where}$

proc $L*$ ≡ ($\underline{bool}$ rec, $\underline{stack}$ $\underline{mark}$ p) :

    $\underline{if}$ rec $\underline{then}$ $\underline{if}$ B $\underline{then}$ S_1 ; $L*(\underline{true}$, p & 1.)

                    $\underline{else}$ S_3 ; $L*(\underline{false}$, p) $\underline{fi}$

  ▯ ¬ rec $\underline{then}$ $\underline{if}$ p ≠ empty

                          $\underline{then}$ $\underline{if}$ $\underline{top}$ p = 1. $\underline{then}$ S_2 ; $L*(\underline{false}$, $\underline{rest}$ p) $\underline{fi}$

                          $\underline{else}$ $\underline{skip}$ $\underline{fi}$ $\underline{fi}$

Obviously the stack p contains only 1. (that is stroke numbers):
it would be sufficient to retain their number by a counter. The sole
purpose of the counter is then to cause termination as soon as it is
0. (The parameter stack can also carry out this task.) In addition
it can be seen that the parameter rec can never again become $\underline{true}$
once it has been actualized by $\underline{false}$. Thus the branch with the guard
¬ rec can be split off to a routine of its own:

        proc $L*$ ≡ ($\underline{nat}$ p) :

           $\underline{if}$ B $\underline{then}$ S_1 ; $L*(p+1)$

                $\underline{else}$ S_3 ; $L_1^*(p)$ $\underline{fi}$,

        proc L_1^* ≡ ($\underline{nat}$ p) :

           $\underline{if}$ p ≠ 0 $\underline{then}$ S_2 ; $L_1^*(p-1)$

                $\underline{else}$ $\underline{skip}$ $\underline{fi}$.

This form corresponds on the whole to those variants of functional inversion which use an additional parameter as a counter in order to
ease the test for termination.

The extension of these methods to the case of three or more calls
in the body of a routine, using ternary etc. marks, is obvious.

4. Conclusion

A specific method of introducing parameter and protocol stacks by
n e e d has been developed in a systematic and formal way. The
transformation process applies to arbitrary kinds of recursions
and hence does not require determining whether the recursion under
consideration is linear.

However, determining linearity and using special properties such
as associativity, commutativity or invertibility of certain operations is still of assistance since it may allow considerable

simplifications. In particular, the combined application of special techniques (like re-bracketing) and general ones (like the method of disentanglement) has proved to be advantageous. For example,
after reshaping a cascade-type recursion into a (simpler) nested recursion, the disentanglement and deparameterization produced a more
efficient result.

The method shown here can be added to the general techniques used in compiler construction for implementing recursive routines. Moreover, it provides a formal proof for the correctness of usual stacking mechanisms.

References

/Auslander, Strong 78/

   M.A. Auslander, H.R. Strong: Systematic Recursion Removal.
   Comm. ACM 21, 127-134 (1978)

/Bauer et al. 78a/

   F.L. Bauer, M. Broy, W. Hesse, B. Krieg-Brückner, H. Partsch,
   P. Pepper, H. Wössner: Towards a Wide Spectrum Language to
   Support Program Specification and Program Development. SIG-
   PLAN Notices 13 (12), 15-24 (1978). Also this volume

/Bauer et al. 78b/

   F.L. Bauer, M. Broy, H. Partsch, P. Pepper, H. Wössner:
   Systematics of Transformation Rules. Technische Universität
   München, Institut für Informatik, Interner Bericht, Dec. 1978.
   Also this volume

/Bird 77/

   R.S. Bird: Notes on Recursion Elimination. Comm. ACM 20,
   434-439 (1977)

/Cooper 66/

   D.C. Cooper: The Equivalence of Certain Computations.
   Comp. J. 9, 45-52 (1966)

A Study on

Transformational Semantics [+)]

P. Pepper

Institut für Informatik
Technische Universität München
Postfach 20 24 20
D-8000 München

Abstract

The semantics of a programming language is specified - relative to a
kernel language - by reducing certain constructs of the language to
more elementary ones by means of definitional transformations.
Parallels to the algebraic specification of abstract data types are
discussed. This approach of "transformational semantics" is illustrated by explaining program variables in terms of purely applicative constructs.

[+)]
Dissertation submitted to the Fachbereich Mathematik der
Technischen Universität München.
This research was carried out within the Sonderforschungs-
bereich 49, Programmiertechnik, München.

/Darlington, Burstall 76/

    J. Darlington, R.M. Burstall: A System which Automatically
Improves Programs. Acta Informatica 6, 41-60 (1976)

/Dijkstra 73/

    E.W. Dijkstra: A Simple Axiomatic Basis for Programming
Language Constructs. Report EWD 372, Technological University Eindhoven, 1973. Also Marktoberdorf Summer School 1973

/Knuth 74/

    D.E. Knuth: Structured Programming with goto Statements.
Comp. Surveys 6, 261-301 (1974)

/Morris 68/

    J.H. Morris: Lambda-calculus models of programming.
Ph. D. Thesis, Project MAC, MIT, MAC-TR-57, Dec. 1968

/Partsch, Broy 78/

    H. Partsch, M. Broy: Examples for Change of Types and Ob-
ject Structures. This volume

/Partsch, Pepper 76/

    H. Partsch, P. Pepper: A Family of Rules for Recursion Re-
moval Related to the Towers of Hanoi Problem. Technische
Universität München, Institut für Informatik, Rep. No. 7612,
1976. Also Inf. Proc. Letters 5, 174-177 (1976)

/Paterson, Hewitt 70/

    M.S. Paterson, C.E. Hewitt: Comparative Schematology. In:
Record of the Project MAC Conf. on Concurrent Systems and
Parallel Computation, New York: ACM 1970, 119-127

/Pepper 78/

    P. Pepper: A Study on Transformational Semantics. Disser-
tation, Munich 1978. Also this volume

/Pepper et al. 78/

    P. Pepper, H. Partsch, H. Wössner, F.L. Bauer: A Transforma-
tional Approach to Programming. In: B. Robinet (ed.): Program Transformations. Proc. of the 3rd International Symposium on Programming, March 28 - 30, 1978, Paris: Dunod 1978

/Wirth 71/

    N. Wirth: The Programming Language Pascal. Acta Informatica
1, 35-63 (1971)

323

Contents

Acknowledgement

I thank Professor F.L. Bauer and Professor K. Samelson for their support and valuable
criticisms. It was especially Professor Bauer who encouraged me to look deeper into
the topic of this thesis.

I am also very grateful to my colleagues from the project CIP at the Technical University Munich. In particular, Helmut Partsch was a stimulating partner in many valuable discussions starting from the time when the first and vague ideas of a formalization of "transformational semantics" and of its application to the introduction of
program variables took shape. Martin Wirsing, too, provided numerous helpful comments
on the subject and on the paper. Manfred Broy and Hans Wössner accompanied the work
with great interest. I also enjoyed some discussions with Franz Geiselbrechtinger and
Rupert Gnatz. Mrs. Erika Heilmann enabled this publication by her speedy and excellent
typing of the manuscript, which made it a pleasure to cooperate with her.

This research was partly carried out within the Sonderforschungsbereich 49, Programmiertechnik, Munich.

Introduction

In the field of the formal specification of programming languages considerable progress has been made since the pioneering work of McCarthy, Yanov, Landin and others.
Whereas in the earlier approaches only parts of programming languages or "toy languages"
containing just a few simple concepts (cf. "Micro Algol" in [McCarthy 66]) have been
dealt with, the methods of denotational and axiomatic semantics nowadays are worked
out so elaborately that "real" programming languages can be fully specified (cf. the
description of PASCAL in [Tennent 77] and in [Hoare, Wirth 73]).

These methods provide a thorough description of the language and thus a rigorous interface between language designer and language implementor: the former has a tool to
formulate exactly his intentions, the latter is enabled to prove that the implementation meets the requirements.

Although being of great help to such skilled workers, these techniques of language description have a major drawback: they tend to become complex and incomprehensible. The
programmer willing to grasp the exact meaning of his program - i.e. the exact semantics
of the language he uses - not only has to conceive the underlying mathematics of the
whole approach, but also has to cope with the specific aspects of the particular description. This also forces him to learn an additional meta-language, which is used to
write down the formulas of the mathematical model in question.

In addition, describing a whole language within one coherent mathematical framework
has the unpleasant effect that the description of any language construct is as complicated as the description of the most complicated one. As an illustrative example
one may regard the *continuations* in denotational semantics: they are needed to handle
goto's , but once introduced they occur in the definition of all other language constructs, too, even in the specification of simple expressions etc.

Under these circumstances it seems promising to reduce the complexity of semantic
specifications by reducing certain language constructs to more elementary ones. In
this way, many constructs can be regarded as *notational variants* of each other and
thus may be covered by the notion of *abstract syntax* (as it will be done in section
1.2). Such constructs are not always just mere variants but often indicate the transition to new concepts.

This can be seen in [Landin 64] or [Landin 66, 66a], where terms like

$$x \cdot (x + 1) \quad \underline{where} \quad x = a + b$$
$$\underline{let} \ x = a + b \ ; \ x \cdot (x + 1)$$
$$(\lambda x. \ x \cdot (x + 1)) \ (a + b)$$

are identified. Whereas the first two lines simply are two different ways of writing down object declarations, the transition to the function application of the third line introduces another concept. This becomes even more obvious in [Burstall 68], where based on Landin's work the variables of ALGOL 60 are explained in terms of the applicative language ISWIM. [Burstall 70] proceeds further into this direction.

The attempt to define certain language constructs in terms of other ones has been used especially for the standard operators of ALGOL 68 and PASCAL , as can be seen from equations like (cf. [van Wijngaarden 75] and [Hoare, Wirth 73])

$$\text{or} \quad \begin{aligned} &\underline{op} + = (\underline{int} \ a, \ b) \ \underline{int} : a - - b \\ &m \ \underline{mod} \ n = m - (m \ \underline{div} \ n) * n \ . \end{aligned}$$

There also have been proposed (recursive) definitions of control constructs, like e.g. Wirth's explanation

$$\underline{while} \ B \ \underline{do} \ S \ \underline{od} = \underline{if} \ B \ \underline{then} \ S \ ; \ \underline{while} \ B \ \underline{do} \ S \ \underline{od} \ \underline{fi}$$

or Dijkstra's

$$\underline{while} \ B \ \underline{do} \ S \ \underline{od} = \lceil \underline{proc} \ P \equiv : \underline{if} \ B \ \underline{then} \ S \ ; \ P \ \underline{fi} \ ; \ P \rfloor \ .$$

This idea can already be found in the design of ALGOL 58 , where not only the for-statement but also the alternative statement have been "precisely described in terms of 'more elementary' statement forms" ([Perlis, Samelson 58], p. 15).

A classical example of this kind is given in the revised report on ALGOL 68 ([van Wijngaarden 75], pp. 65-66), where the "loop-clause"

$$\underline{for} \ i \ \underline{from} \ u1 \ \underline{by} \ u2 \ \underline{to} \ u3 \ \underline{while} \ \text{cond} \ \underline{do} \ \text{action} \ \underline{od}$$

is explained as being equivalent to the "void-closed-clause"

```
            begin int f := u1, int b = u2, t = u3;
            step2:
            if (b > 0 ∧ f ≤ t) ∨ (b < 0 ∧ f ≥ t) ∨ b = 0
                then int i = f ;
                    if cond then action; f + := b; goto step2 fi  fi
      end .
```

This is a very precise specification of all the details characterizing the loop-clause
(in spite of the fact that in some quarters the explanation of a "good" construct like
a loop in terms of a "bad" one like a jump would be regarded bad taste). However,
there is one point missing, viz. the condition that the identifiers f , b and t
must not occur anywhere in u1 , u2 , u3 , cond and action .

As related techniques one might regard those approaches, which extend the Markov algorithm concept to define programming languages (cf. [van Wijngaarden 63, 66], [de
Bakker 67]), but also the *evaluating equations* of [Wirth 63]. Of course, the concept
of *extensible languages* fits directly into this general pattern (cf. e.g [Christensen,
Shaw 69], [Schuman, Jorrand 70]). The *reduction semantics* of [Backus 78], where programs are successively reduced into simpler ones to yield a final "normal form program", is a kind of operational semantics the basic idea of which is rather close to
the approach taken here.

The definition of certain language constructs in terms of others becomes especially
interesting in the environment of a system for program transformations like the one
being studied in the project CIP ("computer-aided, intuition-guided programming") at
the Technical University Munich (cf. e.g. [CIP 77]).

The advantages are manifold: First of all, program transformations provide an exact
formal tool to express the reduction of one term to another one. Secondly, the explanation of the language by successively introducing new constructs can follow the same
lines as the program development should go: from the "high" applicative level to the
"low" machine-oriented level. Furthermore, the proof of the "correctness" of a complex
transformation now may consist of finding a sequence of more fundamental transformations
having the same effect; i.e. the proof can be carried out in a combinatorial instead
of a model-theoretic way.

Because of this strong relationship to the principles of program transformations, the
method of explaining certain language constructs by reducing them to more elementary
ones can be called transformational semantics. It will be used in this paper to introduce not only mere notational variants but also variants leading to new concepts.

As a most prominent example the reduction of an imperative language with program variables and assignments to a purely applicative language will be shown. The basic idea
is the following: Within a given language C (a "wide spectrum language") there will
be distinguished a partial ordering of *sublanguages* (often called *language levels* or
language layers) with a minimal sublanguage C_0.

For any two immediate neighbour languages C' and C'' there will be a small set of
transformations allowing for the reduction of any term of C'' to a term of C' .

To call this approach *transformational semantics* is justified by the following fact:
Let A be a language construct of C' , B be a (newly introduced) construct of C'';
let M_1 and M_2 be the respective meaning-functions of the underlying semantics of
the full language C . Then there is a transformation T mapping B to A , if
$M_1(A) = M_2(B)$. As the respective diagram

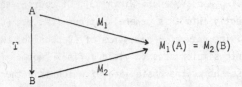

commutes, one can also proceed the other way round: given A , B and M_1 , one requires that the transformation T holds; then M_2 is determined (up to isomorphism).

An example of how this way of proceeding works can be found in [Stoy 77]. Given the
denotational semantics of the if-construct and requiring the transformation

while B do S od = if B then S; while B do S od fi

the semantic equation for the while-construct is derived.

The idea given above in a rather vague and informal way can be formulated very precisely on the basis of the recently proposed *initial algebra semantics* (cf. [ADJ 77]).
This method unifies some of the other techniques for semantic specification by making
explicit use of algebraic properties, especially of homomorphisms from syntax to semantics, which are inherent in most approaches.

By going further into this direction it turns out that the specification of the semantics of a programming language can be done in exactly the same (axiomatic) way as the
specification of abstract data types (cf. e.g. [Guttag 75], [ADJ 76a, 78]).

In this sense, the *transformational semantics* is very close to McCarthy's LISP , where programs are regarded as object structures (cf. [McCarthy 60]). But as in LISP only one particular language and one particular object structure have been used, *transformational semantics* is a true extension of these principles. Section 1 is devoted to these basic algebraic considerations on the theoretical background of the whole approach.

As is well-known from formal logic, the semantics of a language cannot be described fully within the language. (This is similar to the situation in LISP , where an interpreter written in LISP is used to explain the language; this leaves the problem that one still has to understand at least this specific program.) Consequently, there is a (hopefully small) "kernel" C_0 of the language, the semantics of which has to be given in some suitable way. Section 2 describes this kernel.

The following sections 3 to 5 give the transformational definition of some important constituents of CIP-L: the applicative language C_1 , the imperative language C_2 and the language C_3 which introduces non-local variables. Finally, section 6 will show the relationship to the techniques of *denotational semantics* and *axiomatic semantics*.

It is the aim of this paper to study, how far the approach of transformational semantics may lead. The selection of language features included therefore is a compromise between the brevity necessary for presentation purposes and the avoidance of oversimplifications. It is not claimed that the way of proceeding choosen here is the only one possible, it is not even claimed that it is the most "natural" one. I rather would like to call it an experiment, as one of the goals is to test the approach. Consequently, at certain points more emphasis has been given to the discussion of various possibilities of de-, finitions than to the motivation of the choice finally made.

1. Fundamental Concepts

If notions like *sublanguage*, *program-scheme* and *transformation* shall serve as specification tools for defining the semantics of programming languages, they need to be
formalized themselves. Therefore, in the first instance some theoretical background
has to be clarified.

To begin with, the syntactic aspects deal with somewhat "technical" questions like
applicability of transformations etc. The semantic considerations not only define
terms like *correctness of transformations* but also relate the method which is called
here *transformational semantics* to other approaches; for this purpose algebraic ideas
turn out to be best suited.

To make the discussion of the approach of transformational semantics more concrete, a
specific sample language will be defined using these techniques. This language will
be presented briefly in section 1.3. Finally, the notation used throughout this paper
together with some helpful conventions will be given in section 1.4.

1.1. Syntactic Aspects: Programs, Schemes, Transformations

As program transformations are necessarily "syntax-oriented", the notions of formal
language theory are necessary to provide for exact definitions. (However, in the context of transformations it will sometimes be convenient to use other terms than those
known from formal languages.)

The basis for all the definitions in the sequel is the notion of a <u>context-free gram-
mar</u> G = (V, T, R, a) , where V is an alphabet, consisting of the set of <u>terminals</u>
T ⊆ V and the set of syntactic variables (nonterminals) S = V \ T ;
R = {<s, w> [s ∈ S, w ∈ V*} is a set of ordered pairs, called <u>production rules</u>;
finally a ∈ S is called the axiom.

A word w ∈ V* is <u>derived directly</u> from a word v ∈ V*   , in symbols   v ⇒ w   ,
if there are words v', v" , w' ∈ V* and a syntactic variable s ∈ S such that
v = v'sv" , w = v'w'v" and <s, w'> is a production rule in R . The reflexive
transitive closure of ⇒ is denoted by ⇛ .

The language generated by a grammar G is denoted by L(G). A sublanguage is defined
here - more restrictive than usually done - as being the language generated by a
"subgrammar": Let $G = (V, T, R, a)$, $G' = (V', T', R', a)$, where $V \subseteq V', T \subseteq T'$
and $R \subseteq R'$; then L(G) is called a (syntactic) <u>sublanguage</u> of L(G') , in symbols
$L(G) \subseteq L(G')$.

(This means that one gets a sublanguage essentially by deleting some of the productions of the original grammar.)

Now, one can define

A <u>program part</u> p is a word of T* derivable from a syntactic variable $s \in S$:

$$p \in T* \land \exists s \in S : s \overset{*}{\Rightarrow} p .$$

A <u>(program-) scheme</u> σ is a word of V* derivable from a syntactic variable $s \in S$:

$$\sigma \in V* \land \exists s \in S : s \overset{*}{\Rightarrow} \sigma$$

where in addition the nonterminals of σ may be indexed by some index set I. These
(indexed) nonterminals occurring in σ are called <u>scheme-variables</u>.

For any scheme σ there exists the corresponding set of all program parts derivable
from σ : $P_\sigma = \{p \in T* \mid \sigma \overset{*}{\Rightarrow} p\}$ (indeed, each $p \in P_\sigma$ is a program part, as by definition there exists some $s \in S$ such that $s \overset{*}{\Rightarrow} \sigma \overset{*}{\Rightarrow} p$).

The derivation $\sigma \overset{*}{\Rightarrow} p$ associates with each scheme-variable s' of σ a subword p'
of p (the grammar is context-free!); this subword p' is called the <u>instantiation</u>
of the scheme-variable s' .

The reason for adding indices to the scheme-variable of σ is to restrict the set
P_σ to a subset P_σ' by requiring for any program part $p \in P_\sigma'$: if there are two
identical scheme-variables in σ (this implies equal indices), then they must have
identical instantiations within p . (This is analogous to the proceeding of Post
production systems). Thus one has:

A scheme σ is <u>applicable</u> to a program part p , if $\sigma \overset{*}{\Rightarrow} p$ and any two identical
scheme-variables of σ (including their indices) are associated with identical instantiations.

Thus a scheme $\sigma \equiv t_0 s_1 t_1 s_2 t_2 \dots t_{n-1} s_n t_n$ $(t_i \in T^*, s_i \in S)$ is applicable to a program part $p \equiv t_0 a_1 t_1 a_2 t_2 \dots t_{n-1} a_n t_n$ $(t_i \in T^*, a_i \in T^*)$, if $s_i = s_j$ implies $a_i = a_j$. The program part p is then called an <u>instantiation</u> of the scheme σ.

A <u>condition-free transformation rule</u> is an ordered pair (I, O) of program schemes (called input-scheme and output-scheme, resp.), which are both derivable from the same nonterminal $s \in S$; additionally, it is required that any scheme-variable occurring in O must also occur in I.

Thus, a condition-free transformation rule is a post production rule, whereby the scheme-variables are exactly the variables in the sense of Post. However, there are transformation rules which go beyond Post production rules:

A <u>conditional transformation rule</u> is an ordered triple (I, O, P), where I and O are the input- and output-scheme as defined above, and P is a predicate, the free variables of which are the variables of the input scheme I.

Finally, an <u>extended transformation rule</u> is essentially a conditional transformation rule where the restriction that any scheme-variable occurring in O also has to occur in I is abolished: It is permissible now that such a variable from O does not occur in I but in P. (This usually means that P contains an equation, a solution of which gives the appropriate instantiation.)

If the distinction between "conditional", "condition-free" and "extended" is not relevant, one may simply speak of transformation rules or just of transformations.

The following notations have come into use:

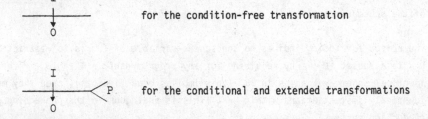

$\dfrac{I}{O}$ for the condition-free transformation

$\dfrac{I}{O} \!\!\!<\!\! P$ for the conditional and extended transformations

If the transformation is valid in both directions (under the same condition), the abbreviations are used

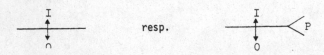

$\dfrac{I}{O}$ resp. $\dfrac{I}{O} \!\!\!<\!\! P$

Remark: It will often be the case that a transformation needs a condition P in one direction, whereas this condition is trivially fulfilled in the other condition (e.g. by the form of the scheme). For the sake of brevity, both transformations will be combined in this case, too:

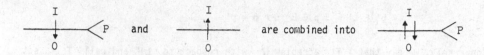

The <u>application</u> of a transformation to a given program part p yields a new program part p' by means of the following process:

(i)   It is tested, whether the input scheme I is applicable to p ; if so, the scheme-variables s_i of I are assigned instantiations p_i .

(ii)   If the transformation is conditional or extended, the predicate P is evaluated using the instantiations p_i for the variables s_i .

(iii)   p' is the result of replacing all variables s_i occuring in the output scheme O by their instantiations p_i .

If either step (i) or step (ii) fails, the transformation is not applicable to p ; the result then is the unchanged original program part p .

The following notations will be used in the sequel:

Let T denote a transformation, T a set of transformations, and let p , p' stand for program parts. Then

$p \overset{T}{\Rightarrow} p'$ means, that application of T to p yields p' .

$p \overset{T}{\Rightarrow} p'$ means, that there exists a finite sequence of transformations
$T_i \in T$ and program parts p_i such that
$$p \overset{T_1}{\Rightarrow} p_1 \overset{T_2}{\Rightarrow} p_2 \Rightarrow \ldots \overset{T_n}{\Rightarrow} p_n \overset{T_{n+1}}{\Rightarrow} p' \quad (T_i = T_j \text{ is allowed})$$

$T(p)$ denotes the set of all program parts p' , for which $p \overset{T}{\Rightarrow} p'$ holds.
(We disregard problems of decidability.)

There is an important relationship between the concept of sublanguages and the concept of transformations: Let $L \subseteq L'$ be two languages and let T , T' be two sets of transformations. We say that " T generates L' from L " and call T a set of <u>generating transformations</u>, iff

$$\forall \, p' \in L' \quad \exists \, p \in L \, : \quad p \overset{T}{\Rightarrow} p'$$

Conversely, we say that " T' accepts L' with respect to L " and call T' a set of <u>reducing transformations</u>, iff

$$\forall \, p' \in L' \quad \exists \, p \in L \, : \quad p' \overset{T'}{\Rightarrow} p \, .$$

(These notions are similar to the concepts of *generative* and *analytic grammar* in formal language theory; cf. [Salomaa 73].)

Although for given languages $L \subseteq L'$ such sets T and T' of transformations always exist - e.g. by collecting all corresponding pairs of programs p' and p - they are not necessarily finite. The interesting questions in this connection therefore are how to get not only a finite but rather a "small" set T , and how to get for a given set T the dual set T' (and vice versa). These questions will not be discussed here in general, but "small" sets T and T' will be given for a collection of sample languages.
(If all transformations are of the form

then this trivially specifies both T and T' at the same time.)

1.2. Semantic Aspects: Algebras, Terms, Equations

So far, everything has been purely syntactical. Hence, the definitions of the last section are too liberal; it will be necessary to restrict the attention to "correct" transformations and to "meaningful" programs only. Therefore, one has to regard semantics, which may be defined as follows:

Let O be a set of (mathematical) objects. Then the <u>semantics</u> of a language $L(G)$ is a computable function $M : \quad L(G) \to [O \to O]$.

This function M associates with each program of L(G) a mapping from O to O ,
called the meaning of this program.

A particular effect of the semantics is that certain programs get the meaning *unde-fined* (i.e. non-terminating) or *error*; this allows to distinguish meaningful programs,
i.e. programs not yielding one of those two "values".

Now, one can also speak of the correctness of transformations: T is called a
correct transformation, if for any meaningful program   p , to which T is applicable, the meanings of p and p' - where the program p' results from the
application of T - are the same, i.e.

$$T \text{ is correct, iff } \forall p, p' : p \overset{T}{\Rightarrow} p' \quad \rangle \quad M(p') = M(p) .$$

Remark: In the case of non-determinacy one does not require that the meanings of the
two programs be equal, but only that the new program is not more ambiguous than the
original one. In the terminology of Wirsing, Broy and Gnatz in [CIP 78b] this essentially says that the "breadth" (i.e. the set of possible values) of p' is contained
in the "breadth" of p and that both p and p' are equally defined:

$$B(p') \subseteq B(p) \quad \wedge \quad d(p') = d(p) .$$

It should be noted that the correctness of a transformation is only defined with respect to meaningful programs. This means that one does not care what happens to
erroneous programs upon application of the transformation.

Nowadays there are essentially three methods for specifying the semantics in use:
In *denotational semantics* the function M is constructed directly (cf. e.g.
[Strachey 66], [Scott, Strachey 71], [Milne, Strachey 76]). In *operational semantics*
M is defined implicitly by specifying an abstract machine; the meaning of a program
then is given by running it on that machine (cf. e.g. [McCarthy 60], [Lucas, Walk 70],
[Reynolds 72], [de Bakker 76], [van Wijngaarden 75]). The so-called *axiomatic seman-
tics* is, strictly speaking, not a semantics but a formal calculus, of which any "ad-
missible" semantics has to be a model (cf. e.g. [Naur 66], [Floyd 67], [Hoare 69],
[Dijkstra 75, 76]).

For obvious reasons, these specifications of the function M all follow the structure
of the syntax: "The semantical definition is syntax directed in that it follows the
same order of clauses and transforms each language construct into the intended
operation on the meanings of the parts" ([Scott, Strachey 71], p. 12).

"This essentially says that syntax is context-free and semantics is a homomorphism" ([ADJ 77], p. 76). This homomorphic character is most clearly exhibited in the *initial algebra semantics* of [ADJ 77], where an attempt is made to unify the diversity of approaches by regarding them from an algebraic point of view.

It has to be clarified how the *transformational semantics* fits into the environment of the other ways of specifying the semantics of programming languages.

Algebraic techniques turn out to be the appropriate tool for providing a sound basis for this approach. Such a sound basis is needed, as the underlying idea of *transformational semantics* - "specify the semantics of a programming language by means of definitional transformations, which reduce certain language constructs to more fundamental ones" - is rather a programme than a definition. There are numerous questions coming along with this approach, like: "Do the transformations specify the semantics in a unique way, at least up to isomorphism, or will there still be a choice of substantially differing variants, just as there are many models satisfying a given axiomatic description?" Other kinds of questions are: "Will finite sets of transformations be sufficient?" "What restrictions are imposed on the form of the transformations or on the kernel of the language?" etc.

Using algebraic techniques, these kinds of questions can be dealt with in a very rigorous and precise manner. Besides, the algebraic view has a further advantage: It is well known that there is a deep connection between data structures and formal languages, and of course this connection becomes even more apparent, if algebraic theories are used as the basic description tool for both of them. Nevertheless, it is somewhat surprising, how far the analogies go: As will be seen in the sequel, the algebraic approach to the specification of the so-called abstract data types and the approach of transformational semantics are identical methods. I will enter into a few of the particulars of these analogies not only because they are interesting on their own but also because they might help to facilitate the understanding.

First, a rough sketch of terminology (for details I have to refer to papers dealing with *initial algebras*, e.g. [ADJ 76], [ADJ 76a] and especially [ADJ 77], [ADJ 78]; a discussion of other than initial algebras together with a treatment of questions of existence can be found in [CIP 78a]; in [Burstall, Goguen 77] a presentation in terms of *algebraic theories* is given, which I will follow in the sequel.)

For describing the algebras involved, one uses a set S of sorts (i.e. symbols for carrier sets) and a signature Σ , i.e. a set of operator symbols (the functionality of which is described by means of the sorts of S). The signature specifies the

<u>well-formed terms</u>, i.e. the terms (also called polynomials) built up from the operator symbols of Σ and respecting their functionalities. The set of all well-formed terms for a given signature Σ is denoted by WFT_Σ . The set of well-formed terms, which contain additionally free variables of a given set Y , is denoted by $WFT_\Sigma(Y)$. Obviously, one has $WFT_\Sigma(\emptyset) = WFT_\Sigma$.

A <u>theory</u> (Σ, E) is a signature Σ together with a set E of equations closed under inference by reflexivity, transitivity and symmetry of equality and by substitution. The equations are of the form $lhs = rhs$, where lhs and rhs are terms of $WFT_\Sigma(Y)$; the variables are implicitly universally quantified. Usually, one also may have conditional equations of the form $e_1 \wedge \ldots \wedge e_n \Rightarrow e_{n+1}$, where the e_i are equations (for more details cf. e.g. [CIP 78a]).

The interpretations of a theory are (heterogeneous) algebras "i.e. structures with one set corresponding to each sort and with an operation corresponding to each operation symbol" ([ADJ 76], p. 3). These operations must obey the equations of the theory. To cut down the variety of admissible models for a given theory (Σ, E) , one regards only the class $Alg_{\Sigma,E}$ of *finitely generated algebras*. This means in particular that any algebra A of $Alg_{\Sigma,E}$ is an epimorphic image of the free word algebra W_Σ (cf. [Birkhoff, Lipson 70]); the elements of the carrier sets of W_Σ are the well-formed terms of WFT_Σ .

Such an algebraic framework is used in [ADJ 77] in the field of the specification of semantics: First, the grammar G is made into an S-sorted operator domain (where S is the set of syntactical variables): Each production

$$p : s_0 ::= t_1 s_1 t_2 \ldots t_n s_n t_{n+1} \qquad (s_i \in S , \ t_j \in T*)$$

becomes an operator symbol

$$p : s_1 \times s_2 \times \ldots \times s_n \rightarrow s_0 .$$

(The terminals may be "forgotten" here, as they are uniquely determined by the name p of the function.) The notion of *abstract syntax* - introduced by McCarthy (cf. [McCarthy 62]) - then can be made more precise by identifying it with the (isomorphism class of the) word algebra W_G .

Now any G-algebra M whatsoever (a set M_s for each nonterminal s and a function $p_M : M_{s_1} \times \ldots \times M_{s_n} \rightarrow M_{s_0}$ for each production p) provides a semantics for the context - free language $L(G)$. The word algebra W_G gives the unique homomorphism $M_M : W_G \rightarrow M$, which assigns "meanings" in M to all syntactically well-formed phrases of the language, and not just to the "sentences" generated from the axiom ([ADJ 77], p. 76).

If in this terminology programs are well-formed terms of $\mathrm{WFT_G}$, then consequently program schemes become elements of the set $\mathrm{WFT_G}(Y)$, where Y is the set of the "scheme-variables" of the previous section. Proceeding further into this direction, a (conditional) transformation now is to be regarded as a (conditional) equation. The notion of "correctness of a transformation" means that the equation is satisfied in the given semantic algebra M .

By prescribing a set T of transformations (i.e. equations) one can restrict the variety of possible semantic algebras from the class of all G-algebras to the class of all (G, T)-algebras. A well-known example for this way of proceeding is the λ-calculus where the set T_{Red} consists of the α- , β- and γ-conversions. (This set is not monomorphic and thus does not determine a unique semantic algebra; apparently the *continuous lattices* of D. Scott have been the first (G_λ , T_{Red})-algebra formally specified, cf. [Scott 72], [Scott 76].)

This way of proceeding may help in particular to cope with the context conditions which are usually needed in addition to a context-free syntax: In analogy to the handling of errors in the field of abstract data types these context conditions can be expressed by means of "error-equations", thus leading to the concept of "error-algebras" (cf. [Goguen 77]; another way of handling errors is favoured in [CIP 78a], where algebras with partial functions are used).

Remark: The ADJ-group favours looking at the algebras of $\mathrm{Alg}_{\Sigma, E}$ together with the homomorphisms between them as a category. In this category they distinct the *initial algebra*, which is (the isomorphism class of) the quotient of the word algebra W_Σ by the least congruence relation satisfying the equations of E . (Analoguously, one gets the *terminal algebra* by regarding the greatest congruence relation satisfying the equations of E .) The word algebra W_Σ then is initial in the category Alg_Σ , and the set $\mathrm{WFT}_\Sigma(Y)$ of well-formed terms including free variables gives rise to an algebra $W_\Sigma(Y)$, which is freely generated by Y , i.e. any family of functions $\theta_s : Y_s \to A_s$ (A_s being the carrier set corresponding to the sort s within an arbitrary algebra A of the category Alg_Σ) extends uniquely to a homomorphism $\bar\theta : W_\Sigma(Y) \to A$. The program schemes then are elements of $W_\Sigma(Y)$, the homomorphism $\bar\theta : W_\Sigma(Y) \to W_\Sigma$ coincides with the notion of an "instantiation of a scheme".

The parallels between the specification of abstract data types and transformational semantics really become striking, if the notions of "expansion/reduct" and "sublanguage" are brought together. An _expansion_ (and conversely a _reduct_) is defined as follows:

Given a triple (S, Σ, E) describing a class $\text{Alg}_{\Sigma, E}$, an expansion is a triple (S', Σ', E') with $S \subseteq S'$, $\Sigma \subseteq \Sigma'$ and $E \subseteq E'$, describing another class $\text{Alg}_{\Sigma', E'}$. The point which is important in our context is the following:

Regard a sort s of S (and thus also of S') and two algebras $A \in \text{Alg}_{\Sigma, E}$ and $A' \in \text{Alg}_{\Sigma', E'}$. The corresponding carrier sets A_s and A'_s are not necessarily isomorphic (for details see [ADJ 78] and [CIP 78a]). However, practical applications usually require this isomorphism for any expansion. (Ways of guaranteeing this by setting up appropriate restrictions for the equations of $E' \setminus E$ have become known under the catchword of _sufficient completeness_, [Guttag 75]). In the sequel, this requirement will be referred to as the _requirement of isomorphism_ (of expansions).

First, to give a better impression of what expansion menas, the example STACK OF NAT shall be regarded. One can go on from NAT to STACK OF NAT by adding a new sort stack, new operator symbols like append, rest etc. and finally new equations like rest(append(s,n)) = s . The claim for isomorphism here means that the carrier sets corresponding to the sort nat in NAT and STACK OF NAT shall be isomorphic.

Now regard the (syntactic) definition of sublanguage given in 1.1: For $L(G) \subseteq L(G')$ one has immediately that G' is an expansion of G with respect to the sorts (i.e. nonterminals) and the operator symbols (i.e. productions). A set T' of transformations takes the role of the equations E'.

Of course, the notion of a sublanguage has to be extended from the purely syntactic view to semantic aspects: Given two languages $L(G) \subseteq L(G')$ together with their semantics M and M', it is natural to require that M is "contained" in M'. This can be made precise in the algebraic framework by the requirement for isomorphism mentioned above:

Given a language $L(G)$ and a semantic G-algebra M, a language $L(G')$ and a semantic G'-algebra M', then $(L(G), M)$ is called a (semantic) <u>sublanguage</u> of $(L(G'), M')$, iff

(i) $L(G) \subseteq L(G')$, i.e. $L(G)$ has to be a syntactic sublanguage of $L(G')$

(ii) there exists an isomorphism φ from M to a "substructure" of M', such that
   - for any syntactic variable (sort) s of G, the corresponding carrier sets M_s and M_s' are identical under φ
   - for any production $p : s_0 ::= t_1 s_1 t_2 \ldots t_n s_n t_{n+1}$ of G the respective functions $p_M : M_{s_1} \times \ldots \times M_{s_n} \to M_{s_0}$ and $p_{M'} : M'_{s_1} \times \ldots \times M'_{s_n} \to M'_{s_0}$ correspond under φ.

This means that given the semantic algebra M of $L(G)$ one has only freedom to specify the carriers $M_{s'}'$ and functions p' for those syntactic variables and productions of G' which are not contained in G.

Usually, one specifies semantic algebras M and M' in a suitable way, i.e. such that they fulfill the sublanguage condition, and then looks for a set of interesting (correct) transformations, especially for expanding or reducing transformations for $L(G)$ and $L(G')$. However, influenced by the proceeding for abstract data types one may also go the other way round, give a set of expanding (or reducing) transformations first and then calculate what kind of semantics they specify.

The algebraic view has the nice effect that all the results stemming from the work on the specification of abstract data types are directly applicable to transformational semantics. In particular, one knows that the desired isomorphism is guaranteed, if the set of transformations is sufficiently complete. If one compares e.g. Guttag's description of this notion (essentially saying that any term of $\text{WFT}_{\Sigma'}$, which is of a sort $s \in S$, must be reducible by means of the equations of E' to a term of WFT_Σ, cf. [Guttag 75]) with the definition of reducing transformations given in section 1.1, one can immediately see that both notions coincide. Thus, one now can define formally:

The approach of <u>transformational semantics</u> means that the semantics M' of a language $L(G')$ is specified relatively to the semantics M of a sublanguage $L(G)$ by means of a *reducing set* T *of transformations* (of course this process may be iterated).

In accordance with the use of abstract data types the transformations of the set T will be called in this paper <u>axiomatic transformations</u> or just <u>axioms</u>. Consequently, the transformations derivable from the axiomatic ones will be referred to as <u>theorems</u>.

From the discussion above it follows that by the definition of transformational semantics the requirement for isomorphism is fulfilled, i.e. that $(L(G),M)$ really is a
semantic sublanguage of $(L(G'),M')$ (for a few very subtle precautions cf. [CIP 78a]).

However, the results gained in connection with abstract data types also tell us that
the "rest" of the semantics M' is n o t determined uniquely. What does this mean?
Remember that the semantic function M' assigns meanings to all phrases of the
language and not only to those derivable from the axiom of the grammar; on the other
hand, the axiom is contained in all sublanguages. Thus the transformational semantics
ensures that the meaning of any "complete" program is fully specified, whereas it
leaves some freedom for the "auxiliary" semantics of program parts (which, as mentioned
earlier, are needed to structure the specification of M' appropriately). To which
degree this freedom extends depends on the set of sublanguages chosen and on the form
of the transformations.

To make this more precise, one has to look more deeply into the mathematics involved.
For not digressing too far, I will refer here to the detailed discussion in [CIP 78a].

It is known that the class $Alg_{\Sigma,E}$ usually contains many non-isomorphic algebras,
two of which are of special interest: the *initial algebra*, where - roughly speaking -
all elements are considered different, if their equivalence cannot be proven from the
axioms, is the "greatest" one, and the *terminal algebra*, where all elements are considered equal, if they cannot be proven different from the axioms, is the "smallest"
one. (The sufficient completeness guarantees that they both exist.)

These differences are totally irrelevant as long as one only asks for the equivalence
of full programs and not for the equivalence of program parts:

To illustrate this, again the example STACK OF NAT can be used: If one looks at
stacks only by considering their top-element (i.e. by the function, which maps stack
to nat), the algebras of $Alg_{\Sigma,E}$ are indistinguishable, i.e. it does not matter
whether stacks are implemented e.g. by means of lists or by means of arrays with
pointers. But as soon as one asks for the equality to two stacks, the different algebras become important. (In the example STACK the different algebras are isomorphic;
there exist, however, simple examples, where the different algebras are non-isomorphic, cf. [CIP 78a].)

For the language to be presented in the subsequent sections this has the following
consequences: the axiom of the grammar is ≪expression≫, but there is also a nonterminal ≪statement≫ standing in particular for assignments. The usual tool for the
semantic description of ≪statement≫ are so-called *states* (cf. e.g. [McCarthy 62],
[Milne, Strachey 76], [Dijkstra 75]). These states are not uniquely determined by the
algebraic approach.

However, in general there is no use in asking, whether two states are equal; the only important question is, which value a certain variable has in the actual state. But for transformations this problem becomes relevant: Regard a transformation $T = (A, B)$, where A and B are two statements. There are essentially two ways of defining the correctness of this transformation; either one requires that the corresponding p r o - g r a m   p a r t s p_A and p_B be equal, or one requires that the f u l l   p r o - g r a m s   surrounding p_A and p_B be equal (the former, of course, implies the latter). In the first case, the validity of the transformation depends heavily on the model chosen for the states. In the second case, the form of the states is irrelevant, as only the properties of expressions determine the correctness of the transformation. This independency of specific models recommends using the second definition. (There is an interesting connection between the two cases: If one selects the terminal algebra of $Alg_{\Sigma,E}$ as the "standard model", then the second of the two equalities above implies the first one, i.e. both definitions coincide, cf. [CIP 78a].)

Having thus answered one of the questions mentioned at the beginning of section 1.2, I would like at least to show how other questions of that kind can be formulated more precisely and also can be dealt with more independently from specific pecularities of the language or the transformations, if the algebraic view is taken.

As an example take the question whether for given languages $L(G) \subseteq L(G')$ and given semantics M , M' (such that the sublanguage relation also holds for the semantics) there exists a finite set T of transformations which generates $L(G')$ from $L(G)$.

First of all, the meaning function $M' : W_{G'} \to M'$ defines a congruence relation $\equiv_{M'}$ on the abstract syntax $W_{G'}$: $t_1 \equiv_{M'} t_2 \Leftrightarrow M'(t_1) = M'(t_2)$.

Also, any set T of transformations defines a congruence relation $t_1 \equiv_T t_2 \Leftrightarrow$ $\ll$ there exists a sequence of transformations from T , such that t_2 is derivable from t_1 or vice versa $\gg$. (This is the least congruence relation satisfying the equations of T , cf. [ADJ 76].) For any set T of c o r r e c t   transformations, one has $t_1 \equiv_T t_2 > t_1 \equiv_{M'} t_2$.

The question mentioned above now can be worded: "Does there exist for a given congruence relation on an algebra A a finite set of equations, which determines this congruence relation?" This is now pure algebraic reasoning and can be worked out in the respective framework (as e.g. [Birkhoff, Lipson 70]) without referring to languages or transformations any longer. This means that one can take advantage of the very powerful methods and results known from algebra (cf. [ADJ 78]).

(I do not intend to discuss such questions here in detail; but e.g. for the above question one simple point now can be seen immediately:

If one regards the congruence classes $[t]_{\equiv_M'}$ of a sort s which lies in G and G' , then each such congruence class must contain at least one term of T_G ; this is a necessary condition for $L(G')$ being definable in terms of $L(G)$.)

The algebraic view also allows to characterize such sketchy notions as e.g. "syntactic sugar" [Landin 66] in a more precise way. Regard the grammar (where the left column shows the usual notation, whereas the right column gives the corresponding algebraic signature):

$$
\begin{array}{llll}
E ::= & \underline{let}\ I \equiv E\ \underline{in}\ E & i: & \underline{Ide} \times \underline{Exp} \times \underline{Exp} \rightarrow \underline{Exp} \\
E ::= & E\ \underline{where}\ I \equiv E & w: & \underline{Exp} \times \underline{Ide} \times \underline{Exp} \rightarrow \underline{Exp} \\
E ::= & I \equiv E\ ;\ E & s: & \underline{Ide} \times \underline{Exp} \times \underline{Exp} \rightarrow \underline{Exp} \\
E ::= & (\underline{\lambda}\ I.E)\ E & l: & \underline{Ide} \times \underline{Exp} \times \underline{Exp} \rightarrow \underline{Exp}
\end{array}
$$

The transformations (written as equations) shall hold

$$
\begin{array}{lll}
i(I, E_2, E_1) & = & l(I, E_1, E_2) \\
w(E_1, I, E_2) & = & l(I, E_1, E_2) \\
s(I, E_2, E_1) & = & l(I, E_1, E_2)\ .
\end{array}
$$

From these equations, it follows e.g. that

$$
i(I, E_2, E_1) \quad = \quad s(I, E_2, E_1)
$$

and so on. One can easily see that all these functions are equal up to permutations of the arguments; s and i even differ only in their terminals. This property offers itself as a more formal specification of the notion "syntactic sugar".

One even may go one step further: These elementary equations define equivalence classes, which may be used to extend the idea of *abstract syntax*: The elements of the *abstract syntax* are the equivalence classes comprising *notational variants* (which may be a better wording than "syntactic sugar"). In this more flexible form the notion of *abstract syntax* even may be used to concretise also the concept of a *coherent family of languages* (cf. [Knuth 74], [Ershov 76]).

In the formal algebraic framework the *abstract syntax* then is the initial algebra not of the class Alg_G but of a class $Alg_{G,E}$, where E is the set of equations specifying notational variants. (As these equations, i.e. transformations, are so simple, they can be applied automatically already by a parser.) In this sense, the languages given in the subsequent sections should be regarded as comprising representatives of equivalence classes of notational variants.

A last remark shall conclude the theoretical background: The approach of transformational semantics is supported, if the language $L(G)$ under consideration has a
direct chain of sublanguages

$$L_1 \subseteq L_2 \subseteq \ldots \subseteq L_n = L(G)$$

where each L_i is definable in terms of L_{i-1} . (I will proceed in this way here.)

However, it should be noted, that this is not mandatory. If a language L_2 shall be
defined in terms of a language L_1 , which is n o t a sublanguage of L_2 , then one
may define a new language L_{1+2} , which is essentially the union of (the grammars of)
L_1 and L_2 :

$$L_{1+2}$$
$$\cup \qquad \cup$$
$$L_1 \qquad \qquad L_2$$

Then one may transform the terms of L_2 within the frame of L_{1+2} into terms of L_1 .
Denotational semantics can be viewed in this way. If e.g. PASCAL shall be defined
in terms of Scott's language LAMBDA , a new language combining PASCAL and LAMBDA
is created, the "metalanguage" P + L . A given PASCAL program p is embedded into
P + L by writing $M[\![p]\!]\rho_0$ (ρ_0 is called the "initial environment"); then the equations are applied until the term $M[\![p]\!]\rho_0$ is transformed into a proper expression of
LAMBDA . An earlier example is [Landin 66] where the language L_{1+2} is ALGOL 60 extended by the Lambda-calculus.

1.3. The Sample Language

The approach taken in this paper is favoured by languages which comprise a wide range
of concepts from applicative to imperative constructs. Such *wide spectrum languages*
are necessary in connection with systems for program development by transformations.
Consequently a language of that kind - called CIP-L - is in the process of being
constructed in the course of the project CIP . (A brief description of this language
may be found e.g. in [CIP 78].)

The language CIP-L is well suited for the purpose of this paper. However, for not making things to excessive, only a subset of it shall be regarded hre, viz. those constructs which are needed for showing possible transitions from the applicative level of expressions, functions and parameters to the imperative level of variables, assignments and loops. Others are left to subsequent studies.

This concentration on a specific problem is the reason for leaving out a great number of - admittedly important - language features. This does concern notational variants like infix-notation, special loops etc. as well as constructs like guarded commands, elsf - cascades, general do ... od - loops etc. The reason for omitting the latter simply is, that the arbitrary number of branches involved brings up some purely technical difficulties for the notation of the transformations, but does not add new aspects for the essential questions discussed in this paper. (Proposals for solving such problems by using techniques similar to regular expressions, as e.g. in [Steinbrüggen 77], show that this can be done in a very clean and formal way but at the expense of the readability of the program schemes.)

The most important of the features left out are the mode - concept and the questions of nondeterminism. As both have to be clarified already on the purely applicative level, they provide prominent examples for the advantages of transformational semantics: If e.g. the semantics of nondeterminism has been given for the kernel of the language (cf. [CIP 78b]), it carries over to all "lower" levels of the language by means of the axiomatic transformations.

The following table gives an overview of the syntax of the language considered in this paper. As usually done in denotational semantics the so-called *syntactic domains* are given together with the syntax (they are the carrier sets of the abstract syntax, i.e. of the initial G-algebra). Some notational conventions will be explained below.

Table I: Full Syntax

Exp	$\ni$ E ::= O I I I E E I if E then E else E fi I(E)*I A I ⌈ G ⌋
Abstr	$\ni$ A ::= (M I)* M : E I Y E
Genexp	$\ni$ G ::= D; E I (var M I)*; S; E
Decl	$\ni$ D ::= F I (M I)* ≡ E I D; D
Fun	$\ni$ F ::= funct I ≡ A I F*
Stat	$\ni$ S ::= (I)* := E I if E then S else S fi I while E do S od I S; S I ⌈D; S⌋ I ⌈(var M I)*; S⌋
Obj	$\ni$ O ::= ≪ object denotation ≫
Ide	$\ni$ I ::= ≪ identifier ≫
Mode	$\ni$ M ::= ≪ mode indication ≫

The regular expressions like $(\underline{var} \, M \, I)^*$ of the extended BNF used here are intended to express tuplings as e.g. $(\underline{var} \, M_1 \, I_1, \, ..., \, \underline{var} \, M_n \, I_n)$, which formally had
to be specified by additional productions as e.g. $T ::= (T')$ and $T' ::= \underline{var} \, M \, I \mid T', T'$.
(For further conventions concerning tuples see the following section.)

Remark: The language given here essentially is a sublanguage of CIP-L . However, the
syntax has been modified in order to meet the particular needs of this paper, as the
interests of easy parsing on the one side and of powerful transformations on the other
side are not always easily balanced. (Finding an acceptable compromise between these
conflicting interests is a major task to be solved for any "mechanical" transformation
system. Of course, for the theoretical considerations of this paper the requirements
of the transformations have been given high priority.)
The nonterminal D comprises function- and object-declarations, as this helps to spare
some axioms. With an additional nonterminal C , the productions

$$\underline{Decl} \ni D ::= F \mid C$$
$$\underline{Const} \ni C ::= (M \, I)^* \equiv E \mid C \, ; \, C$$

would separate the two kinds of declarations.

1.4. Technical Questions and Notational Conventions

The abbreviations for tuples admitted in the syntax are useful for the transformations,
too. They will be employed even more liberally as e.g. in the scheme

$$(I_1, \, I_2)^* := (I_1, \, E_2)^*$$

which should be read as follows: There is a collective assignment like
$(a, \, b, \, c, \, d, \, e) := (a-b, \, b, \, c, \, a+b+c-d, \, e)$ where some of the variables are
assigned their own values. As tuples can be permuted in any order, and as the * -
operator shall indicate arbitrary numbers of components, the example given is an instance of the above scheme. (Formalization of this by means of auxiliary functions is
a trivial exercise.) Sometimes even notations like $(I_1, \, ..., \, I_n)$ will be used for
the sake of readability.

A point which is slightly more problematic comes with productions like

$$p : \quad D \quad ::= D \, ; \, D$$

The definitions given for *program-scheme* and *applicability of program-schemes* in
section 1.1 bring about the difficulty that the structure given by the parsing process does not coincide with the structure required for the transformation: Regard e.g.
the sequence "$F_1 \, ; \, F_2 \, ; \, F_3$" and the scheme "$D \, ; \, F$" .

The parsing order of the sequence may not have the form suited for the application of the scheme, i.e. it may be

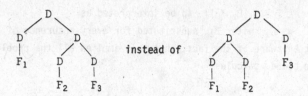

This just means that - again using the algebraic terminology - all functions of this kind are assumed to be associative, i.e. one has *implicit axioms* like

$$p(D_1, p(D_2, D_3)) = p(p(D_1, D_2), D_3) \ .$$

The conditional and extended transformations contain (in addition to the input- and output-scheme) predicates. Throughout this paper essentially two predicates will be used, both of purely syntactic nature (S stands for some syntactic variable):

OCCURS (I in S)   tests whether a given identifier occurs   f r e e l y   in the program part corresponding to S .

M = MODE (S)   tests whether the mode connected implicitly to the program part S is equal to M . (For complicated mode systems this should be weakened to *compatibility* instead of *equality*.)

The formal definition (recursively on the structure of the syntax) will be given together with the respective language levels. There will be an additional abbreviation, viz.

¬ OCCURS (I in S_1, ..., S_n) for ¬ OCCURS (I in S_1) ∧ ... ∧ ¬ OCCURS (I in S_n)

Analogously, ¬ OCCURS (I* in S*) means that no identifier of the tuple I* occurs in any of the components of the tuple S* .

Finally, if an identifier I is contained in the output-scheme but not in the input-scheme, then the condition ¬ OCCURS (I in S) means that a   n e w   identifier has to be introduced, which does not yet occur in the program part corresponding to S .

A very frequent operation in a transformation system is the textual substitution e.g. of an expression for an identifier within another expression. We will denote this here - following the usage of denotational semantics - by

$$E_1[E_2 \ / \ I] \quad \text{to be interpreted as}$$

$$\ll E_1 \text{ with } E_2 \text{ substituted for every occurence of } I \gg .$$

However, we must be aware of the fact, that this implies all the problems of the α-reduction in the Lambda-calculus.

A possible solution - in order to avoid α-reduction - would be to require that all declared identifiers are different. From a pragmatic point of view, this is even natural: As programs usually have been parsed somehow before they are submitted to mechanical transformations, all identifiers can be assumed to be different, viz. indexed by their block-numbers. The only problem then is the backward tree-to-string translation (for showing the program to the user). The so-called Lambda-bar operator of [Berkling 76], which - instead of changing bound variables - protects the free variables, can be used in this process efficiently.

In connection with the α-reduction the essence of the predicate OCCURS can be explained as follows:

OCCURS (I $\underline{in}$ E) is true, if the expression E cannot be replaced by $(\lambda \ I.E)(\Delta)$ - where Δ stands for an arbitrary object - without changing the program.

The symbol "Δ" just introduced will be used at some places in this paper. It might help to get certain normal forms, as illustrated by the following example:
If the function

$$\underline{funct} \ f \equiv (\underline{nat} \ x) \ \underline{nat} \ : \ x + 1$$

shall be extended to an equivalent one with two arguments, this can be done by specifying

$$\underline{funct} \ f' \equiv (\underline{nat} \ x, \ \underline{bool} \ y) \ \underline{nat} \ : \ x + 1$$

and turning any call $f(a)$ into $f'(a, \Delta)$. Here Δ can be replaced by $\underline{true}$ or $\underline{false}$. More generally, for any mode $\underline{m}$, $\Delta_{\underline{m}}$ is defined by (for the notation cf. e. g. [CIP 78])

$$\Delta_{\underline{m}} = \underline{some} \ \underline{m} \ x$$

Therefore Δ is referred to as the "meaningless object". This notational trick will be of some technical help at certain points of the paper.

2. The Kernel Language

As has been mentioned earlier, the semantics of the full language C cannot be expressed totally within the language itself. This means that there remains a "kernel" C_0 , for which the semantics has to be given in some suitable way.

Here, a pure expression language - i.e. a slightly extended (typed) Lambda-calculus - similar to those given e.g. in [Landin 64], [Tennent 76] or [Stoy 77] will serve as the starting point for the whole development. In order to cope with non-determinism, a mathematical semantics like the one given in [CIP 78b] could be used for this expression language.

If only the grammar G_0 is given for this language C_0 , then any algebra of the class Alg_{G_0} is permissible as the semantics. This includes even extreme cases like a model, where every program whatsoever returns one and the same value, or a model, where any program may return any value. In order to keep this variety acceptably small, a few transformations will be given, which are required to hold for C_0 . This set T reduces the class to the smaller one $Alg_{G_0,T}$, where at least these extreme models are excluded. It should be noted that the semantics for all subsequent language levels is defined relatively to the semantics of C_0 . Therefore, the decisions taken here will strongly influence the whole language.

2.1. Syntax of C_0

Table II: Syntax of C_0

<u>Exp</u>	$\ni$ E	::=	O I I I E E I <u>if</u> E <u>then</u> E <u>else</u> E <u>fi</u> I(E)* I A
<u>Abstr</u>	$\ni$ A	::=	(M I)* M : E I <u>Y</u> E
<u>Obj</u>	$\ni$ O	::=	« object denotation »
<u>Ide</u>	$\ni$ I	::=	« identifier »
<u>Mode</u>	$\ni$ M	::=	« mode indication »

The particular symbol $\underline{Y}$ stands for the so-called *paradoxical combinator* of the Lambda-calculus

$$Y \equiv \lambda h. \ (\lambda x. \ h(xx)) \ (\lambda x. \ h(xx))$$

which applied to any expression renders a fixed point of that expression. As can be seen from the syntax, its use is restricted to functions only.

Remark: For the sake of readability, I will often use - especially in this section - the pure λ-notation instead of the typed one, and identifiers like f, g, h for functions and x, y, z for objects. The advantages become obvious, if one compares a lengthy example like

$$((\underline{funct}\ (M)^*\ M_0\ I)\ M_0 : I(E))\ ((M\ I_1)^*\ M_0 : E_0)$$

to its short-hand form

$$(\lambda\ I.\ I(E))\ (\lambda\ I_1.\ E_0)\ .$$

The predicate OCCURS now can be defined recursively as follows:

OCCURS $(I\ \underline{in}\ E)$ is defined by

OCCURS $(I\ \underline{in}\ O)$ = false

OCCURS $(I\ \underline{in}\ I')$ = $(I = I')$

OCCURS $(I\ \underline{in}\ E_1(E_2))$ = OCCURS $(I\ \underline{in}\ E_1)$ $\vee$ OCCURS $(I\ \underline{in}\ E_2)$

OCCURS $(I\ \underline{in}\ \underline{if}\ E_1\ \underline{then}\ E_2\ \underline{else}\ E_3\ \underline{fi})$

= OCCURS $(I\ \underline{in}\ E_1)$ $\vee$ OCCURS $(I\ \underline{in}\ E_2)$ $\vee$ OCCURS $(I\ \underline{in}\ E_3)$

OCCURS $(I\ \underline{in}\ (E_1,\ ...,\ E_k))$ = OCCURS $(I\ \underline{in}\ E_1)$ $\vee\ ...\ \vee$ OCCURS $(I\ \underline{in}\ E_k)$

OCCURS $(I\ \underline{in}\ (M\ I')^*\ M_0 : E)$ =

$\neg$ DECLARED $(I\ \underline{in}\ (M\ I')^*)$ $\wedge$ OCCURS $(I\ \underline{in}\ E)$

where DECLARED $(I\ \underline{in}\ (M_1 I_1,\ ...,\ M_k I_k))$ = $I \in \{I_1,\ ...,\ I_k\}$

OCCURS $(I\ \underline{in}\ \underline{Y}\ E)$ = OCCURS $(I\ \underline{in}\ E)$

The basic manipulation of programs in the Lambda-calculus (and a basic tool in the description of transformations) is the textual substitution of an expression X for and identifier x within another expression E, denoted by $E[X/x]$. This operation is defined inductively following the productions of C_0 :

subst 1 : $O[X/x] = O$

subst 2 : $x[X/x] = X$

$y[X/x] = y$

subst 3 : $(E_1(E_2))\ [X/x] = (E_1[X/x])\ (E_2[X/x])$

subst 4 : $(\underline{if}\ E_1\ \underline{then}\ E_2\ \underline{else}\ E_3\ \underline{fi})\ [X/x] = \underline{if}\ E_1[X/x]\ \underline{then}\ E_2[X/x]\ \underline{else}\ E_3[X/x]\ \underline{fi}$

subst 5 : $(E_1,\ ...,\ E_k)\ [X/x] = (E_1[X/x],\ ...,\ E_k[X/x])$

subst 6 : $(\lambda x.\ E)\ [X/x] = \lambda x.\ E$

$$(\lambda y.\ E)\ [X/x] = \begin{cases} \lambda y.\ E[X/x], & \text{if } \neg\ \text{OCCURS }(y\ \underline{in}\ X) \\ \lambda z.\ E[z/y][X/x], & \text{if OCCURS }(y\ \underline{in}\ X)\ \wedge\ \neg\ \text{OCCURS }(z\ \underline{in}\ E,X) \end{cases}$$

subst 7 : $(\underline{Y}\ E)\ [X/x] = \underline{Y}\ E[X/x]$

Note that subst 6 can be simplified in the special case ¬ OCCURS (x in E) . Then
one has

$$(\lambda y.\ E)\ [X/x] \ = \ \lambda y.\ E \ .$$

For multiple parameters $\lambda y_1, \ ..., \ y_k.$ E the operation subst 6 holds analogously;
now the cases $x \in \{y_1, \ ..., \ y_k\}$ and $x \notin \{y_1, \ ..., \ y_k\}$ have to be distinguished.

2.2. Axioms for C_0

A few axiomatic transformations shall reduce the variety of possible semantic algebras for C_0 (and thus for all subsequent language levels).

Above all, the α- , β- , and η-reduction of the Lambda-calculus shall be valid
here, too. However, with respect to non-determinism (and also to expressions with side-
effects) one has to be careful for the β-reduction.

Axiom 0.1: α - reduction

$$(M\ I_1)^*\ M_0\ :\ E$$
$$(M\ I_2)^*\ M_0\ :\ E[I_2^*/I_1^*]$$
$$\neg\ OCCURS\ (I_2^*\ \underline{in}\ E)$$

Axiom 0.2: β - reduction

$$((M\ I_1)^*\ M_0\ :\ E_0)\ (E_1)^*$$
$$E_0[E_1^*/I_1^*]$$
$$\text{DETERMINATE}\ (E_1^*)$$
$$\text{DEFINED}\ (E_1^*)$$

Two special cases, where E_1^* is guaranteed to be both determinate and defined, can
be distinguished, viz. object denotations and identifiers.

Theorem 0.3: special β - reduction

$$((M\ I_1)^*\ M_0\ :\ E_0)\ (O^*)$$
$$E_0[O^*/I_1^*]$$

Theorem 0.4:   special β - reduction

$$
\frac{((M\ I_1)^*\ M_0\ :\ E_0)\ (I_2^*)}{E_0[I_2^*/I_1^*]}
$$

Note, however, that theorem 0.4 is only true, if a call of a nullary function is not simply written as ... f ... but e.g. as ... f() ... .

It should be noted, too, that the conditions of axiom 0.2 are of semantic nature and usually only decidable for special cases. Therefore, the condition-free theorems 0.3 and 0.4 will be used in this paper wherever possible instead of axiom 0.2.

Axiom 0.5: η - reduction

$$
\frac{(M\ I_1)^*\ M_0\ :\ (E_0(I_1)^*)}{E_0}
$$
$\neg$ OCCURS $(I_1^*\ \underline{in}\ E_0)$

The few rules given above leave considerable freedom for choosing an appropriate semantics. However, one should be aware of the effects certain choices have on the whole language. Regard e.g. a denotational semantics for abstractions (cf. e.g. [Stoy 77], p. 178)

$$
A[\![\lambda I.\ E]\!]\rho = \text{strict } (\lambda\varepsilon.\ E[\![E]\!]\ \rho\ [\varepsilon/I])
$$

$$
\text{where strict } f\ x = \begin{cases} \bot & ,\ \text{if x is } \bot \\ f\ x & ,\ \text{otherwise} \end{cases}
$$

By turning in this way every function into a strict one, one has the effect of *call by value*. This makes the restriction DEFINED (E_1^*) necessary for the β -reduction, whereas a *call by reference* -semantics makes this condition superfluous. The same is true for the condition DETERMINATE (E_1^*) .

Some of the error-handling connected to the context-sensitive parts of the syntax can be put into the form of axiomatic transformations, too. Examples are

Axiom 0.6:   "error-axiom" for identical parameters

$$
\frac{(M_1I_1,\ ...,\ M_nI_n)\ M_0\ :\ E}{\ll \text{error} \gg}
$$
$\exists\ I_i,\ I_j\ \in\ \{I_1,\ ...,\ I_n\}\ :\ I_i = I_j$

<u>Axiom 0.7:</u>   "error-axiom" for mode-compatibility

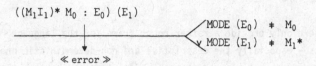

$$((M_1I_1)^* \ M_0 : E_0) \ (E_1)$$

$$\Bigg\langle\begin{array}{l} \text{MODE} \ (E_0) \ \neq \ M_0 \\ \text{MODE} \ (E_1) \ \neq \ M_1^* \end{array}$$

$$\ll \text{error} \gg$$

The "error-propagation" then is accomplished by some kind of strictness, viz.
$f(\ll \text{error} \gg) = \ll \text{error} \gg$ etc. This symbol $\ll \text{error} \gg$ may be regarded as a special
element contained in every mode; it is then part of the language and must not be con-
fused with the element *undefined*, which exists only in the semantics to express non-
termination. (The algebraic theory of abstract data types becomes slightly more complicated, if error-elements are involved, cf. [Goguen 77].)

The above axioms mirror the *basic structure* ([Landin 66]) of the language C_0 (also
called the *language framework* in [Backus 78]). The sets of "primitive" objects together
with their characteristic operations - like e.g. <u>nat</u> , <u>bool</u> , <u>string</u> etc. - then
are built into this framework by means of abstract data types (cf. e.g. [Guttag 75],
[CIP 78a]); this is a slightly more general view of Backus' notion of the *changeable*
parts of a language.

Of course, there has to be at least the particular abstract data type <u>bool</u> comprising the two elements true and false , which is connected to the framework by means
of

<u>Axiom 0.8:</u>   "definition of <u>if</u> - <u>then</u> - <u>else</u> - <u>fi</u> "

$$\text{if true } \underline{\text{then}} \ E_1 \ \underline{\text{else}} \ E_2 \ \underline{\text{fi}}$$

$$E_1$$

$$\text{if false } \underline{\text{then}} \ E_1 \ \underline{\text{else}} \ E_2 \ \underline{\text{fi}}$$

$$E_2$$

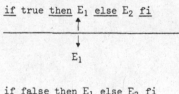

$$\text{if O } \underline{\text{then}} \ E_1 \ \underline{\text{else}} \ E_2 \ \underline{\text{fi}}$$

$$\Big\langle \ O \notin \{\text{true, false}\}$$

$$\ll \text{error} \gg$$

The last of these transformations serves the purpose of error-propagation as well as
that of checking the mode-conformity.

Remark: McCarthy's axioms for the conditional expression ([McCarthy 63]) can be derived from the transformations above by simply substituting all possible combinations
of the values true and false .

The axioms given here only provide a rather rough frame for the language C_0 . Further
language constructs - especially the descriptive and non-deterministic ones of e.g.
[CIP 78] - could be added, but also additional axioms to describe e.g. the mode concept or the error-handling in more detail. For the purpose of this paper, viz. for
the presentation of the general method of transformational semantics, the definition
of the kernel language given so far will suffice.

As has been stated already before, there is one class of problems, which cannot be
handled by axioms of the form given above, namely questions of definedness, i.e. of
non-termination. These questions can only be dealt with in the semantics; any attempt
to include them into the language would lead to numerous paradoxical situations.

3. The Applicative Level

The so-called *applicative languages* comprise expressions - as already introduced in the kernel C_0 - supplemented by function - and object-declarations. They
are often characterized by having the property of *referential transparency* (cf. [White-
head, Russell], [Quine 60]). This essentially means that the only important quality of
an expression is its value; in other words, a subexpression may be replaced by any
other expression having the same value. Such *applicative expressions* were used by
Landin in the definition of ALGOL 60 (cf. [Landin 66]).

The reduction of the applicative language C_1 , which we are going to discuss, to the
pure expression language C_0 can be done by three axioms. Two of them are used to
define function- and object-declarations, resp. The reason for differentiating here
simply is the (somewhat arbitrary) decision that recursive object declarations are not
included in the language. (Thus infinite objects like circular lists etc. cannot be
introduced via object declarations - they can be defined, however, using nullary recursive functions.) The third axiom only serves the purpose of simplifying the arising
block structure in certain special cases.

3.1. Syntax of C_1

The introduction of declarations also requires tools for specifying the *scopes* of the
declared identifiers. Therefore, one needs the segment brackets "⌈" and "⌋" (usually denoted by the symbols begin and end) and the separator within (usually denoted by the semicolon), and obtains the so-called *generalized expressions*.

Table III: Syntax of C_1

Exp	∋ E ::=	O I I I I E E I if E then E else E fi I (E)* I A I ⌈ G ⌋
Abstr	∋ A ::=	(M I)* M : E I Y E
Genexp	∋ G ::=	D; E
Decl	∋ D ::=	F I (M I)* ≡ E I D; D
Fun	∋ F ::=	funct I ≡ A I F*
Obj	∋ O ::=	≪ object denotation ≫
Ide	∋ I ::=	≪ identifier ≫
Mode	∋ M ::=	≪ mode indication ≫

Remark: It is only for the sake of readability that the notation

$$\underline{funct}\ I_1 \equiv A_1,\ \ldots,\ \underline{funct}\ I_k \equiv A_k$$

has been preferred to the form

$$(\underline{funct}\ I_1,\ \ldots,\ \underline{funct}\ I_k) \equiv (A_1,\ \ldots,\ A_k)\ \ ,$$

as the bodies A_i of functions usually tend to be lengthy. For objects, on the contrary, the form of *collective declarations* is used; obviously, the transition between the two notations is just syntactic sugar. The same is true for the use of the semicolon and the comma instead of e.g. Landin's <u>where</u> / <u>and</u> - notation ([Landin 66]).

3.2. Axiomatic Transformations for C_1

Function- and object-declarations are defined by one transformation each:

Axiom 1.1:   FUNCTION-DECLARATION

$$\lceil \underline{funct}\ I_1 \equiv A_1,\ \ldots,\ \underline{funct}\ I_k \equiv A_k\ ;\ E \rfloor$$

$$\big\updownarrow$$

$$((M_1 I_1,\ \ldots,\ M_k I_k)\ M_0 : E)\ (\underline{Y}\ (M_1 I_1,\ \ldots,\ M_k I_k) M_{k+1} : (A_1,\ \ldots,\ A_k))$$

Note that the modes M_i are function modes, which in CIP-L (cf. e.g. [CIP 78]) would be denoted as

$$M_i \ \triangle\ \underline{funct}\ (M_{i1},\ \ldots,\ M_{in_i})\ M_{in_i+1}\ \ ,$$

if the corresponding body is of the form

$$A_i \ \triangle\ (M_{i1} I_1',\ \ldots,\ M_{in_i} I_{n_i}')\ M_{in_i+1} : E_i\ \ .$$

M_0 is the mode of the expression E_0 , and M_{k+1} is just the tuple of all the function modes $(M_1,\ \ldots,\ M_k)$.

(For not making them too unreadable, these explanations have not been specified formally in (the condition part of) the transformation).

Remark: The explicit use of the fixpoint-operator in a declaration like
$\underline{funct}$ $f \equiv \underline{Y}$ ($\lambda f.$ A) is not sufficient, as *mutually recursive* functions cannot be described in this way.

To illustrate the transformation, the standard example of the factorial function may be considered:

$\lceil \underline{funct}$ fac $\equiv$ ($\underline{nat}$ n) $\underline{nat}$:
    $\underline{if}$ n = 0 $\underline{then}$ 1 $\underline{else}$ n × fac(n-1) $\underline{fi}$; E $\rfloor$

is equivalent to (if the expression E has the mode $\underline{nat}$)

  $((\underline{funct}$ ($\underline{nat}$) $\underline{nat}$ fac) $\underline{nat}$: E)
      $(\underline{Y}$ ($\underline{funct}$ ($\underline{nat}$) $\underline{nat}$ fac) $\underline{funct}$ ($\underline{nat}$) $\underline{nat}$:
           ($\underline{nat}$ n) $\underline{nat}$: $\underline{if}$ n = 0 $\underline{then}$ 1 $\underline{else}$ n × fac(n-1) $\underline{fi}$) .

Object-declarations are introduced as abbreviations for parameters of (non-recursive) functions. One should be well aware that the choice of *call by value* or *call by name* semantics for the language C_0 strongly influences the semantics of the object-declaration: If the identifier shall denote the same value throughout its whole scope, then *call by value* is necessary (this is important, if the language comprises non-deterministic constructs).

<u>Axiom 1.2:</u>   OBJECT - DECLARATION

$\lceil$ (M I)* $\equiv$ E$_1$; E$_2$ $\rfloor$

$\neg$ OCCURS (I* $\underline{in}$ E$_1$)

M$_2$ = MODE (E$_2$)

((M I)* M$_2$: E$_2$) (E$_1$)

The first of the two conditions is needed to avoid obfuscated situations like

$\lceil$ $\underline{nat}$ x $\equiv$ 1 ; $\lceil$ $\underline{nat}$ x $\equiv$ 1 + x ; 2 + x $\rfloor$$\rfloor$

where the arrows illustrate the bindings, which would be caused by axiom 1.1 without this condition: In the inner block the same identifier x would denote different objects.

By separating the two axioms above the homogeneousness of objects and functions, which - at least for pragmatical reasons - should be avoided, has not been completely circumvented. There still arise slight problems, if parameter tuples consisting of functions and objects are allowed in the language C_0 , as in this case axiom 1.2 would bring up the mixture again. However, such "mixed" parameter tuples can be forbidden already on the level of C_0 by means of the mode concept. Hence, one should not care about them here.

It is an interesting observation that the axiomatic transformations do not leave much freedom for the syntax of C_1 . As the output-schemes lie in the domain $\underline{Exp}$, the input-schemes have to be in $\underline{Exp}$, too. This makes the productions E ::= $\lceil G \rfloor$ and G ::= D; E necessary (of course, up to the modularization by means of the nonterminal $^\prime G$).

The same is true for the predicate OCCURS and the substitution operation, which have to be extended for the new syntax in a compatible way:

OCCURS (I $\underline{in}$ $\lceil G \rfloor$) is defined by e.g.

$$OCCURS\ (I\ \underline{in}\ \lceil (M\ I')^* \equiv E_1\ ;\ E_2 \rfloor$$
$$=\ OCCURS\ (I\ \underline{in}\ ((M\ I')^*\ M_2\ :\ E_2)(E_1))$$
$$=\ OCCURS\ (I\ \underline{in}\ (M\ I')^*\ M_2\ :\ E_2)\ \lor\ OCCURS\ (I\ \underline{in}\ E_1)$$
$$=\ \neg\ DECLARED\ (I\ \underline{in}\ (M\ I')^*)\ \land\ OCCURS\ (I\ \underline{in}\ E_2)$$
$$\lor\ OCCURS\ (I\ \underline{in}\ E_1)$$

Analogously, one has to define the substitution $E[X/x]$ for the case E ::= $\lceil G \rfloor$, e.g. (where $\underline{m}_i$ is some mode indication)

subst8 : $\lceil G \rfloor$ $[X/x]$
$$=\ \lceil (\underline{m}_1 y_1,\ ...,\ \underline{m}_k y_k)\ \equiv\ E_1\ ;\ E_2 \rfloor\ [X/x]$$
$$=\ (((\underline{m}_1 y_1,\ ...,\ \underline{m}_k y_k)\ \underline{m}_0\ :\ E_2)(E_1))\ [X/x]$$
$$=\ (((\underline{m}_1 y_1,\ ...,\ \underline{m}_k y_k)\ \underline{m}_0\ :\ E_2)\ [X/x])(E_1[X/x])$$

Now, according to the rule subst6 of section 2.1, the two cases $x \in \{y_1,\ ...,\ y_k\}$ and $x \notin \{y_1,\ ...,\ y_k\}$ have to be distinguished. By applying axiom 1.2 again, the former case finally leads to (now writing y_i instead of x)

$$\lceil (\underline{m}_1 y_1,\ ...,\ \underline{m}_k y_k)\ \equiv\ E_1\ ;\ E_2 \rfloor\ [X/y_i]$$
$$=\ \lceil (\underline{m}_1 y_1,\ ...,\ \underline{m}_k y_k)\ \equiv\ E_1\ ;\ E_2 \rfloor$$

(Note that y_i must not occur in the expression E_1 !)

The latter case yields

$$\lceil (\underline{m}_1 y_1, \ldots, \underline{m}_k y_k) \equiv E_1 ; E_2 \rfloor [X/x]$$
$$= \lceil (\underline{m}_1 y_1, \ldots, \underline{m}_k y_k) \equiv E_1 [X/x] ; E_2 [X/x] \rfloor \quad,$$

provided that none of the y_i occurs in X. Otherwise, the respective y_i had to be renamed appropriately.

Analogous derivations have to be done for function declarations. This process has to be carried out for every new language level in the very same way. Therefore, I will refrain from doing these purely mechanical and lengthy derivations in the sequel.

A third axiom for C_1 does not bring up new concepts but only shall allow to omit extensive nestings of block brackets like

$$\lceil D_1 ; \lceil D_2 ; \lceil D_3 ; \ldots ; \lceil D_n ; E \rfloor \ldots \rfloor \rfloor \rfloor$$

by replacing such terms by

$$\lceil D_1 ; D_2 ; D_3 ; \ldots ; D_n ; E \rfloor \quad.$$

However, this omitting of block brackets should not cause name clashes; hence, it will be forbidden to convert e.g.

$$\lceil \underline{nat} \ a \equiv b ; \lceil \underline{nat} \ b \equiv a + 1 ; \lceil \underline{nat} \ a \equiv b + 2 ; a + b \rfloor \rfloor \rfloor$$

into the obfuscated form (where the arrows illustrate the bindings)

$$\lceil \underline{nat} \ a \equiv b ; \underline{nat} \ b \equiv a + 1 ; \underline{nat} \ a \equiv b + 2 ; a + b \rfloor \quad.$$

Although the semantics would be completely clear, the readability and understandability of such constructs would be extremely impeded.

The reason for such prohibitions lies in a basic principle of block structures: If there is a declaration of a certain identifier anywhere in the block, then there must not be any occurrences of this identifier but those referring to that declaration. Remembering axioms 1.1 and 1.2, where the declared identifiers of a block correspond to bindings, whereas the identifiers coming from the "outside" of the block correspond to free variables, one might phrase this principle in a sloppy way as follows:"no identifier must occur bound and free within one and the same block".

The following axiomatic transformation just introduces (removes) one pair of block brackets. To deal with whole sequences of declarations it has to be applied repeatedly "from the inside outward".

Axiom 1.3:   BLOCK BRACKETS

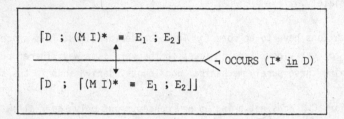

Note that here again a rather arbitrary decision has been taken, viz. that a (system of) function-declaration(s) may only occur at the very beginning of a block. A reason for this decision might be that non-local identifiers should come from outer blocks and not just from a previous declaration. This, of course, is only a matter of taste.

In all previous transformations the predicate OCCURS was only needed for expressions (note that the "full" block $\lceil G \rfloor$ also is an expression). In axiom 1.3 it is applied to another syntactic variable for the very first time. Therefore it cannot be derived from the original specification within C_0 and some axiomatic transformations, but it has to be defined anew reflecting the appropriate intuitive ideas of the "basic principle of block structures" mentioned above.

One wants to express that an identifier occurs in a sequence of declarations, if it is declared or if it occurs free   in one of them. This leads to the definition of OCCURS (I $\underline{in}$ D)

$$\text{OCCURS (I } \underline{in} \text{ } D_1; D_2) = \text{OCCURS (I } \underline{in} \text{ } D_1) \vee \text{OCCURS (I } \underline{in} \text{ } D_2)$$
$$\text{OCCURS (I } \underline{in} \text{ } (M I_1)^* \equiv E) = I \in (I_1)^* \vee \text{OCCURS (I } \underline{in} \text{ } E)$$
$$\text{OCCURS (I } \underline{in} \text{ } \underline{funct} \text{ } I_1 \equiv A_1) = I = I_1 \vee \text{OCCURS (I } \underline{in} \text{ } A_1)$$
$$\text{OCCURS (I } \underline{in} \text{ } F_1, F_2) = \text{OCCURS (I } \underline{in} \text{ } F_1) \vee \text{OCCURS (I } \underline{in} \text{ } F_2)$$

Note that there is an essential difference between the cases OCCURS (I $\underline{in}$ $\lceil D; E \rfloor$) and OCCURS (I $\underline{in}$ D) : If there is somewhere in the sequence D a declaration of the identifier I , then the second predicate yields true, whereas the first one is false, as it only looks at the block "from the outside", i.e. tests for free occurrences of I only. (From a very strict point of view the two predicates should have been named differently, as they have different domains; OCCURSFREE   might have been a more appropriate name for the first one anyhow.)

3.3.   Derived Transformations for C_1

The language C_1 is a well-suited starting point for the development of programs, and there exist a great variety of useful transformations within that language, especially for handling recursive functions (cf. e.g. [Cooper 66], [Darlington, Burstall 76], [CIP 76]). Of special importance are the very elementary transformations like FOLD / UNFOLD   etc.   (cf. e.g. [Burstall, Darlington 75], [CIP 76]). The proofs of these transformations rely heavily - after application of axiom 1.1 - on the properties of the β-reduction and the fixpoint-operator.

In this section there will be presented only a few very simple rules, which are needed for the proofs in subsequent sections. These rules are direct consequences of the axioms for the languages C_1 and C_0 . (The proofs can be found in the appendix.)

Theorem 1.1:   "renaming of object-declarations"

$$\lceil (M\ I_1) \equiv E_1;\ E_2 \rfloor$$

$\neg$ OCCURS $(I_1 \underline{in}\ E_1)$
$\neg$ OCCURS $(I_2 \underline{in}\ E_1,\ E_2)$

$$\lceil (M\ I_2) \equiv E_1;\ E_2[I_2/I_1] \rfloor$$

Theorem 1.2:   "unfolding of object-declarations"

$$\lceil (M\ I) \equiv E_1;\ E_2 \rfloor$$

$\neg$ OCCURS $(I \underline{in}\ E_1)$
DETERMINATE (E_1)

$$E_2[E_1/I]$$

Theorem 1.3:   " importation of object-declarations"

$$\lceil (M_1 I_1)^* \equiv E_1;\ \lceil (M_2 I_2)^* \equiv E_2;\ E_3 \rfloor \rfloor$$

$\neg$ OCCURS $(I_1^* \underline{in}\ E_3)$

$$\lceil (M_2 I_2)^* \equiv \lceil (M_1 I_1)^* \equiv E_1;\ E_2 \rfloor\ ;\ E_3 \rfloor$$

Theorem 1.4:   "importation of an expression into a conditional expression"

$$\lceil (M\ I) \equiv \underline{if}\ E_1\ \underline{then}\ E_2\ \underline{else}\ E_3\ \underline{fi}\ ;\ E_4 \rfloor$$

$$\underline{if}\ E_1\ \underline{then}\ \lceil (M\ I) \equiv E_2;\ E_4 \rfloor\ \underline{else}\ (M\ I) \equiv E_3;\ E_4\ \underline{fi}$$

3.4. Reducibility Theorem for C_1

As has been pointed out in section 1.2, it is of utmost importance that the axioms form a reducing set of transformations. Therefore, it has to be shown here that any program of C_1 can be reduced to a program of C_0 . The following proof will show the necessity of adding a few "error-axioms".

The only new production for the grammatical axiom E is $E ::= \lceil G \rfloor$ with $G ::= D; E$. Therefore, it has to be proved that any term of the kind $\lceil D; E \rfloor \in \underline{Exp}$ can be converted into a "usual" expression. According to the syntax, one has to distinguish the four possible cases

(i)	$\lceil D; E \rfloor$	$=$	$\lceil F; E \rfloor$
(ii)	$\lceil D; E \rfloor$	$=$	$\lceil (M\ I)^* \equiv E_1; E \rfloor$
(iii)	$\lceil D; E \rfloor$	$=$	$\lceil D'; F; E \rfloor$
(iv)	$\lceil D; E \rfloor$	$=$	$\lceil D'; (M\ I)^* \equiv E_1; E \rfloor$

To case (i) axiom 1.1 is directly applicable, whereas in case (ii) one has to observe the restriction that I^* must not occur in E_1. This is accomplished by the

Axiom 1.4: ERROR-AXIOM

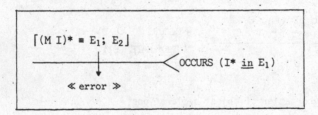

According to the decision taken in axiom 1.3 the case (iii) cannot be handled; one needs the

Axiom 1.5: ERROR-AXIOM

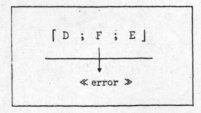

Finally, for the case (iv) one has to observe the condition that I* must not occur in D' , i.e.

Axiom 1.6: ERROR-AXIOM

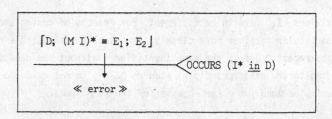

$$\lceil D;\ (M\ I)* \equiv E_1;\ E_2 \rfloor$$

OCCURS (I* in D)

≪ error ≫

With the help of axiom 1.3 and the error-axioms 1.5 and 1.6 one can reduce the cases (iii) and (iv) to the cases (i) and (ii) , thus concluding the proof by structural induction on the lengths of D and D' .

Remark: It is an interesting observation that the error-axioms relate to problems which often are not regarded as questions of the semantics but rather of the context-sensitive parts of the syntax.

4. Program Variables

The language C_1 comprises especially blocks of the form

$$\lceil\; M\; I_1 \equiv E_1 \;;\; M\; I_2 \equiv E_2 \;;\; \ldots \;;\; M\; I_k \equiv E_k \;;\; E_{k+1} \;\rfloor$$

where all identifiers I_j have to be different. For reasons of convenience as well as
for modelling particular machines more closely, one usually weakens this restriction
by permitting the repeated use of the same identifier - without the need for nested
scopes - according to the basic principle: *When an object is not needed any longer,
its identifiers may be used for other objects (of the same mode).*

It has come into use to distinguish between the fixed connection of an identifier to
an object, denoted by the symbol " $\equiv$ " , and the variable connection, denoted by the
symbol " $:=$ " . Thus, the above block reads after the transition to program variables (provided that the respective conditions hold)

$$\lceil\; \underline{var}\; M\; I := E_1 \;;\; I := E_2' \;;\; \ldots \;;\; I := E_k' \;;\; E_{k+1}' \;\rfloor$$

or with an "uninitialized declaration"

$$\lceil\; \underline{var}\; M\; I \;;\; I := E_1 \;;\; I := E_2' \;;\; \ldots \;;\; I := E_k' \;;\; E_{k+1}' \;\rfloor$$

where E_j' stands for $E_j[I/I_{j-1}]$.

Of course, this is not the only possible view of program variables. In the present paper, however, this particular aspect shall be considered as basic. It will be seen
that it brings about all the properties, which usually are claimed for variables. Thus
the approach of regarding program variables as notational variants of certain applicative constructs is compatible with the method of connecting them to states, as it
is done in the semantic fabric of McCarthy or of Floyd/Hoare/Dijkstra.

This chapter will explore several sets of transformations differing in elegance and
range of applicability. It will be one of the aims to keep the axioms as simple as
possible.

Remark: The principle stated above contains the notion "any longer". This presumes the
existence of an ordering "before/after"; such a (partial) ordering is defined in a
natural way inductively on the structure of the language C_1 :
Let $\alpha \lessdot \beta$ stand for " α precedes β ". Then the desired ordering is the (transitive
closure of the) elementwise relation

$$\begin{aligned}
\underline{if}\; E_1\; \underline{then}\; E_2\; \underline{else}\; E_3\; \underline{fi} \;&\Rightarrow\; E_1 \lessdot E_2 \;\wedge\; E_1 \lessdot E_3\\
\lceil D \;;\; E \rfloor \;&\Rightarrow\; D \lessdot E\\
D_1 \;;\; D_2 \;&\Rightarrow\; D_1 \lessdot D_2
\end{aligned}$$

all the other constructs of the language are incomparable. (An interpretation of $\diamond$ in physical time is possible but not unique). In the subsequent axioms, only situations are dealt with where the constructs stand in the relation $\diamond$.

4.1. Syntax of C_2

For the explanation of the basic concept of program variables a rather restricted language will be sufficient. Therefore, at first only blocks containing essentially a sequence of assignments to "local" variables shall be added to the language C_1 . (Note that this prevents side-effects.) Such a restriction to languages where the principles of program variables can be studied without having to care about scope rules and the like is well-known from axiomatic approaches (cf. [Igarashi 64], [de Bakker 69], [Hoare 69], [Dijkstra 75]).

One of the pecularities of the language C_2 is the fact that only uninitialized variable declarations are considered, as they are more generally applicable especially in connection with alternative or repetitive statements. Besides, the transitions from

$$\underline{var}\, M\, I\, ;\quad I := E \qquad \text{to} \qquad \underline{var}\, M\, I := E$$

or from

$$\underline{var}\, M\, I \qquad\qquad \text{to} \qquad \underline{var}\, M\, I := \Delta$$

where Δ is the "meaningless" object of 1.4, are just notational variants. (An extensive discussion of the question of initialization can be found in [Dijkstra 76] pp. 84-93). To a great extent, all this is a matter of taste, as long as the real point, viz. the requirement that variables must have been initialized before they are referred to, is met. This, however, is guaranteed by the axiomatic transformations given below.

Table IV: Syntax of C_2

<u>Exp</u>	$\ni E ::= O \mid I \mid E E \mid \underline{if}\ E\ \underline{then}\ E\ \underline{else}\ E\ \underline{fi} \mid (E)^* \mid A \mid \lceil\, G\, \rfloor$
<u>Abstr</u>	$\ni A ::= (M\, I)^*\, M : E \mid \underline{Y}\, E$
<u>Genexp</u>	$\ni G ::= D;\, E \mid (\underline{var}\ M\ I)^*;\, S\, ;\, E$
<u>Decl</u>	$\ni D ::= F \mid (M\, I)^* \equiv E \mid D\, ;\, D$
<u>Fun</u>	$\ni F ::= \underline{funct}\ I \equiv A \mid F^*$
<u>Stat</u>	$\ni S ::= (I)^* := E \mid \underline{if}\ E\ \underline{then}\ S\ \underline{else}\ S\ \underline{fi} \mid \underline{while}\ E\ \underline{do}\ S\ \underline{od} \mid S\, ;\, S$
<u>Obj</u>	$\ni O ::= \ll \text{object denotation}\gg$
<u>Ide</u>	$\ni I ::= \ll \text{identifier}\gg$
<u>Mode</u>	$\ni M ::= \ll \text{mode indication}\gg$

There is a syntactic predicate ASSIGNED (I <u>in</u> S) which will be used in some of the later transformations. It is defined similar to the predicate OCCURS :

ASSIGNED (I <u>in</u> $(I_1)^*$:= E) = I $\in (I_1)^*$

ASSIGNED (I <u>in</u> <u>if</u> E <u>then</u> S_1 <u>else</u> S_2 <u>fi</u>) = ASSIGNED (I <u>in</u> S_1) $\vee$ ASSIGNED (I <u>in</u> S_2)

ASSIGNED (I <u>in</u> <u>while</u> E <u>do</u> S <u>od</u>) = ASSIGNED (I <u>in</u> S)

ASSIGNED (I <u>in</u> S_1; S_2) = ASSIGNED (I <u>in</u> S_1) $\vee$ ASSIGNED (I <u>in</u> S_2)

4.2. Declaration of Program Variables

One needs a separate axiom to give the semantics of the declaration of program variables. In the generating direction this axiom provides the starting point for the further development, in the reducing direction it is the final step leading from the language C_2 to C_1 . The transformation simply expresses the fact that a variable, to which only one assignment takes place, can be replaced by a constant.

Axiom 2.1:   DECLARATION OF PROGRAM VARIABLES

$$\lceil (\underline{var}\ M\ I)^*\ ;\ (I)^* := E_1\ ;\ E_2 \rfloor$$

$$\updownarrow$$

$$\lceil (M\ I)^* = E_1\ ;\ E_2 \rfloor$$

By application of axiom 1.2 the direct reduction to the level of the language C_0 becomes possible:

Theorem 2.1

$$\lceil (\underline{var}\ M\ I)^*\ ;\ (I)^* := E_1\ ;\ E_2 \rfloor$$

$$\updownarrow \qquad \begin{cases} \neg\ \text{OCCURS (I}\ \underline{in}\ E_1) \\ M_2 = \text{MODE}\ (E_2) \end{cases}$$

$$((M\ I)^*\ M_2 : E_2)\ (E_1)$$

4.3. Successive Assignments

The successive assignments to a previously declared variable have to be introduced by
iterated application of an appropriate transformation rule; for this rule there exist
a great number of equipotent variants which just differ in their "elegance", i.e. in
their technical complexity.

For an easy entrance into the problem, the first rule we want to have exhibits most
accurately the basic idea of the introduction of program variables, i.e. the possibility of reusing (object) identifiers. Unfortunately, this first rule will turn out
not to be powerful enough for all purposes.

$$(*) \quad \frac{\lceil (\underline{var} \; M \; I)* \; ; \; (I)* := E_1 \; ; \; (I)* := E_2 \; ; \; S \; ; \; E_3 \rfloor}{\lceil (M \; I_1)* \equiv E_1 \; ; \; \lceil (\underline{var} \; M \; I)* \; ; \; (I)* := E_2[I_1^*/I^*]; S \; ; \; E_3 \rfloor \rfloor} \quad \begin{array}{l} \neg \; \text{OCCURS} \; (I_1^* \; \underline{in} \; E_2, S, E_3) \\ \neg \; \text{OCCURS} \; (I^* \; \underline{in} \; E_1) \end{array}$$

However, this transformation is not very satisfactory for two reasons: First, the context " $S \; ; \; E_3$ " is only needed to formulate the condition. (Besides, one must allow
S to be empty which brings up formal problems.) Second, the block brackets, which
shall detain the process from "stopping" somewhere in the middle of a block, require
for the additional condition $\neg$ OCCURS ($I^* \; \underline{in} \; E_1$) .

Remark: We could have defined the iterative process of introducing assignments just
as well "from the outside inward", i.e. "from left to right".

When regarding the output-scheme of the above transformation one can see from the
condition $\neg$ OCCURS ($I_1^* \; \underline{in} \; S, E_3$) that the expression $E_2[I_1^*/I^*]$ is the only place, where
I_1^* may occur. This suggests "moving" the declaration to the point, where it is need-
ed, i.e.

$$\lceil (\underline{var} \; M \; I)* \; ; \; (I)* := \lceil (M \; I_1)* \equiv E_1 \; ; \; E_2 \rfloor \; ; \; S \; ; \; E_3 \rfloor$$

This does not even lead to name clashes, as is ensured by the second condition
$\neg$ OCCURS ($I^* \; \underline{in} \; E_1$) . Now everything is safe because of the scope rules. Hence, the
scheme-variables S and E_3 can be omitted.

Note: As I^* neither can occur in E_1 nor in E_2 , the renaming already can be done
on the level of the language C_1 , giving in the output-scheme ($\underline{var} \; M \; I)* \; ; \; (I)* :=$
$\lceil (M \; I)* \equiv E_1 \; ; \; E_2 \rfloor$. This illustrates remarkably the second aspect of variables, viz.
the reusing of identifiers without the need for nested scopes.

In the resulting transformation

$$\lceil (\underline{var}\ M\ I)^*\ ;\ (I)^* := E_1\ ;\ (I)^* := E_2\ ;\ S\ ;\ E_3 \rfloor$$

(**)
_____

$$\lceil (\underline{var}\ M\ I)^*\ ;\ (I)^* := \lceil (M\ I)^* \equiv E_1\ ;\ E_2 \rfloor\ ;\ S\ ;\ E_3 \rfloor$$

the context $\lceil (\underline{var}\ M\ I)^*\ ;\ \ldots\ ;\ S\ ;\ E_3 \rfloor$ has become superfluous. Besides, at the latest in connection with the conditional assignment there will occur situations, where the assignments in question are not immediately preceded by a declaration. For these reasons one chooses as the basic axiom for assignments the more general form

Axiom 2.2:   ASSIGNMENT

$$(I)^* := E_1\ ;\ (I)^* := E_2$$
_____ $\neg$ OCCURS $(I_1^*\ \underline{in}\ E_1, E_2)$
$$(I)^* := \lceil (M\ I_1)^* \equiv E_1\ ;\ E_2[I_1^*/I^*] \rfloor$$ $M = \text{MODE}\ (I^*)$

Note that both schemes now are in the domain <u>Stat</u> , whereas in the transformations (*) and (**) they had been in <u>Exp</u> . The condition is only needed here to avoid name clashes for the newly introduced indentifer I_1^* .

The transformations (*) and (**) now follow immediately from the axiom 2.2. When going back to the level of the language C_1 , one even can do without new identifiers. Application of axiom 1.2 to the output-scheme above yields

$$(I)^* := ((M\ I_1)^*\ M\ :\ E_2[I_1^*/I^*])(E_1)\ .$$

This allows the renaming of I_1^* into I^* , resulting in

Theorem 2.2:

$$(I)^* := E_1\ ;\ (I)^* := E_2$$
_____ $M = \text{MODE}\ (I^*)$
$$(I)^* := ((M\ I)^*\ M\ :\ E_2)(E_1)$$

The axioms 2.1 and 2.2 (or the corresponding theorems 2.1 and 2.2) form the essential basis for the introduction of program variables. However, there is still one drastic restriction inherent in the axioms given so far: Only object declarations having exactly the same modes can be converted into assignments. This means that a block like e.g.

$\lceil$ $\underline{nat}$ a_1 $\equiv$ E_1; $\underline{bool}$ b_2 $\equiv$ $E_2(a_1)$; $\underline{nat}$ a_3 $\equiv$ $E_3(a_1, b_2)$; $\underline{bool}$ b_4 $\equiv$ $E_4(a_3, b_2)$; (a_3, b_4) $\rfloor$

cannot be handled directly. But theorem 1.3 allows to make all modes uniform:

$\lceil$ $(\underline{nat}$ a_1, $\underline{bool}$ $b_1)$ $\equiv$ (E_1, Δ); $(\underline{nat}$ a_2, $\underline{bool}$ $b_2)$ $\equiv$ $(a_1, E_2(a_1))$;

$\quad$ $(\underline{nat}$ a_3, $\underline{bool}$ $b_3)$ $\equiv$ $(E_3(a_2, b_2), b_2)$; $(\underline{nat}$ a_4, $\underline{bool}$ $b_4)$ $\equiv$ $(a_3, E_4(a_3, b_3))$;

$\quad\quad\quad\quad\quad\quad\quad\quad\quad\quad\quad\quad$ (a_4, b_4) $\quad\quad$ $\rfloor$

Now axioms 2.1 and 2.2 are applicable, yielding

$\quad$ $\lceil$ $(\underline{var}$ $\underline{nat}$ a, $\underline{var}$ $\underline{nat}$ $b)$; $(a, b) := (E_1, \Delta)$; $(a, b) := (a, E_2(a))$;

$\quad\quad$ $(a, b) := (E_3(a, b), b)$; $(a, b) := (a, E_4(a, b))$; $\quad$ (a, b) $\rfloor$.

This method is not very satisfactory, as it produces many assignments of the kind $(..., I, ...) := (..., I, ...)$. Although one can prove with the tools provided so far that an assignment $(I)^* := (I)^*$ can be deleted without changing the meaning of the program, one cannot do so, when such a situation occurs only as part of a collective assignment. On the other hand, it would be very tedious to vary the axiom 2.2 appropriately such that it takes care of different modes. Hence, it seems more elegant to add a further axiom deleting $..., I, ... := ..., I, ...$ from collective assignments.

Axiom 2.3:   DELETE ASSIGNMENT

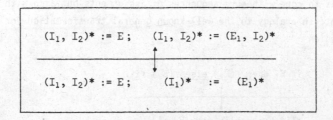

Note that the context is mandatory (for the upward direction), as it ensures the existence of I_2^* as well as its disjointness from I_1^* . (In this transformation the notational conventions of section 1.4 pay.)

Application to the example above yields

$$\lceil (\underline{var}\ \underline{nat}\ a,\ \underline{var}\ \underline{nat}\ b);\ (a,\ b)\ :=\ (E_1,\ \Delta);\ b\ :=\ E_2(a);$$
$$a\ :=\ E_3(a,\ b);\ b\ :=\ E_4(a,\ b);\ (a,\ b)\qquad\rfloor$$

(As has been pointed out in 4.1, the assignment of the "meaningless" object $b := \Delta$ can be avoided by a simple modification of the axioms.)

Remark: Speaking in terms of *state spaces* (cf. e.g. [McCarthy 62], [Dijkstra 75, 76]) the above considerations simply reflect the fact that an assignment to a certain variable leaves all other variables of the state space unchanged. Axiom 2.3 is directly related to McCarthy's rule $a(v, c(v, \xi), \xi) = \xi$ (where a changes the current state ξ for the variable v, and c yields the current value of v in the state ξ).

If one dislikes the "constant" context in axiom 2.3, one may use the variant

Theorem 2.3

$$(I_1,\ I_2)^*\ :=\ (E_1,\ I_2)^*$$

$$I_1^* \cap I_2^* = \emptyset$$
$$\ll I_2^* \text{exists in the surrounding block}\gg$$

$$(I_1)^*\quad :=\quad (E_1)^*$$

Both conditions are needed for the upward direction (a formal specification of the second one would require some expenditure). To prove this theorem one has to consider the context of the assignment, viz. $\lceil (\underline{var}\ M\ I)^*;\ S;\ (I_1)^*\ :=\ (E_1^*);\ \dots\ \rfloor$. Anticipating corollary 2.9 , S can be converted into an assignment $(I)^* := E$, thus providing the context necessary for the application of axiom 2.3. (If S is empty, I_1^* is identical to I^* ; hence, there does not exist a suitable I_2^* .)

4.4. Conditional Assignment

One not only has to cope with pure sequences of assignments but also with the alternative statement. In analogy to the well-known general transformation for the conditional expression

$$\underline{if}\ E_1\ \underline{then}\ f(E_2)\ \underline{else}\ f(E_3)\ \underline{fi}$$

$$f(\underline{if}\ E_1\ \underline{then}\ E_2\ \underline{else}\ E_3\ \underline{fi})$$

(where f is an arbitrary function), the assignment operation can be imported into the condition, too:

__Axiom 2.4:__   CONDITIONAL ASSIGNMENT

$$\underline{if}\ E_1\ \underline{then}\ (I)^* := E_2\ \underline{else}\ (I)^* := E_3\ \underline{fi}$$

$$\downarrow$$

$$(I)^* := \underline{if}\ E_1\ \underline{then}\ E_2\ \underline{else}\ E_3\ \underline{fi}$$

Note that the domain of the two branches of the _if_-clause has changed from __Stat__   to __Exp__ . As in the case of "usual" assignments there are several equipotent variants for this axiom, too (which I am not going to discuss here).

4.5. Repetition

Besides the sequential composition of assignments and the alternative statement, re-petition forms the third essential feature of imperative languages. As representant of this class of constructs the usual _while_-loop shall be introduced here, basing the semantics directly on recursive functions.

Remark: Usually, repetitive control constructs are based on (parameterless) recursive procedures. This is not necessary, however, as one can go back directly to the level of recursive functions.

__Axiom 2.5:__   REPETITION

$$\underline{while}\ E_1\ \underline{do}\ (I)^* := E_2\ \underline{od}$$

$$\downarrow \qquad \neg\ \text{OCCURS}\ (I_1\ \underline{in}\ E_1,\ E_2)$$
$$M = \text{MODE}\ (I^*)$$

$$(I)^* := \lceil \underline{funct}\ I_1 \equiv (M\ I)^*\ M :$$
$$\underline{if}\ E_1\ \underline{then}\ I_1(E_2)$$
$$\underline{else}\ (I)^*\ \underline{fi}$$
$$I_1(I)^* \qquad\qquad \rfloor$$

Again, the condition is needed to avoid name clashes for the newly introduced identifier I_1 of the function. In analogy to the conditional assignment, this restricted form, where the body of the loop is a single assignment, will be sufficient (cf. 4.7).

To avoid renamings within the expression E_2, the identifiers I^* of the program variables have been used for the prarameters of the function, too. This is possible, as the scope rules provide the necessary protection.

In the course of program developments one often has a repetitive function of the form

$$\underline{funct}\ f \equiv (\underline{m}\ x)\ \underline{r}\ :$$
$$\underline{if}\ E_1(x)\ \underline{then}\ f(E_2(x))\ \underline{else}\ E_3(x)\ \underline{fi}\ ,$$

where the body shall be converted into an iteration, yielding

$$\underline{funct}\ f \equiv (\underline{m}\ y)\ \underline{r}\ :$$
$$\lceil \underline{var}\ \underline{m}\ x\ ;\ x := y\ ;$$
$$\underline{while}\ E_1(x)\ \underline{do}\ \ x := E_2(x)\ \underline{od}\ ;\ E_3(x) \rfloor\ \ .$$

In this way, the "interface" of the function f is left unchanged, while internally the recursion is converted into an iteration.

To prove this transformation, one has to use the fact that the original function may be converted into

$$\underline{funct}\ f \equiv (\underline{m}\ y)\ \underline{r}\ :$$
$$\lceil \underline{funct}\ f' \equiv (\underline{m}\ x)\ \underline{r}\ :$$
$$\underline{if}\ E_1(x)\ \underline{then}\ f'(E_2(x))\ \underline{else}\ x\ \underline{fi}\ ;\ E_3(f'(y)) \rfloor$$

(This can be shown within the frame of the language C_0 using e.g. computational induction.) The theorems 1.2 and 1.3 then yield the form

$$\underline{funct}\ f \equiv (\underline{m}\ y)\ \underline{r}\ :$$
$$\lceil \underline{m}\ x \equiv \lceil \underline{m}\ x' \equiv y\ ;\ \lceil \underline{funct}\ f' \equiv \ldots\ \underline{fi}\ ;\ f'(x') \rfloor \rfloor\ ;\ E_3(x) \rfloor\ \ .$$

Now the axioms 2.1, 2.2 and 2.5 immediately give the desired result.

4.6. Comparison to Igarashi's Axioms

To give an impression of the "power" of the axioms presented so far, a few transformations derivable from these axioms shall be presented in this section. As an interesting set of representative transformations one may choose the axiomatic description
of program variables given in [Igarashi 64]. Following [de Bakker 69] the essential
features of this system are - adapted to our notation - the following transformations
(where the function $vars(E)$ gives the set of all variables occurring in the expression E).

Theorem 2.4

The transformations (I1) to (I7) hold :

(I1)

$$S ; I := I \qquad\qquad\qquad I := I ; S$$

$$S \qquad\qquad\qquad\qquad\qquad S$$

(I2)

$$I := E_1 ; S ; I := E_2$$

¬ ASSIGNED $(I$ in $S)$
¬ ASSIGNED $(vars(E_1)$ in $S)$
DETERMINATE (E_1)

$$S[E_1/I] ; I := E_2[E_1/I]$$

(I3)

$$I_1 := E_1 ; S ; I_2 := E_2$$

$I_1 \neq I_2$
¬ ASSIGNED $(I_1$ in $S)$
¬ ASSIGNED $(vars(E_1)$ in $S)$
¬ OCCURS $(I_1$ in $E_1)$
DETERMINATE $(\overline{E_1})$

$$I_1 := E_1 ; S[E_1/I_1] ; I_2 := E_2[E_1/I_1]$$

(I4)

$$I := E_1$$

$E_1 = E_2$

$$I := E_2$$

(I5)

$$\lceil (\underline{var}\ M\ I)^* ; S_1 ; S_2 ; (I_1)^* \rfloor$$

$I_1^* \subset I^*$
¬ ASSIGNED $(I_1^*$ in $S_2)$

$$\lceil (\underline{var}\ M\ I)^* ; S_1; \qquad (I_1)^* \rfloor$$

(I6)

$$I := E_1 \; ; \; \underline{if} \; E_2 \; \underline{then} \; S_1 \; \underline{else} \; S_2 \; \underline{fi}$$

$$\text{———————————————————————} \qquad \text{DETERMINATE } (E_1)$$

$$\underline{if} \; E_2[E_1/I] \; \underline{then} \; I := E_1; \; S_1 \; \underline{else} \; I := E_1; \; S_2 \; \underline{fi}$$

(I7)

$$\underline{if} \; E \; \underline{then} \; S_1 \; \underline{else} \; S_2 \; \underline{fi} \; ; \; S_3$$

$$\text{——————————————————}$$

$$\underline{if} \; E \; \underline{then} \; S_1 \; ; \; S_3 \; \underline{else} \; S_2 \; ; \; S_3 \; \underline{fi}$$

The proofs of these transformations can be found in the appendix.

Note: The transformation (I5) is intended to give as good an approximation to Igarashi's axiom as possible. It tries to capture the notion of the "effect of S_2 on the variables I_1^* ".

Remark: The essential point about Igarashi's axiom system is a completeness result. Again using the trick of (I5) this result can be formulated here as follows: The blocks (i.e. the expressions)

$$\lceil (\underline{var} \; M \; I)^* \; ; \; S_1 \; ; \; (I_1)^* \rfloor$$

and

$$\lceil (\underline{var} \; M \; I)^* \; ; \; S_2 \; ; \; (I_1)^* \rfloor$$

are equivalent, iff they can be transformed into one another by means of (I1) to (I7).

Igarashi's characterization of statements is consistent with McCarthy's approach (cf. [de Bakker 69], [Kaplan 68]). This means that also the axiomatic transformations presented here are compatible with McCarthy's system.

4.7. Reducibility Theorem for C_2

It has to be shown that every program of C_2 can be reduced to a program of C_1 , at least if all variables, to which assignments take place within a certain block, are declared at the beginning of that block. (It will suffice to restrict tuples of variables to at most three components.)

The grammar of C_2 contains the new nonterminal S together with its productions, and the new production G ::= (var M I)* ; S ; E for the nonterminal G already occurring in the grammar of C_1 . Therefore the only construction to be reduced is $\lceil$(var M I)* ; S ; E $\rfloor$.

Lemma 2.5

Any two subsequent assignments can be converted into one assignment.

Proof: Regard

$$(I_1, I_2) := E_1 ; (I_1, I_3) := E_2$$

By axiom 2.2 this is convertible into

$$(I_1, I_2, I_3) := E_1' ; (I_1, I_2, I_3) := E_2' .$$

Now axiom 2.2 yields

$$(I_1, I_2, I_3) := \lceil (M_1I_1', M_2I_2', M_3I_3') \equiv E_1' ; E_2'[I_1'/I_1, I_2'/I_2, I_3'/I_3] \rfloor \bullet$$

Corollary 2.6

Any sequence of assignments can be turned into one assignment.

Lemma 2.7

A conditional statement can be converted into a single assignment.

Proof: Regard e.g. the branch S_1 of

if E then S_1 else S_2 fi .

There are three possibilities:

(a) S_1 is an assignment (by corollary 2.6 this includes sequences);
this is the desired case (see below).

(b) S_1 contains another conditional assignment. Then by structural
induction lemma 2.7 is applicable, giving case (a) .

(c) S_1 contains a <u>while</u>-loop. By lemma 2.8 below this again leads to an assignment and thus to case (a) .

This shows that one finally has a statement like

$$\text{if } E \text{ <u>then</u> } (I_1, I_2) := E_1 \text{ <u>else</u> } (I_1, I_3) := E_2 \text{ <u>fi</u>} .$$

As in the proof of lemma 2.5 this is converted into

$$\text{if } E \text{ <u>then</u> } (I_1, I_2, I_3) := E_1' \text{ <u>else</u> } (I_1, I_2, I_3) := E_2' \text{ <u>fi</u>} .$$

Now axiom 2.4 gives the result

$$(I_1, I_2, I_3) := \text{ <u>if</u> } E \text{ <u>then</u> } E_1' \text{ <u>else</u> } E_2' \text{ <u>fi</u>}$$

Lemma 2.8

An iterative statement can be converted into a single assignment.

<u>Proof:</u>   For the statement S of

$$\text{<u>while</u> } E \text{ <u>do</u> } S \text{ <u>od</u>}$$

one can distinguish again the three cases

(a) S is an assignment. Then axiom 2.5 directly gives the proof.

(b) S contains a conditional assignment. By lemma 2.7 this leads to case (a) . (Note that because of the finiteness of the term S the mutually recursive dependency of lemma 2.7 and lemma 2.8 is admissible.)

(c) S contains a <u>while</u>-loop. Then by structural induction lemma 2.8 is applicable, giving case (a) .

Taking all these results together one has

Corollary 2.9

Any statement S can be converted into an assignment $(I)* := E$.

The rest of the reducibility theorem is trivially proved: Regard

$$\lceil (\underline{var}\ M\ I)^*\ ;\ S\ ;\ E \rfloor$$

By corollary 2.9 this can be turned into

$$\lceil (\underline{var}\ M\ I)^*\ ;\ (I_1)^* := E_1\ ;\ E \rfloor\ \ .$$

If $I^* = I_1^*$, axiom 2.1 gives the final result

$$\lceil (M\ I)^* \equiv E_1\ ;\ E \rfloor$$

Otherwise one needs

Axiom 2.6:   ERROR-AXIOM

$$\lceil (\underline{var}\ M\ I)^*\ ;\ (I_1)^* := E_1\ ;\ E_2 \rfloor$$

$$\ll error \gg$$

$I_1^* \neq I^*$

5. Non-local Program Variables

So far only assignments to variables declared in the same block are admissible. For a more liberal style of programming it is desirable that non-local variables are allowed, too. In order to escape the lot of difficulties coming along with the intro-duction of "expressions with side-effects", the assignment to non-local variables will be admitted only in statements.

5.1. Syntax of C_3

The new language C_3 differs from C_2 only in the productions $S ::= \lceil\ \ldots\ \rfloor$, which allow blocks as statements.

Table V: Syntax of C_3

Exp	$\ni E ::= O \mid I \mid E E \mid \underline{if} E \underline{then} E \underline{else} E \underline{fi} \mid (E)* \mid A \mid \lceil G \rfloor$
Abstr	$\ni A ::= (M I)* M : E \mid \underline{Y} E$
Genexp	$\ni G ::= D; E \mid (\underline{var} M I)*; S ; E$
Decl	$\ni D ::= F \mid (M I)* \equiv E \mid D ; D$
Fun	$\ni F ::= \underline{funct} I \equiv A \mid F*$
Stat	$\ni S ::= (I)* := E \mid \underline{if} E \underline{then} S \underline{else} S \underline{fi} \mid \underline{while} E \underline{do} S \underline{od} \mid S ; S$
	$\lceil D; S \rfloor \mid \lceil (\underline{var} M I)* ; S \rfloor$
Obj	$\ni O ::= \ll object\ denotation \gg$
Ide	$\ni I ::= \ll identifier \gg$
Mode	$\ni M ::= \ll mode\ indication \gg$

The predicate ASSIGNED has to be extended for the new productions appropriately:

$$\text{ASSIGNED } (I \underline{in} \lceil D ; S \rfloor) = \text{ASSIGNED } (I \underline{in} S)$$

note: if I is declared in D and assigned in S, this will
lead to an error.

$$\text{ASSIGNED } (I \underline{in} \lceil (\underline{var} M I_1)*; S \rfloor) = I \notin I_1* \wedge \text{ASSIGNED } (I \underline{in} S) .$$

5.2. Axioms for C_3

In axiom 2.4, an assignment has been imported into a conditional. In a very similar way it can be imported into a block. According to the syntax one needs two axioms for the two cases of *generalized expressions*.

Axiom 3.1:   NON-LOCAL VARIABLES AND DECLARATIONS

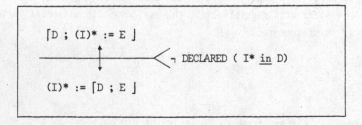

Remark: The axiom 3.1 has severe consequences: First of all, its application (in the upward direction) usually will be the starting point for subsequent applications of the axioms 2.2 to 2.5. Thus, the assignment $(I)* := E$ will become a whole sequence of assignments. This will yield for example

$$\lceil \underline{m} \ c \equiv E_1(x) \ ; \quad x := E_2(x, c) \ ; \ \ldots \ ; \ x := E_n(x, c) \rfloor \quad .$$

According to the axioms the (constant) value of c depends on that value, which the variable x has upon black-entry, and it will be the same in E_2 through E_n. For object-declarations such a property is generally accepted. However, the axiom 3.1 leads to the same property for function-declarations. Regard e.g. the block

$$\lceil \underline{funct} \ f \equiv (\underline{m} \ a) \ \underline{n} : E_1(a, x) \ ; \ x := f(E_2) \ ; \ \ldots \ ; \ x := f(E_n) \rfloor \quad .$$

Here, every call of f depends on the value, which the variable x had upon block-entry, and not on its current value.

If one wants to disallow this, one has to add an appropriate condition to axiom 3.1 forbidding the dependency of functions on variables (as suppressed parameters) - a restriction which has other advantages, too. The consistency of the language requires that such dependencies be reserved for procedures only (cf. 5.4).

The more interesting case is the second one, where a non-local variable can be used to save a local one. This case can be reduced to the first one by means of

Axiom 3.2:   NON-LOCAL AND LOCAL PROGRAM VARIABLES

$$\lceil (\underline{var} \ M_1 I_1)* \ ; \ (I_1, \ I)* := E_1 \ ; \ (I)* := E_2 \rfloor$$
$$\Big\uparrow \qquad \qquad M_2 = MODE \ (I*)$$
$$\Big\downarrow \qquad \qquad \neg \ OCCURS \ (I_2* \ \underline{in} \ I_1*, \ E_1, \ E_2)$$
$$\lceil (M_1 I_1, \ M_2 I_2)* \equiv E_1 \ ; \ (I)* := E_2[I_2*/I*] \rfloor$$

This axiom is a straightforward extension of axiom 2.1. As the conditions only serve the purpose of avoiding name clashes for the newly introduced identifier I_2*, applications of the axioms 3.1 and 1.2 yield a simplified version comparable to theorem 2.1:

Theorem 3.1:

$$\lceil (\underline{var}\ M_1 I_1)^*\ ;\ (I_1, I)^* := E_1\ ;\ (I)^* := E_2 \rfloor$$

$M_2 = \text{MODE}\ (I^*)$

$\neg\ \text{OCCURS}\ (I_1^*\ \underline{in}\ E_1)$

$$(I)^* := ((M_1 I_1, M_2 I)^* M_2 : E_2)\ (E_1)$$

Remark: The input-scheme of axiom 3.2 shows an important peculiarity: The last assignment of the block only concerns the non-local variable $(I)^*$. Of course, this in the only meaningful situation. However, for the reducing direction one has to decide, whether an assignment of the kind $(I_1,I)^* := E_2$ is regarded as an error or as a harmless superfluity. (As the latter would necessitate an additional axiom, the "error-solution" is preferred here. Besides, a program development going from the applicative to the imperative level will never run into this problem.)

The language C_3 is rather restrictive with respect to block brackets, as it does not admit the arbitrary mixture of declarations and commands. One could, of course, be more liberal and delete in a situation like

$$\lceil \underline{var}\ \underline{m}\ x\ ;\ x := E_1\ ;\ \lceil \underline{n}\ c \equiv E_2\ ;\ x := E_3\ ;\ \lceil \underline{n}\ d \equiv E_4\ ;\ x := E_5 \rfloor \rfloor \rfloor$$

the block brackets similar to axiom 1.3. These and other obvious generalizations would require axioms with rather complex conditions and large context. Therefore, they are not included here.

5.3. Reducibility Theorem for C_3

As the language C_3 does not differ very much from the language C_2 , the reducibility is shown quite easily. It suffices to show that corollary 2.9 (stating that every statement S can be converted into an assignment) also holds for the new constructs $S ::= \lceil D;\ S \rfloor$ and $S ::= \lceil (\underline{var}\ M\ I)^*\ ;\ S \rfloor$.

Lemma 3.2

A block $\lceil D;\ S \rfloor$ can be converted into an assignment $(I)^* := \lceil D;\ E \rfloor$.

Proof: By structural induction corollary 2.9 (or lemma 3.2 itself or lemma 3.3 below, depending on the syntactic form of S) is applicable. This gives $\lceil D;\ (I)^* := E \rfloor$. Now axiom 3.1 finishes the proof. (Note that the condition DECLARED $(I^*\ \underline{in}\ D)$ indicates an error-case.)

Lemma 3.3

A block $\lceil (\underline{var}\ M_1 I_1)^* \ ; \ S \ \rfloor$ can be converted into an assignment.

Proof: Again, structural induction allows to convert the block into
$\lceil (\underline{var}\ M_1 I_1)^* \ ; \ (I_s)^* := E \ \rfloor$. If this can be converted into
$\lceil (\underline{var}\ M_1 I_1)^* \ ; \ (I_1, I)^* := E_1 \ ; \ (I)^* := E_2 \ \rfloor$, then axiom 3.2
immediately gives the result (axiom 2.3 plays a central role, here).
If this is not possible, the remark following theorem 3.1 above shows,
which possibilities one has for choosing an appropriate error-axiom. ●

5.4. Further Extensions

The language developed so far should suffice to give an impression of the possiblities
of transformational semantics. Here is not the place to specify the complete semantics
of a comprehensive language like CIP-L ; but I will give at least a few hints, how
the addition of further constructs could be done.

To start with, some comments on the infamous *expressions with side-effects* seem to be
necessary: The language presented here contains certain expressions, which are - with
respect to side-effects - totally harmless, namely those which give the final result
of a block. In

$$\lceil (\underline{var}\ M_1 I_1)^* \ ; \ S_1 \ ; \ \lceil (\underline{var}\ M_2 I_2)^* \ ; \ S_2 \ ; \ E \ \rfloor \rfloor$$

the axioms given so far (especially the error-axiom 2.6) do not allow that an assignment to I_1^* takes place in S_2 , although this would not cause much trouble. Analogously, a construction like

$$\lceil \ldots \ ; \ \underline{if}\ E \ \underline{then}\ S_1 \ ; \ E_1 \ \underline{else}\ S_2 \ ; \ E_2 \ \underline{fi} \ \rfloor$$

is not admissible (a solution within the frame of the language C_3 would be

$$\lceil \ldots \ ; \ \underline{if}\ E \ \underline{then}\ S_1 \ ; \ I := E_1 \ \underline{else}\ S_2 \ ; \ I := E_2 \ \underline{fi} \ ; \ I \ \rfloor \quad) \ .$$

The best way to allow these harmless extensions is to introduce a new syntactic variable in the grammar, which distinguishes them. Then a few axioms will define the
appropriate reductions.

A different matter is the admission of side-effects in any expression (with the well-
known necessary precautions). A closer look into the problems which arise shows that

not only a great number of new axioms would be needed, but that also the existing axioms had to be modified by adding conditions, which guarantee that the expressions involved do not cause side-effects. Thus, the motivation for banning these features from programming languages is reflected in the need for complicated axioms in the transformational semantics.

In contrast to these problems, the concept of *procedures* fits well into the framework presented here, if they are regarded as an analogue to functions, their parameters being program variables - with the difference that they do not deliver a result. The main axiom to establish the link to previous language constructs will be something like

$$\lceil \underline{proc}\ I_1 = (\underline{var}\ M\ I)^* : I^* := E\ ;\ I_1(I)^* \rfloor$$

$$\lceil \underline{funct}\ I_1 = (M\ I)^*\ M : E\ ;\ I := I_1(I)^* \rfloor$$

(with the appropriate variants for recursive situations etc.).

Note that a procedure-call now is a statement. Admitting procedures with results, i.e. allowing procedure-calls as expressions, already would mean the introduction of side-effects with all their consequences.

After the suppression of the (variable) parameters, procedures only serve the purpose of controlling the flow of computation. It is an easy task to derive all loop-constructs from such parameterless procedures (which makes axiom 2.5 superfluous).

It is well known (cf. e.g. [Gill 75]) that the goto-statement can be explained by reducing it to parameterless (recursive) procedures. It is not surprising that quite a number of axioms will be required to do the reduction. The techniques are essentially the same as for the *continuations* of denotational semantics. (It is known from [Böhm, Jacopini 66] that this reduction is always possible. The use of parameterless recursive procedures instead of while-loops makes the transition even more elegant, cf. [Pepper 74].)

A final and very subtle point are special functions which have a program variable as result. They arise with the transition to organized store, e.g. from a variable for an array to an array of variables. A discussion of related problems, centering around the possibility of "selective updating", can be found e.g. in [Gries 78], [Bauer et al. 79].

6. Comparison to Other Methods

In a situation where there exist a number of generally approved methods for the formal description of the semantics of programming languages, the presentation of a new approach is not complete without its comparison to at least some of the existing techniques.

The *transformational semantics* is an algebraic method which specifies abstractly a whole category of models. Therefore it seems suitable to confront it with an approach where the models are constructed directly. A well-known representative of such approaches is the *denotational semantics* of Scott and Strachey.

It will also be instructive to relate the *transformational semantics* to another axiomatic theory. The most prominent candidate for this comparison is the *axiomatic semantics* in the forms given by Hoare and Dijkstra.

Of course, it is not necessary to show the interrelationship of the three methods for the whole language C_3 presented in this paper. For the purpose of comparison it will suffice to select some illustrative examples, for which the consistency of the different descriptions will be proved.

6.1. Denotational Semantics

This is not the place to give a detailed description of the principles of *denotational semantics*; I have to refer to the meanwhile widespread literature, especially to [Milne, Strachey 76], [Tennent 76] and [Stoy 77]. For the purpose of this section a simplified semantics of the language will suffice. In particular, the problems of error-propagation and mode-conformity will be omitted.

Particular emphasis will be given in this section to the demonstration in which way the axiomatic transformations allow to "compute" the semantics of outer language levels from the given semantics of the kernel language. The fact that the transformational approach specifies the semantics only up to isomorphism has the important consequence, that one still has freedom to introduce new functions and domains - thus "modularizing" the description appropriately.

To start with, a simple denotational semantics for the kernel C_0 is given (similar to the ones given in [Tennent 76] or [Stoy 77]) which, of course, has to fulfill the axioms of section 2.2. In the algebraic view this means that the model given below is one of the algebras of the class $Alg_{G,E}$, where G is the grammar of C_0 and

E   the set of axioms for C_0 . (I will follow here the notation which has come into use in *denotational semantics*, although it is not well suited for the algebraic view in all respects.)

The semantic domains and functions for C_0 are

$$o \in \underline{O}$$ basic objects
$$\varepsilon \in \underline{E} = \underline{O} + \underline{F}$$ expressible objects
$$\theta \in \underline{F} = [\underline{E} \to \underline{E}]$$ function objects
$$\rho \in \underline{U} = [\underline{Ide} \to \underline{E}]$$ environments
$$V \in [\underline{Obj} \to \underline{E}]$$ valuation function
$$E \in [\underline{Exp} \to [\underline{U} \to \underline{E}]]$$ meaning-function for expressions
$$A \in [\underline{Abstr} \to [\underline{U} \to \underline{E}]]$$ meaning-function for function objects

The semantics of C_0 then is given by the following equations

(1) $E [\![O]\!] \rho \qquad\qquad = V [\![O]\!]$

(2) $E [\![I]\!] \rho \qquad\qquad = \rho [\![I]\!]$

(3) $E [\![E_1(E_2)]\!] \rho \qquad = (E [\![E_1]\!] \rho)(E [\![E_2]\!] \rho)$

(4) $E [\![\underline{if}\ E_1\ \underline{then}\ E_2\ \underline{else}\ E_3\ \underline{fi}\ ]\!] \rho = \text{cond} (E [\![E_1]\!] \rho,\ E [\![E_2]\!] \rho,\ E [\![E_3]\!] \rho)$

(5) $E [\![E_1, ..., E_n]\!] \rho \qquad = \text{tuple} (E [\![E_1]\!] \rho, ..., E [\![E_n]\!] \rho)$

(6) $E [\![A]\!] \rho \qquad\qquad = A [\![A]\!] \rho$

(7) $A [\![(M_1 I_1, ..., M_n I_n)M_{n+1} : E\ ]\!] \rho = \lambda \delta_1, ..., \delta_n\ .\ E [\![E]\!] \rho'$
$$\text{where } \rho' = \text{update}(\rho, (I_1, ..., I_n), (\delta_1, ..., \delta_n))$$

(8) $A [\![\underline{Y}\ E]\!] \rho \qquad\qquad = \text{fixpoint}(E [\![E]\!] \rho)$

The meanings of the auxiliary functions cond, tuple and fixpoint are the usual ones. The function $\text{update}(\rho, I, \delta)$ yields a new environment ρ' such that $\rho' [\![I]\!] = \delta$.

The language C_1 introduces in particular the new productions $E ::= \lceil G \rfloor$, $G ::= D;\ E$ and $D ::= (M\ I)^* \equiv E$; together with the axiom 1.2 one has to calculate

$$E [\![\lceil (M_1 I_1, ..., M_n I_n) \equiv E\ ;\ E' \rfloor\ ]\!] \rho \qquad\qquad \text{axiom 1.2}$$
$$= E [\![((M_1 I_1, ..., M_n I_n)M_{n+1} : E')(E)\ ]\!] \rho \qquad \text{equ. (3)}$$
$$= (E [\![(M_1 I_1, ..., M_n I_n)M_{n+1} : E']\!] \rho)(E [\![E]\!] \rho) \qquad \text{equ. (6/7)}$$
$$= (\lambda \delta_1, ..., \delta_n\ .\ E [\![E']\!]\ \text{update}(\rho, (I_1, ..., I_n), (\delta_1, ..., \delta_n)))(E [\![E]\!] \rho)$$

the evaluation of E must yield a tuple of n expressible values

$$= (\lambda \delta_1, ..., \delta_n\ .\ E [\![E']\!]\ \text{update}(\rho, (I_1, ..., I_n), (\delta_1, ..., \delta_n)))(\text{tuple}(\varepsilon_1, ..., \varepsilon_n))$$
$$\text{where tuple}(\varepsilon_1, ..., \varepsilon_n) = E [\![E]\!] \rho$$
$$= E [\![E']\!]\ \text{update}(\rho, (I_1, ..., I_n), (\varepsilon_1, ..., \varepsilon_n))\ \text{where tuple}(\varepsilon_1, ..., \varepsilon_n) = E [\![E]\!] \rho\ .$$

The final equation shows that the expression E' is evaluated within a new environment. This means that the object declaration effects a change of the environment. For a suitable modularization one may therefore introduce a new function

$$\mathcal{D} \in [\underline{Decl} \rightarrow [\underline{U} \rightarrow \underline{U}]] \qquad \text{with the equations}$$

(9) $\quad E \, [\![D; E]\!] \, \rho \qquad\qquad\qquad = E \, [\![E]\!] \, \rho' \text{ where } \rho' = \mathcal{D} \, [\![D]\!] \, \rho$

(10) $\quad \mathcal{D} \, [\![(M_1 I_1, \ldots, M_n I_n) \equiv E]\!] \, \rho = \text{update}(\rho, (I_1, \ldots, I_n), (\varepsilon_1, \ldots, \varepsilon_n))$
$$\text{where tuple}(\varepsilon_1, \ldots, \varepsilon_n) = E \, [\![E]\!] \, \rho \qquad .$$

The equations for $D ::= F$ and $D ::= D; D$ can be derived analogously (the latter requiring induction).

In the language C_2 one has to calculate

$$E \, [\![\underline{\text{var}} \, M \, I \, ; \, S \, ; \, E \,]\!] \, \rho$$

(For the sake of brevity, one variable shall suffice for the illustration.) According to corollary 2.9, this is equivalent to

$\quad E \, [\![\underline{\text{var}} \, M \, I \, ; \, I := E_1 \, ; \, E \,]\!] \, \rho \qquad\qquad\qquad\qquad$ axiom 2.1

$= E \, [\![M \, I \equiv E_1 \, ; \, E \,]\!] \, \rho \qquad\qquad\qquad\qquad\qquad$ equ. (9)

$= E \, [\![E]\!] \, \rho' \text{ where } \rho' = \mathcal{D} \, [\![M \, I \equiv E_1]\!] \, \rho \qquad\quad$ equ. (10)

$= E \, [\![E]\!] \, \rho' \text{ where } \rho' = \text{update}(\rho, I, \varepsilon_1)$
$\qquad\qquad \text{where } \varepsilon_1 = E \, [\![E_1]\!] \, \rho$

For the production $S ::= S; S$ one gets analogously

$\quad E \, [\![\underline{\text{var}} \, M \, I; S_1; S_2; E \,]\!] \, \rho \qquad\qquad\qquad\qquad$ corollary 2.9

$= E \, [\![\underline{\text{var}} \, M \, I; I := E_1; I := E_2; E \,]\!] \, \rho \qquad\qquad$ axiom 2.2

$= E \, [\![\underline{\text{var}} \, M \, I; I := [\![M \, I' \equiv E_1; E_2[I'/I]]\!]; E \,]\!] \, \rho \qquad$ axiom 2.1

$= E \, [\![M \, I \equiv [\![M \, I' \equiv E_1; E_2[I'/I]]\!]; E \,]\!] \, \rho \qquad\qquad$ theorem 1.3

$= E \, [\![M \, I' \equiv E_1; [\![M \, I \equiv E_2[I'/I]; E]\!]]\!] \, \rho \qquad\qquad$ equ. (9/10)

$= E \, [\![M \, I \equiv E_2[I'/I]; E \,]\!] \, \rho'$
$\qquad \text{where } \rho' = \text{update}(\rho, I', \varepsilon_1)$
$\qquad \text{where } \varepsilon_1 = E \, [\![E_1]\!] \, \rho \qquad\qquad\qquad\qquad\qquad$ equ. (9/10)

$= E \, [\![E]\!] \, \rho'' \text{ where } \rho'' = \text{update}(\rho', I, \varepsilon_2)$
$\qquad \text{where } \varepsilon_2 = E \, [\![E_2[I'/I]]\!] \, \rho'$
$\qquad\qquad \text{where } \rho' = \text{update}(\rho, I', \varepsilon_1)$
$\qquad\qquad \text{where } \varepsilon_1 = E \, [\![E_1]\!] \, \rho$

Here, ϵ_2 and ρ' may be rewritten (sparing the auxiliary identifier I') into

$$\epsilon_2 = E \, [\![E_2]\!] \, \rho'$$
$$\rho' = \text{update}(\rho, I, \epsilon_1) \quad .$$

One can see here that in the language C_2 the effect of a statement can be described simply by a change of the environment, i.e. the identifier for the program variable is successively connected to new values. This might lead to a new function

$$S \in [\underline{\text{Stat}} \rightarrow [\underline{U} \rightarrow \underline{U}]] \qquad \text{with the equations}$$

(11) $E \, [\![\lceil \underline{\text{var}} \, M \, I; \, S; \, E \, \rfloor]\!] = E \, [\![E]\!] \, \rho'$ where $\rho' = S \, [\![S]\!] \, \rho$

(12) $S \, [\![I := E \,]\!] \, \rho = \text{update}(\rho, I, \epsilon)$ where $\epsilon = E \, [\![E]\!] \, \rho$

(13) $S \, [\![S_1; \, S_2 \,]\!] \, \rho = S \, [\![S_2]\!] \, \rho'$ where $\rho' = S \, [\![S_1]\!] \, \rho$

etc., as can be seen easily from the above derivation. (The declaration $\underline{\text{var}} \, M \, I$ could be used to mark the identifier I within the environment as "assignable".)

This approach can be followed a surprisingly long way (as in principle has already been observed in [Burstall 68]). However, it will fail - or at least be cumbersome - in connection with procedures and non-local program variables. Hence, one may choose already on this level a more suitable modularization by introducing *states* (often also called *stores*), i.e. mappings from so-called *locations* to values. One gets the new domains

$$\sigma \in \underline{S} = [\underline{L} \rightarrow \underline{O}] \qquad \text{states}$$
$$\alpha \in \underline{L} \qquad \qquad \text{locations}$$

The environments and the mapping E now have to be changed:

$$\rho' \in \underline{U}' = [\underline{\text{Ide}} \rightarrow \underline{E} + \underline{L}]$$
$$E' \, [\![I]\!] \, \rho\sigma = \text{cond}(\rho \, [\![I]\!] \in \underline{E}, \, \rho \, [\![I]\!], \, \sigma(\rho \, [\![I]\!]))$$

This further level of indirection causes considerable changes not only in the equations for the new syntactic constructs but also for all existing equations: In addition to the current environment also the current state has to be passed along with the whole computation as a second parameter. (This sensitivity of the whole description to slight changes in some parts is one of the major drawbacks of denotational semantics.)

I am not going to do all the changes here, but will only pick up again the examples above. Instead of changing the environment, an assignment now changes the state:

(12') $S \llbracket I := E \rrbracket \rho\sigma = \text{update}(\sigma, \alpha, \epsilon)$

   where $\epsilon = E' \llbracket E \rrbracket \rho\sigma, \quad \alpha = \rho \llbracket I \rrbracket$

(13') $S \llbracket S_1; S_2 \rrbracket \rho\sigma = S \llbracket S_2 \rrbracket \rho (S \llbracket S_1 \rrbracket \rho\sigma)$

Now, the declaration of a variable serves the purpose of providing a "free" location
for the variable I . (The auxiliary function init yields a new state σ with the
location α .)

In analogy to (9) , one has

(11') $E \llbracket \lceil \underline{\text{var}} \, M \, I; \, S; \, E \rfloor \rrbracket \rho = E' \llbracket E \rrbracket \rho'\sigma$

   where $\rho' = \text{update}(\rho, I, \alpha)$

   where $(\alpha, \sigma) = \text{init}$.

It should be noted that - from the algebraic point of view - one now has a model M_1
which does without states, and another model M_2 which uses states. In M_1 the sort
$\underline{\text{Stat}}$ corresponds to the function space $[\underline{U} \rightarrow \underline{U}]$, whereas in M_2 the sort $\underline{\text{Stat}}$
corresponds to the function space $[\underline{U} \rightarrow [\underline{S} \rightarrow \underline{S}]]$. In addition, M_2 makes use of
auxiliary carrier sets, viz. the set $\underline{L}$ of locations and the set $\underline{S}$ of states together with the corresponding auxiliary operations. Although the two models are totally different, the value of the (generalized) expression

   $E \llbracket \lceil \underline{\text{var}} \, M \, I; \, S; E \rfloor \rrbracket \rho$

is the same in both of them. In other words, if one asks for the equality of two statements S_1 and S_2 , one may get different answers in the two models, although with
any context $\lceil \underline{\text{var}} \, M \, I; \, ...; \, E \rfloor$ the resulting expression has the same value when
either S_1 or S_2 is inserted (cf. the discussion in section 1.2).

In this way, one can proceed for the further languages. The most interesting point
will come with the introduction of procedures. The use of states now allows to ex-
plain them directly as mappings from states to states $[\underline{S} \rightarrow \underline{S}]$. Without states, one
had to associate the procedure declaration with a corresponding function declaration
and to interpret a procedure call as an assignment, the right-hand side of which uses
that function (cf. section 5.4). However, the equations then would become intricate.

6.2. Axiomatic Semantics

In *denotational semantics* "the meaning of a language is defined by establishing a
correspondence between programs and functions of machine states". The *axiomatic
semantics* "introduces a further abstraction, in which memory states are no longer
treated explicitly. They are replaced by propositional formulae, which are regarded

as describing properties of the memory states before and after execution of each part of the program." ([Hoare, Lauer 74]).

An essential characteristic of this approach is that it is only applied to statements. The notation

$$\{P\} \quad S \quad \{Q\}$$

where P and Q are predicates for the program variables occuring in S , should be interpreted: "If the assertion P is true before initiation of the program S then the assertion Q will be true on its completion" ([Hoare 69], p. 577).

In a sense, the axioms and inference rules therefore can be viewed as a tool for the transition from one language - the imperative programming language in question - to another one - the applicative language of predicative expressions. (Dijkstra even uses the statements only as "transformers" for the predicates.) In this respect, the *axiomatic semantics* is similar to the *transformational semantics*. However, there is one essential difference: The combination of statements and assertions can at best be paralleled within the language C_3 , as the predicates used in *axiomatic semantics* are part of the "meta-language", whereas the boolean expressions to which the reduction in *transformational semantics* takes place are part of the programming language itself. This means that the former approach contains a mapping from syntax to semantics where-as the latter only yields a mapping from syntax to syntax. This difference prevents a direct comparison of both methods.

To cope with this difficulty one can in the first instance take advantage of the fact that a wide spectrum language like CIP-L allows to formulate statements and predi-cates within one single frame. As already the kernel language C_0 contains in parti-cular the mode <u>bool</u> together with the usual operations and laws (given e.g. as an abstract data type), the assertions of the axiomatic semantics can be transliterated directly into boolean expressions of C_0 (or of C_1 for easier readability). In this way, an assertion Q about the program variables $I*$ is converted into

<u>funct</u> $Q \equiv (M\ I)* \ \underline{bool} : \ll Q$ regarded as a term of $C_0 \gg$.

Now, a statement S containing the variables $I*$ and its postcondition Q shall be combined into a (generalized) boolean expression $"S; Q(I*)"$.

Note that the piece of text $"S; E"$ is not a proper program part of the language C_3 but rather one of the (harmless) extensions mentioned in section 5.4. But in axiomatic semantics one usually does not care about scope rules and the like anyhow. Hence, one may feel free - at least for the purpose of comparison - to add suitable context where-ever necessary, such that all terms fit into the syntax.

Within the frame of the language C_3 a term

$$\{P\} \ S \ \{Q\}$$

may be converted into (using a newly introduced local variable)

$$P(I^*) \Rightarrow \lceil (\underline{var} \ M \ I_1)^*; \ I_1^* := I^*; \ S[I_1^*/I^*]; \ Q(I_1^*) \rfloor \ .$$

Analogously, Dijkstra's weakest precondition

$$wp(S, \ Q)$$

leads to $\qquad \lceil (\underline{var} \ M \ I_1)^*; \ I_1^* := I^*; \ S[I_1^*/I^*]; \ Q(I_1^*) \rfloor \ .$

This last block will be considered now. By means of corollary 2.9 it is transformed into

$$\leftrightarrow \quad \lceil (\underline{var} \ M \ I_1)^*; \ I_1^* := I^*; \ I_1^* := E_s(I_1^*); \ Q(I_1^*) \rfloor$$

(where the notation $E_s(I_1^*)$ shall express the fact that the expression derived from $S[I_1^*/I^*]$ does depend on I_1^* but not on I^*).
Theorems 2.2 and 2.1 yield successively

$$\leftrightarrow \quad \lceil (\underline{var} \ M \ I_1)^*; \ I_1^* := ((M \ I_1)^* \ M : E_s(I_1^*)) \ (I)^*; \ Q(I_1^*) \rfloor$$
$$\leftrightarrow \quad ((M \ I_1)^* \ \underline{bool} : Q(I_1^*)) \ (((M \ I_1)^* \ M : E_s(I_1^*)) \ (I)^*) \ .$$

The special β-reduction of theorem 0.4 results in

$$\leftrightarrow \quad ((M \ I_1)^* \ \underline{bool} : Q(I_1^*)) \ (E_s(I^*)) \ .$$

which by means of the β-reduction of axiom 0.2 becomes

$$Q(E_s(I^*))$$

(If E_s is not determinate, one may use e.g. the form $\lceil (M \ I_1)^* \equiv E_s(I^*); \ Q(I_1^*) \rfloor$, which results from axiom 1.2, to get the results presented below analogously.)

The boolean expression resulting from this reduction process is a proper term of the language C_0 and will be denoted in the sequel by $RED(S, Q)$, i.e.

$$RED(S, \ Q) \ = \ Q(E_s(I^*)) \ .$$

This function RED has the following properties:

(A1)

$$RED(I := I, Q) = Q(I)$$

(A2)

$$RED(I := E, Q) = Q(E)$$

(A3)

$$RED(S_1; S_2, Q) = RED(S_1, RED(S_2, Q))$$

Proof: By means of corollary 2.9 and theorem 2.2, the left-hand side is equivalent to

$$RED(I := ((M\ I)\ M : E_{s2}(I))(E_{s1}), Q) .$$

The β-reduction of axiom 0.2 gives

$$RED(I := E_{s2}(E_{s1}), Q) .$$

Finally, property (A2) yields $Q(E_{s2}(E_{s1}))$.
The right-hand side becomes by means of corollary 2.9

$$RED(I := E_{s1}, RED(I := E_{s2}, Q)) .$$

By applying property (A2) twice, one gets

$$Q(E_{s2}(E_{s1}))$$

(A4)

$$RED(\underline{if}\ B\ \underline{then}\ S_1\ \underline{else}\ S_2\ \underline{fi}, Q)$$
$$= \underline{if}\ B\ \underline{then}\ RED(S_1, Q)\ \underline{else}\ RED(S_2, Q)\ \underline{fi}$$

Proof: Corollary 2.9, axiom 2.4 and property (A2) yield for the left-hand side

$$Q(\underline{if}\ B\ \underline{then}\ E_{s1}\ \underline{else}\ E_{s2}\ \underline{fi}) .$$

Again corollary 2.9 and property (A2) yield for the right-hand side the equivalent expression

$$\underline{if}\ B\ \underline{then}\ Q(E_{s1})\ \underline{else}\ Q(E_{s2})\ \underline{fi}$$

(A5)

$$RED(\underline{while}\ B\ \underline{do}\ S\ \underline{od}, Q) = h(I)$$
$$\text{where}\ \underline{funct}\ h \equiv (M\ I)\ \underline{bool} :$$
$$\underline{if}\ B\ \underline{then}\ RED(S, h)\ \underline{else}\ Q(I)\ \underline{fi}$$

Proof: The first step again is the application of corollary 2.9:

$$RED(\underline{while}\ B\ \underline{do}\ I := E_s\ \underline{od}, Q) .$$

Now, axiom 2.5 yields

$$RED(I := \lceil \underline{funct} \; h \equiv (M \; I) \; M :$$
$$\underline{if} \; B \; \underline{then} \; h(E_s) \; \underline{else} \; I \; \underline{fi}; \; h(I) \rfloor, \; Q)$$

Using property (A2) , one has the expression

$$Q(\lceil \underline{funct} \; h \equiv (M \; I) \; M :$$
$$\underline{if} \; B \; \underline{then} \; h(E_s) \; \underline{else} \; I \; \underline{fi}; \; h(I) \rfloor)$$

Axiom 1.1 and the rules for C_0 allow the successive transformations first into

$$\lceil \underline{funct} \; h \equiv (M \; I) \; M :$$
$$\underline{if} \; B \; \underline{then} \; h(E_s) \; \underline{else} \; I \; \underline{fi}; \; Q(h(I)) \rfloor$$

and then into

$$\lceil \underline{funct} \; h \equiv (M \; I) \; \underline{bool} :$$
$$\underline{if} \; B \; \underline{then} \; h(E_s) \; \underline{else} \; Q(I) \; \underline{fi}; \; h(I) \rfloor$$

As $h(E_s) = RED(S, h)$, this is the desired form. •

(A6)

$$\boxed{RED(S, \; false) = false}$$

Proof: As false does not depend on I , corollary 2.9 and (A2) immediately give the result. •

(A7)

$$\boxed{Q \Rightarrow R \quad \succ \quad RED(S, \; Q) \Rightarrow RED(S, \; R)}$$

Proof: Follows directly from corollary 2.9 and property (A2) . •

(A8)

$$\boxed{RED(S, \; Q) \wedge RED(S, \; R) = RED(S, \; Q \wedge R)}$$

Proof: By means of corollary 2.9 and property (A2) this is equivalent to the equations

$$Q(E_s) \wedge R(E_s) = (Q \wedge R) \; (E_s) \; ,$$

which simply is an instance of the β-reduction of axiom 0.2. •

(A9)

$$\boxed{RED(S, \; Q) \vee RED(S, \; R) = RED(S, \; Q \vee R)}$$

Proof: Same as for property (A8) . •

Note: For non-determinate expressions E_s the β-reduction of axiom 0.2 is not applicable. A model-theoretic proof (using e.g. the model presented in [CIP 78b]) then would show that property (A8) still holds whereas (A9) has to be changed into an implication.

If one replaces the term RED(S, Q) by the term wp(S, Q) , the properties (A1) to (A9) become essentially those given in [Dijkstra 75, 76] for the predicate transformers. However, this phenomenon of formal similarity should not lead to an identification of RED and wp . There still remains the essential difference that RED(S,Q) stands for a syntactic item whereas wp(S, Q) stands for a semantic one. This difference becomes most apparent for the statement abort (cf. [Dijkstra 75]; in our language this statement can be explained e.g. by the block

$$\lceil \underline{funct}\ f \equiv (\underline{m}\ a)\ \underline{m} : f(a)\ ;\ x := f(x)\ \rfloor\quad,$$

where x is a given program variable of mode $\underline{m}$). In contrast to the weakest precondition wp(abort, Q) = false , the expression RED(abort, Q) is an undefined - i.e. non-terminating - program part.

In order to close the gap between the two methods, one has to use a special semantic function: The function E used in the denotational model of the previous section yields for a boolean expression one of the three possible values tt (for true), ff (for false) or ⊥ (for ≪undefined≫) . To get rid of the value ⊥ , one has to use another function ∂ with

$$\partial(E) = \begin{cases} tt\ , & \text{if}\ E\ [\![E]\!]\ \rho\ =\ tt \\ ff\ , & \text{if}\ E\ [\![E]\!]\ \rho\ =\ ff \\ ff\ , & \text{if}\ E\ [\![E]\!]\ \rho\ =\ \bot\ . \end{cases}$$

This function has the properties that

$$\partial(\underline{if}\ B\ \underline{then}\ Q\ \underline{else}\ R\ \underline{fi}) =$$
$$\partial(B \lor \neg B)\ \land\ (\partial(B) \Rightarrow \partial(Q)) \land (\partial(\neg B) \Rightarrow \partial(R))$$

and that for any recursive boolean function h

$$\partial(h(x)) \quad = \quad tt$$

only if h(x) terminates .

Now, one can give the primitive of the axiomatic theory of predicate transformers an interpretation in terms of the transformational theory:

$$wp(S, Q) = \partial(RED(S, Q)) .$$

Note that

$$\{P\} S \{Q\} = \partial(P) \Rightarrow \partial(RED(S, Q))$$

only is a valid interpretation, if the predicate P cannot be undefined.

The results derived in this section show that all axioms and rules of inference of the *axiomatic semantics* are valid when the primitive has been replaced by the above interpretation. As is pointed out in [Hoare, Lauer 74] this "may be regarded in one of two different lights":

(1) If the *axiomatic semantics* is regarded as the definitive specification of the language, then the *transformational semantics* provides correct (abstract) implementations of the language.

(2) If the *transformational semantics* is regarded as the definitive specification of the language, the *axiomatic semantics* gives a valid proof technique.

In the light of section 1.2, where the *transformational semantics* has been shown to specify a whole category of algebras, the proofs given above even state that all the algebras of the category are valid models for the axiomatic theory. However, from section 1.2 it is also known that all these algebras are defined relative to the kernel C_0 . Thus, it is mandatory that the mode bool (within C_0) and the function ∂ properly reflect the properties of the predicate calculus. Therefore, one either has to give a suitable model for C_0 as a starting point, or one has to give a set of axioms for C_0 which guarantee that all models are suitable (in the final consequence this means that the axioms for the mode bool have to be monomorphic).

7. Concluding Remarks

In [Hoare, Lauer 74] it has been suggested that a computer programming language should be given several separate formal definitions, which should be proved consistent with each other. The definitions should be complementary, in the sense that one of them should assist the implementor and another should satisfy the need of the programmer (cf. [Hoare 78], p. 461). For the latter [Hoare 78] suggests e.g. an operational model involving sets of *traces* the concepts of which are familiar to many programmers. Another class of programmers is more familiar with the Lambda-calculus. Still, a third sort of formal definition is required for the theoretical foundation.

The present paper suggests another possibility for explaining a programming language to the programmer, the reduction of certain language constructs to more elementary ones. This approach, which has been used for the description of languages since the design of ALGOL 58, is given here a sound theoretical basis. It also has been shown to be a rigorous technique for the formal definition of the semantics, which may be used by implementors as well. In particular, the general view of *abstract syntax* allows to build a great variety of notational variants into a language without increasing its complexity.

A main advantage of the *transformational semantics* is that the introduction of new and possibly complex language constructs does not influence the description of the existing ones. On the other hand, one cannot expect that the "genuine logical and semantical irregularities of current languages" ([Hoare 78], p. 136) have simple descriptions in any formal method for the semantic specification. In *transformational semantics* the complexity of a construct can be measured to some degree by the number of axiomatic transformations its description requires.

One even may set up the thesis that for a well designed language it must be possible to describe the semantics (relative to a small kernel or at least relative to a small meta-language) by a few simple axiomatic transformations. If a certain construct requires a bulky set of axioms or if the axioms become rather complicated, then this indicates that the construct does not fit properly into the rest of the language. A typical example for such problems is given by the well-known "expressions with side-effects".

Of course, none of the defining transformations discussed in this paper is cogent (in the sense that it is the only logical choice for the introduction of the new language construct). By varying some of the transformations one may get (from a syntactical point of view) essentially the same language, but with a different semantics. It also is not necessary that the set of axioms be "minimal". For practical purposes, it even may be recommendable to include into the description some derivable theorems which are more illustrative than the axioms.

Appendix : Proofs of Some Theorems

Proof of theorem 1.1:

Immediate consequence of axioms 1.2 and 0.1.

Proof of theorem 1.2:

Immediate consequence of axioms 1.2 and 0.2.

Proof of theorem 1.3 (using the more readable pure λ-notation):

$$\lceil \lambda\ I_1 \equiv E_1 \ ; \ \lceil \lambda\ I_2 \equiv E_2 \ ; \ E_3 \rfloor \rfloor$$

A1.2	$(\lambda\ I_1.\ \lceil \lambda\ I_2 \equiv E_2 \ ; \ E_3 \rfloor)(E_1)$
A0.2	$\lceil \lambda\ I_2 \equiv E_2 \ ; \ E_3 \rfloor [E_1/I_1]$
subst8	$\lceil \lambda\ I_2 \equiv E_2[E_1/I_1] \ ; \ E_3[E_1/I_1] \rfloor$
premise	$\lceil \lambda\ I_2 \equiv E_2[E_1/I_1] \ ; \ E_3 \rfloor$
A0.2	$\lceil \lambda\ I_2 \equiv (\lambda\ I_1.\ E_2)(E_1) \ ; \ E_3 \rfloor$
A1.2	$\lceil \lambda\ I_2 \equiv \lceil \lambda\ I_1 \equiv E_1 \ ; \ E_2 \rfloor ; E_3 \rfloor \rfloor$

Note: As axiom 0.2 is applied in both directions here, the condition DETERMINATE (E_1) can be omitted.

Proof of theorem 1.4:

The proof is analogous to that of theorem 1.3 above, depending on the basic property of the $\underline{if}$ - construct that for any function f the term $f(\underline{if}\ E_1 \ \underline{then}\ E_2 \ \underline{else}\ E_3 \ \underline{fi})$ can be converted into $\underline{if}\ E_1 \ \underline{then}\ f(E_2) \ \underline{else}\ f(E_3) \ \underline{fi}$

Proof of theorem 2.4   (Igarashi's axioms):

The basis of the subsequent proofs is corollary 2.9 stating that any statement   S can be converted into an assignment $(I)* := E$. For the sake of simplicity, it will suffice here to regard only one variable, i.e. $I_s := E_s$. This simplification allows to replace the predicate "ASSIGNED (I $\underline{in}$ S)" by the simpler one "I = I_s" and "ASSIGNED (vars(E) $\underline{in}$ S)" by "OCCURS (I_s $\underline{in}$ E)" .

To start with, simplified versions of (I2) and (I3) shall be proved for later use

$(\overline{I2})$
$$I := E_1; \quad I := E_2$$

$\longleftarrow$ DETERMINATE (E_1)

$$I := E_2[E_1/I]$$

Proof of $(\overline{I2})$:

$$I := E_1; \quad I := E_2$$

A2.2 $I := \lceil (M\ I') \equiv E_1; \quad E_2[I'/I] \rfloor$

T1.2 $I := E_2[I'/I][E_1/I']$

subst $I := E_2[E_1/I]$ ●

$(\overline{I3})$
$$I_1 := E_1; \quad I_2 := E_2$$

$\longleftarrow$ ¬ OCCURS$(I_1 \underline{in} E_1)$
DETERMINATE (E_1)

$$I_1 := E_1; \quad I_2 := E_2[E_1/I_1]$$

Proof of $(\overline{I3})$:

$$I_1 := E_1; \quad I_2 := E_2$$

T2.3 $(I_1, I_2) := (E_1, I_2); (I_1, I_2) := (I_1, E_2)$

A2.2 $(I_1, I_2) := \lceil (M_1I_1', M_2I_2') \equiv (E_1, I_2); (I_1', E_2[I_1'/I_1, I_2'/I_2]) \rfloor$

T1.2 $(I_1, I_2) := \lceil (M_1I_1', M_2I_2') \equiv (E_1, I_2); (I_1', E_2[E_1/I_1, I_2/I_2]) \rfloor$

A2.2 $(I_1, I_2) := (E_1, I_2); (I_1, I_2) := (I_1, E_2[E_1/I_1])$

T2.3 $I_1 := E_1; \quad I_2 := E_2[E_1/I_1]$ ●

The respective generalization to (parts of) collective assignments is obvious and will be used in the subsequent proofs, too.

Proof of $(I1)$:

$$I_s := E_s; \quad I := I$$

T2.3 $(I_s, I) := (E_s, I); (I_s, I) := (I_s, I)$

A2.2 $(I_s, I) := \lceil (M_sI_s', M\ I') \equiv (E_s, I); (I_s', I') \rfloor$

T1.2 $(I_s, I) := (I_s', I')[E_s/I_s', I/I']$

subst $(I_s, I) := (E_s, I)$

T2.3 $I_s := E_s$ ●

For the case $I_s = I$ the first and last step of the proof can be omitted. The variant "I := I; S" is proved analogously.

Proof of (I2) :

Premises: $I_s \neq I$, $\neg$ OCCURS (I_s $\underline{in}$ E), DETERMINATE (E_1)

$\qquad$ $I := E_1$; $I_s := E_s$; $I := E_2$

T2.3	$(I, I_s) := (E_1, I_s)$; $(I, I_s) := (I, E_s)$; $(I, I_s) := (E_2, I_s)$
$(\overleftrightarrow{I2})$	$(I, I_s) := (I, E_s)[E_1/I, I_s/I_s]$; $\qquad$ $(I, I_s) := (E_2, I_s)$
$\underleftrightarrow{subst}$	$(I, I_s) := (E_1, E_s[E_1/I])$ $\qquad$; $\qquad$ $(I, I_s) := (E_2, I_s)$
$(\overleftrightarrow{I2})$	$I_s := E_s[E_1/I]$; $(I, I_s) := (E_2, I_s)[E_1/I]$
$\underleftrightarrow{subst}$	$I_s := E_s[E_1/I]$; $(I, I_s) := (E_2[E_1/I], I_s)$
T2.3	$I_s := E_s[E_1/I]$; $I := E_2[E_1/I]$ $\qquad\qquad$ •

Proof of (I3) :

Premises: $I_1 \neq I_2$, $I_1 \neq I_s$, $\neg$ OCCURS (I_s, I_1 $\underline{in}$ E_1), DETERMINATE (E_1)

$\qquad$ $I_1 := E_1$; $I_s := E_s$; $I_2 := E_2$

T2.3	$I_1 := E_1$; $(I_1, I_s) := (I_1, E_s)$; $I_2 := E_2$
$(\overleftrightarrow{I3})$	$I_1 := E_1$; $(I_1, I_s) := (I_1, E_s)[E_1/I_1]$; $I_2 := E_2$
$\underleftrightarrow{subst}$	$I_1 := E_1$; $(I_1, I_s) := (E_1, E_s[E_1/I_1])$; $I_2 := E_2$
$(\overleftrightarrow{I3})$	$I_1 := E_1$; $(I_1, I_s) := (E_1, E_s[E_1/I_1])$; $I_2 := E_2[E_1/I_1]$
$(\overleftrightarrow{I2})$	$I_1 := E_1$; $I_s := E_s[E_1/I_1]$; $I_2 := E_2[E_1/I_1]$ $\qquad$ •

Note that the case $I_2 = I_s$ is admissible here.

Proof of (I4) :

The proof depends on the fact that the assignment "$I := E_1$; ... " is converted into $((M\ I)\ M_1 : ...\ ) (E_1)$, where the whole program is reduced from the language C_2 to C_0 (cf. section 4.7). Within C_0 the premise $E_1 = E_2$ allows the transition from $((M\ I)\ M_1 : ...\ ) (E_1)$ to $((M\ I)\ M_1 : ...\ ) (E_2)$ - whatever "equality of expressions" means on this level. $\qquad$ •

Proof of (I5) :

It will be sufficient to consider two distinct variables I_1 and I_2 . Then one starts
from the input-scheme

$$\lceil(\underline{var}\ M_1I_1,\ \underline{var}\ M_2I_2);\ (I_1,\ I_2) := E_1;\ I_2 := E_2;\ I_1\rfloor$$

A2.3 $\lceil(\underline{var}\ M_1I_1,\ \underline{var}\ M_2I_2);\ (I_1,\ I_2) := E_1;\ (I_1,\ I_2) := (I_1,\ E_2);\ I_1\rfloor$

A2.2 $\lceil(\underline{var}\ M_1I_1,\ \underline{var}\ M_2I_2);$
$$(I_1,\ I_2) := \lceil(M_1I_1',\ M_2I_2') \equiv E_1;\ (I_1',\ E_2[I_1'/I_1,\ I_2'/I_2])\rfloor;\ I_1\rfloor$$

A2.1 $\lceil(M_1I_1,\ M_2I_2) \equiv \lceil(M_1I_1',\ M_2I_2') \quad \equiv E_1;\ (I_1',\ E_2[I_1'/I_1,\ I_2'/I_2])\rfloor;\ I_1\rfloor$

T1.3 $\lceil(M_1I_1',\ M_2I_2') \equiv E_1;\ \lceil(M_1I_1,\ M_2I_2) \quad \equiv \quad (I_1',\ E_2[I_1'/I_1,\ I_2'/I_2])\ ;\ I_1\rfloor\rfloor$

T1.2 $\lceil(M_1I_1',\ M_2I_2') \equiv E_1;\ I_1'\rfloor$

T1.1 $\lceil(M_1I_1,\ M_2I_2) \quad \equiv E_1;\ I_1\ \rfloor$

A2.1 $\lceil(\underline{var}\ M_1I_1,\ \underline{var}\ M_2I_2);\ (I_1,\ I_2) := E_1;\ I_1\rfloor$ ●

Proof of (I6) :

$$I_1 := E_1;\ \underline{if}\ E_2\ \underline{then}\ I_s := E_{s1}\ \underline{else}\ I_s := E_{s2}\ \underline{fi}$$

A2.4 $I_1 := E_1;\ I_s := \underline{if}\ E_2\ \underline{then}\ E_{s1}\ \underline{else}\ E_{s2}\ \underline{fi}$

T2.3 $(I_1,\ I_s) := (E_1,\ I_s);\ (I_1,\ I_s) := (I_1,\ \underline{if}\ E_2\ \underline{then}\ E_{s1}\ \underline{else}\ E_{s2}\ \underline{fi})$

(I2) $(I_1,\ I_s) := (I_1,\ \underline{if}\ E_2\ \underline{then}\ E_{s1}\ \underline{else}\ E_{s2}\ \underline{fi})\ [E_1/I_1,\ I_s/I_s]$

subst $(I_1,\ I_s) := \underline{if}\ E_2[E_1/I_1]\ \underline{then}\ (E_1,\ E_{s1}[E_1/I_1])\ \underline{else}\ (E_1,\ E_{s2}[E_1/I_1])\ \underline{fi}$

A2.4 $\underline{if}\ E_2[E_1/I_1]\ \underline{then}\ (I_1,\ I_s) := (E_1,\ E_{s1}[E_1/I_1])$
$$\underline{else}\ (I_1,\ I_s) := (E_1,\ E_{s2}[E_1/I_1])\ \underline{fi}$$

(I2) $\underline{if}\ E_2[E_1/I_1]\ \underline{then}\ I_1 := E_1;\ (I_1,\ I_s) := (I_1,\ E_{s1})$
$$\underline{else}\ I_1 := E_1;\ (I_1,\ I_s) := (I_1,\ E_{s2})\ \underline{fi}$$

T2.3 $\underline{if}\ E_2[E_1/I_1]\ \underline{then}\ I_1 := E_1;\ I_s := E_s\ \underline{else}\ I_1 := E_1;\ I_s := E_s\ \underline{fi}$ ●

For the case $I_1 = I_s$ the second and the last step are omitted.

Proof of (I7) :

$$\underline{if}\ E\ \underline{then}\ I := E_1\ \underline{else}\ I := E_2\ \underline{fi};\ I := E_3$$

A2.4 $I := \underline{if}\ E\ \underline{then}\ E_1\ \underline{else}\ E_2\ \underline{fi};\ I := E_3$

A2.2 $I := \lceil(M\ I') \equiv \underline{if}\ E\ \underline{then}\ E_1\ \underline{else}\ E_2\ \underline{fi};\ E_3[I'/I]\rfloor$

T1.4 $I := \underline{if}\ E\ \underline{then}\lceil(M\ I') \equiv E_1;\ E_3[I'/I]\rfloor \underline{else}\lceil(M\ I') \equiv E_2;\ E_3[I'/I]\rfloor \underline{fi}$

A2.4 $\underline{if}\ E\ \underline{then}\ I := \lceil(M\ I') \equiv E_1;\ E_3[I'/I]\rfloor\ \underline{else}\ I := \lceil(M\ I') \equiv E_2;E_3[I'/I]\rfloor\ \underline{fi}$

A2.2 $\underline{if}\ E\ \underline{then}\ I := E_1;\ I := E_3\ \underline{else}\ I := E_2;\ I := E_3\ \underline{fi}$ ●

This concludes the proof of theorem 2.6.

References

[ADJ 76]

J. W. Thatcher, E.G. Wagner, J.B. Wright: Specification of Abstract Data Types Using Conditional Axioms. IBM Research Report RC-6214, September 1976

[ADJ 76a]

A.J. Goguen, J.W. Thatcher, E.G. Wagner: An Initial Algebra Appraoch to the Specification, Correctness, and Implementation of Abstract Data Types. IBM Research Report RC-6487, October 1976

[ADJ 77]

J.A. Goguen, J.W. Thatcher, E.G. Wagner, J.B. Wright: Initial Algebra Semantics and Continuous Algebras. JACM 24, 1, 68-95 (1977)

[ADJ 78]

J.W. Thatcher, E.G. Wagner, J.B. Wright: Data Type Specification: Parametrization and the Power of Specification Techniques. Proc. SIGACT 1oth Annual Symposium on Theory of Computation, 1978

[Backus 78]

J. Backus: Can Programming Be Liberated from the von Neumann Style? A Functional Style and Its Algebra of Programs. CACM 21, 8, 613-641 (1978)

[de Bakker 67]

J.W. de Bakker: Formal Definition of Programming Languages. Mathematical Center Tracts 16, Mathematisch Centrum, Amsterdam (1967)

[de Bakker 69]

J.W. de Bakker: Semantics of Programming Languages. In: Tou (ed.): Advances in Information System Science 2, New York: Plenum Press, 1969

[de Bakker 76]

J.W. de Bakker: Least Fixed Points Revisited. Theoretical Computer Science 2, 155-181 (1976)

[Bauer et al. 79]

F.L. Bauer, H. Wössner: Algorithmic Language and Program Development. Prentice Hall International, London 1979 (to appear)

[Berkling 76]

K.J. Berkling: Reduction Languages for Reduction Machines. GMD, Institut für Informationsforschung, Interner Bericht ISF-76-8, Sept. 1976

[Birkhoff, Lipson 70]

G. Birkhoff, J.D. Lipson: Heterogeneous Algebras. Journal of Combinatorial Theory, 8, 115-133 (1970)

[Böhm, Jacopini 66]

C. Böhm, G. Jacopini: Flow Diagrams, Turing Machines and Languages with Only Two Formation Rules. CACM 9, 5, 366-371 (1966)

[Burstall 68]

R.M. Burstall: Semantics of Assignment. In: E. Dale, D. Michie (eds.): Machine Intelligence 2, 3-20, Oliver and Boyd, Edinburgh (1968)

[Burstall 70]

R.M. Burstall: Formal Description of Program Structure and Semantics in First Order Logic. In: B. Meltzer, E. Michie (eds.): Machine Intelligence 5, 79-98, Edinburgh University Press 1970

[Burstall, Darlington 75]

R.M. Burstall, J. Darlington: Some Transformations for Developing Recursive Programs. Proc. of 1975 Int. Conf. on Reliable Software, Los Angeles 1975, 465-472. Also (revised version)   JACM 24: 1, 44-67 (1977)

[Burstall, Goguen 77]

R.M. Burstall, J.A. Goguen: Putting Theories Together to Make Specifications. Proc. Int. Joint Conf. on Artificial Intelligence 1977

[Christensen, Shaw 69]

C. Christensen, C.J. Shaw (eds.): Proc. of the Extensible Languages Symposium, Boston, Mass., May 1969, SIGPLAN Notices 4, 8 (1969)

[CIP 76]

F.L. Bauer, H. Partsch, P. Pepper, H. Wössner: Techniques for Program Development. Technische Universität München, Institut für Informatik, Internal Report, Sept. 1976. Also in: Software Engineering Techniques. Infotech State of the Art Report 34, 1977

[CIP 77]

F.L. Bauer, H. Partsch, P. Pepper, H. Wössner: Notes on the Project CIP: Outline of a Transformation System. Technische Universität München, Institut für Informatik, TUM-INFO-7729, July 1977

[CIP 78]

F.L. Bauer, M. Broy, R. Gnatz, W. Hesse, B. Krieg-Brückner, H. Partsch, P. Pepper, H. Wössner: Towards a Wide Spectrum Language to Support Program Specification and Program Development. SIGPLAN Notices 13 (12), 15-24 (1978). See also this volume.

[CIP 78a]

M. Broy, W. Dosch, H. Partsch, P. Pepper, M. Wirsing: Abstract Data Types: Some Theoretical Aspects and their Practical Consequences. Technische Universität München (to appear)

[CIP 78b]

M. Broy, R. Gnatz, M. Wirsing: Semantics of Nondeterministic and Noncontinuous Constructs. Proc. International Summer School on Program Construction, Marktoberdorf 1978. This volume.

[Cooper 66]

D.C. Cooper: The Equivalence of Certain Computations. Comp. J. 9, 45-52 (1966)

[Darlington, Burstall 76]

J. Darlington, R.M. Burstall: A System which Automatically Improves Programs. Acta Informatica 6, 41-60 (1976)

[Dijkstra 75]

E.W. Dijkstra: Guarded Commands, Nondeterminacy and Formal Derivation of Programs. CACM 18, 453-457 (1975)

[Dijkstra 76]

E.W. Dijkstra: A Discipline of Programming. Prentice Hall, Englewood Cliffs, N.J., 1976

[Ershov 76]

A.P. Ershov: Problems in Many-Language Systems. Proc. International Summer School on Language Hierarchies and Interfaces, Marktoberdorf 1975, LNCS 46, Berlin-Heidelberg-New York: Springer 1976

[Floyd 67]

R.W. Floyd: Assigning Meanings to Programs. Proc. American Math. Society Symp. in Appl. Math. 19, 19-32 (1967)

[Gill 65]

S. Gill: Automatic Computing: Its Problems and Prizes. Comp. J. 8, 177-189 (1965)

[Goguen 77]

J.A. Goguen: Abstract Errors for Abstract Data Types. Univ. of California at Los Angeles, Comp. Sc. Dept., Semantics and Theory of Computation Report No. 6, May 1977

[Gries 78]

D. Gries: The Multiple Assignment Statement. IEEE Trans. on Software Eng., SE-4, 89-91, March 1978

[Gries 78a]

D. Gries: Current Ideas in Programming Methodology. In: P. Wegner (ed.): Research Directions in Software Technology. (to appear)

[Guttag 75]

J.V. Guttag: The Specification and Application to Programming of Abstract Data Types. Univ. of Toronto, Comp. Syst. Research Group, Techn. Report CSRG-59, Sept. 1975

[Hoare 69]

C.A.R. Hoare: An Axiomatic Basis for Computer Programming.   CACM 12, 10, 576-581 (1969)

[Hoare 78]

C.A.R. Hoare: Some Properties of Predicate Transformers. JACM 25, 3, 461-480 (1978)

[Hoare, Lauer 74]

C.A.R. Hoare, P.E. Lauer: Consistent and Complementary Formal Theories of the Semantics of Programming Languages. Acta Informatica, 3, 135-153 (1974)

[Hoare, Wirth 73]

C.A.R. Hoare, N. Wirth: An Axiomatic Definition of the Programming Language PASCAL. Acta Informatica 2, 335-355 (1973)

[Igarashi 64]

S. Igarashi: An Axiomatic Approach to the Equivalence Problems of Algorithms with Applications. PhD Thesis, University of Tokyo (1964). Reprinted in: Report of the Computer Center Univ. of Tokyo 1, 1-1o1 (1968)

[Kaplan 68]

D.M. Kaplan: Some Completeness Results in the Mathematical Theory of Computation. JACM 15, 124-134 (1969)

[Knuth 74]

D.E. Knuth: Structured Programming with goto Statements. Computing Surveys 8, 261-301 (1974)

[Landin 64]

P.J. Landin: The Mechanical Evaluation of Expressions. Comp. J. 6, 4, 308-320 (1964)

[Landin 66]

P.J. Landin: A Formal Description of ALGOL 60. In: T.B. Steel jr. (ed.): Formal Language Description Languages for Computer Programming. Proc. IFIP Working Conf. 1964, 266-294, North Holland, Amsterdam (1966)

[Landin 66a]

P.J. Landin: The Next 700 Programming Languages. CACM 9, 157-166 (1966)

[Lukas, Walk 70]

P. Lukas, K. Walk: On the Formal Description of PL/1. In: M.I. Halpern, C.J. Shaw (eds.): Annual Review in Automatic Programming 6, 105-182 (1970)

[McCarthy 60]

J. McCarthy: Recursive Functions of Symbolic Expressions and Their Computation by Machine, pt. 1. CACM 3, 4, 184-195 (1960)

[McCarthy 62]

J. McCarthy: Towards a Mathematical Science of Computation. In: C.M. Popplewell (ed.): Information Processing 1962, Proc. IFIP Congress 1962, Amsterdam: North-Holland Publishing Co., 21-28, 1963

[McCarthy 63]

J. McCarthy: A Basis for a Mathematical Theory of Computation. In: P. Braffort, D. Hirschberg (eds.): Computer Programming and Formal Systems. North-Holland Publishing Co., Amsterdam 1963

[McCarthy 66]

J. McCarthy: A Formal Description of a Subset of ALGOL. In: T.B. Steel jr. (ed.): Formal Language Description Languages for Computer Programming. Proc. IFIP Working Conference 1964, 1-12, North Holland, Amsterdam (1966)

[Milne, Strachey 76]

R. Milne, C. Strachey: A Theory of Programming Language Semantics. (2 Volumes) London: Chapman and Hall 1976

[Naur 66]

P. Naur: Proof of Algorithms by General Snapshots. BIT 6, 4, 310-316 (1966)

[Quine 60]

W.V.D. Quine: Word and Object. MIT Press, Cambridge, Mass. (1960)

[Pepper 74]

P. Pepper: Theoretische Ansätze für den Entwurf von Prozessoren für wohlstrukturierten Steuerfluß. Technische Universität München, Diplomarbeit 1974

[Perlis, Samelson 58]

A.J. Perlis, K. Samlson: Preliminary Report - International Algebraic Language. CACM 1, 12, 8-22 (1958)

[Salomaa 73]

A. Salomaa: Formal Languages. New York: Academic Press 1973

[Schuman, Jorrand 70]

S.A. Schuman, Ph. Jorrand: Definition Mechanisms in Extensible Programming Languages. Proc. AFIPS 1970 Fall Joint Computer Conf., 33, 2, 9-20, 1970

[Scott 72]

D. Scott: Continuous Lattices. Proc. 1971 Dalhousie Conference, Lecture Notes in
Mathematics 274. New York: Springer 1972, 97-136

[Scott 76]

D. Scott: Data Types as Lattices. Siam J. Comp. $\underline{5}$, 3, 522-587 (1976)

[Scott, Strachey 71]

D. Scott, C. Strachey: Towards a Mathematical Semantics for Computer Languages.
Oxford University, Computing Lab. Techn. Monograph PRG 6, 1971. Also in: J. Fox (ed.):
Computers and Automata. Wiley, New York, 1971. pp. 19-46

[Steel 66]

T.B. Steel jr. (ed.): Formal Language Description Languages for Computer Programming.
Proc. IFIP Working Conf. 1964, North Holland, Amsterdam (1966)

[Steinbrüggen 77]

R. Steinbrüggen: Reguläre Baumbereiche. Technische Universität München, Internal
Report, August 1977

[Stoy 77]

J.E. Stoy: Denotational Semantics: The Scott-Strachey Approach to Programming Language
Theory. The MIT Press, Cambridge, Mass. and London, 1977

[Strachey 66]

C. Strachey: Towards a Formal Semantics. In: T.B. Steel jr.(ed.): Formal Language Description Languages for Computer Programming. North Holland, Amsterdam, 198-220, 1966

[Tennent 76]

R.D. Tennent: The Denotational Semantics of Programming Languages. CACM $\underline{19}$, 8,
437-453 (1976)

[Tennent 77]

R.D. Tennent: A Denotational Definition of the Programming Language PASCAL. Queen's
University, Kingston, Ontario, Dept. of Computing and Information Sc., Techn. Report
77-47, July 1977

[Whitehead, Russell]

A.N. Whitehead, B. Russell: Principia Mathematica. Cambridge (1910-1913), (2nd ed.
1925-1927)

[van Wijngaarden 63]

A. van Wijngaarden: Generalized ALGOL. In: Symbolic Languages in Data Processing,
Proc. ICC Symp. Rome, 409-419, Gordon and Breach, New York (1962). Also in:
R. Goodman (ed.): Annual Review in Automatic Programming $\underline{3}$, 17-26, Pergamon Press,
New York (1963)

[van Wijngaarden 66]

A. van Wijngaarden: Recursive Definition of Syntax and Semantics. In: T.B. Steel jr. (ed.): Formal Language Description Languages for Computer Programming. Proc. IFIP Working Conf. 1964, 13-24, North Holland, Amsterdam (1966)

[van Wijngaarden 75]

A. van Wijngaarden et al.: Revised Report on the Algorithmic Language ALGOL 68. Acta Informatica $\underline{5}$, 1-236 (1975)

[Wirth 63]

N. Wirth: A Generalization of ALGOL. CACM $\underline{6}$, 547-554 (1963)

Detailization and Lazy Evaluation, Infinite Objects
and Pointer Representation

F. L. Bauer

Institut für Informatik
Technische Universität München

Summary.

Using the concept of "detailization", i.e. introduction of auxiliary denotations, and the strategy of "lazy evaluation" of recursive functions, a collection of linked objects ("nexus of objects") can be described on the applicative level by their constructing functions such that this leads to the introduction of pointers when passing to the procedural, container-oriented level. Examples of such a transformation to pointer representation are discussed, in particular the use of pointer variables and selective updating of composed objects in removing recursion from functions over the objects introduced.

The prevailing concepts in programming: program variables, loops, jumps, pointers have been coined by the dominant organizational form of computers, often vaguely called 'von Neumann machine'. 'Can programming be liberated from the von Neumann style?' asks J. Backus [1][1]. The relative success of LISP, despite its unpalatable parenthesis mountains, and of APL despite its lack of structuring tools, are signs that even practical programming can be done on the functional or applicative level. Moreover, problem specifications originate frequently in a form that connects, when formalized, rather to this level: in the form of predicate calculus. Yet, the instincts of many programmers are suppressed; they do not know that they can not only think in terms of the von Neumann machine, but also in applicative terms. And they have not experienced how much easier this can be.

---

[1] The prevailing style of programming should not be blamed upon von Neumann, although he has contributed to its form [8].

There is no doubt, however, that efficiency considerations still favour the von Neumann machine [1]. Purely applicative programming therefore depends on translation to the von Neumann level. Mechanized translators of this sort are rather inflexible instruments, they often produce relatively inefficient code. Many programmers want to make use of their intuition in order to ameliorate a solution for the von Neumann machine. Thus,

> *if applicative programming should have a chance to*
> *be practically accepted now, it needs a conceptual*
> *bridge to the von Neumann style, such that the pro-*
> *grammer has complete freedom in the choice of his*
> *programming style.*

Not to outlaw the von Neumann style, but to supplement it by applicative programming in coexistence, this should be the goal of whatever liberation one asks for.

In the following we shall show that from certain applicative constructs that have been studied recently (HENDERSON-MORRIS 1976 [10], FRIEDMAN-WISE 1976 [6]), in connection with the philosophy of abstract data types, the concept of pointers can be derived.

Detailized expressions and lazy evaluation

Starting from purely applicative constructs, i.e. lambda expressions, the first step in the direction of the von Neumann machine is d e t a i l i z a t i o n , the decomposition of (large) expressions.

We assume the reader to be familiar with the technique of detailization by introducing auxiliary functions, e.g. to rewrite

$$H(E(x), x) \quad \text{in the form}$$
$$H(f, x) \ \underline{\text{where}} \ \underline{\text{funct}} \ f \equiv E(x) \quad [14] \ .$$

We also assume that he is familiar with the use of non-local parameters, their range being indicated by block brackets [15].

---

[1] Despite attempts to build stack computers, or drastically different approaches like the ones by Magô [16] or by Berkling [4].

Detailization, done in this way can be applied in particular to expressions that involve primitive operations and objects only, i.e. to expressions that define objects in terms of some primitive operations and objects. This includes objects defined by an abstract data type.

Let $succ$ and $twice$ be two unary functions, and consider

$$succ(twice(twice(succ(twice(succ(0))))))$$

This can be completely detailized:

$$\{ f_0 \text{ \underline{where}}$$

$$\text{\underline{funct}} \; f_0 \equiv succ \; (f_1) \; ,$$
$$\text{\underline{funct}} \; f_1 \equiv twice \; (f_2) \; ,$$
$$(*) \qquad \text{\underline{funct}} \; f_2 \equiv twice \; (f_3) \; ,$$
$$\text{\underline{funct}} \; f_3 \equiv succ \; (f_4) \; ,$$
$$\text{\underline{funct}} \; f_4 \equiv twice \; (f_5) \; ,$$
$$\text{\underline{funct}} \; f_5 \equiv succ \; (0) \qquad \}$$

On the applicative level, a call of f_0 means successive insertion, which can be illustrated in the following way, using the double-lined <u>insertion arrow</u> $\Longrightarrow$.

$$succ(\cdot) \overset{f_1}{\longleftarrow} twice(\cdot) \overset{f_2}{\longleftarrow} twice(\cdot) \overset{f_3}{\longleftarrow} succ(\cdot) \overset{f_4}{\longleftarrow} twice(\cdot) \overset{f_5}{\longleftarrow} succ(0) \quad .$$

Similarly, expressions involving n-ary functions can be treated and illustrated as tree structures, a view known particularly from pure LISP.

In a related example using

$$append : \underline{string} \times \underline{char} \to \underline{string}$$

as a primitive operation and

$$empty: \qquad \to \underline{string}$$
$$0 \; : \qquad \to \underline{char}$$
$$L \; : \qquad \to \underline{char}$$

as primitive objects, we consider the expression

$$append(append(append(append(empty,L),L),0),L) \quad ,$$

or, detailized,

$$
\begin{aligned}
\{ f_1 \quad &\underline{\text{where}} \\
&\underline{\text{funct}}\ f_1 \equiv \text{append}\ (f_2,L) \\
(**) \qquad &\underline{\text{funct}}\ f_2 \equiv \text{append}\ (f_3,0) \\
&\underline{\text{funct}}\ f_3 \equiv \text{append}\ (f_4,L) \\
&\underline{\text{funct}}\ f_4 \equiv \text{append}\ (\text{empty},L)\ \}
\end{aligned}
$$

Again this is a detailization of the <u>object generation</u>, and we can say that the generated object is illustrated by

Instead of defining many functions explicitly, they can also be defined recursively, e.g. one per incarnation of a generating function.

To give an example, the function $\quad \text{convert}: N \rightarrow \underline{\text{string}}$,

$$
\begin{aligned}
\underline{\text{funct}}\ \text{convert} \equiv (\lambda a) \\
&\underline{\text{if}}\ a = 0\ \underline{\text{then}}\ \text{empty} \\
&\quad \underline{\text{else}}\ \underline{\text{if}}\ \text{even}(a)\ \underline{\text{then}}\ \text{append}(\text{convert}(a/2),0) \\
&\qquad\qquad \underline{\text{else}}\ \text{append}(\text{convert}((a-1)/2),L)\ \underline{\text{fi}}\ \underline{\text{fi}}
\end{aligned}
$$

can be rewritten, detailizing the result generation:

$$
\begin{aligned}
\underline{\text{funct}}\ \text{convert} \equiv (\lambda a) \\
&\underline{\text{if}}\ a = 0\ \underline{\text{then}}\ \text{empty} \\
&\quad \underline{\text{else}}\ \{f\ \underline{\text{where}} \\
&\qquad \underline{\text{funct}}\ f \equiv \\
&\qquad \underline{\text{if}}\ \text{even}(a)\ \underline{\text{then}}\ \text{append}(\text{convert}(a/2),0) \\
&\qquad\qquad \underline{\text{else}}\ \text{append}(\text{convert}((a-1)/2),L)\ \underline{\text{fi}}\ \}\ \underline{\text{fi}}
\end{aligned}
$$

Then, in each incarnation of convert a new (and different) function f is defined.

For example, convert(13) leads to a result with the illustration

where $f^{(i)}$ means f as defined in the i-th incarnation of convert .

Normal invocation of convert(13) will, however, not retain this detailized structure, it will execute the insertion process and lead to

$$\text{append(append(append(append(empty,L),L),0),L)} \ .$$

What we want is *to keep the detailized structure;* we do not so much want the object itself but rather the rule how to compute the object[1]. This is called <u>lazy evaluation</u> in [10] and corresponds to LANDIN's streams [13]. The result in the example above has to be the computation rule expressed by the construct (**) from above.

An indication <u>lazy</u> can be introduced to mark this situation; a notation we would like to use here is

<u>funct</u> convert $\equiv$ (λa)
     <u>if</u> a = 0 <u>then</u> empty
       <u>else</u> {f <u>where</u>
         <u>lazy</u> <u>funct</u> f $\equiv$
         <u>if</u> even (a) <u>then</u> append(convert(a/2),0)
           <u>else</u> append(convert((a-1)/2),L) <u>fi</u> } <u>fi</u> ,

the semantics of the lazy evaluation being such that the result of convert(13) is

     { $f^{(1)}$ <u>where</u>
     <u>lazy</u> <u>funct</u> $f^{(1)} \equiv$ append($f^{(2)}$,L) ,
     <u>lazy</u> <u>funct</u> $f^{(2)} \equiv$ append($f^{(3)}$,0) ,
     <u>lazy</u> <u>funct</u> $f^{(3)} \equiv$ append($f^{(4)}$,L) ,
     <u>lazy</u> <u>funct</u> $f^{(4)} \equiv$ append(empty,L) }

Infinite objects

This technique allows also [7, 10] the use of infinite objects[2], like

     { a_1 <u>where</u>
     <u>lazy</u> <u>funct</u> $a_1 \equiv$ append(a_2,L)
     <u>lazy</u> <u>funct</u> $a_2 \equiv$ append(a_3,0)
     <u>lazy</u> <u>funct</u> $a_3 \equiv$ append(a_1,0) }

---

[1] 'cons should not evaluate its arguments', [6].

[2] For a treatment of infinite objects as fixpoints of recursion equations, see [17].

more commonly written as

$$(((((((\ldots,0),0),L),0),0),L)$$

This can be illustrated by

(***)

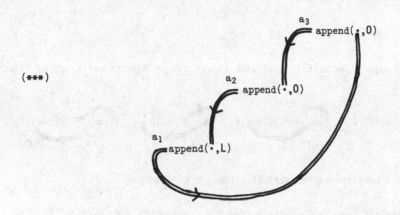

The only difference to finite objects is, that the insertion process cannot be carried out finitely and thus the insertion arrows cannot be eliminated completely; in the example above we are stuck with

$$\{ \ a_1 \ \underline{\text{where}}$$
$$\underline{\text{lazy}} \ \underline{\text{funct}} \ a_1 = \text{append}(\text{append}(\text{append}(a_1,0),0),L) \ \ \}$$

and the illustration contains one indispensible arrow

$$a_1 \quad \text{append}(\text{append}(\text{append}(\ ,0),0),L)$$

As in the case of finite objects, an object contains other (sub-)objects, therefore its illustration describes a whole set of objects. Contrary to finite objects, there is no longer a hierarchical ordering. We say therefore, one _object-diagram_ describes a _nexus_ of objects.

Let

$$\text{top} : \underline{\text{string}} \setminus \{\text{empty}\} \rightarrow \underline{\text{char}} \qquad \text{and}$$
$$\text{rest} : \underline{\text{string}} \setminus \{\text{empty}\} \rightarrow \underline{\text{string}}$$

be the inverse operations to append . Then in the example above,

$$\text{rest}(\text{rest}(\text{rest}(a_i))) = a_i$$

holds, in other words, all a_i are infinite objects.

It is not surprising that this mechanism covers other (infinite) objects like doubly-linked lists. Assume

$$\text{build} : \underline{casc} \times \underline{char} \times \underline{casc} \rightarrow \underline{casc}$$

to be a ternary function, and

$$0 : \rightarrow \underline{casc}$$

a primitive object. We want to deal with those $\underline{casc}$ - objects which can be illustrated like

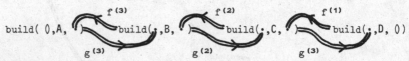

Insertion can only remove one sort of arrows, e.g. lead to

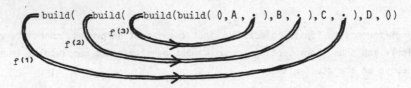

Such objects are obviously created by the following function from $\underline{string}$ to $\underline{casc}$:

$$\underline{funct} \text{ transit} \equiv (\lambda a)\ \text{trans}(a, 0)$$

where the embedding function

$$\underline{funct} \text{ trans} \equiv (\lambda a, \lambda z)$$
$$\underline{if}\ a = \text{empty}\ \underline{then}\ 0$$
$$\underline{else}\ \{f\ \underline{where}$$
$$\underline{lazy}\ \underline{funct}\ f \equiv \text{build}(g,\ \text{top}(a),\ z)$$
$$\underline{lazy}\ \underline{funct}\ g \equiv \text{trans}(\text{rest}(a),\ f)\ \}\ \underline{fi}$$

is a function from $\underline{string} \times \underline{casc}$ to $\underline{casc}$.

Note that for $i > 1$ $f^{(i)} = g^{(i-1)}$. The nexus above is obtained by transit(a), where a ≡ append(append(append(append(empty,A),B),C),D) , with $(f^{(1)}, g^{(1)})$, $(f^{(2)}, g^{(2)})$ and $(f^{(3)}, g^{(3)})$
belonging to the three incarnations of trans , respectively.

Eliminating g in the algorithm above yields

    funct trans ≡ (λa, λz)
        if a = empty then ()
                else {f where
                        lazy funct f ≡ build(trans(rest(a), f), top(a), z) } fi

In a similar way, ring lists and doubly-linked ring lists can be treated.

Pointer representation

On the procedural level, parameterless functions with lazy evaluation lead to a re-interpretation as pointers (see also [12]) in the following way:

A function declaration becomes the generation of a pointer to the object detailized in the body of the function, an invocation of such a function becomes the use of the pointer as a reference to the object in question. nil *is the (universal) pointer to the 0-tuple* () .

Thus, pointer algorithms corresponding to the functions convert or trans can be considered as being mere notational variants of the above. However, the generating operations like append or build are now interpreted as concrete operations cons forming composite objects, and pointers are allowed as components of those objects.

For example,

    funct transit ≡ (λa) trans(a, nil)
    funct trans   ≡ (λa, λz)
        if a = empty then nil
              else {f where
                    pt f ≡ newpt cons(g, top(a), z)
                    pt g ≡ newpt trans(rest(a), f) } fi

Moreover, in pointer interpretation, the arrows (now single-lined) point in a direction opposite to that of insertion arrows. This is the result of another step towards the von Neumann machine: the transition from LANDIN's applicative world [13] to the one of systems programmers: all primitive objects are kept in containers, ('storage cells'), all composite objects are implemented by compositions of containers holding their components. Instead of inserting the content of containers, one points to these containers, and this means obviously in the opposite direction as before. The reader is invited to read the diagrams above in this way.

This has an analogy to the introduction of gotos . Recursive invocations, which are the last action in a function before return , do not need the full control stack organization of a stack machine [9, 11] ; these simple calls can be made parameterless with the help of program variables. The applicative meaning is still insertion of the respective function ('subroutine'); once the program is, however, put into containers the call is replaced by a jump to the location where the 'subroutine' is stored. This also means a reversal of directions.

Interestingly enough, pointers and jumps, which both stem from parameterless functions in particular situations, are finally both represented by addresses in the von Neumann machine. In this way, a bridge connects Quines world of referential transparency with a world that reflects the economic advantages of re-usable storage.

Pointers are normally used on the iterative level. Unfortunately, in our examples convert and trans , the recursive calls are not simple calls; recursion is, although linear, not repetitive. Transition to common iteration requires therefore the techniques of re-bracketing (COOPER [5]). It then leads to the introduction of variables the values of which are pointers, i.e. pointer variables.

In treating convert , we observe that append is a special case of concatenation:
append(T,x) = conc(T, append(empty,x)) .
Concatenation, however, is associative. Thus we obtain [2, 3] , after introducing a variable a for numbers and a variable s for strings, the iterative form

```
funct convert ≡ (λA)
   { (var a, var s) := (A, empty) ;
      while a ≠ 0 do (a,s) := if even(a) then (a/2, stalk(0,s))
                                          else ((a-1)/2, stalk(L,s)) fi
                od ; s                                              }
```

where stalk(x,S) stands for conc(append(empty,x),S) .

Detailization has now to deal with stalk , replacing stalk(x,s) by
f where lazy funct f ≡ stalk(x,s) .

We obtain:

```
funct convert ≡ (λA)
  { (var a, var s) := (A,empty) ;
    while a ≠ 0 do (a,s) := if even(a) then (a/2, f where
                                              lazy funct ≡ stalk(0,s))
                                    else ((a-1)/2, f where
                                              lazy funct ≡ stalk(L,s)) fi
         od ; s                                                          }
```

Thus, convert(13) leads step by step to the following contents of the variable s:

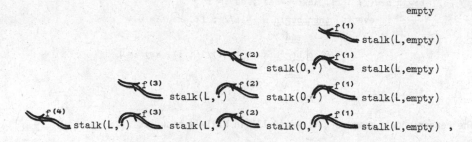

the final content $f^{(4)}$ being the result. Transition to a data structure with pointers is now obvious: Let string be represented by pointers either to the 0-tuple or to a pair (pt string next, char key) , such that the equality cons(S,x) = stalk(x,S↑) holds [1]. Then the particle

$$s := \{ f \text{ where lazy funct } f \equiv \text{stalk}(x,s) \}$$

(cf. the version above) is rewritten as

$$ss := \{ f \text{ where pt } f \equiv \text{newpt cons}(ss,x) \}$$

using a pointer variable ss [or in a more PASCAL-oriented notation and sequentialized form

```
        begin new(f) ; f↑. next := ss ; f↑. key := x ; ss := f end  ]
```

where pt f [or new(f) , resp.,] is interpreted as the 'generation' of a pointer. ss is to be initialized by nil : var pt ss := nil .

---

[1] pt string indicating pointers to string , S↑ denoting the object to which the pointer S points.

Thus we obtain

```
funct convert ≡ (λA)
   { (var a, var pt ss) := (A, nil) ;
     while a ≠ 0 do
     if even(a) then (a,ss) := (a/2, f where pt f ≡ newpt cons(ss,0))
                else (a,ss) := ((a-1)/2, f where pt f ≡ newpt cons(ss,L)) fi
                od ; ss                                                      }
```

[The core of this reads, completely sequentialized, in PASCAL

```
while a ≠ 0 do
     begin new(f) ; f↑. next := ss ; ss := f ;
           if even(a) then begin a := a/2 ; f↑. key := 0
                           end
                      else begin a := (a-1)/2 ; f↑. key := L
                           end ;
     end
```

The reader should compare this to (4.13) in WIRTH's book [18].]

Obviously, the re-bracketing operation, which has led to the replacement of append by stalk , has 'reverted' the data structure: the leading binary digit is now the direct accessible one. This may sometimes be desirable. Otherwise, we have to represent string (again by pointers either to the 0-tuple or to a pair (pt string, char)) such that the equality

$$cons(S,x) \; = \; append(S↑,x)$$

holds.

Selective updating

Thus, if we want to use again the repetitive version of convert , then stalk has to be expressed in terms of append . From the definition

```
funct stalk ≡ (λx, λS)
         if S = empty then append(empty,x)
                      else append(stalk(x, rest(S)), top(S)) fi
```

one obtains in pointer representation

> **funct** stalk $\equiv$ (λx, λS)
>> **if** S = empty **then** f **where** **pt** f $\equiv$ **newpt** cons(**nil**, x)
>>> **else** { f **where**
>>>> **pt** f $\equiv$ **newpt** cons(stalk(x, rest(S)), top(S)) } **fi**

The result of a call stalk(x, S) can be illustrated as

The algorithm for stalk is, however, again non-repetitive; use of this algorithm within the iteration part of convert would mean a perpetual up and down along the nexus. This suggests to preserve in each step the most recent pointer $f^{(n)}$ and to replace in the object to which it points the next-component **nil** by the new pointer $f^{(n+1)}$ (which points to cons(**nil**,x)). But this means, that an element of a composite object is to be altered without touching the other elements.

It is clear that this selective updating is the price we pay for not being forced to touch the pointer connection.

Selective updating is a simple operation only if we work with arrays and records composed from variables, i.e. with organized store, and our example shows why the introduction of pointers is fruitful only if we transgress the strictly applicative style and introduce the typical 'systems programming' concept of organized store.

With the help of a pointer variable tt , s := stalk(x,s) is thus established by

> { **pt** f $\equiv$ **newpt** cons(**nil**,x) ; next **of** tt := f ; tt := f }

except for the very first step, which is simply

> { **pt** f $\equiv$ **newpt** cons(**nil**,x) ; ss := f ; tt := f }   ;

ss delivers the result.

Thus finally

```
funct convert ≡ (λA)
    { (var a, var pt ss, var pt tt) := (A,nil,nil) ;
      while a ≠ 0 do
          { pt f ≡ newpt cons(nil, if even(a) then 0 else L fi) ;
            a := if even(a) then a/2 else (a-1)/2 fi ;
            if tt = nil then ss := f
                        else next of tt := f fi ;
            tt := f
                od ; ss                                              }
```

In a similar way, the algorithm transit can be treated, where casc is represented by a pointer either to the 0-tuple or to a triple

  (pt casc left, char item, pt casc right) .

Using selective updating the algorithm can be simplified to

```
funct trans ≡ (λa, λz)
        if a = empty then nil
                     else pt f ≡ newpt cons(nil, top(a),z) ;
                          left of f := trans(rest(a), f) ;
                          f                                     fi
```

This is still not repetitive; however, recursion can be removed by function inversion, reverting the order of the assignments [2, 3] .

This gives

```
funct transit ≡ (λA)
    { (var a, var pt zz, var pt ss) := (A,nil,nil) ;
      while a ≠ empty do
              { pt f ≡ newpt cons(nil, top(a), zz) ;
                if ss = nil then ss := f
                            else left of zz := f    fi ;
                zz := f
                a := rest(a)                               }
                    od ; ss                                        }
```

There are other ways of eliminating recursion, e.g. using re-bracketing of the operation
cons interpreted as a left singly-linked or a right singly-linked list constructor,
which give other iterative solutions; the ones we tried (MÜLLER) gave slightly more
complicated solutions.

Acknowledgement

I have had a very encouraging discussion with C.A.R. Hoare and stimulating remarks
from A. Perlis, R. London, and D. Luckham. Stephen Zilles gave me a simplification
of the algorithm trans ; I also enjoyed discussions with D. Wise and D. Friedman.
My particular thanks go to B. Möller for critical remarks, and to others of my Munich
colleagues, notably B. Krieg-Brückner who approached the subject in his thesis.

F. L. Bauer

Institut für Informatik
der Technischen Universität München
Postfach 2o 24 2o

D-8ooo München 2
Germany

Literature

1. Backus, J.: Can programming be liberated from the von Neumann style? A functional style and its algebra of programs. Comm. ACM 21, 613-641 (1978)

2. Bauer, F.L.: Vorlesungsskriptum Algorithmische Sprachen, Kap.4. Institut für Informatik der Technischen Universität München, Februar 1978

3. Bauer, F.L., Partsch, H., Pepper, P., Wössner, H.: Techniques for program development. In: Software Engineering Techniques. Infotech State of the Art Report 34. Maidenhead: Infotech International 1977, p. 25-3o

4. Berkling, K.J.: Reduction languages for reduction machines. Gesellschaft für Mathematik und Datenverarbeitung mbH Bonn, Interner Bericht ISF-76-8, Sept. 1976

5. Cooper, D.C.: The equivalence of certain computations. Computer Journal 9, 45 - 52 (1966)

6. Friedman, D.P., Wise, D.S.: CONS should not evaluate its arguments. In: Michaelson, S., Milner, R. (eds.): Automata, Languages and Programming. Edinburgh: University Press 1976, p. 257-284

7. Friedman, D.P., Wise, D.S.: Unbounded computational structures. Softw. Pract. Exper. 8, 4o7-416

8. Goldstine, H.H., Neumann, J. von: Planning and coding problems for an electronic computing instrument, Part II, Volume 1. In: Neumann, J. von: Collected Works, Volume V. Oxford-London-New York-Paris: Pergamon Press 1963, p. 8o-152

9. Haskell, R.: Efficient implementation of a class of recursively defined functions. Computer Journal 18, 23-29 (1975)

1o. Henderson, P., Morris, J.H. jr.: A lazy evaluator. Conference Record of the Third ACM Symposium on Principles of Programming Languages, Atlanta, Jan. 1976, p. 95-1o3

11. Knuth, D.: Structured programming with go to statements. Computing Surveys 6, 261-3o1 (1974)

12. Krieg-Brückner, B.: Concrete and abstract specification, modularization and program development by transformation. Dissertation, Institut für Informatik der Technischen Universität München. TUM-INFO-7805, Jan. 1978

13. Landin, P.J.: A correspondence between ALGOL 60 and Church's lambda notation. Part I: Comm. ACM 8, 89-158, Part II: Comm. ACM 8, 158-165 (1965)

14. Landin, P.J.: The next 7oo programming languages. Comm. ACM 9, 157-166 (1966)

15. Laut, A.: Unterdrückung konstanter Parameter. Institut für Informatik der Technischen Universität München, Interner Bericht, April 1978

16. Magô, G.A.: A network of microprocessors to execute reduction languages. International Journal of Computer and Information Science (to appear)

17. Scott, D.: Data Types as Lattices. SIAM Journal on Computing 5, 522-587 (1976)

18. Wirth, N.: Algorithms + Data Structures = Programs. Englewood Cliffs (N.Y.): Prentice-Hall 1976

Examples for Change of Types and Object Structures [*]

H. Partsch, M. Broy

Institut für Informatik
der Technischen Universität
Postfach 20 24 20
D - 8000 München 2

Abstract

The abstract, algebraic definition of data types by describing their properties
forms a solid formal basis for the specification of computation structures independent of their particular representations. Thus programs can be designed and developed working with objects of an abstractly defined computation structure. The
choice of particular representations (implementations), the releasing of this representation to the "outer world" and the consequences on further program development are demonstrated with examples of joint refinement.

---

[*] This research was carried out within the Sonderforschungsbereich 49, Programmiertechnik, Munich.

Introduction

In the project CIP (cf. [Bauer et al. 77a], [Bauer et al. 77b]) particular emphasis
has been given to appropriate means for defining and handling, i.e. developing, object structures. Usually these are given by means of certain complexes which are made
up of certain data sets and typical operations with characteristic properties (comparable to algebraic laws which hold for the operations). Such modules are called
computation structures ([Bauer 78]) of certain types (or classes [Dahl et al. 68],
clusters [Liskov, Zilles 74], forms [Wulf 74], abstract data types [Guttag 75],
theories [Burstall, Goguen 77]). For the terminology on this subject, a brief summary
of the theoretical foundations and notational conventions we refer to the appendix.

The development of types is usually characterized by a hierarchy of formulations with
decreasing abstraction, with an abstract type definition on the top, and a collection
of machine primitives - in the form of a concrete computation structure - at the
bottom. Intermediate stages in this hierarchy again may be characterized by other
type definitions or concrete computation structures.

Concerning object structures one has an analogous situation: beginning with some mode
declaration defining a certain "abstract" object structure, the program development
proceeds by introducing other mode declarations and finally reaches a level of abstraction where mode declarations describe facilities directly executable on a machine.

Type definitions and mode declarations are closely connected since mode definitions
- as employed in our language CIP-L - correspond to special forms of type definitions.

According to the hierarchy of different formulations we consider the various kinds of
transformations involved in the process of joint refinement, e.g. the change of types,
the transition from types to concrete structures, the transformations of concrete
structures and last not least the transformations of object structures defined by mode
declarations. Our intention is to give an impression of what we are aiming at by means
of illustrative examples rather than to present a complete theory and a formal transformational calculus. However, it should be noted, that from a theoretical point of
view all these transformations may be subsumed under the concept of structural morphisms.

Usually program development does not treat algorithms and data structures in
separate ways but tries to respect their mutual influences on each other. To illustrate this process of joint refinement we give a few examples going through a number of levels of abstraction.

1. Change of Types

The catchword "change of types" means the transition from a given type $\underline{A}$ to a somewhat related type $\underline{B}$. The basic relations involved in this process are essentially of one of the following forms*):

(1) a) $\underline{A} \xleftarrow{\beta} \underline{B}$

   ($\underline{A}$ has more functions or laws than $\underline{B}$, "β-stronger types" [Krieg-Brückner 78])

   b) $\underline{A} \xrightarrow{\beta} \underline{B}$

   ($\underline{B}$ has more functions or laws than $\underline{A}$, "enrichment" [Burstall/Goguen 77])

(2) $\underline{A} \longleftrightarrow \underline{B}$

   $\underline{A}$ and $\underline{B}$ are "weakly equivalent", i.e. they contain different functions, but define the "same" sets of TOI-objects. In other words: There are signatures $\Sigma_{\underline{A}}'$ for $\underline{A}$ and $\Sigma_{\underline{B}}'$ for $\underline{B}$, consisting only of subsets of functions of $\Sigma_{\underline{A}}$ or $\Sigma_{\underline{B}}$ resp., but are sufficient to represent all TOI-objects, and $\Sigma_{\underline{A}}'$ and $\Sigma_{\underline{B}}'$ are strongly equivalent, i.e. they are of the same type (perhaps after trivial renaming).

The relations in (1) are treated in detail in the literature; examples are given in the appendix by the notion of a type membership, where e. g. $\underline{\text{STACK}} \xleftarrow{\beta} \underline{\text{DEQUE}}$ holds. From this example it is already obvious that the addition of functions and laws to those of a given type generally leads to a new type which defines a new set of TOI-objects.

But it is also possible n o t to change the set of TOI-objects by adding a new function (and its laws), namely if that function can be defined in terms of the given primitives.

We demonstrate this using the type $\underline{\text{STACK}}$ (see Appendix A2.2) and by adding a function length, which calculates the length of a $\underline{\text{stack}}$, and a function stalk, which adds a new element to the bottom of a stack; thus $\underline{\text{STACK}}$ becomes a different type $\underline{\text{RLSTACK}}$:

```
funct length ≡ (stack s) nat:
     if isempty(s) then  O
                   else  1 + length(rest(s)) fi

funct stalk ≡ (stack s, m x) stack:
     if isempty(s) then append(empty, x)
                   else append(stalk(rest(s),x),top(s)) fi
```

From these recursive formulations the following laws can be easily derived:

   law L1: length(empty) = O

   law L2: length(append(s,x)) = 1 + length(s)

---

*) More complicated relations between types appear, if in addition we consider the usual operations on relations, e.g. transitive closure.

```
law S1: stalk(empty,x) = append(empty,x)
law S2: stalk(append(s,y),x) = append(stalk(s,x),y)
```

The incorporation of length , stalk and the laws above into the definition of
STACK thus leads to a new type RLSTACK , the laws of which are again sufficiently
complete. Furthermore STACK and RLSTACK obviously define the same set of TOI-
objects.

But there are still other possibilities to turn over from a given type A to another
one B , which is weakly equivalent to A , as can be seen from the following example.
Consider the type definition for equivalence relations on a finite set
m, the elements of which can be tested for equality by an operator eq :

```
type EREL ≡ (mode m) erelat, init, equiv, incorp:
     mode erelat,
     funct erelat init,
     funct (erelat, m, m) bool equiv,
     funct (erelat, m, m) erelat incorp,
     law E1: equiv(init, a, b) = eq(a, b),      *)
     law E2: equiv(incorp(x, a, b), c, d) =
               equiv(x, c, d) ∨ (equiv(x, a, c) ∧ equiv(x, b, d))
                          ∨ (equiv(x, a, d) ∧ equiv(x, b, c)) endoftype
```

As intended, only equivalence relations are objects of mode erelat, since we can
prove by induction the validity of

```
law R: equiv(x,a,a) = true
law S: equiv(x,a,b) = equiv(x,b,a)
law T: equiv(x,a,b) ∧ equiv(x,b,c) ⇒ equiv(x,a,c)  .
```

Additionally we can prove that all possible equivalence relations on m can be
generated by a finite number of applications of incorp to the equivalence relation
init.

Now, as we know from mathematics, equivalence relations define equivalence classes
and each class may be represented by an object of mode m, which is an element of
the class. This knowledge may be used to introduce a function repr , which yields
for a given relation and some object x of mode m the representative for x and
is defined as follows:

---

*) read: "a and b are equivalent with respect to init if and only if eq(a,b)
   holds."

```
funct (erelat, m)m repr,


law R1:repr(init,a) = a ,
law R2:repr(incorp(x,a,b),c) =
         if eq(repr(x,a),repr(x,c)) ∨ eq(repr(x,b),repr(x,c)) then repr(x,a)  *)
                                                             else repr(x,c) fi
```
For this function the important correspondence
```
law ER: equiv(x,a,b) =  eq(repr(x,a),repr(x,b))
```
can be proved and used to define a new type REREL which also describes all equivalence relations on a finite set m:
```
type REREL ≡ (mode m) erelat, init, repr, incorp:
    mode erelat,
    funct erelat init,
    funct (erelat,m)m repr,
    funct (erelat,m,m) erelat incorp,
    law R1: repr(init,a) = a ,
    law R2: repr(incorp(x,a,b),c) =
             if eq(repr(x,a),repr(x,c)) ∨ eq(repr(x,b),repr(x,c)) then repr(x,a)
                                                                 else repr(x,c) fi
                                                                   endoftype
```

Hence EREL and REREL define "essentially" the same object set, i.e. all equivalence relations on a finite set m , where "essentially" means that there are minor differences, e. g. that the TOI of a structure of type REREL has more objects. But the fact that some of them may be identified by means of an additional congruence relation justifies the terminology.

Analogous to the relation between EREL and REREL there are similar connections between the formulations of FLEXARRAY and GREX (see appendix). The proof, however, that there the sets of TOI-objects are the same is much more complicated than in the example above.

---

*) It is also possible to use repr(x,b) but n o t repr(x,a) ⫿ repr(x,b).

2. The Transition from (Abstract) Types to (Concrete) Structures

An abstract type is defined independently of any representation and besides the ex-
clusively intellectual task of specifying such a type, the crucial point is the
transition from a given type to some concrete structure, i. e. to a particular representation of that type in terms of other, more primitive, computation structures.

There are several possible ways to achieve this transition, all of them in the very
end depending on the intuition of the programmer. The differences between these ways
may be characterized by the amount of work that can be done in a formal manner.
A first way to do the job is perhaps one where no formal derivation is involved.

If one already has a representation in mind - e.g. if the type was used for the abstract specification of some given structure, then only the validity of the laws has
to be verified. *) This may conveniently be done by using safe transformation rules
in addition to some induction principles (this is actually the method used by [Guttag
et al. 76 b], though they don't mention the term "transformation").

A more complex task, however, is a formal derivation of a concrete structure from
some given type definition.

In principle the whole word algebra W_Σ may be used to represent TOI-objects. Then
functions with a range different from TOI may be realized by reduction algorithms
which have to be deduced from the given laws. These algorithms are to reduce terms
representing non-TOI-objects to the respective primitive objects; terms representing
TOI-objects remain unchanged.

Obviously this often leads to an inadequate, inefficient implementation, since e.g.
in stack (see appendix 2.2) the term

$$rest(rest(append(append(empty, x), y)))$$

simply represents the empty stack.

Hence additional algorithms should be derived from the laws (in our example e.g.
law R) to reduce also terms representing TOI-objects. Doing so - in some sense -
minimal terms for the representation of the different TOI-objects may be marked
out ("canonical term algebras" cf. [Goguen et al. 77]). In some cases this may
simply be done by not allowing the occurrence of certain function symbols in a term
(e.g. rest in our example stack , see also below).

---

*) To use the word "only" is some kind of understatement because the verification
   of a representation may cause a lot of difficulties especially if it has to be
   proved that a representation is an initial or a terminal algebra of that type.

This technique is supported by a transition from the laws (describing the interaction of functions) to "isolated definitions". To do this, the set of primitive functions is decreased to a subset of constructor functions sufficient to represent all TOI-objects (this actually again means a restriction to a subset of the word algebra w_Σ). These constructor functions now form another type and the remaining functions may be specified in terms of them, e.g. in some descriptive way, by using predicates. These can be derived from the algebraic laws. In general, proceeding in this way requires an introduction of a congruence relation "=" for objects of TOI , i.e. to choose particular congruence classes in w_Σ .

Sometimes it is possible to choose a minimal (but often not uniquely determined) set of constructor functions, such that the corresponding subset of w_Σ represents exactly the set of TOI objects. In this set the corresponding congruence relation "=" coincides with the syntactical identity for the corresponding terms in the subset of w_Σ .

We will illustrate this for the type STACK (cf. Appendix A2.2). First of all we define a reduced type RSTACK (with only constructor functions and a congruence relation):

        type RSTACK ≡ (mode m) stack, empty, append, ≐ :
            mode stack,
            funct stack empty,
            funct (stack,m) stack append,
            funct (stack,stack) bool ≐,

            law EE: (empty ≐ empty) = true,
            law EA: (empty ≐ append(s,x)) = false,
            law AE: (append(s,x) ≐ empty) = false,
            law AA: (append(s,x) ≐ append(t,y)) = ((s ≐ t) ∧ (x = y))
                                                              end of type

Here the identity of terms in the word algebra w_Σ of RSTACK and ≐ coincide. Therefore RSTACK is monomorphic, i.e. all computation structures of type RSTACK are isomorphic. Now descriptive formulations for the non-constructor functions may be derived from the laws. From

        law E: isempty(empty) = true
        law NE: isempty(append(s,x)) = false

we derive by comparison to the laws EE and EA

        funct isempty ≡ (stack s) bool: empty ≐ s

To derive a specification for the function rest we have at our disposal

> law R: rest(append(s,x)) = s,
> law A: ¬ isempty(s) ⇒ append(rest(s),top(s)) = s,

By the application of law A we obtain a possibly ambiguous function:

> funct rest ≡ (stack s: ¬ isempty(s)) stack:
>   some stack t: ∃ m y: append(t,y) ≐ s

Now law R can be proved:

$$
\begin{array}{ll}
\text{(unfold)} & \text{rest(append(s,x))} \qquad\qquad\qquad\qquad\qquad\qquad\qquad \doteq \\
\text{(law AA)} & (\text{some stack } t: \exists \underline{m}\ y: \text{append}(t,y) \doteq \text{append}(s,x)) \doteq \\
& (\text{some stack } t: \exists \underline{m}\ y: (t \doteq s) \wedge (y=x)\ ) \qquad\qquad \doteq \qquad s
\end{array}
$$

Note, that the validity of law R guarantees the determinacy of the function rest. Therefore rest should more precisely be specified by

> funct rest ≡ (stack s: ¬ isempty(s)) stack:
>   that stack t: ∃ m y: append(t,y) ≐ s   .

In a similar way the following specification for top may be derived:

> funct top ≡ (stack s: ¬ isempty(s)) stack:
>   that m y: ∃ stack t: append(t,y) ≐ s

The problem of finding some representation for type STACK is reduced to the simpler task [*]) of finding some representation for type RSTACK and operational formulations for rest and top can be derived from the descriptive ones (for such techniques see [Bauer 78]).

When using techniques like those mentioned above appropriate implementations for types may be derived, which correspond to composed modes formed by direct sum or product. [**])

How to derive more sophisticated implementations (e.g. using pointers etc.) in a systematic way is not clear at all at the very moment. This has certainly to be a field of future research.

---

[*]) It is indeed a "simpler" task, since each function may now be developed independently of the other ones; the occurrence of an existential quantifier in such a restricted way like in top or rest does no harm at all.

[**]) "direct implementation" [Guttag et al. 76a], "derivation of representations of free algebras in terms of standard data structures"[Krieg-Brückner 78]

3. Transformations of Concrete Computation Structures

One of the essential steps in program construction is the transition from one concrete computation structure to another one. Of course there are a lot of transformations each of which in some way connects the theoretical concepts of abstract data types to the properties of concrete computers. From this great variety of transformations we are going to consider two sample representatives which are very frequently used.

Firstly, any recursive data structure can be converted into a more machine-oriented one by introducing references. For example

$$\underline{mode}\ \underline{ls}\quad\equiv\ \underline{empty}\ |\ (\underline{m}\ item,\ \underline{ls}\ trunk)\ ,$$
$$\underline{mode}\ \underline{empty}\ \equiv\ \underline{atomic}\ \{()\}$$

changes to

$$\underline{mode}\ \underline{ls}\quad\equiv\ \underline{ref}\ \underline{lsref}\ ,$$
$$\underline{mode}\ \underline{lsref}\ \equiv\ \underline{empty}\ |\ (\underline{m}\ item,\ \underline{ls}\ trunk)$$

and by using the universal reference $\underline{nil}$ which may be considered to be of mode $\underline{ref}\ \underline{empty}$, i.e. a reference to the object (), we finally obtain

$$\underline{mode}\ \underline{ls}\ \equiv\ \underline{ref}\ \underline{lsr}\ ,$$
$$\underline{mode}\ \underline{lsr}\ \equiv\ (\underline{m}\ item,\ \underline{ls}\ trunk)$$

This transformation establishes the correspondence (for $\underline{ls}$ a)

$$item\ \underline{of}\ a\ \stackrel{\wedge}{=}\ item\ \underline{of}\ \underline{deref}\ a$$
$$trunk\ \underline{of}\ a\ \stackrel{\wedge}{=}\ trunk\ \underline{of}\ \underline{deref}\ a$$
$$\underline{empty}\ ::\ a\ \stackrel{\wedge}{=}\ a\ =\ \underline{nil}$$

Proceeding in this way the structure CSTACK (see appendix) can be transformed into the following structure

```
structure CRSTACK ≡ (mode m) some STACK(m):
       ⌈mode stack ≡ ref rstack,
        mode rstack ≡(stack trunk, m item),
        funct empty ≡ stack : nil,
        funct isempty ≡ (stack s) bool: s = nil,
        funct top ≡ (stack s: ¬ isempty(s)) m: item of deref s,
        funct rest ≡ (stack s: ¬ isempty(s)) stack: trunk of deref s,
        funct append ≡ (stack s, m x) stack: newref rstack:(s,x)⌋
```

Secondly, the storage of a computer can be regarded as a linearly ordered aggregate of single cells, each of which can be "overwritten" individually. Thus a storage is modelled not by a variable for an array but rather by an array of variables, say index array var m. Thus for the structure AGREX (see appendix, A.2.3), we may establish the correspondencies

$$
\begin{array}{ll}
\underline{\text{var}} \; \underline{\text{grex}} \; a & \stackrel{\wedge}{=} \; \underline{\text{index}} \; \underline{\text{array}} \; \underline{\text{var}} \; \underline{\text{m1}} \; a, \; \underline{\text{mode}} \; \underline{\text{m1}} \equiv \underline{\text{m}}|\text{atomic} \; \{\text{virgin}\} \\
a := \text{vac} & \stackrel{\wedge}{=} \; \text{initiate (a), i.e. for all } i \in \underline{\text{index}}: \; a[i] := \text{virgin} \\
a := \text{put}(\underline{\text{val}} \; a, i, x) & \stackrel{\wedge}{=} \; a[i] := x \\
\text{get}(\underline{\text{val}} \; a, i) & \stackrel{\wedge}{=} \; \underline{\text{val}} \; (a[i])
\end{array}
$$

This transformation underlines the subtle difference between single *array variables* [Dijkstra 76, p. 95] and an ALGOL 60-like set of *subscripted variables*.

In our example, the index set index can be quite arbitrary, usually int is chosen for index. This is the case with the kind of flexible array Dijkstra favors [Dijkstra 76]; it can be treated with this technique easily. (For a detailed treatment of Dijkstra's array in terms of types and structures, see appendix.)

4. Transformations of Object Structures (Defined by Mode Declarations)

There are certain types, e.g. those with operations "tupling" and "selecting", which are frequently used and thus are incorporated into the language CIP-L in the standardized form of mode declarations. From this point of view mode declarations are nothing else but a scheme for the construction of types. Therefore it seems to be quite natural to discuss not only the change of types and computation structures but also that of object structures introduced by mode declarations. Logically these changes can be performed formally with the help of the corresponding computation structures. They essentially consist of the following transformation steps:

Given a certain object structure o

(0) encapsulate o in a concrete computation structure co

(1) proceed to the abstract type definition AO

(2) find another representation co' for AO such that co' defines some object structure o' ≠ o

(3) make o' visible to the "outer world" by "releasing" co'.

Steps (1) and (3) may be done completely formally: but the development is rather cumbersome and the result of it not at all surprising, so we refuse to present it here.

Of course, step (2) usually cannot be done automatically, but needs the intuition of the programmer.

We take as an example the bounded left-sequence (see also appendix) defined by

```
mode bls ≡ (ls a: length(a) ≤ N)
where
mode ls ≡ empty | (m item, ls trunk) and mode empty ≡ atomic { () }
```

In steps (0) and (1) eventually one gets

```
type BLS ≡ (mode m, nat n) bls, empty, isempty, top, rest, append, full:
            mode bls,
            funct bls empty,
            funct (bls) bool isempty,
            funct (bls b: ¬ isempty(b)) m top,
            funct (bls b: ¬ isempty(b)) bls rest,
            funct (bls b, m x: ¬ full(b,n)) bls,
            funct (bls,nat) bool full,
            law R: ¬ full(s,n)  ⇒  rest(append(s,x)) = s,
            law T: ¬ full(s,n)  ⇒  top(append(s,x)) = x,
            law A: ¬ isempty(s) ⇒  append(rest(s),top(s)) = s,
            law E: isempty(empty) = true,
            law NE: ¬ full(s,m)  ⇒  isempty(append(s,x)) = false,
            law FE: full(empty,m) = (m=O)
            law FA: ¬ full(s,m)  ⇒  full(append(s,x),m) = full(s,m-1)
                                                            endoftype
```

Note that there are certain simililarities between the types BLS and STACK
(see appendix); nevertheless a definition of BLS like

```
type BLS ≡ (mode m, nat n)  bls, empty, isempty, top, rest, append, full:
            (bls, empty, isempty, top, rest, append) isoftype STACK(m),
            funct (bls,nat) bool  full,
            law FE: full(empty,n) = (n = O)
            law FA: ¬full(s,n) ⇒ full (append(s,x),n) = full(s,n-1)
                                                            endoftype
```

is n o t correct, since it does not reflect neither the correct specification of
append nor the appropriate formulations of the laws R, T and NE .

As already pointed out, step (2) is the crucial one, where the programmer takes the essential decisions. In our example, we want to implement BLS in terms of the abstract type GREX (see appendix) which is based on the mode

$$\underline{\text{mode}} \ \underline{\text{index}} \equiv (\underline{\text{nat}} \ I : 1 \leq i \wedge i \leq n) \ \text{with some natural number} \ n.$$

Thus we get

```
structure GBLS ≡ (mode m,nat n) some BLS (m,n):
    ⌈mode bls      ≡ (index i, grex a),
    funct empty    ≡ bls:(0, vac),
    funct isempty ≡ (bls b) bool: i of b = 0,
    funct top      ≡ (bls b: ¬ isempty(b))m: get(a of b, i of b),
    funct rest     ≡ (bls b: ¬ isempty(b))bls: (i of b-1, a of b),
    funct append  ≡ (bls b, m x: ¬ full(b,n)) bls:
                       (i of b+1, put(a of b, i of b+1, x))
    funct full     ≡ (bls b, nat max) bool: i of b = max ⌋
```

Finally, we can "make transparent" in step (3) both BLS and GREX. Thus, we get the correspondences

$$\underline{\text{mode}} \ \underline{\text{bls}} \equiv (\underline{\text{ls}} \ a : \text{length}(a) \leq n) \stackrel{\Delta}{=} \underline{\text{mode}} \ \underline{\text{bls}} \equiv (\underline{\text{index}} \ i, \underline{\text{index}} \ \underline{\text{array}} \ \underline{m} \ a)$$
$$\underline{\text{mode}} \ \underline{\text{index}} \equiv (\underline{\text{nat}} \ i : i \leq n)$$

bls ()	$\stackrel{\Delta}{=}$ bls(0,vac)
empty :: b	$\stackrel{\Delta}{=}$ i of b = 0
item of b	$\stackrel{\Delta}{=}$ (a of b) [i of b]
trunk of b	$\stackrel{\Delta}{=}$ (i of b-1, a of b)
(x, b)	$\stackrel{\Delta}{=}$ (i of b+1, put(a of b, i of b+1, x))

where we kept the operations vac and put for the sake of simplicity.

5. Joint Refinement

Usually program development proceeds by alternately refining both algorithms and data structures. So in the sequel we will present a few examples of program construction by joint refinement with a special emphasis on the mutual influences between program transformation and changes of object structures. All the examples deal with relatively simple problems, the solutions of which are already known from the literature, in order to concentrate on the way how a solution is developed. However, it should be noted that we are convinced that the methods we suggest apply to more complex problems as well.

5.1. Trees, Tree-Walk and Threaded Trees

The first problem we are considering is to perform a tree-walk, inspecting all nodes of a binary tree in some order, e.g. forming a queue containing the values of nodes in preorder. [*]

First of all we define the type TREE:

```
type TREE ≡ (mode m) tree, emptytree, isempty, construct, left, right, item:
      mode tree,
      funct tree emptytree,
      funct (tree) bool isempty,
      funct (tree, m, tree) tree construct,
      funct (tree t: ¬ isempty (t)) tree left,
      funct (tree t: ¬ isempty (t)) tree right,
      funct (tree t: ¬ isempty (t))  m  item,


      law L:  left (construct (l,i,r)) = l,
      law R:  right (construct (l,i,r)) = r,
      law I:  item (construct (l,i,r)) = i,
      law C:  ¬ isempty(t) ⇒ construct(left(t), item(t), right(t)) = t
      law E1: isempty (construct (l,i,r)) = false,
      law E2: isempty (emptytree)        = true
                                                    endoftype
```

For each structure[**] of type TREE the algorithm then becomes

---

[*] Using postorder or endorder (for the terms see [Knuth 69]) would proceed in an analogous way.

[**] Obviously a representation of type TREE can be obtained by using recursive mode definitions.

```
funct tw ≡ (tree t) queue: treewalk (t, empty) ,
funct treewalk ≡ (tree t, queue q) queue:
        if isempty (t) then q
                        else treewalk (right(t),
                            treewalk (left(t),append (q,item(t)))) fi
```

Note:

In a language allowing variables and explicit sequentialization, this purely functional formulation might read:

```
proc treewalk ≡ (tree t, var queue q):
    if ¬ isempty (t) then q := append (q,item(t));
                        treewalk (left(t),q);
                        treewalk (right(t),q) fi            (end of note)
```

In the function treewalk all subtrees of a given tree t occur during the recursive computation as arguments in an order which is implied by preorder. Thus, a function next can be defined, delivering for a given tree t and for an arbitrary subtree s of t the successor of s (or the empty tree if there is no successor) with respect to preorder. Doing so, the treewalk-algorithm might be simplified to

```
funct tw ≡ (tree t) queue: treewalk (t,t,empty),
funct treewalk ≡ (tree t, tree s, queue q) queue:
        if isempty (s) then q
                        else treewalk (t, next (t,s),  append (q,item(s))) fi
```

At a first glance this seems to be a good idea but with a closer inspection we recognize that an algorithm for next is at least as complicated as one for treewalk itself.

Another idea might be the following:

Under the assumption that each subtree s of a given tree t is characterized by t and a sequence (i.e. a stack) of selections r (right) and l (left) resp. describing a path from the root of t to the root of s , such a formulation of next might - on the basis of the previously defined type TREE - read [*]:

---

[*] Using this version of next involves a slight modification in the function treewalk : the second parameter s now has to be of mode stack .

```
funct next ≡ (tree t, stack s) stack:

    if isempty(s) then if isempty(t) then empty
                          elsf isempty(left(t)) ∧ isempty(right(t)) then empty
                          elsf isempty(left(t)) then append(empty,r)
                                              else append(empty,l) fi
                 else stack s1 ≡ if top(s) = l then next(left(t),rest(s))
                                 [] top(s) = r then next(right(t),rest(s)) fi
                      within
                      if isempty (s1) then if top(s) = l then append(empty,r)
                                           [] top(s) = r then empty  fi
                                      else append (s1,top(s))                fi fi
```

One of the reasons for next being so complicated is the somewhat clumsy way of finding a subtree by walking along the path to its root given by the sequence of selections.

As pointed out in section 4 each recursive object structure may be replaced equivalently by an implementation using references. For the function next this means that subtrees may easily be identified by their corresponding references. Thus, we proceed
from the computation structure using recursive mode definitions to

```
structure TREE ≡ (mode m) some TREE (m):
        ⌈mode rtree ≡ (tree l, m i  , tree r),
         mode tree ≡ ref rtree,
         funct emptytree  ≡ tree: nil,
         funct isempty ≡ (tree t) bool: t = nil,
         funct construct ≡ (tree l, m i, tree r) tree: newref rtree: (l,i,r),
         funct left ≡ (tree t: ¬ isempty(t)) tree: l of deref  t ,
         funct right ≡ (tree t: ¬ isempty(t)) tree: r of deref  t ,
         funct item ≡ (tree t: ¬ isempty(t))  m:    i of deref  t ⌋
```

Now it is obviously simple to select subtrees by direct access via the reference to
it, but it is still rather complicated to implement the function next and nothing
seems to have been gained. The reason is a fundamental one: type TREE as defined
above is n o t the appropriate basis for what we are aiming at; what we really
need is a structure of a type that allows a simple definition of next, i.e. we need
another type definition. Nevertheless the above change to a reference representation
was not in vain, since the following observation can be made:

Upon reaching an empty subtree the algorithm has to backtrack until a node is reached with a subtree not yet visited. For the above representation this means to proceed from an empty reference to some other node. According to the idea of [Perlis,
Thornton 60] such empty references now can be substituted by a special reference,
called *thread*, to the root of the next subtree with respect to preorder.

Thus using the following mode definition

    <u>mode</u> <u>tree</u> ≡ <u>ref</u> <u>rtree</u>,
    <u>mode</u> <u>rtree</u> ≡ (<u>tree</u> l, <u>m</u> i, <u>tree</u> r, <u>bool</u> b)

where the boolean component indicates the presence of a thread, we can define the
basic functions for handling *threaded trees*:

    <u>funct</u> emptytree ≡ <u>tree</u>: <u>nil</u>,
    <u>funct</u> isempty ≡ (<u>tree</u> t) <u>bool</u>: t = <u>nil</u>,
    <u>funct</u> construct ≡ (<u>tree</u> l, <u>m</u> i, <u>tree</u> r) <u>tree</u>:
        <u>newref</u> <u>rtree</u> : <u>if</u> isempty(l) ∨ isempty(r) <u>then</u> (l,i,r,false)
                    [] ¬ (isempty(l) ∨ isempty(r)) <u>then</u> (thread(l,r),i,r,false) <u>fi</u>,

    <u>funct</u> left ≡ (<u>tree</u> t : ¬ isempty(t)) <u>tree</u>:
        <u>if</u> isempty (l <u>of</u> t) <u>then</u> <u>nil</u>
        [] ¬ isempty (l <u>of</u> t) <u>then</u> thread (l <u>of</u> <u>deref</u> t , <u>nil</u>) <u>fi</u>,

    <u>funct</u> right ≡ (<u>tree</u> t : ¬ isempty(t)) <u>tree</u>: r <u>of</u> <u>deref</u> t ,
    <u>funct</u> item ≡ (<u>tree</u> t : ¬ isempty(t)) <u>m</u>: i <u>of</u> <u>deref</u> t ,

    <u>funct</u> next ≡ (<u>tree</u> t : ¬ isempty(t)) <u>tree</u>:
        <u>if</u> isempty (left(t)) <u>then</u> r <u>of</u> <u>deref</u> t
        [] ¬ isempty (left(t)) <u>then</u> l <u>of</u> <u>deref</u> t <u>fi</u>,

    <u>funct</u> thread ≡ (<u>tree</u> t, <u>tree</u> d : ¬ isempty (t)) <u>tree</u>:
      <u>if</u>   isempty (right(t)) ∧   isempty (left(t))
          <u>then</u> <u>newref</u> <u>rtree</u>: (<u>nil</u>, item(t), d, true)
      []   isempty (right(t)) ∧ ¬ isempty (left(t))
          <u>then</u> <u>newref</u> <u>rtree</u>: (thread(left(t),d),item(t),<u>nil</u>,false)
      [] ¬ isempty (right(t))
          <u>then</u> <u>newref</u> <u>rtree</u>: (l <u>of</u> <u>deref</u> t, item(t), thread(right(t),d),false) <u>fi</u>,

    <u>funct</u>   rightisthread ≡ (<u>tree</u> t : ¬ isempty (t)) <u>bool</u>: b <u>of</u> t,

Note that the boolean component b is not essential and may be eliminated, if the
function rightisthread is not required, e.g. if next is only applied in treewalk.

Actually the functions empty, isempty, left, right, item and construct fulfil the
laws of type TREE . The function next , however, may deliver objects of mode
<u>tree</u> different from those generated by the functions above, since the selection
l <u>of</u> <u>deref</u> t may yield a tree s containing a reference (thread) to some tree,
which is n o t a subtree of s. Thus, from a theoretical point of view, next

has to be considered as an additional constructor function. This means that a new type definition is necessary to describe the abstract properties of threaded trees, which is rather complex since it has to reflect the different possibilities of selection by right and left and r of and l of resp. So by a change of type the difficulty of performing a tree-walk in isolated steps, originating from the complex way in which the different parts of the structure are visited, has completely disappeared. The price for this improvement is the somewhat more complicated way to construct tree objects. Yet in an environment where a tree once is built and then mainly tree-walks are performed on it, this means a considerable gain.

5.2. Relations with Particular Properties

Types are not only useful in defining such well-known structures like sets, stacks, queues, deques, trees, etc., but also are capable of defining more difficult structures.

For example we now turn to a type, which may be used to define partial orderings and equivalence relations (cf. section 1). We will demonstrate, that, without having a particular implementation in mind, one is able to control the generation of orderings or equivalence relations which are abstract objects of the corresponding computation structure. These types then may be used for formulating algorithms as well as for transforming them to get certain implementations.

5.2.1. Partial Orderings on a Finite Set and Topological Sorting

Let m be some mode with a finite number of elements, which can be tested for equality by the operation eq. The type of all partial orderings on m is defined by

```
type PORD ≡ (mode m) order, init, isordered, incorp:
     mode order,
     funct order init,
     funct (order, m, m) bool isordered,
     funct (order x, m a, m b : ¬ isordered (x,b,a)) order incorp,
     law I:   isordered (init,a,b) = eq(a,b),
     law NI: ¬ isordered (x,b,a) ⇒
                  isordered (incorp(x,a,b),c,d) =
                      isordered(x,c,d) ∨ (isordered(x,c,a) ∧ isordered(x,b,d)) ·
                                                                    endoftype
```

As intended, all objects of mode <u>order</u> are indeed orderings, since we can prove
(by induction on the number of applications of the function incorp to the ordering
init):

> <u>law R</u>: isordered(x,a,a) = true,
>
> <u>law T</u>: isordered(x,a,b) ∧ isordered(x,b,c) ⇒ isordered(x,a,c),
>
> <u>law A</u>: isordered(x,a,b) ∧ isordered(x,b,a) ⇒ eq(a,b).

Furthermore we can prove that all possible partial orderings on <u>m</u> can be generated
by a finite number of applications of incorp to the ordering init.

As is well-known from mathematics, we now may define an ordering on objects of mode
<u>order</u> by:

> <u>funct</u> isord ≡ (<u>order</u> x, <u>order</u> y) <u>bool</u>:
>   ∀<u>m</u> a, <u>m</u> b : isordered(x,a,b) ⇒ isordered(y,a,b)

(Again the axioms of orderings can be proved.) Such a function may be used to define
a relationship between a partial ordering x and some linear ordering denoted by
linear(x) which is compatible to x , i.e.

> <u>law L</u>: isord(x, linear(x)) ∧ islinear (linear(x))

should hold, where

> <u>funct</u> islinear ≡ (<u>order</u> x) <u>bool</u>:
>   ∀<u>m</u> a, <u>m</u> b :   isordered(x,a,b) ∨ isordered(x,b,a)

This process of computing a linear ordering form a partial one is called "topological
sorting" (cf. [Knuth, Szwarcfiter 74]).
Using a computation structure of type PORD, we are now able to give an "abstract"
formulation for an algorithm which generates a linear ordering from a given partial
one.
We use embedding techniques:

> <u>funct</u> linear ≡ (<u>order</u> x) <u>order</u>:
>   ⌈<u>m</u> max ≡ <u>some</u> <u>m</u> a: ismaximal (x,{<u>m</u> y: true},a) <u>within</u>
>   plinear (x, {<u>m</u> y: true}\{max},max)⌋,

where

<u>funct</u> ismaximal ≡ (<u>order</u> x, <u>set</u> <u>m</u> s, <u>m</u> a) <u>bool</u>:
$$\forall \underline{m}\ b:\ (b \in s \wedge \text{isordered}(x,b,a)) \Rightarrow \text{eq}(a,b),$$

and

<u>funct</u> plinear ≡ (<u>order</u> x, <u>set</u> <u>m</u> s, <u>m</u> a: ismaximal(x,s,a)) <u>order</u>:
   <u>if</u> s = {} <u>then</u> x
        <u>else</u> <u>m</u> b ≡ <u>some</u> <u>m</u> c: ismaximal(x,s,c) ∧ c ∈ s <u>within</u>
          incorp(plinear(x,s∖{b},b),a,b)   <u>fi</u>

Here the ambiguous function plinear computes some weakest partial ordering which is a linear ordering if restricted to elements in s ∪ {a}. ismaximal(x,s,a) indicates, whether a is maximal in comparison to elements in s using the ordering x.

To verify linear, we have to prove that <u>law</u> <u>L</u> holds for linear, i.e.

∀<u>m</u> a, <u>set</u> <u>m</u> s:
(∀<u>m</u> b: b ∈ s ⇒ ¬ isordered(x,b,a)) ⇒
  (isord(x,plinear(x,s,a)) ∧ isplinear(plinear(x,s,a),s ∪ {a}))

where

<u>funct</u> isplinear ≡ (<u>order</u> x, <u>set</u> <u>m</u> s) <u>bool</u>:
  ∀<u>m</u> a, <u>m</u> b: (a ∈ s ∧ b ∈ s) ⇒ ((isordered(x,a,b) ∨ isordered(x,b,a))

The proof can be done by structural induction, i.e. by induction on the number of elements in s.

We know that each subset s of a finite set <u>m</u> can be implemented by a boolean array b, such that

∀<u>m</u> x: (x ∈ s) = b[x].

This transition may formally be accomplished by representing

```
type SET ≡ (mode m) setm, emptyset, iselem, join, delete:
mode setm,
funct setm emptyset,
funct (setm, m) bool iselem,
funct (setm, m) setm join,
funct (setm, m) setm delete,


law E: iselem (emptyset, x) = false,
law I: iselem (join(s,x),y) = if x = y then true
                                        else iselem (s,y) fi,
law D: iselem (delete(s,x),y) = if x = y then false
                                        else iselem (s,y) fi
                                                        endoftype
```

in terms of type GREX (cf. Appendix A2.2):

```
structure SET ≡ (mode m) some SET (m):
┌ structure GREXSET ≡ some GREX (m, bool),
  mode setm ≡ grex,
  funct emptyset ≡ setm: that grex e: ∀m x:
        if isaccessible(e,x)  then get(e,x) = false  else false  fi,
  funct join ≡ (setm g, m x) setm: put(g,x,true),
  funct delete ≡ (setm g, m x) setm: put(g,x,false),
  funct iselem ≡ (setm g, m x) bool: get(g,x)              ┘
```

The representation of GREX by AGREX (cf. Appendix A2.3) leads to a particular representation of SET. If an integer array instead of a boolean array is used, additional information can be expressed by the values of the array components.

Thus we substitute the parameter set m s in plinear by m array nat count, such that count [a] denotes the number of elements b ∈ s, with isordered(x,b,a). We have:

$$\forall m\ a:\ a \notin s \Longleftrightarrow count\ [a] = 0\ \wedge$$
$$count\ [a] = 1 \Rightarrow\ ismaximal\ (x,s,a) \wedge a \in s$$

Note, that this above transition again could be accomplished by using transformations for computation structures. So we obtain the algorithm

```
funct linear ≡ (order x) order:
  ⌈m array nat count ≡ that m array nat  c: ∀m a: c[a] = |{m b: isordered (x,b,a)}|;
   m max ≡ some m a: count [a] = 1;
   plinear (x, alter (x,count,max), max)                                              ⌋
```

where

```
    funct alter ≡ (order x, m array nat count,m max) m array nat:
       that m array nat c: ∀m a: c[a] = if isordered (x,max,a) then count[a] - 1
                                        ⌷¬isordered (x,max,a) then count[a]    fi,

    funct plinear ≡ (order x, m array nat count, m a: count [a] = 0) order:
       if ∀m b: count [b] ≠ 1  then x
                           else m b ≡ some m d: count [d] = 1   within
                                     incorp (plinear (x,alter(x,count,b), b) ,a,b) fi
```

In contrast to the algorithm given in [Knuth, Szwarcfiter 74] the function linear
does not generate all topological sorting arrangements, but only one. But the computation is done in a nondeterministic way, such that each arrangement can be obtained as
a result. The transition to a program computing all orderings is obvious; we only
need to substitute the nondeterministic choice by a for-all-recursion. After recursion removal and some transformations improving efficiency we arrive at an algorithm
organized similarly to that given in [Knuth, Szwarcfiter 74].

5.2.2. Equivalence Relations for Finite Sets

In section 1 two types EREL and REREL are defined analogously to the type
PORD consisting of all equivalence relations over a finite set m . Both of them
contain an operation incorp and thus are suited to define the Fisher-Galler-
algorithm (cf. [Knuth 69], p. 353 - 355) which computes from a finite set s of
pairs (x,y) of mode (m,m) the weakest equivalence relation where all (x,y) ∈ s
are equivalent

```
    funct fishergaller ≡ (set(m,m) s) erelat:
       if s = {} then init
                 else (m a, m b) ≡ some (m,m)c: c ∈ s  within
                      incorp (fishergaller (s∖{(a,b)}), a,b) fi
```

Here the operation incorp is right-commutative; therefore the technique of operand
commutation (cf. transformation RCOMM in [Bauer et al. 77b]) can be applied:

```
funct fishergaller ≡ (set(m,m) s) erelat:
       fg(s,init)
funct fg ≡ (set(m,m) s, erelat e) erelat:
       if s = {}
          then e
          else (m a, m b) ≡ some (m,m) c: c ∈ s  within
                   fg  ( s ∖ {(a,b)}, incorp(e,a,b))  fi
```

Independently of any representation this may be transformed to a loop form [*]
(cf. transformation WHILE in [Bauer et al. 77b]):

```
funct fishergaller ≡ (set(m,m) s) erelat:
       ⌈var set(m,m) vs, var erelat ve) := (s,init);
        while s ≠ {}
           do (m a, m b) ≡ some (m,m) c : c ∈ s;
              (vs,ve) := (vs∖{(a,b)}, incorp(ve,a,b))  od;
        ve                                              ⌋
```

Now we may think of suitable representations for erelat . A first idea is to
represent the equivalence relation by partitions of set m, i.e. by a set of
disjoint sets. This leads to the following representation for EREL :

```
structure PSET ≡ (mode m) some EREL(m):
⌈mode erelat ≡ set set m,
 funct init  ≡ erelat: {set m s: ∃ m x: s = {x}},
 funct equiv ≡ (erelat x, m a, m b) bool: ∃ set m s: s ∈ x ∧ a ∈ s ∧ b ∈ s,
 funct incorp ≡ (erelat x, m a, m b) erelat:
    if equiv(x,a,b) then x
                    else (x∖{class(x,a),class(x,b)})∪{class(x,a) ∪ class(x,b)} fi
 funct class ≡ (erelat x, m a) set m: that set m s: a ∈ s ∧ s ∈ x             ⌋
```

Here each equivalence class is represented by the corresponding set of equivalent
objects.

---

[*] The sequence of transformations is quite arbitrary; the next step might have
    been done first as well.

Analogously to the change of type EREL into REREL, we also could give a computation structure of type REREL similar to PSET. Because repr is a total function on the finite domain m , we can implement it with the help of an array. Since furthermore repr is the only non-constructor function, each element e of erelat is sufficiently-completely characterized by the values of repr(e,x). So we can represent the objects themselves by the array (cf. [Correll 78]).

> structure RARRAY1 ≡ (mode m) some REREL (m):
> ⌈mode erelat ≡ m array m,
> funct init ≡ erelat: that m array m r: ∀m a: r[a] = a,
> funct incorp ≡ (erelat r, m a, m b) erelat:
>   put (r,repr (r,b), a),
> funct repr ≡ (erelat r, m a) m:
>   if r[a] = a then a
>   else repr(r,r[a]) fi   ⌋

In the computation structure above, the array reflects just the order in which the objects are identified. A representation more independent of the generation is obtained if repr is directly represented by the array r .

> structure RARRAY2 ≡ (mode m) some REREL (m):
> ⌈mode erelat ≡ m array m,
> funct init ≡ erelat: that m array m r: ∀m a: r[a] = a,
> funct incorp ≡ (erelat r, m a, m b) erelat:
>   if repr(r,a) = repr(r,b) then r
>   else that m array m x: ∀m c:
>   x[c] = if r[a] = r[c] ∨ r[b] = r[c] then r[a]
>   else r[c] fi,
> funct repr ≡ (erelat r, m a) m: r[a]   ⌋

In structure RARRAY2 the operation incorp is more complicated than in RARRAY1, but the evaluation of repr is done more efficiently. Thus the efficiency of the algorithms formulated using RARRAY1 or RARRAY2 resp., depends on the number of calls occuring for incorp and repr resp. The Fisher-Galler algorithm can be based on both structures.

A "releasing" of the particular representations of the computation structures leads (in addition to recursion removal, to the unfolding of incorp and if m = nat [1..n]) to (using RARRAY1):

```
funct fishergaller1 ≡ (set (m,m) s) erelat:
⌈var set (m,m) vs := s;
 m array var m r;
 for i to n do r[i] := i od;
 while s≠{} do (m a, m b) ≡ some (m,m) c: c ∈ s;
                var m rb := b;
                while r[rb]≠rb do rb := r[rb] od;
                (r[rb],vs) := (a, vs∖{(a,b)}) od;
 r                                                    ⌋
```

and (using RARRAY2) to:

```
funct fishergaller2 ≡ (set (m,m) s) erelat:
⌈var set (m,m) vs := s;
 m array var m r;
 for i to n do  r[i] := i od;
 while s≠{} do (m a, m b) ≡ some (m,m) c: c ∈ s;
                vs := vs\{(a,b)};
                for i to n do if r[a]=r[i] ∨ r[b]= r[i]  then  r[i] := r[a] fi
                                                                            od
                                                                            od;
 r                                                                          ⌋
```

Of course it is more efficient to compute the requested equivalence relation by fishergaller1, but if the function repr(r,x) is often applied to the resulting relation r the second version will be more appropriate.

Now further improvements (for both versions) would be possible if the set of pairs is represented by another structure, e.g. again by an array.

6. Conclusion

In this paper we have stressed some points concerning joint refinement of computation structures and algorithms. The specifications of types by algebraic laws and their implementations are concepts, which may be extremely useful if combined with program transformations. Thus the hierarchies of programs on different levels of abstraction correspond to hierarchies of computation structures leading from pure specifications to various kinds of representations, i.e. implementations. This correspondence is reflected by the sequence of transformations where optimizing transformations and changes of data representations work together like the teeth of a zipper.

Especially the hiding of information supports the independent development of programs and data representations, whereas the "releasing" and subsequent "unfolding" of parts of the implementations of the computation structures opens the door to a wide field of program transformations. Nevertheless, a lot of work has yet to be done in studying these associations.

Acknowledgements: We wish to thank Prof. F.L. Bauer, W. Dosch, P. Pepper, L. Schmitz and M. Wirsing for valuable discussions. We are indebted to R. Gnatz for critically reading the drafts of this paper.

Appendix: Theoretical Background and Notational Conventions

A 1. Object Structures

First of all we give a brief survey of the object structures (and their modes) involved in CIP-L.

From existing modes $\underline{A}$ and $\underline{B}$ new ones may be "composed" by means of the operations

      (i)   disjoint union $(\underline{A} + \underline{B})$

      (ii)   cartesian product $(\underline{A} \times \underline{B})$

      (iii) index mapping $(\underline{A}^{\underline{I}}$ where $\underline{I}$ is some finite index set.)

The use of recursion in building objects, proposed already by McCarthy [McCarthy 63]
and advocated by Hoare [Hoare 73], has been backed theoretically by the work of D.
Scott [Scott 76].

In an ALGOL-like version of CIP-L (cf. [Bauer et al. 77a]), the language in which the
transformations of the CIP system are performed, a notation is used which extends
in a straightforward manner the classical way of introducing composite modes and
selectors.

Let $\underline{m}$, $\underline{m1}$, $\underline{m2}$, $\ldots$, $\underline{mk}$ be sets of objects *(modes)*.

Then

        $\underline{mode}\ s \equiv (\underline{m1} \mid \underline{m2} \mid \ldots \mid \underline{mk})$

means that s is the disjoint union of $\underline{m1}$, $\underline{m2}$, $\ldots$, $\underline{mk}$,

        $\underline{mode}\ p \equiv (\underline{m1}\ s1,\ \underline{m2}\ s2,\ \ldots,\ \underline{mk}\ sk)$

means that p is the cartesian product of $\underline{m1}$, $\underline{m2}$, $\ldots$, $\underline{mk}$ with projection denoted
by the *selectors* s1, s2, $\ldots$, sk,
and

        $\underline{mode}\ \underline{a} \equiv \underline{index}\ \underline{array}\ \underline{m}$

expresses the cartesian power of $\underline{m}$, with projection denoted by the elements of the
index mode $\underline{index}$.

In detail, the canonical operations are, assuming that $xi \in \underline{mi}$, $ai \in \underline{m}$,
$i \in \underline{index}$:

      injection: $\underline{s}\ x \equiv xi$

                  (considers xi as an element of $\underline{s}$, and denotes it by x)

      inspection: $\underline{mi}\ ::\ x$

                  (tests, whether $x \in \underline{mi}$)

      construction: $\underline{p}\ y \equiv (x1,\ x2,\ \ldots,\ xk)$

                  (constructs the cartesian product made from

                  $x1, x2, \ldots, xk,$ and denotes it by y)

projection (selection):   si <u>of</u> y

                            (selects the si-component of y)

      construction: <u>a</u> z ≡ (a1, a2, ..., an)

                            (constructs the cartesian power made from a1, a2, ..., an

                            denoted by z , where n = card (<u>index</u>))

projection (selection):   z[i]

                            (selects the i-th component of z)

The following examples are illustrative

        "Rational numbers" *)

        <u>mode</u> <u>rat</u> ≡ <u>int</u> I (<u>int</u> n, <u>int</u> d)

        "Left sequence"

        <u>mode</u> <u>ls</u> ≡ <u>empty</u> I (<u>m</u> item, <u>ls</u> trunk)

        Here, <u>ls</u> is defined recursively, based on the *primitive* mode <u>m</u>

        (whatever it may be) and consisting of the *elementary* objects ∈ <u>m</u>

        and the *composite* objects ∈ (<u>m</u>, <u>ls</u>) .

There is an important connection between recursive object structures and the structure of certain recursive algorithms defined on them (cf. [von Henke 75]), as can be seen from

        <u>funct</u> length ≡ (<u>ls</u> A) <u>nat</u> :

                <u>if</u> <u>empty</u> :: A <u>then</u> 0

                [] (<u>m</u>,<u>ls</u>) :: A <u>then</u> 1 + length(trunk <u>of</u> A) <u>fi</u> .

There are also trivial ways of defining new object sets by enumeration of "atomic" elements

        <u>mode</u> <u>color</u> ≡ <u>atomic</u> {blue, red, green}

        <u>mode</u> <u>empty</u> ≡ <u>atomic</u> {()}

(Here () is a special object, the *empty tuple*, which is defined by {()} = $A^{\emptyset}$ or by a nullary cartesian product.)

and by restriction (subsets, "submodes"):

---

*) In this representation several different objects represent the same rational
    number, i.e. the same abstract object. Specifications, independent from particular
    representations, are considered in the following section.

"Bounded left-sequence"

mode <u>bls</u> ≡ (<u>ls</u> A : length(A) ≤ N)

For more details, see [Bauer et al. 77a].

A 2. Types and Computation Structures

To begin with we summarize some of the interesting theoretical aspects concerning types and computation structures. From these theoretical considerations we are then able to derive consequences for practical work. One consequence is a notation for both types and computation structures which we expect to be appropriate for the exact formal definition of certain data types as well as for the purposes of program transformations.

A 2.1. Theoretical Aspects

In general a computation structure consists of a family of object sets, called *carriers* ("phyla" [Birkhoff, Lipson 70]), a set of operations defined on these sets and a collection of properties (elsewhere called "axioms") which are valid for the operations. Thus a computation structure is an algebra - usually a heterogenous one ([Birkhoff, Lipson 70]). Typically a computation structure defines a new carrier with new operations on it, which are hierarchically based on carriers and operations of already known structures. Thus we distinguish between the carrier to be defined, called TOI ("type of interest" [Guttag 75] or "principal sort" [Burstall, Goguen 77]) and the primitive carriers $P_1, \ldots, P_n$ which are supposed to be defined elsewhere, i.e. to be well-known. Consequently the set of operations is partitioned into the non-empty, disjoint subsets F_{TOI} and F_p where F_{TOI} comprises all those operations having elements of TOI as arguments or results and F_p concerns only the primitive carriers. In the specification of a computation structure only TOI and F_{TOI} are explicitly given (strictly speaking: denotations for them are given); nevertheless, the P_i as well as F_p are part of the algebra, too.

That is, for a computation structure we specify,

(i) a set Σ consisting of a symbol for TOI[*] and some function symbols (together with their functionalities), called *signature*.

(ii) a set E of properties which are usually written in the form of equations, inequalities and implications in the function symbols and (all-quantified) free variables.

(iii) inference rules which are usually simple reduction rules and therefore omitted.

---

[*] In this paper we suppose having only one TOI , although several TOIs could be treated in an analogous way.

We say for a given algebra A that it is a Σ-*algebra* if for each function symbol in
Σ there exists a "corresponding" operation in A and vice versa. If, additionally,
the properties of E hold for a Σ-algebra A , we say A *is (a model) of type* (Σ,E).

For each signature Σ there exists a special Σ-algebra - the *word algebra* W_Σ [*)] Its
TOI consists of all "well formed" terms which can be generated from symbols for elements of the primitive carriers and function symbols from F_{TOI} by a finite
application of functional composition. A term t from W_Σ is *interpreted*
in a Σ-algebra A , if the function symbols in t are replaced by the
corresponding operations in A and the resulting expression is then evaluated.

For a given type (Σ, E) there are in general a lot of algebras which are not necces-
sarily isomorphic. A first reduction of this set of algebras is achieved by the following *generation principle*:
The set TOI consists exactly of those elements (≠ ω) which may be finitely
generated from the elements of the primitive carriers P_i by a finite number of
applications of functions from F_{TOI} .

For each algebra A from the subset Alg_Σ of all generatable Σ-algebras there exists
an epimorphism $\varphi : W_\Sigma \rightarrow A$ and thus a congruence relation $\equiv_\varphi$ such that A and
$W_\Sigma / \equiv_\varphi$ are isomorphic.

Hence the epimorphism φ associates each term $t \in W_\Sigma$ to that element which is the result of the interpretation of t in A. Two terms t_1 and t_2 are congruent, if and only
if their interpretation in A produces the same result. The set Alg_Σ may be graphical-
ly illustrated by

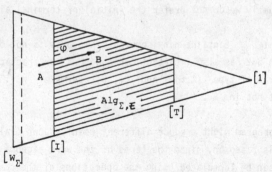

with the following interpretation:

---

*) sometimes also called *term algebra* .

If for two Σ-algebras A and B there exists an epimorphism $\varphi : A \rightarrow B$ then A is to the left of B (Note, however, that this does not imply a linear ordering in the algebras but only a partial one). Vertical (dotted) lines indicate classes of isomorphic algebras. The left edge characterizes the (class of the) word algebra W_Σ, the right edge stands for the class of algebras the. TOI of which is a singleton. The hatched part - denoted by $Alg_{\Sigma,E}$ - comprises the set of all algebras fulfilling the properties of E. If E is inconsistent then $Alg_{\Sigma,E}$ is empty. Left of the hatched area there are all those algebras distinguishing elements which should be equal with respect to E, right of it there are all those algebras, where elements are equal though they should be different with respect to E.

In spite of the generation principle $Alg_{\Sigma,E}$ still comprises usually a lot of non-isomorphic algebras. Therefore some classes of isomorphic algebras of $Alg_{\Sigma,E}$ need to be characterized; obiously, one of the two edges of the hatched area comes in question. In category theory the isomorphic algebras of the left edge are called the *initial algebras*, that of the right edge the *terminal algebras*. Informally they might be characterized in the following way: in an initial algebra all elements are different whose equality cannot be deduced from E; in a terminal algebra all elements are con-sidered to be equal whose inequality cannot be deduced from E. For a complete formal treatment - especially concerning questions of existence - and a detailed discussion of the respective advantages we have to refer to a forthcoming report of our group. In the literature initial algebras are favoured in [Zilles 74], [Goguen et al. 77], whereas terminal ones are preferred in [Guttag 75], [Guttag et al. 76a], [Guttag et al. 76b].

In our approach e a c h algebra from $Alg_{\Sigma,E}$ is called a *computation structure* of type (Σ,E). Usually we do not prefer the initial or terminal algebra.

The fact that $Alg_{\Sigma,E}$ contains non-isomorphic algebras is not only interesting for the theoretician but has also important consequences for practical work: Let A and B be two algebras of type (Σ,E) and t_1, t_2 terms of W_Σ. Then $t_1 = t_2$ may be valid in A but not in B.

Thus, the same program might produce different results upon evaluation depending on the algebra it is based on, since the terms of the word algebra represent exactly the programs which can be formulated using the operations of the computation structure. Therefore, it is quite natural to require that all algebras in $Alg_{\Sigma,E}$ produce the same result upon interpretation of an arbitrary term $t \in W_\Sigma$. Since types should be independent of particular representations, the above requirements for the equality of results may only refer to the primitive carriers P_i and not to TOI. As a result we require that the set E of properties of a type has to be *sufficiently-complete*

(cf. [Guttag 75]), i.e. for each term $t \in W_\Sigma$ with $t \notin$ TOI the result of its interpretation in an arbitrary algebra from $\mathrm{Alg}_{\Sigma,E}$ has to be uniquely determined by E .

For a detailed formal treatment we again refer to our forthcoming report and the work
of J. Guttag, where also (syntactical) criteria are given for testing whether a given
set of properties is sufficiently-complete or not.

It should be noted that the terminal algebra exists, if and only if the set of properties is sufficiently-complete. By the way, we do not require that the set E is minimal. The reason is that properties which are deducible from others in practice often
result in a better understanding of an abstract computation structure.

A 2.2. The Definition of Types

In CIP-L we use a notation somewhat related to that of functions: we consider a type
to be the set (category) of all computation structures that deliver - as a kind of result - an object structure (i.e. the TOI) and a set of operations which are characterized by some kind of assertions.

As a first example we will again use the well-known stack of elements of some mode m .

    type STACK ≡ (mode m) stack, empty, isempty, top, rest, append :

        mode stack ,
        funct stack empty ,
        funct (stack) bool isempty ,
        funct (stack s : ¬ isempty(s)) m top , *)
        funct (stack s : ¬ isempty(s)) stack rest ,
        funct (stack, m) stack append ,
        law R : rest(append(s,x)) = s ,
        law T : top(append(s,x)) = x ,
        law A : ¬ isempty(s) ⇒ append(rest(s), top(s)) = s ,
        law E : isempty(empty) = true ,
        law NE : isempty(append(s,x)) = false   endoftype

Here the object structure stack together with its operations empty , isempty ,
top , rest , and append is exactly what is available from any computation structure of type STACK for the "outer world", i.e. in algorithms handling object structures of mode stack .

---

*) In contrast to [Guttag 75] we prefer to restrict the domain of a function by
   predicates rather than to give equations with undefined elements (ω or error).

The semantics of the operations is given by the laws (which can be named for reasons of accessibility). The syntactic form of these laws originates from all-quantified predicates, e.g. R

from   ∀ stack s : ∀ m x : rest(append(s,x)) = s

where all-quantification is generally assumed and the domain of the free variables is supposed to be completed from the function specifications.

Furthermore, types are allowed to have parameters - either some mode - as in the above example - , some object, or another computation structure.

Our notation also allows us to express relationships between types by the notion of a *type membership*, i.e. a boolean expression that states that an object structure and a set of operations are of some previously defined type. Consider for example the type which arises from STACK by supplementing an additional function length and the associated laws:

    type LSTACK ≡ (mode m) lstack, lempty, islempty, ltop, lrest, lappend, length :

        (lstack, lempty, islempty, lrest, lappend) isoftype STACK (m) ,

        funct (lstack) nat length ,
        law L1 : length(empty) = 0 ,
        law L2 : length(lappend(s,x)) = length(s) + 1   endoftype

From the type membership

        (lstack, lempty, ltop, lrest, lappend) isoftype STACK (m)

functionalities like

        funct (lstack, m) lstack lappend

as well as the associated properties like

        law A : ¬ isempty(s) ⇒ lappend(lrest(s), ltop(s)) = s

can immediately be deduced.

In the example we used in addition the *possibility of renaming*, e.g. ltop for top .

To explain what we mean by relationship of types, consider the following type which models the behaviour of a FIFO-list:

    type QUEUE ≡ (mode m) queue, empty, isempty, top, rest, stalk :

        mode queue ,
        funct queue empty,
        funct (queue) bool isempty ,
        funct (queue q : ¬ isempty(q)) m top ,
        funct (queue q : ¬ isempty(q)) m rest ,
        funct (queue, m) queue stalk ,
        law RE : rest(stalk(empty, x)) = empty ,
        law RNE : ¬ isempty(q) ⇒ rest(stalk(q,x)) = stalk(rest(q), x) ,
        law TE : top(stalk(empty, x)) = x ,
        law TNE : ¬ isempty(q) ⇒ top(stalk(q, x)) = top(q) ,
        law E : isempty(empty) = true ,
        law NE : isempty(stalk(s, x)) = false   endoftype

Now a type DEQUE can be defined as follows:

type DEQUE ≡ (mode m)(deque, empty, isempty, top, rest, append, bottom, upper, stalk:

    (deque, empty, isempty, top, rest, append) isoftype STACK (m) ,
    (deque, empty, isempty, bottom, upper, stalk) isoftype STACK (m) ,
    (deque, empty, isempty, top, rest, stalk) isoftype QUEUE (m) ,
    (deque, empty, isempty, bottom, upper, append) isoftype QUEUE (m)   endoftype

It is fairly obvious that each structure of this type is exactly what Knuth calls a "double-ended queue" ([Knuth 69]).
It should be noted that there is a certain relationship between our notation of type membership and the operations for "building theories" defined in [Burstall, Goguen 77] or [Ehrig et al. 78]. Furthermore, a warning should be given that when using the type membership notation the programmer has to pay great attention not to produce inconsistent systems of properties.

Sometimes a sufficiently-complete description of a certain type requires additional functions,[*)]which should not be at the user's disposal. Such *hidden functions* are treated in the same way as the other ones; the only difference is that their identifiers are not listed in front of the colon and they therefore must not be used outside.

Very often types can be used to express restrictions which cannot be expressed directly by appropriate object structures. The following example gives a well-known problem of this kind:

---

*) cf. [Guttag, Horning 78] or [Linden 78] in reply to [Majster 77].

<u>type</u> GREX ≡ (<u>mode index</u>, <u>mode m</u>) <u>grex</u>, vac, get, put :

    <u>mode grex</u> ,

    <u>funct grex</u> vac ,

    <u>funct</u> (<u>grex</u>, <u>index</u>, <u>m</u>) <u>grex</u> put ,

    <u>funct</u> (<u>grex</u>, <u>index</u>) <u>bool</u> isaccessible ,

    <u>funct</u> (<u>grex</u> g, <u>index</u> i : isaccessible(g, i)) <u>m</u> get ,

    <u>law</u> <u>S</u> : get(put(s,i,x),j) = <u>if</u> i = j <u>then</u> x

                           ⫿ i ≠ j <u>then</u> get(s, j) <u>fi</u> ,

    <u>law</u> <u>NA</u> : isaccessible(vac, i) = false ,

    <u>law</u> <u>A</u> : isaccessible(put(g, i, x), j) = <u>if</u> i = j <u>then</u> true

                                 ⫿ i ≠ j <u>then</u> isaccessible(g,j) <u>fi</u>

                                                        endoftype

This type describes structures with properties like arrays in ALGOL 60, i.e. elements must have been subject to the operation put at least once before selection by get is possible.

Using the above example, we may illuminate the differences between initial and terminal algebras as outlined in section 2.2 of the appendix. For the terminal algebra the property

    <u>law</u> <u>PP</u> : put(put(g, i, x), j, y) = <u>if</u> i = j <u>then</u> put(g, i, y)

                              ⫿ i ≠ j <u>then</u> put(put(g, j, y), i, x) <u>fi</u>

holds - but it does n o t for the initial algebra.

One of the essential goals connected with types is the precise specification of particular classes of structures - including those which are usually described by their implementation. A typical example for this are the various kinds of arrays, e. g. the so-called flexible arrays in ALGOL 68. The necessity for a precise definition of the subtle term "array" has been advocated by Hoare 1972 and Dijkstra 1976.

The essential requirements for arrays which go beyond the trivial case of finite index-sets, are met by the following example of a two-sided flexible array:

<u>type</u> <u>FLEXARRAY</u> ≡ (<u>mode</u> <u>m</u>, <u>structure</u> SINDEX : SINDEX <u>isoftype</u> <u>INDEX</u>)

   <u>flex</u>, hib, lob, get, put, lorem, hirem:

   <u>mode</u> <u>flex</u> ,

   <u>funct</u> (<u>index</u>) <u>flex</u> init ,

   <u>funct</u> (<u>flex</u>) <u>index</u> hib ,

   <u>funct</u> (<u>flex</u>) <u>index</u> lob ,

   <u>funct</u> (<u>flex</u> a, <u>index</u> i : lob(a) ≤ i ∧ i ≤ hib(a)) <u>m</u> get ,

   <u>funct</u> (<u>flex</u> a, <u>index</u> i, <u>m</u> x : pred(lob(a)) ≤ i ∧ i ≤ succ(hib(a))) <u>flex</u> put ,

   <u>funct</u> (<u>flex</u>) <u>flex</u> hirem,

   <u>funct</u> (<u>flex</u>) <u>flex</u> lorem,

   <u>law</u> <u>HI</u> : hib(init(i)) = pred(i) ,

   <u>law</u> <u>LI</u> : lob(init(i)) = i ,

   <u>law</u> <u>PI</u> : pred(lob(a)) ≤ i ∧ i ≤ succ(hib(a)) ➡

               get(put(a, i, x), j) = <u>if</u> i = j <u>then</u> x

                               ⫲ i ≠ j <u>then</u> get(a, j) <u>fi</u> ,

   <u>law</u> <u>HP</u> : hib(put(a, i, x))= <u>if</u> i = succ(hib(a)) <u>then</u> i

                        ⫲ pred(lob(a)) ≤ i ∧ i ≤ hib(a) <u>then</u> hib(a) <u>fi</u> ,

   <u>law</u> <u>LP</u> : lob(put(a, i, x))= <u>if</u> i = pred(lob(a)) <u>then</u> i

                        ⫲ lob(a) ≤ i ∧ i ≤ succ(hib(a)) <u>then</u> lob(a) <u>fi</u> ,

   <u>law</u> <u>OI</u> : lorem(init(i)) = init(succ(i)),

   <u>law</u> <u>II</u> : hirem(init(i)) = init(pred(i)),

   <u>law</u> <u>OP</u> : lorem(put(a,i,x)) = <u>if</u> i = succ(hib(a))   <u>then</u> a

                    ⫲ i = hib(a)   <u>then</u> lorem(a)

                    ⫲ succ(lob(a)) ≥ i > hib(a) <u>then</u> put(lorem(a),i,x) <u>fi</u>,

   <u>law</u> <u>IP</u> : hirem(put(a,i,x)) = <u>if</u> i = succ(hib(a))   <u>then</u> a

                    ⫲ i = hib(a)   <u>then</u> hirem(a)

                    ⫲ pred(lob(a)) ≤ i < hib(a) <u>then</u> put(hirem(a),i,x) <u>fi</u>,

                                              <u>endoftype</u>

<u>where type</u> <u>INDEX</u> is defined by

<u>type</u> <u>INDEX</u> ≡ index, succ, pred, zero, ≤, +, -, ≐ :

   <u>mode</u> <u>index</u> ,

   <u>funct</u> <u>index</u> zero ,

   <u>funct</u> (<u>index</u>) <u>index</u> succ ,

   <u>funct</u> (<u>index</u>) <u>index</u> pred ,

   <u>funct</u> (<u>index</u>, <u>index</u>) <u>bool</u> ≤ ,

   <u>funct</u> (<u>index</u>, <u>index</u>) <u>index</u> + ,

   <u>funct</u> (<u>index</u>, <u>index</u>) <u>index</u> - ,

   <u>funct</u> (<u>index</u>, <u>index</u>) <u>bool</u> ≐ ,

law $\underline{S}$: succ(pred(x)) = x ,

law $\underline{P}$: pred(succ(x)) = x ,

law $\underline{LE1}$: (x ≤ x) = true ,

law $\underline{LE2}$: (x ≤ pred(x)) = false ,

law $\underline{LE3}$: (x ≤ y) = true ⇒ (x ≤ succ(y)) = true ,

law $\underline{LE4}$: (x ≤ y) = false ⇒ (x ≤ pred(y)) = false ,

law $\underline{LE5}$: (succ(x) ≤ succ(y)) = (x ≤ y) ,

law $\underline{A1}$: x + zero = x ,

law $\underline{A2}$: x + y = succ(x) + pred(y) ,

law $\underline{AS}$: (x + y) - y = x ,

law $\underline{E}$: (x ≐ y) = (x ≤ y ∧ y ≤ x) ,

For each structure of type $\underline{FLEXARRAY}$ we are able to define the functions given in
[Dijkstra 76] using an arbitrary index-set of type $\underline{INDEX}$

funct isempty ≡ (<u>flex</u> a) <u>bool</u> succ(hib(a)) ≤ lob(a) ,

funct dom   ≡ (<u>flex</u> a) <u>index</u> : succ(hib(a) - lob(a)) ,

funct low   ≡ (<u>flex</u> a : ¬ isempty(a)) <u>m</u> : get(a, lob(a)) ,

funct high   ≡ (<u>flex</u> a : ¬ isempty(a)) <u>m</u> : get(a, hib(a)) ,

funct hiext ≡ (<u>flex</u> a, <u>m</u> x) <u>flex</u> : put(a, succ(hib(a)), x) ,

funct loext ≡ (<u>flex</u> a, <u>m</u> x) <u>flex</u> : put(a, pred(lob(a)), x) ,

funct shift ≡ (<u>flex</u> a, <u>index</u> k) <u>flex</u> :

      <u>if</u> isempty(a) <u>then</u> init(lob(a) + k)

               <u>else</u> hiext(shift(hirem(a), k), high(a))   <u>fi</u>

As it is advantageous to keep the number of functions defined within a type small, in
order to minimize its complexity, we prefer to define a rather small number of functions within type $\underline{FLEXARRAY}$ and define others in terms of them. Nevertheless, it is
possible to use another basis of functions, e.g. to use only init(0) and shift ,
but this would complicate the laws.

Of course, there are lots of other ways to define the type $\underline{FLEXARRAY}$. For example
we may use the type $\underline{DEQUE}$ and add the functions hib, lob, shift, get, put , i.e.
we may define a flexible array in terms of the basic functions of $\underline{DEQUE}$.

type $\underline{FARRAY}$ ≡ (<u>mode m</u>, <u>structure</u> SINDEX : SINDEX <u>isoftype</u> $\underline{INDEX}$)

   <u>flex</u>, null, lob, hib, get, put, isempty, high, low, hiext, loext,
   hirem, lorem, shift :

(<u>flex</u>,null, isempty, high, hirem, hiext, low, lorem, loext) <u>isoftype</u> $\underline{DEQUE}$ (<u>m</u>) ,

   funct (<u>flex</u>) <u>index</u> lob ,

   funct (<u>flex</u>) <u>index</u> hib ,

   funct (<u>flex</u>, <u>index</u>) <u>flex</u> shift ,

$\underline{\text{funct}}$ ($\underline{\text{flex}}$ a, $\underline{\text{index}}$ i, $\underline{\text{m}}$ x : pred(lob(a)) $\leq$ i $\wedge$ i $\leq$ succ(hib(a))) $\underline{\text{flex}}$ put ,

$\underline{\text{funct}}$ ($\underline{\text{flex}}$ a, $\underline{\text{index}}$ i:lob(a)$\leq$ i $\wedge$ i $\leq$ hib(a)) $\underline{\text{m}}$ get ,

$\underline{\text{law}}$ $\underline{\text{IE}}$: isempty(a) =(hib(a) $\leq$ pred(lob(a))) ,

$\underline{\text{law}}$ $\underline{\text{LN}}$: lob(null) = zero ,

$\underline{\text{law}}$ $\underline{\text{HN}}$: hib(null) = pred(zero) ,

$\underline{\text{law}}$ $\underline{\text{OE}}$: lob(loext(a)) = pred(lob(a)),

$\underline{\text{law}}$ $\underline{\text{IE}}$: hib(hiext(a)) = succ(hib(a)),

$\underline{\text{law}}$ $\underline{\text{ON}}$: lob(hiext(a)) = lob(a),

$\underline{\text{law}}$ $\underline{\text{IN}}$: hib(loext(a)) = hib(a),

$\underline{\text{law}}$ $\underline{\text{LS}}$: lob(shift(a, k)) = lob(a) + k ,

$\underline{\text{law}}$ $\underline{\text{HS}}$: hib(shift(a, k)) = hib(a) + k ,

$\underline{\text{law}}$ $\underline{\text{GS}}$: get(shift(a, k), i) = get(a, i+k) ,

$\underline{\text{law}}$ $\underline{\text{PS}}$: put(shift(a, k),i+k, x) = shift(put(a, i, x), k) ,

$\underline{\text{law}}$ $\underline{\text{P}}$: put(a, i, x) = $\underline{\text{if}}$ i = pred(lob(a)) $\underline{\text{then}}$ loext(a, x)

$\qquad\qquad\qquad\qquad$ [] i = succ(hib(a)) $\underline{\text{then}}$ hiext(a, x)

$\qquad\qquad\qquad\qquad$ [] lob(a) $\leq$ i $\wedge$ i $\leq$ hib(a) $\underline{\text{then}}$ hiext(put(hirem(a),i,x), high(a))

$\qquad\qquad\qquad\qquad\qquad\qquad\qquad\qquad\qquad\qquad\qquad\qquad\qquad\qquad\qquad$ $\underline{\text{fi}}$,

$\underline{\text{law}}$ $\underline{\text{G}}$: get(a, i)   = $\underline{\text{if}}$ i = lob(a) $\underline{\text{then}}$ low(a)

$\qquad\qquad\qquad\qquad$ [] i = hib(a) $\underline{\text{then}}$ high(a)

$\qquad\qquad\qquad\qquad$ [] succ(lob(a)) $\leq$ i $\wedge$ i $\leq$ pred(hib(a)) $\underline{\text{then}}$ get(hirem(a), i) $\underline{\text{fi}}$

$\qquad\qquad\qquad\qquad\qquad\qquad\qquad\qquad\qquad\qquad\qquad\qquad\qquad\qquad\qquad$ $\underline{\text{endoftype}}$

Another rather obvious possibility to define flexible arrays is first to introduce a type $\underline{\text{FLEX}}$ for a one-sided flexible array (which may be based on $\underline{\text{STACK}}$) and then to define the two-sided flexible array in terms of $\underline{\text{FLEX}}$.

A 2.3. The Definition of Computation Structures

Up to now, we have essentially talked about types, i.e. categories. Now we are going to treat *concrete computation structures*, i.e. particular algebras of some type. Given type $\underline{\text{STACK}}$ as defined in section A 2.2. an arbitrary structure   of that type is indicated by

$\qquad\qquad$ $\underline{\text{structure}}$ ASTACK = ($\underline{\text{mode}}$ $\underline{\text{m}}$) $\underline{\text{some}}$ STACK ($\underline{\text{m}}$)

whereas

> structure NATSTACK ≡ some STACK (nat)

characterizes an arbitrary structure of type STACK with natural elements. The
semantics of these computation structures are given by the algebraic laws describing the interaction between their operations, even if additionally there
is a body containing some representation for the operations. Thus interfaces
are kept independent of certain implementations.

Analogous to ls (see section A 1 of the appendix) and its canonical operations, a
concrete computation structure modelling the behaviour of a stack might read:

> structure CSTACK ≡ (mode m) some STACK (m) :
>
> ⌈ mode empty   ≡ atomic {()} ,
>   mode stack   ≡ empty | (stack trunk, m item),
>   funct empty   ≡ stack : () ,
>   funct isempty ≡ (stack s) bool : empty :: s ,
>   funct top   ≡ (stack s : ¬ isempty(s)) m : item of s ,
>   funct rest   ≡ (stack s : ¬ isempty(s)) stack : trunk of s ,
>   funct append   ≡ (stack s, m x) stack :(x, s)   ⌋

Here again the first line specifies what is known to the outside; everything else is
"hidden". This means especially that the implementation, i.e. the algorithmic specification, is not available from the outside and its particular properties must not
be used. From this simple example it also can be seen that each object structure as
defined in section A 1 may be associated with a computation structure in quite a natural
way.

Another example is the concrete structure

> structure AGREX ≡ (mode index, mode m) some GREX (index, m) :
>
> ⌈mode grex ≡ index array ml ,
> mode ml ≡ m | atomic {virgin} ,
> funct vac ≡ grex :
>   that grex g : ∀ index i : ¬ isaccessible(g, i) ,
> funct put ≡ (grex g, index i, m m) grex :
>   that grex k : ∀ index j : j ≠ i ⇒ get(k,j) = get(g,j)
>   ∧ get(k,i) = m,
> funct get ≡ (grex g, index i : isaccessible(g,i)) m : g[i] ,
> funct isaccessible ≡ (grex g, index i) bool : g[i] ≠ virgin ⌋

Note that the body of a concrete computation structure may contain descriptionally formulated functions since by non-algorithmic formulations the particular algebra may be characterized, too.

A formulation like that of structure CSTACK is only meaningful, if CSTACK is indeed a concrete structure of type STACK , i.e. that the functions defined in the body fulfil the laws specified for type STACK .
To show this, induction principles like computational induction are often necessary in addition to the laws of the primitive computation structures.

To show that a concrete structure C is initial (or terminal) with respect to given type T is rather difficult and goes beyond the scope of this paper. Even to find a concrete relation ≡ such that T / ≡ is initial or terminal is difficult as well. However, it should be noted that this latter question is irrelevant if sufficient-completeness is guaranteed.

Literature

[Bauer 78] F.L. Bauer: Design of a Programming Language for a Program Transformation System. This volume.

[Bauer et al. 77a] F.L. Bauer, M. Broy, R. Gnatz, W. Hesse, B. Krieg-Brückner: Notes on the Project CIP: Towards a Wide Spectrum Language to Support Program Development by Transformations. Technische Universität München, Institut für Informatik, TUM-INFO-7722, 1977

[Bauer et al. 77b] F. L. Bauer, H. Partsch, P. Pepper, H. Wössner: Notes on the Project CIP: Outline of a Transformation System. Technische Universität München, Institut für Informatik, TUM-INFO-7729, 1977

[Bauer et al. 78] F.L. Bauer, M. Broy, R. Gnatz, W. Hesse, B. Krieg-Brückner, H. Partsch, P. Pepper, H. Wössner: Towards a Wide Spectrum Language to Support Program Specification and Program Development. SIGPLAN Notices $\underline{13}$ (12), 15-24 (1978). This volume

[Birkhoff, Lipson 70] G. Birkhoff, J.D. Lipson: Heterogeneous Algebras. J. of Combinatorial Theory $\underline{8}$, 115-133 (1970)

[Burstall, Goguen 77] R.M. Burstall, J.A. Goguen: Putting Theories together to Make Specifications. Proceedings of the Int. Joint Conf. on Artificial Intelligence 1977

[Correll 78] C.H. Correll: Proving Programs Correct through Refinement. Acta Informatica $\underline{9}$, 121-132 (1978)

[Dahl et al. 68] O.-J. Dahl, B. Myhrhaug, K. Nygaard: SIMULA 67 Common Base Language. Norwegian Computing Center, Oslo, May 1968

[Dijkstra 76] E.W. Dijkstra:
A Discipline of Programming. Englewood Cliffs, N.J.:
Prentice-Hall, 1976

[Ehrig et al. 78] H. Ehrig, H.J. Kreowski, P. Padawitz:
Stepwise specification and implementation of abstract data types.
In: G. Ausiello, C. Böhm (eds): Automata, Languages and Programming.
Proc. 5th Colloquium, Udine, July 1978. Springer Lecture Notes on
Computer Science 62

[Goguen et al. 77] J.A. Goguen, J.W. Thatcher, E.G. Wagner:
An Initial Algebra Approach to the Specification, Correctness and Implementation of Abstract Data Types. In: R.T.Yeh (ed.): Current trends
in programming methodology, Vol. 3, Data Structuring, N.J.: Prentice
Hall, 1978

[Guttag 75] J.V. Guttag:
The Specification and Application to Programming of Abstract Data Types.
Ph. D. Th., Univ. of Toronto, Dept. Comp. Sci., Rep. CSRG-59, 1975

[Guttag et al. 76a] J.V. Guttag, E. Horowitz, D.R. Musser:
Abstract Data Types and Software Validation.
USC/Information Sciences Institute, RR-76-48 (1976)

[Guttag et al. 76b] J.V. Guttag, E. Horowitz, D.R. Musser:
The Design of Data Type Specifications.
USC/Information Sciences Institute, RR-76-49 (1976)

[Guttag, Horning 78] J.V. Guttag, J.J. Horning:
The Algebraic Specification of Abstract Data Types.
Acta Informatica 10, 27 - 52 (1978)

[von Henke 75] F.W. von Henke:
On Generating Programs from Data Types: An Approach to Automatic Pro-
gramming. In: G. Huet, G. Kahn (eds.): Proving and Improving Programs.
Colloques IRIA, Arc et Senans, 1-3 juillet 1975

[Hoare 72] C.A.R. Hoare:
Proof of Correctness of Data Representations.
Acta Informatica 1: 4, 271-281 (1972)

[Hoare 73] C.A.R. Hoare:
Recursive Data Structures. Stanford University, A.I.Lab.,
Stan-CS-73-400, Oct. 1973

[Knuth 69] D.E. Knuth:
The Art of Computer Programming.
Reading, Mass: Addison-Wesley, 1969

[Knuth, Szwarcfiter 74] D.E. Knuth, J.L. Szwarcfiter:
A Structured Program to Generate all Topological Sorting Arrangements. Inf. Proc. Letters $\underline{2}$, 153-157 (1974)

[Krieg-Brückner 78] B. Krieg-Brückner:
Concrete and Abstract Specification, Modularization and Program
Development by Transformation.
Technische Universität München, Institut für Informatik,
TUM-INFO-7805, 1978

[Linden 78] Th. A. Linden:
Specifying Abstract Data Types by Restriction.
ACM SIGSOFT, Software Engineering Notes $\underline{3}$: 2, 7 - 13 (1978)

[Liskov, Zilles 74] B. Liskov, S. Zilles:
Programming with Abstract Data Types. Proc. ACM SIGPLAN Conf. on
Very High Level Languages, SIGPLAN Notices $\underline{9}$: 4, 50-59 (1974)

[Liskov, Zilles 75] B. Liskov, S. Zilles:
Specification Techniques for Data Abstractions. IEEE Trans. on Software Eng. $\underline{1}$: 1, 7-18 (1975)

[Majster 77] M. Majster:
Limits of the "Algebraic" Specification of Abstract Data Types.
SIGPLAN Notices $\underline{12}$: 10, 37 - 41 (1977)

[McCarthy 63] J. McCarthy:
A Basis for a Mathematical Theory of Computation.
In: P. Braffort, D. Hirschberg (eds.): Computer Programming and
Formal Systems. Amsterdam: North-Holland, 1963

[Perlis, Thornton 60] A.J. Perlis, C. Thornton:
              Symbol Manipulation by Threaded Lists.
              Comm. ACM 3, 195-204 (1960)

[Scott 76] D. Scott:
              Data Types as Lattices. SIAM J. of Computing 5, 522-587 (1976)

[Wulf 74] W. Wulf:
              ALPHARD: Towards a Language to Support Structured Programs.
              Carnegie-Mellon Univ., Pittsburgh, Dept. of Comp. Sc.,
              Internal Report, April 1974

[Zilles 74] S. Zilles:
              Algebraic Specification of Data Types.
              Computation Structures Group Memo 119, MIT, Combridge, Mass.

DEVELOPMENT OF THE SCHORR-WAITE ALGORITHM

Michael GRIFFITHS
Centre de Recherche en Informatique de Nancy
Chateau du Montet
54500 Vandoeuvre-les-Nancy
France

I. INTRODUCTION

The well-known algorithm for marking a graph which dates from [Schorr, Waite, 1967] has been re-programmed recently in a very elegant form. A proof of the result is given by D. Gries in this volume. What is given in this chapter is a derivation of the program, which indicates the path which could be taken to deduce its very elegant final form. The derivation can be treated as a programming exercise from which some personal conclusions may be drawn.

We use the same conventions of representation as in the companion paper by Gries, of which the vital details are the following :

- Each node has an index in the range 1 to n. The representation of a node is by a structure of four fields

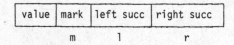

- A node with no left successor or no right successor has value zero in the corresponding l or r field.
- A dummy node 0 exists, and its l and r fields contain zero, its m field containing a mark ; hence $m(0) \neq 0$.

The recursive program with which we start is the standard marking algorithm, which has the following form :

```
procedure mark (x) ;
      if m(x) = 0          {node x is as yet unvisited}
      then m(x):=1 ;
           mark(left(x)) ;     {mark the graph whose root is left (x)}
           mark(right(x))      {mark the graph whose root is right (x)}
      fi
endproc
```

A call of this procedure with the root as parameter will mark all nodes accessible from the root :

    mark (root)

The use of left and right for l and r is an indication of the fact that we wish to treat them as successor functions, leaving open for the moment the concrete representation of the pointers in the fields l and r.

2. ELIMINATION OF RECURSION

The program presented above is that of a standard tree search in prefixed order. Although the marking program applies to a graph, and is thus not limited to tree structures, standard techniques still apply. In particular, nodes already marked are not re-used again to provoke recursive calls. In view of the fact that nodes without successors point to the (marked) dummy node zero, the end of a search chain is indicated by m (x) $\neq$ 0 whether this ending is due to the non-existence of a successor or due to a join of paths by commonality or cycle.

Prefixed traversals have been heavily analysed, for example in [Scholl 1977], amongst others. A node has, in general, a predecessor and two successors :

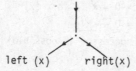

$$\text{left (x)} \qquad \text{right(x)}$$

If x has more than one predecessor, that is that more than one node points towards it, it will be taken into account only the first time, since m (x) will be marked from that point on. A node is visited :

- a first time on arrival from its predecessor
- a second time after marking the graph whose root is left(x)
- a third time after marking the graph whose root is right(x)

It is thus convenient to use m(x) to remember the number of visits already made to x. Hence, initially, we have

$$m (0) \neq 0$$
$$x \neq 0 \Rightarrow m (x) = 0$$

The recursive form of the program is now the following :

```
        procedure mark (x) ;
                if m (x) = 0
                then m (x) := 1 ;
                        mark (left (x)) ;
                        m (x) := 2 ;
                        mark (right (x)) ;
                        m (x) := 3
                fi
        endproc
```

This device allows the iterative form of the procedure to discover which nodes have received which treatment at any moment. It is a common, and useful way of handling traversal problems.

For the iterative forms of the program, that is to say from now on, we use, for compatibility as well as for reasons of elegance, Dijkstra's guarded commands [Dijkstra 1976]. An iterative form is the following :

```
x := root ;
while m (root) ≠ 3                    {m (root) = 3 indicates the end of marking}
do if m (x) = 0
            → m (x) := 1 ;
            if m (left(x)) = 0 → x := left (x)
            ☐ m (left(x)) ≠ 0 → skip
            fi {take left successor if possible}
    ☐ m (x) = 1
            → m (x) := 2 ;
            if m (right(x)) = 0 → x := right (x)
            ☐ m (right(x)) ≠ 0 → skip
            fi {take right successor if possible}
    ☐ m (x) = 2
            → m (x) := 3 ;
            x := pred (x)    {return to predecessor}
    fi
done
```

We have introduced a new function pred, which is the predecessor of a node. At the moment, we have not indicated how to implement pred, and in fact it is this implementation which is one of the keys to the algorithm.

3. DATA STRUCTURE

The above transformation indicates what must be done to the program structure. The idea of implementing a predecessor function is that of Schorr and Waite. It could equally have been deduced from our knowledge of general transformations, since this standard recursive situation is susceptible to treatment if the successor function has an inverse. This point was already discussed in [Griffiths 1976]. This analysis was not available at the time that the idea was first suggested, which must therefore be considered as a piece of inspiration.

The predecessor function is implemented by "turning round" one of the successor pointers. Consider the case of the first visit to a node x. In this case,

m (x) = 0, 1 (x) indicates left (x), r (x) indicates right (x).

After this visit, the following assignments have been carried out :

m (x) := 1 ; x := left (x)

Then, since x follows the left successor chain, l(x) is no longer needed. This "spare" field is used to store the pointer to the predecessor. Similarly, on following the right successor, the other field is temporarily freed. The initial pointers are restored on coming back to the node, that is at the same time that m(x) takes the value 3.

The second critical point in the logic is the decision concerning the organisation of the data with the reverse pointer. The natural solution is simply to put into the "free" field the reverse pointer, and this gives the usual form of the program. We will not study this case. An improved form comes from the apparently uninteresting case in which the l and r fields are exchanged before using the resulting "free" for the reverse pointer. Thus we consider the following situation :

m (x) = 0 or m (x) = 3 : l(x) = left(x), r(x) = right(x)
m (x) = 1   : l(x) = right(x), r(x) = pred(x)
m (x) = 2   : l(x) = pred(x), r(x) = left(x)

We follow this line because of advance knowledge, but a full analysis would follow each of the four possibilities (pred(x) always in l(x), always in r(x), or in the opposite of the case considered). In all cases we need one auxiliary variable, which we call q, in which is kept the preceeding value of x on arrival at a new node.

Hence, the complete description of the values of the fields is as follows :
First visit : m(x) = 0, q = pred(x), l(x) = left(x), r(x) = right(x)

{x is visited after leaving its predecessor}

Second visit : m(x) = 1, q = left(x), l(x) = right(x), r(x) = pred(x)
    {x is visited on returning from marking its left successor graph}

Third visit : m(x) = 2, q = right(x), l(x) = pred(x), r(x) = left(x)
    {after marking the right successor graph}

The final transition puts l and r back to their original values, m(x) to 3 and x
goes back to its first predecessor.

4. FORM OF TRANSITIONS

Consider the first visit to node x, that is the case where m(x) = 0. The next
node to be visited is either the left successor of x, if this left successor exists,
or x itself, ready to try the right successor. This gives us the following
(explanations follow) :

$$m(x) = 0 \land m(l(x)) = 0 \rightarrow$$
$$m(x) := 1$$
$$x, l(x), r(x), q := l(x), r(x), q, x$$
$$m(x) = 0 \land m(l(x)) \neq 0 \rightarrow$$
$$m(x) := 1 ;$$
$$l(x), r(x), q := r(x), q, l(x)$$

The left successor of x is in l(x). Hence the test m(l(x)) = 0 decides whether the
left successor is free to be visited. The multiple assignment assures the successor
function, leaving the values at node x is the correct state. In particular, x takes
the left successor node (l(x)), l(x) takes the right successor (r(x)) in conformity
with the situation corresponding to m(x) = 1, r(x) takes the predecessor value (q),
and q the new predecessor value, that is to say x, which is the node the algorithm
is leaving. However, if the left successor is not followed, then x remains at the
same node, and we simply make the transitions necessary for the values relative to
m(x) = 1. That is l(x) takes the right sucessor (r(x)), r(x) takes the predecessor
(q), and q takes the new, virtual predecessor (l(x)), since m(x) = 1 is reached when
"coming back" after marking the left successor.

Carrying out the same logic for m(x) = 1, where we need to follow the right
successor, we similarly obtain two cases :

```
    m(x) = 1 ∧ m(l(x)) = 0 →
          m(x) := 2 ;
       x, l(x), r(x), q := l(x), r(x), q, x
    m(x) = 1 ∧ m(l(x)) ≠ 0 →
          m(x) := 2 ;
          l(x), r(x), q := r(x), q, l(x)
```

Note that the right successor is in $l(x)$ when $m(x) = 1$, and so the test for taking this successor is the same as in the previous case. In addition, and this is why the choice of representation is so powerful, because of the "rotation" of values amongst $l(x)$, $r(x)$ and q, the multiple assignments turn out to be the same as in the previous case.

Finally, we are not now surprised that we obtain a similar situation when $m(x) = 2$, where the predecessor function is applied :

```
    m(x) = 2 →
          x, l(x), r(x), q := l(x), r(x), q, x
```

Putting all these transitions back into the program, and "factorising" the program where possible, we obtain the elegant program :

```
x := root ; q := 0 ;
while m(root) ≠ 3
do    m(x) := m(x) + 1 ;
      if m(x) = 3 cor m(l(x)) = 0
             → x, l(x), r(x), q := l(x), r(x), q, x
      ☐ m(x) ≠ 3 cand m(l(x)) ≠ 0
             ↦ l(x), r(x), q := r(x), q, l(x)
      fi
done
```

5. CONCLUSION

This exercise was done in order to explain how the program considered may be derived, and to illustrate informally the different techniques which should be acquired and applied by programmers. The techniques fall into two main categories, which are the basic logic needed to produce correct programs, and the transformation and manipulation techniques which may improve them, or adapt them to available equipment. A very large number of research workers have considered different aspects of these problems. To avoid difficulties, let us simply quote E.W. Dijkstra and

F.L. Bauer, who, at this course, may be seen to be representative of what has been seen as two schools of thought.

Of course, in practice, there are also many other so-called schools, many of which allow us to learn new ways of attacking classes of problems. This multiplicity of ideas is positive and fruitful, and the subject is certainly not exhausted. The only danger in the situation would come if the differences between schools was felt as opposition rather than as complementarity. Some readers and students appear to have fallen into this trap in spite of the fact that very few of the research workers themselves are interested in claiming any monopoly of the truth.

The moral we wish to draw is thus that successful programmers will use techniques from different sources as and when the techniques concerned are the most apt to be applied to the problem considered. The difficulty is to choose the right technique at the right moment. There is here a parallel with mathematical theorems, where different proof lines will give proofs of varying elegance and interest. It is not from one example or set of examples that we can establish qualitative hierarchies of methods.

In practical terms, as a professional teacher, the author hopes that his colleagues will make sure that their students receive an education which respects the different contributions made to programming expertise by a demonstration of the essential unity of concept which lies behind a multitude of theories.

REFERENCES

F.L. BAUER, K. SAMELSON (eds.)
    Language Hierarchies and Interfaces
    Springer Verlag, Lecture Notes in Computer Science, 46, 1976

E.W. DIJKSTRA
    Guarded Commands, Non-Determinacy and a Calculus for the Derivation of
    Programs in [Bauer, Samelson 1976]

D. GRIES
    The Schorr-Waite Marking Algorithm
    This volume

M. GRIFFITHS
    Program Production by Successive Transformation
    in [Bauer, Samelson 1976]

P.C. SCHOLL
    Introduction à la Récursivité et aux Arbres
    Université de Grenoble, July 1977

H. SCHORR, W.M. WAITE
    An Efficient Machine Independent Procedure for Garbage Collection in
    Various List Structures
    CACM, Aug. 1967

A DERIVATION-ORIENTED PROOF OF THE SCHORR-WAITE MARKING ALGORITHM

Susan L. Gerhart
USC Information Sciences Institute
4676 Admiralty Way
Marina del Rey, CA 90291

This research was supported by the Defense Advanced Research Projects
Agency under contract DAHC-15-72-C-0308.

Approach

There are many ways to formulate and present program proofs. Some of
the inherent problems are finding and formally stating specifications
and invariants, developing and proving a basis of properties for the
program's data types and problem domain, overcoming the sheer complexity
and length of any proof (formal or informal), and avoiding errors in the
proof. This paper uses an approach orthogonal to that presented in
[Gries], which deals mainly with the final, concrete, fully optimized
program. Instead, our approach stresses finding, stating, and proving
parts of the invariants for the final program in clearly separated
stages of a program derivation from a relatively simple, abstract,
non-optimized program.

This approach is aimed at mitigating some of the inherent problems of
proving. First, factoring and accumulating invariants significantly
reduces the complexity of their proofs by clarifying the proof strategy
and reducing interactions of parts. Second, a derivation is a
presentation device which leads the reader gradually into the complexity
of a fully concrete, perhaps highly optimized, final program and its
proof. Third, by starting programs and assertions at a high level, some
of the proof effort may be applied to other programs which satisfy the
same specifications. Fourth, again by clarifying and proving abstract
versions of a program, there are greater opportunities for proof
carry-over if the task is generalized or specialized or the
specifications otherwise changed. Fifth, the derivation process
suggests that there may be "laws" about the structure of assertions by
which ad hoc assertion generation and proof can be avoided. Sixth,
derivations show why programs are written as they are and suggest ways
they may be constructed more rationally.

Our primary purpose here is to contrast this abstract, derivational
approach with Gries' concrete, monolithic approach. Subsequent
discussion will highlight the motivation for and progression of the
derivation. Moreover, this program is also one of a series of examples

being mechanically verified using the ISI program verifier which is
based on algebraic axioms [Guttag] and rewriting rules. One of the
"advantages" of mechanical verification is that program and proof
complexity becomes tangible and possibly overwhelming. The only
recourse is structuring of programming knowledge, assertions, and
proofs, all of which a good verification system will not only force but
also assist. Our approach shows that and how this may be accomplished.
We will later summarize the experience of this mechanical verification
and the proof achieved.

Summary of the Marking Problem

It is assumed that [Gries] has been read, at least with respect to
the problem description. Our view of the task is a little different
from Gries'. Rather than a graph being marked, we see a transitive
closure being computed. Given a Root and a Relation defining links in a
memory structure, the objective is to compute the transitive closure of
the Relation from the Root. The elements of this transitive closure are
the nodes of the graph, "marking" meaning inclusion in this transitive
closure. This view gives us a familiar mathematical context, relations
and transitive closures, in which to perform much of the needed
reasoning. Therefore, it provides the opportunity for carry-over from
and to other problems using the same concepts. Our only differing
assumption will be that m[0] is initially 3 rather than 0. Gries'
program works all right under either assumption, but the process of
marking 0 could confuse the reader (it did this to me).

We will use sets, sequences, and arrays as data structures (see
Appendix 1a for formal axiomatic specifications of these). Our
SetSequence type uses axioms suggested by [Dahl] extended by set
operations over the elements of the sequences. Additionally defined are
the concepts of Relations and Transitive Closure in terms of the
primitive Rel1(i), denoting the elements related to i in some arbitrary
relation (which may be equated in context to another relation, here
defined in terms of the arrays LO and RO containing the Left and Right
links). Equivalent notation for relations is

$$Rel(a)= Ui: i \text{ in } a: Rel1(i) \qquad Tc(a)= Ui: i \text{ in } a: Tc1(i)$$

Tc1 gives the transitive closure starting from one element for the
relation Rel, i.e. Tc1(i)={i} U Tc(Rel1(i)). The data type defined here
is somewhat specialized to this application, whereas a more elaborate
theory structure would probably separate and then combine these types,
e.g. following the ideas in [Burstall].

The Derivation

Appendix 2 gives the key steps of a derivation of Gries' final
program, starting with a level of sets and purely transitive closure
computation, moving through a level of introducing a stack and pointer
to improve this computation, then introducing an array to show "degree
of marking", and finally embedding the stack into the arrays
representing the graph or relation. We will show and discuss the top
level in most detail, emphasizing the method of transition between

levels, and omit some steps in the latter levels.

A key property of transitive closure is that if Rel(A) <= A then Tc(A)=A. That is, if all the elements immediately reachable from A are in A, then A is its own transitive closure. Versions 0a through 0g exploit this property in the invariant. The basic idea used in the initial program 0a is to keep track of two sets Seen and Unsure, where Unsure <= Seen. The immediate descendents of elements of Seen - Unsure have been "seen", i.e. added to the transitive closure, whereas it is not known whether the immediate descendents of elements in Unsure have been "seen". This is expressed as Unsure <= Seen and Rel(Seen-Unsure) <= Seen. The algorithm selects a Seen element with at least one unSeen descendent and Sees its descendents, making it no longer Unsure. (Select(a, x, pred) assigns some value to x from a which satisfies pred).

Version 0b simply transforms the control structure of 0a to remove the excessive computation of Rel(Unsure) <= Seen from the loop test. The assertion also states that Tc1(Root)=Tc(Seen), which becomes Tc1(Root)=Seen when Rel(Seen-Unsure) <= Seen (from the invariant) together with Rel(Unsure) <= Seen from the loop exit gives Rel(Seen) <= Seen. This assertion follows one of the possible "laws" of assertions: when computing a function $f(x)$ to be the value z, state the invariant as $f(x)=g(y)$, where y are the loop variables and $g(y)=z$ upon exit from the loop.

If the property NoDuplicateElements(Unsure) is invariant, then the Select operation can return the last element and return OtherThanLast to perform deletion on Unsure. Program 0c reflects this. Program 0d then separates Seen into its two parts Unsure and Seen-Unsure, introducing a variable Marks to represent Seen-Unsure. Version 0e then uses Marks U Unsure in place of Seen in expressions and Version 0f deletes Seen entirely from the program, denoting its absence by existential quantification in the assertion. Finally this existential quantification can be deleted by using the equality in the assertion, as shown in Version 0g.

Versions 0d-0g illustrate an important pattern of derivation: (1) introduce a variable and prove invariants for it, while not disturbing the control structure or other variables of the program; (2) use the variable in the expressions of the program, based on the properties proved about and between the new and old variables; (3) delete all assignments to the old variable, while existentially quantifying that variable in the assertion. This treatment of "ghost variables" is both useful and legitimate as shown in [Gerhart78]. Here there is an option whether to change the invariant to use the equality Seen = Unsure U Marks or leave Seen existentially quantified; we choose the former here because the abstraction Seen is close to its representation in terms of Unsure and Marks, getting version 0g. As we will see in the final program, this derivation technique retains the abstractions of the initial programs in parts of assertions, thus ameliorating some of the complexity of the concrete details.

Version 1a shows a control and invariant structure which has been found useful at this level of abstraction and efficiency. The variable Finished is initially FALSE and is set TRUE when the loop is to be exited. Of course, this makes it trivial to prove that the invariant implies the postcondition, but more complicated to prove the invariant. There is no significant difference in the amount of proof required, only when it is done. The advantage of this invariant structure is that final and intermediate conditions are not mixed together. Note that at this level we have started to make extensive use of notation (see Appendix 1b), which significantly reduces the visible (but not logical) complexity of the assertion.

Versions 1b - 1d follow the introduce/delete pattern to replace Unsure by Stack apr p. Version 2 starts to make use of the problem-given definition of Rel, namely two pointers stored in arrays LO and RO, as defined in RelLR(i). The expression Rel1(p) <= Marks U Stack apr p, is broken into a property HasBeenSeen applied to each pointer. The Select operation is implemented by ordering the alternatives in the guards.

Getting further into the details of representation, in Version 3a an array m is introduced to tell the degree of "markedness" of an element. Following the introduce-use-remove pattern described above, assignments are made to m on the various branches and invariants are made about m relative to p, Stack, and Marks. Invariant pinv shows how m[p] tells the amount of marking associated with p. Stackinv shows how m[i] tells which link, LO[i] or RO[i], follows i in Stack apr p and what additional marking information is known. m03inv relates the value m[i] when 0 or 3 to the sets Marks and Marks U Stack apr p. In the two steps 3b and 3c, the properties of m are used to remove the predicate HasBeenSeen or place it at a lower level of branching at which it is then used. After a simple transformation in 3d of factoring assignments to m[p] on all branches into a single increment operation, the variable Marks is removed in 3e. We could define Marks as the set of all elements in [1..n] for which m[i]=3, but instead leave the existentially quantified variable Marks in the invariant.

Version 4 replaces the exit condition Finished by the expression p=VirtualRoot, where VirtualRoot is outside the domain of p during looping; in other words VirtualRoot acts like a sentinel. Finally in Version 5a and 5b, the Stack is embedded in the arrays L and R and the variable q. This is described by the property Rotates which shows where the original values of L and R, those in LO and RO, have been permuted and where the current point in the stack is located. Introducing and using q, L, R permits removal of Stack in 5c. Then the branches of the loop body merge together in 5d and 5e to give Gries' version of the algorithm and program.

The Proof

We haven't yet presented any proof of the algorithm, but we now have at least three choices. We can prove the final program as it stands with the invariants accumulated from the derivation. Alternatively, we can prove first the most abstract program and then prove each of the successors in the derivation using correctness-preserving transformations [Gerhart76]. However, there are many programs in this derivation, so a third alternative is to skip some of these, proving each of several successive key (but not consecutive) programs in the standard way. This third approach is being used in the mechanical verification.

The ISI program verifier, AFFIRM, [Musser] uses the axioms for the defined data types (here RArray and SetSequence), together with rules for propositional logic and conditional expressions, as rewrite rules to reduce formulae. A built-in algorithm analyzes and "improves" sets of axioms and deduces equalities. The user of the system must structure the propositions so that rules can be applied without too much interaction between parts; otherwise the formulae will become too large and lose their original structure. A definition mechanism suppresses details of subformulae until the appropriate moment when the details are brought into play during a proof by invoking the definition. Interactively, the user decides which formulae to try, splits up formulae into smaller subgoals, removes extraneous hypotheses, applies lemmas (which, of course, must then or later be proved), invokes definitions, and calls upon the equality decider. The system applies the rewrite rules and maintains a record of the proof. Thus the overall organization of the proof is the responsibility of the human prover, whereas the details of applying logic and axioms and of recording proofs are the responsibility of the mechanical theorem prover.

It is extremely challenging to find a proof in this system. The need for structuring forces absolute understanding and mastery of the problem. Proofs are quite intelligible, because the division of labor between human and system and the need for structuring break the proof into steps which correspond to what we are used to in rigorous and well-organized mathematical proofs. Lemmas of a general nature are extremely valuable for reducing proof effort and can be accumulated as part of their associated types. As of this writing (November 21, 1978) the proof is not complete, but all parts of it have been attempted and the structuring benefits have been attained. The current barriers to a complete proof are simply performance aspects of the AFFIRM system, e.g. excessively large intermediate expressions, inefficiencies of implementation, and human factors of visual (printing of formulae on terminals and transcripts) and command communication and interaction. We are far enough along to have confidence that there are no major errors in the assertions and that proofs will be relatively straightforward, once the right proof steps are found.

The first choice of proof method mentioned above was tried and discarded because the final program was simply too complex. The second choice was also infeasible because we currently lack the technology for correctness-preserving transformations. The third choice has been successful. Verification conditions (lemmas about paths between assertions) were hand-generated for programs 2, 3e, and 5e (see Appendix 3). The verification conditions for one program are used as lemmas for the next on the parts they have in common. The assertion parts for the introduced data structures are proved in the program where they are introduced. We believe that the (really) interested reader can mentally perform a proof using these lemmas and the structure of the definitions in assertions. Simply break each assertion in a verification condition conclusion into components and find the supporting hypotheses which lead to it. Following the derivation should help convince the reader that the assertions hold, since the assertions only state relations between new and old data structures and are only occasionally changed by the transformations between steps. The reader interested in transformations may want to supply these between steps and argue that correctness is preserved by them. Gries' proof provides more verbal descriptions of why the algorithm works as it does.

Further Observations

Notice the form of the invariant on the final concrete program. It is cleanly partitioned into parts associated with variables and data structures which are not present in the programs, but were clearly important during the derivation. All the manipulation of transitive closures was performed at the highest level with the simplest data structures. The rest of the derivation was all manipulation of additional data structures for the purpose of optimizing the program to embed the stack in the pointer structure. This, of course, is a general operation that can be performed in other algorithms than the Schorr-Waite marking algorithm; isolating the properties of the operation performs part of the proof for further uses. Indeed, the marking algorithms of [Knuth] were proved as a class in [Yelowitz] and the derivation method has been applied to proofs of even more complicated list-copying algorithms in [Lee].

One complication due to the mechanization of the proof is that a formal assertion language does not have the ... notation; we can't avoid describing what goes in the elipsed part, especially the boundary conditions. This informality of notation is clearly an advantage to informal proofs (which of course càn be later formalized, if needed).

Gries' proof has some reasoning about VirtualRoots, e.g. m[VirtualRoot]=2, which seems unnecessary. There may be an error in the proof, or just some extraneous argument.

REFERENCES

[Burstall] Burstall, R. W. and Goguen, J. "Putting Theories Together to Make Specifications", Fifth International Joint Conference on Artificial Intelligence, 1977.

[Dahl] Dahl, O. J. "Can Program Proving Be Made Practical?", Institute of Informatics, University of Oslo, 1978.

[Gerhart78] Gerhart, S. "Two Proof Techniques for Transferral of Program Correctness", Duke University Computer Science Department Technical Report, revised and submitted for publication.

[Gerhart76] Gerhart, S. "Proof Theory of Partial Correctness Verification Systems", SIAM Journal of Computing, Vol. 5, No. 3, September 1976.

[Gries] Gries, D. "The Schorr-Waite Graph Marking Algorithm", Lecture Notes for the International Summer School on Program Construction, Munich, Germany, 1978. (this volume)

[Guttag] Guttag, J. "Notes on Data Abstraction", Lecture Notes for the International Summer School on Program Construction, Munich, Germany, 1978. (this volume)

[Knuth] Knuth, D. The Art of Computer Programming, Vol. I, 1973.

[Lee] Lee, S., Gerhart, S. L., and deRoever, W. P. "The Evolution of List-copying Algorithms", Sixth ACM Symposium on Principles of Programming Languages, January 1979.

[Musser] Musser, D. R. "Abstract Data Type Specification in the AFFIRM System", preliminary report available from Information Sciences Institute, November 1978.

[Yelowitz] Yelowitz, L., and Duncan, A. "Abstractions, Instantiations, and Proofs of Marking Algorithms", Proceedings of the Symposium on Artificial Intelligence and Programming Languages, SIGPLAN and SIGART newsletters, August 1977.

APPENDIX 1A : DATA TYPE AXIOMS

```
type RArray;
declare i, j, k : Integer;
declare a, b : RArray;
interfaces assn(a, i, j),  Empty : RArray;
interface a sub i : Integer;
axiom assn(a, i, j) sub k= if k=i then j else a sub k;
end;

type SetSequence;
declare s, s1, s2 : SetSequence;
declare i, i1, i2 : Integer;
interface null, apl(i, s), apr(s, i), join(s, s1), OtherThanFirst(s),
     OtherThanLast(s), seq(i) : SetSequence;
interface First(s), Last(s) : Integer;
interface Length(s) : Integer;
interface isnull(s),  eq(s, s1) : Boolean;

axioms
    i apl null = null apr i,
    i apl (s apr i1) = (i apl s) apr i1,
    null join s = s,
    (s apr i) join s1 = s join (i apl s1),
    s eq s1 = (s = s1),
    seq(i) = null apr i,
    Length(null) = 0,
    Length(s apr i) = Length(s) + 1,
    First(s apr i)  = if isnull(s) then i else First(s),
    OtherThanFirst(s apr i) = if isnull(s) then null
                              else OtherThanFirst(s) apr i,
    Last(s apr i) = i,
    OtherThanLast(s apr i) = s,
    isnull(null) = TRUE,
    isnull(s apr i) = FALSE;
lemmas
    s join (s1 apr i) = (s join s1) apr i,
    s join null = s,
    s join (s1 join s2) = (s join s1) join s2,
    isnull(i apl s) = FALSE,
    isnull(s join s1) = (isnull(s) and isnull(s1)),
    First(i apl s) = i,
    OtherThanFirst(i apl s) = s;

interface i in s : Boolean;
interfaces s union s1, s diff s1, s int s1 : SetSequence;

axioms
    i in null = FALSE,
    i in (s apr i1) = (i in s or i=i1),
    i in (i1 apl s) = (i in s or i=i1),
    i in (s union s1) = (i in s or (i in s1)),
    i in (s diff s1) = (i in s and ~(i in s1)),
```

```
    i in (s int s1) = (i in s and (i in s1));


define s subset s1 = all i (i in s imp (i in s1));
define s seteq s1 = (s subset s1 and s1 subset s);


interfaces Tc(s),Tc1(i):SetSequence;
interfaces Rel(s),Rel1(i):SetSequence;
define i in Rel(s) = some i1 (i1 in s and i in Rel1(i1));
define i in Tc1(i1) = (i=i1
                        or some i2 (i2 in Rel1(i1) and i in Tc1(i2)));
define i in Tc(s) = some i1 (i1 in s and i in Tc1(i1));


interface NoDuplicateElements(s):Boolean;
axioms
    NoDuplicateElements(null)=TRUE,
    NoDuplicateElements(s apr i)=(NoDuplicateElements(s) and ~(i in s)),
    NoDuplicateElements(i apl s)=(NoDuplicateElements(s) and ~(i in s));
end;


Explanation:
    interface f(x):t declares a function f of type t
    define f(x)=... is the same as giving an axiom except
        that the theorem prover only applies the rule
        under explicit invocation.


Notation used in the text and derivation:
    <= for subset, = for seteq, - for diff, U for union
```


APPENDIX 1B: ASSERTION AND PROGRAM NOTATION


```
type DswNotation;
declare i, j, k : Integer;
interface From1Up, From0Up : SetSequence;
define From0Up = (0 apl From1Up);
note These define the sets [1..n] and [0..n];


note the following concepts are used in versions 0-2 in the derivation;
interface Root : Integer;
interface RootInit : Boolean;
axiom RootInit=(Root in From1Up);


declare p : Integer;
declare Stack, Marks : SetSequence;


define Seeninv(p, Stack, Marks)=(NoDuplicateElements(Stack apr p) and
    Marks union (Stack apr p) subset From1Up);


define Tcinv(p, Stack, Marks)=(
    Rel(Marks)  subset  (Marks union (Stack apr p))
    and Tc1(Root) seteq Tc(Marks union (Stack apr p)));


define TcFinal(Marks)=(Tc1(Root) seteq Marks);
```

```
define TcInvariant(p, Stack, Marks, Finished)=
   if Finished then TcFinal(Marks)
   else Seeninv(p, Stack, Marks) and Tcinv(p, Stack, Marks);


note The Following concepts are used in versions 3 and 4;
interfaces L0, R0 : RArray;

define RelLR(i)=
   (if L0 sub i = 0 then null else seq(L0 sub i)) join
   (if R0 sub i = 0 then null else seq(R0 sub i));

define LRInit=
   all i (i in From1Up imp L0 sub i in From0Up and
                          R0 sub i in From0Up);

define HasBeenSeen(i, p, Stack, Marks)=
           (i~=0 imp i in (Marks union (Stack apr p)));

interface m0 : RArray;  declare m : RArray;

define eqc0=(j=0);  define eqc1=(j=1);  define eqc2=(j=2);

define mInit=(m0 sub 0=3 and all i (i in From1Up imp m0 sub i=0));

define m03inv(p, Stack, Marks, m)=(
   all i (i in Marks imp i in From1Up  and m sub i=3) and
   all j (j in (From1Up  diff (Marks union (Stack apr p)))
        imp m sub j=0) );

interface Stackinv(p, Stack, Marks, m) : Boolean;
define Stackinv(p, Stack, Marks, m)=
   (Stack=null or
   (eqc1(m sub Last(Stack)) and p=L0 sub Last(Stack) or
    eqc2(m sub Last(Stack)) and p=R0 sub Last(Stack)
   and HasBeenSeen(L0 sub Last(Stack), Last(Stack),
                   OtherThanLast(Stack), Marks))
   and Stackinv(Last(Stack), OtherThanLast(Stack), Marks, m) );

define pinv(p, Stack, Marks, m)=(
   eqc0(m sub p)
   or eqc1(m sub p) and HasBeenSeen(L0 sub p, p, Stack, Marks)
   or eqc2(m sub p) and HasBeenSeen(L0 sub p, p, Stack, Marks)
                    and HasBeenSeen(R0 sub p, p, Stack, Marks));

define m03Final(m, Marks)=
   all i (i in From1Up  imp m sub i=if i in Marks then 3 else 0);

define mRootFinal(m)=
   all i(i in From1Up imp m sub i=if i in Tc1(Root) then 3 else 0);

define MarksInvariant(p, Stack, m, Finished)=
   some Marks ( TcInvariant(p, Stack, Marks, Finished) and
      if Finished then m03Final(m, Marks)
      else  pinv(p, Stack, Marks, m) and Stackinv(p, Stack, Marks, m)
         and m03inv(p, Stack, Marks, m));
```

note The following concepts are used in version 5;

interface VirtualRoot : Integer;
declare q : Integer;
declare L, R : RArray;

define RootsInit=(Root in From1Up and ~(VirtualRoot in From0Up));

define Rotated(p, Stack, i, j, k)=(LO sub p=i and RO sub p=j and
        if k=VirtualRoot then p=Root and Stack=null
                        else Stack~=null and k=Last(Stack));

interface LRStackinv(Stack, m, L, R) : Boolean;
define LRStackinv(Stack, m, L, R)=
    (Stack=null or
    (eqc1(m sub Last(Stack))and Rotated(Last(Stack),OtherThanLast(Stack),
        LO sub Last(Stack), L sub Last(Stack), R sub Last(Stack)) or
    eqc2(m sub Last(Stack)) and Rotated(Last(Stack),OtherThanLast(Stack),
        R sub Last(Stack), RO sub Last(Stack), L sub Last(Stack)))
    and LRStackinv(OtherThanLast(Stack), m, L, R));

define LRpinv(p, Stack, m, L, R, q)=(
    eqc0(m sub p) and Rotated(p, Stack, L sub p, R sub p, q) or
    eqc1(m sub p) and Rotated(p, Stack, q, L sub p, R sub p) or
    eqc2(m sub p) and Rotated(p, Stack, R sub p, q, L sub p));

define LRotherinv(p, Stack, L, R)=
    all i (i in (From1Up diff (Stack apr p)) imp
        L sub i = LO sub i and R sub i = RO sub i);

define LRFinal(L, R)=
    all i(i in From1Up imp L sub i = LO sub i and R sub i = RO sub i);

define StackInvariant(p, q, m, L, R)=
    some Stack (
    if p=VirtualRoot then MarksInvariant(Root, Stack, m, TRUE)
                        and LRFinal(L,R)
    else MarksInvariant(p,Stack,m,FALSE) and LRStackinv(Stack,m,L,R)
        and LRpinv(p, Stack, m, L, R, q) and LRotherinv(p,Stack,L,R));

end;

APPENDIX 2: DERIVATION

Version 0a: General computation of Transitive Closure

```
declare Root:Integer; declare Seen, Unsure:SetSequence;
assert Root in [1..n];
Seen, Unsure := seq(Root), seq(Root);
asserting Tc1(Root)=Tc(Seen) and Unsure <= Seen <= [1..n]
               and Rel(Seen - Unsure) <= Seen
do ~(Rel(Unsure) <= Seen) ->
   Select(Unsure, next, ~(Rel1(next) <= Seen));
   Seen := Seen U Rel1(next);
   Unsure := (Unsure U Rel1(next)) - (seq(next));
od
assert Tc1(Root)=Seen;
```

```
Variant |Tc1(Root) - Seen|
```

Version 0b: Select then discard or mark further

```
assert Root in [1..n];
Seen, Unsure := seq(Root), seq(Root);
asserting Tc1(Root)=Tc(Seen) and Unsure <= Seen <= [1..n]
               and Rel(Seen - Unsure) <= Seen
do Unsure ≠ null ->
   Select(Unsure, next, TRUE);
   if Rel1(next) <= Seen -
      Unsure := Unsure - (seq(next))>
   [] ~(Rel1(next) <= Seen) ->
      Seen, Unsure := Seen U Rel1(next),
      (Unsure U Rel1(next)) - (seq(next))
   fi
od
assert Tc1(Root)=Seen;
```

```
Variant |Tc1(Root) - (Seen - Unsure) |
```

Version 0c: Treating Unsure as a list

```
declare Root, next, next1 : Integer; declare Seen, Unsure : SetSequence;
assert Root in [1..n];
Seen, Unsure := seq(Root), seq(Root);
asserting Tc1(Root)=Tc(Seen) and Unsure <= Seen <= [1..n]
     and Rel(Seen - Unsure) <= Seen
     and NoDuplicateElements(Unsure)
do Unsure ≠ null ->
   next := Last(Unsure);
   if Rel1(next) <= Seen ->
      Unsure := OtherThanLast(Unsure)
   [] ~(Rel1(next) <= Seen) ->
      Select(Rel1(next), next1, ~(next1 in Seen));
      Seen, Unsure := Seen apr next1, Unsure apr next1
   fi
od
assert Tc1(Root)=Seen;
```

```
Version Od: Separating Seen into Unsure and Marks and deleting Marks
declare Root, next1:Integer; declare Seen, Unsure, Marks:SetSequence;
assert Root in [1..n];
Seen, Unsure, Marks := seq(Root), seq(Root), null;
asserting Tc1(Root)=Tc(Seen) and Unsure <= Seen <= [1..n]
    and Rel(Seen - Unsure) <= Seen and NoDuplicateElements(Unsure)
    and  Marks = (Seen - Unsure)
do Unsure≠null ->
    if Rel1(Last(Unsure)) <= Seen ->
       Unsure, Marks := OtherThanLast(Unsure), Marks apr Last(Unsure)
    [] ~(Rel1(Last(Unsure)) <= Seen) ->
       Select(Rel1(Last(Unsure)), next1, ~(next1 in Seen));
       Seen, Unsure := Seen apr next1, Unsure apr next1;
    fi
od;
assert Tc1(Root)=Seen;


Version Oe: Using Marks U Unsure in place of Seen
<<omitted>>


Version Of: Removal and existential quantification of Seen
assert Root in [1..n];
Unsure, Marks := seq(Root), null;
asserting  some Seen (Tc1(Root)=Tc(Seen) and Unsure <= Seen <=[1..n]
    and Rel(Seen - Unsure) <= Seen and NoDuplicateElements(Unsure)
    and Marks = (Seen - Unsure) )
do Unsure≠null ->
    if Rel1(Last(Unsure)) <= Marks U Unsure ->
       Unsure, Marks := OtherThanLast(Unsure), Marks apr Last(Unsure)
    [] ~(Rel1(Last(Unsure)) <= Marks U Unsure) ->
       Select(Rel1(Last(Unsure)), next, ~(next in Marks U Unsure));
       Unsure := Unsure apr next
    fi
od;
assert some Seen ( Tc1(Root)=Seen);


Version Og: Removal of Seen
assert Root in [1..n];
Unsure, Marks := seq(Root), null;
asserting  Tc1(Root)=Tc(Marks U Unsure) and
      Rel(Marks) <= Marks U Unsure <= [1..n]
      and NoDuplicateElements(Unsure)
do Unsure≠null ->
    if Rel1(Last(Unsure)) <= Marks U Unsure ->
       Unsure, Marks := OtherThanLast(Unsure), Marks apr Last(Unsure)
    [] ~(Rel1(Last(Unsure)) <= Marks U Unsure) ->
       Select(Rel1(Last(Unsure)), next, ~(next in Marks U Unsure));
       Unsure := Unsure apr next>
    fi
od;
assert Tc1(Root)=Marks;
```

Version 1a: Control structure reorganization to simplify exits

```
assert Root in [1..n];
Unsure, Marks, Finished := seq(Root), null, FALSE;
asserting
   if Finished then Tc1(Root)=Marks
   else Unsure≠null and
      Tc1(Root)=Tc(Marks U Unsure)and Rel(Marks)<=Marks U Unsure<=[1..n]
      and NoDuplicateElements(Unsure)
do ~Finished ->
   if Rel1(Last(Unsure)) <= Marks U Unsure ->
      Unsure, Marks := OtherThanLast(Unsure), Marks apr Last(Unsure)
   [] ~(Rel1(Last(Unsure)) <= Marks U Unsure) ->
      Select(Rel1(Last(Unsure)), next, ~(next in Marks U Unsure));
      Unsure := Unsure apr next
   fi
od;
assert Tc1(Root)=Marks;
```

Version 1b: Introduction of p,Stack
<<omitted>>

Version 1c: Use of p, Stack

```
assert Root in [1..n];
Unsure, Marks, Finished, p, Stack := seq(Root), null, FALSE, Root, null;
asserting
   if Finished then Tc1(Root)=Marks
   else  Unsure=(Stack apr p) and
      Tc1(Root)=Tc(Marks U Unsure <= [1..n]) and
      Rel(Marks) <= Marks U Unsure <= [1..n]
      and NoDuplicateElements(Unsure)
do ~Finished ->
   if Rel1(p) <= Marks U (Stack apr p) ->
      if Stack=null ->
         Unsure, Marks, Finished := OtherThanLast(Unsure),
                                    Marks apr p, TRUE
      [] Stack≠null ->
      Unsure,Marks,p,Stack:=OtherThanLast(Unsure),Marks apr p,
            Last(Stack), OtherThanLast(Stack)
      fi
   [] ~(Rel1(p) <= Marks U (Stack apr p)) ->
      Select(Rel1(p), next, ~(next in Marks U (Stack apr p)));
      Unsure, p, Stack := Unsure apr next, next, (Stack apr p)
   fi
od;
assert Tc1(Root)=Marks;
```

Version 1d: Removal and existential quantification of Unsure
<<omitted>>

Version 1e: Complete Removal of Unsure
```
assert Root in [1..n];
Marks, Finished, p, Stack := null, FALSE, Root, null;
asserting
   if Finished then Tc1(Root)=Marks
   else Tc1(Root)=Tc(Marks U (Stack apr p))
      and Rel(Marks) <= Marks U (Stack apr p) <=[1..n]
      and NoDuplicateElements(Stack apr p)

do ~Finished ->
   if Rel1(p) <= Marks U (Stack apr p) ->
      if Stack=null -> Marks, Finished := Marks apr p, TRUE
      [] Stack≠null ->
         Marks, p, Stack :=   Marks apr p, Last(Stack),
                              OtherThanLast(Stack)
      fi
   [] ~(Rel1(p) <= Marks U (Stack apr p)) ->
      Select(Rel1(p), next, ~(next in Marks U (Stack apr p)));
      p, Stack := next, (Stack apr p)
   fi
od;
assert Tc1(Root)=Marks;
```


Version 2: Instantiating Rel1 and abstracting assertions
```
let Rel1(i)=RelLR(i);
assert RootInit and LRInit;
p, Stack, Marks, Finished := Root, null, null, FALSE;
asserting
   if Finished then TcFinal(Marks)
   else Seeninv(p, Stack, Marks) and Tcinv(p, Stack, Marks)
do ~Finished ->
   if HasBeenSeen(LO[p], p, Stack, Marks) and
      HasBeenSeen(RO[p], p, Stack, Marks) ->
      Marks := Marks apr p;
      if Stack=null -> Finished := TRUE
      [] Stack≠null -> p, Stack := Last(Stack), OtherThanLast(Stack)
      fi
   [] HasBeenSeen(LO[p], p, Stack, Marks) and
      ~HasBeenSeen(RO[p], p, Stack, Marks) ->
      p, Stack := RO[p], (Stack apr p)
   [] ~HasBeenSeen(LO[p], p, Stack, Marks) ->
      p, Stack := LO[p], (Stack apr p)
   fi
od;
assert TcFinal(Marks)
```

Version 3a: Introduction and assertion of m
assert RootInit and LRInit and mInit;
p, Stack, Marks, Finished := Root, null, null, FALSE;
asserting
    if Finished **then** TcFinal(Marks) and mO3Final(m, Marks)
    else Seeninv(p, Stack, Marks) and Tcinv(p, Stack, Marks)
        and pinv(p, Stack, Marks, m) and Stackinv(p, Stack, Marks, m)
        and mO3inv(p, Stack, Marks, m)
do ~Finished ->
    if HasBeenSeen(LO[p], p, Stack, Marks) and
    HasBeenSeen(RO[p], p, Stack, Marks) ->
    Marks := Marks apr p; m[p] := 3;
    if Stack=null -> Finished := TRUE
    [] Stack≠null -> p, Stack := Last(Stack), OtherThanLast(Stack)
    fi
    [] HasBeenSeen(LO[p], p, Stack, Marks) and
    ~HasBeenSeen(RO[p], p, Stack, Marks) ->
    p, Stack, m[p] := RO[p], (Stack apr p), 2
    [] ~HasBeenSeen(LO[p], p, Stack, Marks) ->
    p, Stack, m[p] := LO[p], (Stack apr p), 1
    fi
od;
assert TcFinal(Marks) and mO3Final(m, Marks)

Version 3b: Use of m in first level branches>
<<omitted>>

Version 3c: Use of m in second level branches
assert RootInit and LRInit and mInit;
p, Stack, Marks, Finished := Root, null, null, FALSE;
asserting
    if Finished **then** TcFinal(Marks)
    else Seeninv(p, Stack, Marks) and Tcinv(p, Stack, Marks)
    and
    if Finished **then** mO3Final(m, Marks)
    else pinv(p, Stack, Marks, m) and Stackinv(p, Stack, Marks, m)
        and mO3inv(p, Stack, Marks, m)
do ~Finished ->
    if m[p]=2 ->
    Marks := Marks apr p;   m[p] := 3;
    if Stack=null -> Finished := TRUE
    [] Stack≠null -> p, Stack := Last(Stack), OtherThanLast(Stack)
    fi
    [] m[p]=1 ->
    if m[RO[p]]=0 -> p, Stack, m[p] := RO[p], (Stack apr p), 2
    [] m[RO[p]]≠0 -> m[p] := 2;
    fi
    [] m[p]=0 ->
    if m[LO[p]] = 0 and LO[p]≠p ->
        p, Stack, m[p] := LO[p], (Stack apr p), 1
    [] m[LO[p]]≠0 or LO[p]=p -> m[p] := 1
    fi
    fi od ;
assert TcFinal(Marks) and mO3Final(m, Marks)

Version 3d: Factoring m[p] into an increment
<<omitted>>

Version 3e: Removal of Marks

```
assert RootInit and LRInit and mInit;
p, Stack := Root, null;
asserting some Marks (
   if Finished then TcFinal(Marks)
   else Seeninv(p, Stack, Marks) and Tcinv(p, Stack, Marks)
   and
   if Finished then m03Final(m, Marks)
   else pinv(p,Stack,Marks,m) and Stackinv(p,Stack,Marks,m) and
        m03inv(p,Stack,Marks,m)
do ~Finished ->
   m[p] := m[p]+1;
   if m[p]=3 ->
      if Stack=null -> Finished:=TRUE
      [] Stack≠null -> p, Stack := Last(Stack), OtherThanLast(Stack)
      fi
   [] m[p]=2 ->
      if m[R0[p]]=0 -> p, Stack := R0[p], (Stack apr p)
      [] m[R0[p]]≠0 -> Skip
      fi
   [] m[p]=1 ->
      if m[L0[p]]=0 -> p, Stack := L0[p], (Stack apr p)
      [] m[L0[p]]≠0 -> Skip
      fi
   fi
od;
assert some Marks (TcFinal(Marks) and m03Final(m, Marks))
assert mRootFinal(m);
```

Version 4: Replacement of 'Finished' by 'p=VirtualRoot'

```
assert RootsInit and LRInit and mInit;
p, Stack := Root, null;>
asserting
   if p=VirtualRoot then MarksInvariant(Root, Stack, m, TRUE)
   else MarksInvariant(p, Stack, m, FALSE)
do (p≠VirtualRoot) ->
   m[p] := m[p]+1;
   if m[p]=3 ->
      if Stack=null -> p := VirtualRoot
      [] Stack≠null -> p, Stack := Last(Stack), OtherThanLast(Stack)
      fi
      <<same as 3e>>
```

Version 5a: Introduction of q, L, R

```
assert RootsInit and LRInit and mInit;
p, Stack, q := Root, null, VirtualRoot;
asserting
   if p=VirtualRoot ^then> MarksInvariant(p, Stack, m, TRUE)
   else MarksInvariant(p, Stack, m, FALSE) and LRpinv(p, Stack, m, L, R)
       and LRStackinv(Stack, m, L, R) and LRotherinv(p,Stack)
do p≠VirtualRoot ->
   m[p] := m[p]+1;
   if m[p]=3 ->
      if Stack=null -> p, L[p], R[p], q := VirtualRoot, R[p], q, p
      [] Stack≠null -> p, Stack, L[p], R[p], q :=
                       Last(Stack), OtherThanLast(Stack), R[p], q, p
      fi
   [] m[p]=2 ->
      if m[R0[p]]=0 -> p, Stack, L[p], R[p], q :=
                      R0[p], (Stack apr p), R[p], q, p
      [] m[R0[p]]≠0 -> L[p], R[p], q := R[p], q, L[p]
      fi
   [] m[p]=1 ->
      if m[L0[p]]=0 -> p, Stack, L[p], R[p], q :=
                      L0[p], (Stack apr p), R[p], q, p
      [] m[L0[p]]≠0 -> L[p], R[p], q := R[p], q, L[p]
      fi
   fi
od;
assert mRootFinal(m) and LRFinal(L,R)
```

Version 5b: Use of L[p] in second level branches

```
<<same as 5a>>
do p≠VirtualRoot ->
   m[p] := m[p]+1;
   if m[p]=3 ->
      if Stack=null -> p, L[p], R[p], q := L[p], R[p], q, p
      [] Stack≠null -> p, Stack, L[p], R[p], q :=
                       L[p], OtherThanLast(Stack), R[p], q, p
      fi
   [] m[p]=2 ->
      if m[L[p]]=0 -> p, Stack, L[p], R[p], q :=
              L[p], (Stack apr p), R[p], q, p
      [] m[L[p]]≠0 -> L[p], R[p], q := R[p], q, L[p]
      fi
   [] m[p]=1 ->
      if m[L[p]]=0 -> p, Stack, L[p], R[p], q :=
              L[p], (Stack apr p), R[p], q, p
      [] m[L[p]]≠0 -> L[p], R[p], q := R[p], q, L[p]
      fi
   fi
od;
assert mRootFinal(m) and LRFinal(L,R)
```

```
Version 5c: Compression of m[p]=3 branch and removal of 'Stack'
<<omitted>>

Version 5d: merging m[p]=2, m[p]=1 branches
<<same as 5a>>
do p≠VirtualRoot ->
   m[p] := m[p]+1;
   if m[p]=3 ->
       p, L[p], R[p], q := L[p], R[p], q, p
   [] m[p]=2 or m[p]=1->
       if m[L[p]]=0 -> p, L[p], R[p], q := L[p], R[p], q, p
       [] m[L[p]]≠0 -> L[p], R[p], q := R[p], q, L[p]
       fi
   fi
od;
assert mRootFinal(m) and LRFinal(L,R)




Version 5e (Final Program): Merging m[p]=3 and m[L[p]]=0 branches
assert RootsInit and LRInit and mInit;
p, q := Root, VirtualRoot;
asserting some Stack (
   if p=VirtualRoot then MarksInvariant(p, Stack, m, TRUE)
   else MarksInvariant(p, Stack, m, FALSE) and LRpinv(p, Stack, m, L, R)
       and LRStackinv(Stack, m, L, R) and LRotherinv(p,Stack)
do p≠VirtualRoot ->
   m[p] := m[p]+1;
   if m[p]=3 or m[L[p]]=0 ->
       p, L[p], R[p], q := L[p], R[p], q, p
   [] m[p]≠3 and m[L[p]]≠0 ->
       L[p], R[p], q := R[p], q, L[p]
   fi
od;
assert mRootFinal(m) and LRFinal(L,R)
```

APPENDIX 3: VERIFICATION CONDITIONS

<u>type</u> DswBasis;
<u>declare</u> p, q : Integer; <u>declare</u> Marks, Stack : SetSequence;
<u>declare</u> m, L, R : RArray; <u>declare</u> Finished : Boolean;

<u>note</u> The following vcs are for Program 3e;

<u>define</u> vcTcin= (RootInit and LRInit
                        imp TcInvariant(Root, null, null, FALSE));

<u>define</u> casesTc(p, Stack, Marks, Finished)=
   if HasBeenSeen(LO sub p,p,Stack,Marks)
          and HasBeenSeen(RO sub p,p,Stack,Marks)
   then if Stack=null then TcInvariant(p, Stack, Marks apr p, TRUE)
       else TcInvariant(Last(Stack), OtherThanLast(Stack),
                        Marks apr p, Finished)
   else if HasBeenSeen(LO sub p,p,Stack,Marks) and
           ~HasBeenSeen(RO sub p,p,Stack,Marks)
      then TcInvariant(RO sub p, Stack apr p, Marks, Finished)
   else if ~HasBeenSeen(LO sub p, p, Stack, Marks)
      then TcInvariant(LO sub p, Stack apr p, Marks, Finished)
   else FALSE;

<u>define</u> vcTcaround(p, Stack, Marks, Finished)=
   (RootInit and LRInit and TcInvariant(p,Stack,Marks,Finished)
and ~Finished
    imp   casesTc(p, Stack, Marks, Finished));

<u>define</u> vcTcout(p, Stack, Marks, Finished)=
    (RootInit and LRInit and TcInvariant(p,Stack,Marks,Finished)
and Finished
    imp   TcFinal(Marks));

<u>note</u> The following vcs are for program 3e;

<u>define</u> vcMarksin= (RootInit and LRInit and mInit imp
   MarksInvariant(Root, null, m0, FALSE));

<u>define</u> casesMarks(p, Stack, m, Finished)=
   if eqc2(m sub p-1) then
      if Stack=null then MarksInvariant(p, Stack, m; TRUE)
      else MarksInvariant(Last(Stack),OtherThanLast(Stack),m,Finished)
   else if eqc1(m sub p - 1) then
      if eqc0(m sub (RO sub p))
      then MarksInvariant(RO sub p, Stack apr p, m, Finished)
      else MarksInvariant(p, Stack, m, Finished)
   else if eqc0(m sub p - 1) then
      if eqc0(m sub (LO sub p))

```
      then MarksInvariant(L0 sub p, Stack apr p, m, Finished)
      else MarksInvariant(p, Stack, m, Finished)
   else FALSE;

define vcMarksaround(p, Stack, m, Finished)=
   (RootInit and LRInit and mInit and
   MarksInvariant(p, Stack, m, Finished) and ~Finished imp
   casesMarks(p, Stack, assn(m, p, (m sub p)+1), Finished));

define vcMarksout(p, Stack, m, Finished)=
   (RootInit and LRInit and mInit and
   MarksInvariant(p, Stack, m, Finished) and Finished imp
   some Marks(TcFinal(Marks) and mO3Final(m,Marks)));

define vcMarkspost(m, Marks)=
   (some Marks(TcFinal(Marks) and mO3Final(m,Marks)) imp mRootFinal(m));


note The following vcs are for Program 5e (the final program);

define vcStackin= (RootsInit and LRInit and mInit imp
   StackInvariant(Root, VirtualRoot, m0, L0, R0));

define casesStack(p, q, m, L, R)=
   if eqc2(m sub p - 1) or eqc0(m sub (L sub p)) then
      StackInvariant(L sub p, p, m, assn(L, p, R sub p), assn(R, p, q))
   else  StackInvariant(p, L sub p, m, assn(L, p, R sub p), assn(R, p, q));

define vcStackaround(p, q, m, L, R)=
   (RootsInit and LRInit and mInit and
   StackInvariant(p, q, m, L, R) and p~=VirtualRoot imp
   casesStack(p, q, assn(m, p, m sub p + 1), L, R));

define vcStackout(p, q, m, L, R)=
   (RootsInit and LRInit and mInit and
   StackInvariant(p, q, m, L, R) and p=VirtualRoot imp
   mRootFinal(m) and LRFinal(L,R)
end;
```

IV. SPECIAL LANGUAGE CONSIDERATIONS AND FORMAL TOOLS

Languages as Tools - Interactive Program Construction

Computers are powerful information management tools. Programs are themselves information, and computers can assist in all aspects of their construction. The deficiencies of currently available tools suggest some clear next steps towards an integrated programming environment. It is interesting to speculate about systems for programming in the mid to late 1980's.

Programming languages can have a significant effect on the reliability of the programming process, on the ability to remove or tolerate program faults, and on the possibility of reasoning about programs. These effects are of concern when using a particular language, choosing the language in which to program, and designing new languages.

J. J. Horning

Programing Languages for Reliable Computing Systems

J. J. Horning

Xerox Palo Alto Research Center

PART I—THE RELIABILITY OF THE PROGRAMMING PROCESS

INTRODUCTION

This lecture provides an overview of a series of lectures being presented in an advanced course on computing systems reliability. Many different approaches to obtaining reliability are being considered in that course; they all have in common the need for (at least) nearly-correct programs. The experience of the last thirty years shows that it is generally not easy to produce such programs. This leads us to consider the programming process itself as a major source of difficulty in the development of reliable systems.

It is the goal of *reliable programming* to minimize the number of faults in completed programs. This may involve reducing the number of faults introduced during program construction and/or increasing the fraction of faults that are detected and corrected before the program is put into service. Both management tools and technical tools have been proposed for this purpose, and both can play important roles (although neither is an acceptable substitute for the use of the best available programmers).

Management tools

The structure of the team producing a system may influence the reliability of the programming process. Chief Programmer Teams [Baker 1972, 1975], in addition to various technical tools, impose a definite hierarchical structure on the programming team, with specialized functions and clearly delineated responsibilities. Egoless Programming [Weinberg 1971], while sharing many of the same technical tools, encourages a much more flexible structure and a high degree of shared responsibility. Both techniques require that all programs be read and understood by at least one person besides the author before being compiled.

Parnas [1971] has pointed out that management control of the information flow within a project can significantly affect both system structure and programming reliability. He proposes that formal policies be adopted to ensure that each programmer has access to just the information needed to produce a particular program module, and that systems be structured so that this amount of information will be small.

J. J. HORNING

Finally, management can attempt to keep programmers aware that reliable programming is both practicable and desirable. Methods may range from a substantial (and highly visible) reward structure for producing fault-free programs, down to something as modest as a simple statement in the specifications that reliability is one of the important factors [Weinberg 1973].

Technical tools

Many technical tools to support reliable programming are becoming well-known [ICRS 1975]; several are being discussed in detail by other lecturers in this course. Each of them makes at least modest demands on the language in which programming is done: some demand the availability of particular language features (or the exclusion of others); most require facilities for modularizing a program in such a way that the consequences of particular design decisions can be isolated; some may require even more elaborate support. Excellent expositions of the aims and techniques of "structured programming" are contained in Dahl, Dijkstra, and Hoare [1972], Gries [1974], Dijkstra [1976], and Turski [1978].

This lecture is not primarily concerned with programming methodology; rather, we will be looking at the effects that the programming language can have within a fixed methodology.

The effect of programming languages on programming reliability

The programming language and system used in program development influence the probability of producing correct programs more than any other single tool. Thus it is important to use languages that assist reliable programming. However, newer programming languages are not automatically better in this respect. They are only likely to be so if language designers consciously set out to make them so, and if their customers make reliability a criterion in choosing a language.

Programming reliability was an explicit design goal of the original FORTRAN project [Backus et al. 1957]. However, it has largely dropped from sight in later language design projects (including the various revisions of FORTRAN). This neglect has had serious consequences. The cost of software is soaring past the cost of the hardware on which it runs [Boehm 1973], and dealing with software faults and their consequences (debugging, patching, system integration and test, etc.) has remained the dominant component of software costs. Furthermore, software is undoubtedly the major source of unreliability in most computer systems today.

There are many ways in which a programming language affects the reliability of the programming process, of which we will discuss five: masterability, fault-proneness, understandability, maintainability, and checkability.

If programmers are consistently to produce nearly-correct programs, they must be masters of their programming language. They must know what every construct means and how to use it effectively. The experimental approach to programming ("try it and see what happens") must be ruled out, as must the use of a language so complex that programmers do not understand it in its entirety. "Powerful" features are acceptable only if they are easy to use correctly. Simplicity of the language is a necessary, but not sufficient, condition—the language must encourage the production of simple, yet elegant, programs.

PROGRAMMING LANGUAGES FOR RELIABLE COMPUTING SYSTEMS

Some language constructs are easy to understand, yet are fault-prone in actual use. As will be discussed later, even such seemingly trivial things as the rules controlling the use of the semicolon as a statement separator or terminator can cause order-of-magnitude changes in the number of faults introduced by programmers. After the fault-prone constructs in a language are identified, it is often possible to redesign them and thereby reduce dramatically the number of faults, at no cost in "power," and with little or no inconvenience to the programmer.

Ultimately, the most powerful weapon against incorrect programs is the understanding of those who write and check them. Thus, understandability must be our touchstone. The primary function of any language is communication, and programming languages should be chosen with as much concern for readability as compilability. Programmers need to understand not only the semantics of their language, but also the meanings of particular programs written in the language. It is not sufficient to be able to deduce the computation that will be invoked by a particular set of inputs; it is necessary to be able to see "what is being accomplished" at a higher level of abstraction. The communicative power of the language is largely determined by the degree to which it permits programmers to state their *intentions* along with the instructions needed to carry them out. (Experience has shown that comments and mnemonic variable names are not completely adequate for this communication, especially since they are not uniformly updated when the programmer's intentions change.)

Useful programs are continually modified. Generally, the maintenance process begins even before the program is complete, as its authors respond to changed requirements, new insights, and detected faults or inefficiencies. Maintenance itself must not introduce too many new faults. It is impractical to completely re-analyze a large program after each change, to verify its continued correctness, so we must rely on local scrutiny. A language can be of substantial assistance if it makes it possible to isolate completely the consequences of a change to within a known (and preferably small) region of the source program.

Finally, languages differ widely in the amount and kind of error-checking that their implementations can perform. Such checking always relies on a certain amount of redundancy built into the language (although many kinds of redundancy are of little assistance in error-checking). On those occasions in which programs do contain faults, the promptitude and quality of diagnostics will largely control the speed and certainty of their removal. The ideal is for every likely error in the programming process to transform a correct program into one whose fault is detectable by the system as an error.

INJECTION, DETECTION, DIAGNOSIS, AND REMOVAL OF FAULTS

Fault injection

Faults enter programs in many different ways:

Program specifications may be incomplete or ambiguous, or may simply fail to reflect the customer's intentions.

Program designers may overlook interactions among various parts of the system.

Programmers may misinterpret specifications, design algorithms or data structures incorrectly, or misunderstand some aspects of their programming language.

J. J. HORNING

Mechanical errors during coding, transcription, or entry of the program may introduce faults into the program text.

Faults from many different sources may frequently cause some of the same symptoms, but the chances of the language system providing useful diagnostics increase somewhat as we move down the list, due to the kinds of redundancy available in most languages.

Error detection

We want faults to be detected as errors. All error detection (mechanical or human) is based on redundancy. Thus, the symptom of an error is always an inconsistency between two or more pieces of information that are supposed to agree. For example, a program's output may be compared with its specifications; if the specifications prohibit some outputs, there is a possibility of conflict, and hence of error detection. Similarly, if not all possible inputs to a compiler are acceptable, some programming faults can be detected as errors—the fraction will depend on the amount and kind of redundancy in the source language.

Frequently, if somewhat inaccurately, we name errors by the phase in the programming language system that detects them. Thus, we refer to *lexical errors, syntactic errors, semantic errors, run-time errors,* and *output errors.* Associated with each class of errors are a class of faults most likely to cause them; finally, there are faults not detected by the system at all, called *undetected faults.*

In general, the earlier an error is detected, the less persistent its associated fault will be. The difference between detecting an error at compile time or not is particularly pronounced. For example, Gannon obtained the following results for the average persistence of the faults associated with various classes of errors in the TOPPS and TOPPSII languages [Gannon 1975]:

lexical errors,   1.00 runs;

syntactic errors,   1.34 runs;

semantic errors,   1.24 runs;

run-time errors,   5.78 runs;

output errors,   8.52 runs;

undetected faults, 6.02 runs.

This general pattern was observed even when faults that caused run-time or output errors in TOPPS caused syntactic or semantic errors in TOPPSII. For example, the average persistence of faults in which = was substituted for := (or *vice versa*) was 7.13 runs in TOPPS and 1.42 runs in TOPPSII. Clearly, the amount and location of error detection has a major influence on programming reliability.

Error diagnosis

It is not sufficient to tell programmers that their programs contain one or more faults. To a very large extent, the helpfulness of the diagnostics in locating and explaining detected errors will determine their efficiency in removing faults.

Good error messages will exhibit a number of characteristics:

they will be *user-directed*, reporting problems in terms of what the user has done, not what has happened in the compiler;

they will be *source-language-oriented*, rather than containing mysterious internal representations or portions of machine code;

they will be as *specific* as possible;

they will *localize* the error, and if possible, the fault;

they will be *complete*;

they will be *readable* (in the programmer's natural language);

they will be *restrained* and *polite*.

One of the hardest things to remember in designing error diagnostics is that you don't know what fault *caused* the error. Two or more pieces of information have been found to be inconsistent, but it cannot be said with certainty where the fault lies. The safest strategy is to describe the error (the detected inconsistency) as clearly as possible before attempting to make any suggestion about the nature of the fault. Error symptoms should be described in a positive fashion wherever possible, e.g., "A right parenthesis was expected, but a semicolon was found," rather than "Missing right parenthesis."

The diagnosis of errors detected at run time should follow the same general principles as compile-time diagnosis. However, these standards can only be achieved with some forethought, and many otherwise excellent compilers abdicate all responsibility in this domain to an operating system totally unequipped to deal reasonably with run-time errors—the result is a cryptic message and a memory dump.

It is sometimes argued that efficiency considerations preclude any run-time checking or diagnosis. However, Satterthwaite [1972] has demonstrated that the cost of superb run-time checking and diagnosis can be very modest in a properly-designed system.

Fault removal

The development of systems that automatically remove faults from programs is a problem in artificial intelligence that is well beyond the present state of the art. For the foreseeable future, we must rely on humans to read programs and understand them sufficiently well to spot and correct their faults. Thus our repeated emphasis on program readability.

EMPIRICAL EVIDENCE

We cannot logically prove that particular programming language features will enhance the reliability of the programming process, much less derive the amount of improvement by analysis. However, it is possible to gather empirical evidence that tends to confirm or refute such claims by measuring the amount of improvement (or lack thereof) in actual situations. We can observe programmers at work and examine the programs they create. Experiments can be designed to investigate portions of the programming process, and to reduce the bulk of raw data the simple observation yields. However, experiments also have drawbacks [Weinberg 1971]. The behaviour of the subjects in an experiment may be so constrained that effects that are important in practice never appear.

J. J. HORNING

Experiments

There have been a number of experimental studies of the relationship between programming languages and programming reliability, e.g., [Gould and Drongowski 1972], [Gould 1973], [Sime et al. 1973], [Miller 1973], [Miller 1974], [Shneidermann 1974], [Weissman 1974], [Gannon 1975], [Gannon 1977], [Love 1977]. We will discuss a few of Gannon's results.

TOPPS vs. TOPPSII. Gannon conducted a carefully controlled experiment to measure the effects on reliability of nine particular language design decisions, in the context of a complete programming language. The experiment involved observing the faults in programs written by reasonably experienced programmers (graduate and fourth-year undergraduate students in an operating systems course, including part-time students with industrial experience) using two languages to write rather small (75-200 lines), but fairly sophisticated (i.e., involving concurrency) programs. The languages had equivalent power, and differed only in ways that were expected to affect reliability. None of the subjects had prior experience in either language.

For the purposes of the study, a language was judged to enhance programming reliability if the faults introduced in the programming process were less frequent and less persistent. In addition to this overall comparison, the frequency and persistence of faults attributable to each redesigned feature were compared.

The experiment showed that in the environment studied, several language design decisions affected reliability significantly. The control language, TOPPS, had been used "satisfactorily" in that environment for several years, and each of its "bad" features is shared with other, more widely-used languages. Yet a few simple changes produced striking results.

In using the semicolon as a separator, rather than a statement terminator, TOPPS was following a long and honorable tradition (Algol 60, Pascal, BLISS, etc.). However, the TOPSII form (similar to that of PL/I) led to an order of magnitude reduction in the number of semicolon faults (from 11.4 per program to 1.3 per program). Of course, most semicolon faults are rather trivial (i.e., they generally do not persist more than one run). However, a small modification to the language would have eliminated faults that occurred in more than a quarter of all compilations. It is interesting to note that over 14% of the faults occurring in TOPPS programs during the second half of the experiment were still semicolon faults (compared to 1% for TOPPSII), and that missing semicolons were about as common as extra ones.

At the other end of the scale are four classes of infrequent faults with very high persistence:

	TOPPS	TOPPSII
assignment faults	7.1 runs	1.4 runs
inheritance faults	9.8 runs	1.7 runs
expression evaluation faults	8.6 runs	non-existent
relation-connector faults	11.5 runs	1.0 runs

The persistence of each of these classes of faults in TOPPS was about half the average number of runs needed to complete a program (16.1). It is reasonable to assume that these faults would be even more persistent in larger programs, adding even greater weight to the already significant improvements made by TOPPSII. Furthermore, the relative frequencies of these four classes of faults in TOPPS approximately doubled in the second half of the experiment, making it seem unlikely that they are solely due to unfamiliarity with these language features.

PROGRAMMING LANGUAGES FOR RELIABLE COMPUTING SYSTEMS

The fault of substituting = for := or *vice versa* was statically detectable as an error in TOPPSII, but not in TOPPS. The persistence of these "assignment faults" in TOPPS calls into serious question the treatment of the assignment symbol := as "just another operator." Expression-oriented languages using this convention (e.g., Algol 68) may cause unsuspected reliability problems. Other expression-oriented languages using an assignment operator quite different from = (e.g., ← in APL and BLISS) probably avoid some of these faults, but provide no better error detection.

The TOPPSII restrictions on inheritance of environment reduced the persistence of subtle faults (i.e., those that could not be detected at compile time) at the cost of introducting a few more trivial faults. This would seem to support the claim that the unrestricted use of global variables is harmful [Wulf and Shaw 1973]. However, the TOPPSII inheritance faults that were not detected syntactically had a persistence of 6.7 runs, which demonstrates that its simple restrictions were insufficient to eliminate completely the unreliability due to these faults.

The expression evaluation rules of TOPPS are similar to those of APL. Only two programmers (one in each group) had previously programmed in APL, while all but one had experience using some language (not to mention mathematics) with left-to-right association and traditional operator precedence. Thus, the greater *frequency* of errors in TOPPS may be at least partially explained in terms of prior experience. However, the high *persistence* of these errors seems incompatible with the claims for the benefits of "naturalness" sometimes made for the APL rules. Similarly, errors involving infix relation-connectors (logical operators) seem to be difficult to find and remove.

NT vs. ST. More recently, Gannon [1977] has conducted experiments evaluating the effect of data types on programming reliability. He studied programmer performance on relatively simple problems using a "typeless" language, NT, in which all variables are treated simply as single words, as in BCPL or BLISS, and a statically typed language, ST, with declarations for variables of type integer, string, or integer or string array. Some of the more interesting comparisons were:

	ST	NT
runs to complete program	11.6	19.1
faults in submitted programs	0.2	0.6
faults during first program development	51.7	125.8
faults during second program development	31.4	99.6

LANGUAGE DESIGN FOR PROGRAMMING RELIABILITY

This section surveys several ways in which languages can be designed to improve the reliability of programming. The language designer must make a sensible selection from a multitude of language features that have been proposed, and combine these features into a coherent whole that can be used reliably. "One thing he should not do is to include untried ideas of his own. His task is consolidation, not innovation." [Hoare 1973]

Contraction

Ironically, one of the best ways to improve the reliability of programming is to judiciously reduce the size of the programming language. "The most important decisions in language design concern what is to be left out" [Wirth 1971a]. There are two principal reasons for leaving most language features that been proposed out of any particular language: certain language features are known to have negative effects on reliability, and

J. J. HORNING

simplicity is itself a very considerable virtue.

There is by now an abundant literature on "harmful" language features. Generally, each article identifies a feature that detracts from program structure or readability, and argues that it should be replaced with more restricted (and more easily understood) features. A list of current candidates for removal (some more hotly contested than others) includes:

go to statements [Dijkstra 1968][Knuth 1974], the first publicly proposed candidate;

global variables [Wulf and Shaw 1973];

pointers [Hoare 1975];

selection by position [Ichbiah and Rissen 1971], long parameter lists and case statements are principal offenders;

assignment statements [Strachey 1973], in their unrestricted form they are as de-structuring as go tos;

defaults and implicit type conversions [Hoare 1973], they hide too many program faults;

duplication [Clark and Horning 1973], useless redundancy at its worst.

However, great care must be taken to insure that "harmful" features are not simply replaced by something equally mischievious, and probably more complex; if one "harmful" feature is replaced by several "good" features, the language will expand, rather than contract.

An even more difficult task for the language designer is rejecting enough (separately) *good* features to keep his language as small and simple as it must be. Since languages inevitably grow, it is far better to start with a language that is too small than with one that is even slightly too big.

"A necessary condition for the achievement of any of these objectives is the utmost simplicity in the design of the language. Without simplicity, even the language designer himself cannot evaluate the consequences of his design decisions. Without simplicity, the compiler writer cannot achieve even reliability, and certainly cannot construct compact, fast and efficient compilers. But the main beneficiary of simplicity is the user of the language. In all spheres of human intellectual and practical activity, from carpentry to golf, from sculpture to space travel, the true craftsman is the one who thoroughly understands his tools. And this applies to programmers too. A programmer who fully understands his language can tackle more complex tasks, and complete them quicker and more satisfactorily than if he did not. In fact, a programmer's need for an understanding of his language is so great, that it is almost impossible to persuade him to change to a new one. No matter what the deficiencies of his current language, he has learned to live with them; he has learned how to mitigate their effects by discipline and documentation, and even to take advantage of them in ways which would be impossible in a new and cleaner language which avoided the deficiency.

"It therefore seems especially necessary in the design of a new programming language, intended to attract programmers away from their current high level language, to pursue the goal of simplicity to an extreme, so that a programmer can readily learn and remember all its features, can select the best facility for each of his purposes, can fully understand the effects and consequences of each decision, and can then concentrate the major part of his intellectual effort to understanding his problem and his programs rather than his tool." [Hoare 1973]

Redundancy and error detection

One of the major ways in which programming languages differ is in the amount of error-checking that they permit. Some languages have carried the goal of conciseness to such an extreme that almost any fault will transform a valid program into another "valid" (i.e., not detectably inconsistent program). This is false economy. Not only is a certain amount of redundancy needed for easy readability, but mechanical error detection is one of the most important contributions of high-level languages.

Not all redundancy contributes to error detection. Assembly languages are highly redundant, but since any sequence of valid instructions must be accepted as valid, there are few opportunities for effective error checking. Some forms of redundancy invite faults by requiring that duplicate information be provided. For example, the external attribute in PL/I (like the common statement in FORTRAN) permits separately compiled procedures to share variables. However, if the variables are not declared identically in each of the procedures, the fault may not be detected until run time. By contrast, the mechanisms for separate compilation in the SUE System Language [Clark and Horning 1973] and Mesa [Mitchell *et al.* 1978] require only a single identifier to be duplicated to permit sharing of variables and complete type checking.

To be effective, redundancy must cause likely faults to transform valid programs into detectably erroneous ones. We do not want a compiler to be overly "forgiving." If programmers write statements that do not conform to their stated intentions, it is better to warn them than to interpret the statements "reasonably."

Any form of redundancy will lengthen the program text, thereby increasing the opportunity for "clerical" faults. Thus, we should be careful only to introduce redundancy that leads to the detection of more faults than it causes.

Error detection by humans. To find faults, humans must read programs and spot inconsistencies; these detected errors may take the form of inconsistencies within the program itself, inconsistencies with specifications, or inconsistencies with informal expectations. Relatively little is known about the psychology of program readability [Weissman 1974], but a few general things can be said about inconsistency detection:

> First, it helps if the inconsistent items are close to each other, and the part of the program that must be checked for consistency is small; machines are better at global analysis than humans.

> Second, inconsistency between a pair of items is much easier to see than an inconsistency that is only detectable by simultaneously considering a large number of items.

> Third, direct inconsistencies are more easily detected than those that are only derivable through long chains of inference.

These three considerations help to explain why mandatory declaration, including static typing of variables, contributes so much to human error detection. (It also has other merits, discussed later.) A declaration can collect and make explicit information that is otherwise distributed in implicit form throughout the program. These considerations also justify the use of modularity and explicit interfaces as tools for human understanding.

For easy readability, languages should be "well punctuated," i.e., it should be easy for the reader to directly determine statement types and major subunits, without intermediate inferences (e.g., counting blanks). This generally means the use of distinct structural words (keywords, reserved words) for distinct concepts, and avoidance of the multiple use of symbols unless they serve completely analogous functions (e.g., parentheses for grouping, commas for separating all types of lists). The meaning of a statement should be readily apparent, and unimpaired by elaborate rules for implicit conversions between types or context-dependent interpretations. An effective test of whether a language is "well punctuated" is to try to read and discuss programs over the telephone.

Lexical and spelling errors. Some faults—generally caused by mechanical errors in program preparation—can be detected purely by lexical analysis. Each token class of a language has its own formation rules, any violation of which signals an error. Many faults can be classified as *delimiter faults* involving tokens that start and end with particular symbols (e.g., comments and quoted strings). Failure to terminate such a token with the appropriate delimiter may cause much of the following program text to be inadvertently absorbed into the token. To limit the effects of such faults and speed their detection, some languages bound the length of these tokens, typically by limiting them to a single line.

Many mechanical faults in program production lead to *spelling errors*, in which tokens are well-formed, but undeclared, identifiers. Morgan [1970] claims that 80% of the spelling errors in typical programs involve insertion, replacement, or deletion of a single character, or the transposition of a pair of adjacent characters. In languages that do not require the declaration of identifiers, spelling errors must be treated as implicit declarations. However, mandatory declaration makes it possible to detect many program entry faults at compile time, particularly if programmers are encouraged to use long, dissimilar identifiers. A system such as DWIM [Teitelman 1972] may use several sorts of redundancy to suggest corrections for lexical and spelling errors.

Syntactic errors. Syntactic analysis not only plays a central role in the organization of compilers, it is also the focal point of error detection and diagnosis within compilers. Because syntactic specifications are precise, it is possible to develop parsers that accept exactly the specified languages; because they are formal, it is possible to prove that the parsers detect *any* syntactically invalid program. Typically, syntax provides the most stringent single structure within a programming language; more program entry faults and coding faults can be caught by syntactic analysis than by all other tests combined. The power of syntactic analysis as an error filter, as well as the ease of parsing, is greatly enhanced if the language is well punctuated, as previously discussed.

Static semantic errors. Much of the readability of high-level languages comes from conciseness resulting from the exploitation of context. Redundant non-local information can be used for very effective error checking. Declarations are particularly helpful, since a small amount of easily-supplied additional information can be checked in many places.

The type attribute in declarations is an effective form of redundancy, since the context of each appearance of a data item can be checked against its declared type. Both "typeless" languages (e.g., BLISS and BCPL) and languages with automatic type conversion (e.g., PL/I) defeat type checking, while languages with large numbers of incompatible types (e.g., Pascal) enhance it.

Pointers cause additional problems [Hoare 1975][Wirth 1974a]. By introducing the type pointer and restricting arithmetic operations on objects of this type, many high-level languages have made it possible to detect some of the faults common in the use of pointers in assembly languages. However, in PL/I, pointers may be used to access objects whose types are unknown. This problem can be eliminated by requiring that pointers be declared with the type of data they reference, as is done in Pascal and Algol 68. The further problem, of ensuring that there are no *dangling references* to explicitly freed storage, is more difficult to solve statically.

The declaration of further information about variables may permit easy detection of what would otherwise be subtle "logical" faults. Examples are the *range restrictions* of Pascal, and the provision of types and units for *dimensional analysis* [Karr and Loveman 1978]. This additional information also provides valuable documentation, and may enable the compiler to perform additional optimizations. In general, it helps to explicitly declare information that must otherwise be inferred by examining all uses of a variable.

Programmers can also supply redundant information about their programs by supplying *assertions* or *invariants*. Assertions are logical expressions that are supposed to be true at a particular point in a program, while invariants are intended to hold over a region of the program, such as the body of a procedure. Type declarations may be viewed as simple invariants that involve single variables.

It is common to do most type checking at compile time. By contrast, most compilers that support the assertion feature (e.g., Algol W [Satterthwaite 1972]) generate code to evaluate and test assertions at run time. Euclid, whose design is discussed in another chapter, was designed with the intent that the consistency of programs with their assertions and invariants would be checked statically, by a human or mechanical verifier.

Run-time error detection. Run-time error checking is done for a variety of reasons. Some faults have symptoms that can only be effectively detected at run time. If the cost of undetected errors may be high, or if the program must function more reliably than the compiler, hardware, and operating system that support it, it may be necessary to include redundant checking to duplicate tests made by the compiler. However, it is generally preferable to detect errors at compile time if possible, since the run-time check may be executed thousands or millions of times.

In order to peform dynamic checking, extra information associated with the program and/or data must be preserved and checked for consistency. Some kinds of checking (e.g., subscripts vs. array bounds, case selectors vs. case bounds) require modest overheads, and should almost always be performed, while others (e.g., checking for references to uninitialized variables) are very expensive with most current hardware, and must be very carefully justified to warrant inclusion.

Many systems allow the user to specify the amount of checking to be performed. Typically, full checking is specified during program debugging, and minimum checking during production runs. Hoare [1970] has criticised this practice on the grounds that it is only undetected errors in the production version that are harmful; he likens it to the practice of keeping a fire extinguisher in your car at all times, except when it is being used! Another problem is that the errors caused by subtle faults may disappear or shift when checking code is added to or removed from the program. However, the economic argument is frequently compelling.

Binding time

It is frequently argued that "the advantages and disadvantages of translation-time versus execution-time bindings revolve around [the] conflict between efficiency and flexibility" [Pratt 1975]. However, this ignores the very significant effect that binding times can have on reliability. This springs from two sources: the greater facility that humans have for comprehending and checking static rather than dynamic relationships, and the reduced persistence of errors that are detected at compile time.

The language designer should make provision for binding information at the earliest feasible time. Delayed or dynamic bindings should occur only at the programmer's explicit request, never by default, so that the reliability penalty of increased flexibility

J. J. HORNING

will only be paid when the flexibility is considered useful. For example, the programmer should be able to bind a name to a value either statically (at compile time) or upon block entry, as well as by variable assignment. Because of the key role of static type-checking, all (or almost all) types should be bound at compile time.

"Correctness" is a static (compile-time) property of a program. Thus, it is generally unwise to allow the correctness of a program to depend on assertions that cannot be checked until run time.

Decisions

One of the principal characterisitics of high-level languages is that they take many decisions out of the programmer's hands. This is one of the reasons why they are fiercely resented by so many experienced programmers. However, it is an inevitable consequence of the drive towards conciseness and checkable redundancy, and it is not undesirable.

Every decision takes time, and provides an opportunity for error. A major part of high-level languages' contributions to reliability comes from the errors they prevent (i.e., from the programs that they make it difficult or impossible to write). The language designer should try to restrict the programmer to decisions that really matter, and to get him to record those decisions within the text of the program itself.

In programming there are no decisions that *never* matter. This does not mean that all decisions should always be made by the programmer (writing in absolute hexadecimal!) and none by the compiler. Rather, it means that a programming language may need a very general (and not too frequently used) mechanism for overriding any specific decision (e.g., register or memory allocation, instruction choice) made by the compiler with one made by the programmer. This allows the programmer to be as careful as necessary in the optimization of critical decisions, but allows the compiler to make the routine decisions in a way that results in correct, and generally efficient, programs.

Programming decisions should be recorded *in the program*, independent of external documentation. A good comment convention, and freedom to choose readable, meaningful names can both assist in this process to a certain extent. However, it is better to record decisions in a form that is mechanically checkable for consistency with the rest of the program; all too often, the program is changed, but the comments and names are not. The language designer should favor "self-documenting" features wherever possible. To cite a simple example, the declaration

    type Direction = (North, East, South, West)

is superior to the comment

```
/*      CONVENTION FOR DIRECTION VALUES:        */
/*          NORTH   = 1                          */
/*          EAST    = 2                          */
/*          SOUTH   = 3                          */
/*          WEST    = 4                          */
```

It is shorter. It relieves the programmer of the need to pick numerical values for each of the directions. It ensures that any change to the convention will be consistently reflected throughout the program. Furthermore, type-checking can insure that Direction and integer values are never confused.

PROGRAMMING LANGUAGES FOR RELIABLE COMPUTING SYSTEMS

Structure

A programming language should help the programmer structure his solutions to problems. There are several different kinds of structures that are relevant to the organization of programs. In addition to the traditional topics of *control structures* and *data structures*, we will mention *visual structures*, *historical structures*, *protection structures*, and *recovery structures*.

There seem to be only a small number of fundamental structures for control and data, which can be composed repeatedly to form more complex structures. The main structures for both control and data are

concatenation: statement lists, declaration lists

selection: conditional statements, discriminated unions

fixed-length iteration: do loops, vectors

varying-length iteration: while loops, lists

encapsulation: blocks, records

abstraction: procedures, types.

Omitting any of these structures may force the programmer to awkward (and unreliable) circumlocutions; anything more elaborate can probably be built from these structures fairly easily.

Even so simple a matter as the formatting of the program text on the page can have a profound influence on the reader's ability to comprehend it readily. The visual structure of the text should correspond to the underlying control and data structures in such a way that they are easily visualized. Empirical studies of the "psychological complexity" of programs have sought to quantify the effect of good and bad styles for visual structure (paragraphing) [Weissman 1974]. It seems clear that difficulty in designing a natural and consistent paragraphing style for a programming language is a symptom of more basic flaws [Gordon 1975]. Many compilers now either automatically paragraph source listings or check for consistency between a program's indentation structure and its syntactic structure.

The historical structure of a program is the network of decisions that led to its final form. In principle, this structure includes not only the alternatives chosen, but those rejected, and the reasons for their rejection; few languages provide a reasonable mechanism for recording rejected alternatives. In most current languages, there is a strong temptation for programmers to destroy the historical structure that can be conveniently recorded in their programs. For example, much of the historical structure of a program that has been developed in a top-down fashion by stepwise refinement [Wirth 1971b, 1974b] is visible in its structure of procedures; it may be more "efficient" to eliminate those procedures by expanding out their bodies in-line at the point of call. The result of such premature optimization is often a program that can no longer be safely modified. The language designer (and compiler writer) should ensure that conceptual and historical structures can be retained in source programs with no loss in run-time efficiency, e.g., by making in-line procedure expansion a feature of the optimizer.

As systems get larger, they tend to become more vulnerable to unintended interactions, either accidental or malicious. Programming languages can reduce this vulnerability by providing protection "firewalls" against all but a specified, limited set of interactions. Many protection mechanisms traditionally supplied by operating systems are candidates for inclusion in programming languages [Jones and Liskov 1976].

J. J. HORNING

Truly robust systems must cope with the Dynamic Corollary to Murphy's Law ("Even if it has been shown that nothing can go wrong, something will still go wrong."). Recovery from hardware failures, human errors, problems in the underlying software, etc., is only feasible if advance provision has been made for dealing with exceptional conditions. It is important to clearly separate out the exception-handling portions of a program, so they do not dramatically increase our difficulty in understanding it. We will return to this topic in Part II.

Modularization and interfaces

In order to build or understand large systems, it is necessary to partition them into pieces that can be dealt with more or less independently. Modules are the pieces; interfaces are what separate them, and therefore make modularization useful. An interface defines *what* a module accomplishes, and should provide an opaque barrier between the users of the module, who know *why* the module is used, and the implementation of the module, which says *how* it accomplishes its ends. A useful interface is small ("narrow"), precise, and easily understood.

We want to ensure that a module accomplishes just what is specified in its interface in order to protect against errors, and against the consequences of changes elsewhere in the system. This isolation allows us to focus our attention on one module at a time, to bound the consequences of any change, and to localize the scope both of machine-dependencies and of decisions that may have to be changed.

For maximum effectiveness, modularization and specification should be more than just design tools. The programming language should ensure that conceptual interfaces correspond to those in the actual program. In particular, the interface of a module must include both its explicit effects and any possible side effects, such as changes to non-local variables and error exits. The case against automatic inheritance of global variables [Wulf and Shaw 1973] is largely based on their disastrous effect on the size of interfaces.

REMINDERS FOR LANGUAGE DESIGNERS AND USERS

Simplicity is a considerable virtue.

When in doubt, leave it out.

Correctness is a compile-time property.

The primary goal of a programming language is accurate communication among humans.

Avoid "power" if it's hard to explain or understand.

If anything can go wrong, it will.

Reliability matters.

PART II—LANGUAGE FEATURES FOR FAULT TOLERANCE

INTRODUCTION

Part I addressed the issue of designing a programming language to improve the reliability of the programming process. We now turn to another way in which a programming language can help to improve system reliability: by recognizing that faults are inevitable and providing means to cope with them systematically. Faults may occur in a program, or in the software or hardware of the system on which it runs—whatever the source of the difficulty, the program can contribute to system reliability by keeping faults from becoming failures.

Following the distinctions made by Randell and Melliar-Smith [1977], we will call portions of a program that are explicitly intended to cope with errors *abnormal algorithms*—although it is not at all abnormal for a program to contain them! These can be divided into two classes based on whether they are intended to cope with particular anticipated, but unusual, situations, or are intended as a fallback when something unanticipated occurs. In the former case, *signals* and *exception handlers* provide a useful mechanism; in the latter, *acceptance tests* and *recovery blocks* are more appropriate. We will discuss both in turn, then return to the question of how to justify the complexity that these features add to programming languages.

SIGNALS AND EXCEPTION HANDLERS

Motivation

"Why worry about exception processing? Anyone who has ever built a large software system or tried to write a 'robust' program can appreciate the problem. As programs grow in size, special cases and unusual circumstances crop up with startling rapidity. Even in moderate-sized programs that perform seemingly simple tasks, exceptional conditions abound. Consider a tape-to-tape copy program. Any reasonable programmer will handle an end-of-file condition, since it probably indicates completion of the copying operation. But what about tape errors? End-of-tape? Hung device? Record larger than expected? We could enumerate other possible exceptions, but the point is clear. Exceptions exist even in the simplest problem, and the complexity they induce in large programs can be mind-boggling. ... A look at the (dis)organization of existing large systems should easily convince us that [their] control is essential if we ever hope to make these systems robust, reliable, and understandable. ...

"Although it is obvious that any exceptional condition that arises must be handled if our programs are to be robust, we might wonder whether we need a single, general mechanism to do so. Why not simply test explicitly for an exception at all possible points in the program where it can occur? If this is prohibitively expensive or inconvenient, why not test only at a selected subset of these points? No special mechanism is required here, and the code to detect these exceptions is explicit and under the programmer's control.

"The objections to this *ad hoc* approach should be clear. For some classes of exceptions ... the condition may occur virtually anywhere in the program. Obviously, it is impractical to include an explicit test 'at all possible points' where such exceptions can arise. Polling at 'selected' points may be feasible in principle, but in practice destroys the structural coherence of the source program. Because of timing considerations, it often becomes necessary ... to introduce tests for exceptions into pieces of the program that have nothing to do with the condition being tested. It is then impossible to read and understand such a program segment without understanding the entire structure of which it is a (perhaps very small and localized) part. Explicit polling may suffice in very limited applications but is clearly inadequate for general use. A technique must be found that preserves structural clarity." [Levin 1977]

A recent survey paper discusses exception handling features for programming languages, and identifies several uses for these features:

"Exceptions serve to *generalize* operations, making them usable in a wider variety of contexts than would otherwise be the case. Specifically, exceptions are used:

(a) to permit dealing with an operation's impending or actual failure. Two types of failure are of interest: range failure, and domain failure;

(b) to indicate the significance of a valid result or the circumstances under which it was obtained.

(c) to permit an invoker to *monitor* an operation, e.g., to measure computational progress or to provide additional information and guidance should certain conditions arise. ...

"*Range failure* occurs when an operation either finds it is unable to satisfy its output assertion (i.e. its criterion for determining when it has produced a valid result), or decides it may not ever be able to satisfy its output assertion. For example, a read operation does not satisfy its output assertion when it finds an end-of-file mark instead of a record to read; this is a range failure of the first kind. The second type of failure is exemplified by encountering a parity error when attempting to read a record, since in this case, it is uncertain whether repeated attempts to read will or will not eventually be successful. For a numerical algorithm, evidence of divergence is a range failure of the first kind; failure to converge after a certain amount of effort has been expended would be a failure of the second kind. ...

"Range failure requires the ability to terminate an operation prematurely (with or without production of partial results and with or without the 'undoing' of intermediate results). Range failure also requires the ability to resume the operation when further attempts at completion are deemed reasonable.

"*Domain failure* is a somewhat different type of failure. It occurs when an operation's inputs fail to pass certain tests of acceptability, e.g., the appearance of a letter in a string of digits or the inability to find enough space to satisfy a storage allocation requirement. Domain failure is distinguished from range failure in that domain failure occurs when some *input* assertion is tested and not satisfied, whereas range failure occurs when an output assertion cannot be satisfied." [Goodenough 1975]

PROGRAMMING LANGUAGES FOR RELIABLE COMPUTING SYSTEMS

Although Goodenough considers that "exceptions and exception handling mechanisms are not needed just to deal with errors. They are needed, in general, as a means of conveniently interleaving actions belonging to different levels of abstraction," we will be concerned here only with their use in dealing with errors.

Signals in Mesa

Mesa is a system implementation language developed at Xerox. It contains one of the more general and satisfactory exception handling mechanisms in an implemented language. The following discussion is excerpted from the Mesa Language Manual [Mitchell et al. 1978].

Signals are used to indicate when exceptional conditions arise in the course of execution, and they provide an orderly means of dealing with those conditions, at low cost if none are generated (and they almost never are). Signals work over many levels of procedure call, and it is possible for a signal to be generated by one procedure and be handled by another procedure much higher up in the call chain.

In its simplest form, a signal is just a name for some exceptional condition. Often, parameters are passed along with the signal to help any catch phrase which handles it in determining what went wrong. Finally, it is possible to recover from a signal and allow the routine which generated it to continue on its merry way. This is done by a catch phrase returning a result; the program which generated the signal receives this result as if it had called a normal procedure instead of a signal.

Signals may be *raised* by the detection of hardware or software errors, or explicitly within the program by using a signal statement. Any program which needs to *handle* signals must anticipate that need by providing *catch phrases* for the various signals that might be generated. During execution, certain of these catch phrases will be *enabled* at different times to handle signals. Loosely speaking, when a signal S is generated, the procedures in the call hierarchy at that time will be given a chance to catch the signal, in a last-in-first-out order. Each such procedure P in turn, if it has an enabled catch phrase, is given the signal S, until one of them stops the signal from propagating any further. P may still decide to reject S (in which case the next procedure in the call hierarchy will be considered), or P may decide to handle S by taking control or by attempting to recover from the signal.

Because signals can be propagated right through the call hierarchy, the programmer must consider catching not only signals generated *directly* within any procedure that is called, but also any generated indirectly as a result of calling that procedure. Indirect signals are those generated by procedures called from within a procedure which you call, unless they are stopped before reaching you.

When a catch phrase is called, it behaves like a case statement: it compares the signal code passed to it with each signal value that labels one of its alternatives. If the signal code matches, control enters the statement following the label; if not, the next enclosing catch phrase is tried. The special label any matches all signal codes. When a match is found, the catch phrase is said to have *accepted* the signal. The statement associated with each catch phrase has an implicit *Reject* return as its last instruction; hence if if the statement completes without an explicit control transfer, the signal is rejected and the search for an accepting catch phrase resumes.

Mesa guarantees that all otherwise uncaught signals will be caught at the highest level in the system and reported by the Debugger to the user. This is helpful in debugging because all the control context which existed when the signal was generated is still around and can be inspected to investigate the problem.

Having caught a signal, a catch phrase may transfer control into its containing context by means of a goto, an exit, a retry, or a continue (these are the only forms of "non-local goto" in Mesa). Goto explicitly indicates the next statement to be executed, exit leaves the enclosing iterative statement, retry means "go back to the beginning of the statement to which this catch phrase belongs," and continue means "go to the statement following the one to which this catch phrase belongs."

Another option for a catch phrase is to use the resume statement to return values to the routine which generated the signal. To that routine, it appears as if the signal call were a procedure call that returns some results.

A very important special signal is called *Unwind*. It is generated when a catch phrase has accepted a signal and is about to do some form of unconditional jump into the body of the routine containing it. Immediately preceding such a jump, the catch phrase will generate an *Unwind* signal for every intermediate activation record in the stack, starting from the source of the signal and terminating with the accepting catch phrase. This signal tells that activation that it is about to be destroyed and gives it a chance to clean up before dying, generally by restoring any data structures for which it is responsible to a consistent state and freeing any dynamically allocated storage.

Using Mesa signals

Properly used, Mesa signals go a long way towards meeting the previously discussed objectives for exceptional condition handling. They make it possible to clearly distinguish between normal and abnormal algorithms, and to propagate an error notification to the abnormal algorithm designed to handle it. In many cases, the handling algorithm can be placed at a level in the system where there is sufficient global information to effect a reasonable repair, report the problem in user-oriented terms, or decide to start over.

When designing a system component, it is necessary to anticipate the exceptional conditions that may arise during its operation, and to decide which of them should be reported to its users. It is necessary to document not only the names and meanings of the signals that the component may raise directly or indirectly, but also the names and meanings of any parameters supplied with the signal, whether the signal may be resumed, and if so, what repair is expected and what result is to be returned. Unless all this information is provided, it will be difficult for users to respond correctly to signals. Each programmer must decide which signals to handle via catch phrases, and which to reject (i.e., to incorporate into the interface of his own component).

The "power" and "convenience" of signals arise largely from the possibility of a signal passing through a large number of intermediate levels that need not take explicit account of it. However, the more levels through which a signal passes before being handled, the greater the conceptual distance is likely to be between the signaller and the handler, the greater the care necessary to ensure correct handling, and the greater the likelihood of some intermediate level omitting a necessary catch phrase for *Unwind*.

Jim Morris [private communication 1976] has raised the following warnings about Mesa signals: "Like any new and powerful language feature, Mesa's signal mechanism, especially the *Unwind* option, should be approached with caution. Because it is in the language, one cannot always be certain that a procedure call returns, even if he is not using signals himself. Every call on an external procedure must be regarded as an exit from your module, and you must clean things up before calling the procedure, or include a catch phrase to clean things up in the event that a signal occurs. It is hard to take this stricture seriously because it is really a hassle, especially considering the fact that the use of signals is fairly rare, and their actual exercise even rarer. Because signals are rare there is hardly any reinforcement for following the strict signal policy; i.e. you will hardly ever hear anyone say 'I'm really glad I put that catch phrase in there; otherwise my program would never work.' The point is that the program *will* work quite well for a long time without these precautions. The bug will not be found until long after the system is running in Peoria. ... It should be noted that Mesa is far superior to most languages in this area. In principle, by using enough catch phrases, one can keep control from getting away. The non-local transfers allowed by most Algol-like languages preclude such control. It has been suggested that systems programming is like mountaineering: One should not always react to surprises by jumping; it could make things worse."

It should be apparent that there are some drawbacks to Mesa signals, and users are by no means unanimous in their praise. Speaking from personal experience, there are situations where the use of signals greatly simplifies what would otherwise be a thorny programming problem. However, my own use of signals has turned out to be quite fault-prone, and I have greater difficulty locating and removing signal faults than any other kind. Each signal that is potentially raised by a procedure (directly or indirectly) is an important part of its interface. However, signals are generally the least well documented and least well tested part of the interface, and it is possible for indirect signals to be completely overlooked until they cause catastrophic crashes.

ACCEPTANCE TESTS AND RECOVERY BLOCKS

Motivation

"The variety of undetected [faults] which could have been made in the design of a non-trivial software component is essentially infinite. Due to the complexity of the component, the relationship between any such [fault] and its effect at run time may be very obscure. For these reasons we believe that diagnosis of the original cause of software errors should be left to humans to do, and should be done in comparative leisure. Therefore our scheme for software fault tolerance in no way depends on automated diagnosis of the cause of the error—this would surely result only in greatly increasing the complexity and therefore the error-proneness of the system." [Randell 1975]

Although signals and related exception handling mechanisms can be very effective in dealing with the consequences of certain types of failures, there are two major limitations to their use:

Each likely kind of failure must be anticipated, and suitable handlers provided. Thus, these mechanisms are essentially useless in coping with *unanticipated* faults, such as design faults.

Recovery from failures is entirely under the programmer's control. Although this provides maximum flexibility, it carries with it the responsibility for understanding and compensating for *all* the consequences of each failure—frequently a monumental task. Since failures of the underlying hardware and software should be rare, the recovery code is likely to be the least well tested (and hence most faulty) part of the system.

Thus, to provide a general mechanism for software fault tolerance, we must use language features that do *not* require the programmer to foresee all possible faults and to specify exactly how to recover from each of them. The *recovery block* [Horning *et al.* 1974][Anderson and Kerr 1976] is one such mechanism, which allows the programmer to supply his own error-checking, and to define units for recovery, without being concerned with either the complete set of possible faults or the means of implementing complete recovery.

Components of recovery blocks

It is useful to segment any large program into a set of *blocks* (modules, procedures, subroutines, paragraphs, clusters, etc.), each of which achieves some conceptual operation. Such a segmentation makes it possible to provide a functional description of each block. In documenting, understanding, or verifying a program that uses a such a block, it is normally sufficient to use the functional description, rather than the detailed design of the block. Such blocks also provide natural units for error-checking and recovery; by adding extra information for this purpose, they become recovery blocks. This scheme is not dependent on the particular form of block structuring that is used, or the rules governing the scopes of variables, methods of parameter passing, etc. All that is required is that when the program is executed the acts of entering and leaving each block are explicit, and that blocks are properly nested in time.

A recovery block consists of an ordinary block in the programming language (the *primary alternate*), plus an *acceptance test* and a sequence of *alternate blocks*. The primary alternate is just the program that would have been written had there been no provision for error detection and recovery. The acceptance test is just a logical expression that is to be evaluated upon completion of any alternate to determine whether it has performed acceptably; it is closely analogous to the post-condition of a specification. If an alternate fails to complete (e.g., because of an internal failure or because it exceeds a time limit) or fails the acceptance test, the next alternate (if there is one) is entered. However, *before a further alternate is tried, the state is restored* to what it was just prior to entering the primary alternate. If the acceptance test is passed upon completion of an alternate, any further alternates are ignored, and control passes to the next statement following the recovery block. When no further alternates remain after a failure, the recovery block itself is considered to have failed, and recovery is attempted at the level of the next enclosing recovery block.

This mechanism has some very important characteristics:

It incorporates a general solution to the problem of when and how to switch to redundant software associated with any component, i.e., it deals with both the repair of any damage caused by the failing component and with transferring control to the appropriate spare component.

It provides a method of explicitly structuring the software system which has the effect of ensuring that the extra software involved in error detection and in the spare components does not add to the complexity of the system, and so reduce rather than increase overall system reliability.

It simplifies the task of producing alternate components. There is no need for—indeed, no possibility of—attempts at automated error diagnosis. The system state is reset after an error, deleting all effects of the faulty alternate. Thus, each alternate may be written as though *it* were the primary alternate.

The recovery block scheme does have some disadvantages, as well:

The requirement that the state be restored before proceeding to a further alternate is difficult to implement efficiently on conventional hardware; various hardware aids can make this more feasible.

It is difficult to structure systems of communicating processes in such a way that state restoration is feasible without disastrous "domino effects" as each process forces others with which it has communicated to restore their states.

For systems that communicate with the external world, state restoration may be impossible, even in principle. (This is known as the "please ignore incoming rocket" problem.)

Each of these problems is the object of considerable current research, particularly at the University of Newcastle-upon-Tyne in England. Generally, proposed solutions place only minimal demands on the programming language.

Using recovery blocks

Although there is not yet a great deal of experience in structuring large systems for fault tolerance using recovery blocks, it is clear that two issues are critical to their effective use: the choice of acceptance tests, and the development of suitable alternate blocks.

It was mentioned that acceptance tests are closely akin to post-conditions in specifications. However, it is not generally possible just to carry these post-conditions over from the specification to the program. The minor problem is that the specification language will probably be more general (e.g., including quantifiers) than the logical expressions permitted in the programming language. The major problem is that it is usually nearly as expensive to completely check a post-condition as to achieve it, and the program to do so will probably be as complex and fault-prone as the primary block. Thus it will usually be necessary to choose an acceptance test that is somewhat less stringent than the post-condition. For example, the acceptance test for a sort routine might simply test that the elements of the array are in ascending order and that the sum of the elements in the array has not changed, rather than testing that the output array is a permutation of the input array. Choosing acceptance tests that are sufficiently stringent to ensure that a high percentage of failures are detected, yet sufficiently simple that they are themselves reliable and efficient, is an imperfectly understood art.

Ideally, alternate blocks would be written independently, directly from the functional specification. This should minimize the chance of correlated faults within separate alternates, but it could double or triple the cost of producing the program. In practice, there are a variety of reasons for using alternates that are not completely independent:

In systems undergoing maintenance, the correction of a fault or addition of a feature often introduces a further fault; if the previous version is kept as an alternate, discovery of an error will trigger automatic fallback to the older (and perhaps more robust) version. Of course, this is only feasible if the block's interface has not changed.

It may be more efficient to use a fast heuristic algorithm that "almost always works," and when one of the exceptional cases is discovered automatically fall back to a slower algorithm that really always works.

Among the "acceptable" behaviours for a block may be some that are more desirable than others (e.g., it is valid for a bank cash dispenser either to produce cash for a validated customer or to refuse cash because the validation process has somehow failed, but the former is clearly preferable); a sequence of alternates encompassing the spectrum of acceptable behaviours may be designed together.

J. J. HORNING

One important aspect of recovery blocks is that they provide a straightforward means for testing abnormal algorithms without relying on a sufficient number of failures in the underlying system to test all cases. Since each alternate operates on the same state—and must satisfy the same acceptance test—as the primary alternate, it can simply be substituted for the primary alternate at some stage in system testing, and tested as much as desired. More generally, a system can be "margin tested" by simply arranging for the underlying mechanism to behave as though a certain fraction of the acceptance tests failed (either by initially selecting other than the primary alternate or by rolling back after executing it and the acceptance test).

In addition to initiating recovery, failure of an acceptance test can be made to trigger logging of the error behind the scenes, for off-line analysis. This will be useful data not only for fault isolation and correction, but also for estimating failure rates within the system—and possibly for developing confidence measures in the functioning of the system as a whole.

Recovery blocks are more general than signals, and this generality inevitably exacts an efficiency toll. In circumstances where reliability has a high premium, this may be an acceptable price. However, recovery blocks and signals need not be mutually exclusive. The use of signals to deal with *anticipated* failures, and recovery blocks as a backstop for design faults and other unanticipated failures can be an attractive compromise. Signals will deal with the common cases efficiently and allow for careful programmer control where consequences can be foreseen. Recovery blocks will ensure that nothing will slip through the cracks and that the situation will never get completely out of control; this assurance may permit the signal handlers to be greatly simplified (e.g., no need to worry about what happens if we get a ParityError signal while fielding a DiskError interrupt while attempting to write a page to disk to free a virtual memory page while handling a PageFault interrupt while trying to bring in the non-resident handler for the StorageFull signal while ...).

CONCLUSIONS

Relatively few programming languages contain explicit provisions for fault tolerance. In fact, PL/I is the only widely-used language with extensive exception handling facilities, and these have numerous deficiencies [MacLaren 1977][Levin 1977]. Considering the bias for language simplicity exhibited in Part I, can we justify fault tolerant features that will necessarily increase language complexity? The answer is a qualified "yes."

By careful design, the additional complexity of these features can be kept to a minimum. For example, recovery blocks add very little syntactic or semantic complexity beyond what is already built into almost all current languages. It may be that when signals and exception handling are well understood that they can be provided by features of comparable simplicity [cf. Levin 1977].

Additional complexity is tolerable in a language if the new features remove even more complexity from typical programs. Fault tolerance is not the sort of feature (such as string processing or floating point arithmetic) that can be simply added to a language as a *post facto* package. If it is required, there is just no simple way to program it within a language that does not provide features equivalent to those we have been discussing.

To this point we have stressed the conceptual advantages of a clear separation between normal and abnormal algorithms. However, in practice, the most compelling arguments may be efficiency and robustness. If the programming language makes it

Programming Languages for Reliable Computing Systems

possible to separate normal and abnormal algorithms, quite different implementations may be chosen for each type. For example, in Mesa, signals are very similar to procedure variables; however, since raising a signal is expected to be a relatively infrequent event, a very different implementation technique is used that defers almost all the run-time overhead to the time when the signal is raised—if it isn't, the overhead is avoided. Similarly, it is possible to treat state-saving for recovery blocks quite differently from ordinary assignments—again, reducing average-case overhead.

It can be very important to preserve the redundancy provided by abnormal algorithms in the system at run time. If they are indistinguishably mixed with the normal algorithms, however, even a fairly simple compiler will probably detect some of the redundancies and "optimize" them out of the program entirely. Unless we are to prohibit optimization entirely, there must be some linguistic mechanism for indicating redundancy that is to be preserved.

Finally, unless the system has some way of distinguishing tests that indicate errors from ordinary program tests, it is difficult or impossible for the system to undertake automatic error logging. If the programmer is responsible for error logging, this is another burden of complexity on every program, and another source of program faults.

J. J. HORNING

PART III—LANGUAGES ENCOURAGING PROOFS

INTRODUCTION

Reasoning about programs

In the development of reliable programs, it is not sufficient that a program specify a correct set of computations. The program must also make it possible to understand *why* the computations are correct. Whenever we are concerned with the correctness of computations invoked by a program, we are faced with the problem of reasoning (formally or informally) about that program [McCarthy 1962][Floyd 1967][Dijkstra 1975]. This is not always an easy task; the complexity of many languages makes it virtually impossible to reason with confidence about even very small programs.

Our ability to compose programs reliably, and to understand them, is likely to be highly correlated with our ability to reason about them. Since many of the considerations of language design discussed in Part I were motivated by concern for understandability, it is not surprising that most of them are also applicable here.

It is perhaps less obvious that the ability to reason formally about programs is closely related to the ability to reason about them informally. Formality tends to frighten many programmers; it seems to smack more of mathematical logic than "the art of computer programming." Most practical proofs tend to be rather informal; however, they are more convincing if it is clear that *in principle* they could be reduced to completely formal proofs in a well-understood system. In most languages, this process is complicated by the necessity to consider many possibilities in addition to the "clear meaning" of the program (e.g., suppose that this procedure never terminates, transfers control via an error exit, or destroys the value of a global variable; suppose that this subscript expression overflows, involves division by zero, calls a function that never returns, or produces a value that is out of bounds). It is precisely the "niggling little details" that complicate the reduction to a formal proof that also provide the richest sources of pitfalls in understanding and reasoning informally about programs in these languages.

Incorporation of specifications

One simple, but useful, way in which a programming language can encourage reasoning about programs is by making it easy to incorporate at least partial specifications within the program itself. Of course, comments can always be used for this purpose, but it is better both for the human reader and for the mechanical analyzer if specifications are syntactically recognizable as such. Most commonly, these specifications will take the form of input-output assertions on major program units (such as procedures) and invariant assertions on program loops. The close association of assertions with the program units provides an extremely useful form of documentation for the reader, indicating what assumptions the programmer was supposed to make about the environment, the transformations the program is supposed to effect, and the relations it is to maintain

PROGRAMMING LANGUAGES FOR RELIABLE COMPUTING SYSTEMS

Most programs presented to verifiers are actually wrong; considerable time can be wasted looking for proofs of incorrect programs before discovering that debugging is still needed. This problem can be reduced (although not eliminated) by judicious testing, which is generally the most efficient way to demonstrate the presence of bugs. To assist in the testing process, some languages provide for the compilation of run-time checks for assertions in the program. This checking code provides useful redundancy for program testing. Alternatively, it could be used to initiate the abnormal algorithms discussed in Part II.

Of course, it is generally not feasible to incorporate complete specifications with each program unit. Global properties, such as performance, storage usage, etc., are often best specified and analyzed separately. Furthermore, even specifications that are appropriate to particular program units may need to be written in a richer language than the Boolean expressions of the programming language; for example, quantifiers and auxiliary variables are frequently needed.

Support for proof techniques

Each particular proof technique has its own strengths and limitations. By providing a set of features for which a proof method is especially suited, and avoiding those for which it is not, a language can facilitate proofs in that system. For example, the axiomatic method developed by Hoare [1969] relies on an essential "pun": no distinction is made between a variable and its value. Thus, with this method, it is difficult to simply and precisely formalize programming language constructs that rely on the notion of a variable as a location in memory rather than as merely a name for a value (e.g., reference parameters, equivalence, pointers). A language that avoids such features will simplify the development of axioms for the proof of programs.

An example of where a language can provide a feature needed for a proof technique is provided by Hoare's [1972] approach to the proof of correctness of data representations. This method relies on the maintenance of a specified relationship between the "abstract" and "concrete" values of a data structure by all operations that change it. Proving that such a relationship is maintained is much more straightforward in languages that allow a data structure to be encapsulated together with all the possible operations on it, and that enforce such encapsulations.

LANGUAGES FOR VERIFICATION

Most proof techniques have been demonstrated in connection with "toy" languages, constructed specifically for purposes of illustration. These languages have generally not been implemented, and in any case were not designed for serious programming. The first notable exception was the programming language Pascal [Wirth 1971a], whose design was influenced by verification considerations, and whose formal definition takes the form of a set of proof rules [Hoare and Wirth 1973]. Several newer languages have also been designed with concern for both practical programming and verification.

J. J. Horning

Euclid

Euclid [Lampson *et al.* 1977] is a language for writing system programs that are to be verified. Its design proceeded in conjunction with the development of a set of proof rules [London *et al.* 1978] in the style of Hoare. It provides a good illustration of the practical consequences of attempting to design a realistic language for which proofs will be feasible, and is discussed in separate chapters.

Euclid was evolved from Pascal by a series of changes intended to make it more suitable for verification and for system programming. We attempted to transfer much of the work of producing a correct program, and of verifying that it is consistent with its specification, from the programmer and the verifier (human or mechanical) to the programming language and its compiler. Our changes to Pascal generally took the form of restrictions, which allow stronger statements about the properties of programs to be based on the rather superficial, but quite reliable, analysis that a compiler can perform.

Euclid is currently being implemented by a joint project of the Computer Systems Research Group of the University of Toronto and the Special Systems Division of I. P. Sharp Associates Limited [Sharp 1977]. Both the development of the proof rules and the implementation effort have provided useful feedback on the design of the language and the clarity of the defining report. A significant revision of the latter is currently being contemplated.

CLU

CLU is a programming language under development at the Massachusetts Institute of Technology. It is intended to support the use of three kinds of abstractions in program construction: procedural, control, and data.

> "CLU has been designed to support a methodology ... in which programs are developed by means of problem decomposition based on the recognition of abstractions. A program is constructed in many stages. At each stage, the problem to be solved is how to implement some abstraction (the initial problem is to implement the abstract behaviour required of the entire program). The implementation is developed by envisioning a number of subsidiary abstractions (abstract objects and operations) that are useful in the problem domain. Once the behavior of the abstract objects and operations has been defined, a program can be written to solve the original problem; in this program, the abstract objects and operations are used as primitives. Now the original problem has been solved, but new problems have arisen, namely, how to implement the subsidiary abstractions. Each of these abstractions is considered in turn as a new problem; its implementation may introduce further abstractions. This process terminates when all the abstractions introduced at various stages have been implemented or are present in the programming language in use.

> "In this methodology, programs are developed incrementally, one abstraction at a time. Further, a distinction is made between an abstraction, which is a kind of behavior, and a program, or *module*, which implements that behavior. An abstraction isolates use from implementation: an abstraction can be used without knowledge of its implementation and implemented without knowledge of its use." [Liskov *et al.* 1977]

The clear separation between abstraction and implementation made by CLU is also very helpful in partitioning the problem of program verification; each program module can be verified separately, on the basis of the specifications of the modules that it uses,

PROGRAMMING LANGUAGES FOR RELIABLE COMPUTING SYSTEMS

without concern for their implementation. Note that this style of verification would not be safe if the language did not enforce the separation between abstraction and implementation, so that the only possible interactions are those allowed by the specification.

One of the principal features of CLU is the introduction of *clusters*, program modules that support data abstractions in a fashion analogous to the way that procedures support operational abstractions. A cluster permits a data abstraction to be implemented as a unit containing both a representation for the data object and algorithms for each operation on that object. CLU then allows only the operations within the cluster to access the representation.

A preliminary version of CLU has been implemented. Experience with its use will probably suggest further refinements. A more efficient implementation is being developed.

Alphard

Alphard is a programming language under development at Carnegie-Mellon University. Its designers have set themselves even more ambitious goals than those of CLU. In addition to supporting a programming methodology based on abstraction and verification, Alphard is intended to permit both high-level programming and the convenient description of computer hardware, and is to be amenable to compilation into very efficient code (comparable to "good assembler coding") for present-day computers. Not surprisingly, its design and implementation have not proceeded as rapidly.

The Alphard *form* provides the programmer with a great deal of control over the implementation of data abstractions and of control constructs dealing with data abstractions (e.g., iteration). The primary goal of the form mechanism is to permit and encourage the localization of information about a user-defined abstraction. Specifically, it is designed to localize both verification and modification. Each form contains both a specification part and an implementation part; only the information contained in the specification part may be used outside the form.

A verification methodology is being developed concurrently with the design of Alphard; the designers say that it has provided substantial feedback to the language design itself. Particular attention has been paid to ensuring that there exists a well-understood way to verify both the implementation and use of each type of form. Several examples are contained in a series of papers on the theme of "abstraction and verification in Alphard" [London *et al.* 1976][Shaw 1976][Shaw *et al.* 1976, 1977][Wulf *et al.* 1976a,b].

Dijkstra's guarded command language

One of the most radical approaches to the problem of encouraging proofs has been taken by Dijkstra [1976], who starts from the proposition that verification should not follow programming as a separate activity; rather, the program and its proof should be developed hand in hand. Ideally, the program should be constructed directly from its specifications, with minimum opportunity for error. This topic is covered separately by Dijkstra and Gries, and will not be further pursued here.

J. J. HORNING

PART IV—COPING WITH EXISTING LANGUAGES

INTRODUCTION

The three previous parts of this lecture, by pointing out desirable properties of programming languages, constitute a catalog of inadequacies found in almost all widely-used languages. That most programs are written in languages that cause reliability problems should not be surprising—reliability is not an explicit concern in the initial phases of most projects. Even when reliability is a concern, the programming language is generally selected on some other basis: programmer familiarity, organizational standards, object-code efficiency, or availability; managers and customers do not insist on a language that will contribute to reliability. The major problem, however, is that there is no programming language available today that meets all our criteria; those that come closest tend to be least widely available.

We have already discussed the following common problems:

Most available programming languages are large, complex, hard to master in their entirety, and full of surprises. Languages that have enough features to meet our other requirements are particularly prone to elephantiasis.

All programming languages contain fault-prone features. Many of them do not contain enough checkable redundancy to allow the common faults to be detectable as errors.

Few programming languages incorporate sufficient structure for the construction and maintenance of modular systems. The conceptual structure that guides a program's construction is generally not visible in its text; intended modularity is often not enforced.

Features for fault-tolerance are primitive or non-existent in most widely-available languages. In the major exception (PL/I), the feature itself is so fault-prone that its extensive use does not necessarily contribute to system reliability.

In most languages, it is difficult to reason about programs with any confidence that they actually do what they appear to do in all circumstances. The number of possible special cases, machine limitations, side-effects, etc., is too large to cope with, so only those that happen to turn up during testing are likely to be considered.

Designing and implementing a new language is a difficult and expensive undertaking—in effect, a capital investment. It is rare that a single project has the luxury of specifying a programming language to meet its requirements; most projects must choose from among the already available languages. The key questions become: "Which of the available languages will contribute least to system unreliability?" and "How can that contribution be minimized?" What follows are suggestions for coping with that situation.

MINIMIZING LANGUAGE-INDUCED FAULTS

Style

There are many different ways of using any given language. Some programming styles are less fault-prone than others. It is generally possible to find a style that emphasizes the strengths and avoids the weaknesses of any particular language. An excellent introduction to the general principles of programming style has been written by Kernighan and Plauger [1974]. It may be helpful to develop a more specific style manual for a language or a project.

Language subsetting

Just because a language contains many features that contribute to unreliability does not mean that they must be used. Within even the largest languages it is sometimes possible to discover relatively clean, well-structured subsets; the ability to identify such subsets is not widespread, but should be treasured. A notable example of such subsets is SP/k [Holt et al. 1977]. SP/k is a sequence of nested subsets of PL/I (SP/1, ... , SP/8) designed primarily for teaching purposes. However, as we have previously argued, the clarity and simplicity needed for teaching are also major contributors to reliability. There is anecdotal evidence that programming in SP/6 is more reliable than programming in unrestricted PL/I [Horning and Wortman 1977].

A compiler for a subset language is generally much easier to construct than for the full language; the cost of implementing a language grows more than linearly with the language size [McKeeman et al. 1970]. However, the SP/k experience illustrates that many of the advantages of using a subset are available even without a special subset compiler. Legal SP/k programs will generally compile and run *with the same results* using any PL/I compiler; what is lost by not using the SP/k compiler is the additional checking made possible by the restricted nature of the subset. Thus illegal SP/k programs will generally be accepted by other compilers as "valid," but may produce different meaningless results.

Programmer self-discipline is necessary, but generally not sufficient, to ensure adherence to a chosen subset. Various other supplementary techniques may be used. Enforcement by the compiler, preprocessor, or another checking program (see below) is likely to be the most thorough, but simple management techniques may be all that is needed to achieve compliance.

Preprocessors

It may be possible to considerably improve a widely-available language, such as FORTRAN or COBOL, by adding a relatively small number of structuring features, and imposing more discipline and useful redundancy on the use of the language. Rather than building entire compilers from scratch, it is easier, faster, and more general to write a preprocessor that translates the improved language into the base language. If the preprocessor is written in its own language, the improved language becomes available on all machines where the base language is available.

An example of this approach is the RATFOR (Rational FORTRAN) language and preprocessor [Kernighan and Plauger 1976]. Among the advantages of this approach are its relatively low cost, easy portability, compatibility with existing libraries of programs, minimal programmer retraining, and quick payoff on investment. The disadvantages include the extra cost of preprocessing every time the program is changed, an extra level of language that must be understood (at least) when things go wrong and the compiler produces messages that are not in terms of the preprocessor's language, and the difficulty of accomodating really major language changes (e.g., for fault-tolerance).

Additional checking tools

Rather than checking and transforming a program as part of a preprocessing phase, it is possible to write entirely separate programs whose purpose is to exploit redundancy for error-checking. Checking may range from simple verification that a program conforms to standards that are not checked by the compiler [Culpepper 1975][Bridge and Thompson 1976], to detection of anomalous interprocedural data flow [Fosdick and Osterweil 1976], to determination of whether dimensions and units are used consistently [Karr and Loveman 1978], to full-fledged program verification systems [London 1975].

A study by Boehm et al. [1976] indicates that the biggest potential improvements in software fault detection and correction come from "early application of automated and semiautomated Consistency, Robustness, and Self-Containedness checkers." A prototype Design Assertion Consistency Checker, for example, was given 967 assertions about the inputs and outputs of 186 modules in a large spacecraft software system. At a cost of $30 in computer time, it discovered over 200 genuine inconsistencies in the design (and another 600 inconsistencies in the assertions themselves). Many of the inconsistencies represented faults that "might not have been caught until very late in the testing and integration phase, and are typically the kind of errors which are difficult to correct, as their correction often causes ripple effects into other portions of the software." [Boehm et al. 1975]

Some of the advantages of separating the checking tools from the language processors are the additional modularity of the program production system, the relative ease of adding just a little more checking (without having to redesign either the language or the compiler), the ability to postpone checking until a program is believed to be correct (thereby saving the cost of a lot of checking during program development). The disadvantages are very closely related: because the checker is separate from the compiler, it will probably wind up duplicating many of its functions (certainly lexical analysis of the program, probably partial or complete parsing, and possibly global analysis of control and data flow); because checking may be postponed, faults will generally be detected later, after a greater investment of debugging time.

Manual transformation into implemented languages

"Availability" of a language need not be equated with availability of a compiler for the language. Many programmers who are not satisfied with the languages for which they have compilers use some language they like better for program design and initial coding. After they are confident that this well-structured program represents their intent, they manually transform it into the language that their compiler accepts. This technique is usually most helpful in early stages of program design—no generally-available programming language provides much conceptual assistance in design [cf. McKeeman 1975]. It has definite limitations in later stages of a project: to all the disadvantages of preprocessors are added the slowness, expense, and fault-proneness of the manual transformation.

CHOOSING A LANGUAGE

Selecting a language from among those that are available for use in a given situation is a discouraging process, one of attempting to minimize evils. The traditional criteria, particularly availability, place severe constraints on the choice. When there are two or more languages remaining, however, how should one choose? The following should be taken as hints, rather than firmly established rules:

Compare the languages with the criteria given in Parts I—III. Generally, the "Algol family" of languages conform more closely than those of the "FORTRAN family," which in turn tend to conform better than members of the "PL/I family," which conform better than members of the "COBOL family." Consider, but do not be overawed by, claims that a particular language or dialect is "structured."

Take the simplest available language that will do the job. Additional "power" and complexity are more likely to harm than help reliability.

Consider the available subset compilers and preprocessors very carefully. They may provide a considerable reliability advantage while retaining compatibility with existing systems and minimizing the need for retraining.

Look at the available program development and checking tools. A language with a full set is already a leg up.

"Better the evil that you know than one that you don't." Familiarity with a language may be of considerable assistance in avoiding its worst pitfalls.

ACKNOWLEDGEMENTS

This lecture was based on a series of lectures prepared for an Advanced Course on Computing Systems Reliability given at the University of Newcastle-upon-Tyne, England in August 1978. These notes were slightly condensed from the notes prepared for that course. My ability to focus on these issues was considerably aided by a preparatory meeting of the instructors for that course in October 1977.

I am indebted to discussions within IFIP Working Group 2.3 (Programming Methodology) for many of the ideas expressed throughout these notes.

Part I is based largely on a draft working paper prepared for IFIP Working Group 2.4 (System Implementation Languages) by its subcommittee on reliability, edited by John Gannon and myself. I am grateful to the members of WG 2.4 for their suggestions and criticism, and especially to John Gannon, without whose cooperation and research I could not have formulated the issues so clearly.

My awareness of the issues raised in Part II, and of the approaches discussed, very largely springs from my participation in the Highly Reliable Computing Systems project at Newcastle, and numerous—frequently heated—discussions with many other members of that project over a number of years. My colleagues at Xerox introduced me to Mesa and the practical use of signals in my own programming.

Part III was stimulated by numerous discussions over the years in IFIP Working Groups 2.3 and 2.4 and in the ARPA's informal Quality Software for Complex Tasks working group. The design of Euclid was a team effort; one of its most valuable products for me was an enforced education about verification provided by Ralph London and the other team members. John Guttag and Jim Donahue provided both information and motivation. Finally, my thoughts were focussed by the ACM Conference on

J. J. HORNING

Language Design for Reliable Software [SIGPLAN 1977][CACM 1977].

Part IV is dedicated to the computer manufacturers of the world, whose efforts made it both possible and necessary.

REFERENCES

Anderson, T., and R. Kerr [1976]. "Recovery blocks in action." In *Proc. 2nd International Conference on Software Engineering*, San Francisco, pp. 447–457.

Backus, J. W., R. J. Beeber, S. Best, R. Goldberg, L. M. Haibt, H. L. Herrick, R. A. Nelson, D. Sayre, P. B. Sheridan, H. Stern, I. Ziller, R. A. Hughes, and R. Nutt [1957]. "The FORTRAN automatic coding system." In *Proc. Western Joint Computer Conference*, Los Angeles.

Baker, F. T. [1972]. "Chief programmer team management of production programming." *IBM Syst. J.* **11**, no. 1, pp. 56–73.

——[1975]. "Structured programming in a production programming environment." *IEEE Trans. Software Engineering* SE–1, no. 2, pp. 241–252.

Boehm, B. W. [1973]. "Software and its impact: A quantitative assessment." *Datamation* **19**, no. 5, pp. 48–59.

——, R. K. McClean, and D. B. Urfrig [1975]. "Some experience with automated aids to the design of large–scale reliable software." *IEEE Trans. Software Engineering* SE–1, no. 1, pp. 125–133.

——, J. R. Brown, and M. Lipow [1976]. "Quantitative evaluation of software quality." In *Proc. 2nd International Conference on Software Engineering*, San Francisco, pp. 592–605.

Bridge, R. F. and E. W. Thompson [1976]. "BRIDGES—A tool for increasing the reliability of references to FORTRAN variables." *SIGPLAN Notices* **11**, no. 9, pp. 2–9.

CACM [1977]. Special issue on language design for reliable software. *Comm. ACM* **20**, no. 8, pp. 539–595.

Clark, B. L. and J. J. Horning [1973]. "Reflections on a language designed to write an operating system." *SIGPLAN Notices* **8**, no. 9, pp. 52–56.

Culpepper, L. M. [1975]. "A system for reliable engineering software." *SIGPLAN Notices* **10**, no. 6, pp. 186–192.

Dahl, O.-J. , E. W. Dijkstra, and C. A. R. Hoare [1972] *Structured Programming*. Academic Press, London and New York.

Dijkstra, E. W. [1968]. "Go to statement considered harmful." *Comm. ACM* **11**, no. 3, pp. 147–148.

PROGRAMMING LANGUAGES FOR RELIABLE COMPUTING SYSTEMS

——[1975]. "Correctness concerns and, among other things, why they are resented." *SIGPLAN Notices* **10**, no. 6, pp. 546–550.

——[1976]. *A Discipline of Programming.* Prentice–Hall, Englewood Cliffs.

Floyd, R. W. [1967]. "Assigning meanings to programs." In *Mathematical Aspects of Computer Science*, ed. J. T. Schwartz, American Mathematical Society, Providence.

Fosdick, Loyd D., and Leon J. Osterweil [1976]. "The detection of anomalous interprocedural data flow." In *Proc. 2nd International Conference on Software Engineering*, San Francisco, pp. 624–628.

Gannon, John D. [1975]. "Language design to enhance programming reliability." Technical Report CSRG–47, University of Toronto Computer Systems Research Group. [Summarized in John D. Gannon and J. J. Horning, "Language design for programming reliability." *IEEE Trans. Software Engineering* **SE–1**, no. 2, pp. 179–191.]

——[1977]. "An experimental evaluation of data type conventions." *Comm. ACM* **20**, no. 8, pp. 584–595.

Goodenough, J. B. [1975]. "Exception handling: Issues and a proposed notation." *Comm. ACM* **18**, no. 12, pp. 683–696.

Gordon, Harvey [1975]. "Paragraphing computer programs." M. Sc. Thesis, University of Toronto Computer Science Department.

Gould, J. D. [1973]. "Some psychological evidence on how people debug computer programs." Report RC 4542, IBM Watson Research Center, Yorktown Heights.

——and P. Drongowski [1972]. "A controlled psychological study of computer program debugging." Report RC 4083, IBM Watson Research Center, Yorktown Heights.

Gries, D. [1974]. "On structured programming—A reply to Smoliar." *Comm. ACM* **17**, no. 11, pp. 655–657.

Hoare, C. A. R. [1969]. "An axiomatic basis for computer programming." *Comm. ACM* **12**, no. 10, pp. 576–583.

——[1970]. "The use of high level languages in large program construction." In *Efficient Production of Large Programs*, ed. B. Osuchowska, pp. 81–107, Computation Centre of the Polish Academy of Sciences, Warsawa.

——[1972]. "Proofs of correctness of data representation." *Acta Informatica* **1**, pp. 271–281.

——[1973]. "Hints on programming language design." Technical Report STAN–CS–73–403, Stanford University Computer Science Department.

——[1975]. "Recursive data structures." *Int. J. Comp. Inf. Sci.* **4**, p. 105.

J. J. HORNING

——and Wirth [1973]. "An axiomatic definition of the programming language Pascal." *Acta Informatica* 2, pp. 335–355.

Holt, R. C., D. B. Wortman, D. T. Barnard, and J. R. Cordy [1977]. "SP/k: A system for teaching computer programming." *Comm. ACM* 20, no. 5, pp. 301–309.

Horning, J. J., H. C. Lauer, P. M. Melliar-Smith, and B. Randell [1974]. "A program structure for error detection and recovery." In *Operating Systems*, ed. E. Gelenbe and C. Kaiser, pp. 171–187, Springer-Verlag Lecture Notes in Computer Science 16, Berlin.

Horning, J. J., and D. B. Wortman [1977]. "Software Hut: A computer program engineering project in the form of a game." *IEEE Trans. Software Engineering* SE-3, no. 4, pp. 325–330.

Ichbiah, J. D., and J. P. Rissen [1971]. "Directions de travail pour un atelier de software." Preliminary Report, Compagnie Internationale Pour L'Informatique, Paris.

ICRS [1975]. "Proceedings—1975 International Conference on Reliable Software." *SIGPLAN Notices* 10, no. 6.

Jones, Anita K., and Barbara H. Liskov [1976]. "A language extension for controlling access to shared data." *IEEE Trans. Software Engineering* SE-2, no. 4, pp. 277–284.

Karr, Michael, and David B. Loveman III [1978]. "Incorporation of units into programming languages." *Comm. ACM* 21, no. 5, pp. 385–391.

Kernighan, Brian W., and P. J. Plauger [1974]. *The Elements of Programming Style.* McGraw-Hill, New York.

——[1976]. *Software Tools.* Addison-Wesley, Reading.

Knuth, D. E. [1974]. "Structured programming with go to statements." *Comp. Surveys* 6, no. 4, pp. 261–301.

Lampson, B. W., J. J. Horning, R. L. London, J. G. Mitchell, and G. J. Popek [1977]. "Report on the programming language Euclid." *SIGPLAN Notices* 12, no. 2.

Levin, Roy [1977]. "Program structures for exceptional condition handling." Ph. D. Thesis, Carnegie-Mellon University Department of Computer Science.

Liskov, Barbara, Alan Snyder, Russell Atkinson, and Craig Scheffert [1977]. "Abstraction mechanisms in CLU." *Comm. ACM* 20, no. 8, pp. 564–576.

London, R. L. [1975]. "A view of program verification." *SIGPLAN Notices* 10, no. 6, pp. 534–545.

——, Mary Shaw, and Wm. A. Wulf [1976]. "Abstraction and verification in Alphard: A symbol table example." Technical Report, Carnegie-Mellon University Department of Computer Science and University of Southern California Information Sciences Institute.

528

PROGRAMMING LANGUAGES FOR RELIABLE COMPUTING SYSTEMS

——, J. V. Guttag, J. J. Horning, B. W. Lampson, J. G. Mitchell, and G. J. Popek [1978]. "Proof rules for the programming language Euclid." *Acta Informatica* 10, pp. 1–26.

Love, Tom [1977]. "An experimental investigation of the effect of program structure on program understanding." *SIGPLAN Notices* 12, no. 3, pp. 105–113.

McCarthy, J. [1962]. "Towards a mathematical theory of computation." In *Proc. IFIP Congress 62*. pp. 21–28, North–Holland, Amsterdam.

McKeeman, W. M. [1975]. "On preventing programming languages from interfering with programming." *IEEE Trans. Software Engineering* SE-1, no. 1, pp. 19–26.

——, J. J. Horning, and D. B. Wortman [1970]. *A Compiler Generator*. Prentice–Hall, Englewood Cliffs.

MacLaren, M. Donald [1977]. "Exception handling in PL/I." *SIGPLAN Notices* 12, no. 3, pp. 101–104.

Miller, L. A. [1973]. "Normative procedure specification." In *Proc. 81st Ann. Conv. Am. Psychological Assn.*, Montreal.

——[1974]. "Programming by non–programmers." *Int. J. Man–Machine Studies* 6, no. 2, pp. 237–260.

Mitchell, James G., William Maybury, and Richard Sweet [1978]. "Mesa language manual." Technical Report CSL-78-1, Xerox Palo Alto Research Center.

MOHLL [1975]. *Machine Oriented Higher Level Languages*. ed. W. L. van der Poel and L. A. Maarssen, North–Holland, Amsterdam.

Morgan, H. L. [1970]. "Spelling correction in system programs." *Comm. ACM* 13, no. 2, pp. 90–94.

Parnas, D. L. [1971]. "Information distribution aspects of design methodology." In *Proc. IFIP Congress 71*. pp. 339–344, North–Holland, Amsterdam.

Pratt, Terrence W. [1975]. *Programming Languages: Design and Implementation*. Prentice–Hall, Englewood Cliffs.

Randell, B. [1975]. "System structure for software fault tolerance." *SIGPLAN Notices* 10, no. 6, pp. 437–449.

——, and P. M. Melliar-Smith [1977]. "Software reliability: The role of programmed exception handling." *SIGPLAN Notices* 12, no. 3, pp. 95–100.

Satterthwaite, E. [1972]. "Debugging tools for high–level languages." *Software—Practice and Experience* 2, pp. 197–217.

Sharp [1977]. "Small Euclid transliterator." Technical Report, I. P. Sharp Associates Special Systems Division, Toronto.

J. J. HORNING

Shaw, Mary [1976]. "Abstraction and verification in Alphard: Design and verification of a tree handler." In *Proc. Fifth Texas Conf. Computing Systems.* pp. 86–94.

——, Wm. A. Wulf, and Ralph L. London [1976]. "Abstraction and verification in Alphard: Iteration and generators." Technical Report, Carnegie–Mellon University Department of Computer Science and University of Southern California Information Sciences Institute.

——, ——, and ——[1977]. "Abstraction and verification in Alphard: Defining and specifying iteration and generators." *Comm. ACM* **20**, no. 8, pp. 553–564.

Shneidermann, B. [1974]. "Two experiments in programming behavior." Technical Report 17, Indiana University Computer Science Department.

——[1977]. Special issue on language design for reliable software. *SIGPLAN Notices* **12**, no. 3.

Sime, M. E., T. R. Green, and D. J. Guest [1973]. "Psychological evaluation of two conditional constructions used in computer languages." *Int. J. Man–Machine Studies* **5**, no. 1, pp. 105–113.

Strachey, C. [1973]. Lecture given at IBM Scientific Center, Peterlee, England.

Teitelman, W. [1972]. "Do what I mean: The programmer's assistant." *Computers and Automation* **21**, pp. 8–11.

Turski, W. M. [1978]. *Computer Programming Methodology.* Heyden, London.

Weinberg, Gerald M. [1971]. *The Psychology of Computer Programming.* Van Nostrand Reinhold, New York.

——[1973]. "The psychology of improved programming performance." *Datamation* **18**, no. 11.

Weissman, Laurence M. [1974]. "A methodology for studying the psychological complexity of computer programs." Technical Report CSRG–37, University of Toronto Computer Systems Research Group.

Wirth, N. [1971a]. "The programming language Pascal." *Acta Informatica* **1**, pp. 35–63.

——[1971b]. "Program development by stepwise refinement." *Comm. ACM* **14**, no. 4, pp. 221–227.

——[1974a]. "On the design of programming languages." In *Proc. IFIP Congress 74.* pp. 386–393, North–Holland, Amsterdam.

——[1974b]. "On the composition of well structured programs." *Comp. Surveys* **6**, no. 4, pp. 247–259.

Wulf, W., and Mary Shaw [1973]. "Global variable considered harmful." *SIGPLAN Notices* **8**, no. 2, pp. 28–34.

PROGRAMMING LANGUAGES FOR RELIABLE COMPUTING SYSTEMS

Wulf, Wm. A., Ralph L. London, and Mary Shaw [1976a]. "Abstraction and verification in Alphard: Introduction to language and methodology." Technical Report, Carnegie–Mellon University Department of Computer Science and University of Southern California Information Sciences Institute.

——, ——, and ——[1976b]. "An introduction to the construction and verification of Alphard programs." *IEEE Trans. Software Engineering* **SE–2**, no. 4, pp. 253–265.

PROGRAMMING METHODOLOGY AND LANGUAGE IMPLICATIONS

Michael GRIFFITHS

Centre de Recherche en Informatique de Nancy

Château du Montet

54500 Vandoeuvre les Nancy

France

I. INTRODUCTION

Over the last two or three years, different research groups have produced languages which form a definite generation. The driving force behind these languages has been the revolution in programming habits which followed the discovery of a set of program properties. The programming techniques involved imply that logic which was previously an intuitive idea in the mind of the programmer become an explicit text susceptible to mathematical treatment. It is thus a logical step to creat new programming languages which accept this same mathematical text as supplementary information, and, in turn, that compilers should make use of it.

It may be observed that it is not sufficient to add assertional statements to existing programming languages, except in the form of comments, because of the complexity of the implications on the compiler. Restrictions must also be made on the host language in order to be able to establish the necessary properties. The complexity of establishing these properties in classical languages was considered in [Griffiths, 1976].

In this paper, we consider the set of constraints required and the implications of these constraints on language definitions, with examples from one particular new language. The language chosen is that from the author's own research group, for obvious reasons, but it should be noted that the same concepts are found in other languages of the same general type. A previous synthesis is to be found in [Griffiths, 1977], which used local vocabulary. Several changes will be noted here, since we have made an effort to standardise on the vocabulary which is gradually emerging.

Putting more responsability on the compiler, at the expense of eliminating unsavoury "gimmicks", should, in the long term, allow the demonstration of several global properties, none of which we are able to confirm at this moment in time. An incomplete list of properties would include portability, guarantee of execution and coherence.

Present knowledge should allow us, in a wide sense, to guarantee portability of programs by the elimination of loose points in language design, and by forebidding the use of the term "undefined" in a language definition. This will not, of course, solve the problems of numerical accuracy, word-length or rounding, but would still be a considerable improvement. It is distressing to note that many differences between versions of a language, in particular when considering the reaction of different compilers, are due to non-technical factors.

A guarantee of execution means that any program which compiles successfully will run. This aim is at present unattained, unless we consider that "proved" programs come under this heading. Program proving is, of course, a stronger condition, since it implies a demonstration that the program handed to a compiler solves the problem that was given to the programmer. Execution guarantee merely states that the program always does something which is acceptable on the computer, without considering what the programmer thought.

Coherence is a vague term which implies that the compiler should apply rules of good sense to the program. It includes confirming that all parts of a program are accessible, that calculated values are subsequently used, and so on. Lack of coherence in a program should be an indication of an error on the part of the programmer.

2. IMPORT-EXPORT

Block structure, as invented in ALGOL, has not turned out to be a completely satisfactory way of allowing programs to protect or to share variables and their values. After a period of trying to add new constructs to languages while retaining existing ones, for instance classes in SIMULA [Dahl, Myrhaug, Nygaard, 1968], it was suggested that some of the existing properties of block structures should be disregarded (see, for example, [Wulf, Shaw, 1973] or [Griffiths, 1973]).

Since that date it has become common to require that the program indicate explicitly which variables are available outside their local module (called export variables), and similarly that variables required from elsewhere (import variables) can be accessed only by a parameter - like mechanism. This technique is now sufficiently well-known as to require no further development, although some points of detail still bear discussion.

Our first point concerns some efforts which allow the programmer to use explicit import/export statements or to profit from classical block structure. The mixture must be considered an error, since the advantages of protection by modules are not guaranteed. It is unfortunate that this mixture is proposed in the languages which have been favorably considered in reply to the Ironman report [Dod, 1977]. Security is always dependent upon constraints, which the compiler must be able to verify.

The mere existence of import-export statements is sufficient in assuring the protection of data, but does not forebid ambiguous results, in particular from side effects. Different languages have taken varying decisions when, as a result of function calls, the order of evaluation of operands of an expression would be significant. Consider the simple addition

a + b.

ALGOL 60 requires that the result be that implied by the evaluation of a before that of b ; ALGOL68, however, leaves the choice to the compiler by the use of the term "undefined" in the case where a + b and b + a give different results. We consider that the compiler should reject a program in this case, thus transforming "undefined" into "illegal".

In order to achieve this type of property, we are forced to limit the use of functions in expressions to those which have no side effects. This means that the compiler knows which functions are pure, in the mathematical sense, and which have access to, or change, values which are not local. The result is a classification of procedure and function types :

- utilities. These are pure functions, which return one or more results without access of any kind to data other than parameters. Formal parameters cannot occur on the left of assignments. Obviously, utilities may only call utilities, and always return at least one result.

- functions. They may access outside data, but without changing any non-local values. A module which is a data description will use functions as the means of expressing the relation between abstract and concrete data. Functions may call utilities or other functions, and always return at least one result.

- actions. The dangerous case, where the value of some non-local data is changed. Actions may return results or not, but results are always directly assigned, thus forebidding problems within expressions. Input-output routines are always actions.

If examples are needed, consider the hackneyed one of stacks, in which push and pull are actions, since they change the stack, whereas the operation of examining the top of the stack is a function. Sine, cosine and square root are obvious examples of utilities.

The classification is not just a means of helping the compiler to impose restrictions, although this would be sufficient justification. It is equally important to make the programmer conscious of what he is writing. This view, which is that of an educationalist, is also reasonable outside the academic world : good habits need not necessarily be confirmed to students. In addition to the immediate benefits in standard programming, there are also others which become clear when we consider the use of assertions in the programming language.

3. CONTROL OF VALUES

There are already several languages which are intended as a more logical
support than is normally available when producing programs with verification in
mind. Although the remarks here are directly concerned with MEFIA [Cunin et al,
1978], Alphard [Wulf et al, 1976], Clu [Liskov, Snyder, 1977], Lucid [Ashcroft,
Wadge, 1977] and Euclid [Horning, 1978, Lampson, 1977] are all better known, and
should be studied ; the list is not by any means complete. A vital part of the
technology supported by this class of languages is the use made of assertional
information.

Unfortunately, value properties inside programs are of various types. It is
thus not sufficient to add an <u>assert</u> statement to the language and move on to the
next problem. This remark is not intended as a criticism of PASCAL, which was the
first language to introduce these ideas, since the aims were not the same. To be
useful in a practical world, the devices used by the programmer must correspond to
tests which the compiler will apply or generate in a manner known to the programmer.
Categories of test will include compile-time, run-time and debugging. In some cases
the tests will be implicit, in particular those which are applied by the compiler.

3.1. Compile Time Testing

One of the aims of the languages under discussion is to transfer as much
testing as is reasonable and possible from the run-time system to the compiler.
Standard topics in this region include the following :

- All variables are initialised before use

- For every well-formed set of input data there exists a path through the program
  which is coherent with such other information about the program as may be
  available.

- All references exist. For example all array references have indices within bounds
  and all pointers lead to accessible values.

- Assertions which are merely deductions available from simple manipulations of the
  program text are valid, that is that the programmer has made no trivial logical
  errors in their obtention.
The list is not complete.

Our view on initialisation is that the compiler will consider a program on
which it cannot demonstrate the initialisation of all variables is wrong, even if
the programmer is satisfied. This is not so extreme as it appears, because of the
restrictions imposed on the scope of variables and on assignment. These restrictions
make initialisation easy to prove in general, and also make it more difficult to
write a working program in which initialisation is not obvious to the compiler.

Proving the existence of coherent program paths is no problem in pretty programs, and very difficult in those which use complicated control flow. The solution to the problem thus lies in a mixture of education and simple testing. The testing comes down to the analysis of valid value ranges at different points of the program in order to confirm the existence, for any given set of current values, of a unique path through the segment of program text considered.

Among the tests considered in this list would be that conditionals, expressed as guarded commands, be determinist. For example :

<u>choice</u>   x > 0, ...
         x < 0, ...
<u>endchoice</u>

The keyword <u>choice</u> is simply a syntactic variant of the guarded command. The compiler should be capable, in the given example, of signalling the fact that the case x = 0 is not considered. In general, each possible set of values concerned in the <u>choice</u> conditions should lead to one and only one possibility.

The ranges of values considered may depend on conditions previously established, for example because the <u>choice</u> statement lies inside another, making some condition true, or after a loop, when the condition after <u>while</u> is now false. It is in the combination of such sets of information that it becomes necessary to use sophisticated theorem provers in the general case. To avoid their use, we need to distinguish those cases which need only simple treatment, and find some way of encouraging the programmer to stay inside the boundary. This aspect is still subject to research.

The type of assertion which is a deduction from the program text should also be checked by the compiler, as being subject to "typing errors". An error of this type may cause an apparently proved program to be invalid. An example similar to that used in the choice statement above would be :

<u>while</u> x < 10 <u>do</u> ... <u>done</u> ;
<u>deduce</u> x > 10 ;

The case x = 10 is ignored. Although this "parity" error is not the most frequent, experience shows that it occurs regularly in programs, and its elimination is not difficult.

In general, program incoherence is just one step in the direction of diminishing the number of errors in programs. We believe that it is one of many steps which will be taken steadily, keeping in mind the constant and necessary improvement in programming standards. Perfection is a satisfactory target, but one which is rarely attained by human beings. All additional help and guidance is thus positive.

Amongst others problems to do with the flow of control, there is the classic termination of loops. Proofs in this area, when dealing with a particular case in which proof of termination is possible, are helped by gathering together control information. Thus we suggest that one possible control structure for the loop would be :

first i := ... next i := ... stop ...

Changes of value of the control variable are indicated, and a series is clearly defined. There may be more than one control variable, thus requiring multiple assignments for the initialisation and sequence statements, and the next and stop statements are not necessarily at the start of the loop, as in the suggestion of [Naur, 75].

3.2. Ranges and References

Looking at array references, and in particular at the problem of the validity of indices, one is tempted to take the range concept of PASCAL and generalise it. In so doing, the possible indices of an array become a kind of parameter of the array. For instance :

range r1 = [1 : 10] ;
    [r1] integer tab1 ;
index i in r1 ;

Any reference of the form tab1 [i] is now valid, since i is necessarily in bounds. Of course, this puts the responsability of testing the value of i on to the code generated for assignment, which is necessarily dynamic. Note that assignments to indices are usually less frequent than references which use them, and that optimisation of testing can be done. Consider the simple, and common case of

i := i + 1

Only the upper bound needs testing. Hence the method is more efficient than dynamic bound checking.

This line of thought leads to generalisation, and it should be possible to impose any type of condition on an object. In most of the languages considered, conditions are usually considered as being defined on types, for example :

type posint = integer x, $x \geq 0$

with some suitable syntax. We consider that a better choice is that positive
integers, or any class of objects limited by conditions on their values, have normal
types, but individual conditions :

    integer x cond x ≥ 0

The condition will always be tested on assignment to x.

Comparing this with conditions on types is not simple, since there are some
subtle implications. However, what is clear is that we avoid the potentially numerous
and expensive tests of type compatibility and conversion while leaving most of the
facilities useful to the programmer. The amount of run-time testing may increase,
but usually only in cases that were either impossible or untested when conditions
are put on types.

One important point concerns the initialisation of objects subject to
conditions, as of indices. Since checking the validity of the condition is carried
out at assignment, and not on use, a non-initialised object of this type is not
accepted. This is merely a particular case of the general line, previously mentioned,
on initialisation.

A useful effect of giving names to ranges and conditions is to establish
relationships between objects. Two applications, both relatively common, are
immediate ; they are global assignment and parameter checking. If arrays are to be
manipulated and assigned as single objects, the compiler can do the size checking.
A simple example would be the multiplication of two matrices :

    range r1 = (1 : m), r2 = (1 : p), r3 = (1 : n) ;
    [r1, r2] real a, [r2, r3] real b, [r1, r3] real c ;
    utility matmult ([t1, t2] real mat1, [t2, t3] real mat2) →
                          [t1, t3] real ; c body of matmult c ;
    ...
      c := matmult (a, b)

In the procedure declaration, which in fact is a utility, the input parameters are
decorated with information concerning the sizes of the arrays, and similar information
is available for the result. t1, t2 and t3 are formal ranges which become available
to the inside of the utility as well as establishing the necessary relationship
between input and output. It is thus possible to confirm at compile time that the
assignment in the last line conforms to the required restrictions. This example
illustrates the two applications suggested, but there are, of course, other useful
implications. A more complete discussion of the algorithms involved in testing is
to be found in [Cunin, 1978].

3.3. Run-Time Testing

The preceeding section shows some of the points at which classical techniques of run-time testing are reinforced and made less expensive. In this section we discuss further tests which may add to program security. It is in this area that the generation of languages discussed show the largest differences. At one extreme, we find EUCLID, in which, at least as a first degree of approximation, all assertions in the program are confirmed during execution. Although this is, for the compiler, no more than the similar facility already available in PASCAL, in practice, it is much more applied because of being associated directly with the programming technology used.

The position taken by EUCLID has one important advantage, which is the fact of disposing of a direct instruction to perform a run-time test. This is clear for the user, encouraged by the programming techniques implicity required, and thus immediately, and simply useful. However, we believe that analysis of needs should lead to a more complex, but more general set of statements. We will thus attempt to distinguish several different types of assertion.

A first level of discrimination is whether an assertion should be known to the outside world. There are precisely two such assertions in each unit of program, the pre-condition and the post-condition. The pre-condition is that set of conditions on the input data under which the program is guaranteed to produce the required result. The post-condition is the definition of this result, the combination being the formal specification of the program. All the assertions which figure inside the program text are strictly internal, like temporary variables. They may have two uses, one being the documentation of the proof the proof process used, and the other an aid to debugging, if we allow the use of the term.

This analysis would be easier in an ideal world in which programs were proved by an automatic theorem-prover, in which we need only ask questions about the testing of the pre-condition, which served as axiom for the proof. But this ideal world does not yet exist in practice, and obviously lies some way ahead. We must therefore find a balance, as in any engineering discipline, between security, efficiency and human fallibility. During the period, possibly long, which will elapse before perfection is reached, we must work in several directions.
- Educate programmers so that they use the relevant techniques
- Change languages so that the assertions are left in the text, that is to say recognised by the compiler
- Make the maximum use of the given information in order to reinforce the above attitudes.

In order to leave enough liberty at the program level, there must be a way of indicating whether assertions are tested or not at run-time. A parallel exists with testing of indices in arrays, where a working program guarantees validity, but testing can be useful at some stage of the process. The problem is one of efficiency, where a good example was given by Dijkstra. Consider the program developped which uses dichotomy in looking for an element [Dijkstra 1978]. The whole idea is to minimise the number of vector elements consulted. However, the program depends on the fact that the elements are ordered. To confirm this requires inspection of each element. But, if each element is to be inspected anyway, it is not worth while to use the algorithm. The test becomes an economic disaster. In this case, either we know from elsewhere that the vector is ordered, or the fact is taken on trust. Whether the test is carried out while debugging the program depends on circumstances and the programmer's religion. Assertions must therefore be included in the language, with an indication as to whether they are to be confirmed at run-time, following the desire of the programmer.

This discussion highlights the importance of specifications, with which procedures play the role of theorems, to be combined and used as black-box functions. The only long-term necessary testing should then be of data which comes from outside the program, where it is essential to catch as many typing errors as possible. Whenever data coherence testing is not carried out this should be reflected in the specification. For example, in the case of dichotomy, when a required element is not found, the assertion becomes {either x is not present, or the vector is not ordered}.

It is by the continuing reduction of what we may call the error space that we will one day eliminate program breakdown leading to catastrophes like dumps. The situation is that of a compiler, which must not only accept and translate any correct sequence of characters but also indicate clearly all formal errors, and thus have a predictable (and predicted) response to any sequence whatsoever. Any program should respect these same rules, with a corresponding improvement of dialogue and of security. This means that we consider that it should be impossible for good programs to break down at execution time ; any combination of data which would provoke such a catastrophe being identified, and indicated, in the program prelude.

4. CONCLUSION

The new generation of languages, of which certain members are named in the references, constitutes an attempt to make program tools follow recent improvements in programming technique. No one language is, as yet, satisfactory, but the notions which are common to many of them should become standard over the next few years. This is not to say that we already know the basis of the language to be used in the year 2000, since much more work remains to be done. At least, these new languages have shown up the need to continue thinking about the problem ; the author has hoard several well-known computer scientists suggest that research in programming languages is a dead end. This is obviously untrue, as we need to go much further. Of course, the subject has become much more difficult, and it is no longer possible to publish any set of new keywords in order to be considered an expert.

Future languages will follow improvements in programming, as they always have done. There is no way of imposing better tools without educating programmers in their use. These improvements will follow two directions, which are better control of problem-solving and the reduction of the number of problems to be solved by the identification of standard situations. The first of these has received the more attention, and is gradually converting amateur do-it-yourself programmers to craftsmen. The accumulation of known situations is the computing equivalent of culture, allowing craftsmen to become engineers. This culture is at present insufficiently studied.

Attempts are being made to classify simple program schemes, for example in [Scholl, 1978], but we should try to see further ahead than these. When, little by little, standard modules, or theorems, become available, it will be necessary to have means of putting them together to make new units. It is here that specification becomes most important, not just in its form, but particularly in the means of composing well-defined specifications.

This means that, for the ordinary user of computers, the basic programming language should become irrelevant, because he will dispose of a large number of building bricks which consist of modules which always produce right answers if the pre-conditions are valid. The high-level compiler will confirm the validity of the use of the modules by manipulation of specifications and pre-conditions. The production of basic modules must be as independent as possible of different aspects of programming languages to make them universal. It is by the restriction of gimmicks and precise definitions that the languages used will become mutually compatible. Some of the particular restrictions described in this paper are directed to that end.

Thus, we feel that the future of programming languages is tied up with the classification of problems to be solved and of their "good" solutions. It is from the form of these solutions that we will discover the best form of languages in which to encode them. The search for structured solutions is long-term, even if we now have some idea of what is required.

REFERENCES

ASHCROFT E.A., WADGE W.W. (1977)
 Lucid, A Non-Procedural Language with Iteration
 CACM, Aug. 1977

CUNIN P.Y., GRIFFITHS M., SCHOLL P.C. (1978)
 Aspects Fondamentaux du Langage MEFIA
 Proceedings, Journées AFCET-EDF, April 1978

DAHL O.J., MYRHAUG B., NYGAARD K. (1968)
 The SIMULA 67 Common Base Language
 Norwegian Computer Centre, Oslo, May 1968

DIJKSTRA E.W. (1978)
 This volume

GRIFFITHS M. (1973)
 Relationship between Language Definition and Implementation
 in Software Engineering, ed. F.L. Bauer, LNCS, 30, Springer Verlag, 1973

GRIFFITHS M. (1976)
 Verifiers and Filters
 in Software Portability, P.J. Brown (ed.), Cambridge University Press, 1976

GRIFFITHS M. (1977)
 Language Support for Program Construction
 CREST Advanced Course, Toulouse, Dec. 1977

HORNING J.J. (1978)
 This volume

LAMPSON B.W., HORNING J.J., LONDON R.L., MITCHELL J.G., POPEK G.J. (1977)
 Report on the Programming Language EUCLID
 SIGPLAN Notices, 12, 2, Feb. 1977.

LISKOV B., SNYDER A. (1977)
 Abstraction Mechanisms in CLU
 CACM, Aug. 1977

NAUR P. (1975)
 Programming Languages, Natural Languages and Mathematics
 CACM, 18, 3

SCHOLL P.C. (1978)
 Le traitement séquentiel : une classe de problèmes et une méthode de construction de programmes - Congrès AFCET, Nov. 1978

U.S. Department of Defense (1977)
    Ironman Specifications, 1977

WULF W.A., LONDON R.L., SHAW M. (1976)
    An Introduction to the Construction and Verification of Alphard Programs
    IEEE Trans. Soft. Eng. 4, Dec. 1976

TOWARDS A WIDE SPECTRUM LANGUAGE
TO SUPPORT PROGRAM SPECIFICATION AND PROGRAM DEVELOPMENT *

F. L. Bauer, M. Broy, R. Gnatz, W. Hesse,
B. Krieg-Brückner, H. Partsch, P. Pepper, H. Wössner

Institut für Informatik
der Technischen Universität München
Postfach 202420
D-8000 München 2, Germany

1. Introduction

Source-to-source transformations have been advocated
as a methodological tool for program development (cf.
e.g. [Bauer 73], [Knuth 74], [Burstall, Darlington 75],
[Gerhart 75], [Bauer 76], [Standish et al. 76]).
Once an exact specification of a given problem has replaced an informal description of it, a "contract" is
settled. This contract version frequently happens to
be formulated on a "high level" and may even use non-
algorithmic specification tools. The program should
then be developed step by step applying correctness
preserving transformations. Under the guidance of the
programmer this process is goal-directed: it leads to
program versions which are sufficiently efficient and
adapted to the requirements of a class of machines or
even of a particular machine. The development process
thus involves usually multiple reshapings, e.g. removal
of pure specification constructs (by introducing recursion), simplification of recursion (in particular
transition to iteration), but frequently also more
bulky operations of detailization, if these are not
left to a compiler.

Since most current programming languages do not contain
all the concepts needed for the formulation of the different versions, the programmer is nowadays forced to
use different languages. To avoid the transition from
one language to another, it seems appropriate to have
one coherent language frame covering the whole spectrum outlined above, i.e. a *wide spectrum language*.
(As a former approach to a wide spectrum language [Gei-
selbrechtinger et al. 74], even a family of discrete

language layers turned out not to be flexible enough
to accommodate the requirements of a transformation
system.) If program transformations affect only parts
of a program version, then other parts can remain unchanged, whereas, when switching to another language,
the whole program has to be translated. Moreover, formal problem specifications can be formulated in a single language of this kind, in which non-operational
formulations may coexist with operational ones and
can gradually be eliminated.

This methodology of programming and its support by a
system are investigated in the project CIP (Computer-
aided, Intuition-guided Programming) at the Technical
University of Munich. As a part of this project, a
language which supports program development is currently being designed [Bauer et al. 77a]. This language
must incorporate a variety of concepts, yet still retain a manageable size. It covers coherently the entire spectrum from problem specification tools to machine-oriented languages; it comprises such constructs
as e.g. descriptive expressions and choices, predicates
and quantification (used for abstract specifications
and mode restrictions), recursive modes, recursive
functions and non-deterministic conditionals (for the
applicative formulation of algorithms), and variables,
collective assignments, procedures, iteration, etc.
(for the development towards machine language). According to different collections of constructs used in
the formulation of a program, several particular language "styles" (instead of different languages) can
easily be distinguished.

* This research was carried out within the Sonderforschungsbereich 49 "Programmiertechnik", Munich.

This wide spectrum language is more than an "algorithmic language" in the classical sense, since "programs" may be formulated containing expressions which are not immediately to be executed on any machine. Only certain particular language styles may be executable with respect to a given interpretative system (e.g. a concrete machine) or translatable by a standard transformation ("compiler") into a machine language style.

One of the principles in the design of the language has been to establish transitions between different language styles so as to ease the transformation process. Consequently, transformation rules have considerably influenced the language design. Transformations, while forming a basic stock for the user of the language, can conveniently be used for the language definition itself relative to a language kernel (as has been done in a similar way in the "extensible language" area). In such a way, it can be expected to have reduced the semantics of the full wide spectrum language to an applicative core ("transformational semantics"). Due to lack of space, only a few transformation rules can be presented in this paper (for more information see [Bauer et al. 76], [Bauer et al. 77b], [Broy 77], [Gnatz 77], [Gnatz, Pepper 77], [Partsch, Pepper 77], [Steinbrüggen 77]).

Thus, the main concern is to clarify the abstract concepts of the language, and to indicate their coherence by transformations. Although there is no primary interest in a particular notation, for the following informal presentation an ALGOL-like notation is used ("ALGOL 77"); however, a PASCAL-like notation is also envisaged. "CIP-L" serves as a code-word for the abstract language.

The following stages of a sample development of the problem of computing the quotient and remainder of two natural numbers may give a first impression of CIP-L.

Let the following modes be given:

mode nat = (int x : x ≥ 0), mode pnat = (nat x : x > 0)

1) Specification using a descriptive expression (that...):

```
funct div = (nat a, pnat b)(nat, nat) :
    that (nat q, nat r): a = b × q + r ∧ r < b
```

2) Recursive formulation:

```
funct div = (nat a, pnat b)(nat, nat) :
    if a ≥ b then div(a-b, b) + (1, 0)
             else (0, a)                    fi
```

3) Introduction of program variables, iteration and collective assignment:

```
funct div = (nat a, pnat b)(nat, nat) :
⌈ (var nat vq, var nat va) := (0, a) ;
  while va ≥ b do (vq, va) := (vq+1, va-b) od ;
  (vq, va)                                    ⌋
```

4) Complete sequentialization and use of conditional jumps:

```
funct div = (nat a, pnat b)(nat, nat) :
⌈ var nat vq := 0 ; var nat va := a ;
  L1: if va < b then goto L2 fi ;
      vq := vq + 1 ; va := va - b ;
      goto L1 ;
  L2: (vq, va)                                 ⌋
```

5) Transition to a machine-oriented language style: With the variables AC, QR corresponding to registers, let a description of the machine operations be:

```
mode mint    = int[-2⁴⁸ + 1..2⁴⁸ - 1],
var mint AC, var mint QR,
proc loadAC = (var mint x) void : AC := val x,
proc enterAC = (mint x) void : AC := x,
proc storeQR = (var mint x) void : x := val QR,
proc decrAC = (mint x) void : AC := val AC - x,
proc incrQR = (mint x) void : QR := val QR + x,
proc jumpiflt = (mint x, label L) void :
                if val AC < x then jump(L) fi,
    ⋮
```

In this environment the program reads as follows:

```
mode nat  = (mint x : x ≥ 0),
mode pnat = (nat x : x > 0),
funct div = (nat a, pnat b)(nat, nat) :
⌈ co  AC and QR are used for the
        variables va and vq, resp.  co
        enterQR(0) ; enterAC(a) ;
  L1: jumpiflt(b, L2) ;
      incrQR(1) ; decrAC(b) ;
      jump(L1) ;
  L2: (val QR, val AC)                         ⌋
```

2. Modes and Objects

The notions of "modes" and "objects" are employed in CIP-L in a similar way as in ALGOL 68. Every mode comprises a set of objects characterized by typical operations.

2.1. Construction of Modes, Denotation of Objects

The mode **bool**, consisting of the objects true and false with the usual operations $\land$, $\lor$, $\lnot$, $\to$, and $\leftrightarrow$, is *universal*. Other supporting modes, together with special objects and functions, may be defined explicitly in the form of *abstract computation structures* ("abstract data types" in [Liskov, Zilles 75]), see section 5. For the most frequently used modes of natural and integral numbers, characters, strings, etc., such definitions are available in a particular program environment. All these computation structures contain in particular the *universal relations* "=", the test for identity, and its negation "$\neq$".

In addition, *atomic modes* may be introduced - in analogy to the "enumerated scalar types" of PASCAL - by enumeration of (the denotations of) their elements, e.g.

> atomic {white, blue, green, yellow, red, black} .

For these *atomic objects*, the universal identity relations "=" and "$\neq$" are given. To indicate a linear order for atomic objects, the symbol "," is replaced by "<", e.g.

> atomic {small < medium < large} .

Then, additional operations like "<" , "$\leq$" , succ , and pred are available for the objects of this mode.

New, *composite* modes may be formed by means of the fundamental constructions of union, cartesian product, and index mapping. The new modes then are provided with certain "canonical operations" ([McCarthy 63]):

The *union* of (disjoint) modes is written as

$$\underline{m}_1 \mid \underline{m}_2 \mid \ldots \mid \underline{m}_k \ .$$

The operations *injection* (i.e. considering an element of a *variant* $\underline{m}_i$ as an element of the union) and *projection* (i.e. considering an element of the union as an element of the appropriate variant) need not be denoted explicitly; they can be induced by the mode-specifications of parameters, object declarations, etc. (cf. section 3). The *inspection*, i.e. the test, whether a given object x of the union be-

longs to a certain variant $\underline{m}_i$, is denoted by

$$\underline{m}_i :: x \ ;$$

this operation is necessary to decide whether a projection is allowed.

The *"cartesian" product* is written as

$$(\underline{m}_1, \ \underline{m}_2, \ \ldots, \ \underline{m}_k)$$
or $$(\underline{m}_1 s_1, \ \underline{m}_2 s_2, \ \ldots, \ \underline{m}_k s_k) \ .$$

Note, that the *selectors* s_1, s_2, ..., s_k do not belong to the mode. Note also, that this product is not associative: the three modes

$$(\underline{m}_1, \ (\underline{m}_2, \ \underline{m}_3))$$
$$((\underline{m}_1, \ \underline{m}_2), \ \underline{m}_3)$$
$$(\underline{m}_1, \ \underline{m}_2, \ \underline{m}_3)$$

are different.

The *construction* of an object is denoted by

$$(x_1, \ \ldots, \ x_k) \qquad \text{where } x_i \text{ has the mode } \underline{m}_i$$

and the *selection* of a component by

$$s_i \ \underline{of} \ x \qquad \text{where } x \text{ has the mode}$$
$$(\underline{m}_1 s_1, \ \ldots, \ \underline{m}_k s_k) \ .$$

There is a universal special object, the *empty tuple*, denoted by ( ) ; it is defined to be a nullary cartesian product.

The *index mapping*, written as

> index array $\underline{m}$,

consists of all functions from a mode index to a mode $\underline{m}$. Whereas the *construction* is denoted in the same way as for products, the *selection* is specified in the form

$$x[i]$$

where x is an element of index array $\underline{m}$ and i an element of index .

There are two further ways for building new modes:

The objects of the *set mode*

> set $\underline{m}$

are the elements of the powerset of $\underline{m}$ (more precisely, the powerset of the set of $\underline{m}$ - objects). This mode defines a computation structure for set objects with the usual set operations. (For the denotation of set objects cf. section 3.)

A *submode* characterizes all those objects of a given mode $\underline{m}$ which have a certain property (for the notation see section 3). The functions defined on $\underline{m}$ are also defined - as restrictions - on the submode.

2.2. Mode Declarations

For the sake of convenience, abbreviating mode indications can be introduced by *mode declarations* of the form

mode empty ▪ atomic {()} ,
mode pair ▪ (int x, int y) ,
mode mix ▪ int ∣ bool .

2.3. Recursive Modes

The mode declaration together with the concepts of union and cartesian product allow for the specification of *recursive modes* (cf. [McCarthy 63], [Hoare 73]) such as

or

mode ls ▪ $\underline{m}$ ∣ ($\underline{m}$, ls)
mode lsequ ▪ empty ∣ ($\underline{m}$ item, lsequ trunk) .

The existence of such modes, i.e. of solutions for such "mode equations", is shown in the theoretical work of D. Scott (cf. e.g. [Scott 76]). The first of the above equations describes the mode

$\underline{m}$ ∣ ($\underline{m}$, $\underline{m}$) ∣ ($\underline{m}$, ($\underline{m}$, $\underline{m}$)) ∣ ($\underline{m}$, ($\underline{m}$, ($\underline{m}$, $\underline{m}$))) ∣ ...

Hence, the objects of mode ls include (with x_i of mode $\underline{m}$):

x_1 , (x_1, x_2) , $(x_1, (x_2, x_3))$, $(x_1, (x_2, (x_3, x_4)))$.

An example may demonstrate the use of recursive modes (for the notation see section 3):

funct search ▪ (lsequ s, $\underline{m}$ x) bool :
if empty :: s
then false
else if item of s = x
then true
else search(trunk of s, x) fi fi .

The generalization to mutually recursive declarations is straightforward, as illustrated by the following system of modes (which directly corresponds to a grammar for simple arithmetic expressions):

mode expression ▪ term ∣
(expression, char {'+'}, term) ,
mode term ▪ factor ∣
(term, char {'×'}, factor) ,
mode factor ▪ numeral ∣ identifier ∣
(char {'['}, expression, char {']'}) .

3. Expressions

Expressions are constructs denoting objects of a certain mode. Simple examples are: standard denotations (cf. 2), identifiers denoting parameters, selections and expressions like val x denoting the value of a variable x (see 4.2). Furthermore objects can be denoted either in a constructive way by function applications (cf. 3.1) and conditional expressions (cf. 3.4), or implicitly by descriptive expressions (cf. 3.3).

3.1. Function Declaration and Application

The denotation of a *function* is of the form

$$(\underline{m}_1 x_1, ..., \underline{m}_n x_n) \underline{r} : E$$

where $\underline{m}_1, ..., \underline{m}_n$ denote modes and $x_1, ..., x_n$ identifiers, which may occur free in the expression E. If f stands for this function, and E_i are expressions of modes $\underline{m}_i$, resp., then the *application* of f to $E_1, ..., E_n$ is expressed by

$$f(E_1, ..., E_n) ,$$

forming an expression for an object of mode $\underline{r}$, equivalent to the expression E with all free occurrences of x_i substituted by determinate denotations for objects denoted by E_i ("call-by-value").

By means of a *function declaration* an identifier f for a function may be introduced:

funct($\underline{m}_1, ..., \underline{m}_n$) $\underline{r}$ f ▪ ($\underline{m}_1 x_1, ..., \underline{m}_n x_n$) $\underline{r}$: E

abbreviated by

funct f ▪ ($\underline{m}_1 x_1, ..., \underline{m}_n x_n$) $\underline{r}$: E

where funct($\underline{m}_1, ..., \underline{m}_n$) $\underline{r}$ specifies the functionality (the mode) of f.

If f occurs free in E then this declaration defines, as usual, a recursive function f (for an example, see 2.3).

Functions without arguments are denoted by $\underline{r} : E$; their functionality is specified by funct $\underline{r}$.

Functions with a boolean result are called predicates, their applications are *boolean expressions*.

The modes of the arguments of a function f which are indicated by the functionality of f are, in general, not the exact domain of f. For example, a function sub for the subtraction of two natural numbers a and b is usually undefined for a < b but has the full functionality funct(nat, nat) nat. To express the *restriction of arguments*, an appropriate boolean expression as an explicit *assertion* can be added to the list of formal parameters; in our example:

<u>funct</u> sub = (<u>nat</u> a, <u>nat</u> b : a ≥ b) <u>nat</u> : E .

Functions with one or two arguments can also be declared as *operators* to be used in prefix or infix notation, where the *operator indications* (e.g. + or <u>mod</u>) are notationally distinguished from identifiers for objects as well as from mode indications.

Several functions with the same identifier (or operator indication) can coexist if they have different functionalities.

3.2. Object Declarations

Object declarations $\underline{m}_1 x_1$ = E_1 and *collective object declarations*

$$(\underline{m}_1 x_1, \ldots, \underline{m}_n x_n) = (E_1, \ldots, E_n)$$

introduce the identifiers $x_1, \ldots, x_n$ for the objects denoted by $E_1, \ldots, E_n$. (Note, that the $x_1, \ldots, x_n$ must not occur free in the E_i.)

Object declarations usually occur in a *block*,

$\lceil$ $(\underline{m}_1 x_1, \ldots, \underline{m}_n x_n) = (E_1, \ldots, E_n)$; E $\rfloor$

has by definition the same meaning as the function application

$$((\underline{m}_1 x_1, \ldots, \underline{m}_n x_n) \underline{r} : E)(E_1, \ldots, E_n) .$$

The use of restrictions of arguments of functions may lead to *restricted* object declarations: For the above example sub, the application sub(21, 4) has the same meaning as the block

$\lceil$ (<u>nat</u> a, <u>nat</u> b : a ≥ b) = (21, 4) ; E $\rfloor$.

3.3. Descriptive Expressions for Specification Purposes

Descriptive expressions allow the implicit specification of an object by its properties, i.e. by a certain boolean expression P. If there exists one and only one object x satisfying P then the *object specification*

that $\underline{r}$ x : P

denotes *that* unique object x of mode $\underline{r}$ for which P is true. For example, the subtraction of natural numbers can now be defined by

<u>funct</u> sub = (<u>nat</u> a, <u>nat</u> b : a ≥ b) <u>nat</u> :
that <u>nat</u> x : a = x + b .

Objects of a certain mode $\underline{m}$ may be assembled into a set forming a new object of the mode <u>set</u> <u>m</u> by a *set comprehension*: {$\underline{m}$ x : P} denotes the set of all objects of mode $\underline{m}$ for which P is true. The *enumeration* {$E_1, \ldots, E_n$} and the *interval* [$E_1..E_2$] are abbreviations for special cases.

Set comprehension is also used to define a *submode* of a given mode, e.g.,

<u>nat</u> {<u>nat</u> x : x ≤ 5} ,

abbreviated (<u>nat</u> x : x ≤ 5)

or <u>nat</u> [0..5]

or <u>nat</u> {0, 1, 2, 3, 4, 5} .

Submodes are frequently used for the index mode of an array:

<u>int</u> [-20..+20] <u>array</u> <u>int</u> .

Another kind of forming submodes by comprehension is illustrated by

<u>mode</u> <u>d</u> = (<u>nat</u> a, <u>nat</u> b : a ≥ b) ,

which can be used e.g. in the function declaration

<u>funct</u> sub = (<u>d</u> z) <u>nat</u> :
that <u>nat</u> x : a <u>of</u> z = x + b <u>of</u> z .

Further descriptive tools are the *quantification expressions*

∀ $\underline{m}$ x : P

and

∃ $\underline{m}$ x : P .

As a last descriptive expression, a *choice* denotes an object which is described - but in general not uniquely determined - by a boolean expression P. We use the keyword <u>some</u> for forming choices:

<u>some</u> $\underline{m}$ x : P

provided there exists at least one object x satisfying P.

Choices can be used to define *ambiguous functions* ([McCarthy 63]). Non-deterministic choices (similar to [Dijkstra 75]) go beyond the rules of usual functional calculi; for example, the expressions

$\lceil$ <u>nat</u> x = <u>some</u> <u>nat</u> t : t ≤ 5 ; x + x $\rfloor$

and

(<u>some</u> <u>nat</u> t : t ≤ 5) + (<u>some</u> <u>nat</u> t : t ≤ 5)

are not equivalent.

3.4. Conditional Expressions

The conditional expression (of mode $\underline{m}$) is a modification of Dijkstra's "guarded commands" ([Dijkstra 75]) and has the following general form

$$
\begin{aligned}
&\underline{if}\ B_1\ \underline{then}\ E_1\\
&\mathbb{}\ B_2\ \underline{then}\ E_2\\
&\qquad\vdots\\
&\mathbb{}\ B_n\ \underline{then}\ E_n\ \underline{fi}\ ,
\end{aligned}
$$

where the B_i are boolean expressions and the E_i are expressions (conforming to the mode $\underline{m}$). The object denoted by the conditional expression (its "value") is one of those objects E_i for which the corresponding B_i is true. If no B_i yields true, then (the value of) the conditional expression is not defined.

Following Dijkstra, the boolean expressions $B_1,\ldots,\ B_n$ are called the *guards* of the expressions $E_1,\ldots,\ E_n$, resp.

It is obvious, how the usual (deterministic) $\underline{if}$-$\underline{then}$-$\underline{else}$-$\underline{fi}$-expression, the $\underline{elsf}$[1]-construct and even the $\underline{case}$-construct are defined as abbreviations for special cases.

3.5. Example

As a practical example, we give a function for the (arbitrary) dissection of a nonempty string of characters (() denotes the empty string, ∘ the concatenation):

$\underline{funct}$ diss ≡ ($\underline{string}$ a : a ≠ ())($\underline{string}$, $\underline{char}$, $\underline{string}$):
 $\underline{some}$($\underline{string}$ u, $\underline{char}$ t, $\underline{string}$ v) : a = u ∘ t ∘ v

This ambiguous function can be used to solve a uniquely determined problem, the problem of inserting an element into an ordered string,

$\underline{funct}$ insert ≡ ($\underline{string}$ a, $\underline{char}$ x: isordered(a)) $\underline{string}$:
 $\underline{some}\ \underline{string}$ b : isordered(b) ∧
  ∃ ($\underline{string}$ u, $\underline{string}$ v) : a = u ∘ v ∧
               b = u ∘ x ∘ v ,

the description reflecting rather narrowly how one would explain verbally the problem. The predicate isordered is defined by the following function (where top and rest have the usual meaning):

---

[1] Pronounced "elif".

$\underline{funct}$ isordered ≡ ($\underline{string}$ a) $\underline{bool}$:
 $\underline{if}$ a = ()
  $\underline{then}$ true
  $\underline{else}\ \underline{if}$ rest(a) = ()
       $\underline{then}$ true
       $\underline{else}\ \underline{if}$ top(a) ≤ top(rest(a))
            $\underline{then}$ isordered(rest(a))
            $\underline{else}$ false $\underline{fi}\ \underline{fi}\ \underline{fi}$

A "solution" to the problem of insert, i.e. a function definition from which the descriptive elements $\underline{some}$ and ∃ are eliminated, based on diss, is now

$\underline{funct}$ insert ≡ ($\underline{string}$ a, $\underline{char}$ x: isordered(a)) $\underline{string}$:
 $\underline{if}$ a = ()
  $\underline{then}$ x
  $\underline{else}$ ⌈ ($\underline{string}$ u, $\underline{char}$ t, $\underline{string}$ v) ≡ diss(a);
        $\underline{if}$ x ≤ t $\underline{then}$ insert(u,x) ∘ t ∘ v
        ▯ x ≥ t $\underline{then}$ u ∘ t ∘ insert(v,x) $\underline{fi}$ ⌋ $\underline{fi}$

This version of insert still allows to be implemented by a whole class of algorithms, depending on which implementation of diss is chosen. Various deterministic implementations of diss are obtained by introducing additional conditions, like u = () (linear search) or 0 ≤ length(u) - length(v) ≤ 1 (balanced tree search).

4. Statements

Of course CIP-L would not deserve to be called a wide spectrum language, if the usual machine-oriented concepts like variables, assignments, conditional statements (Dijkstra's guarded commands), jumps, and their collateral or sequential composition were not incorporated as well. Since most of these concepts and the related problems are standard in todays knowledge about programming languages, only some special aspects will be stressed here.

4.1. Sequentialization

Functional composition involves an implicit order for the evaluation of applicative terms. This order is a partial one in the case of multiple-argument functions, since a tuple of arguments is evaluated collaterally. In expressions this order is partly visible when block structure and object declarations are used; it may be totally exposed using the ";" as an explicit sequentialization symbol.

4.2. Variables and Assignments

The introduction of program variables is motivated by the fact that existing machines provide only for a limited number of storage cells or registers (acting as "containers" for objects).

Variables for objects of mode m have the mode var m (and are strictly distinguished from references). The operator val yields the value of a variable, usually its application is understood. As is well-known, the value of a variable may be changed by an assignment; a couple of object declarations can often be replaced by a single (initialized) variable declaration and a sequence of assignments. This abbreviation is useful especially in the case of object declarations arising in recursive situations and necessary for the transition from recursive functions to iterations (cf. 4.4). Hence the introduction of variables may be regarded as a kind of optimizing transformation.

In analogy to a tuple of formal and actual parameters, or to a collective object declaration, a tuple of variables should be declared and initialized collectively, e.g. (var nat vq, var nat va) := (0, a) in section 1, and their values may be changed by a collective assignment (in analogy to a collective parameter linkage), e.g. (vq, va) := (vq + 1, va - b). There is no predefined order for the evaluation of the righthand side (the tuple is collateral) and upon its completion the resulting objects are assigned collectively to vq, va, resp. The decomposition of a collective assignment into a sequence of individual assignments is not at all arbitrary, nor is it equivalent to a clause of collateral individual assignments. In general, additional "temporaries" may have to be introduced, e.g.,

$$(u, v) := (u + v, u - v)$$

can be transformed to

$$\lceil \; \underline{int} \; t = u \; ; \; u := u + v \; ; \; v := t - v \; \rfloor \qquad \text{or}$$
$$\lceil \; \underline{int} \; t = v \; ; \; v := u - v \; ; \; u := u + t \; \rfloor \; ,$$

but obviously n o t to

$$\lceil \; u := u + v \; ; \; v := u - v \; \rfloor$$

nor to a clause of collateral assignments.

A collective assignment can be transformed into collateral assignments, if the individual assignments have no variables *in common*, i.e. if no assignment changes a variable which is used in any of the other assignments; this condition is fulfilled for vq, va

in the div-example (see section 1),

$$\lceil \; vq := vq + 1, \; va := va - b \; \rfloor \quad .$$

A slight modification of this example also shows how justified the restriction is that no variable may occur more than once in the lefthand side of a collective assignment; it would be violated e.g. by

$$(a, a) := (a + a, a - a).$$

4.3. Procedures

Expressions denote objects (without causing any side-effect) and thus only their values are relevant, whereas statements cause side-effects which are relevant in a non-local context. The transition from applicative expressions to constructs with side-effects corresponds to the transition from functions to procedures; their modes are distinguished by the prefix $proc$ instead of $funct$.

In contrast to functions, procedures may have side-effects. Apart from jumps, side-effects are caused by changing variables - either explicitly via formal variable parameters or implicitly via non-local variables (implicit variable parameters).

The mixing of expressions and statements within a procedure with result and side-effects must be handled very carefully, in order to avoid unexpected effects: The duplication of a common "subexpression", for example, may lead to the duplication of the side-effect and thus possibly to an incorrect program - an effect which, of course, does not appear in connection with functions. Care must be taken to specify exactly under which conditions such transformations may be applied; this leads to certain restrictions in the use of the language. Some possible pitfalls can be avoided by restricting oneself to the use of *pure procedures*, i.e. procedures without results - indicated by the symbol $void$ instead of the result mode.

Since procedures are allowed to have variables as parameters, an "alias"-taboo (cf. [Lampson et al. 77]) is required here in connection with the above mentioned restriction for collective assignments: No two (explicit or implicit) variable parameters of a procedure may actually have a variable in common.

As an example for the transition from a purely applicative style to a procedural one, i.e. from functions to procedures, consider the following transformation rule which carries the action over to a parameterless procedure:

```
funct F ≡ (m x) n :          funct F ≡ (m y) n :
  if P1 then E1          ┬   ⌈ var m x := y ;
  ▯ P2 then F(E2) fi         proc G ≡ n :
                                if P1 then E1
                                ▯ P2 then x := E2 ;
                                         G fi ;
                          G                        ⌋
```

4.4. Iteration

The particularly simple form of recursion ("repetitive" recursion) in the transformation above justifies the introduction of a special language construct for iteration, the semantics of which is defined by the transformation

```
proc G ≡ n :               proc G ≡ n :
  do if P1 then E leave  ┬    if P1 then E
  ▯ P2 then S    fi od       ▯ P2 then S ; G fi
```

Here E leave indicates termination of the do...od-iteration with a result value E .

If no call of G is involved within the do...od-construct, the declaration of G may be deleted and a call of G replaced by its body, i.e. the do...od-iteration. Otherwise, recursion is only partially "removed".

It is quite obvious, that the do...od-construct is not restricted to conditionals with two branches; in general, conditional expressions with an arbitrary number of branches (and with or without side-effects) may be used within the do...od-frame, where all the terminating branches are indicated by leave. The extension of Dijkstra's repetitive construct by leave-expressions (for a discussion of such escape constructs cf. e.g. [Knuth 74]), instead of termination by default when none of the guards is true, seems to be appropriate for increased program clarity and is justified by the obvious transformation rules. Note, that several terminating cases can be expressed as well. Also, the use of the conditional is not coupled with the do...od-construct; the "n + 1/2" loop (cf. [Knuth 74]) can be expressed without duplication of text:

    do S1 ; if P then E leave fi ; S2 od .

Some conventional control structures for special cases of iteration have also been included in CIP-L, such as

```
⌈ while P do S od ; E ⌋  →
                 do if P then S else E leave fi od
⌈ do S until P od ; E ⌋  →
                 do S ; if P then E leave fi od  .
```

The usual (static!) for-clause is available, too.

4.5. Labels and Jumps

All recursive versions corresponding to iterations (cf. 4.4) can directly be transformed into the language style of labels and goto's (notice the analogy to the transformation introducing the iteration construct):

```
proc G ≡ n :                     proc G ≡ n :
⌈ g: if P1 then E return    ┬     if P1 then E
   ▯ P2 then S ; goto g fi ⌋      ▯ P2 then S ; G fi
```

This transformation rule can be generalized in the same way as for iterations, even further to systems of mutually recursive procedures in a straightforward way. In this case, it can "remove" recursion if the system is "repetitive", i.e. if every call of a procedure of the system is a *plain call*, that is the l a s t   a c t i o n in the body where it occurs (Germ.: "schlichter Prozedurwechsel"; cf. [McCarthy 62], [Knuth 74]). Thus, a jump is only a notational variant of a plain call of a parameterless procedure.

5. Further Development

There are some further concepts, which are intended to be incorporated into the language and are subject to current work.

References and variables are different concepts in CIP-L. Thus a strict distinction will be made between ref m (references), var m (variables), ref var m (pointers), and var ref var m (pointer variables).

References and variables can be components of composite objects, too ("organized store"). This and further possibilities of treating references and variables like objects open the door to systems programming. Precise rules will restrict the use of selected variables and references to variables in order to guarantee the "alias"-taboo.

A proposal for the introduction of *computation structures* (combining modes and associated operations), comprising the (algebraic) specification of abstract *types* and constructs to express *modularization* for independent development is about to appear ([Krieg-Brückner 78], see also [Pepper et al. 77]).

To describe the *concurrency* of parallel processes and synchronization, additional constructs are necessary. The well-known concepts of signals or semaphores, conditional critical regions, monitors, coroutines, etc. are being considered for a possible incorporation into CIP-L.

Some more machine-oriented concepts at the address level will have to be included. It is an open question how far the design can be extended into the domain of microprogramming and register transfer languages.

Acknowledgement

We thank Mr. M. Woodger and our colleagues F. Geiselbrechtinger, U. Hill, A. Laut, Prof. K. Samelson, and M. Wirsing for their valuable contributions and for critical discussions.

The opportunity to discuss a draft version of this paper which one of the authors had at the meeting of IFIP WG 2.1 in Oxford, U.K., December 16-20, 1977, is also gratefully acknowledged.

References

[Bauer 73]
F.L. Bauer:
A Philosophy of Programming. A Course of three Lectures given at the University of London, October 1973
Also in: Proc. Intern. Summer School on Language Hierarchies and Interfaces, Maktoberdorf 1975
Lecture Notes in Computer Science 46. Berlin, Heidelberg, New York: Springer 1976

[Bauer 76]
F.L. Bauer:
Programming as an Evolutionary Process. Technische Universität München, Institut für Informatik, Rep. No. 7617, 1976
Also: Proc. 2nd Int. Conf. on Software Engineering, Oct. 1976, San Francisco, Ca., 223-234

[Bauer et al. 76]
F.L. Bauer, H. Partsch, P. Pepper, H. Wössner:
Techniques for Program Development. Technische Universität München, Institut für Informatik, Interner Bericht, Sept. 1976
Also in: Software Engineering Techniques. Infotech State of the Art Report 34, 1977

[Bauer et al. 77a]
F.L. Bauer, M. Broy, R. Gnatz, W. Hesse, B. Krieg-Brückner:
Notes on the Project CIP: Towards a Wide Spectrum Language to Support Program Development by Transformations. Technische Universität München, Institut für Informatik, TUM-INFO-7722, 1977

[Bauer et al. 77b]
F.L. Bauer, H. Partsch, P. Pepper, H. Wössner:
Notes on the Project CIP: Outline of a Transformation System. Technische Universität München, Institut für Informatik, TUM-INFO-7729, 1977

[Broy 77]
M. Broy:
Program Development for Steinhaus Type Permutation Generating Programs. Technische Universität München, Institut für Informatik, Rep. No. 7701, 1977

[Burstall, Darlington 75]
R.M. Burstall, J. Darlington:
Some Transformations for Developing Recursive Programs. Proc. of the Int. Conf. on Reliable Software, Los Angeles 1975, 465-472
Also (revised version): J. ACM 24, 44-67 (1977)

[Dijkstra 75]
E.W. Dijkstra:
Guarded Commands, Nondeterminacy and Formal Derivation of Programs. Comm. ACM 18, 453-457 (1975)

[Geiselbrechtinger et al. 74]
F. Geiselbrechtinger, W. Hesse, B. Krieg, H. Scheidig:
Language Layers, Portability and Program Structuring. In: W.L. van der Poel, L. Maarsen (eds.): Machine Oriented Higher Level Languages. Amsterdam: North-Holland 1974

[Gerhart 75]
S.L. Gerhart:
Correctness-Preserving Program Transformations. Conf. Rec. Second ACM Symp. on Principles of Programming Languages, Jan. 1975, 54-66

[Gnatz 77]
R. Gnatz:
Zur Konstruktion von Programmen durch Transformation. Technische Universität München, Institut für Informatik, TUM-INFO-7741, 1977

[Gnatz, Pepper 77]
R.Gnatz, P. Pepper:
fusc: An Example in Program Development. Technische Universität München, Institut für Informatik, TUM-INFO-7711, 1977

[Hoare 73]
C.A.R. Hoare:
Recursive Data Structures. Stanford University A.I. Lab., STAN-CS-73-400, Oct. 1973
Also: Internat. J. Comput. Information Sci. 4:2, 105-132 (1975)

[Knuth 74]
D.E. Knuth:
Structured Programming with go to Statements. Computing Surveys 6:4, 261-301 (1974)

[Krieg-Brückner 78]
B. Krieg-Brückner:
Concrete and Abstract Specification, Modularization and Program Development by Transformation. Dissertation, Technische Universität München, Institut für Informatik, TUM-INFO-7805, 1978

[Lampson et al. 77]
B.W. Lampson, J.J. Horning, R.L. London, J.G. Mitchell, G.J. Popek:
Report on the Programming Language Euclid. SIGPLAN Notices 12:2, Feb. 1977

[Liskov, Zilles 75]
B. Liskov, S. Zilles:
Specification Techniques for Data Abstraction. IEEE Trans. on Software Eng. 1:1, 7-18 (1975)

[McCarthy 62]
J. McCarthy:
Towards a Mathematical Science of Computation. Proc. IFIP Congress 62, München. Amsterdam: North-Holland 1962

[McCarthy 63]
J. McCarthy:
A Basis for a Mathematical Theory of Computation. In: P. Braffort, D. Hirschberg (eds.): Computer Programming and Formal Systems. Amsterdam: North-Holland 1963

[Partsch, Pepper 77]
H. Partsch, P. Pepper:
Program Transformation on Different Levels of
Programming. Technische Universität München,
Institut für Informatik, TUM-INFO-7715, 1977

[Pepper et al. 77]
P. Pepper, F.L. Bauer, B. Krieg-Brückner:
Development of Data-Structures. Technische Universität München, Institut für Informatik, Internal Report 1977

[Scott 76]
D. Scott:
Data Types as Lattices. SIAM J. on Computing $\underline{5}$, 522-587 (1976)

[Standish et al. 76]
T.A. Standish, D.C. Harriman, D.F. Kibler,
J.M. Neighbors:
Improving and Refining Programs by Program Manipulation. Proc. 1976 ACM Annual Conf., Oct. 1976,
509-516

[Steinbrüggen 77]
R.Steinbrüggen:
Equivalent Recursive Definitions of Certain Number
Theoretical Functions. Technische Universität
München, Institut für Informatik, TUM-INFO-7714,
1977

Semantics of Nondeterministic and Noncontinuous Constructs *

M. Broy, R. Gnatz, M. Wirsing

Institut für Informatik
der Technischen Universität
Postfach 20 24 20
D - 8000 München 2

Abstract

The semantics of the nondeterministic and noncontinuous constructs of the descriptive and applicative parts of the wide spectrum language CIP-L is given by defining both, a "breadth - function", characterizing the sets of possible values of ambiguous expressions, and a "definedness - predicate", indicating for such expressions whether all possible evaluations lead to defined values. With the help of the Egli-Milner ordering ambiguous, recursive functions are defined as fixpoints of functionals.

Using these concepts the meanings of quantifiers, ambiguous functions and expressions are based on a mathematical structure satisfying the axioms of two-valued classical logic and set theory.

---

*

This research was carried out within the Sonderforschungsbereich 49,
Programmiertechnik, Munich".

PART I. Definition of the Semantics

The wide spectrum language CIP-L (cf. /Bauer et al. 78/) comprises
full predicate logic including sets, nondeterminacy and nondeterminism
and a number of constructs for the definition of modes, (recursive)
functions etc. We define the semantics of the applicative and descriptive
parts of CIP-L. This semantics serves as a kernel semantics, the semantics
of the remaining parts of CIP-L is defined by definitional transformations
(cf. /Pepper 78/).

1. Introduction

In the wide spectrum language CIP-L nondeterminacy is incorporated to
support the definition of ambiguous expressions and ambiguous functions
(cf. /McCarthy 62/). Nondeterministic constructs such as guarded expressions (cf. /Dijkstra 75/) provide the programmer with sufficient freedom
to delay design decisions during the process of program development, i.e.
the programmer is not yet forced to limit himself to one particular alternative. Furthermore nondeterminism forms an important basis for the definition and analysis of the behavior of parallel processes.

Nondeterminacy and nondeterminism, in addition, serve for modeling
problems and programs the behaviour of which is not uniquely determined:
Certain choice decisions which have to be made during an evaluation of
the program are left to a higher instance - e.g. an erratic demon
(/Dijkstra 75/) or an oracle (/Milner 73/), and should not be analysed
by using methods of statistical behaviour.

In contrast to the definition and use of nondeterminism in artificial
intelligence, where all given possibilities of choices are examined one
after the other (/Floyd 67/) until either a result is obtained or the examination is not successful in all cases, in CIP-L nondeterminism is
understood as in the theory of parallel processes. Each evaluation of
a program containing nondeterministic constructs yields, with the help
of some nondeterministic choice, a particular result or may fail (i.e.
lead to a undefined situation). Independently of the first evaluation a
second one may lead to another result or fail.

In order to describe the semantics of such ambiguous programs, we have
to characterize all possible results of a program. Thus for each expression E the set of possible results B(E) is defined with the help of
a so-called breadth function B: B(E) is called the breadth of E.

As we mentioned above, the evaluation of some expression E may fail,
i.e. may lead to an undefined situation. This fact might be described
by a special object, denoted by ω, such that $\omega \in B(E) \iff$ the interpretation of E may fail (cf. /Plotkin 76/). We prefer, however, to
introduce a definedness predicate d such that

$$d(E) \iff \text{the interpretation of } E \text{ never fails.}$$

In this way both the function B ("breadth") and the predicate d
("definedness") are used to define the semantics of the applicative and
descriptive parts of CIP-L.

Since the descriptive part of CIP-L comprises full predicate logic,
descriptive expressions and "infinite" choices, a mathematical structure
in the spirit of (the semantics of) predicate logic seems indispensible
for our semantics definition. Fortunately this semantics is applicable to
both the descriptive part and the applicative part of the language. Thus
it constitutes a basis for the semantics of the wide spectrum language in
which the semantics of the procedural part is given by "definitional transformations" (cf. /Bauer 78/, /Pepper 78/). Now we have two possibilities
for proving the "theorems" (i.e. the "derived transformations") viz. by
combining definitional transformations into more complex ones ("combinatorial method" cf. /Kreisel, Krivine 67/) or ("semantical") by comparison
of the sets corresponding to premise and conclusion of a derived
transformation ("set theoretical method" cf. /Kreisel, Krivine 67/).

This paper consists of two parts:
The major part is dedicated to the formal definition of the semantics,
followed by some definitional transformations and a few derived transformations that will be proved in the mathematical (semantic) model.

Remark

In the semantics we have eliminated all actual choice decisions necessary
during the interpretation of the program by considering the set of
possible result values. Therefore the semantics of an expression E is
simpler than the "operative" meaning of E in the following sense:
Consider the function

$$\underline{\text{funct}} \; F \equiv (\underline{\text{nat}} \; x) \; \underline{\text{nat}} : 0 \;\|\; 1$$

F might be understood to represent an uncountable number of determinate
functions; most of them are not computable or not primitive recursive,
since all functions g, where

$$\underline{\text{funct}} \; g \equiv (\underline{\text{nat}} \; x) \; \underline{\text{nat}} \; : \; \underline{\text{if}} \; P(x) \; \underline{\text{then}} \; 1 \; \underline{\text{else}} \; 0 \; \underline{\text{fi}}$$

and the predicate P is not recursively enumerable, are "implementations"
(cf. part II,1) of F. The breadth of F is the following set

$$\{ \; (\; \{(x,0) : x \in \mathbb{N}\} \cup \{(x,1) : x \in \mathbb{N}\}, \{(x,\mathbf{T}) : x \in \mathbb{N}\} \;) \; \}.$$

It contains only one pair of primitive recursive sets.

2. Fundamental Concepts

2.1. Syntax

Let CIP-L' be the descriptive and applicative (i.e. nonprocedural) part of
the language CIP-L (cf. /Bauer et al. 78/).

2.2. Determinism, Determinacy

Following /Bauer et al. 77/ we distinguish "determinism" and "determinacy" :

Roughly speaking determinism concerns the syntax, whereas determinacy
concerns the semantics:
We say that an expression E is <u>deterministic</u> if the character string E
does not contain a nondeterministic construct (i.e. E does not contain
finite or infinite choices or guarded expressions. Furthermore every
function application occuring in E must be deterministic.) E is called
<u>determinate</u>, if E has at most one value and if E can be undefined,
then E has no result, i.e. (d(E) = $\mathbf{T}$ $\wedge$ |B(E)| = 1) $\vee$ (d(E) = $\mathbb{F}$ $\wedge$ |B(E)| =0).

Hence a deterministic expression is always determinate, but a determinate expression may be nondeterministic.

It should be noted that in general it is undecidable, whether a nondeterministic expression is determinate or not.

2.3. Universe and Interpretation Functions

2.3.1. Universe

The universe $\mathbb{U}$ is a mathematical structure, satisfying the axioms of the classical predicate calculus, among those the law of "tertium non datur" ("excluded middle") (cf. /Shoenfield 67/). The sets in $\mathbb{U}$ are a model of the ZFC-set theory (i.e. Zermelo-Fraenkel axioms + Axiom of Choice, cf. /Krivine 71/).

The universe is assumed to be "large enough", such that the images of the interpretation function of modes do not exhaust it; even after the definition of the semantics of a new mode or a new object, there should exist infinitely many objects which are not in the range of the interpretation functions.

In particular we might choose a denumerable set for $\mathbb{U}$, for example the set of natural numbers; but this requires a technically complicated "Gödelization" of the expressions which is unsuitable for our purposes.

2.3.2. Modes

We consider a mode $\underline{m}$ as a kind of abstract data type (cf. /Liskov, Zilles 75/, /ADJ 76/, /Guttag 75/, /Burstall, Goguen 77/), consisting of a carrier - also denoted by $\underline{m}$ - and a finite number $f_1, \ldots, f_k$ of canonical functions operating on $\underline{m}$ and possibly some other "known" abstract data types (like $\underline{bool}$ or $\underline{nat}$).

In this sense, the language CIP-L' consists of a hierarchy of (abstract) data types - for which the mathematical semantics approach seems to be more appropriate than the algebraic one and actually forms a basis for the algebraic specification of types (cf. /Partsch, Broy 78/). However for the clarity of presentation we have separated the semantics of the modes into the semantics of the carriers and the semantics of the expressions.

Since in CIP-L submodes may be defined by "comprehension" on predicates and expressions formed by predicates can be nondeterminate, we can theoretically have nondeterminate modes. But these modes do not seem to be an appropriate tool in programming; hence we give first a definition of the semantics of basic modes and only in the appendix a definition of submodes using transformational semantics (cf. /Pepper 78/).

The semantics of basic modes is given by the function U which associates with each mode $\underline{m}$ a set $U(\underline{m})$ in the universe $I\!U$. The CIP-L syntax admits mode definitions like e.g. $\underline{mode}$ $\underline{m} \equiv \underline{set}$ $\underline{m}$, which do not have any solution and therefore would not define a mode. To counter that problem we introduce a "definedness predicate" d for modes, too, yielding false exactly in such cases.

2.3.3. Breadth and Definedness

For every mode $\underline{m}$ we have two interpretation functions $B^{\underline{m}}$ and $V^{\underline{m}}$:

The breadth $B^{\underline{m}}$ associates with every expression E its set $B^{\underline{m}}(E)$ of possible values which is a subset of $U(\underline{m})$. The function $V^{\underline{m}}$ associates with each determinate object denotation x of mode $\underline{m}$ an element $V^{\underline{m}}(x)$ of $U(\underline{m})$. $V^{\underline{m}}$ is defined only for determinate and defined expressions E and plays in a certain way the role of an induction basis in the inductive definition of the semantics of nondeterminate expressions.

In fact we define the breadth B of a determinate and defined expression E by

$$B(E) = \{V(E)\} \land d(E) = \mathbb{T}$$

On the other hand, if $B(E)$ contains exactly one element - let's say $B(E) = \{x\}$ - and $d(E) = \mathbb{T}$ then E is a determinate expression an we define

$$V(E) = x .$$

V is only introduced for the sake of notational convenience. The definition of V for some defined, determinate expression E implies the definition of $B(E)$ and $d(E)$ and vice versa.

Consider e.g. the following expression E

      n! $\div$ (some nat x : x$\leq$n) .

E does not lead to a defined value if one chooses x=0 but for all other
choices E is welldefined. To characterize this situation we introduce the
predicate d(E) which holds if and only if every sequence of choices
during the evaluation of E leads to a defined value (e.g. in the above
case d(E) yields IF. Note, that if d(E) = IF holds an evaluation of E
may, in a not uniquely determined way, either terminate with results from
B(E) or fail. In general this does not imply that the evaluation will
always fail.) d is comparable with the termination operation e of
de Bakker/ de Bakker 76/, but in contrast to de Bakker's e , which is
derived from $\perp$, d is not based on $\perp$.

The definedness predicate does not distinguish between "erroneous" and
"nonterminating" situations. Moreover our interest is in safe programming,
i.e. terminating programs, and not the structure of nonterminating
situations or infinitary processes which can be useful (cf. /de Bakker 77/,
/Arnold, Nivat 77/, /Arnold 78/), too.

2.4.   Notations

We denote by

IM	the set of mode expressions of CIP-L'
ID	the set of determinate object denotations of CIP-L'
/A	the set of expressions of CIP-L'
IU	the universe (the collection of all semantical objects)
U :IM $\to$ IU	the interpretation function for modes
d :IM $\to$ U(bool)	the "definedness-predicate" for modes, U(bool) = {T, IF} ($m = \tau(m)$ has no solution $\leftrightarrow$ d(m) = IF)
$V^{\underline{m}}$:ID $\to$ IU	the interpretation for determinate objects of mode $\underline{m}$
$B^{\underline{m}}$:/A $\to$ IU	the breadth of expressions of mode $\underline{m}$ (the set of possible values)
$d^{\underline{m}}$:/A $\to$ U(bool)	the "definedness-predicate" for expressions of mode $\underline{m}$ ($d^{\underline{m}}$(E) = T $\leftrightarrow$ E is always defined)

Sometimes we write d, B, V instead of $d^{\underline{m}}$, $B^{\underline{m}}$, $V^{\underline{m}}$, if $\underline{m}$ may be derived from
the context.

We denote the logical connectives of the universe by $\lnot, \land, \lor, \Rightarrow \forall, \exists$, the set theoretical operations by

$$\in, \subset, \cup, \cap, \smallsetminus, card, \{:\}$$

and the equality in $\mathbb{U}$ by $=$.

From the context it will always be clear whether we mean the constructs of CIP-L' or those of the semantics.

In the semantics the application of a relation R is defined as usual:

$$R(x) \underset{def}{=} \{y : (x,y) \in R\}$$

In quantified expressions we often write (close to the notation of the language)

$$\forall M \ x : \ldots \quad \text{instead of} \quad \forall x : x \in M \Rightarrow \ldots$$

and $\quad \exists M \ x : \ldots \quad \text{instead of} \quad \exists x : x \in M \land \ldots$

Simultaneous substitution of $x_1, \ldots, x_n$ in an expression E for

$y_1, \ldots, y_n$ is denoted by $E_{y_1 \ldots y_n}^{x_1 \ldots x_n}$.

We denote by $\mathbb{T}$ and $\mathbb{F}$ the objects of the universe which represent the universal constants true and false (cf. 3.1.1). Expressions are denoted by $E, F, P, E_i, F_i, P_i, \ldots$, modes by $\underline{m}, \underline{n}, \underline{r}, \underline{m}_1, \underline{n}_i, \ldots$.

Throughout this paper all problems of name conflicts, such as overloading etc. are disregarded.

2.5. $\mathbb{U}$-expressions

In order to define the semantics of the function applications or quantifiers based recursively on the semantics of "smaller" constructs we have to apply syntactical constructs to semantical terms. Roughly speaking a semantical term represents the semantics of an expression E by a pair (S,b) consisting of a subset S of the universe and a truth value b such that $B(E) = S$ and $d(E) = b$. In analogy to the definition of the semantics of predicate calculus (cf. /Schütte 67/) we extend the interpretation functions to elements and subsets of the universe and to "mixed" constructs:

IU-expressions

Every pair (S, b) where S is some set and b is some truth-value and every syntactically correct CIP-L program is a IU-expression. If in a syntactically correct program an expression of mode $\underline{m}$ is replaced by a IU-expression of mode $\underline{m}$ we obtain again a IU-expression.

The pair (S, b) may be considered as representative for the class of expressions E with $B(E) = S$ and $d(E) = b$.

In the following we define the breadth B and definedness d of all expressions possible in CIP-L'; for the pair (S, b) both functions are simply the (restricted) projector functions:

$$B^{\underline{m}}((S, b)) = S \cap U(\underline{m})$$
$$d^{\underline{m}}((S, b)) = b \wedge S \subseteq U(\underline{m})$$

3. Semantics of Modes

3.1. Inductive Definition of the Semantics

We only give some definitions of the canonical functions of a mode because they have the usual meaning. For each canonical function f we define $d(f) \underset{def}{\equiv} \mathbb{T}$.

(1) bool, Primitive Objects, Conformity Test

Let $\mathbb{T}, \mathbb{F}, a_1, a_2, \ldots, a_n, \ldots$ be pairwise different objects in U which are not yet in the range of U, B, V. For true, false and some primitive object denotations $o_1, o_2, \ldots, o_n, \ldots$ we define now ($i \geq 1$)

$$V^{\underline{bool}}(\text{true}) \underset{def}{\equiv} \mathbb{T}, \quad V^{\underline{bool}}(\text{false}) \underset{def}{\equiv} \mathbb{F}, \quad V(o_i) \underset{def}{\equiv} a_i \; ;$$

$$d^{\underline{bool}}(\text{true}) = d^{\underline{bool}}(\text{false}) = d(o_i) \underset{def}{\equiv} \mathbb{T}.$$

$$U(\underline{bool}) \underset{def}{\equiv} \{\mathbb{T}, F\}; \quad d(\underline{bool}) \underset{def}{\equiv} \mathbb{T}$$

Canonical functions of bool are $\neg$, $\wedge$, $\vee$, $\rightarrow$, $=$. E.g. $\neg$ is of mode funct(bool) bool and defined by

$$V^{\underline{bool}}(\neg(\mathbb{T})) \underset{def}{\equiv} \mathbb{F}, \quad V^{\underline{bool}}(\neg(\mathbb{F})) \underset{def}{\equiv} \mathbb{T}.$$

For each mode m a conformity test :: is defined by ($x \in U$)

$$V^{\underline{bool}}(\underline{m} :: x) \underset{def}{\equiv} \begin{cases} \mathbb{T} & \text{if } x \in U(m) \\ \mathbb{F} & \text{if } \exists M : x \in U(M) \wedge x \notin U(\underline{m}) . \end{cases}$$

(For the extension to nondeterminate expressions see the function application.)

(2) <u>Atomic Modes</u>

$U(\underline{atomic} \{o_1, \ldots, o_k\})$ $\underset{def}{\equiv}$ $\{a_1, \ldots, a_k\}$

$U(\underline{atomic} \{o_1 < \ldots < o_k\})$ $\underset{def}{\equiv}$ $\{a_1, \ldots, a_k\}$

where $o_1, \ldots, o_k$ are identifiers and $k \geq 1$.

For (3) - (9) let $\underline{m}_1, \ldots, \underline{m}_k$ be modes with $d(\underline{m}) = \ldots = d(\underline{m}) = \mathsf{T}$.
Then we define for the new mode $\underline{m}$: $d(\underline{m}) \underset{def}{\equiv} \mathsf{T}$.

If there is an $\underline{m}_i$ $(1 \leq i \leq k)$ with $d(\underline{m}_i) = \mathbb{F}$ then we define the new mode $\underline{m}$ by

$$U(\underline{m}) \underset{def}{\equiv} \emptyset \text{ and } d(\underline{m}) \underset{def}{\equiv} \mathbb{F}.$$

(3) <u>Union</u>

$$U(\underline{m}_1 \mid \ldots \mid \underline{m}_k) \underset{def}{\equiv} \bigcup_{1 \leq i \leq k} U(\underline{m}_i) \quad (k \geq 2)$$

(4) <u>"Cartesian" Product</u>

In contrast to the usual definition in mathematics the "cartesian" product of CIP-L is considered to be not associative. So we define:

$$U(\ (\underline{m}_1, \ldots, \underline{m}_k)\ ) \underset{def}{\equiv} U(\ (\underline{m}_1\ s_1, \ldots, \underline{m}_k\ s_k)\ ) \underset{def}{\equiv} U(\underline{m}_1) \times' \ldots \times' U(\underline{m}_k)$$

where

$$M_1 \times' \ldots \times' M_k \underset{def}{\equiv} \begin{cases} \{[\ ] \times \{\ ]\} & \text{if } k = 0 \\ M_1 & \text{if } k = 1 \\ \{[\ ] \times M_1 \times \ldots \times M_k \times \{\ ]\} & \text{if } k > 1 \end{cases}$$

where [and] are two different objects in $\mathbb{U}$ which are only used for the above purpose.

Other realizations of $\times'$ are possible. It is important to recognize the constituents of the product, i.e. one must have a construction function c and k projection functions p_i which satisfy:

$$p_i \circ c(x_1, \ldots, x_k) = x_i \quad \text{for} \quad 1 \leq i \leq k, x_i \in U(\underline{m}_i)$$

The projection functions p_i are associated with the selectors s_i; but note, that in CIP-L the application of a selector syntactically differs from the function application.

(5) Functions

$$U(\,\underline{funct}\,(\underline{m}_1,\ \ldots,\ \underline{m}_{k-1})\,\underline{m}_k\,) =$$
$$\{\ (g,\ p)\ :\ \ g \subseteq U(\underline{m}_1) \times \ldots \times U(\underline{m}_k)\ \wedge$$
$$p\ :\ U(\underline{m}_1) \times \ldots \times U(\underline{m}_{k-1}) \to \{\,\mathbf{T},\,\mathbf{F}\,\}\ \}$$

Thus every ambiguous function is represented by its graph g and a totally defined predicate p on the domain indicating the definedness.

(6) Sets

$$U(\,\underline{set}\ \underline{m}_1)\ \underset{def}{=}\ \{s:\ s \subseteq U(\underline{m}_1)\}$$

(7) Recursive Modes

Let $\tau(\underline{n})$ be a mode expression with $\underline{n}$ occurring free in τ .

$\tau(n)$ is called isotonic in $\underline{n}$, if for all modes $\underline{m}$, $\underline{m}'$
$$U(\underline{m}) \subseteq U(\underline{m}') \Rightarrow U(\tau(\underline{m})) \subseteq U(\tau(\underline{m}'))$$
holds.

$\tau(\underline{n})$ is called continuous in $\underline{n}$, if for all chains $(\underline{m}_i)_{i\,\in\,\mathbb{N}}$ of modes with $U(\underline{m}_i) \subseteq U(\underline{m}_{i+1})$ for all $i \in \mathbb{N}$

$$\bigcup_{i\,\in\,\mathbb{N}} U(\tau(\underline{m}_i))\ =\ U(\tau(\bigcup_{i\,\in\,\mathbb{N}} \underline{m}_i))$$
holds.

Let $\underline{m}$ be a mode indication introduced by a recursive mode declaration $\underline{mode}\ \underline{m}\ =\ \tau(\underline{m})$. We define

$$U(\underline{m}) \underset{def}{=} \begin{cases} \text{least fixpoint of } U(\underline{m})= U(\tau(\underline{m})) \text{ by set inclusion} \\ \qquad \text{if } \tau(\underline{m}) \text{ is isotonic in } \underline{m} \text{ and this fixpoint exists} \\ \emptyset \qquad \text{otherwise} \end{cases}$$

$$d(\underline{m}) \underset{def}{=} \begin{cases} \mathbb{T} \qquad \text{if } \tau(\underline{m}) \text{ is isotonic in } \underline{m} \text{ and the least fixpoint} \\ \qquad \quad \text{exists} \\ \mathbb{F} \qquad \text{otherwise} \end{cases}$$

3.2. Remarks

The semantics of array modes is omitted here, since we prefer to define it using abstract data types (cf. /Partsch, Broy 78/).

Many mode constructs must be considered harmful, since they are not continuous, not even isotonic and therefore equations of the form $\underline{m} = \tau(\underline{m})$ may not have a solution (set theoretical point of view in contrast to /Scott 70/), e.g. funct($\underline{m}$) $\underline{r}$, set $\underline{m}$ are isotonic but not continuous. But the union and the "cartesian" product are isotonic and continuous, i.e. they guarantee solutions.

Using submodes we can sometimes obtain fixpoint solutions for mode expressions containing nonisotonic or noncontinuous constructs. Then we have to prove the existence of a fixpoint for each special case; often these fixpoints are not submodes of another mode.

4. Semantics of Expressions

4.1. Inductive Definition of the Semantics

Let $P_1, \ldots, P_k, E_1, \ldots, E_k$ be U-expressions of appropriate modes.

(1) Identifier

For each identifier x of mode $\underline{m}$ we choose an element $V^{\underline{m}}(x)$ of $U(\underline{m})$.

$$B^{\underline{m}}(x) \underset{def}{=} \begin{cases} \{V^{\underline{m}}(x)\} & \text{if } x \text{ is an identifier of mode } \underline{m} \\ \emptyset & \text{otherwise} \end{cases}$$

$$d^{\underline{m}}(x) \underset{def}{=} \begin{cases} \mathbb{T} & \text{if } x \text{ is an identifier of mode } \underline{m} \\ \mathbb{F} & \text{otherwise} \end{cases}$$

(2) <u>Tuples</u> $\underline{m} = (\underline{m}_1, \ldots, \underline{m}_k)$

$B^{\underline{m}}((E_1, \ldots, E_k)) \underset{def}{=} B^{\underline{m1}}(E_1) \times' \ldots \times' B^{\underline{mk}}(E_k)$

$d^{\underline{m}}((E_1, \ldots, E_k)) \underset{def}{=} d^{\underline{m1}}(E_1) \wedge \ldots \wedge d^{\underline{mk}}(E_k)$

(3) <u>Finite choice</u>

$B^{\underline{m}}(E_1 \, \mathbb{I} \ldots \mathbb{I} \, E_k) \underset{def}{=} B^{\underline{m}}(E_1) \cup \ldots \cup B^{\underline{m}}(E_k)$

$d^{\underline{m}}(E_1 \, \mathbb{I} \ldots \mathbb{I} \, E_k) \underset{def}{=} d^{\underline{m}}(E_1) \wedge \ldots \wedge d^{\underline{m}}(E_k)$

(4) <u>Guarded Expressions</u>

$B^{\underline{m}}(\underline{if} \; P_1 \; \underline{then} \; E_1$

$\quad \vdots \qquad \vdots$

$\mathbb{I} \; P_k \; \underline{then} \; E_k \; \underline{fi}) \underset{def}{=} \bigcup_{1 \le i \le k \, \wedge \, \mathbb{T} \, \in \, B^{\underline{bool}}(P_i)} B^{\underline{m}}(E_i)$

$d^{\underline{m}}(\underline{if} \; P_1 \; \underline{then} \; E_1$

$\quad \vdots \qquad \vdots$

$\mathbb{I} \; P_k \; \underline{then} \; E_k \; \underline{fi}) \underset{def}{=}$

$\underset{def}{=} \quad \bigwedge_{1 \le i \le k \, \wedge \, \mathbb{T} \, \in \, B^{\underline{bool}}(P_i)} d^{\underline{m}}(E_i) \wedge d^{\underline{bool}}(P_1) \wedge \ldots \wedge d^{\underline{bool}}(P_k) \wedge$

$\exists i : 1 \le i \le n \, \wedge \, \{\mathbb{T}\} = B^{\underline{bool}}(P_i)$

(5) <u>Function Denotation</u>

Every syntactical correct function denotation is a defined, determinate expression.

$\bigvee^{\underline{funct} \, (\underline{m}_1, \ldots, \underline{m}_k) \, \underline{r}} (\, (\underline{m}_1 \, x_1, \ldots, \underline{m}_n \, x_k) \, \underline{r} : E \,) \underset{def}{=} (g, p)$

where

$g = \{ (y_1, \ldots, y_k, z) : (y_1, \ldots, y_k) \in U(\underline{m}_1) \times \ldots \times U(\underline{m}_k) \; \wedge$

$\qquad\qquad\qquad\qquad z \in B^{\underline{r}} \, (E \, {}^{y1, \ldots, yk}_{x1, \ldots, xk}) \}$

$p : U(\underline{m}_1) \times \ldots \times U(\underline{m}_k) \longrightarrow \{\mathbb{T}, \mathbb{F}\}$

where for $(y_1, \ldots, y_k) \in U(\underline{m}_1) \times \ldots \times U(\underline{m}_k)$

$p(y_1, \ldots, y_k) = d^{\underline{r}} \, (E \, {}^{y1, \ldots, yk}_{x1, \ldots, xk})$

(6) Function Application

Let F be a U-expression of mode $\underline{funct}\ (\underline{m}_1, \ldots, \underline{m}_k)\underline{r}$

$$B^{\underline{r}}\ (F\ (E_1, \ldots, E_k))_{\overset{=}{def}}$$

$$\bigcup_{y_1 \in B(E_1)} \cdots \bigcup_{y_k \in B(E_k)} \bigcup_{(g,p)\,\in\,B(F)} \{z: (y_1, \ldots, y_k, z) \in g\}$$

$$d^{\underline{r}}\ (F\ (E_1, \ldots, E_k))_{\overset{=}{def}}$$

$$\forall y_1 \in B(E_1) \ldots \forall y_k \in B(E_k)\ \ \forall(g,p) \in B(F): p(y_1, \ldots y_k)$$

$$\wedge\ d(F) \wedge d(E_1) \wedge \ldots \wedge d(E_k)$$

(7) Infinite Choice

$$B^{\underline{m}}(\underline{some}\ \underline{m}\ x: E(x))\ \underset{def}{=}\ \{y: y \in U(\underline{m})\ \wedge\ T \in B^{\underline{bool}}(E(y))\}$$

$$d^{\underline{m}}(\underline{some}\ \underline{m}\ x: E(x))$$

$$\underset{def}{=}\ \forall U(\underline{m})\ y: d^{\underline{bool}}(E(y))\ \wedge\ \exists!\ U(\underline{m})\ x: \{T\} = B^{\underline{bool}}(E(x))$$

(8) Description

$$B^{\underline{m}}(\underline{that}\ \underline{m}\ x: E(x))\ \underset{def}{=}\ \begin{cases} B^{\underline{m}}(\underline{some}\ \underline{m}\ x: E(x)) & \text{if}\ d^{\underline{m}}(\underline{that}\ \underline{m}\ x: E(x)) = T \\ \emptyset & \text{otherwise} \end{cases}$$

$$d^{\underline{m}}(\underline{that}\ \underline{m}\,x : E(x))$$

$$\underset{def}{=} \forall\,U(\underline{m})\,z : (\,d^{\underline{bool}}(E(z)) \land |\ B^{\underline{bool}}(E(z))\ | = 1\,)\ \land$$

$$\exists\,U(\underline{m})\,y : \forall\,U(\underline{m})\,z : (B^{\underline{bool}}(E(z)) = \{\!\top\!\} \Rightarrow z = y)$$

(9) <u>Existential Quantifier</u>

$$B^{\underline{bool}}(\exists\,\underline{m}\,x : E(x))$$

$$\underset{def}{=}
\begin{cases}
\emptyset & \text{if}\ \exists\,U(\underline{m})\,y : B^{\underline{bool}}(E(y)) = \emptyset \land \forall\,U(\underline{m})\,z : \top \notin B^{\underline{bool}}(E(z)) \\
\{\!\top\!\} & \text{if}\ \exists\,U(\underline{m})\,y : \top \in B^{\underline{bool}}(E(y)) \land \exists\,U(\underline{m})\,z : \mathbb{F} \notin B^{\underline{bool}}(E(z)) \\
\{\!\mathbb{F}\!\} & \text{if}\ \forall\,U(\underline{m})\,y : \{\!\mathbb{F}\!\} = B^{\underline{bool}}(E(y)) \\
\{\!\top,\mathbb{F}\!\} & \text{otherwise}
\end{cases}$$

$$d^{\underline{bool}}(\exists\,\underline{m}\,x : E(x)) \underset{def}{=} \forall\,U(\underline{m})\,y : d^{\underline{bool}}(E(y))$$

(10) <u>Comprehension</u>

$$B^{\underline{set}\ \underline{m}}(\{\underline{m}\ x : E(x)\})$$

$$\underset{def}{=} \{\ S : S \subseteq U(\underline{m})\ \land \forall\,U(\underline{m})\,y : (y \in S \Rightarrow \top \in B^{\underline{bool}}(E(y)))\ \land$$

$$(y \notin S \Rightarrow \mathbb{F} \in B^{\underline{bool}}(E(y)))\ \}$$

$$d^{\underline{set}\ \underline{m}}(\{\underline{m}\ x : E(x)\}) \underset{def}{=} \forall\,U(\underline{m})\,y : d^{\underline{bool}}(E(y))$$

4.2. Examples

(1) Let E be defined by

<u>funct</u> E = (<u>nat</u> x) <u>bool</u> : <u>if</u> x > 0 <u>then</u> (true ⫿ false) <u>fi</u>

then we obtain

$d(\exists\ \underline{nat}\ x : E(x)) = d(\underline{some}\ \underline{nat}\ x : E(x)) = d(\{\ \underline{nat}\ x : E(x)\}) = \mathbb{F}$

$B(\underline{some}\ \underline{nat}\ x : E(x)) = \{U(\underline{nat})\ x : x > 0\}$

$B(\exists\ \underline{nat}\ x : E(x)) = \{\!\top\!\}$

$B(\{\underline{nat}\ x : E(x)\})\ = \emptyset$

(2) Let E' be defined by

<u>funct</u> E' = (<u>nat</u> x) <u>bool</u> :

$\qquad$ <u>if</u> x = 0 <u>then</u> true ⫿ x > 1 <u>then</u> false <u>fi</u>

then we obtain

$d(\underline{some}\ \underline{nat}\ x : E'(x)) = d(\underline{that}\ \underline{nat}\ x : E'(x)) = d(\{\underline{nat}\ x : E'(x)\}) = \mathbb{F}$

$B(\underline{some}\ \underline{nat}\ x : E'(x)) = \{0\}$

$B(\underline{that}\ \underline{nat}\ x : E'(x)) = \emptyset$

$B(\{\underline{nat}\ x : E'(x)\}) = \emptyset$

4.3. Notes

(1) The definition of the semantics of functions may be structured in the following manner: in a first approach only the semantics of function applications is defined and functions are not considered to be independent objects; then a semantical representation of functions is not neccessary. This point of view is sufficient for a wide spectrum of programs. Nevertheless, there are functions which have to be treated like independent objects (e.g. recursive functions). Thus we define the semantics of functions by means of relations.

The definition of the semantics of function applications corresponds to the call-by-value evaluation (i.e. to innermost evaluation rules). We believe this to be a "natural" definition of the semantics of function applications.

(2) 0-ary functions and constants have to be distinguished from each other. Consider e. g. <u>funct nat</u> f = <u>nat</u> : 1 and the constant 1 :
$$B^{\underline{nat}}(1) = \{V^{\underline{nat}}(1)\}$$
where as $B^{\underline{funct\ nat}}(f) = \{(B^{\underline{nat}}(1), \top)\}$

(3) We have defined
$$\top \in B(\exists \underline{m}x : E(x)) \iff \exists U(\underline{m})y : \top \in B(E(y))$$
$$\mathbb{F} \in B(\exists \underline{m}x : E(x)) \iff \forall U(\underline{m})y : \mathbb{F} \in B(E(y))$$
There are other possibilities for the definition of the semantics of quantifiers. For example by the generalization of the semantics of the strict logical connective $\vee$, one obtains a quantified expression $\widetilde{\exists}\underline{m} \, x : E(x)$ which has the value true only if $E(x)$ is defined for <u>all</u> x of $U(\underline{m})$ and if there is an y with $\top \in B(E(y))$. Our quantifier $\exists$ corresponds to a less strict logical connective $\dot{\vee}$. But $\widetilde{\exists}$ and $\dot{\vee}$ can be expressed by $\exists$, $\vee$ and guarded expressions and vice versa.

(4) If and only if E is a totally defined, determinate expression the descriptive expression has a defined value:
$$B(\underline{that} \, \underline{m} \, x: E(x)) \neq \emptyset \iff d(\underline{that} \, \underline{m} \, x: E(x)) = \top$$

(5) For all $\mathbb{U}$-expressions E of mode $\underline{m}$ the following holds:
$$B^{\underline{m}}(E) = \emptyset \Rightarrow d^{\underline{m}}(E) = \mathbb{F}$$
Let F be a syntactical correct function expression of mode $\underline{funct} \, (\underline{m_1}, \ldots, \underline{m_k})\underline{r}$.
Then for all $(g,p) \in B(F)$ and for all $(x_1, \ldots, x_k) \in U(\underline{m_1}) \times \ldots \times U(\underline{m_k})$:
$$p(x_1, \ldots, x_k) \Rightarrow \exists y \in U(\underline{r}) : (x_1, \ldots, x_k, y) \in g.$$

(6)   The breadth function $B^{\underline{m}}$ is <u>not</u> definable in CIP-L' as a canonical CIP-L function.

5.   The Semantics of Recursive Functions

Using the semantics definition of § 3 and § 4 we are able to define ambiguous functions as fixpoints of functionals. But if we wish to distinguish least (or greatest) fixpoints, we must have an order for functions. For this purpose it is convenient to introduce a partial order for deterministic expressions (cf. /Manna 74/).

There are various definitions of an order which may be appropriate from an intuitive point of view. But an analysis of the properties of these definitions shows that the EGLI-MILNER ordering (cf. /Milner 73/, /Plotkin 76/) satisfies the following conditions:

The least fixpoint is the "least defined fixpoint with the smallest breadth" and all constructs of CIP-L' are isotonic and sufficiently distinguishable.

The semantics of CIP-L' can be seen as a "proper" extension of the known semantics for nondeterministic constructs (cf. /de Bakker 76/, /Hennessy, Ashcroft 76/, in a limited way /Plotkin 76/, /Smyth 78/).

5.1. EGLI-MILNER Ordering

Let E_1, E_2 be U-expressions of a mode $\underline{m}$

$$E_1 \subseteq E_2 \underset{def}{\Longleftrightarrow} B^{\underline{m}}(E_1) \subseteq B^{\underline{m}}(E_2) \wedge (d^{\underline{m}}(E_1) \Rightarrow d^{\underline{m}}(E_2) \wedge B^{\underline{m}}(E_1) = B^{\underline{m}}(E_2))$$

Since we consider functions as objects having a pointwise representation, in addition we define a pointwise order for U-functions f,g of mode
<u>funct</u> $(\underline{m}_1, \ldots, \underline{m}_k)$ $\underline{r}$ (cf. /de Bakker 76/):

$$f \subseteq^* g \underset{def}{\Longleftrightarrow} \forall U((\underline{m}_1, \ldots, \underline{m}_k)) \, (y_1, \ldots, y_k):$$

$$f(y_1, \ldots, y_k) \subseteq g(y_1, \ldots, y_k)$$

The above definition can be extended to function expressions F, G in a straightforward way.

5.2. Quotient Structure

The ordering $\subseteq$ induces a congruence relation on the set of U-expressions by

$$E_1 \tilde{=} E_2 \Longleftrightarrow E_1 \subseteq E_2 \wedge E_2 \subseteq E_1$$

The induced quotient structure is an inductive partial ordering (cf. /Plotkin 76/) where <u>some</u> $\underline{m}$ x : false represents the bottom element for each mode $\underline{m}$.

(<u>Proof</u>: $B^{\underline{m}}(\underline{some}\ \underline{m}\ x : false) = \emptyset$ implies $d^{\underline{m}}(\underline{some}\ \underline{m}\ x : false) = \text{IF}$. Hence we
have for all U-expressions E of mode $\underline{m}$: $\underline{some}\ \underline{m}\ x : false \sqsubseteq E$)

From the definition of $\sqsubseteq$ we obtain the following equivalences:

$$E_1 \cong E_2 \leftrightarrow B^{\underline{m}}(E_1) = B^{\underline{m}}(E_2) \wedge d^{\underline{m}}(E_1) = d^{\underline{m}}(E_2)$$

Analogously we define a congruence relation $\cong^*$ on the set of U-functions
by $f \cong^* g \leftrightarrow f \sqsubseteq^* g \wedge g \sqsubseteq^* f$.
From the definition of $\sqsubseteq^*$ we conclude:

$$f \cong^* g \quad \leftrightarrow \quad \forall (y_1, \ldots, y_n) \in U(\underline{m}_1) \times \ldots \times U(\underline{m}_k) :$$
$$B^{\underline{r}}(f(y_1, \ldots, y_k)) = B^{\underline{r}}(g(y_1, \ldots, y_k)) \wedge$$
$$d^{\underline{r}}(f(y_1, \ldots, y_k)) = d^{\underline{r}}(g(y_1, \ldots, y_k))$$

5.3. Isotonicity, Continuity

Let f be a U-function of mode $\underline{funct}(\underline{m}_1, \ldots, \underline{m}_k)\ \underline{r}$.

f is called <u>isotonic</u>

$\underset{def}{\leftrightarrow}$ for all U-expressions E_i, E_i' of mode $\underline{m}_i$ $(i = 1, \ldots, k)$:

$$E_1 \sqsubseteq E_1' \wedge \ldots \wedge E_k \sqsubseteq E_k' \rightarrow f(E_1, \ldots, E_k) \sqsubseteq f(E_1', \ldots, E_k').$$

f is called <u>continuous</u>

$\underset{def}{\leftrightarrow}$ for all chains $(E_{ij})_{j \in \mathbb{N}}$ $(i = 1, \ldots, k)$ of U-expressions
of mode $\underline{m}_i$ with $E_{ij} \sqsubseteq E_{ij+1}$ and $E_{1j}, \ldots, E_{kj}$ of modes
$\underline{m}_1, \ldots, \underline{m}_k$ for all $j \in \mathbb{N}$

$$\underset{j \in \mathbb{N}}{lub}\ f(E_{1j}, \ldots, E_{kj}) = f(\underset{j \in \mathbb{N}}{lub}\ E_{1j}, \ldots, \underset{j \in \mathbb{N}}{lub}\ E_{kj}),$$

where for a chain $(E_j)_{j \in \mathbb{N}}$ of U-expressions $\underset{j \in \mathbb{N}}{lub}\ E_j$ is defined by

$$\underset{j \in \mathbb{N}}{lub}(B(E_j), d(E_j)) .$$

The infinite constructs choice, quantification, descriptive expression and
comprehension are considered as functions with functions as parameters. For
example the isotonicity of the choice

$$E \sqsubseteq^* E' \Rightarrow \underline{some}\ \underline{m}\ x : E(x) \sqsubseteq \underline{some}\ \underline{m}\ x : E'(x)$$
$(E, E'$ U-functions of mode $\underline{funct}(\underline{m})\ \underline{bool})$.

5.4. Notes

(1) For two $\mathbb{U}$-expressions E, E' of mode $\underline{m}$: If $d(E)$ holds, then

$$E \sqsubseteq E' \;\Rightarrow\; E \,\tilde{=}\, E'$$

(2) The least upper bound $\underset{j \in \mathbb{N}}{\text{lub}}(E_j)$ of a chain $(E_j)_{j \in \mathbb{N}}$ of $\mathbb{U}$-expressions

is $\tilde{=}$ - equivalent to the pair $(\underset{j \in \mathbb{N}}{\text{lub}^{\subseteq}} B(E_j), \underset{j \in \mathbb{N}}{\text{lub}^{<}} d(E_j))$, where

$\underset{j \in \mathbb{N}}{\text{lub}^{\subseteq}} B(E_j)$ is the least upper bound of $B(E_j)$ with respect to the set

inclusion and $\underset{j \in \mathbb{N}}{\text{lub}^{<}} d(E_j)$ is the least upper bound of $d(E_j)$ in

$U(\underline{bool})$ with respect to the ordering defined by $\mathbb{F} < \mathbb{T}$.

(3) Breadth of Functions

Consider the following functions f, g, f', g' of mode $\underline{funct(\underline{nat})}$ $\underline{nat}$:

$\underline{funct}\ f \equiv (\underline{nat}\ x)\ \underline{nat} : 0$,
$\underline{funct}\ g \equiv (\underline{nat}\ x)\ \underline{nat} : 1$,
$\underline{funct}\ f' \equiv (\underline{nat}\ x)\ \underline{nat} : \underline{if}\ x = 0\ \underline{then}\ 1\ \underline{else}\ 0\ \underline{fi}$,
$\underline{funct}\ g' \equiv (\underline{nat}\ x)\ \underline{nat} : \underline{if}\ x = 0\ \underline{then}\ 0\ \underline{else}\ 1\ \underline{fi}$

The breadth of $(f \mathbin{\square} g)$ is $\{V(f), V(g)\}$, the breadth of $f' \mathbin{\square} g'$ is
$\{V(f'), V(g')\}$ and these two breadthes are disjoint. But nevertheless
$\forall\, U(\underline{nat})\ x : (f \mathbin{\square} g)(x) \,\tilde{=}\, (f' \mathbin{\square} g')(x)$ and therefore $f \mathbin{\square} g \,\tilde{=}^{x}\, f' \mathbin{\square} g'$ holds.

To see the structure of $\tilde{=}^{*}$ for functions, one can define as breadth'
B' of a function expression F all determinate functions "contained"
in F.

$B'(F) = \{U(\underline{funct(\underline{m})}\ \underline{r})\ h:$
$\qquad \forall U(\underline{m})x : B(h(x)) \subseteq B(F(x)) \land |\ B(h(x))\ | \leq 1 \land$
$\qquad (B(h(x)) = \emptyset \leftrightarrow \neg\, d(h(x)) \land$
$\qquad (\neg\, d(h(x)) \Rightarrow \neg\, d(F(x)))\}$

Then, one can define an ordering $\sqsubseteq'$ for functions in the manner of
/Henessy-Ashcroft 76/ or /Plotkin 76/ by

$F \sqsubseteq' G \underset{\text{def}}{\leftrightarrow} (\forall\, f \in B'(F)\ \exists\, g \in B'(G) : f \sqsubseteq^{*} g) \land$
$\qquad\qquad (\forall\, g \in B'(G)\ \exists\, f \in B'(F) : f \sqsubseteq^{*} g)$

One can prove the following equivalence:

$$F \subseteq^* G \leftrightarrow F \subseteq' G \ .$$

Therefore, $B(F)$ is in some sense a generating set for the "space" $B'(F)$ of determinate functions. If F is of mode <u>funct</u>($\underline{m}$) $\underline{r}$, $\underline{m}$ infinite and $| B(f(x)) | \geq 2$ for an infinite number of elements x of $\underline{m}$, then $| B'(F) |$ is uncountable.

5.5. Isotonicity of Expression Constructs

Proofs of the isotonicity of finite choices, guarded expressions and function applications are known in the literature (cf. e.g. /de Bakker 76/). Hence, although our definition of these constructs is slightly different, we will only prove the isotonicity of "infinite" constructs. Moreover, since these proofs are very similar, we restrict ourselves to the proofs of the isotonicity of infinite choice and comprehension.

Lemma

Let E, E' be $\mathbb{U}$-functions of mode <u>funct</u>($\underline{m}$) <u>bool</u> with $E \subseteq^* E'$. Then

(1) <u>some</u> $\underline{m}\, x : E(x) \subseteq$ <u>some</u> $\underline{m}\, x : E'(x)$

(2) $\{\underline{m}\, x : E(x)\} \subseteq \{\underline{m}\, x : E'(x)\}$

Proof of (1)

a) Let $y \in B(\underline{\text{some}}\ \underline{m}\, x : E(x))$. Then $\mathbb{T} \in B(E(y)) \subseteq B(E'(y))$.
    Thus $y \in B(\underline{\text{some}}\ \underline{m}\, x : E'(x))$.

b) Assume $d(\underline{\text{some}}\ \underline{m}\, x : E(x))$:
    For all $y \in U(\underline{m})$ we have $d(E(y))$ and therefore $d(E'(y))$ and $E(y) \overset{\approx}{=} E'(y)$.
    Since $\overset{\approx}{=}$ is a congruence relation we obtain
    $\underline{\text{some}}\ \underline{m}\, x : E(x) \overset{\approx}{=} \underline{\text{some}}\ \underline{m}\, x : E'(x)$.

Proof of (2)

a) Now we prove $B(\{\underline{m}\, x : E(x)\}) \subseteq B(\{\ \underline{m}\, x : E'(x)\})$:
    Let $S \in B(\{\underline{m}\, x : E(x)\})$. Then for all $x \in U(\underline{m})$
    $B(x \in S) \subseteq B(E(x)) \subseteq B(E'(x))$. Thus $S \in B(\{\underline{m}\, x : E'(x)\})$.
    The proof of 2.b is analogous to the proof of 1.b.   □

5.6.   Continuity of the "Finite constructs"

The proofs of the continuity of finite choice, guarded expressions and
function applications are very similar. We will only prove the continuity
for function application which is slightly more complicated than the others.

Lemma

Let $(f_j)_{j \in \mathbb{N}}$ be a chain of $\mathbb{U}$-functions of mode $\underline{funct}(\underline{m}_1, \ldots, \underline{m}_k) \; \underline{r}$
with $f_j \sqsubseteq^* f_{j+1}$ for all $j \in \mathbb{N}$ and with least upperbound f . In addition
let $(E_{ij})_{j \in \mathbb{N}}$ $(i=1, \ldots, k)$ be chains of $\mathbb{U}$-expressions of mode $\underline{m}_i$

with $E_{ij} \sqsubseteq E_{ij+1}$
and with least upper bounds E_i .

Then $f(E_1, \ldots, E_k) \; \tilde{=} \; \underset{j \in \mathbb{N}}{lub} \; f_j(E_{1j}, \ldots, E_{kj})$

Proof

$\underset{j \in \mathbb{N}}{lub} \; f_j(E_{1j}, \ldots, E_{kj}) \sqsubseteq f(E_1, \ldots, E_k)$ follows from the isotonicity of the
function application (cf. /Kleene 52/, /Manna 74/).

It suffices to show

(*) $f(E_1, \ldots, E_k) \sqsubseteq \underset{j \in \mathbb{N}}{lub} \; f_j(E_{1j}, \ldots, E_{kj})$

Proof of (*)

a) $B(f(E_1, \ldots, E_k)) \subseteq \underset{j \in \mathbb{N}}{lub} \; B(f_j(E_{1j}, \ldots, E_{kj}))$:

    Let $x \in B(f(E_1, \ldots, E_k))$. Then there exist $y_1 \in B(E_1), \ldots, y_k \in B(E_k)$

    such that $x \in B(f(y_1, \ldots, y_k))$. Because of

    $B(f(y_1, \ldots, y_k)) = \underset{j \in \mathbb{N}}{lub} \; B(f_j(y_1, \ldots, y_k))$ there exist natural numbers

    $n, n_1, \ldots, n_k$ such that $y_1 \in B(E_{1n_1}), \ldots, y_k \in B(E_{kn_k})$ and

    $x \in B(f_n(y_1, \ldots, y_k))$.

    Let $n' \underset{def}{=} \max \{n, n_1, \ldots, n_k\}$. Then $x \in B(f_j(E_{1j}, \ldots, E_{kj}))$ for

    all $j \geq n'$. Thus $x \in \underset{j \in \mathbb{N}}{lub} \; B(f_j(E_{1j}, \ldots, E_{kj}))$.

b) Assume $d(f(E_1, ..., E_k))$:

For all $i = 1, ..., k$ $d(E_i) = \underset{j \in \mathbb{N}}{\text{lub}}\, d(E_{ij}) = \mathbb{T}$ holds. Therefore there

exists a natural number n such that for all $j \geq n$: $d(E_{ij}) = \mathbb{T}$

and thus $E_{ij} \tilde{=} E_{in}$ hold. From $d(f) = \mathbb{T}$ we obtain a natural number

$1 \geq n$ such that for all $j \geq 1$

$E_i \tilde{=} E_{ij} \tilde{=} E_{i1}$, $f \tilde{=} f_j \tilde{=} f_1$ and thus

$f(E_1, ..., E_k) \tilde{=} f_j(E_{1j}, ..., E_{kj}) \tilde{=} \underset{j \in \mathbb{N}}{\text{lub}}\, f_j(E_{1j}, ..., E_{kj})$

hold.   □

5.7. Noncontinuity of "Infinite Constructs"

Infinite choices, descriptions, quantifiers, "infinite" function applications and comprehensions are not continuous:

Consider the following chain $(E_j)_{j \in \mathbb{N}}$ of functions:

<u>funct</u> $E_j \equiv$ (<u>nat</u> n) <u>bool</u> :
      if $n < j$ <u>then</u> true <u>fi</u>

The least upper bound of $(E_j)_{j \in \mathbb{N}}$ is represented by

<u>funct</u> $E \equiv$ (<u>nat</u> n) <u>bool</u> : true ,

because $B(\underset{j \in \mathbb{N}}{\text{lub}}\, E_j) = B(E) = \{(g, p)\}$ with $g = p = \{(x, \mathbb{T}) : x \in U(\underline{\text{nat}})\}$.

(1) <u>Infinite choice</u>

$\underset{j \in \mathbb{N}}{\text{lub}}\, \underline{\text{some}}\ \underline{\text{nat}}\ x : E_j(x) \tilde{=} \underline{\text{some}}\ \underline{\text{nat}}\ x :(\text{true} \ [] \ \text{false})$

$\neq \underline{\text{some}}\ \underline{\text{nat}}\ x : \text{true} \tilde{=} \underline{\text{some}}\ \underline{\text{nat}}\ x : \underset{j \in \mathbb{N}}{\text{lub}}\, E_j(x)$.

(2) <u>Quantifiers</u>

$d(\underset{j \in \mathbb{N}}{\text{lub}}\, \exists\ \underline{\text{nat}}\ x : E_j(x)) = \underset{l \in \mathbb{N}}{\text{lub}}\, d(\exists\ \underline{\text{nat}}\ x : E_1(x)) = \mathbb{F}$

$\neq \mathbb{T} = d(\exists\ \underline{\text{nat}}\ x : \text{true}) = d(\exists\ \underline{\text{nat}}\ x : \underset{j \in \mathbb{N}}{\text{lub}}\, E_j(x))$

(3) Comprehension

$$d(\text{lub } \{\underline{nat} \ x : E_j(x)\}) = \text{lub } d(\{\underline{nat} \ x : E_j(x)\}) = \text{lub } \mathbb{F} = \mathbb{F}$$
$$_{j \in \mathbb{N}} \qquad\qquad _{j \in \mathbb{N}} \qquad\qquad\qquad _{j \in \mathbb{N}}$$

$$\neq \mathbb{T} = d(\{\underline{nat} \ x : true\}) = d(\{\underline{nat} \ x : \text{lub } E_j(x)\})$$
$$_{j \in \mathbb{N}}$$

(4) Description

Consider the following chain $(E'_j)_{j \in \mathbb{N}}$:

$$\underline{funct} \ E_j \equiv (\underline{nat} \ x) \ \underline{bool} : \underline{if} \ x = 0 \qquad \underline{then} \ true$$
$$\square \ 0 < x \leq j \ \underline{then} \ false \ \underline{fi}$$

Then $\text{lub } E'_j$ can be represented by
$_{j \in \mathbb{N}}$

$$\underline{funct} \ E' \equiv (\underline{nat} \ x) \ \underline{bool} : \underline{if} \ x = 0 \ \underline{then} \ true \ \underline{else} \ false \ \underline{fi}$$

We have

$$\text{lub } \underline{that} \ \underline{nat} \ x : E_j(x) \ \tilde{=} \ (\emptyset, \mathbb{F}) \ \tilde{\neq} \ (\{0\}, \mathbb{T}) \ \tilde{=} \ \underline{that} \ \underline{nat} \ x : E'(x)$$
$$_{j \in \mathbb{N}}$$

5.8. Notes

(1) If one restricts quantifiers, comprehensions, infinite choices and descriptions to finite modes or to boolean expressions $E(x)$ with different values only for a finite number of elements $x_1, \ldots, x_k$, then these constructs are continuous.

Example: The infinite constructs are continuous for the following chains $(E_j)_{j \in \mathbb{N}}$:

$$\underline{funct} \ E_j \equiv (\underline{nat} \ x) \ \underline{bool} : \underline{if} \ x < 100 \ \underline{then} \ F_j(x) \ \underline{else} \ false \ \underline{fi}$$

where the functions $F_j \ (j \in \mathbb{N})$ are of mode $\underline{funct}(\underline{nat}) \ \underline{bool}$.

(2) The noncontinuity is not a consequence of the introduction of non-
      deterministic constructs but arises whenever the evaluation of an expression
      implies the consideration of an infinite number of elements.

      For example, in a fully deterministic language quantifiers on infinite
      sets are also not continuous.

5.9. Semantics of Recursive Functions

Let τ be an expression of mode

$\underline{funct}(\underline{funct}(\underline{m}_1, \ldots, \underline{m}_k) \ \underline{r}) \ \underline{funct} \ (\underline{m}_1, \ldots, \underline{m}_k) \ \underline{r}$,

i.e. τ is a functional having as parameter and as result a function of
mode $\underline{funct}(\underline{m}_1, \ldots, \underline{m}_k) \ \underline{r}$.

Consider the equation

$g \stackrel{\approx}{=}{}^{*} (\underline{m}_1 x_1, \ldots, \underline{m}_k x_k) \ \underline{r} : \tau(g) (x_1, \ldots, x_k)$,

where g is a free identifier for IU-functions.

The identifier f given by the following recursive declaration

$\qquad \underline{funct} \ f \equiv (\underline{m}_1 \ x_1, \ldots, \underline{m}_n \ x_n) \ \underline{r} : \tau(f) \ (x_1, \ldots, x_n)$

denotes the least fixpoint of the above equation.

5.10. Notes

(1) With this construction to define recursive functions we are always
      considering chains of function objects which are in the $\underline{\sqsubseteq}^{*}$ - order.
      The least upper bounds of these chains are again always ambiguous
      functions but not expressions for functions. Thus the fixpoint of the
      equations is one ambiguous function.

      Note that - even if τ is ambiguous - the term

$\qquad (\underline{m}_1 \ x_1, \ldots, \underline{m}_n \ x_n) \ \underline{r} : \quad \tau(f) \ (x_1, \ldots, x_n)$

      is a determinate expression for a function.

(2) If the functional τ is continuous one can construct the least fixpoint μf
of the equation $f \stackrel{\approx}{=}^* (\underline{m}_1 x_1, \ldots, \underline{m}_k x_k) \underline{r} : \tau(f) (x_1, \ldots, x_k)$

by Kleene's first recursion theorem (cf. /Kleene 52/, /Manna 74/) as usual:
μf is the least upper bound of the following chain $(\tau^i(\Omega))_{i \in \mathbb{N}}$ defined
by induction on i:

$\underline{i = 0}$:

$\qquad$ $\underline{funct}$ $\Omega \equiv (\underline{m}_1 x_1, \ldots, \underline{m}_k x_k) \underline{r} : \underline{some} \ \underline{r} \ z : false$

$\underline{i > 0}$:

$\qquad$ $\underline{funct}$ $\tau^i(\Omega) \equiv (\underline{m}_1 x_1, \ldots, \underline{m}_k x_k) \underline{r} : \tau(\tau^{i-1}(\Omega)) (x_1, \ldots, x_k)$

Ω is the completely undefined function. We have $V(\Omega) = (\emptyset, p_f)$, $d(\Omega) = \mathbb{T}(!)$
where p_f denotes the predicate which always yields $\mathbb{F}$.

For all $(x_1, \ldots, x_k) \in U(\underline{m}_1) \times \ldots \times U(\underline{m}_k)$:

$\qquad$ $B(\Omega (x_1, \ldots, x_k)) = \emptyset$ and $d(\Omega (x_1, \ldots, x_k)) = \mathbb{F}$.

μf can be represented by the pair

$$(g, p)$$

where
$$g = \{(x_1, \ldots, x_k, y): (x_1, \ldots, x_k) \in U(\underline{m}_1) \times \ldots \times U(\underline{m}_k) \wedge$$
$$y \in \underset{i \in \mathbb{N}}{lub} \ B(\tau^i(\Omega) (x_1, \ldots, x_k)) \}$$
and
$$p(x_1, \ldots, x_k) = \underset{i \in \mathbb{N}}{lub} \ d(\tau^i(\Omega) (x_1, \ldots, x_k)) \text{ for all } (x_1, \ldots, x_k) \in U(\underline{m}_1) \times \ldots \times U(\underline{m}_k)$$

5.11. Example: Noncontinuity of $\tau^i(\Omega)$ -chains

To stress the problems of noncontinuous constructs, we give the following
example:

Let $\underline{funct}$ $F \equiv (\underline{nat} \ x) \ \underline{nat} : \tau(f) (x)$

where

$$\tau(F)\ (x) \equiv \text{if } x = 0 \text{ then } F(\text{some nat } z : z > 0)$$
$$[]\ x = 1 \text{ then } 1$$
$$[]\ x > 1 \text{ then } F(x-1) \qquad\qquad \text{fi}$$

We have for all $x \in U(\underline{\text{nat}})$ and all $i \geq 2$

$$B(\tau^i\,(\Omega)\,(x)) = \begin{cases} \{1\} & \text{if } x \leq i \\ \emptyset & \text{otherwise} \end{cases}$$

$$d(\tau^i\,(\Omega)\,(x)) = \begin{cases} \mathbf{T} & \text{if } 1 \leq x \leq i \\ \mathbb{F} & \text{otherwise} \end{cases}$$

$d(\tau^i\,(\Omega)\,(0))$ is false, since there are always natural numbers n contained in $B(\text{some nat } z : z{>}0)$, such that $d(\tau^i\,(\Omega)\,(n)) = \mathbb{F}$

Thus for all $x \in U(\underline{\text{nat}})$

$$B(\text{lub}_i\ \tau^i\,(\Omega)\,(x)) = \{1\}, \quad d(\text{lub}_i\ \tau^i\,(\Omega)\,(x)) = \begin{cases} \mathbf{T} & \text{if } x \geq 1 \\ \mathbf{F} & \text{if } x = 0, \end{cases}$$

but

$$B(\tau(\text{lub}_i\ \tau^i\,(\Omega))\,(x)) = \{1\}, \quad d(\tau(\text{lub}_i\ \tau^i\,(\Omega)\,(x)) = \mathbf{T}.$$

Therefore τ is not continuous.

If in the definition of τ we set $z \geq 0$ instead of $z > 0$, then the new τ is continuous due to the fact that now

$$d(\tau(\text{lub}_i(\Omega))\,(0)) = d(\text{lub}_i\ \tau^i\,(\Omega)\,(0)) = \mathbb{F}$$

holds.

Note that it is impossible to give an operative realization of the above some-expression without any reduction of its breadth or loosing its definedness.

Part II. Transformation Rules and Semantics

1. Rule of Implementation

The formal definition of the semantics of the expressions of CIP-L' forms the basis for the verification of transformation rules. Moreover we believe that a <u>transformation calculus</u> (having combinatorial semantics) should be developed together with set theoretical semantics. We then have the possibility of model theoretic proofs which are often simpler than combinatorial ones.

Program development often starts from ambiguous functions or expressions. Besides equivalence transformation rules which transform programs to ones with equal breadth and definedness, we want to apply transformations reducing the breadth of given programs. Doing so, we finally may end with unambiguous functions (or expressions) or completely deterministic programs. This direction in program development can be formalized by introduction of the "implementation relation" - which is nothing but a particular partial order on functions and expressions of CIP-L'.

Definitions

(1) $\sqsubseteq_I$ - Ordering

Let E_1, E_2 be expressions of mode $\underline{m}$.

$$E_1 \sqsubseteq_I E_2 \underset{\text{def}}{\leftrightarrow} B^{\underline{m}}(E_1) \subseteq B^{\underline{m}}(E_2) \wedge (d(E_2) \rightarrow d(E_1)) .$$

Let f, g be $\mathbb{U}$-functions of mode $\underline{\text{funct}}(\underline{m}_1\ x_1,\ \ldots,\ \underline{m}_k\ x_k)\ \underline{r}.$

$$f \sqsubseteq^*_I g \underset{\text{def}}{\leftrightarrow} \bigvee (y_1,\ \ldots,y_k) \in U(\underline{m}_1) \times \ldots \times U(\underline{m}_k):$$
$$f(y_1,\ \ldots,\ y_k) \sqsubseteq_I g(y_1,\ \ldots,\ y_k)$$

Let E, E' be expressions

$$E \cong_I E' \underset{\text{def}}{\leftrightarrow} E \sqsubseteq_I E' \wedge E' \sqsubseteq_I E .$$

$=^*$ is defined analogously.

Remark: In program development for functions we are in general interested in the $\sqsubseteq^*_I$ - relation.

(2) <u>Rule of Implementation</u>

Let E, E' be expressions.

"E implements E' under the condition P"
(represented by the following diagramm)

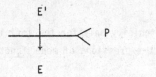

$$\underset{\text{def}}{\leftrightarrow} \begin{cases} P \Rightarrow E \sqsubseteq^{*}_{I} E' & \text{if E and E' are } \mathbb{IU}\text{-functions} \\ P \Rightarrow E \sqsubseteq_{I} E' & \text{otherwise} \end{cases}$$

(3) <u>Rule of Equivalence Transformation</u>

Let E, E' be expressions.
"E is equivalent to E' under the condition P"
(represented by the following diagramm)

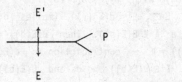

$$\underset{\text{def}}{\leftrightarrow} \begin{cases} P \Rightarrow E \approx_{I} E' & \text{if E and E' are } \mathbb{IU}\text{-functions} \\ P \Rightarrow E \approx_{I} E' & \text{otherwise} \end{cases}$$

<u>Notes</u>

(1) The orderings $\sqsubseteq_{I}$ and $\sqsubseteq$ induce identical congruence relations on
CIP-L expressions. In contrast to $\sqsubseteq$ maximal elements exist for the
ordering but minimal do not.

(2) The $\sqsubseteq_{I}$ -relation permits the derivation of an operative semantics:
Each reduction of the breadth by transformations anticipates some choice
which actually should be performed during an evaluation of the program.
This shows the relationship between program development by transformation and symbolic evaluation (simplification).

Correctness of Transformations

(1) Lemma

All finite and infinite constructs of CIP-L' are isotonic with
respect to the $\sqsubseteq_I$ -ordering.

Proof:

We show the isotonicity only for the infinite choice:
Let E, E' be U-expressions of mode $\underline{funct}(\underline{m})\ \underline{bool}$
with $E \sqsubseteq_I^* E'$.
Then $\underline{some}\ \underline{m}\ x : E(x) \sqsubseteq_I \underline{some}\ \underline{m}\ x : E'(x)$ is valid, too.

Proof:

(a) $B(\underline{some}\ \underline{m}\ x : E(x)) \subseteq B(\underline{some}\ \underline{m}\ x : E'(x))$
can be proved exactly as for $\sqsubseteq$, the Egli-Milner ordering.

(b) Assume $d(\underline{some}\ \underline{m}\ x : E'(x))$:
Thus for all $y \in U(\underline{m})$ $d(E'(y))$ and there exists an element
$b \in U(\underline{m})$ with $\{\mathbb{T}\} = B(E'(b))$.
Since $E \sqsubseteq_I^* E'$ $d(E'(y))$ implies $d(E(y))$ for all $y \in U(\underline{m})$.
Suppose $\mathbb{T} \notin B(E(b))$. Then $B(E(b)) = \emptyset$ and
$d(E(b)) = \mathbb{F}$ - contradiction to $d(E(b)) = \mathbb{T}$.
Hence $\mathbb{T} \in B(E(b))$ holds and $B(E(b)) \subseteq B(E'(b)) = \{\mathbb{T}\}$
implies $\{\mathbb{T}\} = B(E(b))$.
Therefore $d(\underline{some}\ \underline{m}\ x : E(x))$ holds.

□

(2) Definition

A program (expression) E in CIP-L' is called partially correct with
respect to some predicate P, if all $x \in B(E)$ satisfy $P(x)$; E is
called totally correct if $d(E)$ holds, too (compare /Manna 74, p. 165/).

(3) Corollary

If an expression E is partially (totally) correct, then a transformation
substituting a subexpression S of E by an expression S' such that
$S' \sqsubseteq_I S$ preserves the partial (total) correctness.
Such transformations may even generate totally correct programs from
partially correct ones.

2. Definitional Transformations

In the same way as extensions by definitions of theories are used in logic
(cf. /Shoenfield 67/), we can introduce new syntactic constructs by <u>defini-
tional transformations</u>:

(1) <u>if - then - else - fi</u>

    <u>if</u> P <u>then</u> E <u>else</u> E' <u>fi</u>

    def ——$\ddagger$——

    ⌈ <u>bool</u> p ≡ P;
      <u>if</u> p <u>then</u> E
     ▯ p <u>then</u> E' <u>fi</u> ⌋

Knowing the semantics of the defining expression we are able to write
down the semantics of the new construct:

$$B(\underline{if}\ P\ \underline{then}\ E\ \underline{else}\ E'\ \underline{fi}) = \begin{cases} B(E) \cup B(E') & \text{if } \{\mathbb{T}, \mathbb{F}\} = B(P) \\ B(E) & \text{if } \{\mathbb{T}\} = B(P) \\ B(E') & \text{if } \{\mathbb{F}\} = B(P) \\ \emptyset & \text{if } \emptyset = B(P) \end{cases}$$

$$d(\underline{if}\ P\ \underline{then}\ E\ \underline{else}\ E'\ \underline{fi})$$

$$= d(P) \wedge (\mathbb{T} \in B(P) \Rightarrow d(E)) \wedge (\mathbb{F} \in B(P) \Rightarrow d(E')) \wedge |B(P)| = 1$$

(2) Object Declaration

The nonrecursive introduction of identifiers for objects ("object
declaration") can be defined by transformations, e.g.:

⌈<u>m</u> x ≡ E_1 ;
        E_2⌋

——$\ddagger$——$\langle$ ∀ U(<u>m</u>) x : x ∈ $B(E_1)$ ⇒ <u>r</u> :: E_2

((<u>m</u> x) <u>r</u> : E_2) (E_1)

(3) Universal Quantifiers

The universal quantifier is defined by:

$$\forall \underline{m} \, x : E(x)$$

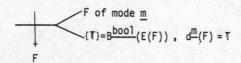

$$\neg \, \exists \, \underline{m} \, x : \neg \, E(x)$$

Thus the semantics of $\forall \underline{m} \, x : E(x)$ is

$B(\forall \underline{m} \, x : E(x))$

$$= \begin{cases} \emptyset & \text{if } \exists \, U(\underline{m}) \, z : B(E(z)) = \emptyset \land \forall \, U(\underline{m}) \, y : \mathbb{F} \notin B(E(y)) \\ \{\mathsf{T}\} & \text{if } \forall \, U(\underline{m}) \, z : B(E(z)) = \{\mathsf{T}\} \\ \{\mathsf{F}\} & \text{if } \exists \, U(\underline{m}) \, z : \mathbb{F} \in B(E(z)) \land \exists \, U(\underline{m}) \, y : \mathsf{T} \notin B(E(y)) \\ \{\mathsf{T}, \mathbb{F}\} & \text{otherwise} \end{cases}$$

$d(\forall \underline{m} \, x : E(x)) = \forall \, U(\underline{m}) \, y : d(E(y))$

3. Derived transformations

(1) Elimination of Choice

$\underline{\text{some}} \, \underline{m} \, x : E(x)$

F of mode $\underline{m}$

$\{\mathsf{T}\} = B^{\underline{bool}}(E(F))$, $d^{\underline{m}}(F) = \mathsf{T}$

F

Proof:

$B(E(F)) = \{\mathsf{T}\} \Rightarrow B(F) \subseteq B(\underline{\text{some}} \, \underline{m} \, x : E(x))$.

Because of $d(F) = \mathsf{T}$, the condition $d(\underline{\text{some}} \, \underline{m} \, x : E(x)) \Rightarrow d(F))$ holds always.

(2) Elimination of Nested Choice

$\underline{\text{some}} \, \underline{m} \, x : E(\underline{\text{some}} \, \underline{n} \, y : F(y,x), x)$

$\underline{\text{some}} \, \underline{m} \, x : \exists \, \underline{n} \, y : \underline{\text{if}} \, F(y,x) \, \underline{\text{then}} \, E(y,x) \, \underline{\text{else}} \, \text{false} \, \underline{\text{fi}}$

Proof

We denote $E(\underline{\text{some}}\ \underline{n}\ y : F(y, x), x)$ by $C(x)$, $\exists\ \underline{n}\ y : \underline{\text{if}}\ \dots\ \underline{\text{fi}}$ by $D(x)$.

a) $B(\underline{\text{some}}\ \underline{m}\ x : C(x)) = B(\underline{\text{some}}\ \underline{m}\ x : D(x))$:

For all $a \in U(\underline{m})$ we have: $a \in B(\underline{\text{some}}\ \underline{m}\ x : D(x))$

• ↔ there exists some b with $\top \in B(F(b, a))$ and $\top \in B(E(b, a))$.

↔ $\top \in B(E(\underline{\text{some}}\ \underline{n}\ y : F(y, a), a))$

↔ $a \in B(\underline{\text{some}}\ \underline{m}\ x : C(x))$.

b) Assume $d(\underline{\text{some}}\ \underline{m}\ x : C(x))$:

From the definition of $d(\underline{\text{some}} \dots)$ we obtain for all $b \in U(\underline{m})$ •
and all $c \in U(\underline{n})$ $d(F(c, b))$ and $(\top \in B(F(c, b)) \rightarrow d(E(c, b)))$.
Therefore for all $b \in U(\underline{m})$:

(*) $d(\exists\ \underline{n}\ y : \underline{\text{if}}\ F(y, b)\ \underline{\text{then}}\ E(y, b)\ \underline{\text{else}}\ \text{false}\ \underline{\text{fi}})$.

Moreover there exists an element $b' \in U(\underline{m})$ such that
$\{\top\} = B(E(\underline{\text{some}}\ \underline{n}\ y : F(y, b'), b'))$.

Thus $\displaystyle\bigcup_{c\ :\ \top \in B(F(c, b'))} B(E(c, b')) = \{\top\}$

and hence there exist $c', c'' \in U(n)$ with

$\top \in B(F(c', b'))$, $\top \in B(E(c', b'))$, $\top \in B(F(c'', b'))$, $F \in B(F(c'', b'))$.

But this means that

(**) $\{\top\} = B(\exists\ \underline{n}\ y : \underline{\text{if}}\ F(y, b')\ \underline{\text{then}}\ E(y, b')\ \underline{\text{else}}\ \text{false}\ \underline{\text{fi}})$.

(*) and (**) together imply $d(\underline{\text{some}}\ \underline{m}\ x : D(x))$.

(3) <u>Relation between Choice and Description</u>

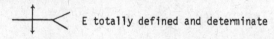

that $\underline{m}\ x : E(x)$

E totally defined and determinate

$\underline{\text{some}}\ \underline{m}\ x : (E(x) \wedge \forall\ \underline{m}\ y : (E(y) \rightarrow y = x))$

The proof is obvious.

(4) Sequentialisation of Guarded Expressions

$$
\begin{array}{l}
\underline{if}\ P_1\ \underline{then}\ E_1 \\
\quad \vdots \qquad \vdots \\
\square\ P_k\ \underline{then}\ E_k\ \underline{fi}
\end{array}
\qquad \xrightarrow{\quad\quad} \qquad
\begin{array}{l}
\underline{if}\ P_1\ \underline{then}\ E_1 \\
\square\ \neg P_1\ \underline{then}\ \underline{if}\ P_2\ \underline{then}\ E_2 \\
\quad\quad \vdots \qquad\qquad \vdots \\
\square\quad P_k\ \underline{then}\ E_k\ \underline{fi}\ \underline{fi}
\end{array}
$$

$$|B^{\underline{bool}}(P_1)| = 1$$

Proof

Denote the expression on the left by C, the other by D.

a) $B(D) \subseteq B(C)$:

Let $a \in B(D)$. Then either $\top \in B(P_1)$ and $a \in B(E_1)$ or there
is a $j \in \{2, \ldots, k\}$ such that $\top \in B(P_j)$ and $a \in B(E_j)$.
Therefore $a \in B(C)$.

b) Assume $d(C)$:

Then $d(P_i)$ holds for all $i = 1, \ldots, k$. Therefore
$B(P_1 \vee \neg P_1) = \{\top\}$ and $d(P_1 \vee \neg P_1) = \top$ and we obtain $C \stackrel{\approx}{=} D$

Note

$\xrightarrow{\quad}$ is a reflexive and transitive relation. For expressions consisting
of unquantified boolean expressions and guarded expressions one can construct
a finite set T of transformations such that T is complete in the following
sense:

Let E, E' be expressions. Then $E' \sqsubseteq_I E$ holds if and only if there
exists a finite sequence of transformations of T (more exactly of transformation instances of T) of the following form:

$$
E \xrightarrow{\quad} E_1,\ E_1 \xrightarrow{\quad} E_2,\ \ldots,\ E_{k-1} \xrightarrow{\quad} E_k,\ E_k \xrightarrow{\quad} E'.
$$

Concluding Remarks

The mathematical semantics given in this paper comprises coherently
descriptive constructs for specifications and algorithmic constructs such as
recursive functions etc. The combination of these constructs with nondeterminacy
and nondeterminism leads to a rather powerful language. Since the main idea of
a wide spectrum language is a flexible combination of different "styles", it
is necessary to give a coherent semantics for all possible mixtures, i.e. to
treat all expressions like nondeterminate expressions. As demonstrated, this
involves no specific problems . Nevertheless, the definition of recursive
functions should be restricted in order to avoid infinite quantifications,
choices etc., since, in general, these constructs are not continuous.

With the help of definitional transformations the semantics for the remainder
of the language CIP-L can be based on the semantics defined so far (cf. /Pepper
78/). Furthermore - compatible to the given mathematical semantics - an operational semantics can be defined for the operational parts of CIP-L.

Acknowledgements:

We wish to thank H. Osswald for valuable discussions. We are indebted to
W. Hesse, B. Möller and P. Pepper for critically reading the drafts of this
paper.

Appendix

A. Submodes and Parameter Restriction

In CIP-L submodes may be defined using predicates.

Let $\underline{m}_1, \ldots, \underline{m}_{k+1}$ be some modes and P be some welldefined determinate boolean expression with $x_1, \ldots, x_n$ occuring free in P. Then a submode may be defined with the following semantics

$$U((\underline{m}_1 \, x_1, \ldots, \underline{m}_k \, x_k : P)) \underset{def}{=}$$

$$\{(y_1, \ldots, y_k) \in U(\underline{m}_1) \times \ldots \times U(\underline{m}_k) : \mathbb{T} = V^{\underline{bool}}(P \begin{matrix} y1, \ldots, yk \\ x1, \ldots, xk \end{matrix})\}$$

Submodes of functions may be formulated using the predicate to indicate the restriction of a function

$$U(\underline{funct} \, (\underline{m}_1 \, x_1, \ldots, \underline{m}_k \, x_k : P)\underline{m}_{k+1}) =$$

$$\{ (g, q) \in U(\underline{funct}(\underline{m}_1, \ldots, \underline{m}_k) \, \underline{m}_{k+1}) :$$

$$\forall (y_1, \ldots, y_n) \in U(\underline{m}_1) \times \ldots \times U(\underline{m}_k):$$

$$\mathbb{F} = V^{\underline{bool}}(P \begin{matrix} y1, \ldots, yk \\ x1, \ldots, xk \end{matrix}) \;\Rightarrow\; q(y_1, \ldots, y_n) = \mathbb{F} \;\wedge$$

$$\forall r \in U(\underline{m}_{k+1}):(y_1, \ldots, y_k, r) \notin g \}$$

In the above definition only determinate expressions P have been allowed. Nevertheless the semantics of submodes using nondeterminate expressions can be defined by reducing it to nondeterminate expressions which perhaps gives a "raison d'être" for these constructs.

Let $\underline{mode} \; \underline{sm} = (\underline{m} \, x : Q)$

We have

$$(\underline{sm} \, x) \, \underline{r} : E \;\;\text{⧓}\;\; (\underline{m} \, x : Q) \, \underline{r} : E$$

$$(\underline{m}_1 \, x_1, \ldots, \underline{m}_k \, x_k : P) \, \underline{m}_{k+1} : E \;\;\text{⧓}\;\; (\underline{m}_1 \, x_1, \ldots, \underline{m}_k \, x_k) \, \underline{m}_{k+1} :$$
$$\underline{if} \; P \; \underline{then} \; E \; \underline{fi}$$

some <u>sm</u> x : R   ←|→   <u>some</u> <u>m</u> x : if Q <u>then</u> R <u>else</u> false <u>fi</u>

∃ <u>sm</u>   x : R   ←|→   ∃   <u>m</u> x : if Q <u>then</u> R <u>else</u> false <u>fi</u>

∀ <u>sm</u>   x : R   ←|→   ∀   <u>m</u> x : if Q <u>then</u> R <u>else</u> true <u>fi</u>

B.   Notes on the Axiom of Choice

The Axiom of Choice states that for every family F of nonempty sets, there is a "choice function" f such that $f(S) \in S$ for each set S in the family F .

In 1904 this axiom was formulated first by Zermelo in a letter to David Hilbert (/Zermelo 04/). Hilbert himself presented a "transfinite axiom" in a lecture given at the "Deutscher Naturforscher Kongreß" in Leipzig 1922 /Hilbert 23/; later in 1927 in Hamburg he defined a choice function ε_x by the following axiom (/Hilbert 27/)

(1) $A(a) \rightarrow A(\varepsilon_x : A(x))$

He commented: "In the case, where A can be satisfied by at least one thing, then $\varepsilon(A)$ is one of these things".

The axiom (1) is not the full axiom of choice, since $\varepsilon(A)$ and $\varepsilon(A')$ may be different for equivalent predicates A and A' . But together with Ackermann's axiom (/Ackermann 24/)

$$(\forall x : A(x) \leftrightarrow A'(x)) \rightarrow \varepsilon_x : A(x) = \varepsilon_x : A'(x)$$

one obtains exactly the choice function used in set theory. Note that in
the semantics of CIP-L we only have

$$(\forall \underline{m} x : A(x) \leftrightarrow A'(x)) \Rightarrow B(\underline{\text{some}} \; \underline{m} x : A(x)) = B(\underline{\text{some}} \; \underline{m} x : A'(x))$$

The existence of a "global" set theoretical choice function cannot be
proved by the usual Zermelo-Fraenkel axioms; the Axiom of Choice is independent of these. The existence of a "local" or "finite" choice (used by
/McCarthy 62/, /de Bakker 76/, /Dijkstra 75/ etc.), however, can be proved
by these axioms. The situation for the infinite choice construct used in
CIP-L is rather delicate:

An operational definition of the <u>some</u>-construct requires the Axiom of Choice (1)
whereas the semantics of <u>some</u> is defined without it.

This can be illustrated by the independence proof of the (Countable) Axiom
of Choice (cf. /Jech 73/). We will only give the proof idea:

Consider an infinite set of unordered pairs, let's say an infinite set of
pairs of shoelaces. Then for each finite subset of these pairs of laces
we can choose a lace from each pair by a
finite method, e.g. by listing all chosen
laces ("finite choice"). The pairs themselves can be ordered, thus we obtain a
method for enumerating the whole set of
pairs of laces ("Breadth of the infinite
choice"). But because the laces of each
pair are unordered, we cannot simply say,
"Choose the first (second) lace", there-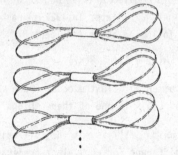
fore we must explicitly state for each pair which of the laces we will choose.
Hence, for an infinite set of unordered pairs the choice cannot uniquely be
made using finite specifications. In this situation one needs the "global"
Axiom of Choice (more exactly the Countable Axiom of Choice) to be able to
prove the existence of choice methods ("operative meaning of infinite choice").

Nevertheless, this problem will not appear for object sets defined by
abstract data types, since we always can define orders on those finitely
generated objects.

References

/Ackermann 24/   W. Ackermann: Die Widerspruchsfreiheit des Auswahlaxioms. Göttinger Wiss. Nachrichten, Math. - Phys. Klasse, 246 - 250, 1924

/ADJ 76/   J. A. Goguen, J. W. Thatcher, E. G. Wagner: An Initial Algebra Approach to the Specification, Correctness and Implementation of Abstract Data Types. IBM Research Report RC - 6487, 1976

/Arnold, Nivat 77/   A. Arnold, M. Nivat: Non Deterministic Recursiv Schemes. Fundamentals of Computation Theory. Poznan 1977. Lecture Notes in Computer Science 56, 12 - 21, 1977

/Arnold 78/   A. Arnold: Schémas de programmes récursifs non déterministes avec appel "synchrone". Laboratoire de Calcul, Université des Sciences et Techniques de Lille, Publication № 105, 1978

/Bauer et al. 77/   F. L. Bauer, H. Wössner, H. Partsch, P. Pepper: Algorithmische Sprachen. Vorlesungsskriptum, Technische Universität München 1977, Kap. 1

/Bauer et al. 78/   F. L. Bauer, M. Broy, R. Gnatz, W.Hesse, B. Krieg-Brückner H. Partsch, P. Pepper, H. Wössner: Towards a Wide Spectrum Language to Support Program Specification and Program Development. SIGPLAN Notices 13 (12), 15-24 (1978). See also this volume.

/Bauer 78/ F. L. Bauer: Prealgorithmic Formulations by Means of Choice

and Determination. In: this volume.

/Burstall, Goguen 77/   R. M. Burstall, J. A. Goguen: Putting Theories To-gether to Make Specifications. Proc. of the Int. Joint Conf. on Artificial Intelligence 1977

/de Bakker 76/   J. W. de Bakker: Semantics and Termination of Nondeter-ministic Recursive Programs. 3rd International Colloquium on Automata, Languages and Programming, Edinburg, 1976

/de Bakker 77/   J. W. de Bakker: Semantics of Infinite Processes using generalized trees. Math. Foundations of Computer Sciences 1977, Tatrănska Lomnica.Lecture Notes in Computer Sciences 53, 240 - 247, 1977

/Dijkstra 75/   E. W. Dijkstra: Guarded Commands, Nondeterminacy and Formal Derivation of Programs. CACM 18, 453 - 457, 1975

/Floyd 67/   R. W. Floyd: Nondeterministic Algorithms, JACM 14, 636 - 644, 1967

/Guttag 75/   J. V. Guttag: The Specification and Application to Programming of Abstract Data Types. Ph. D. Th., Univ. of Toronto, Dept. Comp. Sci., Rep. CSRG - 59, 1975

/Hennessy, Ashcroft 76/   M. Hennessy, E. A. Ashcroft: The Semantics of Non-determinism. 3rd International Colloquium on Automata, Languages and Programming, Edinburg 1976

/Hilbert 23/   D. Hilbert: Die logischen Grundlagen der Mathematik. Math. Ann. 88, 151 - 165, 1923

/Hilbert 27/   D. Hilbert: Die Grundlagen der Mathematik. Abh. math. Seminar d. Hamburger Universität VI, Heft 1/2.

/Jech 73/   T. J. Jech: The Axiom of Choice. North-Holland, Amsterdam,
      68 - 71, 1973

/Kleene 52/   S. C. Kleene: Introduction to Metamathematics. North-Holland,
      Amsterdam 1952

/Kreisel, Krivine 67/   G. Kreisel, J. L. Krivine: Elements de logique
      mathématique. Dunod, Paris 1967

/Krivine 71/   J. L. Krivine: Introduction to Axiomatic Set Theory.
      Reidel, Dordrecht 1971

/Liskov, Zilles 75/   B. Liskov, S. Zilles: Specification Techniques for
      Data Abstraction. IEEE Trans. on Software Eng. $\underline{1}$:1, 7 - 18, 1975

/Manna 74/   Z. Manna: Mathematical Theory of Computation. McGraw - Hill,
      New York 1974

/McCarthy 62/   J. McCarthy: A Basis for a Mathematical Theory of Computation.
      P. Braffort, D. Hirschberg (eds.) Computer Programming and Formal Systems.
      North-Holland, Amsterdam 1963

/Milner 73/   R. Milner: Processes: A Mathematical Model of Computing Agents.
      Logic Colloquium 73, North-Holland, Amsterdam 1973

/Partsch, Broy 78/   H. Partsch, M. Broy: Examples for Change of Types and
      Object Structures. In: this volume.

/Pepper 78/   P. Pepper: A Study on Transformational Semantics.
      In: this volume.

/Plotkin 76/   G. D. Plotkin: A Powerdomain Construction. SIAM J. on Computing 5,
      452 - 486, 1976

/Schütte 67/   K. Schütte: Einführung in die mathematische Logik. Vorlesungs-
      ausarbeitung, Universität München 1967

/Scott 76/ D. Scott: Continuous Lattices. Toposes, Algebraic Geometry and
      Logic. F. W. Lawvere, Ed., Springer-Verlag Notes, vol. 274, Berlin 1970

/Shoenfield 67/   J. R. Shoenfield: Mathematical Logic. Addison - Wesley,
      Reading, Massachusetts 1967

/Smyth 78/   M. B. Smyth: Power Domains. J. of Computer and System Sciences 16,
      23 - 36, 1978

/Zermelo 04/   E. Zermelo: Beweis, daß jede Menge wohlgeordnet werden kann.
      Math. Ann. 59, 514 - 516, 1904

NOTES ON TYPE ABSTRACTION

John Guttag
Computer Science Department
University of Southern California
Los Angeles, California 90007

Abstract

This paper, which was prepared to accompany a series of lectures
given at the 1978 NATO International Summer School on Program
Construction, is primarily tutorial in nature. It begins by discussing
in a general setting the role of type abstraction and the need for
formal specifications of type abstractions. It then proceeds to examine
in some detail two approaches to the construction of such
specifications: that proposed by Hoare in his 1972 paper "Proofs of
Correctness of Data Representations," and the author's own version of
algebraic specifications. The Hoare approach is presented via a
discussion of its embodiment in the programming language Euclid. The
discussion of the algebraic approach includes material abstracted from
earlier papers as well as some new material that has yet to appear.
This new material deals with parameterized types and the specification
of restrictions. The paper concludes with a brief discussion of the
relative merits of the two approaches to type abstraction.

Notes on Type Abstraction

Introduction

A key problem in the development of programs is reducing the amount of complexity or detail that must be considered at any one time. Two common and effective approaches to accomplishing this are decomposition and abstraction.

One decomposes a task by factoring it into sub-tasks each of which can be treated independently. Unfortunately, for many problems the smallest separable sub-tasks are still too complex to be mastered in toto. The complexity of such problems must be reduced via abstraction. By providing a mechanism for separating those attributes that are relevant in a given context from those that are not, abstraction serves to reduce the amount of detail that one need come to grips with at any one time.

One of the most significant aids to abstraction used in programming is the self-contained subroutine. It performs a specific, arbitrarily abstract, function by means of an unprescribed algorithm. Thus, at the level where it is invoked, it separates the relevant detail of "what" from the irrelevant detail of "how." Similarly, at the level of the implementation, it is usually unnecessary to complicate the "how" by considering the "why," i.e., the exact reasons for invoking a subroutine are rarely of concern to its implementor. By nesting subroutines, one may develop a hierarchy of abstractions.

Unfortunately, the nature of the abstractions that may be conveniently achieved through the use of subroutines is limited. Subroutines allow us to abstract single events. Their applicability is thus limited to problems that are conveniently decomposable into independent functional units. Type, or data, abstraction is not amenable to such an attack.

The large knot of complexly interrelated attributes associated with a data object may be separated according to the nature of the information that the attributes convey about the data objects that they qualify. Two kinds of attributes, each of which may be studied in isolation, are:

(1) those that describe the representation of objects and the implementations of the operations associated with them in terms of other

objects and operations, e.g., in terms of a programming language's primitive data structures and operations;

(2) those that specify the names and define the abstract meanings of the operations associated with an object.

Though these two kinds of attributes are in practice highly interdependent, they represent logically independent concepts. At most points in a program one should be concerned solely with the latter. The user of a data object should have no more interest in the details of its implementation than does the user of a high level language in the details of the object code produced by the compiler.

If at a given level of refinement one is interested only in the effect of the operations associated with certain data objects, then any attempt to abstract data must be based upon those characteristics, and only those characteristics. The introduction of other attributes, e.g., a representation, can only serve to cloud the relevant issues. Here, we will use the term "abstract type" to refer to a class of objects defined by a representation-independent specification.

On the other side of the fence, those responsible for providing an implementation of an abstract type need to be isolated from consideration of exactly how objects of the type are to be used. This isolation takes place at two levels: On a conceptual level this isolation involves a reduction in the number of concerns that must be dealt with at any one time. On a more concrete level, it involves the assurance of the validity of data type induction (called generator induction elsewhere, e.g., [Spitzen 75]). Consider a type, T. Let f1, ...,fn be the set of all operations that have as their range values of type T. Let $P(t)$ be any predicate on values of type T. If the truth of P for all arguments of type T of each fi implies the truth of P for the results of applications of that fi, then it follows that P holds for all values of type T. Assuming strong type checking, the validity of this principle follows by induction on the number of computation steps used to generate any value of type T. The data type induction principle is analogous to that of complete induction over the integers. The basis step of the induction occurs when one shows that P holds for the results of those fi with no arguments of type T.

Most of the recent work on incorporating abstract data types into programming languages has emphasized the use of strong typing and class-like constructs to provide isolation for the implementors of abstract types. In Euclid, for example, the author of a module may assure the validity of data type induction through careful use of the import and export lists. If no "var" globals are imported, the value of any instance of the module is a function of the values of the data structures that are local to the module and global to the module routines. If furthermore no portion of the data structure is exported as "var," the principle of data type induction is established.

It is certainly possible to use abstract types as a programming tool without actually making provision for them in the programming language. There are, however, several advantages to be gained from having a facility for the definition of abstract types within a programming language. Perhaps the most significant of these is that it increases the likelihood that the program text will accurately reflect the thought processes that led to its construction. Thus the program should be easier to read and comprehend, particularly for those who were not involved in its construction.

A second reason for the inclusion of facilities for the definition of abstract types within a programming language is to permit type checking. Much has been written about the benefits to be gained from extensive type checking. [Gannon 75] and [Morris 73] contain particularly good discussions. Morris suggests that type checking serves two distinct purposes: authentication and secrecy. By authentication, he means that type checking can be used to prevent programs from attempting to perform operations on values of other than the appropriate type: trying to divide one queue by another, for example. What Morris calls secrecy has often been called protection or security. Its purpose is to prevent users from writing programs that depend upon the particular representation chosen for a type. If one can actually define a type Queue, rather than merely a data structure to be used as a queue, the compiler can prevent the user from modifying or accessing values of type Queue except through the operations provided as part of that type. This inhibits him from destroying the integrity of the data structure (thus allowing data type induction), and from writing programs that rely upon the representation of the type (thus allowing the substitution of a different representation).

The specification of abstract types

The class construct of SIMULA 67 [Dahl 68] has been used as the starting point for much of the more recent work on embedding abstract types in programming languages, e.g., Clu, Alphard and Euclid. While each of these offers a mechanism for binding together the operations and storage structures representing a type, they offer (within the base language) no representation-independent means for specifying the effect of the operations. The only representation-independent information that one can supply in the language proper are the domains and ranges of the various operations. One can, for example, define a type Queue (of Integers) with the operations:

```
new:     --> Queue
add:     Queue X Integer --> Queue
front:   Queue --> Integer
remove:  Queue --> Queue
empty?:  Queue --> Boolean.
```

Except for intuitions about the meaning of such words as Queue and front, the operations might just as easily be defining type Stack as type Queue. The domain and range specifications for these two types are isomorphic. To rely on one's intuition about the meaning of names can be dangerous even when dealing with familiar types; when dealing with unfamiliar types, it is almost impossible. What is needed, therefore, is a language for specifying the semantics of the operations of the type.

This language must be a formal one. An informal language, such as a natural language, is often not efficient -- either for the communication of abstractions or for their creation. (This is not to say that informality has no role to play in the abstraction process. At times the high connotational content of an informal language makes it a valuable tool for both creative thinking and the communication of the fruits of that thought.)

Unlike formal languages, informal languages do not force precision. In fact, it is only by dint of great care and expertise that it is possible to write precise specifications in a notation as informal as a natural language. Thus, at times, an informal language may prove more a hindrance than a help in organizing one's thoughts. The problem is compounded when one attempts to use an informal notation for communicating an abstraction to others. Not only might the specification be underdefined, hence ambiguous, but the language in which the specification is stated will almost certainly be ambiguous. If all goes well, someone will perceive the ambiguity, and it will be resolved. More often, the people involved will merely form their own, different, conceptions of the abstraction. Of course, the use of a formal language is no guarantee that specifications will be unambiguous or even consistent. It is, for example, quite possible to specify ambiguous grammars or empty languages in BNF. What a formal language does provide, are objective criteria for recognizing ambiguity and inconsistency, thus increasing the likelihood that such failings in a specification will be recognized.

A good formal specification technique is a technique that facilitates the production of good formal specifications. Good specifications may take many forms, but all of them have certain attributes in common. A good specification must be restrictive enough to ensure that nothing unacceptable to the specifier will meet the requirements imposed by the specification. Yet it must also be sufficiently general to ensure that few, if any, acceptable entries are precluded. And finally, a good specification must be well tailored to its intended application. In most cases this implies that it must be perspicuous enough to facilitate communication among people, and at the same time suitable for purely formal reasoning.

That a good specification must be sufficiently restrictive (or specific) is a statement that should need no justification. It is the assumption that lies at the base of most arguments in favor of formal specifications. The importance of the generality criterion is less obvious. It is not essential to ensure that no acceptable model is precluded, but whenever one introduces unnecessary constraints one runs the risk of eliminating some of the more desirable (e.g., efficient or elegant) solutions to the problem at hand. That a certain tension exists between the goals of generality and restrictiveness is clear. The use of weakest pre-conditions [Dijkstra 76] to specify a programming language represents one attempt to strike an optimal balance between the two. Often, however, it is counterproductive to strive for this optimal

balance -- for to do so may lead to less elegant and less useful
specifications. In these cases, one must be willing to accept some loss
of generality.

There are many possible approaches to the formal specification of
abstract types. Most, however, can be placed in one of two categories:
operational or definitional. In an operational specification, instead
of trying to describe the properties of the abstract type, one gives a
recipe for constructing it. One begins with some well-understood
language or discipline and builds a model for the type in terms of that
discipline.

The operational approach to formal specification has many
advantages. Most significantly, operational specifications seem to be
relatively (compared to definitional specifications) easily constructed
by those trained as programmers -- chiefly because the construction of
operational specifications so closely resembles programming. For
abstract types containing a small number of moderately simple operations
(i.e., operations readily expressible in the modelling domain),
operational specifications seem to offer a sufficient degree of
perspicuity. As the operations to be specified grow more complex,
however, operational specifications tend to get too long to serve as an
adequate tool for communication among people. As the number of
operations grows, problems arise because the relations among the
operations are not explicitly stated, and inferring them becomes
combinatorially harder. This can be reflected in the difficulty in
reasoning about programs that use the type. A final serious problem
associated with operational specifications is that they often force one
to over specify the abstraction. By introducing extraneous detail they
are likely to associate non-essential attributes with the type.

The extent to which an operational specification is unnecessarily
restrictive depends upon the level of abstraction achieved by the
specification. With an operational specification, one must infer the
properties of the abstract type from the properties of the operational
model. In general, one can infer properties other than the necessary
ones. Loosely speaking, the greater the number of inessential
properties that may be inferred, the lower the level of abstraction.
The level achieved depends largely upon the level of abstraction of the
language in which the specification is given. A Pascal implementation
of an abstract type, for example, scarcely qualifies as an abstract
specification. The Vienna Definition Language allows more abstract
specifications. Parnas's state machine model [Parnas 72] seems to allow
still higher levels of abstraction.

In a definitional specification, one explicitly lists properties
that the values and operations forming the abstract type are to have.
The primary advantage of this mode of specification is that it tends to
define the type quite generally, in that only essential characteristics
need be specified. The specification is thus an abstraction
encompassing a relatively large (compared to an operational
specification) class of implementations. In addition to increasing the
generality of the specification, the absence of superfluous detail tends
to increase the clarity of the specification. If the type has many
operations, the ability to state explicitly the relationships among the

operations makes the specification a better tool for formal reasoning.

There are an enormous number of formalisms that can be used to construct definitional specifications. The two most prominent approaches (in programming) are the axiomatic specifications of Hoare [Hoare 69] and Scott's lattice theoretic approach to mathematical semantics [Scott 70]. The axiomatic approach is the more widely used of the two; nevertheless mathematical semantics offers several advantages. Donahue [Donahue 76] cites two advantages as particularly notable: Firstly, mathematical semantics is a more powerful specification technique because the domain of discourse is far less limited. Secondly, by virtue of the fact that the notion of a computation appears explicitly, a mathematical semantics definition seems to provide considerably more guidance for implementors.

These apparent advantages, however, are in reality two-edged swords. Just as a well-designed programming language should encourage its users to write better programs by constraining the programs they may write, a well-designed specification language should place severe constraints on the specifications its users may write. Thus, the freedom of expression offered us by mathematical semantics may be more a bane than a boon. The explicit appearance of the notion of a computation saddles mathematical semantics definitions with some of the same over-specification problems associated with operational specifications. This will almost certainly lead to problems if one is interested primarily in proof theoretic (rather than model theoretic) properties of the type being specified. For these reasons, we shall be concentrating on axiomatics in the remainder of these lectures.

We shall look at two axiomatic approaches to the specification of abstract types: first the approach suggested by Hoare in [Hoare 72] and then algebraic axioms [Guttag 75]. Today, variants of Hoare's method predominate, e.g., [Wulf 76] and [London 78]. The algebraic approach does, however, seem to be gaining some currency, e.g., [Dahl 78].

The <u>Hoare approach (as embodied in Euclid)</u>

As stated above, Hoare's approach has enjoyed widespread use. Most of its users have departed in some ways from the notation originally used by Hoare. Here, we shall use the notation of Euclid's [Lampson 78] modules. We begin by looking at an example from "Proof Rules for the Programming Language Euclid," [London 78]. The module <u>smallintSet</u> provides the abstraction of a set of integers in the range 1-100. The abstract operations are insertion and removal of individual elements and a membership test. When a variable of type <u>smallintSet</u> is declared, it is initialized to the empty set. The set will be represented by a Boolean array, S, of 100 elements,

S: <u>array</u> 1..100 <u>of</u> Boolean

where S(i) = i belongs to the set.

```
type smallintSet =
    pre true
    module smallSet
    abstract invariant true
    concrete invariant true
    exports (insert,remove,has,:=)
    var S: array 1..100 of Boolean

    procedure insert (i: integer) =
        pre 1≤i≤100 and smallSet=smallSet'
        post smallSet=smallSet' union {i}
        begin S(i) := true end insert

    procedure remove (i: integer) =
        pre 1≤i≤100 and smallSet=smallSet'
        post smallSet=smallSet' - {i}
        begin S(i) := false end remove

    function has (i: integer) returns hasResult: Boolean =
        pre 1≤i≤100
        post hasResult = (i ∈ smallSet)
        begin hasResult := S(i) end has

    initially
        post smallSet = {}
        begin for j in S.indexType loop S(j) := false
                                end loop end initially

    abstraction function setValue returns resultSet = imports (S)
        begin resultSet = {j | S(j) and 1≤j≤100} end setValue

end smallintSet
```

The module is a mechanism for providing encapsulation and the support of type abstractions, and as such provides distinct pictures to its users and its implementors. To the user the module presents a picture intended to deal only with those properties pertinent to the

```
true {var S:array 1..100 of Boolean
     begin for j in 1..100
                loop S(j):=false end loop end} setValue(S) = { }.
```

We replace setValue by its definition, and this proof becomes straightforward.

Premise 3: Verify that the body of each exported procedure is correct, i.e., that the conjunction of the procedure's pre-condition and the concrete invariant is a sufficient pre-condition to ensure that the body of the procedure will establish its post-condition and preserve the concrete invariant. Not surprisingly, this premise bears a strong resemblance to that of the procedure call rule. It differs only in the presence of the module invariant and the need to use the abstraction function. This need arises from the fact that the pre- and post-conditions deal with abstract objects, while the body of the procedures deal with concrete ones. Looking at insert, the verification condition generated is:

$$1 \leq i \leq 100 \text{ and } setValue(S) = setValue(S') \text{ and } true$$
$$\{S(i) := true\}$$
$$setValue(S) = (setValue(S') \text{ union } \{i\}) \text{ and } true.$$

Again, using the definition of setValue, the verification of this premise is trivial.

At this point let us pause in our analysis of the individual premises, and look a bit more closely at the way we have been using the abstraction function setValue. Notice that we have been using the substitution of setValue(S) for smallSet as a device to convert predicates in the abstract domain of smallintSets to predicates in the concrete domain of arrays. We thus seem to be using setValue as a mechanism for moving from the abstract to the concrete -- despite the fact that the functionality of setValue goes the other way, from the concrete to the abstract. That we use a mapping that goes in this direction is crucial, since the mapping in the other direction may not be a function. Consider, for example, a type Bounded Queue (with a maximum length of three). An implementation of this type might be based on a ring-buffer and top pointer. Given this implementation we might well discover that a queue containing the elements A, B and C in that order has the attainable concrete representations:

```
→A --> B --> C                          >B --> C --> A—   .
```

In this example, the concrete representation of a particular abstract value is not a function of that value, but is rather a function of the history of insertions and deletions from the queue. The realization that the mapping from abstract to concrete may be one to many, and the circumvention of this apparent problem through the use of an abstraction function (called a "representation" function by Hoare) represents the essence of the substantial insight and contribution of [Hoare 72].

Premise 4: Verify that the body of each exported function is correct. Premise 4 is analogous to premise 3 except that the concrete

ways in which the abstraction can be used. These "abstract" properties are captured in the pre- and post-conditions associated with <u>initially</u>, <u>finally</u>, and the exported routines. The implementor of the module must deal not only with the user's view, which defines the object he must implement, but also with the module's data structures and the bodies of the module's routines. The abstraction function is the bridge between the two perspectives with which the implementor must deal.

In general, the abstraction function maps a sequence of concrete identifiers to an abstract identifier. In the above example, setValue maps the array S to the smallintSet resultSet. If, for example, S were to have the value false in all positions except the 31st and 40th, we could deduce from the definition of the abstraction function, setValue, that resultSet =

$$\{j \mid S(j) \text{ } \underline{and} \text{ } 1 \leq j \leq 100\} = \{31, 40\}.$$

To see exactly how Euclid modules work, let us examine the structure (but not the details) of the proof rule given for modules in [London 78]. The rule contains a conclusion and eight premises. We now explain the structure of the rule and describe the purpose and workings of each premise.

The conclusion of the rule involves the instantiation of a module identifier in a scope. Premises 1-5 are properties required of the module definition. These properties, which must be verified only once for each module definition, deal with the internal consistency, or well-formedness, of the definition. Premise 6 states that the instantiation pre-condition is met; this must be proved each time a variable of the module type is declared. Premise 7 tells us that we may use the information contained in the module definition (which we verified in connection with premises 1-5) to prove what we need to show about uses of variables of the module type. Thus the module rule has the structure:

$$1,2,3,4,5,$$
$$6,$$
$$[7.1, 7.2, 7.3, 7.4] \mid\mid-- P\{x.initially; S; x.finally\}R$$

$$P\{\underline{var} \text{ } x:T(a); S\}R \text{ } \underline{and} \text{ } Post-of-finally$$

We now describe each premise in a bit more detail. In premises 1-5, the substitution of a call of the abstraction function for the name of the module converts a predicate on the abstract identifier to one involving concrete identifiers.

Premise 1: Show that the concrete invariant implies the abstract invariant. In our example, since each invariant is the constant true, this is trivial. Had we chosen the slightly more interesting abstract invariant cardinality(smallSet) $\leq$ 100, we would have arrived at the verification condition:

$$true => cardinality(\{j \mid S(j) \text{ } \underline{and} \text{ } 1 \leq j \leq 100\}) \leq 100.$$

Premise 2: Show that the module pre-condition across the declaration of the module's local variables and the body of initially establishes the post-condition of initially and the concrete invariant. Again, to show that the invariant will hold is trivial. To show that the post-condition of initially is established we must prove:

invariant is assumed to be preserved, since Euclid functions are guaranteed to be side-effect free.

Premise 5: Show that the body of _finally_ establishes the post-condition of the module. (There is no _finally_ in our example.)

Premise 6: Show that at the point where a variable of the type is declared, the state implies the module pre-condition with the actual parameters substituted for the formals.

Premise 7: This premise deals with reasoning about uses of the module variable, x, in the scope S. In showing that the state at the point where x is declared implies a pre-condition that is sufficient to ensure the truth of R after executing the body of _initially_ followed by S and the body of _finally_, we may use the four formulas 7.1-7.4. These formulas give the properties of the module procedures, functions, initially and finally respectively. Formulas 7.1 and 7.2 correspond to the conclusions of the procedure and function call rule; the only difference is that the abstract invariant may be used in proving the pre-conditions and is assumed following the calls. (This is the source of much of the utility of the module construct. It allows us to prove theorems using data type induction.) Formula 7.3 treats x.initially as a parameterless procedure call that establishes the invariant. Formula 7.4 treats x.finally as a parameterless procedure call for which the abstract invariant may be used in establishing its pre-condition. (If x is declared to be an array of modules or a record containing modules, then x.initially and x.finally must be replaced in 7.3 and 7.4 by a sequence of calls to initialization and finalization routines respectively.)

Conclusion: The conclusion of this proof rules simply states that if all of the premises have been shown to hold, one may conclude that if P holds before executing the statements: _var_ x:T(a); S, then R and the post-condition of finally will hold upon exiting the scope in which x is declared. An example of the application of this proof rule to prove some properties of a program containing our example module definition is contained in [London 78].

The above may strike the reader as excessively complicated. That would be an accurate appraisal of the situation. Part of the complexity of the above discussion (and more importantly the proof rule behind it) stems from the linguistic eccentricities of Euclid and the fact that we are dealing with partial rather than total correctness. (The latter issue is most relevant to the part of the rule dealing with the module's functions, and is manifested in the complexity, not dealt with here, of clauses 4 and 7.2.) Much of it, however, reflects more fundamental problems with the basic approach. Despite the fact that the various operations of type smallintSet are intricately related to one another, these relationships are not directly expressed in the (abstract) specification of the type. Rather, we supply stand-alone pre- and post-conditions for each operation. This leads us to introduce a third domain of discourse in which to express the meanings of the operations. In our example, we want to supply the programmer with the abstraction smallintSet. We implement this abstraction using the Euclid primitives array, Boolean and integer. We specify it using the (presumed well-defined) third domain of discourse supplied by the operations on

mathematical sets. To prove the correctness of our implementation of
smallintSet, we must map a Euclid data structure onto mathematical sets.
To reason about programs that use type smallintSet, we must reason in
terms of mathematical sets. This can be a serious problem. Presumably,
one introduces an abstraction primarily because one feels that some
advantage is to be gained by thinking in terms of it. Perhaps little is
lost when one is forced to reason in terms of mathematical sets rather
than smallintSets. They are, after all, rather similar abstractions.
For the sake of argument, however, let us assume that our domain of
already well-understood types doesn't include mathematical sets. It may
well prove to be the case that the programmer is forced to reason in
terms of some abstraction quite different from that he wished to
introduce into his program. If this is the case, then much of the
rationale for introducing the type abstraction is lost.

Algebraic specifications

An algebraic specification of an abstract type consists of three
parts: a syntactic specification, a semantic specification, and a
restriction specification. The syntactic specification provides the
syntactic and type checking information: the names, domains, and ranges
of the operations associated with the type. The semantic specification
is a set of axioms which defines the meaning of the operations by
stating their relationships to one another. The restriction
specification deals with pre-conditions and exception conditions. The
word "algebraic" is appropriate because the values and operations can be
regarded as together forming an abstract algebra. [Goguen 75] and
[Zilles 75] have strongly emphasized the algebraic approach, developing
a theory of abstract types as an application of many-sorted algebras.
Implementations are treated under this approach as other algebras, and
the problem of showing that an implementation is correct is treated
through showing the existence of a homomorphic mapping from one algebra
to the other. We shall in these lectures, as we have in our own
research, de-emphasize the use of algebraic terminology and methods,
preferring instead the terminology and methods of programming and logic.

At the heart of any specification technique lies the specification
language. We begin by assuming a base language with five primitives:
functional composition, an equality relation (=), two distinct constants
(true and false), and an unbounded supply of free variables. From these
primitives one can construct a richer specification language. Once a
type abstraction has been defined, it may be added to the specification
language. One might, for example, want to include a type Boolean with
an if-then-else operation defined by the axioms:

$$\text{if-then-else}(\text{true},q,r) = q$$
$$\text{if-then-else}(\text{false},q,r) = r.$$

Throughout we shall assume that the expression if-then-else(b,q,r),
which we will write as **if** b **then** q **else** r, is part of the specification

language.   We shall also assume the availability of infix Boolean
operators as needed.   The axiomatization of these operators in terms of
the if-then-else function is trivial.   Finally, we shall assume the
availability of type Integer with the standard operations.

Let us now look at a simple example (with no restriction
specification).   Consider a type Bag (of Integers) with the operations:

```
empty-bag:      --> Bag
insert: Bag X Integer --> Bag
delete: Bag X Integer --> Bag
member-of?:     Bag X Integer --> Boolean.
```

There are, of course, many ways to implement type Bag.   Some (e.g., a
linked list representation) imply an ordering of the elements, some
don't (e.g., a hash table implementation).   These details are not
relevant to the basic notion of what a bag is.   A bag is nothing more
than a counted set, and a good axiomatic definition must assert that and
only that characteristic.   The axioms below comprise just such a
definition.

```
declare b:Bag, i,i':Integer

1) member-of?(empty-bag,i) = false
2) member-of?(insert(b,i),i') = if ?=?(i,i')
                                      then true
                                      else member-of?(b,i')
3) delete(empty-bag,i) = empty-bag
4) delete(insert(b,i),i') = if ?=?(i,i')
                                 then b
                                 else insert(delete(b,i'),i)
```

As an interesting comparison, consider the following specification
of type Set:

```
empty-set:       --> Set
insert: Set X Integer --> Set
delete: Set X Integer --> Set
member-of?       Set X Integer --> Boolean

declare s:Set, i,i':Integer

1) member-of?(empty-set,i) = false
2) member-of?(insert(s,i),i') = if ?=?(i,i')
                                      then true
                                      else member-of?(s,i')
3) delete(empty-set,i) = empty-set
4) delete(insert(s,i),i') = if ?=?(i,i')
                                 then delete(s,i')
                                 else insert(delete(s,i'),i).
```

Except for the change in the then clause of axiom 4, this
specification is, for all intents and purposes, the same as that for
type Bag.   The two specifications thus serve to point out the
similarities and isolate the one crucial difference between type Set and

type Bag.

Once one has constructed a specification, one must address the question of whether or not one has supplied a sufficient number of consistent axioms. The partial semantics of the type is supplied by a set of individual statements of fact. If we can use the statements to derive an equation that contradicts the axioms of one of the underlying types used in the specification, the axioms of the specification are inconsistent. Ultimately, any inconsistent axiomatization is characterized by the fact that it can be used to derive the equation true = false. If, for example, one were to add the axiom:

> member-of?(delete(b,i),i') = <u>if</u> ?=?(i,i')
>
> > > <u>then</u> false
> > > <u>else</u> member-of?(b,i)

to the specification of type Bag, one would have created an inconsistent specification. There would exist values of type Bag for which it would be possible to prove both member-of?(b,i) = true and member-of?(b,i) = false, depending upon which of the axioms one chose to use. Member-of?(delete(insert(insert(empty-bag,3),3),3),3) is an example of an expression for which such a contradiction could be derived.

Determining the consistency of an arbitrary set of equations is in theory an unsolvable problem. In practice, however, it is often relatively simple to demonstrate consistency. The construction of a model is perhaps the most widely used technique. To show that an axiomatization of an abstract type is consistent, it suffices to construct an implementation of the abstraction that can be proved correct using a consistent proof theory. From a practical point of view, this is often the best way to demonstrate consistency. The chief drawback to this approach is that if the specification is inconsistent, it is possible to expend considerable effort trying to construct a model that does not exist. This problem can be avoided by proving the consistency of a specification prior to attempting to implement it. This can be done by treating the equations of the specification as left to right rewrite rules, and demonstrating that they exhibit the Church-Rosser property. Informally, a set of rewrite rules is Church-Rosser if whenever one applies a rewrite rule to reduce a term, and then a rule to reduce the resulting term, etc. until there is no longer an applicable rule, the final result does not depend upon the order in which the rules were applied. That is to say, the final result is independent of the order in which one chooses to apply the rules. A useful method for proving that a set of rewrite rules exhibits this property is presented in [Knuth 70].

Having established the consistency of a set of axioms, one should next address the question of its completeness. The notion of a complete axiom set is a familiar one to logicians. The exact definition used depends upon the environment in which one is working. The statements that a complete axiom set is "one to which an independent axiom cannot be added," or "one with which every well-formed formula or its negation can be proved as a theorem," or "one for which all models are isomorphic (i.e., the axiom set is categorical)," are all common. Our notion of completeness is equivalent to none of these statements, thus we introduce the qualifier "sufficiently" to differentiate it from these other, more common, concepts. [Guttag 78] discusses sufficient-completeness at length and with some formality. Here we treat it only briefly and relatively informally.

The syntactic specification of a type, T, defines a free word algebra. The set of words, L(T), contained in this algebra is a set of expressions that may occur in a program that uses the abstract type. For an axiomatization of a type to be sufficiently-complete, it must assign meaning to certain ground (i.e, without variables) terms in this language. We begin by partitioning the operations of the type into the sets S and O, where S contains exactly those operations whose range is the type being specified, the type of interest. Looking at type Bag, for example, S = {empty-bag,insert,delete} and O = {member-of?}. Intuitively, S contains the operations that can be used to generate values of the type being defined, and O the operations that map values of the type into other types. The need for operations to generate values of the type of interest is clear, thus S will always be non-empty.

In principle, one could define a type for which O were empty. Such a type, however, would be singularly uninteresting. With no way to partition the values of the type of interest (O empty implies no predicates) or to relate these values to values of other types, no value of the type could be distinguished from any other value. For all one could observe, every value of the type of interest would be equivalent to every other value of the type. For all intents and purposes, there would be only one value of that type. The ability to distinguish among the values of the type of interest thus rests solely upon the effects that these values have when they appear in the argument lists of the operations contained in O. It is this observation that lies at the root of our definition of sufficiently-complete.

For any abstract type T, and any axiom set A, A is a sufficiently-complete axiomatization of T if and only if for every ground word of the form o(x1,...xn) contained in L(T) where o is a member of O, there exists a theorem derivable from A of the form o(x1, ...,xn) = u, where u contains no operations of type T. The above axiomatization of type Bag, for example, is sufficiently-complete because it can be used to reduce any word in the set: {member-of?(b,i) | b is either empty-bag or any sequence of inserts and deletes applied to empty-bag and i is any integer} to either true or false.

It can be shown that the problem of establishing whether or not a set of axioms is sufficiently-complete is undecidable. If, however, one is willing to accept certain limitations, it is possible to state reasonable conditions that will be sufficient to ensure sufficient-completeness. Such conditions are discussed in [Guttag 78].

Before leaving the issue of sufficient-completeness, we should make it clear that while sufficient-completeness is a weaker completeness criterion than is generally used, there are circumstances in which it is still too strong. Consider, for example, adding an operation

        choose: Set --> Integer

defined by the single equation

member-of?(s,choose(s)) = true

to type Set.   Our axiomatization of type Set would no longer be
sufficiently-complete, since it would be impossible to prove that a word
such as choose(insert(insert(empty-set,3),2)) is equal to any particular
integer.   Nevertheless, this may well be exactly the specification
needed.   If we have no reason to care which value the choose operation
selects, any sufficiently-complete axiomatization would be unnecessarily
restrictive.   Given this not sufficiently-complete specification, we
interpret choose as a not fully specified function.   That is to say,
given an arbitrary value of type Set, s, the value of choose(s) is not
predictable. However, we require that choose be a function, i.e., that
for all values, s and s1, of type Set

s=s1 => choose(s)=choose(s1).

In some circumstances, even this may be too restrictive. Insisting that
choose be a function of sets, may preclude the most efficient
implementation of the operation. If, for example, we implement sets as
linked lists, it may prove convenient to return the last element added
to the list. If one wishes to allow this flexibility, one must specify
choose as a relation rather than as a function.   At this point, it
should be noted that we believe that in practice the need for
specifications that are not sufficiently-complete is relatively limited,
and that routinely checking the sufficient-completeness of a
specification is a useful activity.

We turn now to a somewhat more comprehensive example:

      <u>type</u> Stack[element-type: Type, n:Integer]
      <u>where</u> ( )

      <u>syntax</u>

      newstack: --> Stack
      push: Stack X element-type --> Stack
      pop: Stack --> Stack
      top: Stack --> element-type
      isnew: Stack --> Boolean
      replace: Stack X element-type --> Stack
      *depth: Stack --> Integer

      <u>semantics</u>

      <u>declare</u> stk:Stack, elm:element-type

      1) pop(push(stk,elm)) = stk
      2) top(push(stk,elm)) = elm
      3) isnew(newstack) = true
      4) isnew(push(stk,elm)) = false
      5) replace(stk,elm) = push(pop(stk),elm)
      6) depth(newstack) = 0
      7) depth(push(stk,elm)) = 1 + depth(stk)

      <u>restrictions</u>

      <u>pre</u>(pop,stk) = ~isnew(stk)
      <u>pre</u>(replace,stk,elm) = ~isnew(stk)
      isnew(stk) => <u>failure</u>(top,stk)
      <u>failure</u>(push,stk,elm) => depth(stk)≥n

In this example, the lowercase symbols in the first line are free variables ranging over the domains indicated, i.e., n ranges over the set of integers and element-type over the set of types. This tells us that we can have a type Stack of any type of elements (but all elements in a stack must be of the same type). What we have defined is thus not a single abstract type, but rather a type schema. The binding of element-type to a particular type and n to a particular integer, e.g., Stack[Real,18], reduces the schema to the specification of a single abstract type. The empty <u>where</u> clause indicates that the choice of which type to bind element-type to and which integer to bind n to is completely unrestricted. In general, however, we provide for <u>where</u> clauses such as:

where n>0 and element-type has

    op: element-type X element-type --> element-type
    const: --> element-type

    declare e1,e2:element-type

    op(e1,e2) = op(e2,e1)
    op(e1,const) = e1.

The second portion of this where clause restricts the types to which element-type may be bound. I.e., it may be bound only to types that contain some nullary operation and some binary predicate exhibiting those properties specified in the two equations. It would thus be possible to bind element-type to type Integer, with op bound to + and const to 0, or to type Set, with op bound to union and const to the empty set, e.g.,

Stack[Set with (union,empty-set) as (op,const), 18].

The * preceding depth in the syntactic specification of type Stack indicates that depth is an auxiliary function. Auxiliary functions, which have also been called hidden functions, may not appear as part of programs using the abstraction. They are part of the specification of the abstraction, but not of the abstraction itself. As [Thatcher 78] proves, the introduction of auxiliary functions is necessary if one relies on equations as the basis of a specification technique. Even when not strictly necessary, however, the introduction of an auxiliary function may greatly simplify and clarify a specification -- much the same way the introduction of a non-essential procedure can simplify and clarify a program.

The restriction specification serves two purposes. A pre-condition specification limits the applicability of the axioms. In the absence of a restriction specification, the weakest pre-condition (wp) associated with each function, f, of the abstract type is (roughly speaking) defined by

wp(x:=f(Y),Q) = (axioms => Q(f(Y) for x)).

If a pre-condition, pre(f,Y), is added to the specification of the abstraction, it becomes:

pre(f,Y) and (axioms => Q(f(Y) for x)).

The formula pre(replace,stk,elm)=~isnew(stk), for example, indicates that axiom 5 holds only if ~isnew(stk). This is equivalent to replacing axiom 5 by the conditional equation

~isnew(stk) => (replace(stk,elm) = push(pop(stk),elm)).

(For a careful discussion of conditional equations see [Thatcher 78].) Notice that the burden of checking (or proving) the pre-condition lies with the user of type Stack. The implementor of the type need not insert a check in the implementation of replace.

Failure specifications, on the other hand, place a burden on the implementor of the type. A formula of the form P(X) => failure(g,X) states that if the operation g is invoked with arguments X such that P(X), then g must fail, i.e., failure is required. By this we mean that g must not terminate normally. Formally,

failure(f,Y) => wp(f(Y),Q)=false.

It may abort, loop or even (if the programming language permits it) execute a jump to some external routine. A failure specification thus serves to restrict the domain of an operation. Isnew(stk) => failure(top,stk), for example, combines with the syntactic specification of top to tell us that top is a partial function that accepts a stack as its argument and is defined if and only if that stack is not empty. Note that this is not equivalent to using the syntactic specification

$$top: \quad Stack - \{newstack\} \longrightarrow element\text{-}type.$$

This would imply that top would never be called with newstack as the actual parameter, thus absolving the implementor of top from having to insert in his code a check on the suitability of the argument passed to it.

A formula of the form failure(g,X) => $P(X)$ states that if the operation g is invoked with arguments X and fails to terminate normally, then $P(X)$ must have been true at the point where g was invoked. That is to say failure is optional if $P(X)$ is true, but must not occur if $P(X)$ is not. The formula failure(push,stk,elm) => depth(stk)$\geq$n, for example, gives the implementation of push the option of failing whenever the depth of the resulting stack would exceed n.

Initially, we had hoped to limit ourselves to one form of failure specification. In particular, we had hoped to limit ourselves to the specification of optional failures and pre-conditions. It seemed that if a condition, $P(X)$, were sufficient to guarantee failure, then ~$P(X)$ should be used as a pre-condition, obviating the need for the failure specification. However, just as one can take comfort in knowing that the definition of a programming language guarantees that subscript errors will be reported, the programmer who uses type Stack may take comfort in knowing that should he try to compute the top of newstack, his computation will not proceed. This security is particularly important if the program using type Stack has not been formally verified, for then there is no guarantee that the specified pre-conditions hold at the point of invocation. The need for optional failure specifications is more pervasive. It stems from our desire to make our specifications as unrestrictive as possible. When dealing with capacity constraints, in particular, it is often the case that the specifier of the type needs only to establish a bound, and the exact choice of where to fail is best left to the implementor of the type. The implementor of type Stack, for example, might find it convenient to allow the depth of the stack to reach the first power of two not less than n. A related example involves the specification of a type Number with restriction specifications dealing with overflow and underflow. In some applications, it is crucial that calculations be carried out in exactly the precision asked for. In other applications, one need only require that the precision used be at least as great as that requested. The use of an optional failure specification in the latter case may allow a significantly more efficient implementation of type Number.

A few closing comments

For verifications of programs that use abstract types, both algebraic and Hoare-like specifications of the types used provide rules of inference that can be used to demonstrate consistency between a program and its specification. That is to say, the presence of axiomatic definitions of abstract types provides a mechanism for proving a program to be consistent with its specification, provided that the implementations of the abstract operations that it uses are consistent with their specifications. Thus a technique for factoring the proof is provided, for the axiomatic definitions serve as the specification of intent at a lower level of abstraction. For proofs of the correctness of representations of abstract types, the axiomatic specifications provide the minimal set of assertions that must be verified. A lengthy discussion of the use of algebraic axioms in program verification appears in [Guttag 76]. Discussions of the use of Hoare-like specifications in program verification appear in [Hoare 72] and [Wulf 76].

Any discussion of the relative merits of these two specification techniques in program verification must be highly subjective. One can invent arbitrarily many examples for which one or the other approach is clearly more convenient. Those examples favoring the Hoare-like approach are characterized by the choice of a type abstraction that is closely related to a type available in the underlying specification language. Those examples favoring the algebraic technique are characterized by the choice of a type abstraction that is not readily represented by a type available in the underlying specification language. These two classes of examples illustrate two facts:

Fact 1: If there exists some domain of discourse about which a great deal is known, and the abstraction we wish to provide is readily mapped into that domain, then a great deal is to be gained by performing that mapping and reasoning in terms of the better understood domain.

Fact 2: If we are forced to map the desired abstraction into a dissimilar domain and then reason in terms of that domain, we will have lost any advantage we had hoped to gain by introducing the abstraction.

Given these two facts, any evaluation of the relative utility of these two approaches to type abstraction must be based upon a subjective evaluation of the way in which type abstraction will be used. In particular, one must address the question of what kinds of abstractions will prove most useful. Will they be primarily close variants of a small set of currently well-understood abstractions? Or, given suitably imaginative programmers, will they often be quite distinct from any already well-understood abstraction? These are questions to which only experience can provide answers.

Acknowledgments

The discussion of Euclid modules is derived in part from [London 78]. Both the exposition of the module rule and my understanding of it can, to a great extent, be attributed to many hours spent discussing the subject with Ralph London. The discussion of algebraic axioms is in part a condensation of material appearing in earlier papers and in part a preliminary discussion of work currently in progress. I thus owe a significant debt to my past and present collaborators: Jim Horning, Ellis Horowitz and Dave Musser. I would also like to thank the participants of the Summer School on Program Construction, whose response to my lectures led to substantial revisions in these notes.

This work was supported in part by the National Science Foundation under grant MCS78-01798 and the Joint Services Electronics Program monitored by the Air Force Office of Scientific Research under contract F44620-76-C-0061.

References

[Dahl 1968]
Dahl,O.J., Nygaard,K., and Myhrhuag,B., "The SIMULA 67 Common
Base Language," Norwegian Computing Centre, Forskningsveien
1B, Oslo (1968).

[Dahl 1978]
Dahl,O.J., "Can Program Proving Be Made Practical?" Institute
of Informatics, University of Oslo, Norway, (1978).

[Dijkstra 1976]
Dijkstra,E.W., A Discipline of Programming, Prentice-Hall,
(1976).

[Donahue 1976]
Donahue,J.E., "Complementary Definitions of Programming Language
Semantics," Lecture Notes in Computer Science, vol. 42, Springer-Verlag,
(1976).

[Gannon 1975]
Gannon,J.D., Language Design to Enhance Programming Reliability,
Ph.D.Thesis, University of Toronto, Department of Computer
Science (1975), available as Computer Systems Research Group
Technical Report CSRG-47.

[Goguen 1975]
Goguen,J.A., Thatcher,J.W., Wagner,E.G., and Wright,J.B.,
"Abstract Data-Types as Initial Algebras and Correctness of
Data Representations," Proceedings, Conference on Computer
Graphics, Pattern Recognition and Data Structure, (May 1975).

[Guttag 1975]
Guttag,J.V., The Specification and Application to Programming
of Abstract Data Types, Ph.D. Thesis, University of Toronto,
Department of Computer Science (1975), available as Computer
Systems Research Group Technical Report CSRG-59.

[Guttag 1976]
Guttag,J.V., Horowitz,E., and Musser,D.R., "Abstract Data
Types and Software Validation," USC Information Sciences Institute
Technical Report, (1976).

[Guttag 1977]
Guttag,J.V., "Abstract Data Types and the Development of Data
Structures," Communications of the CACM, vol. 20, no. 6, (June 1977),
pp. 396-404.

[Guttag 1978]
Guttag,J.V., and Horning,J.J., "The Algebraic Specification
of Abstract Data Types," Acta Informatica, 10,1, pp. 27-52 (1978).

[Hoare 1969]
Hoare, C.A.R., "An Axiomatic Basis for Computer Programming,"
CACM, vol. 12, no. 10 (October 1969), pp. 576-580.

[Hoare 1972]
Hoare, C.A.R., "Proofs of Correctness of Data Representations,"
Acta Informatica, vol. 1, no. 1 (1972), pp. 271-281.

[Knuth 1970]
Knuth,D.E., and Bendix,P.B., "Simple Word Problems
in Universal Algebras," Computational Problems in Abstract Algebras,
J.Leech, Ed., Pergamon Press, (1970), pp.263-297.

[Lampson 1978]
Lampson,B.W., Horning,J.J., London,R.L., MItchell,J.G.,
Popek,G.J., "Revised Report on the Programming Language Euclid,"
Xerox Research Center, to appear. An earlier version appeared in
SIGPLAN Notices 12, 2 (February 1977).

[London 1978]
London,R.L., Guttag,J.V., Horning,J.J., Lampson,B.W.,
Mitchell,J.G., and Popek,G.J., "Proof Rules for the Programming
Language Euclid," Acta Informatica, 10,1, pp. 1-26 (1978).

[Morris 1973]
Morris,J.H., "Types are not Sets," ACM Symposium on the
Principles of Programming Languages, (October 1973), pp. 120-124.

[Parnas 1972]
Parnas,D.L., "A Technique for the Specification of Software
Modules with Examples," CACM, vol. 15, no. 5 (May 1972),
pp. 330-336.

[Scott 1970]
Scott,D., "Outline of a Mathematical Theory of Computation,"
Proceedings of the Fourth Annual Princeton Conference on Information
Science and Systems, (1970), pp. 169-176.

[Spitzen 1975]
Spitzen,J., and Wegbreit,B., "The Verification and Synthesis
of Data Structures," Acta Informatica, vol. 4, (1975), pp.
127-144.

[Thatcher 1978]
Thatcher,J.W, Wagner,E.G., and Wright,J.B., "Data Type
Specification: Parameterization and the Power of Specification
Techniques," Proceedings SIGACT Tenth Annual Symposium on Theory
of Computing, (May 1978).

[Wulf 1976]
Wulf,W.A., London,R.L., and Shaw,M., "An Introduction to the
the Construction and Verification of Alphard Programs," IEEE
Transactions on Software Engineering, SE-2, 4, (December 1976),
pp. 253-265.

[Zilles 1975]
Zilles,S.N., "Abstract Specifications for Data Types," IBM
Research Laboratory, San Jose, California, (1975).

SOME THEORETICAL ASPECTS OF PROGRAM CONSTRUCTION

Claude PAIR

Institut National Polytechnique
de Lorraine
Porte de la Craffe
B.P.3308
54042 NANCY CEDEX
France

INTRODUCTION

The subject of this School is "Program Construction". We can see construction of a program as a process going from a <u>specification</u> to a <u>program</u>.

<u>What is a specification</u> ? Just a text. Now, what is the meaning of this text ? In fact, it is a mapping[(*)] from input to output.

<u>What is a program</u> ? Just a text. The meaning of this text is a mapping which, for each input, leads to a computation.

The problem of programming is,given a specification, to build a program which computes the corresponding mapping[(*)] :

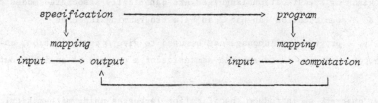

<u>figure 1</u>

[(*)] The precise sense of the word "mapping" can be discussed : is it necessarily functional, i.e. one-valued, in other words deterministic ?

Example

- Specification (gcd) :

for input a, b
find output d such that
$div(d,a)$ *and* $div(d,b)$ *and* $\forall x(div(x,a)$ *and* $div(x,b) \Rightarrow div(x,d))$

- Program :

$a,b := input$;
while $b \neq 0$ do $r := a$ mod b ;
$\qquad\qquad\quad a := b$;
$\qquad\qquad\quad b := r$
$\qquad\quad$ od ;
$d := a$

We have to deduce the program from the specification or to prove the commutativity of
the previous diagram (fig. 1). The difference between specification and program lies :

- in the kind of meaning : a specification does not express a method of computation
- sometimes, in the data structure : for the specification, data are relevant to the
  problem only, they can be abstract, algebraic... ; for a program they are closer to
  the hardware.

A specification must be expressed in a language, called a specification language. A
program is expressed in a language, called a programming language.

The difference between a specification language and a programming language is in its
type of semantics : in both cases the meaning of a sentence is a mapping, with a set
of inputs as domain : the range is a set of outputs in the first case, a set of computations in the second case.

In fact, this difference between specification language and programming language is
not very precise :

- to some kinds of specification languages are canonically associated modes of computations ; so a specification language can be a programming language.

- conversely, a programming language can be used to give a specification, and a very
admissible point of view is to see the semantics of a program as an input-output mapping.

In the next chapter, we introduce specification languages using mathematical logic.
Then a more restricted kind of specification (explicit specifications or recursive
schemes) is introduced and studied.

It must be noted that the question of building a specification from an idea of the
problem to be solved, can be a very difficult one. It will not be examined here.

SPECIFICATION LANGUAGES

In the introduction, we gave an example of specification :
(1) $div(d,a) \wedge div(d,b) \wedge \forall x(div(x,a)$ and $div(x,b) \Rightarrow div(x,d))$
where a, b are the inputs and d the output. The problem is stated for the set N
of natural numbers. More generally, a specification is stated for some set D,
the domain of the problem.

We shall now explore this type of specification. It can give an idea of what a specification language can be. In fact, we present here more "models" of specification languages than true specification languages : a specification language will contain more
"syntactic sugar", for example abbreviations, and be adapted to a specific domain. Our
"models" can be seen as "kernel languages" into which specification languages can be
translated.

1. Syntax

The alphabet contains :
- logical connectors, like $\wedge$, $\Rightarrow$.
- quantifiers, like $\forall$.
- variables : they can be bound, like x in the previous specification, or free, like
  a, b, d ; there are two kinds of free variables, inputs and outputs.
- symbols denoting relations, like div ; each relation has an "arity" : for example,
  div is a binary relation, i.e. a relation whose arity is 2.
- in general, symbols denoting functions, each of them having an arity ; e.g., in N,
  addition and multiplication, with arity 2, square, with arity 1, etc.
- symbols denoting constants of D, e.g. $0,1,\ldots$ in N.

With this alphabet can be built :
- terms, with constants, variables, functions (according to their arity), like
  $plus(mul(b,q),r)$
- atoms, with relations applied to terms, like $div(p,a)$ or $eq(a,plus(mul(b,q),r))$
  where eq is a binary relational symbol (interpreted by, for example, equality)
- formulas, obtained by the combination of atoms with connectors and quantifiers according to normal rules.

In fact, in this case a specification is a formula of an applied first order predicate
calculus, with relational and functional symbols denoting, respectively, relations and
functions on the set D, and in particular 0-ary functions denoting elements of D.

2. Semantics
Our example specification means :

for a, b given in D, find d in D such that the formula (1) is true.

For example, with 12 for a and 15 for b, the formula is true with 3 for d.

More generally, an <u>interpretation</u> of the considered first order predicate calculus is given, using D as the domain of interpretation : functional symbols of arity n are interpreted as functions from D^n into D, relational symbols of arity n as n-ary relations in D^n, i.e. n-ary functions from D^n into $\{true, false\}$. Thus a formula without free variables can be interpreted as true or false. For a specification S with a, b as input variables and d as output variable, the meaning is :

for u, v given in D, find w in D, such that $S^{a\ b\ d}_{u\ v\ w}$ is interpreted as true.

$S^{a\ b\ d}_{u\ v\ w}$ is the formula obtained by replacing a by u, b by v, d by w in S. It is a formula without free variables.

3. Remarks and generalizations

3.1. Those formulas which are always interpreted as true after replacement of their free variables by arbitrary elements of D, are called valid formulas, or theorems. They can be obtained in a purely syntactical manner, by <u>demonstrations</u> deducing them from <u>axioms</u> by <u>rules of inference</u>.

An axiom is a formula, for example

$$div(a,b) \wedge div(b,c) \Rightarrow div(a,c)$$
$$div(3,12)$$

Examples of rules of inference :

$$\frac{p \quad p \Rightarrow q}{q} \quad \textit{(from formulas p and $p \Rightarrow q$, deduce q)}$$

$$\frac{p}{\forall x\ p}$$

No other rule of inference is necessary. Of course, enough axioms must be given to allow deduction of all valid formulas from the axioms by the use of the rules of inference.

3.2. The problem to be specified can in fact be given not only for one domain D, but for a whole class of "similar" domains : for example the g.c.d. problem is given not only for integers, but also for polynomials of 1, 2, ... variables. The same symbols are used, only their interpretation will be different. The axioms are the same.

In this case, one works in a <u>formal system</u>, which is an applied first order predicate calculus with equality, characterized by :
- its relational and functional symbols
- its axioms.

This allows the definition of theorems, deduced from the axioms by repeatedly apply-ing the rules of inference. All this is purely syntactic.

Then a _model_ of this formal system can be defined as an interpretation on a domain D, which interprets the axioms (and from this, the theorems) as being true for each set of values given to the free variables.

For more details, the reader will consult the relevant texts of mathematical logic.

A specification can be given as a formula in this kind of formal system, which can be called an _abstract data type_.

Semantics of the specification refer to a particular model. The specification is interpreted as a relation between inputs and outputs in the domain D of this model.

3.3. The problem can use simultaneously, not only one domain D, but n different domains D_1, D_2, ..., D_n. For example, to specify a problem on stacks, two domains are needed : the domain of stacks and the domain of stack elements.

Syntactically, variables, constants, functions, relations will have _sorts_ (or _types_), to restrict the allowed terms and atoms. For example, in the case of stacks,

$$top(push(s,a))$$

will be a correct term, but

$$push(top(s),a)$$

will not.

Semantically, an interpretation for a corresponding formal system (3.2) will use n domains.

The presence of the domain $B = \{true, false\}$ can prevent the distinction between relations and functions, a relation being a function into B. In this case, it is sufficient to keep the equality relation, denoted by = . For example, the relational symbol _div_ will be replaced by a functional symbol _div_ and the atom $div(a,b)$ will be written $div(a,b) = true$.

Equality is characterized by the axiom of "substitutivity" : for a formula α and terms t and t' : $\qquad\qquad\qquad t = t' \Rightarrow (\alpha \Leftrightarrow \alpha')$
where α' is deduced from α by substituting t' for an occurrence of t. From this axiom can be deduced the symmetry and transitivity of equality.

4. A specification language

To conclude, a specification language can be the language of formulas of an applied, many-sorted, first order predicate calculus with equality, where within the free va-riables are distinguished input variables and output variables.

A specification defines a relation between inputs and outputs in a model of this formal system. The model can be fixed or arbitrary : in this case, the specification states a problem for an abstract data type, defined by the formal system. An example is given in annex (§ A1,A3).

Of course, this is not the only possible kind of specification language. It has the merit of being general enough and well-known.

But,now, for a given specification, arise three successive problems :
a) existence : for each input, does it exist an output ?
b) uniqueness : for each input, is the output unique ?
            if not, can some particular output be chosen ?
c) effectiveness : how to compute the chosen output ?

In fact, we cannot   hope to solve these problems in the general case. Take for example the famous problem of FERMAT : find natural integers x, y, z, n, such that
$$n > 2 \wedge x^n + y^n = z^n.$$

It is possible to try, in turn for some order, all quadruples (x,y,z,n). If a solution exists, this is an algorithm, but certainly not a feasible one. And if no solution exists, the process will never end and we will never know if a solution really exists ... In fact, this is the case, nobody knows...

5. A radical restriction to study these problems

5.1. A specification can often be given as a set of definitions : definitions of the outputs in terms of intermediate results, definitions of these intermediates in terms of others intermediates... and of the inputs. The intermediates have to be quantified by an existential quantifier. The simplest case of definition of a result x is an equality $x = \tau$ where τ is a term.

We thus arrive at the idea of specifications of the following type :
$$\exists r_{p+1} \cdots \exists r_q \quad (r_1 = \tau_1 \wedge \cdots \wedge r_p = \tau_p \wedge \cdots \wedge r_q = \tau_q)$$
where $r_1, \ldots, r_p$ are the outputs, $r_{p+1}, \ldots, r_q$ the intermediate results, $\tau_1, \ldots, \tau_q$ are terms.

To study the previous problems, the quantifiers can be removed :
$$r_1 = \tau_1 \wedge \cdots \wedge r_q = \tau_q$$

Indeed, for given inputs, the p-tuples $(r_1,\ldots,r_p)$ of outputs for the first specification are made up of the first p components of the q-uples $(r_1,\ldots,r_p,\ldots r_q)$ of outputs for the second one.

We refer to such a specification as an explicit specification, because each unknown is <u>explicitly</u> defined by a term.

Example : $p = gp + t$

$gp = nb * up$ *(nb, up, pct are inputs)*

$t = gp * pct$

5.2. We define a dependence relation δ in $\{r_1,\ldots,r_q\}$: $r_i \, \delta \, r_j$ iff r_j occurs in the term τ_i.

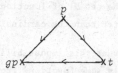

Graph of δ for the example

<u>figure 2</u>

If the graph of δ has no cycle, there exists one and only one solution and it can be computed by successive replacements. This is the case for the example. Hence our three previous problems are solved. But this case is very restricted, it is the elementary school case!

5.3. The more general case, where the graph has a cycle, is well-known in computer science if some r_i are functions : it is the case of recursion.

Example : $d = x(a,b)$
$$\hat{x} = \lambda u \, \lambda v \; (\underline{if} \; v = 0 \; \underline{then} \; u \; \underline{else} \; x(v,mod(u,v)))$$

Is this specification a formula in the first order predicate calculus ?

a) <u>if</u> ... <u>then</u> ... <u>else</u> ... can be seen as a function of 3 arguments, the first being boolean :

$$cond(b,u_1,u_2) = if \; b \; then \; u_1 \; else \; u_2$$

which can be axiomatized by :

$$cond(true,u_1,u_2) = u_1$$
$$cond(false,u_1,u_2) = u_2$$

b) the use of the λ-notation is not necessary : the second equation can be written :

$$x(u,v) = cond(eq(v,0),u,x(v,mod(u,v)))$$

c) but here x is a variable and in the first order predicate calculus, there is no variable of type "function" ; if x is a variable, $x(a,b)$ is not a well-formed term.

A solution is to use (constant) functions "apply", the first argument of which is interpreted as a function : $apply(x,u)$ is interpreted as $x(u)$; $x(a,b)$ is denoted by $apply2(x,a,b)$, etc.

But here arise some difficulties. If we try to give an interpretation with one domain D, the first argument of (the interpretation of) apply is an element of D, but also an arbitrary function from D to D. The set D^D of functions from D to D is included in D ; but its cardinal is strictly greater than the cardinal of D!

Two solutions can be tried to prevent this impossibility :
- for the interpretation, keep only some functions from D into D, for example D being enumerable, an enumerable set of such functions ; this is the idea of SCOTT for giving a model of λ-calculus with "computable" functions (see 5.5).
- introduce more than one domain, that is several sorts ; the simplest case is to use a sort of "individuals" and sorts of functions, with $0,1,2, \ldots$ arguments of sort individual and a value of sort individual ; here we are in the case of a predicate calculus of second order. This could be generalized, but we shall study this case.

5.4. So our explicit specification will be of the form :

$$\bigwedge_{i=1}^{n} \forall x_1 \ldots \forall x_{m_i} \quad f_i(x_1,\ldots,x_{m_i}) = \tau_i$$

- f_i is a variable of type function with m_i arguments $(m_i \geq 0)$.
- τ_i is a term in which as free variables can occur only $x_1,\ldots,x_{m_i},f_1,\ldots,f_n$ and the input variables.

Example :
$$d = f(a,b)$$
$$f(u,v) = \underline{if} \ v = 0 \ \underline{then} \ u \ \underline{else} \ f(v,mod(u,v))$$
($\wedge$ will be omitted, together with the universal quantification on u,v).

For this kind of specification (also called recursive specification or recursive scheme) we shall study the three problems of existence, uniqueness and computation of a solution.

The restriction on specifications to obtain recursive specification makes also arise an important problem, that of transforming a general specification (in terms of predicate calculus) into a recursive one (see annex, A2,A4,A6). A recursive specification can indeed be viewed as an intermediate between a general specification and a program.

5.5. Remark : the problem of types (or sorts) of functions can be stated for programming languages : briefly, LISP is a language without types, like λ-calculus ; in Algol 60, there is only one type of function, irrespective of the arguments ; in Algol 68, functions are apparently fully typed ; however, recursive modes allow a mode declaration like :   _mode lambda = proc(lambda) lambda_

which is the mode of λ-calculus values. In fact all these languages are consistent, despite the previous remark on the difficulty of interpretation without types, because the considered functions are only some of the possible functions, that is computable ones. This was the intuition of SCOTT for giving a model of λ-calculus.

APPLICATION OF FIXPOINT THEORY TO RECURSIVE SPECIFICATIONS

We have to study the problems of —existence

—uniqueness or choice

—computation

of solutions, for a recursive specification.

The interpretation of this specification is a <u>fixpoint system</u> the unknowns of which are n functions of 0, 1, 2, ... p arguments :

$$f_i(x_1,\ldots,x_{m_i}) = \tau_i\ (x_1,\ldots,x_{m_i},f_1,\ldots,f_n) \quad for\ 1 \le i \le n$$

also written as

$$f_i = \lambda x_1\ \ldots\ \lambda x_{m_i}\ \tau_i(x_1,\ldots,x_{m_i},f_1,\ldots,f_n)$$

It is possible to take uniformly $m_i = p$, by adding dummy arguments. If the domain of individuals of the interpretation is D, a solution is an element of $E = (D^p \to D)^n$ when $D^p \to D$ is the set of functions from D^p into D.

The fixpoint system can be considered as a unique fixpoint equation in E, the unknown f of which is the vector $(f_1,\ldots,f_n)$. We denote it by

$$f = \tau(f) :$$

τ is the mapping transforming $f = (f_1,\ldots,f_n)$ into the vector having as components the n functions

$$\lambda x_1\ \ldots\ \lambda x_p\ \tau_i(x_1,\ldots,x_p,f_1,\ldots,f_n).$$

6. Some examples

An example with 2 equations was given in 5.4. See also annex. The examples below are only systems with one single equation, to study problems of existence and uniqueness.

6.1. $a = \underline{if}\ a = 0\ \underline{then}\ 1\ \underline{else}\ 0$
A fixpoint equation has not necessarily a solution.

6.2. $f(x) = \underline{if}\ x = 0\ \underline{then}\ 0\ \underline{else}\ f(x+1)$
Domain : $\mathbb{N}$. Solution : $f(0) = 0$; $f(1) = f(2) = f(3) = \ldots$, arbitrary value. A fixpoint equation can have more than one solution.

6.3. $f(x) = \underline{if}\ x = 0\ \underline{then}\ 1\ \underline{else}\ f(x-1)+2$
In $\mathbb{N}$, an unique solution : $f = \lambda x.\ 2x+1$
In $\mathbb{Z}$ (set of integers), an infinity of solutions :

$$f = \lambda x \; \underline{if} \; x \geq 0 \; \underline{then} \; 2x+1 \; \underline{else} \quad 2x+b$$

where b is arbitrary.

6.4. $f(x) = \underline{if} \; x = 0 \; \underline{then} \; 1 \; \underline{else} \; |f(x-1)+2|$ in domain $\mathcal{L}$.

$f(x) \geq 0$ for every x. So the function is also defined as in 6.3. There is a solution in $\mathbb{N}$, but in $\mathcal{L}$, no solution can be everywhere positive.

In $\mathcal{L}$ no total function is a solution, but if we accept <u>partial</u> function, there is a solution

$$f = \lambda x \; \underline{if} \; x \geq 0 \; \underline{then} \; 2x+1 \; \underline{else} \; undefined.$$

The graph of this function is given by figure 3.

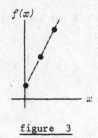

figure 3

7. Partial functions and the undefined value

To increase the possibility of a solution, we shall accept partial functions. That is to say, we introduce into the domain D a new value, ω , and a partial function f will be made total by extending it : $f(x) = \omega$ if f is not defined for x.

In the previous example, a solution is :

$$f = \lambda x \; \underline{if} \; x \geq 0 \; \underline{then} \quad 2x+1 \; \underline{else} \; \omega$$

with the conventions :

$$|\omega+2| = \omega$$

$$\underline{if} \; \omega \geq 0 \; \underline{then} \; u \; \underline{else} \; v = \omega$$

to define the function for ω, and also

$$\underline{if} \; true \; \underline{then} \; u \; \underline{else} \; \omega = u.$$

For example 6.1, there now exists a solution : ω.

In other words, our domains will always contain a special constant ω, and corresponding axioms will be :

$$g(\dots,\omega,\dots) = \omega$$

for each (constant) basic functional symbol g, but for $cond$:

$$cond(\omega,u_1,u_2) = \omega$$

$$cond(true,u_1,u_2) = u_1 \quad (even \; for \; u_2 = \omega)$$

$$cond(false,u_1,u_2) = u_2 \quad (even \; for \; u_1 = \omega)$$

cond is a special function which can be defined even if one argument is undefined.

Remark : it is sometimes interesting to introduce basic functions having this property. For example in $B = \{true, false, \omega\}$ use two functions <u>and</u>, <u>or</u>, with

$$\underline{and}(false, \omega) = \underline{and}(\omega, false) = false \; ; \; \underline{or}(true, \omega) = \underline{or}(\omega, true) = true.$$

8. How to find a solution ?

Let us return to example 6.3.

At the beginning, I know nothing. I can only draw the axes of the graph.

At first glance, I see that $f(0) = 1$. I know one point of the graph.

Knowing $f(0) = 1$, I can see that $f(1) = 3$ and know 2 points of the graph.

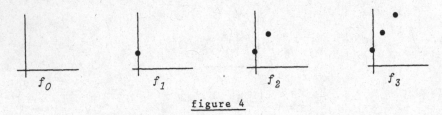

figure 4

I can continue and, after n steps, I shall know $f(0), f(1), \ldots, f(n-1)$. And if I am
clever, I shall see the solution : $f(x) = 2x + 1$ for $x \geq 0$.

At each step, the function is more defined. f can be seen as the "limit" of an infinite sequence of functions :

$$f_0 = \lambda x \; \omega$$
$$f_1 = \underline{if} \; x = 0 \; \underline{then} \; 1 \; \underline{else} \; \omega$$
$$f_2 = \underline{if} \; x = 0 \; \underline{then} \; 1 \; \underline{else} \; \underline{if} \; x = 1 \; \underline{then} \; 3 \; \underline{else} \; \omega$$
$$\cdots$$

To make this more precise, we shall use some notation :

- $f \sqsubseteq g$ means f is less defined than g, i.e. $f(x) = \omega$ or $f(x) = g(x)$ for all x, a graph
  of f is contained into graph of g : $\sqsubseteq$ is a (partial) ordering.
- the minimum element for this ordering is the function always equal to ω ; it will be
  denoted by $\perp$ (called "bottom").

The f_i form an increasing sequence for the ordering

$$\perp = f_0 \sqsubseteq f_1 \sqsubseteq f_2 \sqsubseteq \cdots$$

f is the <u>least upper bound</u> of this sequence : $f = \sqcup f_j$. This mean that :

a) $\quad\quad \forall j \; f_j \sqsubseteq f$

b) $\quad\quad \forall j \; f_j \sqsubseteq g \; \Rightarrow \; f \sqsubseteq g$

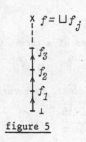

figure 5

Note also that f_j is obtained by substituting f_{j-1} into the right hand side of the definition of f :

$$f_j = \lambda x \ \underline{if} \ x = 0 \ \underline{then} \ 1 \ \underline{else} \ f_{j-1}(x-1)+2$$

9. Structure of the domains

The basic domain D (completed by ω) is ordered by

$$\forall \ x \ \epsilon \ D \qquad \omega \sqsubseteq x$$

(ω is less defined than every value, fig.6).

figure 6

The set of partial functions $D \rightarrow D$, and more generally $D^p \rightarrow D$ is also ordered by the ordering "less defined than", with a minimum element $\bot$, the never defined function. It possesses an important property :

each ascending sequence $f_0, f_1, \ldots, f_j, \ldots$ has a least upper bound, $\sqcup f_j$.

Indeed, if for $x \ \epsilon \ D$, one of the f_j is defined $(f_j(x) \neq \omega)$, all the $f_{j+k}(x)$ are equal to $f_j(x)$ and $(\sqcup f_j)(x) = f_j(x)$; else $(\sqcup f_j)(x) = \omega$. In other terms,

$$(\sqcup f_j)(x) = \sqcup f_j(x) \qquad \text{(least upper bound in } D\text{)}.$$

An ordered set with this property is called inductive. The set $E = (D^p \rightarrow D)^n$ is also an ordered inductive set, for the order defined by :

$$(a_1,\ldots,a_n) \sqsubseteq (b_1,\ldots,b_n) \Leftrightarrow \forall \ k \ \epsilon \ [1,n] \ a_k \sqsubseteq b_k.$$

It possesses a minimal element $(\bot,\bot, \ldots ,\bot)$, still denoted by $\bot$.

10. Fixpoint theorem

We have to study the existence of a solution for a fixpoint equation $f = \tau(f)$ in an inductive set with a minimal element ⊥.

Paragraph 8 leads to the definition of a recursive sequence :

$$f_0 = \perp \qquad\qquad f_j = \tau(f_{j-1})$$

a) It is clear that $f_0 \sqsubseteq f_1$. To deduce, by recursion, that $f_{j-1} \sqsubseteq f_j$, it is sufficient that the functional τ be <u>monotonic</u> :

$$f \sqsubseteq f' \;\Rightarrow\; \tau(f) \sqsubseteq \tau(f')$$

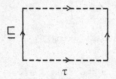

<u>figure 7</u>

b) If this is true, $\sqcup f_j$ exists. It will be a solution, a <u>fixpoint</u>, if

$$\tau(\sqcup f_j) = \sqcup \tau(f_j)$$

because $\sqcup \tau(f_j) = \sqcup f_{j+1} = \sqcup f_j$. This hypothesis (for every ascending sequence) is called the <u>continuity</u> of τ.

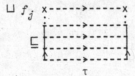

<u>figure 8</u>

So the existence of a fixpoint is shown if τ is monotonic and continuous. In fact, a continuous function is necessarily monotonic : consider a sequence of two elements $f, f', f', f', \ldots$, with $f \sqsubseteq f'$ (see figures 7 and 8).

We have demonstrated the fixpoint theorem :

A fixpoint equation $f = \tau(f)$ in an inductive set with a minimum element ⊥ admits, if τ is continuous, a solution, which is the least upper bound of the infinite sequence :

$$f_0 = \perp \qquad\qquad f_j = \tau(f_{j-1})$$

<u>Remarks</u> :

1. It is not true that, conversely, a monotonic function is continuous : consider the functional :

$$\tau = \lambda f \qquad \underline{if}\ \forall x \in \mathbb{N}\ f(x) \neq \omega\ \underline{then}\ 1\ \underline{else}\ 0$$

and the sequence :

$$f_j = \lambda j \ \underline{if} \ x \le j \ \underline{then} \ 0 \ \underline{else} \ \omega.$$

2. In fact, it can be shown that the hypothesis of monotony is sufficient to ensure the existence of a fixpoint. But the determination of a fixpoint by the previous method of "successive approximation" must be generalized.

3. It is not necessary to start with $f_0 = \perp$, but only with $f_0 \sqsubseteq \tau(f_0)$. Then is found a fixpoint f verifying $f_0 \sqsubseteq f$. An application is given in annex (A5).

The problem is now : can we be sure that, for a recursive specification, the hypothesis of continuity is true ? It is in fact the case, and we shall now give a sketch of the demonstration.

11. Continuity of τ for a recursive specification

11.1. Basic functions and *cond* are monotonic for each of their arguments : *in D,* $x \sqsubseteq y \ and \ x \ne y \ implies \ x = \omega$ (§ 9, fig. 6). Then a function h is monotonic if $h(\omega) = \omega$ or $h(\omega) = h(y)$, for every y.

It is the case for a basic function g because $g(...,\omega,...) = \omega$ (§ 7). It is also the case for each argument of *cond* :

$$cond(\omega, u_1, u_2) = \omega$$
$$cond(b, \omega, u_2) = \omega \ or \ cond(b, \omega, u_2) = u_2 = cond(b, y, \omega)$$
$$cond(b, u_1, \omega) = \omega \ or \ cond(b, u_1, \omega) = u_1 = cond(b, \ u_1, y).$$

It would be also the case for the functions *and*, *or* introduced in § 7, remark.

11.2. The f_j of the approximation sequence are monotonic : this is immediate by induction on j, for f_j is obtained by a composition of monotonic functions.

Thus, we shall not work in the whole set of functions from D^p into D , but only in the set of the monotonic functions from D^p into D : it is this set which is in fact denoted by $D^p \to D$. It is also the set of functions from D^p into D which are continuous for each argument, because in D increasing sequences have at most 2 elements, and thus continuity is equivalent to monotony.

11.3. We have to prove $\quad \tau(\sqcup f_j) = \sqcup \tau(f_j)$

i.e. $\qquad\qquad\qquad \forall x \quad \tau(\sqcup f_j)(x) = (\sqcup \tau(f_j))(x)$

From § 9 $\qquad\qquad\qquad (\sqcup \tau(f_j))(x) = \sqcup (\tau(f_j(x)).$

Using the notation $\qquad \tau(f)(x) = \alpha(f, x)$

we have to prove $\qquad\quad \alpha(\sqcup f_j, x) = \sqcup \alpha(f_j, x)$

i.e. continuity of α for its first argument.

11.4. α is obtained by a composition of basic functions and *cond*, which are continuous
and of *"apply"* functions :

$$apply(f,x) = f(x) \; ;$$

apply is continuous for its first argument :

$$(\sqcup f_i)(x) = \sqcup f_i(x) \qquad \text{by definition of } \sqcup \text{ (§ 9)}$$

and for its second argument :

$$f(\sqcup x_i) = \sqcup f(x_i)$$

because we are working on a domain of monotonic functions (11.2).

It is easy to prove that a composition of continuous functions is continuous.

12. What fixpoint is found by successive approximation ?

The fixpoint theorem of § 10 builds a fixpoint f be approximation :

$$f_0 = \bot \qquad\qquad\qquad f_j = \tau(f_{j-1}),$$

when τ is monotonic.

Let g be another fixpoint : $g = \tau(g)$. We see that $f_0 \sqsubseteq g$ and consequently, as τ is
monotonic, $f_1 \sqsubseteq \tau(g) = g$, and more generally be recursion $f_j \sqsubseteq g$. Therefore

$$f = \sqcup f_j \sqsubseteq g.$$

f is the least fixpoint of τ.

> A fixpoint equation $f = \tau(f)$ admits, if τ is continuous (it is the case for the
> explicit specifications), a least solution :
> $$f = \sqcup f_j \quad where \quad f_0 = \bot \quad and \quad f_j = \tau(f_{j-1}).$$

For example, $a = \underline{if} \; a = 1 \; \underline{then} \; 1 \; \underline{else} \; 0$ admits ω and 1 as solutions : the least solution is ω.

Moreover, in example 6.3 for domain $\mathcal{L}$, the least solution is

$$f = \lambda x \; \underline{if} \; x \geq 0 \; \underline{then} \; 2x+1 \; \underline{else} \; \omega$$

This is the solution found by successive approximations (§ 8).

So we have solved our first two problems for explicit specifications :

> Theorem : for a recursive specification in a domain completed by ω, there exists
> a least defined input-output mapping.

Thus, the answer to the problem of existence is : yes, but if we accept partial function ; and for the problem of uniqueness : no, but we can choose a particular solution:
the least fixpoint. It is this solution that we consider to be defined by the recursive specification.

13. Remark on the use of fixpoint systems in computer science

Fixpoint systems are used in many chapters of computer science. Let us give some
examples.

13.1. Context-free grammars define languages by fixpoint systems. For example,
arithmetic expressions with variables, integers and operators +, -, *, are defined
by the system :

$$
\begin{aligned}
E &= E + T \cup E - T \cup T \\
T &= T * F \cup F \\
F &= V \cup N \cup (E) \\
V &= L \cup VL \cup VC \\
N &= C \cup NC \\
L &= \{a, b, \ldots, z\} \\
C &= \{0, 1, \ldots, 9\}
\end{aligned}
$$

This system has one unique solution. This is not the more general case. The set of
languages is ordered by the inclusion relation, and is inductive. The languages defined by a context-free grammar are those of the least fixpoint of the system.

13.2. Now, let us see how to define the semantics of a programming language with
procedures. The set V of processed values contains basic values, for example integers
(set Z) but also procedure values. If we limit ourselves to procedures with one parameter, a procedure value is a mapping from $V \times S$ into S, where S in the set of "states".
A state can be viewed as a mapping giving values to identifiers :

$$
S = Id \to V.
$$

We are then led to write equations like :

$$
V = \mathit{Z} \cup (V \times S) \to S
$$
$$
S = Id \to V.
$$

Thus, the domains necessary to express the semantics of the language are given by a
fixpoint system.

We had already seen this for the semantics of λ-calculus, the domain D of which must
verify
$$
D = B \cup (D \to D)
$$
where D is the set of basic values.

Finding a solution for this kind of fixpoint systems is not easy, because we are not
in a general frame which is an inductive set. In fact, we should have to work in the
class of all sets, which is not a set. From that arises the impossibility seen in
§ 5.3. In fact, if we interpret $A \to B$ as the set of continuous functions from A into
B (A and B being inductive sets), these systems have a least fixpoint (for inclusion
of sets).

Let us return to the definition of the semantics of a programming language : we have to define the meaning of each construct : generally, this depends on the meaning of constructs which are included in this construct (and eventually on the meaning of the procedures denoted by identifiers included in it). It results that the "semantic mapping" is defined recursively, i.e. by a fixpoint equation.

13.3. The set of binary trees labeled by an alphabet A is solution of the equation:
$$T = nil \cup A \times T \times T$$
where nil is interpreted as the empty tree.

The sets of multirooted trees and rooted trees, M and R , labelled by A , are defined by :
$$R = A \times M$$
$$M = nil \cup R \times M$$

The linear lists are also defined by a fixpoint equation.

13.4. The modes of an Algol 68 program can be defined by a fixpoint system.

14. Computation of the output of a recursive specification for a given input

14.1. We have solved two of the three problems stated in last chapter ; we are sure of existence of a solution and we have chosen one : that defined by the least fixpoint. The third problem (computation) can appear solved by § 8.10. In practice, this is not true : § 10 allows the finding of a global solution ; but one problem is to compute an output for given inputs.

See for instance how § 8.10 would solve the problem of finding $f(12,15)$ where
$$f(u,v) = \underline{if} \; v = 0 \; \underline{then} \; u \; \underline{else} \; f(v,mod(u,v)).$$

It builds successive increasing domains where f is defined, until $(12,15)$ is in the domain :
$$D_0 = \emptyset$$
$$D_1 = \{(u,v) \mid v = 0\}$$
$$D_2 = D_1 \cup \{(u,v) \mid mod(u,v) = 0\}$$
$$D_3 = D_2 \cup \{(u,v) \mid mod(v,mod(u,v)) = 0\}$$
$$D_4 = D_3 \cup \{(u,v) \mid mod(mod(u,v),mod(v,mod(u,v))) = 0\}$$

$(12,15)$ is in D_4, but D_4 contains an infinity of pairs, for instance $(13,0)$ or $(1214, 612)$.

14.2. Computation by derivation.

It is of course better to compute $f(12,15)$ using the equation defining f :
$$f(12,15) = \underline{if} \; 15 = 0 \; \underline{then} \; 12 \; \underline{else} \; f(15,mod(12,15))$$

$$= f(15,mod(12,15))$$
$$= f(15,12)$$
$$= \underline{if}\ 12 = 0\ \underline{then}\ 15\ \underline{else}\ f(12,mod(15,12))$$
$$= f(12,mod(15,12))$$
$$= f(12,3)$$
$$= \underline{if}\ 3 = 0\ \underline{then}\ 12\ \underline{else}\ f(3,mod(12,3))$$
$$= f(3,mod(12,3))$$
$$= f(3,0)$$
$$= \underline{if}\ 0 = 0\ \underline{then}\ 3\ \underline{else}\ f(3,mod(3,0))$$
$$= 3$$

This is in fact a <u>proof</u> using theorems on integers (e.g. $mod(15,12) = 3$, $\neg 15=0$), axioms on conditional (§ 5.3), the definition of f, substitutivity and transitivity of equality.

It is equivalent to consider this as a <u>formal derivation</u>, starting with the term to be computed $f(12,15)$ and using as a <u>rewriting rule</u> the replacement of a term t by t' if $t = t'$ is :

  i) a theorem for the domain D equating a term t without conditionals and an element t' of D.

 ii) an axiom on the conditionals :

$$\underline{if}\ a = a\ \underline{then}\ t1\ \underline{else}\ t2\ =\ t1$$
$$\underline{if}\ a = b\ \underline{then}\ t1\ \underline{else}\ t2\ =\ t2$$

   where a and b are distinct elements of the domain D.

iii) deduced from the equation $f(u,v) = \tau$ by substitution of terms for u and v.

Thus, a derivation is a sequence of terms $t1$, $t2$, ..., tn : we write $t1 \overset{*}{\succ\!\!-} tn$. Then, $t1 = tn$ is a consequence of the specification.

As a computation is a proof, it results that if $f(a,b) \overset{*}{\succ\!\!-} d$, where a,b,d are elements of D, for each fixpoint, $f(a,b) = d$; this is true in particular for the least fixpoint : $lfp(a,b) = d$. Consequently :
- d is unique (independent of the particular derivation) ;
- if the function φ is defined by :

$$\varphi(a,b) = d\ \ \text{if}\ f(a,b) \overset{*}{\succ\!\!-} d$$

$$= \omega\ \ \text{if this holds for no}\ d$$

φ is less defined than each fixpoint, especially the least fixpoint lfp :

$$\varphi \sqsubseteq lfp.$$

In other words, if a computation by derivation yields a result, this is a value of the least fixpoint ; no other fixpoint is attainable by this computation. But conversely, is each value of the least fixpoint attainable ?

14.3. For a fixpoint equation
$$f = \tau(f)$$
it can be shown that the previous function φ verifies
$$\tau(\varphi) \sqsubseteq \varphi$$
where $\tau(\varphi)$ is the result of substitution of f by φ in $\tau(f)$.

This can be proved by <u>structural induction</u> on the term $\tau(f)$, i.e. : if the theorem is true for all subterms τ' of τ , it is true for τ itself.

From this result, we can deduce that the successive approximations $f_0, f_1, \ldots, f_j,$ $\ldots$ leading to the least fixpoint, verify :
$$f_j \sqsubseteq \varphi .$$

This is done by recursion on j . It is true for $j = 0 : f_0 = \bot$. And
$$f_{j-1} \sqsubseteq \varphi \quad \text{implies} \quad f_j = \tau(f_{j-1}) \sqsubseteq \tau(\varphi) \sqsubseteq \varphi$$
for τ is monotonic.

It results $lfp = \sqcup f_j \sqsubseteq \varphi$

and, from 14.2 $lfp = \varphi.$

<u>Theorem</u> : the function φ computed by derivation is the least fixpoint.

We can now give another interpretation of $lfp(x) = \omega$: it means that no derivation stops.

The preceding study can easily be generalized to a system of n equations : to replace φ is considered a n-tuple of functions computed by derivation starting with the n left hand sides of the equations.

14.4. Deterministic computations.

The preceding method of computation has an important drawback : it is not deterministic; of course, if two different derivations lead to a result, it is the same result ; but one of them can lead to a result and the other be infinite!

In the preceding example, for instance, in the term
$$\underline{if} \ 15 = 0 \ \underline{then} \ 12 \ \underline{else} \ f(15, mod(12,15))$$
we can replace the term $f(15, mod(12,15))$ according to the definition of f ; and if we go on replacing the terms $f(\ldots)$, we go into an infinite computation.

One idea is to restrict the order of application of the rewriting rules (i), (ii), (iii), of 14.2. The risk is of getting a computed function strictly less defined than the least fixpoint.

It is probably natural to begin with rule (i) to get simplifications ; the order of application of (i) to the different possible terms is immaterial ; we can for example choose left to right.

Then, we can simplify conditionals (rule(ii)) : the application of (ii) before (iii) avoids the previous difficulty.

Then, we apply rule(iii), and there we have to choose a term beginning by an unknown function.

In the previous example, no choice was necessary at this stage, but this is not always the case and the choice is not immaterial, as we shall now see.

Example : $f(x,y) = \underline{if}\ x = 0\ \underline{then}\ 1\ \underline{else}\ f(x-1,f(x-y,y))$
$\qquad\qquad f(2,1) = \underline{if}\ 2 = 0\ \underline{then}\ 1\ \underline{else}\ f(1,f(1,1))$
$\qquad\qquad\qquad\ = f(1,f(1,1)).$

We can replace the outside f : this leads to
$$f(0,f(1-f(1,1),f(1,1)))$$
and then to 1 with the same strategy.

But if we choose ever to replace the innermost f, it leads to
$$f(1,f(0,f(0,1)),f(1,f(0,1)),f(1,1),f(0,f(0,1)),f(0,1),1$$
which is much longer. The reason is that we have computed useless terms.

The two previous strategies are the simplest ones :
- replace the leftmost outermost
- replace the leftmost innermost
occurrence of an unknown function.
They are respectively referred to by <u>call by name</u> and <u>call by value</u>, because of similar features in programming languages.

We have seen that call by value can compute useless terms. It is not only a matter of optimality : it is possible that computation of these useless terms gives no result and goes into an infinite computation.

Example :
  system $\left|\ \begin{array}{l} r = f(a,u(a),b) \\ f(x,y,z) = \underline{if}\ x \geq 0\ \underline{then}\ g(y)\ \underline{else}\ h(z) \\ u(x) = \underline{if}\ x = 0\ \underline{then}\ 1\ \underline{else}\ u(x-1) + 2 \end{array}\right.$

If $a < 0$, the computation of the argument $u(a)$ is infinite.

In this case, call by value leads to a function stricty less defined than the least fixpoint. It can be said that call by value is not <u>safe</u>.

Call by name does replacement only for useful terms. Thus it can be thought that it is safe. In fact, it can be shown that it computes effectively the least fixpoint.

<u>Theorem</u> : the function computed by call by name is the least fixpoint.

<u>Remarks</u> :

a) It was shown by DE ROEVER that every recursive scheme can be transformed into a recursive scheme in which each argument is always useful : in this case, call by value is safe. The idea is to partition the domain of a function into domains where some arguments are useful and the others not (for f in previous example, x, y are useful for $x \geq 0$, and x, z for $x < 0$) ; the function is then the least upper bound of functions defined in these domains and undefined elsewhere (in the example $f = f1$ $\sqcup$ $f2$ with $f1(x) = \underline{if}\ x \geq 0\ \underline{then}\ g(y)\ \underline{else}\ \omega$, $f2(x) = \underline{if}\ x < 0\ \underline{then}\ h(z)\ \underline{else}\ \omega)$.

b) Call by name computes only useful terms. But this does not mean that call by name is optimal, because it can compute several times the same argument for the same call. One improvement is, when a term is computed for a replacement, to replace it in all of its occurrences : this is a compromise between call by name (arguments are computed only when needed) and call by value (they are computed only once).

14.5. Return to our example of gcd :

$$f(u,v) = \underline{if}\ v = 0\ \underline{then}\ u\ \underline{else}\ f(v,mod(u,v))$$

or more generally

$$f(x) = \underline{if}\ c(x)\ \underline{then}\ e(x)\ \underline{else}\ f(g(x))$$

(x can be one or several parameters). We have already said that, if we apply first rule of rewriting (i), then (ii), there is no other choice. Call by name and call by value lead to the same computation, which computes the least fixpoint :

$$f(x_0), f(x_1), \ldots, f(x_k)$$

where $x_0 = x$, $x_i = g(x_{i-1})$

until $c(x_k)$ if such a k exists ; then the result is $e(x_k)$.

This leads to the notion of iteration and to iterative specification languages like LUCID, mathematical model of which is recursive functions. It is a step towards programming languages.

The relation between recursive specifications and iterations, according to the form of recursivity, is important to study, but we cannot treat it here. In the annex, we transform general specifications into recursive ones which are in fact recurrent ($f(i)$ expressed in terms of $f(i-1)$) and so lead to iteration.

15. A conclusion

Recursive specifications allow us to answer our three problems of existence, choice and computation of a solution. They are, in this respect, a convenient specification language.

We can say that we have given two types of semantics for recursive specifications.
In the first case (fixpoint semantics or <u>denotational</u> semantics), a recursive specification denotes a function, its least fixpoint. In the second, a specification and
an input define computations : this second type of semantics can be called <u>operational</u>.
The two types are compatible, and can be said to be <u>complementary</u>, because the function denoted, i.e. the least fixpoint, is also the function computed when input runs
through its domain (fig. 9), at least if the computation rule used is safe.

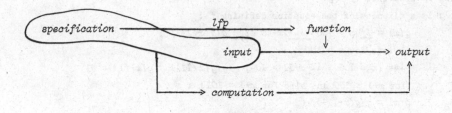

<u>figure 9</u>

An important question is whether the given semantics, using partial functions, are
those intended (see an example in annex   ,A5).

An other essential question is how to <u>obtain</u> a recursive specification from a more
general one, like those considered in the previous chapter. More particularly, how to
<u>transform</u> a recursive specification into another one, for example considered as better
for computations ? At least, how to <u>prove</u> that a recursive specification satisfies another specification ? For this, properties of the least fixpoint have to be proved.

We now consider briefly some ideas arising from these questions.

16. Properties of the least fixpoint

16.1. A famous example by Mc CARTHY.

$$f(x) = \underline{if}\ x > 100\ \underline{then}\ x{-}10\ \underline{else}\ f(f(x{+}11))$$

a) Let us first see the solution by successive approximation :
   - f_1 is defined in $[101, +\infty[: f_1(x) = x{-}10$
   - $f_2(x)$ is defined for $x{+}11 \geq 101$ and $x{+}11{-}10 \geq 101$, i.e. $x \geq 100$:
     $$f_2(100) = f_1(101) = 91\ ;$$
     recall that $f_2(x) = f_1(x)$ if $x \geq 101$.
   - $f_3(x)$ is defined for $x{+}11 \geq 100$ and $f_2(x{+}11) \geq 100$, i.e. $x \geq 99$:
     $$f_3(99) = f_2(100) = 91.$$

- $f_4(x)$ is also defined for
  - $x + 11 = 99$ if $f_3(99) \geq 99$: this is not true
  - $f_3(x+11) = 99$, i.e. $x = 98$: $f_4(98) = f_3(99) = 91$.

b) It seems that, for $x \leq 100$, $f(x)$, if defined, equals 91 . Let us try to compute $f(95)$:

$$f(95) = f(f(106)) = f(96) = f(f(107)) = f(97) = f(f(108)) = f(98).$$

But $\qquad f(98) = f_4(98) = 91.$

c) Let $g(x) = \underline{if}\ x > 100\ \underline{then}\ x-10\ \underline{else}\ 91$

We wish to show that $f = g$.

First g is a fixpoint of the equation defining f :

$\qquad g(x) = \underline{if}\ x > 100\ \underline{then}\ x-10\ \underline{else}\ g(g(x+11))$:

. obvious for $x > 100$

. else $(x \leq 100)$, if $x+11 > 100$, $\quad g(g(x+11)) = g(x+1)\ = 91$

(for $x+1 \leq 100$ and also for $x+1 = 101$) :

$g(x) = g(g(x+11))$.

. else if $x+11 \leq 100$, $g(g(x+11)) = g(91) = 91 = g(x)$.

Thus, f being the least fixpoint, $f \sqsubseteq g$.

d) To show $f = g$, it is sufficient to show $f(x) = \omega \Rightarrow g(x) = \omega$, that is here $f(x) \neq \omega$ for every $x \neq \omega$.

- obvious for $x > 100$

- else, if $x+11 > 100$, $f(x) = f(x+1)$

$\qquad$ if $x+11 \leq 100$ (i.e. $x \leq 89$) $f(x) = f(f(x+11))$

Then, a descending induction proves the result :

- for $x > 100$, $f(x) \neq \omega$

- for $100 \geq x > 89$, $f(x+1) \neq \omega \Rightarrow f(x) \neq \omega$

- for $x \leq 89$, $f(x+11) \neq \omega \Rightarrow f(x+11) = g(x+11) = 91$

thus $f(91) \neq \omega \Rightarrow f(x) \neq \omega$.

e) Remarks : the method of induction consists of reducing the case x to *simpler* cases: we denote by $y \prec x$ the fact that the case y is simpler than the case x ; here $y \prec x$ means $y > x$; for ordinary induction, $y \prec x$ means $y < x$. The idea is that a descending chain $x_1 \succ x_2 \succ \ldots \succ x_n \succ \ldots$ is necessarily finite. Then, to show a property $P(x)$ for all x , it is sufficient to show :

$\qquad (\forall y\, (y \prec x \Rightarrow P(y))) \Rightarrow P(x).$

For example, for a property on lists, the induction can been on length ; for trees on depth, for formulas on length or depth. For that reason, this kind of induction is often called <u>structural induction</u> : it was referred to for terms in 14.3.

The proof of $f(x) = g(x)$ by descending induction could well be done directly and this would be simpler. But the method used can be generalized to proofs of the correction of recursive specifications.

16.2. A method for proving the correction of a recursive specification.

A problem being given by a specification S , we have found an explicit specification R and we wish to prove that R is a specification for the same problem.

We can prove that $R \Rightarrow S$: that means that every fixpoint solution of R, is a solution of S , in particular the least fixpoint. This is a strong assertion, but it has two drawbacks :
- it would be sufficient to prove that the <u>least</u> fixpoint is a solution for S.
- moreover, the direction of the deduction, from R to S, is opposite to the direction of the construction, from S to R ; as the construction is generally done in **several** steps, it would be better to prove $S \Rightarrow R$ during the construction.

$S \Rightarrow R$ means that each solution g of S verifies R, i.e. is a fixpoint of R . Then, for the least fixpoint lfp :
$$lfp \sqsubseteq g.$$

If now we prove that lfp is everywhere defined, necessarily
$$lfp = g.$$

Thus, the proof is performed in two parts :
a) find the explicit specification R by proving that $S \Rightarrow R$; this can often be done by answering two questions :
    - is it a simple case where the result is immediate ?
    - can we reduce every other case to a "simpler" case ?

b) prove that the least fixpoint is defined everywhere ; for example by structural induction ; that often means that the process of reducing a case to a simpler case is always finite.

Before giving examples, we must however observe the limitation of the method : first, it is assumed that S has a solution ; second, if lfp is everywhere defined, there exists no other fixpoint ; then, as each solution of S is a fixpoint, S has only one solution. So the method is applicable only to problems having one and only one solution ; the existence of a solution of S must be known, or proved by another method. With this restriction, the method proves the equivalence of S and R, and the unicity of the solution.

16.3. Example of gcd.

Specification (S_0) :
    $div(d,a) \wedge div(d,b) \wedge \forall x(div(x,a) \wedge div(x,b) \Rightarrow div(x,d))$.
We assume the existence and unicity of d, given a and b. To go towards an explicit specification, we express d as a function of a and b:
(S_1) $\exists f$ $[d=f(a,b) \wedge$

        $div(f(u,v),u) \wedge div(f(u,v),v) \wedge \forall x(div(x,u) \wedge div(x,v) \Rightarrow div(x,f(u,v)))]$

Thus $S_1 \Rightarrow S_0$.

We remove the quantifier (cf. 4.1), getting a specification (S_2) with outputs d and f :
$$d = f(a,b) \wedge S$$
with (S) :
$$div(f(u,v),u) \wedge div(f(u,v),v) \wedge \forall x(div(x,u) \wedge div(x,v) \Rightarrow div(x,f(u,v))).$$
We know the existence and unicity of f.

All this is only a technique to introduce an intermediate result, here f, in order to go towards an explicit specification. Now we work on (S) and transform it into an explicit specification by the preceding method.

The case is simple and the result immediate when $v = 0$:
$$S \Rightarrow f(u,0) = u$$
(proof : $S \Rightarrow div(f(u,0),u) \wedge \forall x (div(x,u) \Rightarrow div(x,f(u,0)))$
$$\Rightarrow div(f(u,0),u) \wedge div(u,f(u,0))$$
$$\Rightarrow f(u,0) = u).$$

Now, reduce every other case to a simpler one :
$$S \Rightarrow f(u,v) = f(v,mod(u,v))$$
(proof : $S \Rightarrow S^{u\ v}_{v\ mod(u,v)}$ and use unicity). The pair $(v,mod(u,v))$ can be considered simpler than (u,v) because $mod(u,v) < v$.

Then :
$$S \Rightarrow f(u,v) = \underline{if}\ v = 0\ \underline{then}\ u\ \underline{else}\ f(v,mod(u,v)).$$

It remains to be proved that the explicit definition of f implies :
$$f(u,v) \neq \omega \quad \text{for}\ u \neq \omega\ \text{and}\ v \neq \omega .$$
This can be done by structural induction using our simplicity relation :
$$(u_1,v_1) \blacktriangleleft (u_2,v_2) \Leftrightarrow v_1 < v_2 ;$$
for pairs of natural integers, each descending chain is finite.

16.4. Scott's rule for the least fixpoint.

In fact, we have not really taken care of the first drawback outlined in 16.2, for the previous method applies only when the fixpoint is unique.

To show a property $P(f)$ for the least fixpoint, we have to use one of its definitions, for example its construction by successive approximation. If :

      i) $P(\perp)$ is true

      ii) $P(g) \Rightarrow P(\tau(g))$

          then $P(f_j)$ is true for every approximation f_j.

Now, if P is such that for an ascending sequence (f_j), $P(\sqcup f_j)$ is deduced from

$\forall j\ P(f_j)$, then the two conditions (i) and (ii) are sufficient to prove $P(f)$. This hypothesis is general enough : it is true, for example, if P is a predicate without quantifiers, or contains only universal quantifiers at the beginning.

Example :

For the least fixpoint of
$$f(u,v) = \underline{if}\ v = 0\ \underline{then}\ u\ \underline{else}\ f(v,mod(u,v))$$
prove $P(f)$:
$$f(u,v) = \omega \vee div(f(u,v),u) \wedge div(f(u,v),v) \wedge$$
$$\forall x\ (div(x,u) \wedge div(x,v) \Rightarrow div(x,f(u,v))).$$
(the quantifier could be at the beginning).

    i) $P(\perp)$ is obvious.

    ii) $\tau(g)(u,v) = \underline{if}\ v = 0\ \underline{then}\ u\ \underline{else}\ g(v,mod(u,v))$.

We suppose $P(g)$ and we prove $P(\tau(g))$:

    - if $v = \omega$, then $\tau(g)(u,v) = \omega$

    - if $v = 0$ and $u = \omega$, then $\tau(g)(u,v) = \omega$

    - if $v = 0$ and $u \neq \omega$, then $\tau(g)(u,v) = u$ and
$$div(u,u) \wedge div(u,0) \wedge \forall x\ (div(x,u) \wedge div(x,0) \Rightarrow div(x,u))$$

    - if $v \neq \omega$ and $v \neq 0$, $\tau(g)(u,v) = g(v,mod(u,v))$; the induction hypothesis $P(g)$ implies, substituting v for u and $mod(u,v)$ for v :
$$g(v,mod(u,v)) = \omega \vee div(g(v,mod(u,v)),v) \wedge div(g(v,mod(u,v)),mod(u,v)),$$
$$\wedge\ \forall x\ (div(x,v) \wedge div(x,mod(u,v)) \Rightarrow div(x,g(v,mod(u,v)))).$$
But, from theorems of arithmetic :
$$div(z,v) \wedge div(z,mod(u,v)) \Rightarrow div(z,u)$$
$$div(x,u) \wedge div(x,v) \Rightarrow div(x,mod(u,v))$$
so that $P(g)$ implies $P(\tau(g))$.

The assertion $P(f)$ is not very interesting in itself, and as in 16.3, it remains to prove that for $u \neq \omega$ and $v \neq \omega$, $f(u,v) \neq \omega$. This cannot be proved by Scott's rule, because it is not true for the successive approximations.

A BRIEF BIBLIOGRAPHY

On mathematical logic

A.CHURCH. *Introduction to mathematical logic*. Vol.1, Princeton University Press(1956).

S.KLEENE. *Introduction to metamathematics*. Van Nostrand (1952).

J.SHOENFIELD. *Mathematical logic*. Addison Wesley (1967).

On fixpoint theory

W. DE ROEVER. *First order reduction of call by name to call by value*. Arc et Senans IRIA Symp. (1975), pp. 413-434.

C.LIVERCY. *Théorie des programmes*. Dunod (1978).

Z.MANNA. *Mathematical theory of computation*. McGraw-Hill (1974).

Z.MANNA, J.VUILLEMIN. *Fixpoint approach to the theory of computation*. Comm. ACM 15 (1972), pp. 528-536.

Z.MANNA, S.NESS, J.VUILLEMIN. *Inductive methods for proving properties of programs*. Comm. ACM 16 (1973), pp. 491-502.

G.PLOTKIN. *LCF considered as a programming language*. Arc et Senans IRIA Symposium (1975), pp.234-261.

D.SCOTT. *The lattice of flow diagrams*. Symp. Semantics Alg. Lang., Lecture Notes in Math. 188, Springer (1971), pp.311-366.

D.SCOTT. *Lattice theoretic models for λ-calculus*.IFIP W.G.2.2 Bulletin 5 (1970).

D.SCOTT. *Continuous lattices*. Oxford Mono. PRG7, Oxford University (1972).

J.VUILLEMIN. *Syntaxe,sémantique et axiomatique d'un langage de programmation simple*. Thèse, Université de Paris 6 (1974).

Others

E.ASHCROFT, W.WADGE. *Lucid, a non procedural language with iteration*. Comm. ACM 20 (1977), pp. 519-526.

R.BURSTALL. *Proving properties of programs by structural induction*. Comp. Journ. 12 (1969), pp. 41-48.

R.BURSTALL, J.DARLINGTON. *A transformation system for developping recursive programs*. JACM 24 (1977), pp. 44-67.

E.DIJKSTRA. *Hierarchical order of sequential processes*. Acta Inf.1 (1971),pp.115-138.

J.GUTTAG, E.MOROWITZ, D.MUSSER. *The design of data type specifications*. Report ISI/RR, University of Southern California (1976).

R.TENNENT. *The denotational semantics of programming languages*. Comm. ACM 19 (1976), pp. 437-453.

ANNEX

The problem of the philosophers

It is a well-known problem. Some philosophers are sitting around a table and can be in two different <u>states</u> : "thinking" or "eating". To eat (spaghetti) two forks are necessary, but there exists only one fork between each pair of neighbours, so that

the desire of a philosopher to eat cannot necessarily be immediately satisfied.

A1. A specification

a) The <u>data structure</u> contains the set P of philosophers, a relation of neighbourhood:
$$nei : P \times P \to B$$
($B = \{true, false\}$), with axioms :
$$nei(p,q) = nei(q,p)$$
$$\neg\ nei(p,p)$$
We forget every other property on neighbourhood, so that the specification is more general than the problem.

In the data structure are also found the input and the output . An <u>input</u> is an infinite sequence of demands of philosophers asking for their state to be changed. It is formalized as a function
$$d : N \to P :$$
$d_i = p$ means that at "time" i, philosopher p asks for his state be changed.

An <u>output</u> is an infinite sequence of boolean vectors giving the successive states :
$$eats : N \to (P \to B)$$
$eats_i(p)$ means that, at time i, p is eating.
$eats_0(p) = false$ (another possibility would be to consider $eats_0$ as an input).

An axiom of mutual exclusion must be stated :
$$\neg\ (nei(p,q) \wedge eats_i(p) \wedge eats_i(q)).$$

b) The specification can be given as a conjunction of implications :

(1) $eats_i(d_i) \Rightarrow \neg\ eats_{i+1}(d_i)$

(2) $eats_i(p) \wedge p \neq d_i \Rightarrow eats_{i+1}(p)$

(3) $eats_{i+1}(p) \Rightarrow eats_i(p) \vee waits_i(p)$

with :
$$waits_i(p) = \exists j(p=d_j \wedge j\leq i \wedge \forall l(j \leq l \leq i \Rightarrow \neg eats_l(p)))$$

(1) means that to stop eating is effective when requested ; (2) that eating continues until stop eating is requested ; (3) that nobody can eat if he has not made a request.

To complete the specification, we give a condition for non-starvation. For example, there is no universal starvation with :

$$(4) \quad waits_i(p) \Rightarrow \exists q \; eats_{i+1}(q) :$$

if somebody waits at i, somebody eats at $i+1$.

It is clear that to obtain this specification, some work must be done, for example abstracting the use of forks into the neighbourhood relation. In the sequel, we shall transform the specification and prove by that the existence of a solution. The interest of the exercise is to make our transformations as automatic as possible and for that, reasoning in as primitive a fashion as possible. In particular every idea must come from the specification.

A2. Transformation into a recursive specification

We wish to express $eats_{i+1}$ from $eats_i$, i.e. to obtain an expression for $eats_{i+1}(p)$. (1), (2) and (3) are equivalent to :

$$\underline{if} \; p \doteq d_i \wedge eats_i(p) \; \underline{then} \; eats_{i+1}(p) = false$$
$$\underline{else} \; \underline{if} \; eats_i(p) \; \underline{then} \; eats_{i+1}(p) = true$$
$$\underline{else} \; \underline{if} \; \neg waits(i,p) \; \underline{then} \; eats_{i+1}(p) = false$$

This can also be transformed into :

$$\underline{if} \; p = d_i \wedge eats_i(p) \quad \underline{then} \quad eats_{i+1}(p) = false$$
$$\underline{else} \; \underline{if} \; eats_i(p) \vee \; \neg waits_i(p) \; \underline{then} \; eats_{i+1}(p) = eats_i(p)$$

One case remains to be studied : $waits_i(p)$, which implies $\neg eats_i(p)$. It has to be chosen so that (4) is verified . For that, two cases:

- if there does not exist p such that $waits_i(p)$, (4) is verified and the definition is complete.
- otherwise, we have $waits_i(p_0)$ for some p_0 and we must find q such that $eats_{i+1}(q)$, respecting mutual exclusion :

$$\forall p \quad \neg (nei(p,q) \wedge eats_{i+1}(p))$$

. a choice is $q = p_0$ if $\forall p \; \neg (nei(p,p_0) \wedge eats_{i+1}(p))$
. otherwise, $\exists p(nei(p,p_0) \wedge eats_{i+1}(p))$ and (4) is verified.

Then, (4) and mutual exclusion are verified with :

$$eats_{i+1}(p) = false \; (= eats_i(p)) \; \text{ if } waits_i(p) \text{ and } p \neq p_0$$
$$eats_{i+1}(p_0) = \forall p \quad \neg (nei(p,p_0) \wedge eats_{i+1}(p)).$$

Index $i+1$ can be removed from the right-hand side because $nei(p,p_0)$ implies $p \neq p_0$

and then $\quad eats_{i+1}(p) = eats_i(p) \wedge p \neq d_i.$

Finally, the specification is verified with

$$eats_{i+1}(p) = eats_i(p)$$
$$except\ for\ p = d_i \wedge eats_i(d_i) : eats_{i+1}(p) = false$$
$$for\ one\ p_0\ such\ that\ waits_i(p_0),\ if\ any :$$
$$eats_{i+1}(p_0) = \forall p \ \neg(nei(p,p_0) \wedge eats_i(p) \wedge p \neq d(i)).$$

Here, transformation is very simple and requires only simple logical reasoning.

Remark :

The definition of $waits_i$ can also be transformed into a recurrent one :

$$waits_i(p) = (waits_{i-1}(p) \vee p = d_i) \wedge \neg eats_i(p)$$

with $\qquad waits_0(p) = (p = d_0 \wedge \neg eats_0(p)).$

A3. Other specifications

(4) can be criticized from two points of view :

- it does not ensure optimal use of resources : in the previous solution, one p_0 at most is chosen at time i to begin eating.
- it prevents universal starvation, but not individual starvation.

To express the fact that resources are used as much as possible, (4) can be replaced by : $\qquad$ (5) $\quad waits_i(p) \wedge caneat_{i+1}(p) \Rightarrow eats_{i+1}(p)$

$$with \quad caneat_{i+1}(p) = \forall q \ \neg(nei(p,q) \wedge eats_{i+1}(q)).$$

It is clear that (5) implies (4).

Individual non-starvation is expressed by :

$$(6) \quad \neg eats_i(d_i) \Rightarrow \exists j(j > i \wedge eats_j(d_i)):$$

if somebody asks to eat, he will eat at some time afterwards. But to make this possible, a complementary hypothesis is necessary, for some philosophers could eat for ever, preventing others from eating. Thus we introduce a new axiom on input to express the fact that after a time i, each philosopher will ask for a change of state :

$$\forall p \quad \forall i \quad eats_i(p) \Rightarrow \exists j(j > i \wedge d_j = p).$$

A4. Transformation of the specification for optimal use of resource

The beginning of § A2, working on (1), (2), (3) is still valid. The case $waits_i(p)$ and specification (5) remain to be studied : if $waits_i(p)$, by mutual exclusion, then

$$eats_{i+1}(p) = caneat_{i+1}(p).$$

Thus we obtain immediately :

$$eats_{i+1}(p) = \underline{if}\ p = d_i \wedge eats_i(p)\ \underline{then}\ false$$

$$\underline{else} \ \underline{if} \ eats_i(p) \ \wedge \ \neg \ waits_i(p) \ \underline{then} \ eats_i(p)$$
$$\underline{else} \ caneat_{i+1}(p)$$

with
$$caneat_{i+1}(p) = \underset{q \ \in \ P}{\Lambda} \ \neg \ (nei(p,q) \ \wedge \ eats_{i+1}(q)).$$

Changing i into $i-1$, we obtain a recursive specification. This is not as simple as in
§ A2, because, $eats_i$ being given, $eats_{i+1}$ is defined by a fixpoint equation.

A5. Study of the fixpoint equation

If we suppose that boolean functions $\wedge$, $\neg$ are undefined for an undefined argument,
$caneat_{i+1}(p) = \omega$ if $eats_{i+1}$ is not a total function. Then, the solution by successive
approximation gives :
- first approximation of $eats_{i+1}$: $\bot$, function undefined for each p
- second approximation :

$$\lambda p \ \underline{if} \ p = d_i \ \wedge \ eats_i(p) \ \underline{then} \ false$$
$$\underline{else} \ \underline{if} \ eats_i(p) \ \vee \ \neg \ waits_i(p) \ \underline{then} \ eats_i(p)$$
$$\underline{else} \ \omega$$

- third approximation : idem ; thus we have the least fixpoint.

Thus, except for the very particular case where nobody is waiting at time i, we do
not obtain a total function.

Even if p has an eating neighbour $q \neq d_i$ at time i, the solution does not show that
$eats_{i+1}(p)$ is false. This is a consequence of $false \ \wedge \ \omega = \omega$.

To prevent this difficulty, we now state (§ 7, § 11.1)
$$false \ \wedge \ \omega = \omega \ \wedge \ false = false.$$

But this is not enough to obtain a least fixpoint defined everywhere. The reason is
that, in general, the equation has several solutions which are total functions, i.e.
not comparable for the order "less defined". Consequently, the least fixpoint, less
defined than each of them, cannot be a total function and is not the intended solution.

The problem is to build, from the least fixpoint, more and more defined solution, until
a total function is found.

Let us denote the equation $g = \tau(g)$, with

$$\tau(g)(p) = \underline{if} \ p = d_i \ \wedge \ eats_i(p) \ \underline{then} \ false$$
$$\underline{else} \ \underline{if} \ eats_i(p) \ \vee \ \neg \ waits_i(p) \ \underline{then} \ eats_i(p)$$
$$\underline{else} \ \underset{q \ \in \ P}{\Lambda} \ \neg \ (nei(p,q) \ \wedge \ g(q)).$$

Let g be a partial function, fixpoint of the equation. A fixpoint strictly more defined
than g can be built by successive approximations starting with g' such that (§10,

remark 3)

$$g \sqsubset g' \sqsubseteq \tau(g')$$

($g \sqsubset g'$ means $g \sqsubseteq g'$ and $g \neq g'$). If we find such a g', the same process will be iterated from the new fixpoint, until a fixpoint is found which is a total function : as we are working in a finite domain, this will be the case after a finite number of repetitions of the process.

To find g' :
- as $g \sqsubset g'$, g' is defined for some p_0 such that $g(p_0) = \omega$, and thus $waits_i(p_0)$ and $nei(p_0,q) \wedge g(q) \neq \omega \Rightarrow g(q) = false$; we take for example $g'(p_0) = true^{(*)}$.
- $\tau(g')(p_0)$ must be true ; it is iff

$$nei(p_0,q) \Rightarrow g'(q) = false.$$

- thus we choose g' as an extension of g by

$$g'(p_0) = true \qquad \text{and} \qquad g'(q) = false \text{ for } nei(p_0,q);$$

$\tau(g')$ has the same values as g' for p_0 and those q ; and, as $g \sqsubset g'$ implies $\tau(g) = g \sqsubseteq \tau(g')$, we can conclude that $g' \sqsubseteq \tau(g')$.

In other words, we have found that among those philosophers who are waiting and whose next state cannot be deduced from the known states by application of mutual exclusion and of (5), we can choose one, make him eat and repeat the process until every philosopher has his state defined.

Here, transformation has required knowledge about fixpoint theory.

A6. Transformation of the specification to avoid individual starvation

Specification : (6) $\quad \neg eats_i(d_i) \Rightarrow \exists\, j(j > i \wedge eats_j(d_i))$.

Axiom : $\qquad\qquad \forall p \; \forall i \; \exists\, j \; (j \geq i \wedge d_j = p)$.

An existential quantifier in the specification can be removed by introducing a new function : here $beg(i)$ is a time after i when d_i eats. We replace (6) by

$\qquad$ (7) $\quad \neg eats_i(d_i) \Rightarrow beg(i) > i$

$\qquad$ (8) $\quad \neg eats_i(d_i) \Rightarrow eats_{beg(i)}(d_i)$

Moreover, it can be supposed that $beg(i)$ is the first integer verifying (7) and (8).

In the same way, the axiom introduces a function ch : if $eats_i(p)$, $ch(i,p)$ is the first demand of change after (or equal to) i. ch is given, but beg must be found.

First, we build a definition of $eats_{i+1}$: here again, the start of § A2 is valid to satisfy (1), (2), (3) and the case $waits_i(p)$ remains to be studied. In the defini-

---

(*) choice $g'(p_0) = false$ leads to a slightly more complicated process.

tion of $waits_i$, there is an existential quantifier : here too, we introduce a function $j(p,i)$ to replace it :

$$p = d_{j(p,i)} \wedge j(p,i) \leq i \wedge (j(p,i) \leq l \leq i \Rightarrow \neg eats_l(p)).$$

Then, if $waits_i(p)$, $eats_{i+1}(p)$ is true iff $i+1$ is the least $l > j(p,i)$ such that $eats_l(p)$. Thus, the definition of beg implies :

$$waits_i(p) \Rightarrow eats_{i+1}(p) = (i+1 = beg(j(p,i))).$$

From this, the definition of $eats_{i+1}(p)$ can be written :

$$eats_{i+1}(p) = \underline{if}\ p = d_i \wedge eats_i(p)\ \underline{then}\ false$$
$$\underline{else}\ \underline{if}\ eats_i(p) \vee \neg waits_i(p)\ \underline{then}\ eats_i(p)$$
$$\underline{else}\ (i+1 = beg(j(p,i)))$$

or $\quad eats_{i+1}(p) = \underline{if}\ p = d_i \wedge eats_i(p)\ \underline{then}\ false$
$$\underline{else}\ \underline{if}\ waits_i(p) \wedge beg(j(p,i)) = i+1\ \underline{then}\ true$$
$$\underline{else}\ eats_i(p)$$

Conversely, this definition and (7) imply (8).

We must now find a definition of beg such that (7) and mutual exclusion are verified.

For mutual exclusion at $i+1$ (supposing mutual exclusion at i), let p, q be two neighbours. Two properties are to be verified :

a) $\quad waits_i(p) \wedge waits_i(q) \wedge beg(j(p,i)) = i+1 \Rightarrow beg(j(q,i)) \neq i+1$:

this leads to the supposition $beg(j(p,i)) \neq beg(j(q,i))$; we can for example choose beg "increasing" on neighbours, i.e. :

$$j < j' \wedge nei(d_j, d_{j'}) \Rightarrow beg(j) < beg(j').$$

b) $\quad waits_i(p) \wedge beg(j(p,i)) = i+1 \wedge eats_i(q) \Rightarrow d_i = q$

equivalent, from the definition of ch, to :

$$waits_i(p) \wedge beg(j(p,i)) = i+1 \wedge eats_i(q) \Rightarrow ch(i,q) \leq i.$$

We have to introduce beg into the right-hand side : as $eats_i(q)$, let k be the beginning of the corresponding eating time of q :

$$k \leq i \text{ and } k = beg(j(q,k)) \text{ and } ch(i,q) = ch(k,q) ;$$

the right-hand side is then :

$$ch(beg(j(q,k)),q) \leq beg(j(p,i)) - 1$$

with $beg(j(q,k)) = k \leq i < i+1 = beg(j(p,i))$

and, as beg is increasing on neighbours : $j(q,k) < j(p,i)$.

Property (b) will be verified if

$$j' < j \wedge nei(d_j, d_{j'}) \Rightarrow ch(beg(j'), d_{j'}) + 1 \leq beg(j)$$

This formula and (7) lead to a definition for beg :

$$beg(j) = max(j, \max_{j' \in E(d_j)} ch(beg(j'), d_{j'})) + 1$$

where $E(p) = \{j' \mid j' < j \wedge \neg eats_{j'}(d_{j'}) \wedge nei(d_j, d_{j'})\}$

beg is increasing on neighbours.

The existence of beg and thus of a solution is now proved. But we have no recursive specification for beg. We wish to transform the previous definition.

To compute the maximum of a set of natural integers, if the cardinal of the set can be found, it is possible to run through the natural integers, each time a number of the set is met decreasing the cardinal, until its value falls to zero.

Here, the j' such that $ch(beg(j'),d_{j'}) > j > j'$ are :
- those such that $beg(j') > j$: they verify $waits_j(d_{j'})$
- those such that $beg(j') < j < ch(beg(j'),d_{j'})$: they verify $eats_j(d_{j'})$.

The number of elements of $E(d_j)$ which are superior to j is then known : with $p = d_j$,
$$prior(p,j) = card \ \{q \mid nei(p,q) \land (waits_j(q) \lor eats_j(q))\}$$
Now, for $i \geq j$:
$$prior(p,i+1) = \underline{if}\ eats_i(d_i) \land nei(d_i,p)\ \underline{then}\ prior(p,i) - 1\ \underline{else}\ prior(p,i).$$

And finally :
$$eats_{i+1}(p) = \underline{if}\ p = d_i \land eats_i(p)\ \underline{then}\ false$$
$$\underline{else}\ \underline{if}\ waits_i(p) \land prior(p,i+1) = \overline{0}\ \underline{then}\ true$$
$$\underline{else}\ eats_i(p)$$

It is also possible to remark that the second case happens only for
$$eats_i(d_i) \land nei(d_i,p) \lor \neg eats_i(d_i) \land p = d_i.$$

Here, logical reasoning, especially on quantifiers, was more complicated than in A2. We have not written all the details of the demonstrations ; the transformation is somewhat long, but we have used no hidden or ad hoc idea; the most difficult one is probably how to find a maximum, but it is general enough. We have shown how existential quantifiers lead to the introduction of intermediate results. Finally, a good solution is obtained.

ACKNOWLEDGMENT

I am grateful to M. GRIFFITHS for his aid in preparing the manuscript.